HENRY FIELDING

POLITICAL WRITER

Henry Fielding: Political Writer

Thomas R. Cleary

An accurate and comprehensive study of the political aspects of Fielding's art has been sorely needed. As a result of decades of work by literary scholars and a series of great historians, such a study is finally possible. This volume addresses that need, and, in the light of a recent revival of interest in Fielding's work, it arrives most opportunely. The author offers here a wide-ranging focus and a firm grip on the shifting complexities of Fielding's political situations—the loyalties and enmities, factional alignments and fractious rhetoric—that allow a satisfactory understanding of Fielding's political writing. Political writing in Fielding's day, as in ours, was topical, concerned with evanescent problems and day-to-day needs that were familiar to contemporaries, but that are now recaptured only with greatest difficulty. This study constitutes a thorough reconstruction of Fielding's political context and extricates from the context Fielding's own political endeavours. Cleary's work will make many of Fielding's previously unstudied works accessible to students and scholars of eighteenth-century English literature.

A necessary point of reference to both literary specialists and historians concerned with eighteenth-century England.

Thomas R. Cleary teaches in the Department of English at the University of Victoria.

HENRY FIELDING

POLITICAL WRITER

Thomas R. Cleary

Wilfrid Laurier University Press

Canadian Cataloguing in Publication Data

Cleary, Thomas R. (Thomas Raymond), 1940–
    Henry Fielding: political writer

Includes index.
Bibliography: p.
ISBN 0-88920-131-5

1. Fielding, Henry, 1707-1754 – Political and social views.
I. Title.

PR3458.P6C63   1984   823'.5   C84-098493-6

Contents

*To those who have always mattered
more than Fielding—
Elizabeth, Ruth, Caroline,
Matthew, and Stephen.*

List of Abbreviations

Appleton—Henry Fielding, *The Historical Register and Eurydice Hissed*, ed. W. Appleton (Lincoln, NE, 1967).

Atherton—Herbert M. Atherton, *Political Prints in the Age of Hogarth* (Oxford, 1974).

Baker, *PAF*—Sheridan Baker, "Political Allusion in Fielding's *The Author's Farce, Mock Doctor*, and *Tumble-Down Dick*," *PMLA* 77 (1962), 221-31.

B-B, "Bedford"—M. C. Battestin (with R. R. Battestin), "Fielding, Bedford, and the Westminster Election of 1749," *Eighteenth Century Studies* II (1977/78), 143-85.

Battestin, "FCP"—Martin C. Battestin, "Fielding's Changing Politics and *Joseph Andrews*," *Philological Quarterly* 39 (1960), 39-55.

Cleary, "Case"—Thomas R. Cleary, "The Case for Fielding's Authorship of *An Address to the Electors of Great Britain* (1740) Re-opened," *Studies in Bibliography* 28 (1975), 308-18.

Cleary, "Jacobitism"—Thomas R. Cleary, "Jacobitism in *Tom Jones:* The Basis for an Hypothesis," *Philological Quarterly* 52 (1973), 239-51.

Cleary, "Paper War"—Thomas R. Cleary, "Henry Fielding and the Great Jacobite Paper War of 1747-49," *Eighteenth-Century Life* 5, no. 1 (1978), 1-11.

Coley, *JJ*—Henry Fielding, *The Jacobite's Journal and Related Writings*, ed. W. B. Coley (Middletown, CT and Oxford, 1975).

Coxe, *Pelham*—William Coxe, *Memoirs of the Administration of the Right Honourable Henry Pelham*, 3 vols. (London, 1829).

Cross—Wilbur Cross, *The History of Henry Fielding*, 3 vols. (New Haven, 1918).

Diary—John Perceval, 2nd Earl of Egmont, *Diary of Viscount Perceval, Afterwards Earl of Egmont*, 3 vols. (London, 1920-23).

DNB—*The Dictionary of National Bibliography*, ed. Sir Leslie Stephen and Sir Sidney Lee, 22 vols. (London, 1937-38).

Dudden—F. Homes Dudden, *Henry Fielding, His Life, Works and Times*, 2 vols. (Oxford, 1952).

ECS—Eighteenth-Century Studies.

Foord—Archibald Foord, *His Majesty's Opposition: 1714-1830* (New Haven, 1964).

Godden—G. M. Godden, *Henry Fielding: A Memoir* (London, 1910).

Goldgar—Bertrand A. Goldgar, *Walpole and the Wits* (Lincoln, NE, 1976).

Grundy—Isobel M. Grundy, "New Verse by Henry Fielding," *PMLA* 87 (1972), 213-45.

Henley—Henry Fielding, *The Complete Works of Henry Fielding, Esq.*, ed. W. E. Henley, 16 vols. (London, 1903).

Hervey, *Memoirs*—John, Lord Hervey, *Memoirs*, ed. J. W. Croker, 2 vols. (London, 1884).

Irwin—William Irwin, *The Making of Jonathan Wild* (New York, 1941).

JA—Henry Fielding, *Joseph Andrews*, ed. Martin C. Battestin (Middletown, CT and Oxford, 1967).

Laprade—William T. Laprade, *Public Opinion and Politics in Eighteenth-Century England, to the Fall of Walpole* (New York, 1936).

Locke, *TP*—Henry Fielding, *The True Patriot*, ed. Miriam A. Locke (Baton Rouge, 1964).

Loftis—John Loftis, *The Politics of Drama in Augustan England* (Oxford, 1963).

Marchmont—*A Selection from the Papers of the Earls of Marchmont*, ed. Sir G. H. Rose, 3 vols. (London, 1831).

Miller, *Misc*—Henry Fielding, *Miscellanies, by Henry Fielding, Esq., Volume One*, ed. Henry Knight Miller (Middletown, CT and Oxford, 1972).

MLN—*Modern Language Notes.*

MLQ—*Modern Language Quarterly.*

MLR—*Modern Language Review.*

Morrissey, *GSO*—Henry Fielding, *The Grub-Street Opera*, ed. L. J. Morrissey (Edinburgh, 1973).

Morrissey, *TT*—*Tom Thumb and the Tragedy of Tragedies*, ed. L. J. Morrissey (Edinburgh, 1970).

N&Q—*Notes and Queries.*

Owen—John B. Owen, *The Rise of the Pelhams* (London, 1975).

Phillimore—Robert Phillimore, *Memoirs and Correspondence of George, Lord Lyttelton*, 2 vols. (London, 1845).

Plumb—J. H. Plumb, *Sir Robert Walpole: The King's Minister* (London, 1961).

P.Q.—*Philological Quarterly.*

Roberts, *GSO*—Henry Fielding, *The Grub-Street Opera*, ed. Edgar V. Roberts (Lincoln, NE, 1968).

TJ, Battestin—Henry Fielding, *Tom Jones*, ed. Martin C. Battestin (Middletown, CT and Oxford, 1975).

Thomas—P.D.G. Thomas, *The House of Commons in the Eighteenth Century* (Oxford, 1971).

Wiggin—Lewis M. Wiggin, *The Faction of Cousins: A Political Account of the Grenvilles*, 1733-63 (New Haven, 1958).

Wilkes—John W. Wilkes, *A Whig in Power: the Political Career of Henry Pelham* (Evanston, IL, 1964).

Woods, *AF*—Henry Fielding, *The Author's Farce (Original Version)*, ed. Charles B. Woods (Lincoln, NE, 1966).

Wyndham—Maud Wyndham, *Chronicles of the Eighteenth Century*, 2 vols. (London, 1924).

Yorke, Hardwicke—P. C. Yorke, *The Life and Correspondence of Philip Yorke, Earl of Hardwicke* (Cambridge, 1913).

Acknowledgements

I must begin by thanking teachers who awakened and deepened my interest in the eighteenth century and Henry Fielding: Gerald A. Barker and A. Robert Towers, Jr. of Queens College, CUNY, and Louis A. Landa and Henry K. Miller, Jr. of Princeton University. Over the years (too many) spent in writing and revising this study I have also been helped by a surprising number of strangers who extended aid out of generosity and love of knowledge. William B. Coley of Wesleyan University and John B. Shipley of the University of Illinois at Chicago offered especially useful hints at what were to me important moments.

I am indebted to my colleagues John Money and Terry Sherwood, the former for sharing his historical enthusiasm and expertise, the latter for friendship that extended to listening to authorial complaints, often breathless and lengthy. Patrick Grant volunteered to read my manuscript in a version that was hundreds of pages longer than the one that went to the printer. He read with his usual speed, precision, and insight, made many corrections and suggestions, and said kinder things than an outsized, rough manuscript deserved.

I owe special thanks to Donald Greene of the University of Southern California. He offered encouragement and approval at a crucial moment in the struggle to find a publisher for a long, scholarly manuscript in times receptive mainly to short, critical ones. This was doubly gratifying because his own *The Politics of Samuel Johnson* remains the finest political study of an eighteenth-century author.

I am indebted to the helpful staff of the MacPherson Library at the University of Victoria. For hospitality and co-operation I must also thank the staffs of the Princeton University Library, the British Library, the Bodleian Library and the William Andrews Clark Memorial Library.

I would like to thank the publishers of *Philological Quarterly, Studies in Bibliography*, and *Eighteenth-Century Life* for permission to include in this study material that originally appeared (in somewhat different form) in those journals.

Henry Fielding: Political Writer has been typed, corrected, revised, and retyped a number of times. Several typists have struggled at length with my inconsistencies and obscurities. I would like particularly, however, to acknowledge the good humour and hard work of Eleanor Lowther, Jacqueline Crouch, and Susan Meisler.

Good copy editing is, I imagine, both difficult and unthanked. I would like to extend warm thanks to Janet Shorten of Wilfrid Laurier University Press for her painstaking efforts and forbearing civility in the face of my many sins and assaults on Priscian.

My investigations have been supported by research and travel grants from the University of Victoria, by a research grant and a leave grant from the Canada Council, and by the Department of English at the University of Victoria. Without this support I would not have been able to carry my work to completion. I would, finally, like very gratefully to acknowledge that this book has been published with the help of a grant from the Canadian Federation for the Humanities using funds provided by the Social Sciences and Humanities Research Council of Canada.

University of Victoria   *T.R.C.*
Victoria, B.C.
May 1, 1983

Introduction

An accurate and comprehensive study of the political aspects of Fielding's art is sorely needed and, as a result of decades of work by literary scholars and a series of great historians, beginning with Sir Lewis B. Namier, such a study is finally possible. There has been an intense revival of interest in Fielding among scholars and readers; a dozen or more excellent books and many articles have illumined the form and style of Fielding's novels and other prose and the moral, spiritual, and social attitudes that are implicit in all of his work, from the early plays, through the novels and journals, to the late legal and social tracts. But toward the elucidation of the often complexly ironical and topical political content of much of his work, there have only been gestures, some helpful, some less so, and all limited in scope to one or a few works. No study offers anything like the comprehensiveness of focus and the firm grip of the shifting complexities of the political situations, loyalties, and enmities; factional alignments; and factious rhetoric that would allow a satisfactory understanding of Fielding's long involvement in political writing.[1] A study with these strengths has become increasingly necessary as our interest in Fielding and our understanding of other aspects of his life and work have grown, and will be ever more essential as the Wesleyan-Oxford edition of his works moves toward completion, forcing its editors to consider and attempt adequately to explain the political content of works which have been little studied and allowing a relatively broad readership to examine works which have hitherto been the domain of specialists and the occasional writer of a learned thesis.

An understanding of Fielding's political output or of the aims and significances of given individual works or groups of works is not always easily achieved. Political writing in his day, as in ours, was topical, concerned with evanescent problems and day-to-day needs that were familiar to contemporaries, but that are now recaptured only with difficulty. It was extraordinarily dependent on ironies, half-truths, exaggerations, conventional rhetorical distortions, and varieties of self-interest and loyalty (or disloyalty) that contemporaries could fathom, relish, and even discount. Even the informed modern may find them difficult to

analyze and the less informed may find them hopelessly confusing. The scholar concerned with eighteenth-century political writing
must attempt to recapture the intelligent contemporary's informed,
critical, and ultimately realistic view of the relationships between the
writer and current events, and between the writer's assertions and what
passed for truth in the shadow world of political life. Why is he saying it?
What individual, political group, or principle is he supporting or attacking? What, exaggeration aside, does he actually mean or hope to
achieve? Is it true? Is it a slander? Is it overtly or subtly ironic and, if so,
how? These are the questions one frequently must try to answer despite
the lapse of over two hundred years.

One problem to be eased, if never really solved, is the almost total
lack in Fielding's case of the kinds of evidence (MSS, letters, diaries,
reasonably unbiased or circumstantial contemporary commentary on the
man or his political utterances) that have afforded insight into the
political motivations and methods of other great authors of the period,
notably Pope and Swift. We have, for the most part, only his works and
the possibility of creating an informative background against which to
view them by delving into the publications and actions of Fielding's
political and literary friends and foes and into contemporary and modern
analyses of the political history of Fielding's time. But here, again,
Fielding presents special problems. His political work is as diverse as the
length of his career and the constantly changing situations and motivations that produced it would suggest. He produced a richer body of
drama between 1728 and 1737 than many a writer has in a lifetime; during his later career he penned all or a large part of the essays in four
periodicals, and wrote several political tracts as well as his novels and a
number of impressive works with political content that are less easy to
classify. Much of his work is heavily political and all but a few works
have some tinge of politics. Each political work, indeed nearly every allusion, requires us, if we are to understand it adequately, to consider its
relationship not only to Fielding's ambitions and needs, hatreds and
loyalties; we also (particularly with reference to works written after 1735)
must consider changing realities of domestic and foreign politics and the
skirmishings and confrontations between three administrations and their
oppositions or (and this is often confusing) between dissident elements
within those three administrations and oppositions. This will be a full-
length, detailed study: anything less would surely not fully illuminate,
and might obscure, its subject.

In depicting Fielding's activities against such a political backdrop,
traditional historical simplifications (e.g., "Whig" *versus* "Tory," "Opposition" *versus* "Administration," "Country" *versus* "Court,"
"Jacobite" *versus* "Hanoverian") must be used with extreme caution
and careful qualification. One must use some convenient terminology or
choke on circumlocutions, but one must not ignore the greys behind the
verbal blacks and whites. A failure to see past the bipartisan myths of an
outmoded historiography continued to render some accounts of

Fielding's political activities misleading. Even less promising is the assumption, frequently implicit in earlier criticism, that Fielding (being a man of genius and benevolence, and a favourite of ours) *must* have exerted far greater influence over the minds of his contemporaries and the march of political events than he (or indeed any other political writer of his time) did; *must* have been above political hack-work for gain or in the hope of preferment; *must*, unlike his opponents, have been concerned with the good of the nation, with high-flown constitutional questions, to the exclusion of narrow partisan aims or the desire to benefit himself or his friends and patrons; and *must*, consequently, always have been fair-minded, generous, and right. Literary genius does not imply moral perfection, and the moral flexibility necessary in the rough-and-tumble world of eighteenth-century politics or partisan authorship was incompatible with the sentimental moral prudery with which we often approach favourite authors. To use only one very relevant example, Irvin Ehrenpreis' biography of Swift makes it clearer with each volume that one's ability to credit the political poses of a well loved author lessens radically with the firming of one's grasp on the personal and civic facts. In Fielding's case one soon learns that though he could admire, as well as smile at, Parson Adams' political naïveté, Adams' innocence was a characteristic he could not and did not maintain as a political author. One must describe the malleability of principle and truthfulness and on occasion the seaminess of contemporary politics and political writing, including Fielding's, as one finds them, however one admires Fielding and wishes to view him as a "true patriot" and a more perceptive version of Squire Allworthy. To those who may be disturbed, I can offer the succinct justification of unvarnished biography offered two decades ago by Leon Howard to Melvillophiles: ". . . in the long run, it may be well to recognize the fact that memorable literature is something which has risen above the frailties of its human origin rather than descended from some perfect inspiration."

This study will depend more heavily than the credits will indicate on the work of historians, but it will also incorporate a great deal of essential and very specific evidence they do not provide that bears upon Fielding's political aims and activities. It will, of course, examine in detail works by Fielding normally accorded little attention by scholars; tracing, for example, Fielding's satiric campaigns in pamphlets, poems, and periodicals as well as in novels and drama. It will consider the activities of other writers who shared Fielding's views or opposed them at various points in his career. For example, the most peculiar pattern of reaction of the *Daily Gazetteer* to Fielding's *Champion* and of Fielding's opposition enemies during his "anti-Jacobite" phase, 1747-49, will form a significant part of the evidence supporting my interpretation of these periods in Fielding's career. Though we do not often think of him in that way, one of Fielding's realms of action was the nether world of partisan journalism for extended periods between 1739 and 1748. He was a propagandist, a foot-soldier, though a skilled one, in the inbred, vital, but ephemeral "paper wars" that characterized politics "outside doors" (as the eighteenth century described the broad spectrum of political activity outside the Houses of Parliament). And if his activities as a propagandist are to be understood, if their texture and aims are to be recaptured, we must descend from the relatively lofty literary-political realm of Pope, Swift, and Bolingbroke; of Pulteney, Chesterfield, and Lyttelton; of the author of *Joseph Andrews, Tom Jones*, and *Amelia;* and observe the cut and thrust of "John Trott-Plaid, Esq." and the editor of *Old England* at close range. Only thus will aspects of the "history" of Fielding's political career take on the concreteness needed to balance its superposition, elsewhere in this study, upon the backdrop of the broad foreign and domestic patterns of the politics of his time.

Chapter One

Prolegomena: George Lyttelton, the Broad-Bottoms, and the Pattern of Fielding's Political Career

The turning point of Henry Fielding's political career was the latter half of 1735, when the faction he would support for the rest of his life first took form. The catalyst for this event was the dismissal two years earlier, on June 14, 1733, of one of England's wealthiest, proudest, and most influential aristocrats from his post as Colonel of the King's Own Horse (Red). Richard Temple, Viscount Cobham, Lord Lieutenant of the County of Buckingham, and master of the great house of Stowe, had formerly supported the ministry, but opposed Walpole's Excise Bill of 1733. This dismissal was his punishment. Cobham's response was angry and effective, in great part because a crop of his young nephews and one of their talented friends from Eton days—collectively dubbed "Cobham's Cubs"—were entering politics at the time.[1]

One of Lord Cobham's sisters had married Richard Grenville of Buckinghamshire, who died in 1727, leaving behind a daughter and five sons, whom Cobham adopted as his protégés and heirs. The two oldest sons, Richard and George Grenville, embarked on their long political careers during the first flush of their uncle's anger and naturally joined the clique that was coalescing around him. Another nephew was George Lyttelton, son of another of Cobham's sisters, and a figure of extreme importance in this study since he was Fielding's principal political friend and patron for the better part of two decades. Lyttelton first won a seat in Commons in the general election of 1734, and began to bloom into a first-class debater and satirist just in time for the birth of the new Cobhamite faction.[2] The brilliant young William Pitt was not a nephew, but he had been at Eton with George Lyttelton, Richard Grenville, and

1

George Grenville, and Lord Cobham had bought him a commission in the King's Own Horse (Red). Pitt even had a family connection, his older brother, Thomas Pitt, having married George Lyttelton's sister Christiana in 1727, though the force of this would be negated when Thomas remained a ministerialist after 1735. Inevitably, he later confirmed his solidarity with the "faction of cousins" by marrying Richard and George's only sister, Hetty Grenville.

The birth of the new faction, the "Cousinhood," was signalled in the late summer of 1735 when Lord Cobham invited all of his nephews to Stowe, recently said by Pope himself in the *Epistle to Burlington* to be "A Work to wonder at." William Pitt also attended, his first visit to Stowe. It was a council of war, during which the Cobhamites dedicated themselves to opposing Walpole and his corrupt system in every way possible, their aims being to bring him utterly down and force political reform. They would not settle for the kind of "conventional accommodation" (the ministry finding places and favours for a few leaders of the opposition as the price of peace without the reformation of corruption or an alteration of measures) covertly favoured by William Pulteney, Lord Carteret, and others.[3] The future would call their sincerity on this issue in question—in 1741-42 and 1744—but in 1735 it gave them a rallying point and a sense of superiority to opposition colleagues. It also seemed desirable to form a closer alliance with the restive Prince of Wales, whose intimate and trusted advisor young George Lyttelton had already become, and to encourage the Prince to move into open opposition to his hated father's ministry. Lord Hervey noticed as early as 1733 that Frederick was moving toward the Cobham group.[4] In 1735 he dismissed George Bubb Dodington, who urged political moderation, as his chief advisor and replaced him with George Lyttelton. By 1737 the efforts of Lyttelton and his friends in Parliament in support of the demands of the newly married Prince for a decent allowance would secure his firm alliance through the earlier 1740s.

The faction already possessed considerable voting strength in Parliament (provided by members of the complexly interrelated Temple, Grenville, Lyttelton, and Pitt clans, and such side growths as the Wests and Wyndhams) and it soon formed alliances with the talented and influential. One ally was the rich, able Duke of Bedford, who will rival George Lyttelton in importance in the chapters in this study dealing with the last half-decade of Fielding's career, when he became a most generous benefactor of the writer-magistrate. The Bedford alliance was eventually cemented in 1745 in typical "family faction" style, when Richard Lyttelton, George's younger brother, married the much older Lady Rachel Russell, Bedford's widowed sister. Lord Chesterfield, also punished for opposing Excise, became a very close collaborator, though he was a natural "lone wolf" and never quite became (or wished to become) "family." Chesterfield would march with the Cobhamites through two periods in opposition and several years in place, only breaking with them (and being dropped by Fielding) in 1748. For briefer periods close working relationships, duly reflected in Fielding's work, were also maintained with George Dodington and the Duke of Argyll.

The new faction had an attractive ideology and the backing of the most celebrated ideologue of the day, Lord Bolingbroke. His Patriot theories called for the eradication of government through and by party or faction, in favour of rule by "true Patriots" under a "Patriot King" and with the support of an uncorruptly elected Parliament of gentlemen voting independently in the "National Interest," free of partisan prejudice or influence. These theories were impractically idealistic, and a bit odd coming from as sly an old political fox as Bolingbroke, whose chequered past included years as a most skilled party intriguer and an only partly reversed attainder for Jacobite treason. However, they were stirring in an age that knew deep corruption, still thought of "party" as a dirty word (one's friends were always "independent patriots," one's enemies members of a faction), and found the idea of formed parliamentary parties (especially a "formed opposition") theoretically and constitutionally unacceptable, though practically essential. Cobham's young followers used the rhetoric of "Patriotism" from the first, earning the nickname "Boy Patriots," and continued to do so even during periods in the 1740s when their behaviour was extraordinarily unidealistic and factious. A modified version of Bolingbroke's idealism, known as "Broad-Bottom" theory, was even more useful in the new faction's struggle against Walpole and toward its members' inclusion in the ministry in the name of reform. Its central tenet was that since the eradication of party was presently unlikely, the best answer to present evils (the King's channelling of patronage and power through and to Robert Walpole, an unconstitutional "sole" or "prime" minister, straddling the executive and the legislature at the head of a faction) would be a grand coalition of the best men of all parties. This would be signalled by the appointment of a coalition ministry with a "broad bottom"—that is, including the leaders of all of the present factions within the ministerial and opposition camps.[5] The Broad-Bottom plan gave the new faction a goal and a rhetoric that it would retain in opposition until first Walpole and then Lord Carteret (who in 1742 had entered the ministry dominated by Walpole's ex-henchmen and backed by the Walpole faithful in Parliament in a classic "conventional accommodation") had been forced from office. Thereafter, they would continue half-sincerely to take pride in the fact that the government they served in from late 1744 to Fielding's death was a modified "Broad-Bottom Ministry," the obstinate Country Tories, the Prince of Wales's following, and Lords Bath and Granville (our friends Pulteney and Carteret) abstaining. It at least partly fulfilled the dreams of a faction-destroying coalition of all factions and the avoidance of concentrated power in the hands of a subject, a prime minister, "one hated Man." That Lord Bolingbroke opposed this ministry on Broad-Bottom or Patriot grounds is a poignant irony generated by the collision of ideals with ambitions which Bolingbroke could not share, as the partial pardon he received in the 1720s did not

allow him to sit in Lords or take an active part in political life. I will normally refer to Fielding's faction as the "Broad-Bottoms" (rather than
using its other nicknames, the "Cousinhood," the "Grenvilles," the
"Cobhamites," "Cobham's Cubs," or the "Boy Patriots"), and the
long lasting importance of Broad-Bottom theory in its speeches and propaganda, including that written by Fielding, justifies this preference.

Most interestingly from our point of view, the Broad-Bottoms
always placed very heavy emphasis on the literary side of the assault on
Walpole, just as Bolingbroke and his Scriblerian friends had done since
the mid-1720s. Bolingbroke himself remained active as a political
essayist, though he withdrew from writing for the famed *Craftsman* in
1735, at roughly the time the Cobhamites formed up for battle, as a
result of a quarrel with its co-inspirer, William Pulteney. Though the
Broad-Bottoms would collaborate with Pulteney until he turned his coat
and became anathema in 1742, neither they nor Bolingbroke trusted him
or doubted he would sell them and the opposition Tories out the moment
he saw a way to achieve his ambition for office and honours. Meanwhile,
Lyttelton was not only the chief link between the Broad-Bottoms and
Bolingbroke (maintaining a close three-way correspondence with him
and Lord Chesterfield), but also an important political author in his own
right. The *Persian Letters* of 1735 was a major contribution to the opposition chorus, immediately seen to be influenced by Bolingbroke, and he
wrote influential pamphlets through the late 1730s. In 1737 he and Lord
Chesterfield established a splendid new journal, *Common Sense*, which
promoted Bolingbrokean, Broad-Bottom, reformist views while blackening the ministry.[6] They wrote for it and surely subsidized it, with the
result that it soon became the most distinguished opposition journal as
the *Craftsman* entered its lengthy post-Bolingbrokean decline. Not until
Fielding established *The Champion* in 1739 would it have an equal in
quality, and *The Champion* remained at a peak of quality and potency
for a relatively brief time. With Lyttelton as its recruiter, the faction
soon gained strong literary auxiliaries. James Thomson was a dependent
of Lyttelton's and his idealistic (if a bit tedious) poem, *Liberty* (1735-36),
and a series of political plays were important items of Broad-Bottom
propaganda. David Mallet and other writers strengthened Lyttelton's ar-
tillery, making it the most formidable in the opposition, aside from the
unrivalled brilliance of the survivors from the Harley-Bolingbroke years,
Pope and Swift. But Lyttelton's greatest recruit and the most formidable
and faithful of Broad-Bottom writers was Henry Fielding, a very experienced and successful dramatic satirist, though he was not yet thirty
years old. His Broad-Bottom plays of 1736-37 were devastating and
popular enough to help determine the ministry to tighten the censorship,
and though he would be forced off the stage in 1737, he would continue
to defend the Broad-Bottoms and smite their enemies and rivals through
the 1740s and earlier 1750s. His recruitment was rapid; if an attribution I
will argue for in Chapter Three is correct, it was first signalled as early as
December 20, 1735, when he urged in a *Craftsman* lead essay the con-

tinuation of the good fight against Walpole. It was also perfectly predictable and natural.

Fielding had attended Eton with Lyttelton, Pitt, and the Grenvilles. Poverty and the need to earn a living had prevented Fielding from attending a university (aside from his brief stay at Leyden), going on the "Grand Tour," or adopting the life of a leisured gentleman. However, he had not lost touch with Lyttelton, the heir to considerable wealth and by 1732 a star rising over the horizon as an intimate of the Prince of Wales and the Cobham circle. Indeed, the evidence is that Lady Mary Wortley Montagu and George Lyttelton were the only distinguished connections the young gentleman-writer had, bright spots at a time when players and hack-writers were his acquaintances.[7] Fielding addressed poetry to Lyttelton in the earlier 1730s and would seem to have liked and admired him, but Lyttelton was then not in a position that would incline him to act as political patron for Fielding or anyone else. A friendship with the Prince of Wales was collateral for a political future, and it was to be expected that Lyttelton, nephew of Cobham and the able son of a minor Walpole placeman, would enter and shine in Commons. Nonetheless, Lyttelton was not elected a member of Parliament until 1734, and would (given his father's and uncle's support of the ministry) surely not have become an opposition politician with a motive for recruiting political satirists if his uncle had not opposed the Excise, been dismissed, and forged a factious instrument of vengeance at the right time.[8] The political significance of Fielding's friendship with Lyttelton remained purely potential through 1734 and, the evidence indicates, even the first half of 1735.

During his first seven years as a writer—very prolific ones—Fielding had no political affiliation and thus no consistent political aims or direction, as will be demonstrated (and literally charted) in Chapter Two. That Fielding was a lover of his country and liberty, and that he despised dishonesty and corruption in public as well as private life are beyond doubt. But he was always a realist (as were most of his contemporaries in the tight, oligarchically smug world of the ruling classes), sure that the national interest would fare at least no worse and his personal interests a great deal better if he and his patrons were on the winning side in the partisan struggles of the day. He certainly saw that neither Walpole nor his enemies had a corner on either virtue or vice, that the possession of office, not the absolute rightness or wrongness of debated measures or moralities, was the basis of their strife. Critics have often assumed that opposition orientation (the opposition seen as a vague corporate entity, somewhat akin to a modern opposition party, rather than the eclectic and unstable alliance of factions, pressure groups, and disgruntled individuals it actually was) was natural for, and adopted early by, Fielding. This will not stand up a moment under close examination; it will not be upheld by an unbiased reading (in the order in which they were written) of the works and variant versions of works he wrote between early 1728 and early 1735. Equally false is the more moderate notion that he consistently evolved into a more violently political author with an increasing Walpole bias in these years. In fact, impelled by motives and pressures that will be explained in Chapter Two, he behaved most inconsistently for seven years, alternating abuse and eulogy of Walpole and opposition leaders, incurring censorial wrath one year and eulogizing Walpole the next, change following change of direction. He became alternatively free with political abuse and shy of it, following public taste and his own whim, trying to fill theatres while avoiding censorship. He repeatedly dragged his coat in the hope (always vain, I am sure) of attracting patronage from either Walpole or an opposition grandee. In short, he was a young man with all the talents required to become a most potent voice of opposition or the ministry, but one without a political cause or affiliation, and his inconsistency showed it. The obvious reason is that Lyttelton and the Broad-Bottoms were not yet factors in politics. One of the ironies of Fielding criticism has been that some critics have been overeager to force consistency on his behaviour before 1735, while others see him as an apostate during his years of steady adherence to the Broad-Bottoms, insisting that he "changed parties" in 1741-42 and admitted it in *The Opposition: A Vision*. In fact his seeming inconsistencies in Walpole's last weeks in office merely reflect the conflicting strategies and concepts of the future (for Fielding's *Vision* is about the near future, not the present) that absorbed the Broad-Bottoms as they strove against rivals in the opposition for the fruits of success when Walpole fell or was forced to shore up his majority by compromising with one of the ambitious opposition factions.

After 1735 Fielding's task as new partisan was clear and he performed brilliantly. *Pasquin* created a stir comparable to the *Beggar's Opera* sensation of 1728, and the *Historical Register* dealt laughing blows to the ministry. As co-manager of the Haymarket Theatre, with James Ralph, Fielding also staged plays of greater violence by others. Here again, it is clear that his allegiance was very specifically to the Broad-Bottom faction, not merely to that figment of the bipartisan mind, "*The* Opposition." One result is that the anti-ministerial satire in his plays of 1736-37 is regularly balanced by equally severe satire on opposition hypocrites and Tory boobies. As is now widely recognized, the opposition then was—as always under George II—a conglomeration of factions and individuals, distrustful at best and prone to rivalry. The Country Tories provided the most votes (as they had done for years and would continue to do through the 1750s) but were very unambitious, distrustful of office holders and seekers, and aware that their allies would desert them whenever office beckoned. They believed in a "Country Party Programme": the need for annual, not septennial Parliaments, strict legislation forbidding placemen and government pensioners to sit in large numbers in Parliament, a foreign policy designed to encourage merchant trade and backed by a very aggressive naval threat to the Spaniards and French. Others only pretended to believe in this "Programme": every ambitious faction in allegiance with the Tories in the

1730s and 1740s had to espouse such measures while in opposition, but rejected them upon entry into office. In addition, before the Broad-Bottoms materialized, there were special-interest factions (e.g., representatives of the London trading classes), the personal followings of men like William Pulteney and Lord Carteret, many smaller cliques, and a variety of more-or-less unconnected individuals. In the latter 1730s the Broad-Bottoms were a new unity within the amorphous conglomerate, which was strengthened as well by the movement of the Prince of Wales and his household into open opposition in 1736-37. Some men could be counted in more than one category—Lyttelton and Pitt were major placemen in the Prince of Wales's household as well as leading Broad-Bottoms.[9] However, it was normal for even such fence-sitters to have a prime affiliation (far narrower and clearer than merely to "opposition") that dictated their behaviour whenever a crisis or a rebuilding of the ministry forced them to choose. Pitt and Lyttelton finally chose the Broad-Bottom connection over the Prince in the 1740s. Fielding learned to despise Pulteney and Carteret more than Walpole while they were still ostensibly on the same side, and he attacked them as worse than Walpole after the Prime Minister fell. The Tories were always ready to desert their temporary allies when their motivation seemed excessively factious. Thus, a play in which Fielding savaged the likes of Pulteney and the Tories, as well as Walpole, for factionalism, corruption, and hypocrisy was quite consistent with his opposition allegiance as well as with the Bolingbrokean idealism of his faction.

After the Licensing Act of 1737 and some time to lick his wounds while studying law, Fielding resumed the attack on Walpole in a Broad-Bottom spirit in *The Champion*, helped by his ex-Haymarket partner, James Ralph. Calling for solidarity against Walpole in one breath and in the next condemning all faction or teasing Tories or insisting on real reform, not just a change in ministers ("measures," not "men"), Fielding was behaving precisely as one would expect a writer with his particular connections to do. At times, as in the "Address to the Electors," published as a long series of *Champion* essays in late 1740, Fielding rivalled Lyttelton or Bolingbroke himself as an espouser of Patriot theory.[10] The same bias is apparent in the spate of pamphlets and other works he put out in 1741 and even in *The Opposition: A Vision* (December, 1741). Fielding freely admitted his authorship of *The Opposition: A Vision* in 1743, at a time when he remained close to the Broad-Bottoms. Its mysteries clear considerably, as hinted earlier, if one recalls (1) that the Broad-Bottoms had come to hate Pulteney and Carteret of the fast-dissolving opposition at least as much as Walpole by late 1741; (2) that they were half convinced that Walpole would survive in the new Parliament by recruiting one of the groups within the old opposition at the cost of posts for its leaders; and (3) that they were intent upon insuring that (whether Walpole fell or triumphed by dividing his enemies) they, not Pulteney and Carteret, would move into the ministry. Certainly, Fielding was wrong (Walpole fell and Pulteney and Carteret triumphed) and he may *seem* to have turned his coat, but his pamphlet was a reflection of his Broad-Bottom loyalties and a position fleetingly adopted in December 1741 by his patrons, not a betrayal of those loyalties.

Fielding's continuing attachment to the Broad-Bottoms is apparent in *Joseph Andrews* and the *Miscellanies*, for it dictated the broadening of the kind of satire formerly aimed at Walpole to blacken Pulteney and Carteret. Fielding became a voice of the "new" opposition (really the "old" one, less Pulteney, Carteret, and the Prince of Wales), indignantly rejecting the "new" Carteret-Pelham coalition, known as the "Wilmington Ministry." Though Walpole was gone, his followers dominated the "new" ministry and maintained their solidarity under the Duke of Newcastle and his brother, Henry Pelham. The really new aspect of the ministry was the inclusion, as one of the Secretaries of State, of Lord Carteret. Anti-Carteret indignation and chagrin at his failure to fight for changed policies or reformed methods after the ministerial reconstruction were standard emotions among opponents of the ministry and Fielding expressed both in 1742-43. Even at the end of its career in opposition (at the precise moment in late 1744 when it closed with the Pelham brothers in the coalition known as the "Broad-Bottom Ministry" and helped force Carteret from office) the faction enjoyed Fielding's support. The extreme anti-Hanover rhetoric of *An Attempt Toward a Natural History of the Hanover Rat* is very like that which Lyttelton and Pitt employed in Commons during the preceding two years and which Chesterfield employed in the new journal he established in 1743, *Old England*.[11]

In 1745 Fielding again demonstrated his Broad-Bottom loyalty. In late 1744 he had sounded very like a Jacobite in mocking "Hanover Rats" and the pernicious effects of "Hanoverian" diplomatic and military policies upon the prosecution of the War of the Austrian Succession. Then the Broad-Bottoms entered the ministry (against the wishes of the King, who favoured Carteret over the Pelhams and their new allies), and within a year the Jacobite invasion of 1745-46 began. Fielding's anti-ministerialism and anti-Hanoverianism vanished utterly. He established *The True Patriot*, in which he hailed George as the best of kings, the Hanoverian Succession as essential to England's liberties and religion, and the once-scorned policies of the ministry at home and abroad (which were little altered) as justified by circumstances. And he did more, for there was a war on in the council chamber as well as on foreign and domestic battlefields. The ministry, with its majorities, and Granville, backed by the king, were vying to destroy one another, while the nation fought both an invasion and a European war. In the early run, under the darkest Jacobite threat, Fielding had to limit his partisanship to the odd sly hint, but the moment the "cabinet crisis" of 1746 forced the king permanently to drop Lord Granville, he converted his obtrusively nonpartisan journal into a propaganda organ for the Broad-Bottom ministry. The metamorphosis Fielding went through between late 1744 and early 1746 might seem surprising to a naïve believer in the myth of simple bipartisanship in eighteenth-century politics, but it was actually the logical result of his attachment to a faction that had found the right moment to sell out for places and was equally determined to repel the Stuart invader and continue in office despite the hostility of George II (who theoretically had the right freely to choose his ministers or "servants"), Carteret, and the weak, Tory-dominated opposition in Commons. One is certain Fielding would have become an opposition writer once more if the ministry his patrons had joined had not survived in 1746, but he was fortunately not forced to do so.

Fielding helped his ministry while it faced the first great challenge to its security: the rivalry with Carteret, which ended in the cabinet crisis of 1746. Thereafter, he rallied to help it over the two further crises that remained before it was completely secure: the election of 1747 and the ending of the War of the Austrian Succession in 1748. He published *A Dialogue Between a Gentleman from London . . . and an Honest Alderman of the Country Party* at the time of the election of 1747, called a year early, as the Parliament (elected in 1741 and still in existence despite two changes in the ministry) did not need to be dissolved until 1748 under the Septennial Act. The ministry won a commanding majority, good for seven years. Since it already had a near-monopoly on debating talent, it was extraordinarily secure after the election; its only vulnerability was in foreign policy. The war on the continent had dragged on for over half a decade, unwinnable, yet unendable without accepting treaty terms from the French that would give the opposition fine opportunities for complaint. After the election, and some final worrying over the relative wisdom of continuing a dismal war or risking a disappointing peace, the ministry chose the latter course at the end of 1747, and Fielding almost simultaneously established *The Jacobite's Journal*. During the months of negotiation, the success and then the precise results of which could not safely be anticipated by a ministerial spokesman, he vilified the opposition as Jacobites, republicans, and hypocrites, just as every ministry's writers had done for decades whenever the real issues were too tender for much touching. Then he metamorphized into a celebrator of the ministry's virtues and the peace terms it had obtained, discontinuing his journal soon after the final treaty was publicized and accepted.

In the years 1746-48, though Fielding was only called away from his work on *Tom Jones* at crisis periods, he was as dedicated a propagandist for the ministry that had absorbed his patrons as the *Gazetteer* writers had been under Walpole. During these years Lyttelton and the Duke of Bedford (who had become the most highly placed of the ministerial Broad-Bottoms with his appointment in 1748 as co-Secretary of State with Newcastle) arranged Fielding's appointments as magistrate in London and Middlesex, and began the financial arrangements that would allow him to take up his magisterial duties. He clearly had earned his preferment, and would work very hard and effectively for his money, but he gratefully dedicated *Tom Jones* to Lyttelton and handsomely acknowledged Bedford's goodness in it. He also imposed anti-Jacobite, anti-opposition satire of the *Jacobite's Journal* variety on his novel, probably in a late revision carried out in the first half of 1748,[12] and he continued to serve his patrons after its publication, defending governmental severity in the Bosavern Penlez case and taking Bedford's side in the Westminster by-election of late 1749.[13] After nearly fifteen years of service Fielding had seen the political struggles of his patrons crowned with some success and his own permanently, if modestly, rewarded through the good offices of Lyttelton and Bedford.

In dealing with Fielding's years as a ministerialist we must remember that eighteenth-century ministries, like their oppositions, were backed by often uneasy alliances of factions and individuals, not the solidity of a modern majority party. Even Walpole never had under discipline nearly enough votes to win a division in a full House of Commons on a controversial issue, though his employment of patronage gave him a solid core group (the "Walpole Whigs" or "Old Corps") large enough to serve as the basis for a majority at times of crisis and keep him in office, provided he could win over a certain number of less disciplined or amateurishly independent cliques and individuals.[14] After his fall, though the Pelhams inherited the "Old Corps" and knew how to use it, ministries were obviously coalitions between elements that were potentially or actually in rivalry. The ministerial coalition was, after all, "rebuilt" twice between the elections of 1741 and 1747. Fielding was not just a ministerialist, as has been said, but a supporter of the Broad-Bottom wing (the "junior partners") in the ministerial coalition, for all the praise he heaped upon Henry Pelham and other "senior partners." As we will see in later chapters this gave peculiar twists to his ministerial work between 1745 and 1749; whenever a Broad-Bottom required defence or praise, he would go all out though the occasion might be trivial from the standpoint of the general ministerial situation.

Fielding's loyalty-within-a-loyalty had a more extreme, negative effect on his writing in the 1750s. His political position was then rendered ambiguous by the very firmness of his factional loyalty and his personal commitments to George Lyttelton and to the Duke of Bedford, who was a great landowner and power in Fielding's London jurisdiction and the source of income-supplementing favours. Bedford even quietly allowed Fielding rent-free tenure of his court and residence in Bow Street.[15] The ministry was secure and seemed solid after the peace crisis passed in late 1748. It had also been more closely compacted in early 1748, when Lord Chesterfield resigned (without going into opposition) and the Duke of Bedford became one of the Secretaries of State, the highest post enjoyed by a Broad-Bottom. However, present security can breed ambition and worry about the future, and in 1751 the Broad-Bottoms (working through Lyttelton and Pitt, Frederick's old dependents) were caballing with the Prince of Wales when Frederick suddenly died and killed their hopes of greater power in the next reign. Worse, they were caught in the act by the King and the Pelhams. Though the rest survived, embarrassed and chastened, the Duke of Bedford was sacrificed, forced to resign, in June 1751. From then on, as we will see in Chapter Seven, Fielding had one patron in opposition—for Bedford was not one to resign as tamely as Chesterfield had in 1748—and another patron, Lyttelton, still in office, along with the rest of the Broad-Bottoms. Even in this difficult situation Fielding managed to write according to his loyalties, but in the works, including *Amelia*, he published in the remaining three years of his life he had to avoid either attacking opposition to an extent likely to irritate Bedford (who had the tact to recruit James Ralph as his propagandist,[16] leaving Fielding free to avoid offence) or the slightest appearance of criticizing the ministry. The same attachments that had made him an opposition firebrand in the later 1730s and earlier 1740s and a strong anti-opposition voice in the later 1740s made him a most cautious political commentator in his last years. It was not merely old age, contentment, or the new dignity of his magistracy that took the political violence out of Fielding in the 1750s: he was walking the finest of lines between patrons divided by the vagaries of political alignment.

This study will demonstrate in detail that Fielding's political career cannot be understood unless one focusses upon the narrow, realistic realm of faction and personal obligation the eighteenth-century politicians and propagandists inhabited. We must move behind the pretences and the rhetoric of those involved and beyond the anachronistic, fictitious party dualisms that historians used to believe in and literary scholars are only now learning sufficiently to distrust. It was not an idealistic world or one in which men at war over office actually differed as much as they pretended on matters of national interest, constitutional questions, or political morality, nor was it a world really built around conflicts between "Whig" and "Tory," "Court" and "Country," "Hanoverian" and "Jacobite," "*The* Ministry" and "*The* Opposition," or even the "Ins" and the "Outs."[17] The dualistic nature of parliamentary voting, "Aye" *versus* "Nay," and the terminology used by contemporaries—often loosely or disingenuously—in rallying and abusing friends and foes, as well as our own bipartisan habits of thought, may suggest a falsely simplistic picture. However, Fielding's was a world of shifting alliances in which even a politician or a writer who loved England was apt to be most essentially influenced at moments of hard choice by attachments to relatively narrow circles of friends and patrons. In his early years Fielding lacked a firm attachment of this kind and behaved accordingly. Then for twenty years he navigated the political shoals according to a very firm commitment to a faction and patrons within it, moving parallel to Lyttelton and the Broad-Bottoms as they changed directions and alliances.

Chapter Two

Fielding's Early Career: 1728-35

1. The Pattern

The first difficulty in approaching the political aspects of Fielding's early career may be called the "Tory view" of eighteenth-century literary history. This assumes that writing for the opposition was the normal, respectable course for a satirist in Walpole's England. A corollary is that deviation from this pattern by a writer of genius was just that, a deviation which tended to yield to the natural opposition bent of literary talent with the passage of time. Fielding *ought* immediately to have joined the best writers of the 1720s and 1730s in execrating Walpole's corruption and paying homage to the patriotic idealism of Walpole's enemies, and otherwise good scholars have over-emphasized the anti-Walpole bias of some early works, and ignored the obvious pro-ministerial bias of others. Some have detected, in the teeth of plain evidence, a more or less steady evolution in the years before 1736 from political neutrality or unreliability to an anti-Walpole commitment. The "Tory view" of literary history must be rejected not only because it is wrong, but also because Fielding's early political writing can only be falsified by it.

It is understandable that political satire in the late 1720s and 1730s is automatically associated with opposition to Walpole. Jonathan Swift's *Gulliver's Travels*, the political poems Alexander Pope produced in the decade or so following the publication of the original version of the *Dunciad* in 1728, and John Gay's *Beggar's Opera* have all outlived the narrow partisan issues with which they are, in part, concerned. Their genius understandably eclipses the lesser political or politically tinged works that poured from the pens of opposition and ministerial writers during this period of extraordinary obsession with politics among the literary. Even below these peaks most of the works which continue, at least

13

sometimes, to be reprinted and read also fall within the opposition category: e.g., Thomson's *Liberty*, Fielding's *Tragedy of Tragedies, Pasquin*, and *Historical Register*, and Lyttelton's *Persian Letters*. Further yet from the tastes of common readers, the balance of quality (as well as quantity) even in partisan journalism greatly favours opposition. The opposition's premier journal, the *Craftsman* (founded in 1726 and maintained at a very high level of quality until the mid-1730s under the editorship of Nicholas Amhurst, and with the inspiration and contributions of Lord Bolingbroke and William Pulteney) offered a blend of witty elegance and partisan venom. It was matched in the first half of the century only in two much earlier and shorter-lived ministerial journals, the *Examiner* of Swift and the *Freeholder* of Addison. In the decade and a half following its establishment, the *Craftsman's* quality was only briefly rivalled (and I think never equalled) in the early runs of the two opposition journals that took up the slack when it began to deteriorate in the closing years of the 1730s: Lyttelton and Chesterfield's *Common Sense* and the *Champion* of Fielding and James Ralph.

Though the quality of its argumentation and style is underestimated by modern literary scholars (who usually seem to have little first-hand knowledge of it), the ministry's *Daily Gazetteer* never really approached the standards of the best opposition journalism. The many lesser government journals that slogged away before their demise in the amalgamation of 1735 that spawned the *Gazetteer* are in depressing contrast to the *Craftsman*. There were ministerialists who could argue persuasively in pamphlets as well as debate, and make opponents wince with their barbs— John, Lord Hervey, or Robert Walpole himself when he was occasionally tempted to answer his critics in print. But here too the literary advantage of the opposition was marked; it could hardly be otherwise with the talented William Pulteney, Lord Carteret (after 1730), Lord Chesterfield (after 1733), and George Lyttelton (after 1735) voting in the minority, and Lord Bolingbroke joining in from his half-disenfranchised sidelines and enheartening the inner councils of opposition. It was nearly always true in the eighteenth century (one exception is probably the period 1710-14) that opposition sought and enjoyed a stronger press than ministry, indeed that its literary strength was in roughly inverse proportion to voting strength in Parliament. As an anonymous wag of 1734 succinctly observed, it was proverbial "that Losers will speak."[1] In the 1730s the gap was unusually great, owing partly to the continuation in opposition of the men of genius—Swift, Pope, Bolingbroke, and friends—who had been associated with the Harley-Bolingbroke ministry, and partly to Walpole's habits of forcing politicians of conspicuous eloquence and ability—men like William Pulteney and Lord Carteret—out of office and ignoring literary talent.

The literary brilliance of the opposition in the age of Walpole may, in short, explain the "Tory myth." But it must not obscure Fielding's dubiety about the relative attractiveness of a commitment to ministry or opposition before 1735. Nor should it distort the pattern that is apparent in an overview of the many works he produced during this period. Fielding expressed a general contempt for the rascality of politicians on *either* side of the partisan skirmishings of the time that he probably really felt. A similar attitude surfaces periodically throughout his long career. However, this gave way briefly, alternatively, and repeatedly to (1) sharp satire on the opposition and eulogy of Walpole; (2) satire on Walpole, the ministry, and even the royal family; (3) a careful, even ostentatious avoidance of political questions. Fielding's early work clearly shows several things. First, he was interested in obtaining patronage from either side, though in all probability neither the ministry nor the opposition ever solicited or rewarded his aid, and though his considerable income from the stage, at least after 1730, must have rendered a patron more a desire than a necessity. Second, he had no firm political allegiance during these years, normally employing political satire on the ministry or the opposition to appeal to the tastes of audiences, the first consideration for a professional dramatist, as well as to signal his willingness to accept patronage. Third, he was initially more inclined to support the ministry than its opponents, ready indeed to contemplate attacking Walpole's opponents in a poem of 1729 (which he wisely left unpublished) with a libellous bluntness only equalled—if at all—in his career by the satire on another opposition in *The Jacobite's Journal* in 1747-48. Finally, Fielding obviously did *not* evolve, in the sense of moving steadily or consistently toward opposition or even in the direction of greater involvement with politics between 1728 and 1735. His metamorphosis into a major enemy of the ministry between 1735 and 1736 was sudden, a sharp change of direction (or more precisely discovery of a direction) resulting from the new factor stressed in Chapter I, the inclusion of old friends and future patrons in the Broad-Bottom wing of the opposition that took shape in the fall of 1735.

If one shades one's eyes against the glamour of the opposition satirists, the reasons for the prolonged hesitation of the ambitious (and, at least at first, impecunious) young Fielding over supporting ministry or opposition and his gestures toward soliciting government patronage are not difficult to fathom. Lady Mary Wortley Montagu was Fielding's cousin and friend, and the only personal patron or advisor from whom he had a reasonable hope of support or a good word in the right ears. She was an admirer of Walpole and an increasingly caustic critic of the great opposition wits who had been her friends. It was to the fascinating Lady Mary that Fielding, not much more than a boy, despite his talent, at twenty years of age, dedicated his first play, the relatively apolitical *Love in Several Masques* (1728). It was to her that he addressed his first major political satire in 1729 (recently recovered by Isobel Grundy among Lady Mary's papers),[2] an extended blank verse poem which violently assaults the leading opposition wits, Swift, Pope, Bolingbroke, and Gay, and which she may have advised him not to print. As noted earlier, George Lyttelton only entered Parliament after the election of 1734, and would not have exerted pressures in the direction of opposition. Though it is not primarily political, a poem (again unpublished until discovered by Isobel Grundy) Fielding addressed to Lyttelton as late as the spring of 1733 is somewhat slanted against the opposition. This is not surprising since Lyttelton's father was a Walpole placeman[3] and the son's future opposition patron, Lord Cobham, remained a majority voter until he revolted at the height of the Excise crisis. Lady Mary, in short, was Fielding's most promising potential avenue to patronage, the only connection at all likely to aid him in obtaining an obvious *desideratum* for a young man in his circumstances, the patronage of a "Great Man."

The lucrative possibilities of satire on the model of John Gay's *Beggar's Opera* were obvious. It enjoyed record runs in early 1728, almost immediately before the appearance of *Love in Several Masques*, and would repeatedly influence Fielding's later opposition drama and prose. However, Fielding surely saw the dangers symbolized by the banning in late 1728 of Gay's *Polly*, a fate that later overcame Fielding's first really violent opposition play, *The Grub-Street Opera*, in 1731, and ended Fielding's career as an opposition dramatist in 1737. In addition, considerable financial and patronage rewards might be earned by a writer lucky enough to win ministerial support or employment. Despite his genteel background (his father, though unable to aid him much financially, finally rose to the rank of Lieutenant-General in 1741), Fielding was a professional. He was dependent upon the profits from his writing for a living, a fact that differentiates him sharply from Pope, Swift, and Bolingbroke, who would have been embarrassed at the thought of writing political satire for money. Government patronage was not, all evidence indicates, very easy to attract for a writer with the "sin of wit," owing to the relative invulnerability of any ministry with a comfortable majority to opposition criticism and the peculiarly thick skin of Robert Walpole under such criticism. The most a writer could normally hope for was a laborious position with a government journal, an employment Fielding would have felt was beneath him in the early 1730s. Writers as unlikely as Edward Young (in his unspeakably inept patriotic odes) nonetheless scrambled after the patronage given to those who won ministerial favour during this period. Fielding may have learned slowly that opposition patrons were, of necessity, far more approachable by those less ready to engage in dogged political hack-work than such men as William Arnall and James Ralph. Fielding's friend from 1729 onward, and later his literary and business associate, Ralph was a ministerial journalist until the many ministerial journals were consolidated into the "official" organ, *The Daily Gazetteer*, in 1735.[4] Significantly, what little evidence there is suggests that the rewards offered by the ministry to journalists might have enticed Fielding if he had not found the theatre so profitable. Records—which have miraculously survived—of expenditures from the Secret Service Fund to buy and distribute by post copies of government journals in 1733-34 indicate, for example, that the government bought 2050 copies a week of the *London Journal* from May 11 to June 8, 1734 at a total cost of £272 1s.8d., and spent £3,435 to purchase and distribute copies of William Arnall's *Free Briton* between January 1733 and January 1734.[5] It is impossible to determine whether any comparable support was extended to ministerial apologists in other genres, but these were enormous figures in the penny and shilling world of the eighteenth-century author. Then, too, a young gentleman determined by becoming a hackney writer not only to avoid becoming a hackney coachman (as he joked to Lady Mary), but also to find the means to live genteelly might have reflected that Swift became Dean of St. Patrick's and Addison became a Secretary of State only after successful stints as ministerial apologists.

Finally, it seems more than possible that Fielding was not immune (particularly with Lady Mary as older woman-confidante) to the envy and sensitivity to imagined or actual rebuffs that young writers are prone to feel toward established authors and the socially and intellectually desirable, but often impenetrable, circles in which they move. A very young man hoping to establish and enrich himself as a writer in a literary epoch dominated by the Scriblerians—Pope, Swift, Bolingbroke, and Gay—might almost be forgiven such feelings, particularly if, as it happened in Fielding's case, his first play appeared with modest success during the triumphant initial run of Gay's *Beggar's Opera*. It is easy to read as the product of such envy "An Original Song Written on the Appearance of the Beggar's Opera" which Fielding wrote in 1728 and modern scholarship has rescued from deserved obscurity. It was not yet within Fielding's power to equal the success of Gay's play and he was not yet prepared to pay it the compliment of imitation as he would repeatedly from 1730 onwards. After drawing a brief satiric picture of the horror of Shakespeare, Addison, Dryden, and Wycherley at Gay's "famous play," the song ends with this ineptly sarcastic jab at the play's popularity:

> Now all the mob from town and court;
> Came for to see this hotch potch sport;
> To see this famous play, which ran both night and day
> Call'd the Beggar's Opera—Oh brave Gay![6]

Fielding's scorn coexisted with attempts to associate his fledgling efforts with the greater works of the literary giants. His first published work, *The Masquerade: A Poem* (1728), appeared under the pseudonym "Lemuel Gulliver, Poet Laureate to the King of Lilliput" and several of his early plays appeared under the pseudonym "Scriblerus Secundus." Even the poem of 1729 implies vacillation: in it Fielding compliments Pope by adopting the mock-epic form and the techniques of the *Dunciad*, while satirizing his dullness. The poem perhaps remained unfinished because Fielding faced his inability to satirize Pope in Pope's manner. Writing so inferior to the satires of those it attacks could not earn him more than the amused contempt of its targets or a place in the next version of the *Dunciad*, perhaps alongside his friend James Ralph.

Fielding did not even begin tentatively to assume the role of gadfly to the Prime Minister that many vaguely associate with his early dramatic work until mid-1730. Despite a sprinkling of anti-Walpole hits in the 1739 version of *The Author's Farce* (the presence of which may seem surprising now that we know about his poetic fragment of 1729), he began really to indulge in satire on the ministry only in the last of his four plays of 1730, *Rape upon Rape; or, The Justice Caught in his Own Trap*. Moreover, the first and quite discrete chapter in the tale of his development as an anti-ministerial writer was very short-lived, begun in June 1730 when *Rape upon Rape* first appeared, continued in *The Tragedy of Tragedies*, and concluded under pressures of government censorship with the ironically masked near-sedition of *The Grub-Street Opera* (or *Welsh Opera*) of mid-1731. It was followed by a phase, lasting for over four years, during which he veered, without consistent direction, from political quiescence to pro-Walpole eulogy to anti-Walpole satire and back to quiescence. Opposition was not a natural or a consistent orientation for Fielding in the first seven years of his stage career. If one resists the urge to over-emphasize every item of anti-Walpole satire or to imagine a consistent tendency to evolve toward opposition in these years, one is left with a very complex, if more accurate, picture. The young Fielding was extraordinarily prolific as well as politically flexible. Counting the various versions of some items, he produced twenty-four comedies and farces in the seven years ending in 1735, when he was only twenty-eight. His brilliant Etonian friends, Lyttelton and Pitt, merely on the threshold of their political careers in the mid-1730s, were late bloomers compared to him. Successive works reveal striking variations not only in Fielding's political bias but in his degree of interest in political matters. All of Fielding's early plays are "miscellaneous" (a term he uses to describe his writing for the *Champion* in 1740), blending satire on many targets, buffoonery, serious didactic argument, parody, witty comedy, song, and dance. Some plays are very political, others less so, others not at all. The result is a maze that requires a plan.

The purpose of the chart that follows is simple: to indicate at a glance the degree of political interest and bias of Fielding's major early works. It is straightforwardly chronological, except as noted, arranging works according to the month and year of their first performance or (in the case of works Fielding left unpublished) their composition. Items on the extreme left are strongly pro-opposition or anti-ministerial, items on the extreme right are strongly pro-Walpole or anti-opposition, and items in the centre are politically neutral, either because they scant or ignore politics or because they satirize both ministry and opposition. Those between either extreme and the centre are dominated by degrees of the bias represented by their distance from the neighbouring extreme. Items with a considerable political focus are printed in italics, less political items are in Roman type, and the titles of wholly or nearly apolitical ones are in Roman type and placed in square brackets. In the two cases where a work and its dedication are separately charted, the implication is that each seems to have its own political tendency. A question mark after a work indicates (1) that I am not certain about the propriety of its

	Opposition (or Anti-Ministerial)	Neutral, Balanced, or Apolitical	Ministerial (or Anti-Opposition)
1728		(Jan.) [The Masquerade, a Poem] (Feb.) Love in Several Masques	
1729			Long unpublished fragment (2 cantos) of a mock-epic poem[a]

1730[b]	(June) Rape upon Rape } or, The
	                 } Justice
	 (Dec.) The Coffee-House } Caught
	         Politician
		(Feb.) The Temple Beau
		 (Mar.) The Author's Farce; original version?
		 (Apr.) Tom Thumb: A Tragedy
		 (May) Tom Thumb. A Tragedy by Scriblerus Secundus }}?
			?

1731	(Mar.) The Tragedy of Tragedies;
	     or The Life and Death of
	     Tom Thumb the Great
	 (Apr.) The Welsh Opera?
	 (Aug.) The Genuine Grub-Street Opera } ?
	 (Summer)[c] The Grub-Street Opera
		(Mar.) [The Letter Writers]
		 ?	

1732[d]		(Jan.) The Lottery (Feb.) The Modern Husband[e]? (June) The Old Debauchees (June) The Covent-Garden Tragedy (July) The Mock Doctor?	Dedication to Sir Robert Walpole

1733		(Mar.) [The Miser]?
		 (Apr.) [Deborah; or, a Wife for
		         You All]
			(Feb.-Apr.) "An Epistle
			     to Mr. Lyttelton"
			     (unpublished)

1734	(Jan.) The Author's Farce; revised version? Dedication to Lord Chesterfield	(Jan.) [The Intriguing Chambermaid] (Apr.) Don Quixote in England?[f]	
1735		(Jan.) [An Old Man Taught Wisdom] (Feb.) [The Universal Gallant]	

[a] This poem and the "Epistle" of 1733 have recently been uncovered among the papers of Lady Mary Wortley Montagu.

[b] By early 1730 a draft of Don Quixote in England and The Temple Beau had been rejected by the Drury Lane Company and Fielding had worked on The Wedding Day (performed first in 1743); by the fall he had drafted The Modern Husband (performed 1734).

[c] The title page of The Grub-Street Opera says it was published in 1731, but recently scholars have conjectured that it was not actually published until the 1740s or 1750s. (I accept L.J. Morrissey's argument that it was published in 1755.)

[d] I do not include the "letter" from "Philalethes" in The Daily Post for July 31, 1732, which is often attributed to Fielding; neither the argument from style nor the argument from content sufficiently suggests his authorship.

[e] First drafted, shown to Lady Mary Wortley Montagu, and even "puffed" by The Craftsman in September, 1730; dedication surely written in 1734.

[f] The "Election scenes" added to the play in 1734 are its most political material.

classification; or (2) that, as in the case of the *Welsh/Grub-Street Opera*, it presents an anomalous mixture of political attitudes, and yet, on balance, cannot be classified at the centre of indifference; or (3) that, though I am confident about its placement, there is sufficient scholarly debate about its political significance to require detailed adjudication in a later chapter. The cumbersome procedure of a chart will I hope seem justified by the present nebulousness of our concept of Fielding's early political activities and by the odd patterns in those activities that only such a chart can readily reveal.

2. The Young Wit, 1728-30

The Masquerade of 1728, which Fielding published under the pseudonym Lemuel Gulliver on the day *The Beggar's Opera* opened, is relatively apolitical. Some lines might be construed in a partisan way, but it is distortive to do so: for example, his statement that Count Heidegger, masquerade-master, was thrown out of hell because of his ugliness and made by Satan "First minister of 's Masquerade" is aimed primarily at Heidegger and masquerades and only secondarily at Walpole. Fielding's concern to associate himself with Swift, who so recently had published the greatest prose satire in the language, does not indicate a desire to endorse the politics of the "Tory wits." Even the "Song" which, as noted earlier, satirizes *The Beggar's Opera* ignores its politics. Only the major work of 1728, *Love in Several Masques* (first performed February 16; printed February 23), includes political satire, and it is relatively sparse and directed about equally at the government and its opponents. It is a regular comedy, no more than lightly tinged with non-partisan (or more accurately, "bipartisan") political badinage, a strikingly unpolitical play in a capital excited by Gay's Newgate opera and soon to take sides over the banning of Gay's *Polly*.

In *Love in Several Masques* Sir Positive Trap is an anti-ministerial country squire, the first in a long line of courtier-hating country boobies in Fielding's work that culminated in Squire Western. Sir Positive's "Country" bias is apparent in his pride in being a baronet, an "English" title, and his withering contempt for "Coronets," titled courtiers. The "Country Interest" is again jabbed in Lord Formal's answer to Merital's hope that "good principles" will "engage some [lady] or other to chuse me." He sneers, "It would as soon engage a Country Borough to chuse you Parliament-Man."[7] The motivations of ambitious opposition leaders are also questioned when it is predicted that the wife of a satirist of women will say: "Like a detracting Courtier in disgrace . . ./ he only wants a Place" (p. 52). On the other side, the ridiculously foppish, cynical Lord Formal is an insulting caricature of a courtier, an ignoramus whose praise of "that divine Collection of polite learning written by Mr. Gulliver" implies that he has not read or could not understand *Gulliver's Travels*. The final and most pointed thrust in the play epitomizes its political balance. Sir Positive Trap, comically reflecting the landed economic prejudices of his class, asks Merital, "Does your Estate lie in Terra Firma or in the Stocks." Merital's answer cleverly combines standard satiric allusions to Walpole's supposed favouring of the "Moneyed Interest" and the minister's nickname, "Brass": "In a stock of Assurance, Sir. My Cash is all Brass, and I carry it in my forehead, for fear of pickpockets" (p. 67).

The political satire in this non-partisan play is merely the first trace of the audience-pleasing technique that Fielding began to employ more extensively in *The Author's Farce* of 1730 and wittily defined (albeit with an opposition stress) in 1737. Asked about the best subject for a successful play, the First Player in *The Historical Register* answers:

> First Player.
>> Why no subject at all, sir, but I would have a humming deal of satire, and I would repeat in every page that courtiers are cheats and don't pay their debts, that lawyers and rogues, physicians, blockheads, soldiers, cowards, and ministers -------
> Second Player.
>> What, what, sir?
> First Player.
>> Nay, I'll only name 'em, that's enough to set the audience a-hooting.[8]

1729

When he wrote *Love in Several Masques* Fielding was not firmly set upon a career as a professional dramatist; he soon left for the University of Leyden, enrolling on March 16, 1728. When he returned to London in mid-1729, he could not afford further leisure or formal education—his father might promise, but could not pay, an allowance adequate for a young gentleman. He had the energy of a twenty-one-year-old who has found a vocation. Before the end of 1729 he offered plays drafted abroad to the Drury Lane Company, which turned them down. As noted earlier, he also wrote, probably in the late summer and fall, the ambitious poem preserved by Lady Mary, who had experienced the first of the many pains which would be inflicted by her former Scriblerian friends upon the appearance of Pope's original *Dunciad* in May 1728. If the lengthy fragment of this effort recently unearthed by Isobel Grundy had been printed instead of buried among Lady Mary's voluminous literary memorabilia, contemporaries would have noted a striking alteration of the witty, uncommittedly good-humoured author of *Love in Several Masques* into a scurrilous champion of Walpole and enemy of the "Tory wits." There would also have been no modern theorizing about Fielding's native leanings toward opposition or assertions that later compliments to Walpole *must* have been ironical. The mock-epic fragment (it has no title) is blunt, slanderously partisan ministerial propaganda, dwelling upon the danger supposedly posed by self-serving opposition spokesmen, dubiously loyal to the Present

Establishment in Church and State. It treats the continuation in power of Sir Robert at the head of a loyal "Whig" ministry as the only guarantee of the Hanoverian, Protestant *status quo.*

The exaggerated fears about the safety of the Constitution expressed in the poem are not, of course, to be taken seriously. Fielding certainly recovered from them by 1730, and he was not again to pretend to worry about the loyalty of an opposition until 1746-48, when he was writing as the apologist of a ministry beleaguered by quite loyal foes. In 1729, as in 1748, the themes in question—the disloyalty and designs upon the Establishment of a "Tory" (read "Jacobite") dominated opposition and the necessity of preserving the ministry to preserve that Establishment—were the common cant of anti-opposition writers. They were as predictable as the opposition writers' continual insistence upon the patriotic intent of their attacks on a corrupt ministry that had come between the People and the King, whom they distinguished from his ministers. Only confusion results from the assumption—one that flaws Isobel Grundy's otherwise sound introduction to the text of the rediscovered poem—that "Walpole's importance to Fielding rested largely on his assuring the Hanoverian Succession." It is very difficult to maintain such an assumption in view, first, of the general employment of this rhetorical chimera by ministers and their apologists from 1714 through the 1750s and, second, of Fielding's intermittent but sometimes very severe criticism of the minister after 1730. Grundy is forced to suggest that Fielding was so ignorant of Walpole's actual political methods in 1729 that he sincerely idealized Walpole as a "constitutional hero." This impression, she suggests, "could not withstand any first-hand knowledge of the minister's dirty methods in the day-to-day exercise of power." Repeating the false assertion of J. R. Brown that Fielding gradually became an opponent of the minister as his political knowledge grew between 1730 and 1736, she concludes that "the gradual sharpening of Fielding's satire from the good humour of the 1730s to the intensity of 1736 is therefore a natural development."[9] The development of Fielding's satiric bent as a dramatist reveals no such consistent evolution. His attitude toward Walpole may have changed for the worse during these years, though the "Dedication" to Walpole of *The Modern Husband* of 1732 indicates the untrustworthiness of such an assumption. But the most acceptable conclusion seems to be that the poem of 1729 was written by an ambitious young man hoping possibly to curry ministerial favour and certainly to please Lady Mary Wortley Montagu. He was aware that Walpole was neither a lily-white bastion of endangered Hanoverianism and Protestantism nor the devil incarnate slandered in the opposition press, and determined (at least until good sense and, I would guess, good advice from Lady Mary changed his plans) to flatter the minister and blacken his enemies in broad enough strokes to win ministerial favour. Flattering a prospective patron and libelling his enemies were venial and very common sins in Fielding's day, and I would sooner admit that Fielding was guilty of it than picture him as the kind of upright imbecile who could literally believe (at least until a year later!) the extreme assertions about Walpole and the opposition wits offered in his poem.

The rediscovered draft fragment of the poem consists of three cantos in heroic couplets, the first of 194 lines, the second of 253 lines, and the third of 161 lines. It begins, without the ceremony of an invocation, with a lament addressed by the Goddess Dulness [sic] to her favourite son Codrus (Alexander Pope) in which she bemoans the decline of her dominion over England since it became a Protestant nation, since "The Monkish days! Those glorious Days of Rhime!" (p. 219). The incursion of wit upon the province of Dulness since the accession of George II ("that hated Sun arisen in the West") in 1727 is lamented with particular bitterness in lines that offer a fulsome and somewhat inappropriate compliment to the King and Queen:

> Look up, my Son, and see it's Glories shine.
> See Pallas boast the Smiles of Caroline
> While George and she Wit's brightest Patrons reign
> Vain all our Efforts! all our Hopes are vain! (p. 221)

"Never," Dulness grimly concludes, "shall England more my God head own / While such a Race expect the British throne" (p. 221), and she charges Codrus with altering the Succession. Thus, the poem first associates opposition authorship with a desire to alter the Establishment in Church and State.

Codrus and Bernardus (the publisher, Bernard Lintot) decide to call a meeting of the Grub-Street "Nobles." First, Codrus visits the nether throne of the god Rhime, who acknowledges that he begot Codrus upon Dulness, praises the soporific effect of his work, and ironically compliments John Gay's plays. Rhime laments that "Caleb" (i.e., the writers of *The Craftsman*, ostensibly written by "Caleb D'anvers, Esq.," and more specifically, Lord Bolingbroke, its co-inspirer with William Pulteney) does not use rhyme in Codrus' manner:

> Oh! that great Caleb would my power Confess
> His Nonsense and his Lies in Metre dress
> W------- [Walpole] himself might then be taught to fear
> And England view her fancied dangers near
> Charm'd with sweet Sounds the world might give the Praise
> (Which they deny his Politicks)—t' his Lays. (p. 225)

"Canto 2nd" begins with Dulness' arrival at Codrus' "Lofty Garret." She appears in a dream, as "L.B—" (Lord Bolingbroke) to Codrus, who has fallen asleep reading his own work. She rebukes his sloth ("No Chains of Slumbers should thy Eye-lids keep / Let it be still thy Readers lot to sleep" [p. 227]), asks how he can sleep when Gay's *Beggar's Opera* and *Polly* ("Sure none ee're took so Low a Road to Fame" [p. 228]) serve her cause, and orders him to form "a writing Company"—"some fam'd like thee for Nonsense and for Noise" (p. 228). The scene then shifts to a meeting of the "Grubstreet Bards," which oc-

cupies the rest of "Canto 2nd" and "Canto 3rd," which Codrus opens
by relaying Dulness' instructions. They may reflect Fielding's anti-
Scriblerian jealousy: "She bids us in a Company unite / And suffer none
besides ourselves to write" (p. 229).

   The major political focus of the poem becomes apparent when the
"Company" argues over who has done most toward Dulness' re-
establishment, paralleled throughout with the re-establishment of
Roman Catholicism and absolute Stuart rule. First Caleb (Bolingbroke;
The Craftsman) brags:

> What Floods of ink have from our Goose quill fell
> Whatever Feuds in jarring Factions rage,
> All, all arose from our exclaiming Page.
> Squires [i.e., the "Country" opposition] thoughtless of
>   their Hounds and Drink I've made
> Priests of the Gospel—Shop-keepers of Trade.
> Not Orpheus (tho more tuneful was his song)
> Could draw more stupid senseless things along
> For what each Saturday my Papers speak
> The Realm my echo murmurs all the Week. (p. 230)

Ilar (John Gay) objects that the *Craftsman's* political satire is too witty:

> . . . tho thy Stile be often dull 'tis true
> Thy great Invention proves thee of another Crew.
> On me the Goddess should her Bays bestow
> My thoughts, my Stile, my subject all were low.
> Plain, open! Scandal, spoke my New[gate] Muse
> My Satyr did not railly but abuse
> Dull, senseless Libel level'd at the great
> ....
> Wit certainly might stand tho W[alpole] fell. (p.230)

   Caleb's answer is the centre of the political satire in the three cantos.
His witty assaults on the government are designed to reintroduce
"Popery," eliminating all the "Learning, Wit, and Knowledge" that pros-
per in a free state:

> Were Popery once Master of the Ball
> How soon must Learning, Wit and Knowledge fall
> Wit (like a Summer Flower) can only thrive
> By Liberty's warm Beams preserv'd alive
> And should the Star of Popery arise
> The Star of Liberty must quit the Skies
> But ah! it labours to ascend in Vain
> By G---- [God or George?] depress'd beneath an Iron Chain.
>   (pp. 230-31)

Caleb says his real aim is to destroy the King by destroying Walpole, in the
hope of profiting from political chaos:

> Then knows not Ilar to what mightier End
> All my seditious, Lieing Writings Tend
> Look through the long Record of Ages past
> The M----[inister] first falls the K----[ing] at last

....
May all the Powers! to send that Day conspire
While we enjoy the Plunder of the Fire. (p. 231)

Though colourable, if untrue, in the case of Bolingbroke (fairly recently returned from exile for Jacobite treason in Queen Anne's last days) the implication that the *Craftsman* aimed to overturn the Establishment in Church and State is absurd. It is a perfect example of the hyperbolic rhetorical fiction, so dear to ministerial authors, that enmity toward the ministry implied enmity toward the Establishment. More plausible, and probably closer to Fielding's perception of the opposition's feet of clay, is Caleb's concluding statement. It includes an extended panegyric upon Walpole's services to the nation, unambiguous and stressed enough to serve as a signal for patronage. It is not dissimilar to the dedication to Walpole Fielding prefixed to *The Modern Husband* in 1732, and it may justify believing that Fielding really did write two comic *Epistles to Walpole* in 1730 and 1731 (only published in the *Miscellanies* of 1743), and that the compliment to Walpole's foreign and domestic policies in the 1730 *Epistle* was not ironical.[10] Caleb also "frankly" admits he wishes to bring Walpole down in order to force himself into the post thus vacated (here Caleb probably represents all the ambitious leaders of opposition, including William Pulteney, co-backer of *The Craftsman*, and Lord Carteret, whose relationship with the opposition was becoming closer, though he remained Lord Lieutenant of Ireland until 1730):

The Man whom publick Statues should reward
Against the Gibbet carefully should guard
For Scandal by the disaffected Mouth
Is Sown and Scatter'd like the Gree[cian]'s Tooth
....
W[alpole] thy services shall be vain
Thy place will be our certain Prize—for that
You know, my Friends, I'm chiefly aiming at. (pp. 231-32)

Enraged by Caleb's boasts, Codrus angrily insists on his own merits, combining again religious and political heterodoxy: "Has he at W[alpole] struck—have not my Darts / Been boldly thrown at much superior Hearts / And has he Aim'd at one Religion's Fall / I by my Writings will extirpate all." Then Ochistes (Jonathan Swift) attempts to mediate the dispute:

To Caleb's Lot P[rime] M[inister] is due
But Poet L[aureate] shall devolve on you
Our Self the S[ee] of C[anterbury] fills
Physician [John Arbuthnot] be the Poet read in Bills
Ilar and Fog—shall Sec [i.e., Secretaries of State] be
D---- W----n will with C[hancellor] agree. (p. 232)

"Fog" is either Nathaniel Mist, editor of *Mist's Weekly Journal* until he fled abroad to avoid prosecution in 1728, or Charles Molloy, editor of *Fog's Weekly Journal*. Molloy's essays, James Ralph later implied, occasionally revealed disloyalty. "D---- W----n" is probably the Duke of Wharton, a Jacobite whose violent attack from exile on Walpole in *Mist's Weekly Journal*, August 24, 1728, led to its suppression.[11] Their inclusion is a final libellous association of opposition and Jacobitism. The second canto ends in low comedy as Codrus, a Lilliputian to the Gulliverian Ochistes, sputters about his superiority until Ochistes nearly squeezes him to death between his giant thumbs.

In "Canto 3rd" Grub-Streeters try to overcome their jealousies, Ilar suggesting that they choose the new Prime Minister by lot, Ochistes, Codrus, and Caleb each arguing he deserves the post. Finally (p. 237) Codrus begs, "Let us no longer talk—but act for fame," and displays a copy of "The Se[quel] to the B[eggar's] O[pera]" (Gay's *Polly*). He implies it was written collaboratively by the Scriblerians, and suggests that the relative popularity of the contributions of each contributor determine the new Prime Minister:

> As all in this have shewn our utmost Powers
> So he—whose Song shall gain the most Encores
> P---- M---- in future times shall be,
> And by his Name we call the C----. (p. 237)

Fielding briefly and apolitically satirizes the pantomimes and Harlequinades that were the speciality of John Rich's company, which had performed Gay's *Beggar's Opera* and rehearsed *Polly* before performance was forbidden in December 1728, but he soon returns to politics. The fragment ends with a sneer at the suppression of *Polly* as a defeat for the opposition wits, depicting Rich's decision to drop the play as a result of a warning from the "God of Pantomime" not to risk presecution by performing it. The caution to Rich came on December 2, 1728 from the Duke of Grafton, Lord Chamberlain, in the form of an order to suspend performance until he examined it, and was followed by a final ban on performance ten days later. But Fielding's fanciful version of events attempts to rob Gay of the aura of anti-Establishment heroism that descended on him when governmental power prevented the performance of his play, making *Polly* a resounding success and symbol of opposition defiance upon publication. The final couplet of the poem is wittier than much of Fielding's first extended political satire:

> The Gods resolve no Nonsense shall be sung
> In any but the Soft Italian Tongue. (p. 239)

Charles B. Woods suggested that Fielding "had the reputation of belonging to the outskirts of Walpole's camp" in 1731;[12] if rumours about this poem were current, it is not hard to see why.

1730

In 1730, back from Leyden, Fielding hit his stride as a dramatist with a flair for amusing variations on the irregular forms—ballad opera, farce—that were replacing traditional five-act comedy, particularly at the non-patent Haymarket and Goodman's Fields theatres. London in 1730 had five or six theatres, more than it had supported in a century, and steady demand for new plays and farces.[13] When Drury Lane, which had put on *Love in Several Masques* in 1728, rejected both *Don Quixote in England* (unperformed until 1734) and *The Temple Beau*, the latter was performed at Goodman's Fields in January 1730. (Fielding also began *The Wedding Day* in late 1729, though it was put on only in 1743, perhaps because of discouragement from Drury Lane.) Fielding's "*annus mirabilis*" witnessed the performance and publication of *The Temple Beau, The Author's Farce* (written in late 1729), *Tom Thumb: A Tragedy*, and *Rape upon Rape; or, The Justice Caught in His Own Trap*, as well as an expanded version of *Tom Thumb* and a second run of *Rape upon Rape* under the title *The Coffee-House Politician; or, The Justice Caught in His Own Trap*. The clever *Author's Farce* ran forty-one performances in the spring and summer of 1730, the most successful opening season since *The Beggar's Opera* in 1728. The two 1730 versions of *Tom Thumb* ran for months (the second version alone for forty nights between April 24 and June 22), and a third, heavily revised version, *The Tragedy of Tragedies; or, The Life and Death of Tom Thumb the Great* would draw audiences in April and May, 1731.[14] From our point of view, however, it is significant that Fielding did not achieve his early successes in 1730 by satisfying the contemporary taste for political satire, particularly on Walpole and the Court. *The Temple Beau* is rather innocuous. *The Author's Farce* and both 1730 versions of *Tom Thumb* are only slightly less so. They are certainly not "anti-ministerial," though they have been misinterpreted by some critics as early signs of a drift into opposition. A considerable interest in politics and an intention to assault Walpole are first apparent in the play with which Fielding closed the year, *Rape upon Rape*. It foreshadows the experiment with political satire, including severe anti-ministerial and anti-Court material, that Fielding would begin with *The Tragedy of Tragedies* and sustain until the censor acted against the *Welsh/Grub-Street Opera*. In fact, *Rape upon Rape* is not predominantly a political, much less an anti-government, play, and even the satires of 1731 are not the work of an opposition playwright, but of an unaffiliated wit laughing at opposition hypocrisy as well as Walpolian corruption and the absurdities of the Court. In 1730-31 Fielding did not move into opposition. He merely returned to his natural attitude of neutral contempt for contemporary party politics briefly abandoned in the anti-opposition poem of 1729.

The Temple Beau

The Temple Beau, a five-act, "regular" comedy of manners in the general vein of *Love in Several Masques*, opened, with a prologue by James Ralph, on January 26, 1730 at the theatre established in 1729 in Goodman's Fields (Fielding's first association with the non-patent theatres), and was published with his name on the title page five days later. The play is basically non-political, concerned, as Winfield Rogers has suggested, with the follies and vices of social "pedants."[15] Its satire on coquettes, beaus, and misers is mingled at times with satire on English society as viciously avaricious that in other plays (*The Beggar's Opera* and Fielding's own *Pasquin*, for example) could form part of an assault on a corruptive ministry. But here it has no such partisan valence: even jabs at the "South-Sea" fiasco and stock-jobbery—frequent in opposition satire on Walpole's corrupt favouring of the "Moneyed Interest"—seem without partisan intent. Only a song in Act II, which some evidence suggests may have been an afterthought,[16] focusses on politics and condemns both Whig and Tory partisanship and the very influence of party:

> The Man who by reason
> His life doth support,
> Ne'er rises to Treason
> Ne'er sinks to a Court
> By Virtue, not Party
> Does Actions commend,
> My Soul shall be hearty
> Towards such a Friend.

The Author's Farce

This successful play first appeared on March 30, 1730 at the "Little Theatre" in the Haymarket (a fortunate move since the Goodman's Fields theatre was soon to be temporarily closed by royal order as a corruptive nuisance in its neighbourhood), and was published at "five o'clock in the Afternoon" of the following day. It followed the second run of the mad, "exquisitely bad" *Hurlothrumbo* by Samuel Johnson of Cheshire, which had played over thirty nights in 1729. *The Author's Farce* was the most successful of a spate of irregular plays (influenced by Gay) that opened in early 1730, including Gabriel Odingsell's *Bayes' Opera* (which opened the same night at Drury Lane) and James Ralph's *The Fashionable Lady; or, Harlequin's Opera*. Inaugurating a pattern revived in *Pasquin* and adapted in Fielding's novels, *The Author's Farce* is an interesting variant on the play-within-a-play, *Rehearsal* format, the "frame Play" deriving from Farquhar's *Love in a Bottle*, and the internal play, the mock-puppet show called "The Pleasures of the Town," incorporating hints, in the opinion of Charles B. Woods, from Lucian, Buckingham, Gay, Pope, Jonson, Dryden, Congreve, and Regnard.[17] It is a "satura," an almost plotless "potpourri . . . in which songs, dances, verbal parody and vignette scenes, attacking corrupt politicians or stupid theatre are jumbled together."[18] Its structure could accommodate incidental partisan, as well as social, religious, and artistic satire. This was later demonstrated by the insertion of thrusts at Walpole, a fiscal scandal in the Charitable Corporation, the Excise scheme of 1733, and governmental corruption at the election of 1734 in a revised version performed at Drury Lane in 1734. But the degree to which Fielding lent political overtones to it in 1730 has been exaggerated. Sheridan Baker has contended that the "first [1730] version is hardly less political than the second [1734]," and that the original contains many "threads of the anti-Walpole satire that Fielding worked into this stage burlesque with increasing frequency," but Charles B. Woods has rightly concluded that there is "little political satire in the 1730 text."[19] The political satire in the 1730 play is insufficient in context to justify considering it partisan. The play has only a few more political moments than *Love in Several Masques*, and in the spirit of the song from *The Temple Beau* they primarily ridicule the practices of the political booksellers and hacks of Grub Street rather than the ministry. It appeared (like the second 1730 version of *Tom Thumb*) under the pseudonym "Scriblerus Secundus," but its Scriblerian amusement at the moral, social, and artistic failings is seldom political. The author who had contemplated savaging the opposition wits in 1729 did not so rapidly adopt a "Scriblerian," anti-Walpole bias.

At long intervals in the frame play and the puppet show, there is stock mockery of courtiers and Justices of the Peace, but to consider these as significant assaults on the "Court" or the "Country party" would be to imply political intent in many apolitical plays of the earlier eighteenth century. More specific partisan material is rare. The four minor examples of anti-Walpole or anti-government satire are: (1) Witmore's statement that he is as sickened by talk of true love and the Muses in a garret as by "honesty talked at court, conscience at Westminster, politeness at the university" (p. 17); (2) Marplay's rejection of a play because the author has "no interest" and "interest sways as much in the theatre as at court and you know it is not always the companion of merit in either" (p. 26); (3) Bookweight's reply to a translator who protests he knows no Latin ("Not qualified!—If I was an Emperor thou should'st be my Prime Minister" [p. 32]); and (4) Luckless' introduction into the cast of his puppet show of "a bookseller who is the prime Minister of Nonsense" (p. 47). Here the audience laughed at recognizable political hits, cleverly combined with satire on hacks, theatre managers, and booksellers, the denizens of a world daily experienced by Fielding. However, they bulk exceedingly small in the play's potpourri; again Fielding was merely "naming" a minister "to set the audience a-hooting." The only other item that might have been applied to Walpole is a passage satirizing a rise in theatre prices and Marplay's (i.e., Colley Cibber's) imperviousness to hissing. It might have been viewed as satiric of Walpole's imposition of high taxes, employment of bribery, and notorious capacity to ignore satire. But probably no such meaning was intended in 1730, high prices and Cibber's effrontery being sufficient and, in context, more likely satiric marks. After his failure to place plays at Drury Lane, Fielding had reason to satirize Cibberian practices, and the brazen Colley was a standard target. In 1734, after Walpole's vain attempt to force the Excise Bill of 1733 through the legislature despite overwhelming protests, history nurtured the partisan possibilities of this scene and Fielding exploited them. But the revision must not colour our view of the original.

Though Sheridan Baker treats it as anti-Walpole, it would be far easier (if one felt compelled to specify a partisan target) to read as anti-opposition Luckless' ironical compliment to Bookweight and his hacks: "Who can form to himself an idea more amiable than of a man at the head of so many patriots working for the benefit of their country" (p. 33). The spokesmen of opposition (specialists in high-flown, "constitutional" rhetoric in the *Craftsman's* manner) were already ironically called "patriots." In fact, this "compliment" to "patriotism" was probably intended to mock the general rampancy of hypocrisy in political life and Grub-Street journalism, but the ease with which it could be interpreted as a sneer at, say, William Pulteney underscores the inappropriateness of an anti-Walpole reading. *The Author's Farce* of 1730 is the play of a young man without a real stake in politics or real animus; it is not much more politically charged than *The Temple Beau*. Its real political focus, the empty, self-generating, self-serving nature of party strife, not the sins of Walpole, is clear in its best political satire:

> Bookweight:—Do you consider, Mr. Quibble, that it is above a fortnight since your Letter from a Friend in the Country was published? Is it not high time for an Answer to come out? At this rate, before your Answer in [sic] printed your Letter will be forgot. I love to keep a controversy warm. I have had authors who have writ a pamphlet in the morning, answered it in the afternoon, and compromised the matter at night. (p. 29)
> ....
> Scare[crow]. Sir I have bought you a Libel against the Ministry.
> Book[weight]. Sir I shall not take any thing against them (for I have two in the Press already).
> Scare[crow]. Then, sir, I have another in Defense of them.
> Book[weight]. Sir, I never take any thing in Defense of Power. (p. 31)

Baker's conclusion (PAF, p. 222) that such dialogue constitutes the "first open slur Fielding ever made against Walpole's ministry, equivocal though it is" is unacceptable.

Baker's further suggestions (PAF, pp. 222-26) that there are far more extensive, subtler anti-ministerial elements also outrun the evidence. Encouraged by anti-Walpole innuendo in the 1734 version of *The Author's Farce*, he reads assaults on Grub Street as "ambiguous" slurs on Walpole, and unconvincingly argues that there are three separate and extended anti-Walpole parallels (constituting a kind of intermittent triple allegory) running through the original version. He bases his allegorical readings on weak internal evidence and dubiously relevant or anachronistic external evidence. He assumes (1) that partisan use by Fielding of a given type of satire or satire on a given individual in, say, 1737 or the early 1740s implies that the same kind of satire or mockery of the same man in his early plays must be partisan; (2) that the partisan use by other authors of satire resembling that in *The Author's Farce* must be regarded as evidence of partisan intent in the latter; (3) that Fielding could count on audiences to identify the most obscure satiric allusions to the ministry.

Baker assumes that audiences (recalling an ephemeral partisan skirmish a year earlier) would have read a very equivocal thrust at the hissing of Cibber's *Love in a Riddle* on January 7, 1729 (if one was intended) as anti-ministerial since Cibber's play was damned because he was "suspected of using his political influence to get Walpole to suppress Gay's *Polly*." Working from a single hint in the play (Marplay's remark that "Interest sways as much in the Theatre as at Court") and the fact that Walpole and Cibber (represented by Marplay) and the worlds theatrical and political were sometimes satirically compared by opposition satirists (including Fielding, *over a decade later*), Baker treats much of the satire on Cibber as co-manager of Drury Lane as satiric of Walpole's corrupt and inept leadership. Such a reading of *some* of the anti-Cibber satire *in the 1734 version* is justified. Alterations in the play, the times, Fielding's political hopes, and Cibber's appointment as Poet Laureate in November 1730 assured that. But Baker's reasoning about the 1730 version is weak: to isolate an example, it is unacceptable to propose that because *Mist's Weekly Journal* satirized Walpole by satirizing Cibber during the 1720s, and because Fielding employs the same technique in the 1734 version of *The Author's Farce* and the *Historical Register* of 1737, satire in the original *Author's Farce* on Cibber must be anti-ministerial. Similarly, Baker suggests a running parallel between Bookweight, master of his hacks, and Walpole, leader of the ministerial majority: "A man at the head of his country, driving his shop of [political] writers looks very much like Walpole." However, grounds for such a reading are non-existent, aside from his observation that Luckless introduces into his puppet show a second Bookseller (*not* Bookweight), "who is the Prime Minister of *Nonsense*." As in the case of Cibber-Walpole, Fielding *could* have used Bookweight as a reductive parody of the minister, but did not.

Next Baker suggests that the least political part of the 1730 version, the puppet show called "The Pleasures of the Town," has strong anti-Walpole overtones (though far weaker ones than the puppet show in the 1734 revision). An obscure pamphlet of 1715 associates Walpole with Punch and Judy, Punch is Walpole in a pamphlet serialized in an opposition journal in 1742, ten lines in Fielding's opposition tract *The Vernoniad* (1741) describe the world as Walpole's puppet show, and *Jonathan Wild* (1743) compares politics and a puppet show, "Where it is the Master of the Show who dances and moves everything." This seems to Baker to render it "quite possible that Fielding intends Luckless' show to cast some shadow on the political scene as well as the theatrical, intimating that Walpole's England is not unlike a puppet show about the Court of Nonsense on the nether side of Hell" (Baker, *PAF*, p. 223). The next sentence converts this possibility into a certainty: Fielding's Punch and Joan "undoubtedly satirize Walpole." Baker then discusses a seemingly irrelevant alteration in the Drummer's announcement of the Puppet show, stresses that by belabouring the text Fielding can be shown to confuse the character "Somebody" with Punch, and that "Quidam" (which means "Somebody") in *The Historical Register* of 1737 represents Walpole. Finally, he assumes that the marital squabbles of Punch and Joan *must* represent Walpole's troubles with his wife because a battle between Jonathan Wild and his wife described by Fielding a decade later does so. One must concur with Charles B. Woods, who allows that the strong anti-Walpole element Baker detects in the 1734 puppet show is there but observes that, with reference to the 1730 version, "if Professor Baker's line of reasoning were followed, every stage production of the Walpole era that presented Punch and Judy or Harlequin would be politically suspect" (*AF*, p. xv). In truth, the 1730 *Author's Farce* is basically not a political, certainly not an opposition, play, even though Fielding found it easy in 1734 to adapt it to satirize Walpole's Excise fiasco of 1733, government electoral corruption in 1734, and speculation scandals in the Charitable Corporation.

Tom Thumb: A Tragedy

This successful two-act farce (it ran with *The Author's Farce* through June) appeared in two versions in 1730: *Tom Thumb: A Tragedy*, first performed on April 24, and published on April 24 or 25, and *Tom Thumb: A Tragedy* (by "Scriblerus Secundus"), first performed on May 1, performed with certain additional scenes on May 7, and finally published (presumably in early May) with a new preface, prologue, and epilogue. Both versions broadly parody seventeenth-century heroic drama and its fustian descendants, from *The Conquest of Grenada* to *Sophonisba*, and each satirizes, in good *satura*-fashion, targets from silly courtiers to Colley Cibber to bad physicians. The notion that either 1730 version of the farce is anti-Walpole must be dismissed. L. J. Morrisey's otherwise excellent introduction to his edition of *Tom Thumb* and *The Tragedy of Tragedies* of 1731 insists on the anti-Walpole bias of the earlier as well as the later play,[20] but (like Baker's reading of the original *Author's Farce*) Morrissey's interpretation is a result of the natural, though false, assumption that political overtones in a revision imply the like on the original.

Neither 1730 version seems to have struck contemporaries as political. The intelligent, knowledgeable Earl of Egmont discusses the opening performance of the original *Tom Thumb* without mentioning political satire. Looking at the play from the viewpoint of more experience on July 11, 1730, the *Grub-Street Journal* seems to consider satire upon bad tragedies, not political mockery, the play's central interest:

> The Comical Tragedy of *Tom Thumb* having had so great a run (this being the 33rd day) he raised the envy of some unsuccessful Poet against the Author, and Occasioned the following Parody.

Act I, sc. 1. pag. 1,

Dood. When Good $^{Y\ Thumb}_{man\ F\text{---}g}$ first brought this *Thomas* forth,

The *Genius* of $^{our\ Land}_{the\ Bard}$ triumphant reign'd;

Then, then O $^{Arthur}_{F\text{----}g}$ did thy Genius reign.

Nood. They tell me it is whisper'd $^{in}_{from}$ the $^{books.}_{mouths.}$

Of all our Sages, that this mighty $^{Hero,}_{Piece,}$

By $^{Merlin's\ art}_{On\ Folly's\ self}$ begot, has not a $^{bone}_{joke}$

Within $^{his\ skin,}_{its\ leaves,}$ but is a lump of $^{gristle.}_{nonsense.}$

Dood. Would Arthur's subjects were such $^{gristle}_{nonsense}$ all;
        If F----s pieces prove

He then $^{might}_{will}$ break the $^{bones}_{hearts}$ of ev'ry foe.

This being apprehended, by the greater part of the Members present, to be design'd as a Satire upon the Author, for whom they have a great value; they were against the inserting of it in our journal. But I observed to them, that let it be designed as it would, it was in reality a Panegyric, which the two last lines evidently shewed. And that even the two preceding lines, which seemed to carry in them the greatest reflection, had really none upon this performance, but upon the Plays which were ridiculed by it.

Nothing in the poem or the Grub-Streeter's commentary on it suggests that the Prime Minister was among Fielding's "foes." The only hint I have located that anyone was even possibly reading the play politically in 1730 is the twentieth item in a long, ironical list in the pro-administration journal *The Free Briton* (October 8, 1730) of the charges levelled by the opposition against Walpole: "XX. That he subscrib'd for *Thirty Books of Hurlothrumbo* and was present *Three* several Nights at the Tragedy of Tom Thumb." Though hardly a compliment to Fielding's play, only tortured logic could construe it as a sign that *The Free Briton* considered *Tom Thumb* politically unfriendly. Indeed, the notice may imply that Walpole enjoyed the play sufficiently to draw opposition scorn for his irregular tastes; Walpole had subscribed for thirty copies of *Hurlothrumbo* in 1729.

Morrissey's idea that *Tom Thumb: A Tragedy* is anti-ministerial seems to have grown out of suggestions by G. M. Godden, Wilbur Cross, and F. Homes Dudden that *The Tragedy of Tragedies; or, The Life and Death of Tom Thumb the Great* of 1731 *(not the earlier play)* would have been regarded by contemporaries as anti-Walpole. Their arguments, objections other scholars have raised against them, and certain hitherto ignored evidence really bear upon the question of political satire in the 1731 play, *The Tragedy of Tragedies;* in this connection, however, a brief *résumé* of the state of the case up to 1952 (the date of Dudden's biography) will prove useful. Godden's *Memoir* (1910) cited as evidence that *The Tragedy of Tragedies* "carried some political significance in Fielding's day," a notice occasioned by a revival of it in the *London Daily Post* (March 29, 1742) that describes it as "a Piece at first calculated to ridicule some particular Persons and Affairs in Europe (at the Time it was writ) but more especially in this Island." Though he ignored Godden's "new" evidence, Wilbur Cross continued in the same direction. He said of *The Tragedy of Tragedies* (rather confusingly referred to as "Tom Thumb the Great"):

> "Tom Thumb the Great," besides being a burlesque of current tragedy, was a hit at Sir Robert Walpole, the Great Man, as he was called in irony by his enemies. Fielding reduced the Prime Minister to a pigmy, to the delight of the audience, making the little man more powerful than men, giants and the gods combined, and then throwing doubt upon his claims to have killed the giants at all. And yet the political import of the farce was not direct enough to occasion interference on the part of the Government. No one could quite say that Tom Thumb was intended for Walpole.

Cross's reading was contradicted by both James T. Hillhouse and Mabel D. Hessler as unsupported by real evidence in the play, but F. Homes Dudden reiterated it in more detail. He maintained that material in all versions of the play would have been taken as satiric of Walpole in *The Tragedy of Tragedies* because of the new epithet (my italics) appended to the hero's name in its sub-title ("Or, the Life and Death of Tom Thumb *the Great*"):

> In the literature of the Opposition this appellation was consistently applied to Walpole: the mere mention of 'Great Man' in any kind of public utterance was sufficient to direct attention to Walpole. When Fielding, therefore, brought upon stage a personage styled 'The Great,' a contemporary audience would immediately suspect that an allusion to Walpole was intended. When, further, this 'great' personage was represented as the most famous man in the kingdom, a pillar of the State, a friend of the King, favoured by the Queen, acclaimed by the Court party, hated and feared and plotted against by the Opposition (Lord Grizzle)—when his name was associated with 'peace and safety' (Walpole's declared policy) and with fox-hunting (Walpole's favourite sport)—the suspicions of the audience would be deepened into practical certainty.

Dudden declared that the audience would have seen the posing of the little hero as a false "great man" as a sign that "the play was purposely satirizing the Great Minister," and noted the *Daily Post* notice of 1742 as corroboration, then reversed himself (in the absence of contemporary comment on the political aspects of the play) and left open the question of anti-Walpole intent in *The Tragedy of Tragedies*.[21] There the case for an anti-Walpole interpretation of *The Tragedy of Tragedies* rests, as far as real evidence or argument is concerned. Nothing in it bears directly upon the 1730 version of *Tom Thumb*. Indeed, the principal strength of

Dudden's discussion, though he does not make it wholly clear, is its recognition that the insertion of "The Great" in the 1731 subtitle could lend anti-ministerial overtones to old material which would not have been there in the absence of such a hint. It remained for more recent critics to ignore Dudden's point, politicizing as yet innocent passages in the 1730 version as opposition satire.

Baker's discussion (Baker, *PAF*, p. 231) of *The Author's Farce* begins by observing that "Fielding's veiled aspersions of Walpole as the great Man of his *Tom Thumb* (April 24, 1730) is accepted as his first political satire on the stage." He conflates the first 1730 version of *Tom Thumb: A Tragedy* with *The Tragedy of Tragedies*, though he cites the discussions by Godden and Cross, Hillhouse and Hessler, all four of whom were discussing *The Tragedy of Tragedies*. The same confusion and misreading flaw John Loftis' brief remarks on *Tom Thumb* of 1730 in *The Politics of Drama in Augustan England* (p. 104): "Tom Thumb *the great*, the giant killer, the upholder of peace, the favourite of the queen, the successful lover—could all of this be innocent of innuendo?" Morrissey follows Baker and Loftis, suggesting (Morrissey, *TT*, p. 4) that "there were references throughout [the original version of Mar. 24, 1730] that the audience would have identified." He offers as proof only (1) the suggestion that the "verve and . . . burlesque" of the play seem insufficient to explain its popularity, so that it must have contained political satire; and (2) a selection from Dudden's list of items that audiences of *The Tragedy of Tragedies* (keyed for political innuendo by the reference to Tom Thumb as "the Great,") might have interpreted an anti-ministerial: "There are references to fox-hunting, Walpole's favourite pastime, and to peace and safety, the mainstay of Walpole's foreign policy; the Queen favours Thumb, the 'Preserver of [the] Kingdom,' as Caroline favoured Walpole." Dudden is cautious about so interpreting these items even in *The Tragedy of Tragedies* and never hints that audiences in 1730 would have interpreted them politically. Morrissey's political reading of the original *Tom Thumb*, in short, is unacceptable, as are his suggestions about the two additions Fielding made to his farce in the second 1730 version: "The two bailiff scenes were added to the text, increasing the honour of the fiery tempered hero and probably suggesting Walpole's trouble with the city merchants. A single additional speech was given to the King at the end of II.VIII, where his maggot simile might be a nasty new thrust at Walpole" (p. 5). The probability of these readings is wholly dependent on the false assumption that the original version was seen as anti-Walpole. Both versions of 1730 are innocent, though Fielding found it easy to give his farce a political dimension in 1731. The anti-ministerialism of Fielding's first three dramatic offerings in 1730—the original *Author's Farce* and two versions of *Tom Thumb*—is a creation of their critics.

3. A Political Experiment in Four Phases, 1730-31

The publication in June 1730 of *Rape upon Rape* signalled the beginning of a temporary abandonment of the detached and balanced view of contemporary politics that characterizes Fielding's earlier plays. It satirizes Walpole more consistently and directly, and alludes to matters (e.g., the Treaty of Seville of 1729 and two celebrated trials for rape) embarrassing to the ministry in 1730. It is Fielding's first anti-ministerial play (insofar as it is political), and the first published work into which he wove really topical political satire. In this respect it is best grouped with the plays of 1731 that with increasing rashness attack not only the prime minister, but the royal family. In 1731 *The Tragedy of Tragedies* broadly hinted ridicule of Walpole, King George, and Queen Caroline, as well as the leaders of the opposition, and *The Welsh Opera* so openly mocked the royal family, as well as ministry and opposition, that the Lord Chamberlain prevented the staging of the revised version known as *The Grub-Street Opera*. The reasons Fielding began his first real "experiment in political satire" (to use Wilbur Cross's apt phrase) in mid-1730 are unclear. Perhaps Fielding and the management of the Haymarket Theatre (where the first of the two versions of *Rape upon Rape* and all of the plays of 1731 were put on) may have felt that daring political satire would draw audiences. But one explanation must be ruled out. This experiment is not a sign that he had been recruited, even temporarily, by the opposition. While *The Tragedy of Tragedies* and the *Welsh/Grub-Street Opera* are severe in their treatment of Walpole, they are at least as harsh to the leaders of the opposition. Fielding's "experiment" involved a new political sharpness, but it was not, in a narrow sense, partisan.

Rape upon Rape; or, The Justice Caught in His Own Trap

Closing Fielding's first full season as a dramatist with a return to "regular" comedy, this rough-edged play was performed and published under two titles: *Rape upon Rape; or, The Justice Caught in His Own Trap* (first performed at the Haymarket and published on June 23) and *The Coffee-House Politician; or, The Justice Caught in His Own Trap* (first performed at the Theatre-Royal in Lincoln's Inn Fields, perhaps because of some passing friction with the Haymarket management, on November 30 and published on December 17, 1730). However, only the title change and the disclosure of Fielding's authorship (the first version was published anonymously) differentiate the two versions. Probably the play was revived when Fielding decided to withhold his new comedy, *The Modern Husband*. Presumably begun after his departure from London in June for his annual summer visit to Salisbury and East Stour, *The Modern Husband* was well advanced when he returned to London. He showed all or part of it to Lady Mary in September and managed to get it "puffed" in the *Craftsman*—"We hear that the Town will shortly be diverted by a Comedy of Mr. Fielding's call'd 'The Modern Husband,' which is said to bear a great Reputation"—and *The Grub-Street Journal*. However, *The Modern Husband* was not staged until 1732. *Rape upon Rape* may have been renamed because the Theatre-Royal found the original title *risqué* ("low" in contemporary jargon) or Fielding may have wished to stress the funniest comic character in it, Sir Politick Wouldbe. The introduction of the word "politician" into the title, innocent in itself, may remind us that political satire (even pointed anti-ministerial satire) is more important in this play than any other of 1730.

It seems ironical that anti-Walpole readings have been forced on *The Author's Farce* and *Tom Thumb*, while details deserving political exegesis in *Rape upon Rape* (as I shall call it for the sake of convenience) have been virtually ignored. Both Wilbur Cross and F. Homes Dudden briefly analyze the central comic-satiric underpinnings of the play, noting its satire upon the biased greed of the courts (embodied in Justice Squeezum, eventually exposed by the exemplary Justice Worthy) and its mockery of Sir Politick Wouldbe's quixotic ruling passion for "politicks" and the absurdities of contemporary newspapers. But they see in *Rape upon Rape* nothing equivalent to the anti-Walpole satire they detect in *The Tragedy of Tragedies*. Sheridan Baker ignores the play, and only very recently has one scholar, Bertrand Goldgar, begun to explore its topical political content.[22] Yet *Rape upon Rape* is more anti-ministerial than the works that flank it chronologically.

In interpreting *Rape upon Rape*, one does not have to depend—as is the case with *The Tragedy of Tragedies*—on quite as tricky an argument as that audiences would have been sufficiently primed by an epithet added to the title ("Tom Thumb *the Great*") to trace political parallels, even though, as noted, the revised title *does* stress the political. The Prologue would have alerted any audience in 1730 that parts of *Rape upon Rape* were likely to be applicable to Walpole. Spoken by Mr. Paget (the actor who played Justice Worthy, exemplar and authorial mouthpiece), it first laments that contemporary satirists, unlike those of ancient Greece, are afraid to attack the "Mighty Villain," and promises that "the Heroick Muse Who sings Tonight/ . . . dares the Lyon in his Den."[23] Whether or not one interprets "Lyon" as a clever way of naming the head of the government (embodiment of the "British Lion"), there is significant excess in the phrase "Mighty Villain" as a description of the play's contemptibly minor villain, Justice Squeezum. Before the end of the Prologue, the audience's nose for anti-ministerial innuendo in the play's treatment of the "Mighty Villain" would have been further stimulated by Worthy's justification of emphasizing the corruption of a mere Justice of the Peace:

> They only Reverence to Pow'r is due,
> When *Publick Welfare* is its only View:
> ....

Who 'gainst those *Traytors* fights defends the *Publick Cause.*

More appropriate to an attack on cabinet ministers than a fictitious magistrate, this recalls the rationalizations by opposition spokesmen throughout the century of attacks on the King's ministers as in the best interests of King and country. The constant attempts by administration supporters (including Fielding in 1729 and 1747-48) to depict opposition assaults as seditious, as signs of disaffection from the Present Establishment, had constantly to be countered, and in 1730 a strong attack on "factious" libelling in the Crown speech at the opening of the Parliament stirred up extraordinary slanging matches on this issue between the opposition's *Craftsman* and the ministry's *Free Briton*, which peaked in the weeks before Fielding's play opened.[24]

The Prologue hints satire on Walpole, perhaps interwoven with satire on the sins of the Justice named in the title, a pattern similar to *The Beggar's Opera*'s combined assault on corrupt thief-catchers and the ministry. A similar hint is placed at the very end of the play. Worthy's closing denunciation of venality in the courts—"Golden Sands too often Clog the Wheels of Justice"—is capped by this epigram: "No Reverence that Church or State attends, / Whose Laws the Priest or Magistrate offends." "Magistrate" was a meaningfully ambiguous term in 1730, signifying, among other things, the wielder of supreme power in the state (the "Supreme Magistrate"—the King or the leader of the ministry), as well as humbler members of the Bench. The Epilogue's association of such a loss of "Reverence" for the Present Establishment in Church and State and the misbehaviour of a Squeezum seems overstrained. The couplet's style and content mesh happily, however, if Walpole is introduced into the equation, and spectators leaving the theatre with it ringing in their ears would have had little difficulty in properly applying it.

Though the body of the play is not so obviously anti-ministerial, its anti-ministerial tendencies would have been recognizable to a forewarned and reminded audience. For one thing, the portions of the play dealing with Squeezum's court strikingly recall the Walpole-Peachum / Lockit, Westminster-Newgate parallels in *The Beggar's Opera* two years earlier. Fielding was later to employ Gay's comparison very openly in *The Champion* to satirize both Walpole and judicial inequity, and he weaves *Beggar's Opera* motifs into *Rape upon Rape* in a similar way. Justice Squeezum verges on quotation from Gay's play at times (". . . if you cannot pay for your Transgressions like the Rich, you must suffer for them like the Poor"—p. 26), and his dialogue as well as his behaviour recall the central political themes of *The Beggar's Opera*. One pronouncement in Act II, scene ii develops a strong partisan tang:

> The laws are Turnpikes, only made to stop People who walk on Foot, and not to interrupt those who drive through them in their Coaches.— The Laws are like a Game at Loo, where a blaze of Court Cards is always secure, and the Knaves are the safest Cards in the Pack. (p. 216)

Other items may be read as anti-Walpole. Cloris' statement about the "rights" of a wronged wife (". . . it hath been ever my Opinion that a Husband, like a Courtier, who is above doing the Duties of his Office, should keep a Deputy"—p. 2) may have been interpreted as a hit, among other things, at Walpole's notorious family difficulties. And certainly Walpole's Sinking Fund (as well as Sir Politick and "projectors") is laughed at when Wouldbe says building a machine to transport ships over the Isthmus of Suez would be ". . . a Method to pay off the Debts of the Nation without a Penny of Money" (p. 3).

There may also be sly anti-government, though not specifically anti-Walpole, overtones elsewhere in the play. Rape was much in the news in 1730 as a result of two cases that embarrassed the government. As Bertrand Goldgar has noted, the notorious Colonel Charteris (satirized as a vicious lecher by Pope, Arbuthnot, and Hogarth) was convicted on February 17, 1730 of raping a young girl, but pardoned after a token imprisonment: a stunning example of the influence of money, earned in his case through card-sharping and shylocking, over English justice satirized in *Rape upon Rape*.[25] In addition, Swift's obviously partisan "An Excellent new Ballad: or, the True En---sh D---n to be Hang'd for a R-pe" was printed in the *Grub-Street Journal* June 11, 1730, twelve days before the opening of Fielding's play. It immortalizes a Church of Ireland dean, freshly appointed by the English authorities, who was condemned for brazenly raping a young girl. The two rape cases and anti-ministerialism are blended wittily in a letter of Swift's to the Earl of Oxford, dated August 28, 1730: "There is a fellow here from England, one Sawbridge, he was last term indicted for Rape. The plea he intended was his being drunk when he forced the woman; but he bought her off. He is a Dean and . . . I am confident you will hear of his being a Bishop; for in short, he is just the counterpart of Charteris, that continual favourite of Ministers."[26] Fielding's emphasis on rape stirred political depths.

In the play's Epilogue, Fielding also archly yoked rape and a particularly unpopular diplomatic measure taken by the government in late 1729 and violently debated in Parliament and the press through 1730:

> Oh! May your Youth whose Vigour is so parlous,
> To Italy be wafted with *Don Carlos*.

One clause of the Treaty of Seville (signed November 9, 1729 by England, France, and Spain) permitted Don Carlos of Spain to garrison Parma and certain Tuscan cities to enforce his claim to parts of Northern Italy. Beholden to the "Trading Interests" and enraged by interference with English trade, the opposition preferred war with Spain. It was unsatisfied by the defensive alliance with France and Spain and the renewal of the *Asiento* (the right to send one trading ship a year to Spanish America) that England obtained in return for the Don Carlos agreement and other concessions. The "wafting" of the Spaniard occasioned partisan invective that Robert Walpole himself answered in one of his rare political pamphlets, the "Observations upon the Treaty between the

Crowns of Great Britain, France, and Spain" of 1730. The political gossip between Fielding's Sir Politick and Dabble (Act I, scene i) refers to Don Carlos' garrisoning of the Italian cities (they ponder its prudence), and briefly considers England's problems with Spain over possession of Gibraltar (a necessity for the continued safety of English trade to the Mediterranean) and the possibilities for peace and war. The whole scene and the Epilogue focus on the same diplomatic questions as William Pulteney's blistering criticism of the Treaty of Seville in the debate on the Address from the Throne. Pulteney expressed horror at secret articles in the treaty and the government's pusillanimity in sending commissioners to Spain (rather than the reverse) to negotiate trade arrangements, but his violence peaked in attacks on the authoritarian harshness of imposing Don Carlos on unconsenting Parma and Piacenza and demands for information about the safety of Gibraltar, not covered in the treaty, though essential to England. Parma, Piacenza, and Gibraltar were not names the ministry's friends were apt to mention by choice in June 1730.[27]

Rape upon Rape also includes less partisan political satire like that in the *Author's Farce*. Wild political theorizing, the uninformed political fascinations of coffee-house gossips and Grub-Street journalists, are laughed at uproariously. Sir Politick lives in terror of an invasion of England by the Turks, and cares more about the supposed illness of the Dauphin than the elopement of his daughter. He recommends that Hilaret read political newspapers ("all that come out: about forty every Day, and some days fifty; and of a *Saturday* about four-score"), and laments that he has read only *"The London Journal, The Country Journal,* the *Weekly Journal,* Applebee's *Journal, the British Journal*, the British *Gazetteer, The Morning Post, The Daily Post*, the Daily *Post-Boy, The Daily Journal, The Daily Courant, The Gazette, The Evening Post, The Whitehall Evening Post, The London Evening Post*, and *The St. James Evening Post"* (all actual papers of the day) and hastily consults the *Lying Post*. Wouldbe reads aloud vague and contradictory news items from his "bibles" and assures Hilaret that they will teach her "as much of politics as—any Man that comes to our Coffee-House." Fielding was already honing the mockery of the learned political ignoramus that would culminate in Aunt Western's speeches in *Tom Jones*.[28]

Rape upon Rape is not a very partisan play (though it is Fielding's most political play before 1731), much less a sign that Fielding had drifted toward an opposition allegiance by the summer of 1730. The flaws in an opposition drift theory have already been suggested, but it may be useful here to stress that George Lyttelton, still on the Grand Tour, seems to have approved of the agreement by the government his father served to the Treaty of Seville.[29] However, *Rape upon Rape*, rather than the original *Author's Farce* or *Tom Thumb: A Tragedy*, was the first tentative phase of a political experiment carried to a violent climax the following season. Indeed, though its anti-ministerial needling is less daring, *Rape upon Rape* is singularly lacking in the anti-opposition ridicule which characteristically balances the sharper satire on Walpole and the Court in the experiment's later phases.

The Tragedy of Tragedies; or, The Life and Death of Tom Thumb the Great

The general nature of the arguments G. M. Godden, Wilbur Cross, F. Homes Dudden, and L. J. Morrissey have advanced in favour of a political reading of *The Tragedy of Tragedies* has, perforce, been noted in my critique of Morrissey's political reading of *Tom Thumb: A Tragedy*. But it is necessary to restress (with Cross and Dudden) the absolute dependence of a political interpretation of *The Tragedy of Tragedies* upon the existence of new hints, external to its action or dialogue, that would have primed audiences or readers in 1731 to look for political satire in patterns, characterizations, dialogue, and details that would have seemed politically innocent in 1730. There are enough such hints (though they are not numerous) to have encouraged them to do so and to justify a political interpretation of the revised play. Much of the apolitical satire in the 1730 versions was susceptible to subtle political electrification; all that was required were signs that Tom Thumb *might* represent Walpole or King Arthur and Queen Dollallolla *might* represent King George and Queen Caroline, as well as the overblown characters in fustian tragedy. James T. Hillhouse was technically correct in denying that the "dialogue" in *The Tragedy of Tragedies* justified interpreting it as a satire upon contemporary political figures. Its topical political overtones are only apparent because of broad hints that are not part of the "dialogue" *per se*, and that acted in 1731 on the often unaltered material of the earlier versions of Fielding's farce as catalysts do in chemical reactions, allowing aesthetic satire to fuse with political.

Given the political possibilities of Tom Thumb at the court of King Arthur in *Tom Thumb: A Tragedy*, the addition of the epithet "the Great" to the subtitle of the *Tragedy of Tragedies* might alone be described (as it is by Cross and Dudden) as a sufficient warning to audiences of anti-Walpole intent. But there were other pointers. Fielding had inserted anti-ministerial barbs in his last play, *Rape upon Rape*. A *Tragedy of Tragedies* was also performed together with the very political *Welsh Opera* in late April 1731, after its original afterpiece, *The Letter-Writers*, failed. Most significantly, it was sold on opening night at the Haymarket Theatre (March 24, 1731) in an edition that includes a significantly expanded list of the *Dramatis Personae*. The 1730 editions simply list the characters and the actors; the 1731 list offers capsule characterizations calculated to create suspicions that Walpole was to be mocked, along with the royal family, the courts, and both sides in the struggles between the ministry and its enemies. As recently as 1976, Bertrand Goldgar has cited the relevant satiric *Dramatis Personae* of 1731 as if they were printed with the 1730 versions, but they were not:

King Arthur, a passionate sort of King, Husband to Queen Dollallolla, of whom he stands a little in Fear, Father to Huncamunca . . . .

Tom Thumb *the Great*, a little Hero with a great Soul, something violent in his Temper, which is a little abated by his love for *Huncamunca*.

Lord Grizzle, Extremely zealous for the Liberty of the Subject, very
cholerick in his Temper, and in Love with *Huncamunca*.

Noodle   Courtiers in Place, and consequently of the Party that is
Doodle   uppermost.

Foodle, A Courtier that is out of Place, and consequently of that Party
that is undermost.

Queen Dollallolla, Wife to *King Arthur*, and Mother to *Huncamunca*,
a Woman entirely faultless, saving that she is a little given to Drink, a
little too much a Virago Towards her Husband, and in Love with *Tom
Thumb*.

These are accurate capsule characterizations, but the details they
stress strongly imply a desire to suggest analogies between the play's action and contemporary politics. They may explain in part why the *Daily
Post* much later remembered that the play originally was considered
satiric of "particular persons"; the journalists would only have had to
glance at the list of characters to revive scandalous recollections. The
possible effect of again calling Tom Thumb *"the Great"* is obvious
enough. Stressing King Arthur's passionate nature and fear of his wife
might recall the opposition's continual slurs on the extra-marital liaisons
of George II and his supposed domination by his wife. Queen
Dollallolla's faults similarly recall opposition mockery of Queen
Caroline's coarseness (in her cups or out), domination of her husband,
use of wifely influence to aid Walpole, and supposed unqueenly feelings
for the Prime Minister. All broadly hint satire on the royal family, as
well as Walpole. Though contemporaries could not know it until part
way through the play's run, Fielding's next play, *The Welsh Opera*, was
to include very sharp and dangerously obvious satire on the same targets,
and would first signal this in its subtitle, "The Gray Mare the Better
Horse," and title page epigram: ". . . a Batchelor Cobler, is happier than
a Hen-peck'd Prince." Surely no audience would have viewed *The
Tragedy of Tragedies* as "a Dramatization of Lord Hervey's *Memoirs*"
(John Loftis' description of *The Welsh Opera*),[30] but similar possibilities
might well have crossed a contemporary's mind as he encountered first
the new subtitle, then the *Dramatis Personae* added to the play by the
writer of *Rape upon Rape*. And it must have seemed a more cautious
essay in the kind of near-seditious ridicule offered in *The Welsh Opera*
when, in late April, the farces began to run as a double bill.

Similarly, the descriptions of "Tom Thumb the Great" and Lord
Grizzle might well have suggested to contemporaries that their struggles
figured forth Walpole's struggles with either the leaders of the opposition (William Pulteney, whose battles with Walpole are obviously
mocked in the conflict between Robin and William in *The Welsh Opera*,

seems the most likely candidate) or Lord Townshend (Walpole's brother-in-law and former ally, who had quarrelled with the Prime Minister and resigned from the ministry on May 15, 1730). Indeed contemporaries might well have viewed Grizzle as a reductive symbol for *both* Pulteney and Townshend. L. J. Morrissey (without referring to the *Dramatis Personae*) has suggested that Grizzle may represent Townshend and has, in support of this conjecture, noted that Fielding altered his play in 1731 to stress the open breach between Thumb and Grizzle. The "something cholerick" in Thumb's temper and the "very cholerick" disposition of Grizzle seem to Morrissey to fit Townshend and Walpole, but Pulteney was always violent in his rhetoric, and, more importantly, had been involved in a bloody duel with Lord Hervey on January 25, 1731. The fact that Thumb's temper is "a little abated by his love for Huncamunca" and that Grizzle is in love with her might be taken (though the parallels are inexact) as a reference to the fact that Townshend and Walpole both loved one woman, Walpole's sister and Townshend's wife. But his extreme zeal "for the Liberty of the Subject" can only be read as the broadest of hints that Grizzle, who leads the rebels in the play, is a comic symbol of the leaders of opposition (again it fits Pulteney best), rather than Townshend, and thus as an indication (reinforced by the descriptions of Foodle, Doodle, and Noodle) that the party struggles at the court of King Arthur mock all participants in the party struggles at the court of King George. It cannot be proven that theatregoers and readers caught all these hints, in the total absence of known contemporary comments implying that the play was so interpreted, but the evidence provided by additions to the 1731 version provides more than a reasonable warrant for such a reading. Dudden was too cautious in concluding, after revealing clearly enough his own conviction that the play is political, that the question of its political intentions must be left open. Indeed, if one accepts the idea that the specific details we have been discussing served as catalysts allowing partisan interpretation, almost every aspect of the play, from pointed details to the very nature of its mock-solemn burlesque of the "heroic" court of King Arthur, can be viewed as having served in part as a delicious parody of political life under George II. The fact that the same material may not have been political, because it would not have been seen to be, in the 1730 version is not a problem, as odd as that may seem.

It is plausible to assume (as Dudden and Morrissey do) that audiences in 1731 saw hidden edges in the description of Thumb by Noodle as the "Pillar of our State" (I,i) and by King Arthur as the "Preserver of my Kingdom" (I,ii), and that a doubly ironic allusion to Walpole's cautious and unpopular diplomatic policies (and position as the King's agent in Parliament) would have been detected in the King's expression of confidence in Thumb's ability to put down the rebellion led by Grizzle: "In Peace and Safety we may stay, / While to his Arm we trust the bloody Fray." Opposition resentment at the Treaty of Seville had hardened into rejection of Walpole's diplomatic policy by 1731, because of the discovery in 1730 that France was refortifying Dunkirk in defiance of earlier treaties and the signing on March 16, 1731 (eight days before the first performance of *The Tragedy of Tragedies*) of the Treaty of Vienna, the first version of the so-called Pragmatic Sanction. The Treaty of Vienna further complicated England's diplomatic situation by obliging her—in alliance with Austria and Spain—to guarantee the Succession of the Austrian Princess, Maria Theresa, to her father's throne and possessions. It would enmesh England in a general European war a decade later. The opposition also rejected clauses giving strategic advantages to Spain and trading advantages to Austria's Ostend Company. Walpole's opponents demanded an "English" policy of freeing trade from Spanish interference, by war if necessary, in March 1731. Finally, Morrissey and Dudden's weak-sounding suggestion that a reference to fox-hunting in I,v would have been seen as a satiric allusion to Walpole's "favourite pastime" seems justified, not only because Walpole's habit of playing the bluff squire was frequently mocked, but also because the reference is made in a context with political applicability. Grizzle weaves it into an attempt to convince the Queen that Thumb's supposed rescue of the state was a trick:

> I tell you, Madam, it was all a trick,
> He made the Giants first, and then he kill'd them;
> As Fox-hunters bring Foxes to the Wood.
> And then with Hounds they drive them out again.

It is tempting to see all of this as a parody of one of the constants of contemporary partisan rhetoric: the ministry (especially Walpole) or Tom Thumb insisting that its enemies were dangerous Jacobites against whom vigilance was necessary and the opposition (especially Pulteney) or Lord Grizzle scoffing at this political trickery. When this play appeared the ministry and the opposition, Walpole and Pulteney, were locked—as I have suggested in dealing with *Rape upon Rape*—in a crossfire of Jacobite charges and rebuttals that was hot even by the standards of the 1730s.

Thus far, but no farther, elaborating suggestions of previous scholars can take us. L. J. Morrissey (*TT*, pp. 4-6, 112) sees other political satire in the play, but the readings he offers are less than convincing. There seems no connection between an allusion to the "King of Brentford" in II,iii and Walpole's control of the elections in 1727. Tempting but unlikely are suggestions that the King's expression of indebtedness to the victorious Thumb ("what Gratitude can thank away the Debt,/ Your Valour lays upon me?") and the difficulty Thumb reports in getting the giants through the palace gates in I,iii satirize, respectively, Walpole's "handling of public funds" and "Walpole's difficulties in getting the city merchants willingly to accept . . . The Treaty of Seville." There seems no basis for the hypothesis that Glumdalca, the giant Queen, represents the Queen of Spain and was added to the play in 1731 in order to introduce satire on the Treaty of Seville. The addition

(Glumdalca recalling Glumdalclitch, Gulliver's favourite Brobdingnagian) was surely meant to capitalize on the humorous possibilities of introducing a giant lady into the play's love plot. On the positive side, Morrissey ignores two items found in all versions of the play that would in all likelihood have seemed political in 1731. Suspicious audiences could not have overlooked the anti-Walpole possibilities of the Queen's prediction in I,v that ". . . little Thumb will be a great Man made." It was, indeed, the one item that might momentarily have suggested intent to mock the minister in 1730. More important is a droll political thrust in the exchange between King Arthur and his queen in I,ii that ends with the King's reference, noted earlier, to Thumb as "Preserver of my Kingdom." The King announces his intention to get drunk with the Queen, and she, "tho' already half seas over," bravely vows to match him:

> If the capacious Goblet overflow
> With *Arrack-Punch*—'fore George! I'll see it out.

It is hard to believe that spectators primed to see parallels between Arthur and George, Dollallolla and Caroline would have missed Dollallolla's naming of the King of England. If a significant stare at the ridiculous Arthur accompanied the oath, this must have been one of the hilarious high points of the play's political comedy.

The Welsh Opera

The Welsh Opera, Fielding's third play of 1731 (counting an apolitical three-act farce by "Scriblerus Secundus," *The Letter-Writers; or, a New Way to Keep a Wife at Home*,[31] which ran briefly after its opening on March 24 as the original afterpiece of *The Tragedy of Tragedies*), was the culmination of his first, increasingly daring experiment with strong political ingredients. He had obliquely satirized the minister and his policies in *Rape upon Rape*, and adapted *The Tragedy of Tragedies* to accommodate satire on the Court and the minister, as well as the opposition. Finally he satirized the royal family (as well as the politicians) so openly and pungently in *The Welsh Opera* that the Lord Chamberlain, *ex officio* censor of the stage, prevented the performance of the revision of the play known as *The Grub-Street Opera*.

As noted, John Loftis has observed that the satire on the royal family in both *The Welsh Opera* and *The Grub-Street Opera* is as scandalous as Lord Hervey's gossip about Court life. L. J. Morrissey (*GSO*, p. 3) has rightly said that "it is no wonder" the government suppressed *The Grub-Street Opera*. In 1731 political daring got the Haymarket Theatre in deep trouble, and Fielding, its principal playwright, had a foretaste of his permanent exclusion from the stage by the Licensing Act of 1737. Presented ten times as an afterpiece to *The Tragedy of Tragedies* between late April and early June, *The Welsh Opera* was one stimulant to government reprisals against the Haymarket. The government's reaction took the shape of an effective (if not an actual) ban on *The Grub-Street Opera* in early or mid-June and the firm banning of Richard Mountfort's *The Fall of Mortimer*, a violent opposition play that replaced *The Welsh Opera* as afterpiece to *The Tragedy of Tragedies*. In July constables raided performances of Mountfort's play which were being staged in defiance of the ban, and later in the season the theatre was forced to close until February 1732. His involvement no doubt cost Fielding money, banned plays being bad business for a dramatist, though sometimes a windfall for alert printers. Part of what seems to have been a concerted attempt to silence the government's less temperate critics (the publisher of the *Craftsman* was arrested in May and again in June, 1731), this harassment encouraged a temporary avoidance of political risk that coincided with Fielding's migration, between the 1731 and 1732 seasons, from the Haymarket to the slightly more decorous Theatre-Royal in Drury Lane.

Unlike most of Fielding's plays, *The Welsh Opera* was not published on or soon after opening night. Perhaps Fielding was dissatisfied with his weakly plotted farce, and decided not to print it until amplified and revised. He seems to have done some minor revisions (it was advertised on May 19 in *The Daily Post* as having "several alterations and additions") on the original two-act farce after only a few performances, and he went to work on the three-act version eventually called *The Grub-Street Opera* almost immediately after *The Welsh Opera* opened. In a letter to the *Daily Post*, June 28, 1731, he may also have disowned the only published edition of *The Welsh Opera* (London: J. Rayner) as the "incorrect and spurious" work of a "notorious Paper Pyrate." This edition of *The Welsh Opera* probably reproduces an acting script that was sold to Rayner by an actor. It was printed in June, long after *The Welsh Opera* had been withdrawn and after the performance of *The Grub-Street Opera* had been prevented. *The Welsh Opera* had, technically, not been treated as an offensive play by the Lord Chamberlain, though it and *The Fall of Mortimer* surely generated the resentment visited on *The Grub-Street Opera* and the Haymarket company. If Fielding took the trouble to deny in the *Daily Post* that he had authorized publication, his motivation may not have been anger at literary piracy alone, but a desire to lessen governmental resentment. By the next season Fielding would complete a retreat from the risks of anti-government satire. As we will see later, he seems never to have authorized the publication of *The Grub-Street Opera* during his lifetime. Though it preserved a creation embarrassing to its author, and enjoyed nothing like the vogue of *Polly*, the tardy edition of *The Welsh Opera* represents (reasonably closely, one would assume) the only form of the farce seen by a contemporary audience.[32] Its prefatory material reveals Fielding in a temporary mood of angry defiance against the authorities. Its publication was the culmination of Fielding's first experiment in anti-ministerial and anti-court (as well as anti-opposition) satire.

The published version of *The Welsh Opera* bears a subtitle em-

phasizing the most dangerous satire in the play, Fielding's mockery of
Queen Caroline's supposed dominance over King George: "The Gray
Mare the Better Horse." A song in the play re-emphasizes the studied in-
sult to both George and Caroline:

> For where the gray mare
> Is the better horse, there
> The horse is but an ass, sir.

Lest the royal applicability of this ribaldry be missed, a title-page
epigram and a preface (surely by Fielding), found only in *The Welsh
Opera*, not in either edition of *The Grub-Street Opera*, advertise the
play's comic approach to sedition. The epigram is extraordinarily blunt:
". . . a Batchelor Cobler, is happier than a Hen-peck'd Prince." The
preface is blunter. After alluding to the repression of *The Grub-Street
Opera* by "certain Influence which hath been very *prevailing* of late
Years" (possibly meaning the Queen, as well as the Lord Chamberlain
and Walpole), it promises that the play will interest many who have "a
domineering Wife, who will aspire at wearing the Breeches, tho' G-d help
the Man whose hard lot it is to fall under *Petticoat Government*."
Having joked about the relative pleasures of a "Presbyterian Lecture" (a
foretaste of the play's mockery of the Queen's religious pretensions) and
a "Curtain Lecture" (a wife's nagging behind the bed curtains), it goes
so far as this: "We have known in History, that even *Sovereign Princes*
have not been exempted from such *Female Furies;* even one of the most
arbitrary Emperors of Turkey had a *Roxolana* that held his Nose to the
Grindstone."[33]

These prefatory additions were meant to stress the mockery of the
royal family. If *The Tragedy of Tragedies* insinuates scorn for George
and Caroline, *The Welsh Opera*, particularly as published, roars forth its
ridicule of royalty and the censorship. Moreover, the play itself is a
political satire with obvious seditious implications. Its plot (insofar as
plot is discernible) is dual. Its upper or "high" plot concerns a Welsh
Squire named Sir Owen Apshinken and his wife, during a crisis
precipitated by the clandestine courtship and marriage of his empty-
headed, beauish, fumblingly amorous son, Master Owen Apshinken.
The squire obviously represents King George, Madam Apshinken Queen
Caroline, and Master Owen the Prince of Wales. The squire-king is
described as a good man and a generous landlord, which may reflect
Fielding's actual feelings about George, or, more likely, the tendency of
satirists and opposition politicians to blame Caroline or Walpole, rather
than the King. Unfortunately, he allows his wife to run the estate as long
as he is supplied with tobacco (perhaps a symbol for the mistresses
George kept with his wife's enforced approval) and music (George's
abiding artistic passion). The squire's formula, "Let her govern while I
smoke," incorporates a particularly gross insult if tobacco represents
George's mistresses.

His wife's "petticoat government" is unsatisfactory. She desires intellectual, as well as connubial, dominion. She devotes much time to debating theology with her flattering chaplain, Parson Puzzletext, who has been tentatively and futilely identified with a number of contemporary Churchmen who pursued success by dignifying the theological fascinations of Queen Caroline with their attention.[34] More seriously, she delegates authority over the estate to Robin, the butler, who clearly represents Walpole. He maintains his hold over his mistress and the estate by liberally stocking the wine cellar that is her delight. This recalls, of course, the slurs upon Caroline's addiction to the coarser pleasures in Fielding's characterization of Queen Dollallolla, but it also represents Walpole's consistent satisfaction of the royal couple's heavy demands upon the treasury with unprecedented and ever-rising allowances. To cite but one especially relevant example, he obtained a Civil List of £100,000 for Caroline upon her husband's accession in 1728.[35] Ensured control by his services to his mistress and the indifference of his master, Robin is able to loot the estate at will, stealing spoons, shaving plate, overcharging his employers for provisions, and commandeering purposely created excesses of beer. Robin is the ''Robin'' (or ''Honest Bob'') of anti-Walpole caricatures, a domineering servant who enriches himself and his cronies by looting the treasury with the tacit approval of his royal master and, especially, Queen Caroline.

Master Owen is a more insulting caricature of Frederick, Prince of Wales, a hapless, trouble-making figure. Despised by his parents (Caroline's attitude toward her son was more negative than Madam Apshinken's, though the latter regards Master Owen as a mental defective), he was courted and used by ambitious opposition politicians during his more than two decades as potential heir to the throne. In the late 1730s Fielding would support opposition politicians close to Frederick, but in 1731 Frederick and Fielding were both unaligned, and the former was a natural target. Master Owen is ineffectively amorous (as was the young Frederick, who paid one father £1500 for the enjoyment of his daughter in 1730), a ridiculous beau of dubious sexual potency and a desperate pursuer of the state of matrimony. As Puzzletext says, Owen is ''almost half a man, and more than half a beau.''[36] The major complications of the play are caused by his clandestine attempts to wed Molly, daughter of one of his father's tenants, and it ends with the grudging, after-the-fact acceptance of the marriage by his parents. Though the squire is pacified by a song and Owen and Molly are left in bliss, Frederick did not succeed in marrying until 1736 (then had to fight his parents with opposition backing to obtain even the shreds of a married prince's dignities), and could not have gained his father's acquiescence in a marriage of his own planning. The play cleverly suggests two embarrassing episodes in the battle over Frederick's marital desires, one of the standing jokes of the 1730s. In 1730, the King prevented Frederick from betrothing himself to Princess Sophia of Prussia, and in 1731 the Prince was involved in a lame-brained scheme to marry one of his father's subjects, Lady Diana Spencer, niece of the Duchess-Dowager of Marlborough and later briefly (she died in 1735) married to the Duke of Bedford. Like Master Owen, Frederick seems seriously to have contemplated a secret marriage, royal approval being out of the question, forcing Walpole to take measures to abort his plan.[37] The happy conclusion of Master Owen's courtship should perhaps be read as an acidulous anticipation of the possibility that George, Caroline, and Walpole might someday be faced with a quite unacceptable Princess of Wales. Fielding's "high" plot is perhaps best epitomized in air XXVII, where "Clown," "Squire," and "King" are equated: "Love makes a Clown a 'Squire, / Would make a 'Squire a King."

The "lower" plot, concerned with the love and power struggles of the servants, is even more political. Robin's manipulation and fleecing of his employers obviously allegorizes the opposition's assaults on the nature and source of Walpole's influence over the King and Queen and his corrupt diversion of government funds to enrich himself and his supporters. As important and less obvious is a broad parody throughout of the battles between Walpole and his supporters (specifically John, Lord Hervey: John, the groom) and the leaders of the opposition (specifically, William Pulteney, Walpole's most vocal critic: William, the coachman). The treatment of Robin is predictable: he is not only dishonest, but brazenly so, and confident of continued indulgence from his employers. Edgar V. Roberts has declined to term *The Welsh Opera* an opposition play on the grounds that its satire on the minister is less vitriolic and personal than that in the vicious *Robin's Panegyric: or, the Norfolk Miscellany* (1731).[38] But the real point is that it is too balanced to be termed an opposition play: in isolation, its treatment of Robin would justify describing it as typical anti-Walpole satire, but the treatment of Robin's rivals makes it too double-edged to be treated as an opposition play or a sign that Fielding owed any allegiance to opposition in 1731. Fielding remained neutral. He wrote an apolitical epilogue for Theobald's *Orestes* at the same time that *The Welsh Opera* opened, even though Theobald dedicated his play to Walpole, and the low plot of the *Welsh Opera* reveals the contempt for both the opposition and the ministry that is apparent in every early political work but *Rape upon Rape* and the anti-Scriblerian poem of 1729. William the groom (William Pulteney and, by extension, the leaders of the opposition) comes off at least as badly as Robin in the slanging matches that dominate the low action after Master Owen (a glance at the Prince of Wales's function as a troublemaker and catalyst for battles between ministry and opposition) causes trouble by forging love letters from Susan (William's beloved) to Robin and William to Sweetissa (Robin's mistress and intended bride, representative of Walpole's mistress and eventual second wife, Maria Skerrett).

Robin answers William's threats to expose him by pointing out that William too has looted his master's goods and shared in the proceeds of the butler's peculations. Not only Pulteney, but such opposition spokesmen as Lord Carteret (who held office as late as 1730), had served in ministries led by Walpole, a fact often treated as proof of their hypocrisy in attacking the corruption they once shared. Robin also accuses William, with obvious justification, of being motivated by a desire for his post (and greater opportunities for theft), not devotion to his master. Walpole and ministerial apologists scorned Pulteney's hypocritically patriotic scrambling after power and status, and many of his opposition allies in the 1730s also saw it. He would cry out against the government until it met his price, as it finally was to do (at the moderate cost of a peerage) in 1742. In 1731 Fielding saw that the leaders of the opposition were hypocritical rogues attacking a more brazen one, and he as yet had no allegiance to tilt the balance against Walpole. Satiric balancing is everywhere apparent in *The Welsh Opera*. Even when it parodies the famous duel between John, Lord Hervey and William Pulteney early in 1731 (in the ineffectual scuffle in Act II, scene iii between Will and Robin, John and Thomas) it mocks all participants equally. Fielding's view of both sides is, however, most directly expressed in Susan's attempt to make peace between the feuding servants by pointing out that her master can afford to lose the goods they steal, and urging that they "stand by one another, for let me tell you, if matters were to be too nicely examined into, I am afraid it would go hard with us all." Susan's conclusion captures Fielding's attitude toward party politicians: ". . . were we all to have our desserts, we should be finely roasted indeed."

Probably *The Welsh Opera* reveals deeper contempt for William (or Pulteney) than Robin (or Walpole), though Fielding's preference for the corrupt Prime Minister over his opponents only becomes patent in *The Grub-Street Opera*. Throughout the original farce, while both are rogues, William compounds his sins with a hypocritical pretence of disinterested devotion to his master's interests and seems far less able, morals aside, than the efficient butler. William's pretences of superior virtue and disinterestedness ("when Master thinks fit,/ I am ready to quit/ A Place I so little regard, sir;/ For while thou art here,/ No merit must e'er/ Expect to find any reward, sir.") are mocked by Robin and even William's beloved Susan. They precisely parody the kind of patriotic rhetoric which was Pulteney's specialty. William's mockery of Robin's lack of enthusiasm for fist-fighting (which is meant to recall the opposition's assault on Walpole's peace policies toward the Spaniards) is countered with a warning, not answered by William, that the coachman's rashness (the opposition's war policies) may someday endanger his master and mistress: "You are such a headstrong devil that you will overturn the coach one day or other, and break both Master and Mistress' necks. It is always neck or nothing with you." More explicit is a song comparing the railings of failed courtiers (including, in 1731, Pulteney, Carteret, and Lord Bolingbroke) to that of impotent old lovers:

> The worn-out rake at pleasure rails,
>   And cries, 'tis all idle and fleeting;
> At court, the man whose int'rest fails,

> Cries, all is corruption and cheating:
> But would you know
> Whence both these flow,
> Though so much they pretend to abhor them?
> That rails at court,
> This at love's sport,
> Because they are neither fit for 'em, fit for 'em,
> Because they are neither fit for 'em.

Clearly, Fielding, who had in the past and would in the future (e.g., in *The Opposition: A Vision*) prefer Walpole to a man like Pulteney, meant to imply that the opposition's leaders were no more honest and much less able than the Prime Minister. Even at the height of his first flurry of anti-ministerial satire, Fielding was not drifting toward opposition allegiance.

The Grub-Street Opera

The three-act *Grub-Street Opera* is a much better play than the two-act *Welsh Opera*. It is so much improved that the impossibility of staging it (for there is no evidence of a performance of either of the two versions of the play that have come down to us, *The Genuine Grub-Street Opera* and *The Grub-Street Opera*) must have infuriated Fielding. Indeed, he never had even the satisfaction of seeing the best version of his play published. Edgar V. Roberts suggested some years ago that only *The Genuine Grub-Street Opera* was printed in 1731 or indeed in the 1730s. L. J. Morrissey has since argued very convincingly in the superb textual introduction to his edition of the play that the final, longest, most polished version, *The Grub-Street Opera*, was only published in 1755, by Andrew Millar, though its title-page indicates publication in 1731 by J. Roberts. Though Morrissey is not certain that the revisions that distinguish this text from *The Genuine Grub-Street Opera* were carried out in 1731, it is clear that those with political impact were in the text when the young Fielding decided not to risk publishing it.[39] From a political rather than an artistic standpoint *The Grub-Street Opera* is not changed enough to require very extended discussion. The expansion in length and tightening of structure is more extensive in *The Grub-Street Opera*, though there is much added material and new tightness even in the pirated version, which probably was based on a script sold, again to J. Rayner, by an actor after the play's banning. The revisions greatly improve the play. The elimination of the revelations of Goody Scratch as a *dea ex machina* to produce a happy ending, the provision of a more plausible motivation (a passion for Sweetissa) for Master Owen's trouble-making among the servants, and the introduction of Molly's father, Mr. Apshones, into the action were all very welcome. But the basic political difference between *The Welsh Opera* and either *Grub-Street Opera* is that the revisions give us more of Sir Owen and Madam Apshinken (who appear in only four scenes in the original) and allow a more leisurely development of the "political" squabbles between the ser-

vants. In the new third act, Sir Owen sings a marvelous song in praise of
"a pipe of Tobacco," the Apshinkens have their most comical argument,
and Madam Apshinken engages in a droll theological discussion with
Parson Puzzletext. But the political change is generally in degree, not in
kind. It is simply more of the same sort of ridicule of George and
Caroline found in the many passages retained in Acts I and II from *The
Welsh Opera*. This quantitative increase in the royal satire is, moreover,
balanced by the dropping of the subtitle, title-page epigram, and preface
that had added stringent, obtrusive mockery of the royal pair in the
published *Welsh Opera*. The pattern is generally similar in the revisions
of the "lower" plot; the basic implications of the intrigues and debates
between the servants are unchanged, though the political satire is
generally expanded in a dramatic structure allowing more scope for
reductive disputation.

     One exception to the pattern of expansion without significant altera-
tion is a passage in Act III that may allude to Queen Caroline's supposed
role in the retention of Walpole in office upon the accession of George II
in 1728. The opposition, which had courted George and Caroline while
he was Prince of Wales, anticipated his dismissal when George I died.
Walpole was asked to surrender his tokens of office, but George II soon
sensibly asked the minister who controlled Parliament and had proven
ability to do the "King's Business" to resume his offices. George
recognized Walpole's value, though he had encouraged the opposition
during his minority. However, the opposition considered Caroline's influence crucial, a misconception that grew into a conviction as the
Queen, as well as the King, came increasingly to rely on Sir Robert. Her
supposed role in his reinstatement is surely suggested in Act III, scene v,
where Robin informs her that he is to be turned away and William made
butler. Having been informed by William of his dishonesty, the squire
has sent Robin a notice of dismissal, requiring "an account of the
plate." Madam storms out to "see whether I am a cipher in this house or
no," and Puzzletext assures Robin that he is safe with "her ladyship" as
his friend.

     This addition sharpens the anti-court, anti-Walpole edge of the
play, but additions to Act I, scene v of *The Grub-Street Opera (not The
Genuine Grub-Street Opera)* considerably palliate the satire on Walpole
and aggravate the treatment of Pulteney in a scene that originally treated
the former severely. Sweetissa and Margery discuss the "virtues" of their
lovers, the former singing (Air IX) of her satisfaction with the proceeds
of Robin's thievery—and her confidence that he will escape punishment:
"Let halter tie up the poor cheat,/ Who only deserves to be banged;/
The wit who can get an estate,/ Hath still too much wit to be hanged." In
The Welsh Opera these sentiments (echoing *The Beggar's Opera* and
Fielding's *Rape upon Rape*) are presented uncomplicatedly. In *The
Grub-Street Opera*, Sweetissa's song is thus introduced:

     Sweet. I know you are prejudiced against him [Robin] from what

> William says; but be assured that all is malice; he is desirous of getting his place.
>
> Marg. I rather think that a prejudice of yours against William.
>
> Sweet. O Margery, Margery! an upper servant's honesty is never so conspicuous, as when he is abused by the under servants.— They must rail at someone, and if they abuse him he preserves his master and mistress from abuse.

Lest the significance of this be missed, Sweetissa hastily insists on finishing her song that she does not "speak this on Robin's account! For if all my master's ancestors had met with as good servants as Robin, he had enjoyed a better estate than he hath now." A more favourable view of Walpole is apparent here than that in *The Welsh Opera*, though *The Grub-Street Opera* is still certainly not complimentary to Walpole, in other than a comparative sense. It is conceivable that these additions were not made until late in Fielding's career, perhaps in the early 1750s, before he gave his manuscript to Millar for posthumous publication. In later years he was inclined to more positive attitudes about Walpole and far more negative ones about Pulteney than in 1731. However, I believe these changes were made in 1731, before Fielding concluded it was prudent to shelve his play as unperformable and too risky to publish. Assuming they were inserted in 1731, these speeches re-emphasize the impropriety of classifying *The Grub-Street Opera* (or *The Welsh Opera*) as an opposition play. They may signal the beginning of the process that made Fielding a politically innocuous playwright and a praiser of Walpole by 1732. It is clear that J. R. Brown is correct in seeing these revisions as "apologetic," added by an author who was "at this time, more a looker-on at politics than an active participant in party warfare," who was "not overjoyed at finding his play taken as an outright attack on the ministry."[40] Ever inclined to look with at least as jaundiced an eye on Walpole's foes, Fielding had just had a sharp lesson (the banning of his play and the persecution of the Haymarket) in the dangers of anti-administration satire. An evolution away from anti-ministerialism was a natural reaction for a professional writer without sustaining opposition connections. His next play with anti-ministerial potential, *The Modern Husband* of 1732, not only eschews the application of very tempting details and patterns to Walpole, but was published with a fulsomely complimentary, apparently straightforward dedication, "to the Right Honourable Sir Robert Walpole, Knight of the Most Noble Order of the Garter." There was never a chance of the tragical *dénouement* envisioned by Orator Henley's *Hyp Doctor*, which said the Haymarket players would next perform at Tyburn, offering a play by "Doeg Fielding" entitled "Tyburn in Glory, or Thespis in a Cart, tying in one knot the beginning and the end of Tragedy."[41] However, there were consequences of a less fatal kind in mocking kings, queens, princes, and even ministers, and Fielding did not again tempt censorship until time and new opposition obligations gave him new reasons for doing so in 1736.

4. A Retreat from Politics, 1732-33

There was a sharp break in Fielding's career between the *Grub-Street Opera* and the theatrical season of 1732. He moved from the Haymarket, along with the cream of its company, to Drury Lane, and turned away from dangerous anti-court satire. For the next two years (with two exceptions, a dedication to Walpole and a poem left unpublished that insults the leading opposition wits, though not on overtly political grounds) he cultivated an indifference to politics unmatched until his old age. This change is the more striking because England became a political battleground in these years as Walpole's plan to replace such difficult-to-collect sources of revenue as customs duties with internal excise taxes was introduced, debated, and withdrawn under pressure, and the government and the opposition geared up for the general election in 1734. Its opponents treated the excise scheme as a threat to liberty and property, involving armies of excise agents with the right of search and seizure. Partisan journalists and print-makers produced invective and argument to match the violent debate on the excise in Parliament. The battle began in 1732, reached frenzy with the debates on the Excise Bill in the first half of 1733, and reverberated through the election that followed Walpole's abandonment of the attempt to force his scheme through an unwilling House of Commons. The nation rang to the cry "Liberty, Property and No Excise!," the *Free Briton* and the *Craftsman* battled, Lords Cobham and Chesterfield opposed the Excise Bill and lost the places that tied them to the government, and Walpole finally conceded "this dance it will no longer go." But Fielding observed a most pregnant silence. He avoided politics generally through six plays, and dedicated *The Modern Husband* to Walpole, probably to ensure that nothing in it would be interpreted as anti-ministerial. His retreat was near-total, conscious, and obvious.

The Lottery: A Farce

The Lottery, a ballad opera, was first performed on New Year's Day, 1732 and published a week later, in a version that incorporated some innocuous songs from *The Grub-Street Opera*. It ran after February 1 in a revised version, pruned of most of the material from the 1731 play. The revision, as Edgar V. Roberts has said, "set the pattern for his ballad operas during the next three years at Drury Lane: happy, lightly satirical, and for the most part nonpolitical."[42] A charming, slight piece, enlivened by songs, it satirizes dishonest brokers dealing in tickets in the government's joint-stock lottery, and ridicules those who hoped to make their fortunes by buying them. But the fact that lotteries were a controversial method by which the government eked out its funds does not in itself make such satire political. Lotteries, as F. Homes Dudden argues, were always one of Fielding's pet hatreds. Wit, clever plotting, good songs, and social and moral satire, not political satire, made this play a success. Fielding, who also provided an epilogue during January 1732 for *The Modish Couple* (a play ostensibly written by Captain Bodens, but actually the work of Lord Hervey and the Prince of Wales), had backed far away from censorable political satire in six months.

Certain minor items in *The Lottery* might be politically interpreted, but their importance is slight. Fielding criticizes cringing courtiers and the beggaring of brave officers who were on half-pay because of the peace policies favoured by the government. Fielding no doubt knew the latter problem first-hand as the impecunious son of a half-pay general, but his satire on it here is no more partisan than that in *Amelia*, which focusses on the plight of half-pay officers in the early 1730s. *The Lottery* includes only two examples of more pointed political satire. One song parallels political bribery, electoral corruption, and prostitution:

> When the Candidate offers his Purse,
>   What Voter requires what he meant?
> When a great Man attempts to disburse,
>   What little Man ask'd his Intent
> When the Lover has nam'd the Maid
> And thus has ask'd good Mother's Aid,
> Who, but a Novice in the Trade
>   Wou'd ever ask his Meaning?

The other example, a satiric reference to the Charitable Corporation (". . . a method invented, by some very wise Men, by which the Rich may be charitable to the Poor and be Money in the Pocket by it") may be partly a reaction to advance rumours (the Corporation's financial practices were first attacked during 1731 in Parliament) about a major fiscal scandal that surfaced in the Commons approximately a month after *The Lottery* opened. Three directors of the Corporation (designed to lend "small sums" to the "industrious poor" at legal interest to keep them out of the hands of usurers), Denis Bond, Archibald Grant, and Sir Robert Sutton, were to varying degrees involved in a looting of the Corporation's funds that began in the late 1720s and left the Corporation bankrupt, with net liabilities of over £450,000, by the end of 1731. These M.P.s (Bond and Grant being utter scoundrels, Sutton a victim, in part, of his carelessness and gullibility) were expelled from the House as a result of an investigation by a Commons Committee (dominated by the opposition) between the time a complaint was lodged by Sir Thomas Robinson on February 3, 1732 and the following May. They had turned to crime because they were deeply in debt to the mastermind behind the swindle, a stockbroker named George Robinson, who bought a seat in Commons in late 1731, but never sat in the House. Robinson took at least £200,000 when he and the Corporation's warehouse-keeper, one Mr. Thomson, fled unpunished abroad, though he was expelled from the House and his property in England confiscated.[43] Though all of this came out slightly after *The Lottery* was published, it is reasonable to see as political Fielding's sharp dig at the "uncharitable charity" of the Corporation's directors. It resembles Pope's dig at Denis Bond in the *Epistle to Bathhurst* of 1731: "Bond damns the Poor, and hates them from his heart" (1.102). The scandal embarrassed a ministry associated since the South Sea Bubble with peculation and jobbery, and in *The Author's Farce* of 1734, Fielding would hammer partisanly at the dishonesty of the directors. However, such political hints do not make *The Lottery* political. Fielding did not need a partisan motivation to ridicule corruption or the making of a profit out of relieving the deserving poor. No play in Fielding's canon up to 1732 is less concerned with politics than *The Lottery*.

The Modern Husband

Fielding's first "regular" comedy in five acts since 1730, *The Modern Husband*, opened at Drury Lane on February 14, 1732 and was published a week later. The work of several years ("puffed" in *The Craftsman* not long after it was sent to Lady Mary Wortley Montagu on September 4, 1730), it was rejected by audiences and critics as indelicate, even pornographic. It arraigns a particularly degraded social and moral vice. Mr. Modern, who has eased his financial difficulties in the past by allowing Lord Richly to bed with his willing wife for money, plans to "discover" Richly in his wife's bed and extort a large bribe from the peer. Richly is cloyed with Mrs. Modern, but willing to pay well for her aid in procuring for him the beautiful and virtuous Mrs. Bellamant. The Moderns almost ruin Mrs. Bellamant, principally because Mr. Bellamant (a foolish and weak but basically good man, really in love with his wife) has been conducting a secret affair with Mrs. Modern. A variation on Mr. Modern's original plan, a "discovery" of Mr. Bellamant with Mrs. Modern, nearly succeeds, and the sordid scheming of the play only just allows a happy ending for the Bellamants. Such vice in a comedy repelled audiences and critics, though Fielding probably had hoped that the moral seriousness and severity that dominates the play would justify depicting the vice. He would have similar problems upon the publication of *Amelia*, which recalls *The Modern Husband* in certain aspects of its plot, themes, and characterizations as well as its time setting, the earlier 1730s.

Ironically, *The Modern Husband* is politically fascinating because Fielding failed to exploit its obvious receptivity to political overtones and actively discouraged readers from imposing such overtones upon it. If Fielding had inserted the slightest hint (in the manner of *The Tragedy of Tragedies*) of anti-ministerial intent in *The Modern Husband*, audiences and readers might well have interpreted the satire on the depraved Lord Richly as a severe ironical attack on Walpolian political corruption. Whether Lady Mary saw political significance, overt or potential, in the scenes from the play that Fielding seems to have submitted to her in September 1730 is not discoverable, though if she had she would have discouraged its performance. However, the opposition's *Craftsman* "puffed" the play in September 1730, as one "said to bear a great reputation," which may indicate an expectation of anti-ministerial satire.[44] Timing alone suggests that if the play had been produced (and published, *sans* dedication to Walpole) in September or October, 1730, receptive details or patterns in it would have invited anti-Walpole interpretation. *Rape upon Rape* was performed and published that summer, foreshadowing the anti-ministerial satire of 1731.

The play of 1730 is lost, but the version of *The Modern Husband* printed in 1732 seems too well organized and stylistically and tonally consistent to have been extensively revised. It includes much that Fielding could have given an anti-ministerial turn in the rash mood apparent in *Rape upon Rape* and the plays of 1731, however politically innocuous this material may seem in the light of the dedication to Walpole ultimately prefixed to it. Ignoring such ambiguous details as the notice that Mr. Modern was impoverished by the collapse of the South Sea Bubble, the temptations to associate Walpole and Lord Richly are considerable. He is not only an immoral rogue, but a corrupt and corrupting "great Man"—a "Mighty Villain," as Fielding put it in the prologue to *Rape upon Rape*. Captain Merit must bribe his way into Richly's levee since, as Captain Bravely says, "the Servants of a great Man are all great Men." The notion that these references to the varieties of "great Men" may originally have been intended as a slap at Walpole and his sycophants is reinforced a few lines later, when Captain Merit bitterly observes: "What an abundance of poor Wretches go to the feeding the Vanity of that Leviathan, one great Rogue."[45] Lord Richly's behaviour also illustrates one of the political skills that most infuriated Walpole's enemies: he has learned that to corrupt and control his suppliants he has only to promise a favour, not perform it. He promises everyone something—even Merit—but assures his sycophants he never will deliver. He calls his levee "a Paradise of Fools," and boasts (while he considers offering Bellamant a place in exchange for his wife's virtue): "I have made twenty such Men subscribe themselves Cuckolds by the prospect of one Place, which not one of them ever had." His "fools," we are told, "are not caught like Fish in the Water by a Bait, but like the Dog in the Water by a shadow" (p. 50). All of this recalls the frequent satire of Walpole as a great man who had perfected the use of "promises" as "bribes." The technique, as his biographer, J. H. Plumb, points out, was actually one of his essential skills as an organizer of majorities.[46]

With the slightest encouragement, in short, audiences could have seen Richly as a type of Walpole, corrupting supple husbands as the minister corrupted electors and M.P.s, and Bellamant, who resists the temptation of a place in exchange for his wife's and his own honour, as a symbol of political purity and opposition. Had Bellamant's final denunciation of Lord Richly—"Where Grandeur can give License to Oppression, the people must be Slaves, let them boast what Liberty they please" (pp. 67-68)—been thundered from the stage of Drury Lane in the fall of 1730, audiences would have had as good cause to apply it politically as

Justice Worthy's attack on official villainy at the end of *Rape upon Rape:*

> No Reverence that Church or State attends,
> Whose Laws the Priest or Magistrate offends.

Though Fielding all but openly asks for a reward, I agree with F. Homes Dudden that there is little likelihood that he hoped to attract Walpole's patronage by dedicating *The Modern Husband* to him. Walpole was unlikely to favour the author of the plays of 1731. But any shadow of an excuse for viewing the dedication as ironical evaporated, it seems to me, with the rediscovery of Fielding's anti-opposition poems of 1729 and 1733. I believe Fielding added the dedication to *The Modern Husband* as a safety measure, to present readers from seeing anti-ministerial satire in parts of the play that may originally have been intended to convey it and that continued to invite interpretation dangerous to Fielding and Drury Lane. If, as suggested, the "puffing" of the play in the opposition's *Craftsman* in 1730 implied an expectation of anti-Walpole content, the fact that Fielding found *The Grub-Street Journal* (see the essay by "Dramaticus," March 30, 1732) contemptuous of the play after it appeared with the dedication to Walpole almost surely bears an opposite significance. It is difficult to envision a surer preventive against anti-ministerial interpretation than the dedication to Walpole:

> Protect therefore, Sir, an Art from which you may promise your self such notable Advantages; when the little Artifices of Your Enemies, which you have surmounted, shall be forgotten, when Envy shall cease to misrepresent your Actions, and Ignorance to misapprehend them. The Muses shall remember their Protector, and the wise Statesman, the generous Patron, the stedfast Friend, and the true Patriot; but above all that Humanity and Sweetness of Temper, which shine thro' all your Actions, shall render the Name of SIR ROBERT WALPOLE dear to his no longer ungrateful Country . . . . that you may continue to preserve us from our Enemies abroad, and to triumph over your Enemies at home, is the sincere Wish of,
>
> > Sir,
> > Your most obliged,
> > Most obedient humble Servant,
> > Henry Fielding.

The Old Debauchees and *The Covent-Garden Tragedy*

L. J. Morrissey has said, "Fielding seems to have lost interest in political satire"[47] by the opening of *The Covent-Garden Tragedy* on June 1, 1732. He might have set the date earlier. Both the *Covent-Garden Tragedy* (a mock-solemn, two-act farce, hissed off the stage after one performance) and *The Old Debauchees* (a crude comedy incorporating violent anti-Catholic satire that opened the same night and fared somewhat better) are innocent. Fielding revived *The Old Debauchees* (with the subtitle "The Jesuit Caught") in 1745-1746, as part of the assault during the "Forty-Five" on the Catholicism of the Stuarts. The play's satire on the Inquisition, Catholic superstition, and the Machiavellian attempts of the heroine's Jesuit confessor to seduce her (recalling Father Girard, the French Jesuit tried in October 1731 for seducing a young virgin by sorcery) resembles satire in Fielding's much later anti-Jacobite journalism. This should not, however, obscure the play's original avoidance of politics in favour of bigoted scurrility. There was no more political scandal to titillate the audience at Drury Lane on June 1, 1732 than on the opening night of *The Modern Husband*.

Morrissey's emphasis on the political innocuousness of *The Covent-Garden Tragedy*, rather than the other half of the double bill, is apt. A lukewarm burlesque of Ambrose Phillips' *Distressed Mother*, it not only ignores politics, but was published (on June 24, 1732) with a prefatory parody of *Grub-Street Journal* criticisms of the play, which implies Fielding's belief that attacks on it reflected resentment at his failure to satirize the government. *The Grub-Street Journal* was not highly political by contemporary standards, but its bias was to opposition, and it became hostile to Fielding in 1732. After mocking the style and morality of *The Modern Husband* on March 30, it treated *The Covent-Garden Tragedy* as scenes from a brothel on June 8 and 15, suggesting Mr. Fielding knew his subject. On June 29, perhaps newly irked by Fielding's "answer"-prologue, it attacked *The Lottery, The Modern Husband*, and *The Covent-Garden Tragedy* as ill-written smut, and disputed the *Daily Post's* assertions (June 2, 15, 16) that *The Old Debauchees* was a hit. It briefly criticized *The Modern Husband* on July 13, and on July 20 violently attacked *The Covent-Garden Tragedy* and *The Old Debauchees* as indecent and said Fielding's final play of 1732, *The Mock Doctor; or, the Dumb Lady Cur'd* (an adaptation of Molière's *Le Médecin Malgré Lui*), had "most execrably murdered" the French original. The battle went on until September, fueled by replies from Fielding's friends, including a letter from "Philalethes" in *The Daily Post* for July 31 which some have attributed to Fielding himself, though its style (like and yet unlike his) and lavish praise of Fielding's birth, learning, and character suggest that a friend (perhaps James Ralph, who often wrote somewhat like Fielding) defended him.[48]

The attacks on *The Covent-Garden Tragedy* and other plays of 1732 never focus on their avoidance of political satire (a journalist could not openly complain about that!), and Fielding *did* revenge himself for the attack on *The Modern Husband* when he made Leathersides, the porter-pimp in *The Covent-Garden Tragedy*, stand for one of the authors of *The Grub-Street Journal*. But there must have been another reason for *The Grub-Street Journal's* extraordinary concentration on damning Fielding in 1732. It had teased him as early as June 1730, parodying *Tom Thumb*, but it never, earlier or later, showed such an interest or the same severity, even though his plays of, say, 1731 were at least as irregular and sometimes nearly as indecent. Wilbur Cross rightly said that Fielding was "regarded as fair game by the Grubeans in their lighter mood" until his shift to Drury Lane, dominated by the Cibbers, and to eulogy of Walpole made him the target of "those heavier shafts of Grub-Street wit that were aimed to kill."[49] Fielding, who knew well the secret springs of contemporary paper warfare, implies that *The Grub-Street Journal*'s sudden enmity was a result of his metamorphosis into a political neutral.

The Grub-Street critic in Fielding's pre-emptive parody ("*A Criticism* on the *Covent-Garden Tragedy*, originally intended for the *Grub-Street Journal*") vows to prejudice the public against it. He admits that his envy has been aroused by Fielding's successes, and ridicules with hilarious ineptitude ("Horase" and "Aristuttle" are his authorities) Fielding's violations of the rules of tragedy. His absurd definition of tragedy, however, includes one item (my italics) meant to imply the *Grub-Street Journal*'s intolerance of plays without anti-ministerial satire: ". . . a thing of five Acts, written Dialogue-wise, consisting of several fine Similies, Metaphors, and Moral Phrases, *with here and there a speech upon Liberty* . . . . it must contain an Action, Characters, Sentiments, Diction, and a Moral." The Grub-Streeter momentarily praises the play's first five lines as promising good things to come:

> Who'd be a Bawd in this degen'rate Age!
> Who'd for her Country unrewarded toil!
> Not so the Statesman scrubs his plotful Head,
> Not so the Lawyer shakes his unfeed Tongue,
> Not so the Doctor guides the doseful Quill.

The third line is the only item in *The Covent-Garden Tragedy* (except for Mother Punchbowl's remark that Captain Bilkum and Stormandra deserve "The fate of greater Persons") that even hints political ridicule. Fielding's Grub-Streeter stresses his disappointment at the non-fulfillment of its anti-ministerial and anti-court promise: "What did I not expect from such a Beginning? But alas! What follows? No fine Moral Sentences, not a Word of Liberty and Property, no Insinuations, that Courtiers are fools, and Statesmen Rogues." "Liberty and Property" were becoming the cry of opponents of Walpole's excise plans in 1732. If avoiding them was a dereliction to *The Grub-Street Journal*, Fielding's *Covent-Garden Tragedy* must have seemed as faulty as *The Modern Husband*, even before he dedicated the latter to Walpole on its publication two weeks after opening night. Both failed, *The Covent-Garden Tragedy* disastrously, and the opposition's antagonism toward a "deserter" was probably one cause.

The Mock Doctor and The Miser

Fielding ended the 1732 season and opened the 1733 season with adaptations of Molière's *Le Médecin Malgré Lui* and *L'Avare: The Mock Doctor* and *The Miser*. His interest in Molière (the *Old Debauchees* is indebted to *Tartuffe*) was, doubtless, a result of his involvement with an edition of the *Select Comedies of Molière* published in

1732 and "puffed" in the preface to *The Mock Doctor*, though the process that turned *Le Médecin Malgré Lui*, a farce of three acts, into *The Mock Doctor*, a charming one-act ballad opera, was hardly translation. Neither of Fielding'd adaptations is political, though it will be necessary to demonstrate the innocence of *The Mock Doctor*, and it is just possible that *The Miser* has political overtones.

The Mock Doctor; or, The Dumb Lady Cur'd (first performed as an afterpiece to *The Old Debauchees* on June 23 as a replacement for the failed *Covent-Garden Tragedy*) is as apolitical as its immediate predecessors. It differs structurally from Molière's play and imposes satire on a contemporary quack, Dr. John Misaubin, upon the original's more general satire on quackery, but no political satire is added. However, Sheridan Baker has suggested that subtle satire on Walpole, a "political quack," is implicit in the play's satire on Misaubin and his kind. His case is similar to that for his complexly allegorical, anti-Walpole reading of the original *Author's Farce*. He begins by noting that one of Fielding's characters is named "Robert," and concludes (though the name is retained from Molière) that " 'Squire Robert,' could not avoid suggesting Walpole, no matter how innocently presented." He traces extraordinarily complex associations between characters in the play and Walpole that audiences would, he thinks, have recognized. He notes that Walpole was depicted as a quack distributing medicine (or bribes) in an obscure ballad republished (having originated in a pamphlet called *The Empiric*) on November 13, 1731 in *Fog's Weekly Journal*, and that in 1740 (*The Champion*, June 17) Fielding was to compare Walpole with a quack doctor. Misaubin and his famous useless "pill" were common satiric butts, the play never clearly hints anti-Walpole intent, and the dedication of the play to Misaubin overwhelmingly particularizes its target; nonetheless, Baker sees anti-Walpole intention in the play's treatment of Misaubin.

As further "corroboration" he offers two suggestions. First, he notes (1) that Squire Robert is caught up in a marital argument that resembles the squabbles of Punch and Judy in the traditional puppet-show; (2) that Molière's treatment of a similar scene may have been influenced by the Italian Harlequin tradition (though he does not show that Robert is a recognizable Harlequin in Fielding's play); (3) that the frontispiece of Volume II of the 1731 reprint of the Craftsman depicts Walpole as a Harlequin; and (4) that *Craftsman* essays reprinted in the same volume (nos. 74 and 78 published in the 1720s but reprinted in the volume in question) develop the comparison and propose an "entertainment" called "The Mock Minister; or Harlequin a Statesman;" and (5) that in *Tumble-Down Dick* Fielding was to associate Walpole with "Harlequin in his Dr. Faustus aspect." Baker's suggestion about *Tumble-Down Dick* will be examined later. For now, it is sufficient to stress that an audience would have had to strain in 1732 to see Robert as a Harlequin, then perform a feat of memory and imagination to associate the Craftsman's quack-minister comparison with *The Mock*

Doctor. Baker's second corroboration is weaker. He notes that "Orator" Henley had triumphed in *The Hyp-Doctor* (a paper favouring Walpole) on July 15 and 22, 1731 over Fielding's difficulties with the censor, and that Fielding alludes to Henley's paper and depicts the "Orator" following Walpole (who is scattering bribes) in *The Champion* for, respectively, February 14, 1740 and December 13, 1739. It is unclear how these skirmishes between Henley and Fielding bear upon the question of associating Misaubin and Walpole in *The Mock Doctor* in 1732. In sum, the case for a political reading rests on the weakly supported assertion that Misaubin's quackery would have recalled obscure satires on Walpolian corruption as quackery and that satire on the "Orator" was automatically satire on Walpole because the *Hyp-Doctor* was ministerial. Baker contends that, though Fielding was "somewhat chastened after the *Grub-Street Opera*" (a considerable understatement), he "could not possibly have missed the fact that he was admitting anti-Walpoliana, from quack doctor to mock minister, into the apparently innocent *Mock Doctor*." One must accept, without qualification, Baker's answer to his own rhetorical question: "Did Fielding translate Molière to satirize Walpole? Obviously not."[50]

The Miser, a five-act comedy based upon Molière's *L'Avare*, opened on February 17. On April 6 Fielding introduced a short piece called *Deborah; or, A Wife for You All* as an afterpiece to *The Miser*, but it was never published and one can only conjecture that it was a miniature ballad-opera burlesquing both Handel's unpopular *Deborah* and perhaps an operatic version (not by Fielding) of *The Tragedy of Tragedies* entitled the *Opera of Operas*, which opened at the Haymarket on May 31. *The Miser* offers an early glimpse of Fielding's skill as an adapter. He heavily altered the original—dropping and adding scenes, changing the plot and lightening the moral tone—and yet produced a comedy that holds together admirably and ran for twenty-six nights. But it cannot be assigned political significance with assurance, though certain aspects offer some temptations to a political interpreter.

Its dedication to the Duke of Richmond (a courtier who received the Garter in 1726 and was Lord of the Bed-Chamber in 1733) surely does not imply a desire to curry ministerial favour. Richmond was actually noted for the benevolence it attributes to him, and Fielding (who perhaps experienced his benevolence) later dedicated two generally non-partisan works to him, "Of Good Nature" (*Miscellanies*, 1743) and *An Enquiry into the Causes of the Late Increase of Robbers* (1751). Two patterns in the play itself, however, are intriguing. The machinations of its "clever servants" are intermittently compared to the schemes of party politicians. Ramallie refers to himself as a "party-coloured gentleman." Another servant boasts thus of exacting multiple bribes: "Fools only to one Party will confide,/ Good Politicians will both Parties guide,/ And, if one fails, they're fee'd on t'other Side." This is political, though non-partisan and unimportant. More interesting, but less certain, is a possible running allusion to the financial and marital troubles between George II and Frederick, Prince of Wales. The Son of Lovegold, the miser, is named Frederick and he clashes with his father over money and marriage. The name Frederick (unlike Robert in the *Mock Doctor*) is *not* carried over from Molière, whose son is called Cléante. Though it was natural to change the name (Cléante is a very French name without a common English equivalent), the choice of Frederick is suggestive. Fielding's Frederick waits for his father's death with something of the impatience felt by every Hanoverian heir and his adherents. Ramallie asks, "Do you think my Master's Father will live forever?" The tension between father and son might be interpreted as a variant of the squabbles of the Apshinkens in *The Welsh Opera* and "party-coloured" Ramallie as another insult to scheming opposition politicians. The evidence for such interpretation, however, is too shaky for confident assertion; it is merely a possibility or a direction for future investigation. It has three obvious weaknesses. First, no one in the eighteenth century, or since, seems to have detected political satire in *The Miser*. Secondly, Fielding may have chosen the name Frederick by chance or because of an unconscious (and unexploited) perception of resemblances between the Lovegolds and George and Frederick. Finally, the battles between King and Prince over the latter's female entanglements had become a standing joke by 1730-31, but those between Lovegold *père* and *fils* most precisely resemble those between George and his heir after Frederick married in 1736 (an event which was followed by intense bickering over the Prince's insistence on a separate and regal residence and an increased income), rather than in 1732.

Whether one assumes that the allusion to Frederick and George (which would give the play a slight anti-opposition bias, all things considered) is a figment or that its subtlety hitherto precluded detection, Fielding's *Miser* is consistent with the elaborate caution of Fielding's temporary retreat from political risk after being censorially gagged in 1731. This is particularly true as it was his major stage offering in a spring that saw the beginning of the excise crisis. The same caution, blended with a tendency to express contempt for the spokesmen of opposition *in private*, is apparent in "An Epistle to Mr. Lyttelton occasioned by two Lines in Mr. Pope's Paraphrase on the first Satire of the 2nd Book of Horace." He probably wrote this poem between mid-February and April 1733, though it was unknown until Isobel Grundy found it among Lady Mary Wortley Montagu's papers. Its major purposes were to compliment George Lyttleton, whose poem *Advice to a Lady* was circulating in manuscript at the time (written in 1731, it was finally published in *The Universal Spectator* on March 10, 1733), and to defend Lady Mary from Pope's attack on her, as Sappho, in lines 83-84 of the poem mentioned in its title. However, its anti-opposition bias is clear. That Pope was associated with the opposition and Lady Mary with Walpole does not in itself imply that the poem is partisan, nor do its compliments to the wives of the Earl of Shaftesbury, the Duke of Richmond, and Lord Hervey. But anti-opposition bias becomes overt when

Fielding's satire on Pope for using his great gifts to slander Lady Mary is broadened to include not only Swift, but Lord Bolingbroke, as writer, and William Pulteney, as orator:

> The bad Man eclipsed the Poet's [Pope's] Worth.
> But oh! Can Homer's fire, can Virgil's Art,
> Ballance the Horrours of an evil Heart.
> Can Wit for wild Barbarity atone?
> What Swift has writ for half what
>   E_____[?] has done?
> Me, the Benevolence that joys to please,
> The heart that triumphs in another's Ease,
> The more one Action of a Wade delights
> Then all that Poulteney speaks,
>   and St. John [Bolingbroke] writes.
>   (11. 65-71)

Isobel Grundy's conclusion that this expresses Fielding's "reservations about politicians in general"[51] is inadequate, though he certainly had such reservations. The fact that makes the poem a perfect close to Fielding's retreat from politics, 1732-33, is not that it satirizes the leading voices of opposition, but that is *was not published*. Though rumours may have reached the Scriblerians and may have even evoked a minor response from Swift,[52] this poem remained a private gift to an injured lady and a compliment to an important friend.

5. A Tentative Return to Politics and Dramatic Disasters, 1734-35

When the 1734 season opened, Fielding must have been far less confident than in the glory days of 1730-31. His attempted recovery after the banning of *The Grub-Street Opera* had not proved very successful, for two of the five plays he introduced in 1732 had failed amid hisses and he had achieved nothing approaching the success of his earlier farces. He may have been driven to translate plays for the *Select Comedies of Molière* by financial pressures in 1732. In 1733 *Deborah; or, A Wife for You All* was performed only once (as a benefit for Mrs. Clive, Fielding's favourite actress), and was not published. *The Miser*, though it succeeded, was no *Tom Thumb* and did not balance the reverses of 1732. His silence for the rest of 1733 may reflect the disruption of the Drury Lane Company, which was deserted by most of its best actors because of a dispute between Theophilus Cibber, who led a migration to the Haymarket, and its new manager, John Highmore, with whom Fielding sided.[53]

Fielding's two major productions in 1734, a revised version of *The Author's Farce* and the hurriedly revamped ballad opera, *Don Quixote in England* (based on a comedy written in 1728 at Leyden and turned down by Drury Lane in 1729),[54] both bespeak desperation and a decision once more to risk political satire. The 1734 *Author's Farce* includes new satire not only on Theophilus Cibber, but also on Walpole's Excise defeat in 1733, predictions of extraordinary corruption and violence in the general election due in 1734, and an acid allusion to the Charitable Corporation scandals of 1732. *Don Quixote in England*, Fielding tells us in the preface to the published version, was revived in order to help Highmore's beleaguered remnant at the Drury Lane Company, though it eventually played at the Haymarket. It was altered to accommodate satire on electoral corruption, a timely subject since it opened in April as the election loomed, and was published on April 18, the day the election writs were issued.[55] It was also dedicated to Lord Chesterfield, an important post-Excise recruit to opposition, in terms suggesting that its author shared Chesterfield's animosity toward Walpole.

Despite these seemingly obvious symptoms of a reawakening interest in politics and of a trend toward opposition, *The Author's Farce* of 1734 is not very political and the more political *Don Quixote in England* (its dedication aside) is certainly not, in a simple sense, partisan, for it is as critical of the opposition as of Walpole, even in the added scenes dealing with the impending election. Indeed, the inapproporiateness of seeing a simple *rapprochement* with the opposition in these plays is not only apparent when one analyzes their political content, but is also implicit in another, basically unpolitical work. The hesitancy of Fielding's return to political satire and the confusion of his political hopes and loyalties are obvious in the prefatory material to the published version of *The Intriguing Chambermaid*. A charming, successful two-act farce (based on Reynard's *Le Retour Imprévu*), it was Fielding's only wholly new offering in 1734 about which we know very much. Though it opened (obviously as a showcase for Mrs. Clive) on the same night (January 15, 1734) as the revised *Author's Farce*, to which it served as an afterpiece,[56] it is absolutely non-political. A deeper political mystery is apparent in the published version.

The dedication to Mrs. Clive compliments Chesterfield as "one of the finest Judges" of drama and "the greatest man of his age." This naturally has been viewed as one more symptom of the desire for opposition patronage signalled by the two major plays of 1734 (though not the *Intriguing Chambermaid*) and the dedication of *Don Quixote*. However, it is immediately followed by a dedicatory poem "To Mr. Fielding, occasioned by the Revival of the *Author's Farce*," by an "unknown Hand," which notes, among other things, that when Fielding displays "the politician" none can fail to be amused and angered "when he reflects that such grave Heads, so late/ controul'd our Senate, and inflam'd our State." The target is not immediately identifiable since it best fits the opposition's role in the Excise crisis, while the play being praised mocks Walpole's failure. But the closing exhortation of the poem makes it clear that the opposition is the poem's political target and implies not only that Fielding's hope is still for support from Walpole but also—odd as it may seem—that the revised *Author's Farce* ought to earn him the minister's favour:

> Proceed, even thus, proceed, bless'd Youth to charm,
> Divert our Hearts, and Civil Rage disarm,
> Til Fortune, once not blind to Merit, smile
> On thy Desert, and recompense thy Toil;
> Or Walpole, studious still of Britain's Fame,
> Protect thy Labours, and prescribe the Theme,
> On which, in Ease and Affluence, thou may'st raise
> More noble Trophies to thy Country's Praise.[57]

There seems no excuse for dismissing this (any more than the dedication of *The Modern Husband*) as ironical. Its tenor and publication with *The Intriguing Chambermaid* surely signify the confused desperation of Fielding's dreams of patronage and the half-heartedness at best of his drift toward the anti-Walpole camp in 1734.

The Author's Farce (1734)

The revision of *The Author's Farce* for its revival in January 1734 was "almost conscientiously thorough, scarcely a page being left untouched."[58] This left the play less coherent and somewhat less gay, which may explain its failure and the fact that it was not printed until 1750, but the revision added political savour. Fielding incorporated satire on Theophilus Cibber (Colley's son and the "villain" at Drury Lane) in the new character, Marplay Jr., indignant allusions to the shocking elevation of Colley (Marplay Sr.) to the Laureateship, and stringent mockery of Italian opera. He also added (by cleverly revising some scenes and inserting others) satiric allusions to Walpole and political ills often blamed on the minister. The added political material does not radically shift the play's satiric balance or make it a "political" play, in the sense that *The Grub-Street Opera* or even *Don Quixote in England* are political, but it is obvious and sharp.

Fielding's revision accidentally eliminated some minor partisan items in the original, while adding others (e.g., "A pretty woman will be sooner earnest to part with her beauty, than a great man with his power"), but the general politicizing pattern is best captured in three examples. Sheridan Baker's assumption that Punch, the "puppet," reductively represented Walpole in 1730 and that the parallel was merely emphasized in 1734 is false. (Indeed, to recapitulate, the general analogies between Walpole and Punch, the Marplays, and Bookweight that Baker suggests seem no more apparent in the 1734 play than in the original.) The revisions *add* (as opposed to *re-emphasize*) anti-Walpole innuendo. A case in point is the scene in which Punch states his intention to seek a seat in Parliament (an allusion to the impending election), and observes that he "is very well known to have a very considerable Interest in all the Corporations in *England;* and for Qualification, if I have no Estate of my own, I can borrow one." (Woods, *AF*, p. 98) The reference is not specifically to Walpole; it indeed fits his lieutenant, the Duke of Newcastle, better.[59] However, its satire on the electoral methods of one with universal influence over electoral "corporations" as well as its possible reference to scandals of 1732-33 in the Charitable Corporation[60] (which are newly satirized earlier in the revised play) makes its general implications fairly clear. Any lingering doubt is immediately allayed by Punch's rejoinder to Luckless' questions about the sufficiency of his qualifications as a candidate: "Ay, why then I'll turn great Man, that requires no Qualification whatsoever." Even more revealing is the conversion, with one simple insertion, of Marplay's boasts in 1730 about his imperviousness to hissing into mockery of Walpole's vain efforts in favour of the Excise Bill. Originally this scene simply mocked Colley Cibber's greed and effrontery. However, in 1734 Marplay Sr. stands suddenly for Walpole as well when Fielding adds to his rhodomontade a vow to make the town swallow a farce it has damned: "Let's see which will be weary first, the town of damning or we of being damned." (Woods, *AF*, p. 90) The movement of history since the original run of *The Author's Farce* (the Excise defeat in 1733 and Cibber's elevation to the Laureateship in late 1730) and Fielding's new desire to mock Walpole combined to produce an amalgam of anti-Cibber and anti-Walpole satire which audiences would not have missed.

The most striking political alteration is the insertion into the scene on the river Styx in Act III (the first, in 1730, of Fielding's many satiric, Lucianic dialogues of the dead) of these exchanges (Woods, *AF*, pp. 95-96) between the Director, a new character, Charon, and a Sailor:

Director. Mr. Charon, I want a boat to cross the river.

Charon.   You shall have a place, sir; I believe I have just room for you unless you are a lawyer, and I have strict orders to carry no more over yet: Hell is too full of them already.

Director. Sir, I am a Director.

Charon.   A Director, what's that?

Director. A Director of a company, sir. I am surprised that you should not know what that is; I thought our names had been famous enough on this road.

Charon.   Oh Sir, I ask your pardon. Will you be pleased to go aboard?

Director. I must have a whole boat for myself, for I have two wagon loads of treasure that will be here immediately.

Charon.   It is as much as my place is worth to take anything of that nature aboard.

Director. Pshaw, pshaw, you shall go snacks with me and I warrant we cheat the devil. I have been already too hard for him in the other world. Do you understand what security on bottomry is? I'll make your fortune.

Charon.   Here take the gentleman, let him be well fettered and carried aboard. Away with him!

Sailor.   Sir, here are a wagonload of ghosts arrived from England that was knocked on the head at a late election.

> Charon. Fit out another boat immediately. But be sure to search their
> pockets that they carry nothing over with them. I found a
> bank bill of fifty pound t'other day in the pocket of a
> cobler's ghost who came hither on the same account.

The Director most obviously recalls the looters of the Charitable
Corporation, but he also stands for the jobbery in stocks, insurance, and
credit (the "Moneyed Interest") that Walpole's government was criticized for favouring. His question "Do you understand what security on
bottomry is?" alludes to allegations of dishonesty made in 1731 against
officials of the East India Company, and his surprise that Charon does
not know what a director is ("I thought our Names had been famous
enough on this road") was probably meant to recall the South Sea Bubble with which Walpole was forever associated by his enemies. The
passage focusses upon the supposed safety provided under Walpole for
financial tricksters to fleece the nation and escape with their loot. Behind
it lay memories of the South Sea disaster and its aftermath, reinforced by
the East India scandals of 1731, and revived (despite the severe punishment of some offenders) in the furor over the Charitable Corporation in
1732-33. It recalls as well the lines in Swift's sharp *On Poetry: A Rapsody* of 1733 which satirize Directors, recall the South Sea scandals, and
depict the bribery of Charon. Combining such satire with the allusions to
electoral violence and bribery produced a far headier political brew than
anything in the original *Author's Farce*. Contemporaries would certainly
have viewed the passage as anti-ministerial, election-year satire, despite
the fact that the source of the cobler's "bank bill of fifty pound" is not
specified, particularly because the next major change in the play is the
addition of Punch's declaration of intent to seek a seat in Parliament.
This, as noted, involves more satire on electoral corruption and an
almost direct insult to Walpole's qualifications for office.

Don Quixote in England

Don Quixote in England was prepared for performance at
Drury Lane in February 1734, but withheld temporarily. It was put on at
the Haymarket in April, after a reunion between the Drury Laners (now
managed by Charles Fleetwood) and the Haymarket rebels. The dedication to Chesterfield added upon publication hints strong anti-ministerial
bias, and *Don Quixote* is certainly much more political than *The
Author's Farce*, primarily because Fielding added scenes satirizing electoral misconduct as the general election campaign of 1734 entered its
final stages. Surprisingly, however, the political satire in the play does
not reveal the anti-ministerial bias suggested by the dedication. Even the
new election scenes can only be described as either non-partisan or slightly more biased *against* the opposition's Country wing than the ministry.
As published, it seems to be another case where Fielding's political intentions are peculiarly mixed. The kind of anomaly apparent in *The Intriguing Chambermaid* resurfaces.

The dedication "To the Right Honourable Philip Earl of Chester-field, Knight of the most Noble Order of the Garter," elaborately suggests opposition bias. Fielding hopes that the intention of some scenes—obviously the new election scenes—"cannot fail of recommending them" to Chesterfield, "One who hath so gloriously distinguished Himself in the Cause of Liberty, to which the Corruption I have here endeavoured to expose, may one Day be a very fatal Enemy."[61] In 1734, Chesterfield's defence of "Liberty" could only refer to his resistance to the Excise Bill, which cost him the lucrative, minor posts that had rewarded his support of the ministry in the Lords, driving him into opposition. Fielding then insists that freedom of the stage is as important as freedom of the press. "Examples work quicker and stronger on the Minds of Men than Precepts," so that "a lively Representation of the Calamities brought on a Country by general Corruption might have a very sensible and useful Effect on the Spectators."

"General Corruption" was part of the standard jargon of opposition through the 1730s and 1740s. Inveighing against it on the eve of the 1734 general election in a dedication to Lord Chesterfield had to suggest that Fielding's play would probably accuse Walpole of corrupting the nation, perhaps to the point (to complete the usual accusation) where constitutional checks upon his power and the Crown's were being rendered inoperative. The allusion to freedom of the stage would, moreover, have suggested the opposition's resistance to the government's desire to strengthen the Lord Chamberlain's censorial power. Early in 1735, in fact, the opposition narrowly missed helping Walpole to impose new controls. Sir John Barnard, the London opposition stalwart, introduced a bill to ratify and confirm, but not to enlarge, the Lord Chamberlain's powers.[62] He hoped to limit the number of theatres in London since his constituents objected to the immoral influence of the non-patent Goodman's Fields Theatre. However, the crafty Walpole introduced an amendment increasing the censorial powers of the Lord Chamberlain, along the lines of the licensing clause of the notorious Act of 1737. Barnard, faced with a possibility he had not envisioned, hurriedly withdrew the bill.

Fielding's dedication closes with a compliment to Chesterfield as an opposition hero, whose generosity as a patron and "true Patriotism" are lauded by anti-ministerial authors: ". . . to be celebrated by them, and applauded by the more discerning and worthy, are the only Rewards which true Patriotism (a Word scandalously ridicul'd by some) can securely expect." Fielding was asking for patronage and celebrating Chesterfield's sacrifice of places in opposing the Excise. The dedication seems to promise a powerful assault on the minister who had punished such noble independence; it is the most open and loaded hint of willingness to embrace an opposition allegiance in Fielding's work between 1728 and the opening of *Pasquin* in 1736.

The play itself is a strange mixture from a political point of view. It includes both vague and sharp anti-ministerial satire; for example, the dispute between the Don and an innkeeper in the opening scene patriotically satirizes Spanish absolutism (there knights are "above the law") and Spain's failure to seize Gibraltar, but meanders into more partisan channels. The unwisdom of Walpole's appeasement of Spain at a time when England is cursed with a standing army in time of peace (the essence of many an opposition barb) is alluded to in the innkeeper's parting comment: ". . . if I ever suffer a *Spaniard* to enter my Doors again, may I have a whole Company of Soldiers quartered on me; for if I must be eaten up, I had rather suffer by my own Country Rogues, than Foreign ones" (pp. 1-2). One cannot say for certain when this opening scene was written, but Fielding implies in the preface that, aside from adding the election scenes, he merely dusted off in 1734 scenes that had lain on his shelf since late 1728. The political satire in the first scene may have been six years old, for it precisely recalls the foreign policy preoccupations of critics of the ministry of 1728—the difficulties with Spain over trading rights and Gibraltar that led to the unpopular Treaty of Seville in 1729. A few pages later Fielding may mock Walpole more directly but not more topically. Don Quixote thinks he sees a giant, "Toglogmoglogog Lord of the Island of Gogmagog, whose Belly hath been the Tomb of above a Thousand strong Men" (pp. 4-5), and Sancho recognizes that it is only a drunken country squire (the marvellously comic squire Badger) come courting with his dogs. This may be a slur on Walpole's dominion over England, capped by mockery of his tendency to ape the country squire and his adulterous courtship of Maria Skerrett.

However, these passing examples (all in early scenes) of anti-ministerial mockery are greatly overbalanced by satire on the electoral corruption sure to be employed by *both* sides in the general election. If these scenes and the opposition-charged dedication to Chesterfield were the principal additions made to the play (very naturally, since the election writs were issued on the same day it opened), they seem irresolvably contradictory from a partisan point of view. Three items in the election scenes would have been viewed as anti-ministerial: (1) the sardonic comment that "one Man gets an Estate, by what another gets a Halter" (p. 13); (2) the marvelous song "The Roast Beef of Old England," probably written by Richard Leveridge (a verse included in the version of the song in *The Grub-Street Opera* remembers when "our Soldiers were brave and our Court ["courtiers" in 1734] were good," and a verse new in 1734 anticipates the day when "Mighty Roast Beef shall command on the Main"); and (3) Sancho's vow, "If ever I do lay my fingers on an island more, I'll act like other wise Governors, fall to plundering as fast as I can, and when I have made my Fortune, why, let them turn me out if they will" (p. 39). But the chief stress is on the disastrous corruption of electors and candidates, regardless of allegiance; the candidates, Sir Thomas Loveland and Mr. Bouncer, and the electors they corrupt, seem, respectively, to represent and to favour the Country Interest. Loveland's name suggests the landed bias of Country opposition and Don Quixote, urged on by electors opposed to Loveland and Bouncer, is thought to be in the Court Interest (p. 18). Thus, the satire is more directly aimed at opposition than ministry when we learn that the only jewels owned by Guzzle's wife are "two bobs . . . which were given her by *Sir Thomas Loveland* at his last Election." (p. 11) The same is true in the marvellous scenes where the Mayor, innkeeper, Guzzle, and Mr. Retail reveal their corrupt political philosophy. Though willing to vote for anyone for a sufficient bribe, they are basically adherents of the Country Interest. The mayor says, "when we invite a Gentleman to stand, we invite him to spend his Money for the Honour of his Party; and when both Parties have spent as much as they are able, every honest Man will vote according to his Conscience" (p. 19). Sir Thomas Loveland and Mr. Bouncer are the incumbents, the town's "Conscience" having in the past finally dictated a Country vote. The mayor indicates that, when the money is spent and the beer drunk, it will probably do so again:

> I never gave a Vote contrary to my Conscience. I have very earnestly recommended the Country-Interest to all my Brethren: But before that, I recommended the Town-Interest, that is, the Interest of this Corporation, and first of all I recommend to every particular Man to take a particular care of himself. And it is with a certain way of Reasoning, That he that serves me best, will serve the Town best, and he that serves the Town best, will serve the Country best.

No wonder that when Guzzle longs for the annual elections demanded by the Country members, Loveland is horrified: "The Kingdom would not be able to supply us with Malt." Fielding was to make the same point as a ministerial propagandist on the eve of the election of 1747,[63] and in 1734 the election scenes bring the charge of electoral corruption more directly home to the Country Interest than the Court Interest. A neater insult to the Country members, whose continual cry was for annual parliaments and against coruption, than Loveland's rejoinder to Guzzle, is hard to imagine, though this does not, of course, imply that *Don Quixote in England* is not also satiric of ministerial corruption.

The anti-Country satire in the election scenes looks forward not only to the satire on the boozy folly of opposition squires in Fielding's ministerial *Jacobite's Journal* and *Tom Jones*, but to the satire on Country as well as Court corruption Fielding produced in 1736-37 as spokesman for the Broad-Bottom, "Patriot" wing of the opposition. But 1734 was not 1747 or even 1736 and Fielding may have tried to change the balance of the play and please Chesterfield. He does this finally in a song that expresses not an opposition bias, but an even-handed contempt for both the ministry and its opponents that probably was close—as I have suggested before—to his real perception of political realities in the 1730s:

> All Mankind is mad, 'tis plain;
>   Some for Places,
>   Some Embraces;
>   Some are mad to keep up Gain,
> And Others mad to spend it.

>   Courtiers we may Madmen rate,
>   Poor Believers
>   In Deceivers
>   Some are mad to hurt the State
>   And others to mend it.

Scholars have suggested that Lord Chesterfield did not respond favourably to the dedication of *Don Quixote in England*.[64] Clearly, he did not, as the unpolitical nature of Fielding's next two plays indicates. The reason surely was that the play was unlikely to please a newly dismissed opposition *grandee* who was infuriated at Walpole and eager to see him defeated in the election. Chesterfield prided himself on being above party (the common cant of most politicians) even before he allied himself with the new Broad-Bottom group in the ministry in 1735. He was never closely associated with the Country wing of the opposition. However, this would not have helped Fielding's case very much in 1734, though the young writer may have been gullible enough to think so. Chesterfield, the aristocrat, may have shared Fielding's contempt for many Country candidates and electors. Chesterfield, the realist, would have shared his conviction that the political hypocrisy of Walpole's opponents matched the minister's. But it is extremely unlikely that Chesterfield, the angry politician, would have looked with favour on a play implying that Country candidates were as likely to employ bribery in the coming election as Court candidates. It was politically essential to confine one's doubts about allies to the privacy of correspondence and gossip. One had to maintain the fiction of solid trust between dissident, ambitious lord and independent, unambitious country squire with particular care at election time, the septennial test of ministry and opposition strength.

In the first play of his "high" opposition phase, *Pasquin* of 1736, Fielding was to serve opposition patrons by satirizing the corrupt electoral practices of both Country and ministerial candidates. But *Pasquin* is a very different play, written in very different circumstances. Its satire on indirect bribery by Country candidates is more than balanced by satire on direct bribery by Court candidates, and the balance is swung most definitely against the latter when Court candidates are declared elected though they have lost the election. To take the choice out of the hands of electors, however corrupt, and transfer it to a perpetually rigged parliamentary committee (which was the procedure in contested elections) was to disrupt the operation of representative government to an extent not even envisioned in *Don Quixote in England*. Moreover, in 1736 Fielding was attempting (with enormous success as it turned out) to win back audiences that had rejected so many of his plays since 1731 and to please old friends from Eton days, not a distant and cynical opposition lord. He could count by 1736 on a sympathetic hearing for satire on the general corruption attending partisan electioneering on either side from his natural patron, George Lyttelton, and even, ironically enough, from Chesterfield. Lyttelton was then a committed member of the

Broad-Bottom faction in opposition, allied with the other "Boy Patriots" (William Pitt and the Grenville brothers) and Chesterfield beneath the banners of Bolingbroke's idealistic, anti-party theories. But Chesterfield, co-inspirer of the Broad-Bottom journal *Common Sense* in 1737, would have felt very differently during the hardfought election campaign of 1734 about balanced satire in a play by a young man still tainted by his dedication of *The Modern Husband* to Walpole in 1732. I do not think there is any truth in either *The Grub-Street Journal*'s vague classification of Fielding in 1734 as one of the writers obligated to Walpole or (looking slightly ahead) Fielding's grouping with Edward Young, Theobald, Welsted, and Frowde as a praiser of the minister in Joseph Mitchell's *A Familiar Epistle to Walpole*.[65] But those interpretations indicate the dubiety of his reputation.

An Old Man Taught Wisdom and *The Universal Gallant*

Fielding's plays of 1735 are almost totally apolitical. Angered by failure in the election of 1734 and heartened by the recruitment of Chesterfield and Lord Cobham, the opposition redoubled its efforts against Walpole in Parliament and the press in 1735. The ministry responded by consolidating its propaganda apparatus, fusing its various journals into the *Daily Gazetteer* (thereafter the more or less official organ of ministerial opinion and apology as long as Walpole remained in office), and insuring this paper's wide, daily distribution by post throughout the kingdom. But in all of this Fielding, who had married Charlotte Craddock on November 9, 1734 during a lengthy vacation from the theatre and London, took no obvious part. He had flirted with Chesterfield, and his Eton friends, Lyttelton and Pitt (who won his Commons seat in a by-election in 1735), were gravitating toward the centre of the new Cobham group in opposition. Lyttelton's *Persian Letters*, with their severe reflections on the ministry, were a major contribution to the opposition's campaign in 1735, and by the end of 1735 Thomson's *Liberty* (though less overtly partisan) would indicate the direction that friendship with Lyttelton would normally dictate and that Fielding would follow brilliantly in *Pasquin*. Indeed, as I will argue in Chapter III, there may be evidence in print that Fielding was committed to Lyttelton's faction and the assault on Walpole by November and December, 1735. But in the two plays he produced in the spring of 1735 Fielding gave no sign whatever of following up the dedication or the election scenes to *Don Quixote in England* or closing with his Cobhamite friends.

His first offering of 1735, a farce called *An Old Man Taught Wisdom; or, the Virgin Unmask'd* (opened January 17; published January 23) is utterly unpolitical, and enjoyed a modest success. His five-act comedy, *The Universal Gallant; or, the Different Husbands*, hissed on opening night, February 19, and forced off stage after its third performance, was equally free of politics.[66] Indeed, in the season's work the only temptation to political speculation is the dedication of *The Universal Gallant* to "His Grace Charles Duke of Marlborough." Charles Spencer, who had succeeded to the dukedom two years earlier, was in opposition in 1735,[67] though he was to begin a long and successful career as a courtier in 1738. But Fielding probably meant to stress the Duke's generosity, not his resistance to tyranny (in contemporary jargon, Walpole), when he said: "Poverty has imposed Claims on Mankind equal with Tyranny and Your Grace has shewn as great an Eagerness to deliver Men from the former as your illustrous Grandfather [John Churchill, 1st Duke of Marlborough, a perennial hero of Fielding's] did to rescue them from the latter." This would not have sounded very political at the head of a play without the slightest tinge of opposition sentiment. When Fielding later praised a Marlborough, the grand old Duchess Dowager, for supporting "patriotic" opposition (in *A Full Vindication of the Dowager Duchess of Marlborough* of 1742) the partisan point, while not stated directly, was made abundantly clear. Fielding surely hoped the Duke of Marlborough (noted for generosity amounting, his enemies said, to profligacy) might make him a gift in return for the compliment that would make up in part for the deserved failure of *The Universal Gallant*. It is impossible to say whether Marlborough did; but Fielding received good financial news at about this time. His mother-in-law, Mrs. Craddock, died, leaving as much as £1500 to Charlotte in a will executed on February 2, 1735 and proved on February 25, less than a week after *The Universal Gallant* was published.

It has been suggested by his biographers, from Arthur Murphy's time, that Fielding, who had always spent much of the summer and early autumn in Salisbury or at the family estate in East Stour (in which he had a one-sixth interest), considered life as a gentleman-farmer ("bidding adieu to all the follies and intemperances of the town") after the death of Mrs. Craddock. If so, the young writer (he was still only twenty-seven) changed his mind, and he may have used an unusual period of secure leisure to recharge his energies and begin to work on *Pasquin*. But in the present connection, it must be emphasized that if Fielding had retired in 1735, he would *certainly* not be thought of (if anyone ever did think of him) as a dangerous baiter of Walpole's ministry. Only hindsight allows us to see the season of 1735 as a lull before the storm of anti-ministerial satire Fielding unleashed in 1736-37 as a leading playwright and co-manager of the Haymarket theatre. The political silence observed during the last season before he became "Pasquin" is a final rebuttal to the idea that Fielding evolved from neutrality to opposition between 1728 and 1736.

Chapter Three

Pasquin and the Haymarket: 1736-37

The year 1735 was a series of ups and downs for Fielding, and a divide between epochs in his theatrical career. Without a real political commitment from 1728 to his departure from London after the failure of *The Universal Gallant*, he returned in late 1735 a firm friend of the new Broad-Bottom ("Boy Patriot" or "Cobhamite") wing of the opposition, probably with *Pasquin* in mind or under his arm. How different in intention and success *The Universal Gallant* and *Pasquin* were! Fielding returned to impudent, irregular drama, and achieved a success overshadowing that of 1730. *Pasquin* and the other irregular plays he offered at the Haymarket theatre in 1736 and 1737—*Tumble-Down Dick, The Historical Register*, and *Eurydice Hiss'd*—made him more formidable politically than any dramatist in the eighteenth century except John Gay. The *Universal Gallant* debacle of February 1735 coincided with Mrs. Craddock's bequest to Charlotte Fielding.[1] This perhaps supplied motive and means for what Fielding did the following winter. He had tried, with indifferent results, to find a formula for stage success since 1731: avoiding politics much of the time, signalling his harmlessness to Walpole in 1732, gingerly trying anti-ministerial as well as anti-opposition satire, and appealing confusedly to Lord Chesterfield in 1734. But the hissing of the apolitical *Universal Gallant* may have been the final straw: could censorial banning or harassment be any costlier or more embarrassing? On the other hand, £1500 allowed Fielding a lengthy rest in the country with his new wife, to ponder years of moderate success mingled with failure, and to compose the kind of play needed to recoup. Return to battle was likely urged by George Lyttelton, just entering into opposition intrigue. Moreover, whatever remained of £1500 no doubt helped Fielding to organize his own company at the

Haymarket before the 1736 season and to convince James Ralph, an old friend and a professional, to risk joining the venture.

We need not take literally the hyperbolic complaints in the advertisements and dedication of *The Universal Gallant* that its hissing reduced him to poverty and deprived his family of bread.[2] Fielding always tended toward sensationalism in this area, and Arthur Murphy and others have discussed his financial sufferings. Probably his sense of an adequate income for a gentleman, an Etonian, and the eldest son of a general was chronically superior to his situation. If he ever experienced actual want, it was between the passage of the Licensing Act in 1737 and his elevation to the magistracy in 1748, not in 1735. Still, he could not have organized his own company in the spring of 1735 or earlier. When he offered *Pasquin* to the patentee-managers of Covent Garden and, possibly, Drury Lane in late 1735 or early 1736,[3] he very likely anticipated rejection of such a brew of political satire and theatrical parody. But he did not need to be as concerned as he would have been in previous seasons. Denied a patent theatre and an established company, he was not obliged to bow and rewrite, but could put on *Pasquin* himself and profit from its sensational popularity—sixty nights was only its first run. He was to enjoy being "Great Mogul" of the "Great Mogul's" company, as well as the playwright of the hour. A mature, indeed a battle-scarred, twenty-nine-year-old, Fielding was ready to gamble in 1736 and able to do so.

Aside from what he called the "itch of scribbling" (a phrase, we will see, he used even in 1735) and the boredom of country life, the final push that sent Fielding back to London's Haymarket was surely political. I have described the family meeting held in September 1735, amid the patrician wonders of Lord Cobham's Stowe, which signalled the mobilization of Cobham's "personal" opposition clique. Cobham's "Boys" and Fielding's schoolmates, George Lyttelton, William Pitt, Richard and George Grenville, were newly placed in Commons, ready to help Cobham toward revenge on Walpole for the insult of 1733 and themselves toward positions of power and profit. Their chances of success were greatly enhanced by a relationship—already close, soon to become intimate—with the Prince of Wales, whose battles with his father and Walpole they would fight, and whose prestige and patronage they would enjoy. They had associates in Lords who helped make them a respectable and potentially very important political force: among others, Lord Chesterfield (who in 1737 would help Lyttelton found the journal *Common Sense*) and the ambitious, wealthy Duke of Bedford. And they could vaunt the idealistic conception of government by a coalition of true patriots (above party ties and prejudices, free of corruption) of Bolingbroke's Broad-Bottom theories, and a related commitment to bringing down Walpole's political machine *in toto*, rather than forcing themselves into power under Walpole or within his corrupt system. Broad-Bottom Patriotism (however questionable the sincerity of Lord Bolingbroke or its ambitious adherents) was a marvelous rhetorical basis for opposition in Parliament and in the poetry, pamphlets, journal essays, and plays that the Broad-Bottoms and their literary allies poured forth. A numerically minor wing of the opposition, the Broad-Bottom faction was blessed with talent, but Fielding became its most talented, prolific, and dangerous literary warrior. He was unlikely to resist for long the temptation to join schoolfellows setting out on the road to distinction in company with great and witty older men under the banners of an ideology that seemed to promise more than the uninspiring "politics as usual" that was so natural to Pulteney and Carteret as well as Walpole. In short, Fielding found a cause and natural patrons in the aftermath of the meeting at Stowe. He would never abandon this commitment: through all the changes of political alignment and disappointments of the next decade and a half, he would follow the Broad-Bottoms.

There may be still-detectable preliminary signs from the closing months of 1735 of the metamorphosis revealed at the opening of *Pasquin* in March 1736. The first is an insult to Fielding in *Seasonable Reproof*, an anonymous poem. Published in November 1735 with a dedication to the Duke of Argyll (not yet a convert to opposition), it presumably was composed during the Broad-Bottoms' preparations for the winter parliamentary session. The relevant passage has often been quoted:

> F_____g who *yesterday* appeared so rough,
> Clad in *coarse Frize*, and plaister'd down with *Snuff*.
> See how his *Instant* gaudy Trappings shine;
> What *Play-house Bard* was ever seen so fine!
> But this, not from his Humour flows, you'll say,
> But mere *Necessity*—for last Night lay
> In Pawn, the Velvet which he wears to-Day.[4]

However, the timing of this allusion and its possible political significance have been blurred. Wilbur Cross assumed, reasonably enough, that the sudden change in Fielding's dress from "coarse Frize" to "Velvet" in 1735 was a result of the bequest from Mrs. Craddock, coming after the *Universal Gallant* failure. But Cross unfortunately went on, though he observed that the satiric poem appeared in November, to slight the significance of a time-lag of eight months between the bequest and the publication of *Seasonable Reproof*: "At this time [i.e., February] an anonymous maker of verses took Fielding as an example of the violent changes to which fortune subjects those dependent on her." Cross then insisted there was no "bitterness" in these lines, which were "only Grub Street's vivid way of saying that he could buy a new suit when a play succeeded [Fielding produced none between the *Universal Gallant* and *Pasquin* the following year]; but must wear his old clothes if it met disaster." This will not do, but no better explanation has since been put forward.[5]

When one assumes that the satire's timing is important, intriguing possibilities open. Fielding's prosperity was surely due to the February bequest, but the satirist probably would not have known this, for it was a private matter and Fielding had been in the country for months. In the fall of 1735, in the atmosphere of political recruitment and drumbeating before the opening of Parliament, Fielding reappeared in London. (The usual assumption that he did not return from East Stour until early 1736 is pure guesswork and little plausible in the light of his establishment of a theatre and performance of a new play so soon after the 1736 season began.) If he was in splendid new clothes and obviously in funds this might well have led an unfriendly writer to suspect that his sudden prosperity reflected the generosity of a patron. Suspicion would centre on the active new opposition group which included so many of his friends, as well as Lord Chesterfield, whom he had courted in the dedication to *Don Quixote in England*. The possibility that the anonymous poet meant to imply a political insult becomes more solid if one reads on in *Seasonable Reproof*, for the poem is obviously anti-opposition, and it moves *immediately* from the sneer at Fielding to mockery of a nobleman (not named) who sits in the House of Lords "with a *Peerlike Pride*," takes snuff, cries "Pox, let's divide," then repairs to his "sharpers" and a "whore." No one aware of Lord Chesterfield's sexual misbehaviour (including taking a new mistress almost simultaneously with taking a new wife) and gaming losses in this period[6] will doubt that he is the satirized peer. The passage in *Seasonable Reproof* may be the first of the many, many attacks on Fielding stimulated by the political loyalties he formed in 1735, a rebuke to a political allegiance which was rumoured, though its first major result, *Pasquin*, would not appear for another four months. Biographically, it implies not simply that Fielding's stage income was precarious, but that he was seen as newly committed to Broad-Bottom opposition.

A more direct foreshadowing of Fielding's new opposition role may be an unsigned lead essay (a "letter" to the editor) in *The Craftsman* for December 20, 1735. Its style and content as well as its timing suggest Fielding's authorship, though no one has previously connected him with it. Assuming I am right in viewing the "Philalethes" letter in the *Daily Post* for July 31, 1732 as the work of a friend of Fielding's, this may be Fielding's earliest periodical essay as well as the first published signal of his new opposition orientation. The stylistic argument for his authorship must begin with the fact that it "passes" the standard "hath" test: Fielding's preference for the auxiliary form "hath" (somewhat unusual and obsolescent in his time) rather than "has" is well known and nearly consistent. It can provide strong negative evidence and some degree of positive evidence. If "has" is used, the likelihood is greatly against his authorship. The consistent use of "hath," in a piece that bears in its style or content other corroboratory indications of his hand, is a major prop to an attribution. "Hath" is everywhere used in this essay, and this is important, though inconclusive, especially since other contributors to *The Craftsman* sometimes used it. In addition, the style of the essay in every other way suggests Fielding's. It begins with a subordinate construction ("As you are now entered . . .") that will strike a chord with anyone who has read many of his later periodical essays, where the use of "As . . . ," "There are [is] . . . ," "It hath been said . . . ," and a few other rhetorical "ice breakers" is habitual. As one proceeds, Fielding's habits are suggested by: the lengthy, additive flow of the sentences; the characteristically heavy employment of initial grammatical and logical connectives (one finds, sticking to paragraph, as opposed to sentence, beginnings, "However," "Nay," "Or, if," "For Instance," "Again," "For my Part," "But," "But, in all Events"—within the paragraphs there are many, many more); the suspensive constructions; the diction and choice of imagery.[7] The "Fieldingesque" style and content of this piece are not fully apparent unless one reads all of it, but the resemblances are sometimes especially strong. The essay, for example, urges *The Craftsman* on in the fight against the ministerialists with witty irony:

> Again; what an *agreeable Variety* would Mrs. Osbourne's works [those of James Pitt] afford Us; whether We consider the *Matter*, of which they are composed, or the *Style*, in which they are written? All her *Discourses*, as she calls them, are so distinct, and follow one another in such a regular methodical Order, that nobody can read them without finding his Understanding wonderfully enlighten'd, and his Ideas grow as clear as her own.
>
> Then, as to *Humour* and *Ridicule*, I pity *Cervantes, Rabelais* and *Swift*, as well as the Proprietors of their Works, if that Triumvirate of prodigious Wits, the Hyp-Doctor, the Corn-Cutter and *Sir A.B.C.* should club the Offspring of their Brains together, and oblige the World with a Collection of their *inimitable Drollery*.
>
> I know it hath been frequently objected against *these Gentlemen*, that they have acted a very ungenerous Part towards *You*, to whom most of them owe their *Bread*, and even their Being, as *Authors*. This hath been the common Complaint of all Persons in *your Case;* and, indeed, was never more just than at present; for no Writer had ever such Legions of Adversaries professedly retain'd against Him, for so many Years together; and it is certain that the moment *You* lay down your Pen, They must return to their primitive Obscurity. Nay, I am firmly persuaded that if their Patron had no other Reason to desire your Silence, He would heartily rejoice in any Opportunity of dropping *Them;* who, like *other Mercenaries*, are apt to grow troublesome and mutinous, if not constantly *humour'd* and fed with *Plunder* . . . .
>
> For my Part, I look upon a *popular Author* in much the same Light with the *Minister* Himself, against whom He draws his Pen. *Both of Them* have not only their *Envyers* and *Competitors*, who are eternally endeavouring to depreciate and supplant Them; but likewise a Crowd of *Dependents* and *Followers*, who expect more than it is either prudent or possible for Them to perform; and yet look upon every Disappointment as an Instance of *their Selfishness*, or an Insult to their *own Understandings*. I cannot tell, Mr. *D'Anvers*, whether You have had any Occasion to make this Reflection yourself; but I could name *one of your present and most industrious Defamers*, whom I have formerly heard expatiate as warmly in *your Commendation;* and upon enquiring a little into this Alteration in his Language, I could find no other Cause for it, than your refusing to publish several *Papers*, which He had sent You; upon which He immediately resolved to revenge such an heinous Affront, by applying to the *other Side*, and met with that Encouragement from *Them*, which *You* had so unpolitickly deny'd Him.

> You may, perhaps, think such a Method of Proceeding unreason-
> able; but it is natural to Mankind, when They are once seized with the
> Itch of Scribbling; and, to tell you the Truth, I begin to grow so fond
> of *this Letter*, which I am now writing to You, that if you should not
> publish it in your *next Paper*, I don't know whether I may not be
> tempted to give it Another Turn, and send it to the Gazetteer.

The prose style is not the only "Fieldingesque" aspect of these
paragraphs, though it perfectly reflects his stylistic habits. Their ridicule
of ministerial journalists anticipates *The Champion* (and, with a change
to opposition targets, *The Jacobite's Journal*), and he elsewhere
chuckled over the "Itch of Scribbling."[8] But the most striking evidence is
implicit in a comparison of the passage beginning "then, as to *Humour*
and *Ridicule* [in itself a classic Fielding pairing], I pity *Cervantes,
Rabelais* and *Swift* . . . if that Triumvirate of prodigious Wits . . . ,"[9]
with literary assessments Fielding wrote in later journals. His often-
quoted obituary on Swift in *The True Patriot* for November 5, 1745 says,
"He possessed the talents of a Lucian, a Rabelais, and a Cervantes . . . ," and in *The Covent-Garden Journal* for February 4, 1752
Fielding admires "that great triumvirate, Lucian, Cervantes and Swift
. . . . they all endeavoured with the utmost Force of their Wit and Humour
to expose and extirpate those Follies and Vices which chiefly prevailed in
their several Countries." (The replacement of Rabelais reflects the aging
Fielding's changing taste, often remarked in other connections; he goes
on to accuse Rabelais and Aristophanes of immorality.) Fielding's habit
of reusing phraseology, anecdotes, or ideas is well known.[10] I believe this
is an example of it.

This essay is significant as Fielding's earliest extant journalism and
the first acknowledgement of his alliance with Lyttelton and the Broad-
Bottoms. It probably was written while he was writing *Pasquin*. It reveals
a renewed interest in politics (the concluding paragraphs discuss details
of foreign policy) and a sharp anti-ministerial bias consistent with
publication in *The Craftsman*. When it appeared, Lyttelton's opposition
clique was readying its first assault on Walpole in Parliamant, and beginning to churn out the literary attacks that would continue as long as
Walpole survived in office. Bolingbroke's *Dissertation upon Parties*, the
most celebrated element of the Broad-Bottom Patriot Scripture, had
already appeared serially in *The Craftsman*, but pamphlet editions were
still producing political reverberations. Earlier in 1735 Lyttelton's *Persian Letters* had been branded a "libel on the present Government" and
Lyttelton had been called the pupil of "the Author of the *Dissertation
upon Parties*."[11] Thomson's *Liberty* (dedicated, naturally, to Frederick,
Prince of Wales) had begun to appear, tracing through four parts the
history of "Liberty" from ancient to modern times, and warning that
"the felon Hand" of "dark Corruption" might finally destroy
England's constitutional freedoms. *Liberty* would close ("The
Prospect," Part V, 1736) with a rosy vision of England as it might be
(flourishing morally, socially, artistically, religiously, and economically)

without Walpole and ruled according to Patriot principles. *The Christian Hero*, a new play offered at Drury Lane in 1735 by George Lillo, of *George Barnwell* fame, was overtly Broad-Bottom: "To Night we sing/ A Pious Hero/ and a Patriot King."[12] The increasing polarization of the literary world was completed by the establishment in 1735 of the *Daily Gazetteer*, the editor of which, James Pitt, is ridiculed in a play upon his pen-name, "Mother Osbourne," in Fielding's *Crafstman* essay. It would have been as natural for Fielding to begin the attack on Walpole in *The Craftsman* as it was to serve the Broad-Bottoms at the Haymarket in 1736. The die was cast; Fielding was launched into his second phase.

1736

The "Little Theatre" in the Haymarket eked out a varied existence (always on the edge of respectability and viability as an undersized, non-patent house) between the run of Fielding's *Don Quixote in England* in 1734 and early 1736. French comedians played there during the spring of 1735, followed by young comedians from the Drury Lane company who put on older plays through February 1736. Once Covent-Garden and perhaps Drury Lane refused Fielding's new play, this junior company was ready-made for reorganization into "The Great Mogul's Company of Comedians" before the opening on March 5 of *Pasquin: A Dramatick Satire on the Times: Being the Rehearsal of two Plays, viz. A Comedy call'd, The Election; and a Tragedy call'd, The Life and Death of Common-Sense.*[13]

The political tenor of "A Comedy Call'd The Election" was surely no surprise to those who remembered the "election scenes" added to *Don Quixote in England* in 1734 and knew of his Broad-Bottom associations. Bolingbroke and his political pupils obsessively dwelt upon the necessity for honest, as well as party-free, elections, and the dangers electoral corruption posed to the Constitution and ultimately to liberty. These were standard themes in the Broad-Bottom rhetorical-intellectual *milieu* in which *Pasquin* grew. The *Dissertation upon Parties* was constantly advertised in *The Craftsman* throughout these years and its theories were echoed fervently during 1736 in *The Fatal Consequence of Ministerial Influence: Or the Difference between Royal Power and Ministerial Power Truly Stated* and, later, in *The Importance of an Uncorrupted Parliament Considered in Three Letters Addressed to the Electors of Great Britain* (1740), as well as in George Lyttelton's *Letter to a Member of Parliamant from a Friend in the Country* (1738), and Fielding's own *Address to the Electors of Great Britain* (1740). During 1736 Bolingbroke sent from his voluntary exile in Chanteloup the first version of *Letters on the Spirit of Patriotism* for perusal by his political friends.[14] Though unpublished until years later, it circulated widely. As an unaligned author Fielding had always scorned both political extremes as either mindless or corrupt and hypocritical: "The Election" shows what had to result when this tendency coincided perfectly with the ideological and rhetorical preferences of political friends and patrons. Its depiction of an election in a country borough as a cynical travesty determined by the indirect bribery of the Country zealots of opposition, Sir Harry Fox-Chase and Squire Tankard, the more direct bribery of the Court candidates, Lord Place and Colonel Promise, and the utter bribability of the electors is a highly coloured dramatization of the Broad-Bottom conception of the awful *status quo*. It convinced the Earl of Egmont that Fielding was now "a protege of Lyttelton and the Cobham group."[15]

The Court candidates persuade electors with a squeeze of the hand, a euphemism for bribery later frequently used by Fielding (along with the term "touching") in *The Champion* and elsewhere:

> *Lord Place.* Gentlemen, you may depend on me; I shall do all in my power. I shall do you some services which are not proper at present to mention to you; in the mean time, Mr. Mayor, give me leave to squeeze you by the hand, in assurance of my sincerity.

The point is emphasized when the rehearsal is interrupted by its author, Trapwit:

> *Trapwit.* You, Mr. that act my Lord, bribe a little more openly if you please, or the audience will lose that joke, and it's one of the strongest in my whole play.
>
> *Lord Place.* Sir, I cannot possibly do it better at the table.
>
> *Trapwit.* Then get all up, and come forward to the front of the stage. Now, you gentlemen that act the Mayor and Alderman, range yourselves in a line; and you, my Lord, and the Colonel, come to one end, and bribe away with right and left.
>
> *Fustian.* Is this wit, Mr. Trapwit?
>
> *Trapwit.* Yes, Sir, it is wit; and such wit as will run all over the kingdom.[16]

"The Election" is the most single-mindedly political piece Fielding had written since 1731. It includes other satire (especially the "rehearsal" business interspersed within it), but politics is its *raison d'être*. The promises, favours, and payments every enemy saw as the key to Walpole's sway are directly, repeatedly satirized, and the comic veneer is very thin over the idea that Walpole has made corruption universal—"all over the kingdom." Trapwit ironically insists the play must be dated "before the Bill of Bribery and Corruption" to be believable, but it brings on stage the kind of political corruption that obsessed opposition and that was rendered as still life in so many of the anti-ministerial prints and broadsides of the age.[17]

The play is not simply an assault on Court corruption. This would have been alien to Fielding and Broad-Bottom theory and rhetoric. He promises in the Prologue that "The Election:" "Brings a strange Groupe of Characters before you, / And thus shows you here at once both *Whig* and *Tory;* / Or Court and Country you may call 'em; / But without Fear and Favour he will maul 'em!'' (p. 170). The direct ministerial bribery is more than balanced by the indirect bribery of the Country candidates, Fox-Chase and Tankard (names suggesting the two main "occupations" of the booby Country squire). They go on a buying spree that indicates why candidates ruined their fortunes in contested elections, and win a majority of the electors in the end. Trapwit brags about this: ". . . now, Mr. Fustian, I shall show you the Art of a Writer, which is, to diversify his Matter, and do the same thing several Ways. You must know, Sir, I distinguish Bribery into two kinds; the direct and the indirect . . . . call Sir *Harry* and the Squire'' (p. 174). The Country pair *speak* as if they depend on the honesty of the electors and local attachments, but the electors vote according to their pockets, and the candidates *act* cynically. Sir Harry wishes the Company to drink the toast "Liberty, Property, and No Excise" with him (one of several indications that the play is a tardy satire on the 1734 election). The Mayor and aldermen say they disapprove of "Party Healths," which he correctly assesses as a sign that they have been bribed. He reminds them courtiers rob the nation for bribe-money, and will take bribes once elected: "If you would be served faithfully, you must choose faithfully; and give your Vote on no Consideration but Merit; for my Part, I would as soon suborn an Evidence at an Assize, as a Vote at an Election." His speech nobly summarizes the main points of the opposition's attacks on electoral corruption (serving double-duty, the lecture is meant to teach political morality as well as set up a satiric undercutting of opposition hypocrites), but his behaviour soon hilariously belies it. He goes on a spree of gift-giving (can he send his neighbours some wine or some venison?) and purchases whatever the aldermen sell, even ordering bricks from the mayor to build a new house he does not need. This wonderfully comic confrontation of pious rogues ends with the mayor himself proposing a toast to "Liberty and Property, and no Excise," and Sir Harry's crowning irony: "Give me thy Hand, Mayor; I hate Bribery and Corruption: if this Corporation will not suffer itself to be bribed, there shall not be a poor Man in it." Harry ruefully observes later, ". . . tho' I have not bribed a single vote, my Election will stand me in a good Five Thousand Pounds" (pp. 175-77, 187).

Ministerial writers so frequently stressed the importance of the kind of indirect bribery Harry Fox-Chase uses that a "letter" from "Courtly Grub, Esq." in *The Craftsman* for March 15, 1735 attempted to reduce the charge to absurdity by sarcastically agreeing with it. Yes, said Grub, "*pecuniary Influence* is not the only Specis of *corrupt Influence*," for there are other kinds, "such as Living and Dealing in the *Neighbourhood, Charity, Hospitality*, and in short all that natural Interest, which commonly attends the Possession of a *large Estate* and a *good Character*." Fielding's Broad-Bottom patrons discountenanced the employment of corruption by either side or in any form. Thus, Fielding's attack on Country (as opposed to Court) corruption is, unlike Courtly Grub's, both serious and consistent with his friendships within the opposition during Walpole's last Parliament. For our part, it is not enough to recognize the pattern of satire on both sides seen at least hazily by such critics as John Loftis: "He [Fielding] handled the subject (electoral corruption) boisterously, with an implied acknowledgement that the Country party was not above adroit manoeuvring of its own; but his comedies were nevertheless well calculated to serve the opposition and *Pasquin* at least had a huge success."[18] We must understand that balanced satire served *his* opposition, that it reflected a typical attitude of the Broad-Bottom faction.

The alternation of satire on Court and Country corruption in the scenes we have examined is repeatedly paralleled in briefer form. In the second act of "The Election" two mobs are egged on by Country toasts and Court promises ("Gentlemen, we'll serve you"), then warm up for a fist-fight in a shouting match of meaningless party slogans: "Down with the Rump! No Courtiers! No Jacobites! down with the Pope! no Excise! a Place and a Promise! a Fox-Chase and a Tankard" (p. 185). Elsewhere the Squire and the Mayor sagely discuss sobriety and neglect of Trade among courtiers: "*Squire.* [drunk] A Man that won't get drunk for his country is a Rascal./ *Mayor.* So he is, Noble Squire; there is no Honesty in a Man that won't be drunk—a Man that won't drink is an Enemy to the Trade of the Nation" (p. 186). This parody of opposition attacks on ministerial indifference to "Trade" is balanced in Lord Place's assurances to the mayor's wife that he understands the depressing aspects of merchant life: "I hope we shall have no such People as Tradesmen shortly; I can't see any use they are of; if I am chose, I'll bring in a Bill to extirpate all Trade out of the Nation" (pp. 180-81). Similarly, when the mayor's wife favours the Court on grounds reflecting the illogic of ministerial "Jacobite" propaganda ("I am a friend to My Country; I am not for bringing in the Pope") her husband enunciates his brand of opposition patriotism: "I will have the Place first, I won't take a Bribe, I will have the Place first; Liberty and Property!—I'll have the Place first" (pp. 182-83). The double ironies climax along with the struggle in the borough. The indirect bribe seems to prove mightier than the direct: a majority votes Country, though the Mayor votes for Place and Promise. But the Mayor returns the Court candidates, to the delight of most of the corporation (as well as the government, which won most struggles over elections), for a controverted election means expense-paid travel to London for them and their wives.

In short, if "The Election" obviously *does*, as the Earl of Egmont said of *Pasquin*, make "the usual points against the court,"[19] it also makes many of the usual points against opposition. It stresses the total venality of the electoral *status quo*, the roughly equal rascality of Court and Country politicians, and the necessity of replacing the system of party prejudice and corruption that was characteristic of the age. It is also a Broad-Bottom play, not simply an opposition play, in another respect. It reflects a concern that was to grow steadily in importance to the Broad-Bottoms after 1736 and to dominate much of Fielding's political satire in the earlier 1740s. As was stressed in Chapter One, an abiding worry of the

Broad-Bottom group was that its ambitious allies (men like William Pulteney and Lord Carteret) would desert them in a scramble for office, without regard to friendship, ostensible principles, or reform, when Walpole met their price. This fear was as constant in the Broad-Bottoms' public and private utterances as scorn for Country hypocrisy. It echoes through the letters of Bolingbroke, Chesterfield, and Lyttelton, and explains why Broad-Bottom literature was characterized not only by balanced satire on the corruption of Court and Country, but also by "anticipatory satire" on the expected apostasy of Pulteney, Carteret, and the other believers in "conventional accommodation" and "Whig reunion."

Two linked scenes in "The Election" are not only scornful reminders of past conversions of "patriots" into placemen or pensioners, but also warnings to future coat-turners. In Act III the Mayor asks Fox-Chase and Tankard about the result if the ostensible Country goal, the downfall of the present, corrupt government, were ever reached: "if these courtiers be turn'd out, who shall succeed them?" (p. 187). The answer, though the Mayor cannot quite follow it, perfectly evokes the pattern that Lord Bolingbroke remembered from 1733-34, when Walpole wobbled but managed to save himself: ". . . the *object* of his *succession* interposed to the sight of many, and the *reformation* of the *government* was no longer their point of view."[20] Sir Harry Fox-Chase stands unmistakably for all those whom Bolingbroke, Lyttelton, and Fielding expected to abandon reform for profit when he rationalizes the cynical scramble for spoils after a storming of the Treasury: "I love my Country, but I don't know why I may not get something by it as well as another; at least to re-imburse me — And I do assure you, tho' I have not bribed a single Vote, my Election will stand me in a good Five Thousand Pounds" (p. 188). This is the germ of the politics of "conventional accommodation" which Pulteney, Carteret, and the other "riper Patriots" favoured and Bolingbroke, Chesterfield, and the Broad-Bottom "Boys" condemned. The Mayor re-emphasizes the pattern in explaining to his wife the Country candidates' absurd promise of an Ambassadorship if the election goes the right way:

> Mrs. Mayor. What, is Sir Harry going to change Sides then, that he is to have all this Interest?
>
> Mayor.   No but the Sides are going to be changed, and Sir Harry is to be—I don't know what to call him, not I,—some very great Man; and as soon as he is a very great Man, I am to be made an Ambassador of. (p. 188)

Roughly the same concern about false brethren is apparent in a debate between Miss Stitch, pro-Country and a reader of *The Craftsman*, and "Miss," the Mayor's daughter, Lord Place's future bride and a reader of *The Daily Gazetteer*. They debate Walpole's peace policies: Miss Stitch wonders, *Craftsman* style, whether Spain can be trusted, Miss rebukes her, *Gazetteer* fashion, for endangering, through such criticism, the interests of her country. Miss Stitch's rejoinder is witty (it includes a poke at the *Gazetteer*'s free postal distribution, an early example of a grievance oft-aired by Fielding) and hints every opposition spokesman's protestations of loyalty to nation and king, though not to bad ministers: "Perhaps, Madam, I have a Heart as warm in the Interest of my Country as you can have; tho' I pay Money for the Papers I read, Madam, and that's more than you can say" (p. 191). However, Miss Stitch breaks the fan Valentine gave her as she argues, and cries out, "Oh, my poor dear Fan! — I wish all Parties were at the Devil, for I am sure I shall never get a Fan by them." Then she swiftly accepts a new fan from Miss in return for convincing Valentine to vote for the Court candidates. It has been suggested that the scene allegorizes the enlistment of the effeminate Lord Hervey—"Lord Fanny"—into the ministry, partly through the intercession of Queen Caroline.[21] But this seems too exclusive an interpretation, particularly since Hervey was "bought" between 1728 (when he received a pension of £1000 per annum) and 1730 (when he became Vice-Chamberlain), ancient history in 1736. Instead, it is a ludicrous vision of the sham patriotism and expected apostasy of the ambitious allies of the Broad-Bottoms. "The Election" expresses the same triple distrust Bolingbroke confided to Lyttelton in 1740: ". . . I see likewise, and have long seen, not only the incessant endeavours of the Court to traverse this wise and honest scheme [the "coalition of all parties" and all "true patriots," the "Broad-Bottom"], and the dull obstinacy of the Tories that is proof, even against long and uniform experiences, but what is worse, the avowal of a principle directly contrary to this, of a coalition, and national union, by men who engaged to promote it, and whose consideration has arisen from it; they seem to have no view but that of preparing one faction to succeed another."[22] Miss Stitch's closest relative in Fielding's earlier drama is William, the groom (representative of Pulteney) in *The Welsh Opera*. John, Lord Hervey, already a Walpole henchman in 1732, was treated as such in the character named John in the same play. The political untrustworthiness she exemplifies would be satirized with growing directness from *The Historical Register* of 1737 to *The Opposition: A Vision* of 1741 as suspicion yielded to certainty.

"The Election" was the centre of critical attention and praise during *Pasquin*'s early run, the "tragic" half of the double rehearsal being relatively ignored.[23] This would not seem to demand explanation. "The Life and Death of Common Sense" is not as entertaining. Its rather trite satire on fustian tragedy (one of many examples of a rich parodic tradition) is sometimes funny, but aside from a few passages of dialogue between Fustian, Sneerwell, and Trapwit, it never approaches the wild humour of *Tom Thumb*. Its satire on the "improving" of plays by Cibber and Rich, the managers of the patent theatres, too often degenerates into neo-classical lecturing foreign to Fielding's own practices. It never measures up to Buckingham's *Rehearsal* or even Fielding's *Author's Farce*, and it is not mysterious that audiences would slight it. What *does*

require explanation is a sudden rise in its relative popularity in mid-run
that brought it more into public favour than "The Election" and moved
Lyttelton and Chesterfield to call their new journal *Common Sense* in
1737. It is a genuine oddity that first the "comedy," then the "tragedy"
sustained *Pasquin* through the greatest first season since *The Beggar's
Opera.*

The key to this mystery is political. I think that Fielding always intended "The Life and Death of Common Sense" to be seen as a
stringent, oblique criticism of Walpole's corruptive system and a plea for
Bolingbrokean political sanity, but audiences initially reacted insuffi-
ciently. The sprinkling of obvious partisan touches were soon com-
mented on by the Earl of Egmont[24] and presumably noticed by others:
allusions to pending legislation affecting trade and clerical livings—a
Mortmain bill and a tithe bill—and the total inactivity and uselessness of
England's land forces under Walpole's peace policies. But Fielding's real
assault was implicit in the broad depiction of England as corrupt and
sliding into cultural degeneracy, with Cibber its Laureate and religion,
law, and medicine declining into priestcraft, pettifoggery, and quackery.
This would seem a massive condemnation of the results of
"Robinocracy" and resulting "universal corruption," recalling the *Dunciad* and *Gulliver's Travels,* once audiences were given a nudge in the
right direction. The use of such social, moral, and aesthetic satire and (to
use A. D. McKillop's words) the "lofty abstractions of ethics"[25] to condemn Walpole was a constant in opposition literature, as Maynard
Mack's analysis of the technique at its subtlest in Pope's later poetry has
recently made even clearer. This was especially true in Broad-Bottom
writing. Lyttleton's *Persian Letters* are perhaps too direct to quite fit into
this category. However, Thomson's *Liberty,* almost precisely contemporary with *Pasquin,* reads most of the time as a rather platitudinous
celebration of freedom and condemnation of tyranny until one is alerted
by a few overt passages (and the fact of its dedication to the Prince of
Wales) to see it as an oblique but strong satire on Walpole's subversion
of the Constitution. Similarly, Richard Glover's *Leonidas,* published in
1737 (though dated 1734) with a preface acknowledging a "sense of
obligations" to Lord Cobham, might seem a non-partisan summons to
heroic action (though it is a classic party piece, advertised for years in
every opposition journal from *Common Sense* to Fielding's *Champion*)
if one comes to it out of context and without due suspicion. There was
terrific potential for political interpretation in Fielding's mock-tragedy
from the first. For example, the killing of Queen Common-Sense during
her battles with the forces of Queen Ignorance by Firebrand, corrupt
arch-priest of the Sun, and her triumphant resurrection bear many
resemblances to the departure from England and triumphant return of
freedom in Thomson's *Liberty.* Indeed, the resemblances are close
enough to explain why Fielding addressed his own poem called *Liberty* to
George Lyttelton at some point in the later 1730s, though he did not
publish it until the *Miscellanies* of 1743. But Fielding's oblique approach

in "The Life and Death of Common Sense" seems to have left audiences and critics indifferent.

Fielding soon remedied this awkward situation. Wilbur Cross long ago noted that the popularity of the tragedy seems to have resulted from "a short humourous advertisement" of its virtues in the playbill for the benefit night of the actor who played Fustian, Trapwit having had his turn:

> Mr. Fustian desires the Audience (notwithstanding his brother Trapwit's unfair Advertisement to the contrary) to take particular Notice of the Tragedy, there being several New and very deep Things to be spoke by the Ghost of Tragedy, if the Cock does not crow him away too soon.
>
> N.B. *As Mr.* Fustian *is the first Poet that ever cared to own, that he brought Ignorance upon the Stage, he hopes all her Friends will excuse his calling in particular upon them, and favour him with their Company along with the Friends of Common Sense, which he hopes will be the Foundation of a Coalition of Parties.*[26]

One could not advertise Broad-Bottom bias more clearly—*"which he hopes will be the Foundation of a Coalition of Parties"*—or much more openly call upon political friends to applaud the tragedy as a satire in tune with "The Election," though different in technique. We have seen the politicizing effect of adding "the Great" to Tom Thumb's name and, perhaps, the de-politicizing effect of the dedication of *The Modern Husband* to Walpole. This advertisement seems to be another instance of Fielding directing audience reaction. Interest in *Pasquin* was restimulated when the play was published—after running thirty nights to packed houses—on April 8, two days after the advertisement appeared. (One specific determinant of the date of publication may have been the scheduling of an anti-Fielding afterpiece, *Marforio, a Theatrical Satyr*, which had its only performance on April 10 at the Covent-Garden theatre.) *Pasquin*'s publication encouraged re-evaluation of the tragic parody. On April 3, "The Prompter" in *The Grub-Street Journal* suddenly praised Fielding highly in a context which makes it clear that "Common Sense" was a major reason, and "The Prompter" reported on April 22 that the tragedy has become more popular than the comedy.[27] The interpretation of *Pasquin* that led to the naming of the journal *Common Sense* had become fashionable.

It is difficult to explain in the abstract what audiences found to relish politically once warned, though the tragedy is full of passages capable of deliciously insulting interpretation if the actors stressed the right words or gestured significantly, and a partisan claque applauded every stroke which could be construed as in favour of "Liberty." For example, one exchange between Firebrand (easily seen as Walpole), chief priest (read chief minister) of the Sun (read King), and Queen Common Sense is interpretable as satire on Walpole as perverter of the Constitution and the natural love between the king and the people. Thus interpreted, it recalls one of the *Craftsman* essays implying analogies between, say, Walpole and Wolsey and George II and Henry VIII. Common Sense complains of seeing a ghost in a dream, and Firebrand immediately gives this a turn suggestive of Walpole's supposed exclusion of all but the corruptly sycophantic from patronage:

> *Firebrand.*
>   And if such Toleration
>   Be suffered, as at present you maintain
>   Shortly your court will be a court of ghosts.
>   Make a huge fire and burn all unbelievers,
>   Ghosts will be hanged ere venture near a fire.
> *Queen Common Sense.*
>   Men cannot force belief upon themselves.
>   And shall I then by torture force it on them?

Firebrand answers, "The Sun will have it so," and Common Sense objects, "How do I know that?" Once the hint was given, the ensuing debate could be taken as anti-Walpole political satire, as well as an attack on priest-craft recalling *Tale of a Tub*. It strikes the typical opposition balance between devotion to the King and disdain for his minister:

> *Firebrand.*
>   Why I, his priest infallible, have told you.
> *Queen Common Sense.*
>   How do I know you are infallible?
> *Firebrand.*
>   Ha! do you doubt it? Nay, if you doubt that,
>   I will prove nothing — but my zeal inspires me,
>   And I will tell you, Madam, you yourself
>   Are a most deadly enemy to the Sun,
>   [This is best read as a parody of the favourite "Jacobite" and republican" smears of ministerial oratory and the anti-opposition press]
>   And all his priests have greatest cause to wish
>   You had never been born.
> *Queen Common Sense.*
>   Ha! Sayst thou, Priest?
>   Then know, I honour and adore the Sun!
>   And when I see his light, and feel his warmth,
>   I glow with flaming gratitude toward him;
>   But Know, I never will adore a priest,
>   Who wears pride's face beneath religion's mask,
>   And make a pick-lock of his piety
>   To steal away the liberty of mankind.
>   But while I live, I'll never give thee power. (pp. 214-15)

When Common Sense accused the arch-priest of enmity to freedom and promised his exclusion from power, the opposition must have cheered. They must have cheered louder at the politically charged lines (my italics) woven into Common Sense's dying speech:

> Oh! Traitor, thou [Firebrand-Walpole] hast
>   murdered Common Sense.
> Farewell, vain World! to Ignorance I give thee.
> Her leaden sceptre shall henceforward rule.
> Now, Priest, *indulge thy wild ambitious thoughts,*

Men shall embrace thy schemes, till thou hast drawn
All worship from the Sun upon thyself:
Henceforth all things shall topsy-turvy turn;
Physic shall kill, and *Law enslave the world:*
Cits shall turn beaus, and taste Italian songs,
While courtiers are stock-jobbing in the city.
Places, requiring learning and great parts,
Henceforth shall all be hustled in a hat.
And drawn by men deficient in them both.
Statesmen—but oh! cold death will let me stay
No more—and you must guess et caetera. (p. 224)

Fielding's other play of 1736, *Tumble-Down Dick; or, Phaeton in the Suds*, is shorter, slighter, and much less concerned with politics. Sheridan Baker has declared himself "astonished that scholarship has missed the anti-Walpole implications" of this work of Fielding's "high 'political' period."[28] But though it formed a double bill with *Pasquin* and retained its rehearsal format and the characters Fustian and Sneerwell, *Tumble-Down Dick* has only a few mild political touches. It concentrates mockery on (1) a pantomime called *The Fall of Phaeton*, by one Pritchard (given names unknown); (2) the whole sub-dramatic "entertainment" genre (which could combine elements of farce, pantomime, fustian eloquence, dance, song, the spectacular use of costume, stage machinery, puppets, and other interesting novelties); and (3) John Rich, manager of the Covent-Garden theatre, the most successful deviser of, and performer in, "entertainments." Politics aside, Fielding had reasons to satirize all three. As Covent-Garden manager, Rich had rejected *Pasquin*, as Fielding complained in the satiric dedication to "John Lun Esquire," Rich's stage name, added to the published version of *Tumble-Down Dick*.[29] He had also put on *Marforio*, the attack on *Pasquin*, on April 10 while Fielding was completing *Tumble-Down Dick*. Rich's "entertainments" made him almost as general a butt as Colley Cibber, and few writers disliked them more than Fielding did. Pritchard's *Fall of Phaeton* (a pantomime adaptation of Ovid's account of the death of Phaeton, Apollo's son, who let the horses run away with the sun chariot, nearly burned heaven and earth, and was struck down by Jupiter) typified the bastardization of drama that Fielding execrated. John Rich's most famous role had him hatching from a giant egg,[30] and Pritchard's piece was a prime example of the "drama" that (along with Italian opera) challenged the drawing power and theatrical *venues* of comedy, tragedy, and even the unconventional drama in which Fielding dealt.

The political innocuousness of *Tumble-Down Dick* obviously did not signal a withdrawal from Broad-Bottom activism; it was the afterpiece to *Pasquin*, after all. Indeed, Fielding's opposition connections and a particular political resentment may have spurred his non-political ridicule of Pritchard's play. Wilbur Cross, with his enviable instinct for truths about Fielding that he could not totally elucidate, vaguely suspected that Fielding's attack on *Fall of Phaeton* was not unrelated to the fact that "the concluding speeches of Jupiter and Phaeton . . . clearly pointed to the reconciliation between King George and his rash undutiful son." Cross then backed away, merely noting that "at the first opportunity, Fielding thrust in his 'Tumble-down Dick.' "[31] F. Homes Dudden and others have since ignored the possibility that Pritchard's insult to Frederick may have been important to the Prince's Broad-Bottom dependents and thus to Fielding. This is understandable, for there is not a single detail or pattern in *Tumble-Down Dick* that can be construed as a defence of Frederick or a rebuke to Pritchard for insulting the Prince or an allusion to the fact that he did so. We have only the facts that Pritchard took the King's side against the Prince, and that Fielding soon singled out *The Fall of Phaeton* for non-political ridicule in the afterpiece to *Pasquin*. A single identifiable allusion to the criticism of the Prince in *Tumble-Down Dick*, would, I think, justify a confident assertion of political motivation. But there is none, and the most I can do is record my strong *suspicion* that *Tumble-Down Dick* was intended to revenge Frederick without ever openly acknowledging that he had been injured.

If the opportunity had been unambiguous it seems very likely that Fielding would have loved to please his friends and the Prince by ridiculing George II, who did not achieve a reconciliation with his son in 1736 like that Pritchard imagined. Frederick's marriage to the Princess Augusta of Saxe-Gotha finally was solemnized on April 6, three days before *Tumble-Down Dick* opened, no thanks to Frederick's father. George Lyttelton and William Pitt then distinguished themselves in Commons by insulting the King and Walpole in sarcastic speeches in favour of a somewhat ironical motion of thanks to the King for arranging the marriage, which was introduced, not accidentally, by William Pulteney.[32] But such Leicester House strokes had to be left to the politicians. Fielding could only insult Pritchard. The Phaeton myth really does not lend itself to satire on the man symbolized by Apollo rather than Phaeton; Phaeton is the proud young fool reaching above himself in Ovid or any adaptation. Thus to politicize the tale in 1736 was to treat Frederick more roughly than George. In any case, Frederick could never appreciate being "defended" in a parody that reduces Phaeton to the bastard son of an "Oyster-wench" by an Apollo who lords it over the night-watch in the round-house or, worse, a "Serjeant in the foot-guards." This would most satisfyingly insult King George and Queen Caroline, but *lèse-majesté* is a spreading offence, royalty being familial. Fielding could not insult the King without tarnishing the Prince. Indeed, Fielding was probably nervous on opening night that some might see dangerous allusions where none were intended. He had an embarrassing "past" to live down as a writer close to men who were close to the Prince, for he had ridiculed Frederick, in the guise of Master Owen Ap-shinken, as an impotent boob in *The Welsh Opera*. This may not have been held against Fielding in 1736, but he may have had qualms about the ease with which an audience seeing *Pasquin* and *Tumble-Down Dick* one after the other might reason that if Firebrand, Priest of the Sun, allegorically represents Walpole and the Sun represents the King in *Pasquin*, then Apollo (the Sun god) must also represent George in his conflicts with Frederick-Phaeton.

In the afterpiece Haymarket audiences actually saw there is little of political interest. Air III laughingly complains about the Gin Act of 1736, and broadens this mockery in two stanzas to include allusions to the useless or under-used armed forces that suggest the many criticisms of Walpole's peace policies toward Spain:

> 'Twas Gin that made the train-bands so stout,
>   To whom each castle yields;
> This made them march the town about,
>   And take all Tuttle Fields.
>
> ....
> 'Tis Gin, as all our neighbours know,
>   Has served our Army too;
> This makes them make so fine a show,
>   At Hyde Park, at review.

Its last stanza echoes the satire on corruption in *Pasquin:*

> But what I hope will change your notes,
>   And make your anger sleep;
> Consider, none can bribe his votes
>   With liquor half so cheap.

Though it seems to me quite wrong to assume that Harlequin here or elsewhere in Fielding's work necessarily represents Walpole,[33] the pervasiveness of bribery under his government is suggested in passing when a Justice is bribed to acquit Harlequin of picking a poet's pocket of a play (a very Rich-like, rather than Walpolian offence), and Machine thus justifies the probability of this:

> Fustian. Pray, how is this brought about, sir?
> Machine. How, sir! Why, by bribery. You know, sir, or may know,
>   that Aristotle, in his book concerning entertainments, had
>   laid it down as a principal rule, that Harlequin is always to
>   escape; and I'll be judged by the whole world if ever he es-
>   caped in a more natural manner. (p. 21)

Air II ends with a thrust an audience just exposed to *Pasquin* might have viewed as directly anti-Walpole:

> Great Courtiers palaces contain,
>   Poor courtiers fear a jail;
> Great parsons riot in champagne,
>   Poor parsons sot in ale;
> Great whores in coaches gang,
>   Smaller misses
>   For their kisses
> Are in Bridewell banged;
>   Whilst in vogue
>   Lives the great rogue,
> Small rogues are by dozens hanged. (p. 16)

Even if these desultory allusions to Gin, bribery, and the success of "the great rogue" are read as anti-Walpole, they were tame stuff at the Haymarket in 1736. Moreover, the only really overt political applications of the farce's parody, some lines of the song (Air V) sung by the assembled cast as the curtain descends, are even-handed. They condemn the knavery of all parties (my italics). They are also oddly unconnected with the rest of *Tumble-Down Dick*, though they fit the concerns of *Pasquin* perfectly and rounded off the theatrical evening with some appropriateness:

> You wonder, perhaps, at the tricks of the stage,
> Or that Pantomime miracles take with the age;
> But if you examine *court, country, and town,*
> There's nothing but Harlequin feats will go down.
> > Derry down, & c.
> From Fleet Street to Limehouse the city's his range,
> He's a saint in his shop, and a knave on the 'Change;
> At an oath, or a jest, like a censor he'll frown,
> But a lie or a cheat slip currently down.
> > Derry down, & c.
> *In the country he burns with a politic zeal,*
> *And boasts, like a knight-errant, to serve commonweal;*
> *But once returned member, he alters his tone,*
> *For, as long as he rises, no matter who's down.*
> > Derry down, & c.
> *At court, 'tis as hard to confine him as air,*
> Like a troublesome spirit, he's here and he's there;
> All shapes and disguises at pleasure puts on,
> *And defies all the nation to conjure him down.*
> > Derry down, & c.

It is obvious that the Broad-Bottom author of *Pasquin* wrote this, insulting "false Patriots," perhaps slapping at the Prime Minister at the end, but this cannot alter the verdict that *Tumble-Down Dick* is not a very political, much less an anti-ministerial, work.

When Fielding left for the country at the end of the spring theatrical season of 1736, he was riding the very crest of success and notoriety as playwright and theatre manager. *Pasquin* had run an astounding thirty nights before it was published, then played to full houses for twenty more consecutive nights (omitting Sundays), and extended its first run to sixty nights (the longest since *The Beggar's Opera*) by the author's benefit night, May 26. Mrs. Charke, who played Lord Place, recalled that she earned sixty guineas on her benefit night,[34] and Fielding's income in 1736 must have been large enough to satisfy even his apparently expensive style of life. He profited as Haymarket entrepreneur as well as playwright. *Tumble-Down Dick* succeeded as afterpiece during *Pasquin*'s later run, and Fielding's triumph was probably even a bit embarrassing. *The Astrologer*, by his friend and colleague James Ralph, could not be put on at the Haymarket in 1736; there simply was not room for it.[35] On his return in this year to Salisbury and East Stour (where he now had control of one sixth of the family estate, the trust having been dissolved and a division having been made on February 7) he must have felt like the Fielding pictured in a friendly print ("The Judgement of the Queen o' Common Sense. Address'd to Henry Fielding Esq.") which has him kneeling before the goddess while she pours gold into his lap.[36] Since the spring of 1735 his financial and professional standing had risen remarkably.

The last days of the spring season of 1736 augured continuing success and foreshadowed more political aggressiveness at the Haymarket in 1737. George Lillo's fine, grim tragedy of common life, *Guilt its own Punishment; or Fatal Curiosity*, opened in place of *Pasquin* on May 27, and ran for six nights with *Tumble-Down Dick* or Thomas Phillip's *The Rival Captains; or The Imposter Unmasked* as comic afterpiece.[37] Fielding respected the humble, talented Lillo. He not only produced Lillo's tragedy and supplied it with a prologue, but also praised it in Lillo's obituary in *The Champion* as "a Masterpiece in its Kind, and inferior only to Shakespeare's best Pieces."[38] In fact, it is vastly superior to most of what passed as tragedy in the eighteenth century, including Lillo's better-known *George Barnwell, or the London Merchant*. It still possesses a stark, inevitable power, and could lend serious distinction to a company that had proved itself pre-eminent in comedy and satire. It also bore political overtones perfectly in keeping with Fielding's Broad-Bottom biases. As has been noted, Lillo's *London Merchant* of 1731 had opposition material grafted upon its tragic *corpus*. His less successful second tragedy, *The Christian Hero* of 1735, included touches appropriate in a Broad-Bottom manifesto: it glorified resistance to tyranny, and in particular sang of a "Patriot King" and urged audiences to "Quit either Faction, and, like Men, unite/ To do their King and injured Country right." *The Fatal Curiosity* also was made to accommodate such political touches, though they have little relevance to its action or themes.[39] For example, in mourning Walpole's peace policies (the "shame of this pacific reign" in which "Poor England" submits to Spanish "Insolence") *The Fatal Curiosity* nicely rounded off the Haymarket's first season as a Broad-Bottom theatre.

The Haymarket continued to put on plays two or three days a week during the summer of 1736 to finance the actors between seasons; *Pasquin, Tumble-Down Dick, Fatal Curiosity*, and *The Rival Captains* were the most frequently played. Gay's *Beggar's Opera*, always very popular while Walpole lasted, was put on twice, once with Fielding's *Mock Doctor* and once (August 2) with a new farce, *The Deposing and Death of Queen Gin, with The Ruin of Duke Rum, Marquee de Nantz, and the Lord Sugarcane. Queen Gin*, a take-off on Fielding's own "Life and Death of Common Sense" includes funny but harmless ridicule of the new Gin Act and "a Certain Gentleman in Power," Walpole.[40] But in this Fielding probably took no active part, and there is no evidence he returned to London until after Christmas, in time to prepare for 1737.

1737

Fielding's successes in 1736 made the other London theatres more receptive to political satire. Drury Lane staged Robert Dodsley's *The King and the Miller of Mansfield* (which the *Daily Gazetteer* was eventually to couple with Fielding's *Historical Register* as offensively anti-ministerial) the same year and revived it in 1737. In 1737, Lincoln's Inn Fields put on a play by Francis Lynch called *The Independent Patriot* that reads like a dramatization of a Broad-Bottom pamphlet. Its title character, Medium, attacks both sides, though his position is clearly anti-ministerial, vows never to vote against Walpole out of "Pique or Prejudice," and stands for voting according to conscience alone. The play is strongly biased against Walpole, for all its satire on hypocritical opposition Patriotism. This appeared odd to John Loftis,[41] but it is no more peculiar than the same combination in *Pasquin* and Fielding's main political effort of 1737, *The Historical Register*.

Fielding and Ralph reassembled the "Great Mogul's Company" in January 1737, and staged two plays, now lost, *The Defeat of Apollo* and *The Fall of Bob, alias Gin*. The latter surely ridiculed the Gin Act again, and anticipated the fall of "Bob" Walpole.[42] But, amazingly, Fielding's first play of 1737 was a politically innocuous one-act farce, *Eurydice, or the Devil Henpeck'd*, which opened on February 19 at *the Drury Lane theatre*. The reasons for this double reversal of form we can only ponder. Drury Lane and the Haymarket were converging in 1737, artistically as well as politically. *The King and the Miller of Mansfield* not only re-opened at Drury Lane, but was put on at the Haymarket on March 2, 1737.[43] Fielding was later in the spring to imply that he had never been really happy with the mediocre facilities and company at the Haymarket, and he may have wanted to try a minor work at Drury Lane. This does not, however, explain why he would follow up *Pasquin* with a mediocre, unpolitical farce like *Eurydice*. Even the unattractive notion that political circumspection was required by Drury Lane seems ruled out by *The King and the Miller of Mansfield*. Certainly, when his farce failed Fielding admitted (in the chidings of Pillage's nurse in *Eurydice Hiss'd*)[44] that he had been foolish to abandon a rich political vein. If there was more than simple bad judgment behind *Eurydice*, failure cut short whatever manoeuvre it portended, and sent him back to the Haymarket and the political barricades.

On February 19, opening night, the footmen in the Drury Lane audience objected to certain aspects of *Eurydice* and attempted to hiss it from the stage. Others forced the footmen from the theatre, but they got back in and the Riot Act was read. The hissing seems to have stemmed from resentment at slurs on "beaus" (especially the appearance of the "Ghost of a military beau"), not political antagonism. It did not utterly discourage Fielding and Fleetwood. But when the footmen caused more trouble at the second performance, the farce was permanently withdrawn and left unpublished (perhaps because J. Watts, the bookseller, reconsidered bringing it out when he heard the hisses) until 1743. Then it appeared in *The Miscellanies* as *Eurydice, A Farce: As it was d-mned at the Theatre Royal in Drury Lane*. Though Fielding soon made clever political use of *Eurydice* in *Eurydice's Hiss'd*, he must have initially been frustrated by a debacle recalling the *Universal Gallant* failure of February 1735.

Fielding retreated to the Haymarket, elaborating the "Great Mogul" joke by taking the names of actual "moguls," "Koulikan" and "Theodore of Corsica." An irregular company was his natural home, and his love for mock-epic, comical posing was an instinct that would be reflected in the elaboration of *personae* in his later journalism and novels. As noted, on March 2, less than two weeks after the *Eurydice* riot, he put on *The King and The Miller of Mansfield*. The Drury Lane management perhaps loaned it to tide him over. This was followed, on March 9, by *A Rehearsal of Kings; or, the Projecting Gingerbread Baker, with the unheard of Catastrophe of MacPlunderkan, King of Roguomania, and the ignoble Fall of Baron Tromperland, King of Clouts* and then by an obscure piece called *Sir Peevy Pet*, neither of which is extant. The subtitle of *A Rehearsal of Kings* seems to promise satire on Walpole as MacPlunderkan, and perhaps George II as Baron Tromperland, King of Clouts. They may partly explain Mrs. Eliza Haywood's recollection that the specialty of "Fielding's Scandal Shop" was "certain drolls, or more properly, invectives against the Ministry."[45] Lillo's *Fatal Curiosity* was also revived while Fielding readied new plays.

Though its date has been questioned, it now is clear that *The Historical Register for the Year 1736* opened on March 21, 1737 and was an immediate success. Fielding promised in *The Daily Advertiser* for March 15 to open it with a "short and very merry farce, called *The Damnation of Eurydice*"[46] (obviously a version of the farce that actually opened on April 13 as *Eurydice Hiss'd*), but *The Historical Register* was first coupled with Lillo's *Fatal Curiosity*. It was a nicely balanced programme: a somber, brooding, proven tragedy and a wild new comic satire in three acts. The extremely loose format and title of the latter parodied a popular, annual news compendium, *The Historical Register*, that had been appearing since 1716 and is now often used as a short-cut to major events by historians. Fielding's new play also offered several political scenes strongly reminiscent of *Pasquin*.

The Historical Register is "miscellaneous," satirizing social, artistic, personal, and moral, as well as political targets. It is a *satura* or *potpourri*, to use again L. J. Morrissey's apt wording.[47] Its format parodies a popular news publication. Its "rehearsal" technique allows ridicule of the practices of actors, authors, and theatre managers, as well as bad drama. It laughs at beaus, fine ladies, auctions, Italian opera, soldiers, and clerics. It mocks the Cibber family: Colley's unspeakable "improvement" of Shakespeare's *King John*, the behaviour on and off stage of the blustering, inadequate Theophilus, and the unsuccessful fight of Susanna, Theophilus' wife, to wrest the role of Polly in *The Beg-*

gar's Opera away from Kitty Clive, her rival for pre-eminence at Drury Lane.[48] All of Fielding's best plays were satiric, parodic miscellanies—his mind and art tended toward the inclusive—but none were more various than this, his last major effort and success as a dramatist. The first player describes the pattern in Act I:

> Second Player.
> > Ay, prithee, what subject woudst thou write on?
> First Player.
> > Why no subject at all, sir, but I would have a humming deal of satire, and I would repeat in every page that courtiers are cheats and don't pay their debts, that lawyers are rogues, physicians, blockheads, soldiers, cowards, and ministers—
> Second Player.
> > What, what, sir?
> First Player.
> > Nay, I'll only name 'em, that's enough to set the audience a-hooting. (p. 13)

However, the series of scenes rehearsed before Mr. Medley (the appropriately named author), Lord Dapper, and the critical Sourwit go a great deal farther than naming ministers. The Earl of Egmont confided to his diary on opening night: "It is a good satire on the times and has a good deal of wit."[49] He and the rest of the audience could not mistake, from Act I on, the fact that Fielding was up to his old political tricks.

Sourwit asks early in the play how Medley's "political" and "theatrical" themes are connected, and Medley replies: "When my politics come to a farce, they very naturally lead to the playhouse where, let me tell you, there are some politicians too, where there is lying, flattering, dissembling, deceiving, and undermining, as well as in any court in Christendom" (p. 16). Before one has finished deciding whether theatrical politicians—the Cibbers—or parliamentary ones are the prime targets, the rehearsal of "The Historical Register" (the play-within-the-play called *The Historical Register*) begins. After a "Prologue" that turns out to be a senseless "Ode to the New Year," parodying Colley Cibber's laureate odes ("This is a day in days of yore, / Our fathers never saw before:/ This is a day, 'tis one to ten,/ Our sons will never see again"—p. 17), comes the "scene of the politicians." Five politicians "in the island of Corsica, being at present the chief scene of politics of all Europe" (p. 18) ply their trade; in this scene the play's anti-ministerialism is patent.

The "scene of the politicians" very wittily satirizes the indifference to the national welfare in foreign affairs and the greed and corruption constantly imputed to the Walpole ministry. The first politician, who represents Walpole, the secret intriguer, says nothing: ("He's a very deep man, by which, you will observe, I convey this moral, that the chief art of a politician is to keep a secret . . . . That little gentleman, yonder in the chair, who says nothing, knows it all."—p. 19). The others *very* briefly try to plan a defence of Corsica from the Turks, conclude they "know nothing of the matter" (one imagines the audience applying this to

Horatio Walpole and the Duke of Newcastle), then obey the Fifth Politician: "Hang foreign affairs, let us apply ourselves to money" (pp.
19-20). Medley has his actors repeat this: "over again—and be sure to
snatch hastily at the money" (p. 20). Then they imposed a new tax on ignorance, the only thing (aside from learning and poverty) "not taxed
already." The passage satirizes the greed of the government and, in particular, the Excise Bill. This became especially clear after April 13, when
the Excise defeat in 1733 was nightly ridiculed in the other half of the
double bill, *Eurydice Hiss'd*. Ministerial corruption and incompetence in
foreign affairs are also emphasized in Medley's explanation of the immediate and permanent departure of the five politicians after they vote
for the tax: "They have finished the business they met about, which was
to agree on a tax. That being done, they are gone to raise it, and this, sir,
is the full account of the whole history of Europe, as far as we know of
it, comprised in one scene" (p. 21). The critic Sourwit's horrified reaction refers implicitly to a crisis which the opposition accused Walpole of
mishandling, the War of the Polish Succession (1733-35), a dynastic
struggle in which France and Spain strove against the Emperor of
Austria, but which England managed to avoid: "The devil it is! Why you
have not mentioned one word of France, or Spain, or the Emperor!"

The satire in the rest of Act I is generally innocuous, but the auction
scene in Medley's second act has an admixture of political matter, revealing the same roughly equal balance between criticism of false opposition Patriotism and the government that characterized *Pasquin*.
Christopher Hen (the name is that of a skilled London auctioneer) offers several political items on "Monday the 21st day of March" (the actual opening night; one assumes that the date was changed nightly), including "a most curious remnant of political honesty . . . . It will make
you a very good cloak. You see it's both sides alike so you may turn it as
often as you will" (p. 30). This goes for five pounds to Lord Both-Sides
"Lot 2. A most delicate piece of patriotism" occasions debate:

> First Courtier.
>> I would not wear it for a thousand pound.
>
> Hen.
>> Sir, I assure you several gentlemen at court have worn the same.
>> 'Tis a different thing within to what it is without.
>
> First Courtier.
>> Sir, it is prohibited goods. I shan't run the risk of being brought
>> into Westminster Hall for wearing it.
>
> Hen.
>> You take it for the old patriotism, whereas it is indeed like that in
>> nothing but the cut, but, alas! sir, there is a great difference in the
>> stuff. But, sir, I don't propose this for a town suit. This is only
>> proper for the country. Consider, gentlemen, what a figure this
>> will make at an election. Come—five pound? One guinea?
>> [*Silence.*] Put patriotism by.
>
> Banter.
>> Ay, put it by. One day or other it may be in fashion. (p. 30)

Obviously, this distills much of *Pasquin* and Broad-Bottom rhetoric. Other lots neatly pair John Rich and the ministry's journalists: "Lot 5 and Lot 6. All the wit lately belonging to Mr. Hugh Pantomime, composer of entertainments for the playhouses, and Mr. William Goosequill, composer of political papers in defense of a ministry" (p. 32). These do not sell, though they comprise "near three hundred volumes in folio." Mr. Banter reasons, "The town has paid enough for their works already" (p. 33). With reference to Goosequill's work this is another jab at the subsidizing and free postal distribution of *The Daily Gazetteer*.[50] Naturally, "Lot 8. A very considerable quantity of interest at court" (p. 33) goes for £1000. Even Lord Dapper, a spectator at the rehearsal, bids on it during an eager contention that symbolizes the patronage game, and in which Hen stands for Walpole. Banter stresses this in sniffing at the £1000 bid: "Damn me, I know a shop where I can buy it for less" (p. 34). All the cardinal virtues "having almost gone for eighteen pence to a Gentleman who thought he was getting "a *cardinal's* virtues'' (p. 34), "a little Common Sense" (Lot 10) attracts no bids, but produces "a most emphatical silence," which recalls the condemnation of the *status quo* in the tragic segment of *Pasquin* and foreshadows much in Lyttelton's *Common Sense*.

In the remainder of Medley's second Act, Pistol (Theophilus Cibber) appeals to the town in the conflict, noted earlier, over whether his "great consort" should "represent the part/of Polly Peachum in *The Beggar's Opera*." He is loudly hissed; Fielding was ever a fan of Kitty Clive. But Pistol interprets this as a yes, hissing being the applause always accorded to his family—"Those glorious hisses which from age to age/ Our family has bourne triumphant from the stage" (p. 37). This insults each of Fielding's Cibberian targets, Theophilus, Colley, and Susanna. But it also slyly insults Walpole (Pistol calls himself "Prime Minister theatrical"), the second foreshadowing in *The Historical Register* of the satire in *Eurydice Hiss'd* on Walpole's attempt to force the Excise Bill through Commons. The two layers of intention are underscored in a lecture Medley delivers immediately before Pistol's declaration:

> You may remember I told you before my rehearsal that there was a strict resemblance between the states political and theatrical. There is a ministry in the latter as well as the former, and I believe as weak a ministry as any poor kingdom could ever boast of. Parts are given in the latter to actors with much the same regard to capacity as places in the former have sometimes been, in former ages, I mean. And though the public damn both, yet while they both receive their pay, they laugh at the public behind the scenes. And if one considers the plays that come from one part, and the writings from the other, one would be apt to think the same authors were retained in both.[51] (p. 36)

We cannot treat all satire in the play on the Cibbers or theatrical practices an anti-Walpole. Fielding was no simple-minded allegorist. But some passages (e.g., when "Pistol runs mad and thinks himself a Great

Man"—p. 35) deserve such a double reading, for they fuse political with theatrical criticism.

The final act begins with theatrical mockery that periodically broadens to embrace politics. The prompter, the First Player, and the bastard son of Apollo (who seems here at the beginning to represent Theophilus Cibber) are trying to cast Shakespeare's *King John*.[52] The casting of the English Lords is left to the prompter by Apollo, since their parts are "of little consequence" (p. 40). The point is the role of the "safe" House of Lords under Walpole. The unnecessary, as well as un-constitutional, nature of Walpole's role as Prime Minister is slyly hinted at in their discussion of the script:

> Apollo.
>> . . . *Robert Faulconbridge*. What is this *Robert*?
>
> Prompter.
>> Really, sir, I don't well know what he is. His chief desire seems to be for land, I think. He is no considerable character. Anybody may do him well enough, or if you leave him quite out the play will be little the worse for it. (p. 41)

In *The Champion* (e.g., June 7, 1740) Fielding would similarly play upon Walpole's name and nicknames, "Robin" and "Bob." The theme of a prime minister's uselessness or obnoxiousness within the balanced mechanisms of Constitution and government was popular in opposition writing as long as Walpole remained at the Treasury.

Much more directly anti-ministerial is the next scene, in which Ground-Ivy (i.e., Colley Cibber, who had tried to "improve" Shakespeare's play) declares Shakespeare's *King John* "won't do," and sets about altering it. The prompter is nervous about this "as Shakespeare is so popular an author" and Ground-Ivy "so unpopular." Ground-Ivy scorns such argument, however, and Walpole's general per-sistence in forcing unpopular legislation through Parliament and his vain insistence on the Excise Bill in the teeth of Commons resistance in 1733 again leap suddenly into focus through the surface satire on the Cibbers:

> Ground-Ivy.
>> . . . I can tell you, Mr. Prompter, I have seen things carried in the House against the voice of the people before today.
>
> Apollo [who here becomes Walpole, as well as—or instead of—Theo-philus Cibber for a moment].
>> Let them hiss. Let them hiss and grumble as much as they please, as long as we get their money.
>
> Medley.
>> There, sir, is the sentiment of a Great Man, and worthy to come from the great Apollo himself. (p. 43)

Ridicule of the Cibbers immediately reasserts itself, when Pistol (Theophilus in another guise) drives Ground-Ivy (Colley) from the stage. Indeed, though it was cut out after the first performance, this was originally followed by a comic confrontation between the two Pollys: Susanna Cibber and Mrs. Clive, competitors for the role in *The Beggar's*

Opera.[53] Thus, Medley's "article from the theatre" ends unpolitically.

At the very end of the play Fielding inserted his strongest political scene, one that at least balances the scene of the politicians in Act I, and that shows emphatically that while this play is always anti-ministerial, it is not simply an *opposition* play, but a *Broad-Bottom* play. Medley tells the critic Sourwit that placing "my Politicians and Patriots at opposite ends of my piece" is designed to show "the wide difference between them." He began with the Politicians to signify "that they will always have the preference in the world to Patriots," and ended with the Patriots "to leave a good relish in the mouths of my audience" (p. 45). There is irony on irony in this. The remark about the preference of Politicians over Patriots is straightforward satire, but the Patriots leave anything but a "good relish." The real point of the first and last political scenes in Medley's "Historical Register" is that there is little difference—aside from greater hypocrisy—between the Politicians (the ministerial clique) and too many insincere opposition Patriots. It is the same double insult that dominates "The Election" in *Pasquin.* Sourwit asks whether his "Dance of Patriots" does not seem "to turn patriotism into a jest." Medley speaks for Fielding and his patrons in answering that opposition hypocrites are a greater danger to the "whole play," the Constitution of England, than Walpole's tools:

> So I do. But don't you observe I conclude the whole with a Dance of Patriots, which plainly intimates that when patriotism is turned into a jest, there is an end to the whole play. (p. 45)

The "scene of the Patriots" is, of course, set in Corsica, that amusing fiction never being quite abandoned, and involves four Patriots and a character named Quidam, who represents Walpole. Medley explains that there are only four Patriots, as opposed to the five Politicians, to show they are "not so plenty." But we miss one of the play's many ironical symmetries and blurrings of political polarities if we fail to notice that Quidam was played by one "Mr. Smith," who also played one of the Politicians (the silent, Walpolian one?) in Act I. The Patriots are worse dressed than the Politicians, and free with the ringing "Trading Interest" slogans of England's opposition: "Prosperity to Corsica!"; "Liberty and Prosperity!"; "Success to trade!" The crying of slogans is not over, however, before the selfishness of their allegiance is patent. "Fourth Patriot. 'Ay, to trade—to trade—particularly to my shop!' " (p. 46). It is not surprising that a character (whom we later learn is Quidam) *"standing in the wings laughs loudly"* at this. Greed will make it easy to corrupt such Patriots; he regards their protestations precisely as Walpole did those of the ambitious in opposition.

The First Patriot next drinks a meaningless health to peace. He is, says Medley, "The noisy Patriot, who drinks and roars for his country and never does good or harm in it." The "cautious" Second Patriot vaguely agrees with the first, *sub rosa*, and the third, "self-interested Patriot" thus rationalizes calling for war:

> Look 'ee, gentlemen, my shop is my country, I always measure the
> prosperity of the latter by that of the former. My country is either
> richer or poorer, in my opinion, as my trade rises or falls; therefore,
> sir, I cannot agree with you that a war would be disserviceable. On the
> contrary I think it the only way to make my country flourish; for as I
> am a sword-cutler, it would make my shop flourish, so here's to war!

The "indolent Patriot," who wakes at the end of a fray, rouses himself
only to toast both peace and war, "I do not care which" (p. 47).
Quidam[54] enters, drinks with them, pours gold on the table, and con-
vinces them, as they snatch it up, that the nation is prosperous and their
protests unjust. They thought they were poor, but now they are rich and,
as Lord Chesterfield was to say in 1741 about the buying off by Walpole
of the false Patriots of opposition, "there's an end to opposition." The
Patriots dance out after Quidam, and Medley's final comment to Sourwit and Lord Dapper focusses on the financing by the taxpayer of
general corruption under Walpole. It also resembles the mayor's decision
in *Pasquin* to return defeated Court candidates:

> Sir, everyone of these Patriots have a hole in their pockets, as Mr.
> Quidam the fiddler there knows, so that he intends to make them
> dance till all the money is fallen through, which he will pick up again
> and so not lose one halfpenny by his generosity; so far from it, that he
> will get his wine for nothing, and the poor people, alas! out of their
> own pockets pay the whole reckoning. (p. 49)

"The Historical Register" opens with satire that one might call simply
anti-ministerial, taken by itself, but Act II carefully balances satire on
Walpole and on hypocrite opposition. The last Act is also balanced: even
while satirizing false brethren, Broad-Bottom writers were primarily
determined to destroy Walpole. Walpole finally is shown to be at the centre of the spreading cancer of corruption. The false Patriots are his victims, though they too victimize the public.

Following the pattern set with *Pasquin* and *Tumble-Down Dick* in
1736, Fielding linked the two halves of a bill by reusing two characters
from *The Historical Register* in *Eurydice Hiss'd or A Word to the Wise*,
which opened as afterpiece on April 5. Sourwit and Lord Dapper are the
audience for a rehearsal of Mr. Spatter's new tragedy, "the damnation
of *Eurydice*." It depicts—in a parody of *de casibus virorum* tragedy—
the fall from theatrical eminence of Mr. Pillage into failure and alcoholic
stupor. At the simplest level it laughs about what happened to Fielding's
Eurydice, but Fielding alerts the audience even before the rehearsal
begins that Pillage also stands for Walpole. Spatter says his play conveys

> . . . the instability of human greatness and the uncertainty of friends.
> You see here the author of a mighty farce at the very top and pinnacle
> of poetical or rather farcical greatness, followed, flattered, and adored
> by a crowd of dependents. On a sudden, Fortune changing the scene,
> and his farce being damned, you see him become the scorn of his ad-
> mirers and deserted and abandoned by all those who courted his favor
> and appeared the foremost to uphold and protect him. (p. 55)

On opening night the Earl of Egmont came away from the Haymarket sure that the *Eurydice Hiss'd* was an "allegory on the loss of the Excise Bill" and "a satire on Sir Robert Walpole." The performance seems to have been a gathering of opposition forces; Egmont records that Prince Frederick himself was there, clapping "when any strong passages fell . . . especially when in favour of liberty."[55] He had much to applaud. The brief *Eurydice Hiss'd* is the most thoroughly political, most steadily anti-Walpole of Fielding's five plays of 1736-37. It is probably accurate to say it is the most single-mindedly partisan work he had yet written, aside from the unpublished anti-opposition poem of 1729. *The Welsh Opera, Pasquin,* and *The Historical Register* all balance satire on the ministry with satire on elements of the opposition. Here Walpole is unrelentingly mocked. The specifically Broad-Bottom elements in the play are the lectures on political virtue and the need to rise above party, prejudice, and corruption spoken by Honestus, a Broad-Bottom Patriot sage. The play rebukes Walpole's whole system as partisan, corruptive, and dangerous to liberty, mocks his failure with the Excise Bill, and envisions the loss of his majority in Commons and fall into neglected obscurity. It celebrates the greatest opposition victory to date, that of 1733, and foresees the achievement of a greater.

As the rehearsal begins, Sourwit observes that Mr. Pillage is "a very odd name for an author." But it is perfect for Walpole as the opposition saw him, and Sourwit is assured he "will not remain long in that opinion" (p. 55). Pillage's first speech unmistakably identifies him with Walpole, the centre of a vast swirl of sycophants and place-seekers at all times and a minister continually compared by opposition writers with Cardinal Wolsey, as well as Buckingham, Sejanus, and other historical types[56] of the evil advisor or minister:

> Who'd wish to be the author of a farce,
> Surrounded daily by a crowd of actors,
> Gaping for parts and never to be satisfied;
> Yet, say the wise, in loftier seats of life,
> Solicitation is the chief reward,
> And Wolsey's self, that mighty minister,
> In the full height and zenith of his power,
> Amid a crowd of sycophants and slaves,
> Was but perhaps the author of a farce,
> Perhaps a damned one too. 'Tis all a cheat,
> Some men play little farces and some great. (pp. 55-56)

Pillage holds a levee, as "a very Great Man" (p. 56), that represents Walpole's broad use of patronage and bribery to cultivate majorities. Actors are promised parts, as voters and M.P.s were promised places and favours. A bribe is given "out of the office" (i.e., the secret service fund) to ensure that one actor will clap (vote favourably) when the House (both the Commons and the Haymarket) hisses. An actor asks for money to buy a ticket to the theatre (i.e., requests funds to help him buy a place in Commons), but is brusquely turned down, even though he was previously promised aid. Two printers (government contractors? those who hoped for places in the Excise service in 1733?) bid for the right to publish the farce, and one succeeds by bribing Pillage (Walpole, corrupt as well as corruptive). Finally, a Poet (the ministerial writers) is bribed to stand by Pillage's farce. The Poet assures the *farceur* that "we will make more noise than they," and Pillage agrees to do something in the way of a part (a sinecure?) for the Poet's *protégé*, a "handsome, genteel young gentleman" (a specific allusion now obscure). The levee serves as a summary of the patronage system, as well as the theatrical world, and leaves Pillage very confident:

> Then I defy the town, if by my friends,
> Against their liking, I support my farce,
> And fill my loaded pockets with their pence,
> Let after-ages damn me if they please. (p. 59)

It is a very sharp opposition satire indeed.

The Broad-Bottom tang of the play is provided by the next character to enter, Honestus, a critical playgoer, the antithesis of the sycophant actors and paid clappers. Asked by Pillage for his vote (applause from the pit and "Aye" in the Commons), he answers:

> Faith, sir, my voice shall never be corrupt.
> If I approve your farce, I will applaud it;
> If not, I'll hiss it, though I hiss alone. (pp. 59-60)

He represents—surely—both those who refused to be bullied or cajoled into voting for the Excise in 1733 (especially Cobham and Chesterfield, sheet anchors of the Broad-Bottom faction) and all the Patriots who in 1737 opposed Walpole, not out of personal hatred or prejudice, at least in theory, but as true lovers of their country. Pillage hopes "to see the time/ When none shall dare to hiss within the house," a dream reproducing the worst nightmares of Bolingbroke about the withering of the Constitution and the utter corruption of the Legislature. Honestus' answer could serve as a motto for many a Broad-Bottom tract from the hand of Bolingbroke or Lyttelton or Fielding: "I rather hope to see the time when none/ Shall come prepared to censure or applaud,/ But merit always bear away the prize." Pillage is confident that he has "so many friends/ that the majority [a term placing the theatre in the background and Commons in the foreground] will sure be mine." This draws from Honestus a "Curse on this way of carrying things by friends,/ This bar to merit, by such unjust means./ A play's success or ill success is known/ And fixed before it has been tried i' the house" (p. 60). Honestus goes on to lament high theatrical prices (high taxes and the Excise) and complain that the people do not even get "good tragedy" (government) for their money, but paltry Harlequin "tricks and juggling."[57] (p. 61) Honestus reminds Pillage that as theatre manager (first minister), he is a public servant, who pays his actors (placemen, voters) from the "people's pockets." The dramatized political essay ends with the refusal of a bribe, always Pillage's final argument, as it was Quidam's:

Pillage.
>   If you assist me on this trial day,
>   You may assure yourself a dedication.
Honestus.
>   No bribe—I go impartial to your cause,
>   Like a just critic to give worth applause,
>   But damn you if you write against our laws. (p. 62)

With the kaleidoscopic variability typical of Fielding's use of allegorical characters, Pillage temporarily represents only Fielding, not Walpole, in the next scene. There he gives in very easily when his Muse chides him for creating *Eurydice*, a whorish offspring, rather than another play like *Pasquin*, their legitimate child. He decides to write a good anti-ministerial play (presumably *The Historical Register*, surely being composed when *Eurydice* failed). Should he fail, he exclaims, "mayest thou forsake me, mayest thou then inspire/ The blundering brain of scribblers who for hire/ Would write away their country's liberties" (p. 63). Her reply mocks the mediocre verse of "Newgate" Thomas Purney and the odes of Cibber, then grows very serious: ". . . sooner starve, ay, even in prison starve,/ Than vindicate oppression for thy bread,/ Or write down liberty to gain thy own." Small wonder that the *Gazetteer*, whose writers are the target here, would relish the destruction of Fielding's stage career by the Licensing Act, and that Sourwit observes "this merry tragedy . . . growing sublime." Spatter allows that he was carried away—"Talking of liberty made me serious in spite of my teeth" (p. 64)—capping an exchange that undoubtedly drew sustained cheers from the Prince of Wales and his followers at the Haymarket.

Then develops the catastrophe, the damnation of *Eurydice* (or the past failure of the Excise Bill or the future collapse of Walpole's ministry) by the Town (or parliament and the nation):

>   The pit is crammed, I could not get admission,
>   But at the door I heard a mighty noise,
>   It seemed of approbation and of laughter.
>   . . . At first the pit seemed greatly pleased,
>   And loud applauses through the benches rung,
>   But as the plot began to open more
>   (A shallow plot) the claps less frequent grew
>   [this fits the failure of Excise better than that of *Eurydice*]
>   Till by degrees a gentle hiss arose;
>   This by a catcall from the gallery
>   Was quickly seconded. Then followed claps
>   And long 'twixt claps and hisses did succeed
>   A stern contention: victory hung dubious.
>   So hangs the conscience, doubtful to determine,
>   When honesty pleads here and there a bribe.
>   At length from some ill-fated actor's mouth
>   Sudden there issued forth a horrid dram,
>   And from another rushed two gallons forth.

The audience, as it were contagious air,
All caught it, halloed, catcalled, hissed and groaned. (p. 66)

Here the employment of the Eurydice-Excise parallel is perfect; in general and in detail, Fielding mocks the process by which in 1733 Walpole's safe majority so dwindled by second reading of his bill that he had to admit defeat—"This dance it will no farther go"—and avoid a division that might have destroyed him.

After his fall a drunken Pillage describes his own error to Honestus, underlining the play's idealistic politico-theatrical point: ". . . had I trusted/ to the impartial judgement of the town,/ And by the goodness of my piece had tried/ To merit favor, nor with vain reliance/ On the frail promise of uncertain friends/ produced a farce like this—friends who forsook me,/ And left me nought to comfort me but this [he drinks]" (pp. 67-68). Pillage's drunkenness may, as has sometimes been suggested, vaguely allude to Walpole's love of wine or (though I doubt it) the Gin Act of 1736 or even, given Fielding's mood of wry self-deprecation, indicate the way he dealt with his failure at Drury Lane in February. But it also reiterates the Broad-Bottom emphasis on the radical badness of Walpole's party-patronage system, carrying all "by friends." It goes beyond ridicule of the Excise failure to envision the day when his supporters (seeing him totter and overborne by the clamour of the nation against him) will leave him to a worse fate (impeachment and hemp were often mentioned) than drunken oblivion. The election of 1734 made it clear that the Excise had not seriously undermined Walpole's sway, but Fielding, Chesterfield, Cobham, and Lyttelton hoped for a final collapse like that in *Eurydice Hiss'd*.

Even before *The Historical Register* and *Eurydice Hiss'd* opened it is probably that the forces that would drive Fielding from the stage in 1737 were beginning to stir. Fielding's plays did not in themselves cause the ministry to pass the amendment to the Vagrants Act generally known as the Stage Licensing Act of 1737, but his success as an anti-ministerial satirist in 1736 and 1737 and the example the Haymarket set made it worthwhile to defy criticism and tighten regulation of the stage. In 1735, as we have seen, the ministry only half-heatedly pressed for a tighter stage act when John Barnard, voice of the London merchants, suggested an amendment designed to close the Goodman's Fields Theatre. The ministry proposed an amendment to Barnard's amendment that would have required the prior licensing of plays by the Lord Chamberlain (with it, Barnard's measure, if passed, would have approximated that made law in 1737), but did not prevent the horrified Barnard from withdrawing his proposal.[58] In 1737, faced with an opposition strengthened by the Broad-Bottoms and a surge of theatrical satire encouraged by Fielding and the Haymarket, the ministry moved with determination to grasp greater control of the stage.

The sharpening of the opposition literary attack, led by Fielding, is symbolized by the establishment of *Common Sense*, a major landmark in the increasing polarization and volume of political debate in 1737. Designed "to rebuke Vice, correct Errors, reform Abuses, and shame Folly and Prejudice without regard to anything but Common Sense," this quintessentially Broad-Bottom journal implicitly credited the author of *Pasquin* with inspiring its establishment and fighting the same evils in its first essay, February 5, 1737. Its seventh and eighth issues would carry as powerful, as scurrilous an attack on Walpolian corruption (and the King's co-operation with his minister's corruptive patronage) as ever appeared in the Walpole years: the notorious "Vision of the Golden Rump." In the "Vision" (perhaps best known from a print based on it, "The Festival of the Golden Rump")[59] Walpole ushers the ambitious and greedy to kiss the rump of a cloven-footed eastern idol—George II—which excretes showers of gold. In May 1737 a lost play, *The Golden Rump*, was passed on to the ministry by the manager of Lincoln's Inn Fields (it may have been a ministerial "plant") and was used in Commons as evidence of the need for tighter theatrical censorship. This should not obscure, however, that this political dynamite was first detonated in *Common Sense* on March 19 and 21, 1737. *The Historical Register* opened at the Haymarket on March 21. A minister reading the "Vision of the Golden Rump" in *Common Sense* in the morning and seeing *The Historical Register* in the evening must have marvelled at the vigour of the literary corps of the new Broad-Bottom wing of opposition and pondered partially silencing it, particularly since Drury Lane and Lincoln's Inn Fields seemed increasingly inclined to emulate the Haymarket. Step by step the movement to limit political satire on stage was linked to the activities of Fielding, his literary friends, and their opponents. *Eurydice Hiss'd* opened on April 13, and on April 14 *The Daily Gazetteer* reported that George Lyttelton was actively recruiting dramatists to slander the government. As the weeks passed and the ministry's plans solidified, *The Daily Gazetteer* warmed to the task of attacking Fielding and hinting his danger, while Fielding (now politically committed, unwilling to back away under the threat of censorship as he had in 1731) fought back, flaunting the political aspects of his plays.

The battle over the tightening of stage legislation began for Fielding on May 7, 1737, with a sharp attack upon *The Historical Register* and its author in a "letter-essay" signed by "An Adventurer in Politics" (perhaps Lord Hervey)[60] in *The Daily Gazetteer*. Making the standard distinction between the freedom allowed in England and tight censorship in France, the "Adventurer" avoids attacking freedom of speech or the press, but condemns as an evil requiring action "the bringing of *Politicks* on the *Stage*." He reviews the sharpening of Fielding's satire from the generality of *Pasquin* to the direct anti-ministerialism of *The Historical Register*, giving the facts fairly accurately as far (but *only* as far) as he goes, and then adding a decidedly unfriendly twist:

> The *Election* (a *Comedy in Pasquin*) laid the Foundation for introducing Politics on the Stage; but as the Author was general in his

> Satyr, and exposed with Wit and Humour, the Practices of *Elections*,
> without coming so near, as to point *any Person* out, he was not then
> guilty of the fault he has since committed; tho I cannot think him
> *Praiseworthy*, for turning into Ridicule and making light of one of the
> *gravest* Evils our Constitution is subject to.

This clever admission of extenuation pre-empts Fielding's favourite
theme (the last sentence is based upon a line, cited above, from *The
Historical Register*), the anti-Constitutional gravity of corruption. It is
followed by less qualified criticism of *The Historical Register* and
Fielding's allegiance to Lyttelton, Chesterfield, Bolingbroke, and the
other Broad-Bottoms. After *Pasquin*, Fielding gave

> his Genius unlimited Scope, in this Vein, in which it has been made evi-
> dent since, he was secretly *buoy'd up* by some of the *greatest Wits* and
> *finest Gentlemen* of the Age, who letting their Passions get the Better
> of their more mature Reflections, have patronized a Method of
> Writing [they] themselves, were they in the Administration would be
> the first to discountenance.
>   *The Historical Register* then, appeared to the Town, under the
> *Patronage* of the *Great*, the *Sensible*, and the *Witty* in the Opposi-
> tion.

Having thus branded and flattered Fielding, the "Adventurer" makes
his real point,[61] that Fielding has demonstrated the dangerous "Power of
such Exhibitions, *to make a Minister appear Ridiculous to a People.*"
This compliment to Fielding's satiric skill also indicates why Fielding's
future on stage was soon to be curtailed by Act of Parliament.
    The essayist finally faces the balanced nature of the satire in *The
Historical Register* and weakly tries to convert virtue into sin by blurring
the obvious ironies in Fielding's use of the terms "Patriot" and
"Patriotism" and (not entirely without justice) seeing the satire on the
Patriots as a last insult to Walpole:

> It may be said here, in favour of the Author, that in the Close of his
> Register [the auction scene is ignored], he has treated the Patriots no
> better than the Politicians. But this, instead of extenuating only
> doubles his Crime, for, I think, to turn *Patriotism*, the noblest of
> Characters, into a Jest, equally blameable, and that neither should
> have any place on the Stage. But perhaps these Patriots have consented
> to have themselves play'd, only to *exhibit that* Impudent Fellow, *who
> can stand their* Hisses, and *laugh in his Sleeves at them.*

Eurydice Hiss'd is criticized for treating government as a farce, threatening the very foundations of society, and exposing the present ministry
before Europe, for a "true Patriot" would never "endeavour to render
his country contemptible: He would rather strive to hide its Weaknesses.
He would try at a Cure, but by such Means as would not lay the Wound
too open." In short, the Stage is no place for "Politicks or Religion."
The press produces too much criticism of the ministry, and if the political
abuse of the stage goes on,

> . . . the very Gentlemen themselves, who now personally support it,
> tho' perhaps, in their own Minds they can't justify their Conduct in so
> doing, may themselves, in process of Time, be the Objects of such Ex-
> hibitions, and afford themselves as Publick Spectacles of Derision on a
> Stage to the lowest of Mankind. And who then can they blame? For
> the *very Poet* that now prostitutes the Muses to their private Passions,
> may serve those of a future Opposition to a future Ministry.

There was some truth to this closing warning. If Fielding had been
active in a loosely regulated theatre between 1742 and 1744 (when he remained faithful to the disappointed Broad-Bottoms in opposition), he
would have treated Pulteney and Carteret as roughly as he did Walpole
in 1737.[62] But the crucial point of the *Gazetteer* essay was semi-officially
to hint that the licentiousness of the stage would not much longer be
tolerated. Otherwise the essay is pretty standard, though unusually well-
written ministerial journalism. With minor adjustments Fielding was to
make all of the same points in his attacks on the "licentiousness" of the
opposition press when he assumed the role of the chief ministerial
apologist in the later 1740s: an example is the essay in *The Jacobite's
Journal*, no. 26, where he sears the opposition press for committing the
high crime of *"scandalium magnatum"* in satirizing the chief servants of
the Crown and the King himself. But whereas Fielding only dared to hint
the need for a tighter rein on the freedom of the press, and then retreated
into a fever of disclaimers, the "Adventurer in Politics" was pointing
toward a looming and forbidding reality. Within three weeks the Licensing Act would be introduced in Commons. In less than two months it
would be law and Fielding would be casting about for a new career.

In 1731 Fielding attempted to placate the censor by eschewing
authorially approved publication of any version of his offensive play,
and then avoiding political satire for a considerable time. In 1737 he was
hardened to fight, rather than flex, by his real attachment to an opposition faction. It would have been embarrassing to give way after posing as
"Pasquin," chief theatrical defender of liberty and political honesty, so
ostentatiously for two seasons. He must also have recognized that no accommodation would help this time. He was *persona non grata*, and a
stringent stage act amendment would be passed in 1737 no matter what
he did. Indeed, no stage career may have seemed preferable to one
diminished and anti-climactic. The kind of plays that had offended were
his *forte*, and if he could no longer stage them, it is understandable that
at the age (for all his experience) of only thirty, journalism and a new
career as a lawyer seemed better alternatives. Fielding went down
fighting in 1737, and then turned completely away from literature for a
time.

Only five days after the "Adventurer in Politics" essay Fielding's
Historical Register and *Eurydice Hiss'd* were published in a single-
volume edition giving every indication of hurried editing and typesetting.
The implication that this was a reaction to the attack in *The Gazetteer*, a
flaunting of the offending works, is crystallized into certainty by

Fielding's "Dedication to the Public." Really a political essay rebutting
the *Gazetteer*, it repeats *The Historical Register*'s crime, offering a
criticism of the raising of prices at Drury Lane by Charles Fleetwood that
begs (point by point) also to be read as a criticism of Walpole's corrupt
political system, based on buying votes with the proceeds from ever-rising
taxes:

> . . . I cannot help thinking his [Fleetwood's, Walpole's] manner of
> proceeding somewhat too arbitrary, and his method of buying actors
> [voters, M.P.s] at exorbitant prices to be of very ill consequence. For
> the town [the nation] must reimburse him these expenses [the cost of
> bribery, the Civil List, etc.], on which account those advanced prices
> [taxes] so much complained of must be always continued; which,
> though the people in their present flourishing state of trade and riches
> [a heavy irony insisted on in the parenthetical comment in the next
> clause] may very well pay, yet in worse times (if such can be supposed)
> I am afraid they may fall too heavy, the consequence of which I need
> not mention. Moreover, should any great genius produce a piece [law
> or policy] of most exquisite contrivance, and which would be highly
> relished by the public, though perhaps not agreeable to his own taste or
> private interest, if he should buy the chief actors, such play, how-
> ever excellent, must be unavoidably sunk, and the public lose all the
> benefit thereof. Not to trouble the reader with more inconveniences
> arising from this *argumentum argentarium* [the "silver" argument,
> Quindam's specialty], many of which are obvious enough, I shall only
> observe that corruption hath the same influence on all societies, all
> bodies, which it hath on corporeal bodies, where we see it always pro-
> duce an entire destruction and total change. For which reason, who-
> ever attempteth to introduce corruption into any community doth
> much the same thing [the Fleetwood-theatrical element in the satiric
> dualism has about vanished], and ought to be treated in much the same
> manner with him who poiseneth a fountain, in order to disperse a con-
> tagion, which he is sure everyone will drink of.

Fielding next ironically "rebuts" the *Gazetteer's* aspersions, attacking the ministry in self-defence. He expresses disbelief that *The
Historical Register* was not recognized to be "a ministerial pamphlet,
calculated to infuse into the minds of the people a great opinion of their
ministry, and thereby procure an employment for the author, who had
been often promised one, whenever he would write on that side." The
jest is based on the careful balancing of anti-ministerial and anti-
opposition satire in *The Historical Register*, but was never meant even
momentarily to confuse a reader. It allows Fielding simultaneously to
mock the *Gazetteer* and Walpole. He goes on ironically to insist that the
"scene of the politicians" ridicules "the absurd and inadequate notions
persons among us, who have not the honor to know 'em, have of the
ministry and their measures." He hopes the *Gazetteer* did not mean to
find "any resemblance," it being hardly "a compliment to any M----y as
to suppose that such persons have been ever capable of the assurance of
aiming at being at the head of a great people, or to any nation, as to
suspect 'em contentedly living under such an administration." He recalls

a wag ["An Adventurer in Politics"] who pointed to an ass on a sign, and cried out to his short-sighted friend ["Bob" Walpole], "Bob! Bob! Look yonder! Some impudent rascal has hung out your picture on a signpost." Bob complained to the landlord before a smiling mob about the likeness. Possibly the sign of the ass may have been meant to suggest and rub in "The Vision of the Golden Rump" or (more precisely) the offensive print, "The Festival of the Golden Rump," which affronted Walpole from many a signpost and wall. If showing the play called *The Golden Rump* to the Commons helped get the Licensing Act through, Walpole unfortunately laughed last.

Fielding next argues that "turning patriotism into a jest" should have pleased a ministry so industrious in doing so, and challenges "all the ministerial advocates to show me, in the whole bundle of their writings, one passage where false patriotism (for I suppose they have not the impudence to mean any other) is set in a more contemptible and odious light than in the aforesaid scene." This, of course, implies that ministerial writers slander true Patriots along with the false in opposition, while his play exposes the false Patriot as well as the venal minister or placeman in the name of true Patriotism. Indeed, Fielding means to emphasize that his play is harder on the false Patriot precisely because he so values true Patriotism: "The politicians are represented as a set of blundering blockheads rather deserving pity than abhorrence, whereas the others are represented as a set of cunning self-interested fellows who for a little paltry bribe would give up the liberties and properties of the country." This somewhat whitewashes the "scene of the politicians," and skirts the obvious fact that Quidam plays the tempter and confuser in the "scene of the Patriots." However, the latter point is soon made in a Broad-Bottom diatribe against the corruption of "false Patriots":

> Here is the danger, here is the rock on which our constitution must, if it ever does, split. The Liberties of a people have been subdued by the conquest of valor and force, and have been betrayed by the subtle and dextrous arts of refined policy; but these are rare instances, for geniuses of this kind are not the growth of every age, whereas if a general corruption be once introduced and those who should be the guardians and bulwarks of our liberty [the members of the legislature] once find, or think they find, an interest in giving it up, no great capacity will be required to destroy it; on the contrary, the meanest, lowest, dirtiest fellow [Walpole], if such a one should have ever the assurance, in future ages, to mimic power and browbeat his betters, will be as able as Machievel himself could have been, to root out the liberties of the bravest people.

This denunciation of perilous corruption could have come from Bolingbroke at his thundering best, but the next touch is purest Fielding:

> But I am aware I shall be asked who is this *Quidam* that turns patriots into ridicule and bribes them out of their honesty? Who but the Devil could act such a part? Is not this the light wherein he is everywhere described in scripture and the writings of our best divines? Gold hath always been his favourite bait, wherewith he fishes for sinnes, and his

laughing at the poor wretches he seduceth is as diabolical an attribute as any. Indeed it is so plain who is meant by this *Quidam* that he who maketh any wrong application thereof might as well mistake the name of Thomas for John, or Old Nick for Old Bob.[63]

Under the threat of censorship Fielding was not in a mood of conciliation. After some further comic protestations of ministerial intent and some sly satire on "a certain person . . . sometimes the author, often the corrector of the press, and always the patron of the *Gazetteer*" (probably Lord Hervey), he ends with a vow to continue fighting the battle against Walpole and corruption. Indeed, he suggests that if literary freedom is not curtailed, he will try to improve the Haymarket's facilities as a forum for satire on these evils. There is wishful bravado in this combative declaration from a man with a theatrical life expectancy of a few weeks:

> The very great indulgence you [the public] have shown my performances at the little theatre, these last two years, have encouraged me to the proposal of a subscription for carrying on that theatre, for enlarging it and procuring a better company of actors. If you think proper to subscribe to these proposals, I assure you no labor shall be spared, on my side, to entertain you in a cheaper and better manner than seems to be the intention of any other. If nature hath given me any talents at ridiculing vice and imposture, I shall not be indolent nor afraid of exercising them while the liberty of the press and stage subsists, that is to say, while we have any liberty left among us.

But the clock continued to tick away on Fielding and the "Little Theatre" in the Haymarket. On May 20 Commons ordered the preparation of an amendment to the Vagrant Act,[64] roughly equivalent to Barnard's bill of 1735, *with* the Walpolian rider, the so-called "licensing" requirement that had caused Barnard to retreat. It was designed to regulate "theatrical entertainments, which from their excess, fill both town and country with idleness and debauchery; and, from being under no restraint exhibit to the publick encomiums on vice, and laugh away the sober principles of modesty and virtue." It restricted the theatres not within the verge of the Court to those already legally permitted in the City of Westminster and its "Liberties," which effectively closed the non-patent theatres, including the Haymarket, and reinforced the oft-breached monopoly of the more controllable, patented Drury Lane and Covent-Garden theatres. It also prohibited the acting for "hire, gain, or reward" of any play or dramatic performance not previously sanctioned by letters-patent from the Crown or (the normal route) granted a licence by the Lord Chamberlain, *ex officio* censor, who was to receive a copy of every play at least two weeks prior to performance.[65] The preparation order was tantamount (for all the objections sure to pour from the opposition) to an assurance of passage before Parliament rose in June. Fielding, with little to lose, defended himself and assaulted the *Gazetteer* and its masters again the following day, May 21, in a "letter-essay" signed "Pasquin" in *Common Sense.*

"Pasquin" makes it clear ("As I have yet no Vehicle of my own, I shall be obliged to you if you will give the following a Place in the next Stage'') he is pondering the establishment of his own journal, though in the event this plan did not bear fruit for two and a half years. This implies Fielding's recognition that the more familiar and lucrative theatre would soon be closed to him as manager or playwright. The "Pasquin" essay retraces many of the arguments in the "Dedication to the Public." Fielding insists again that it was his right and duty, rather than a prostitution of the theatre and betrayal of his country, to expose "a general Corruption (one of the greatest Evils (you are pleased to own) our Constitution is subject to)." He ironically reiterates the sly theatrical-political indictment of Walpole in *The Historical Register* and *Eurydice Hiss'd* ("Mr. Penkethman [a player in *The Burlesque of Alexander*] never was so ridiculous a Figure, as when he became *Penkethman the Great*"). In a passage designed to acknowledge and solicit aid from his political friends, he also glories in the opposition connections sneered at by the *Gazetteer* and his freedom from obligations to the ministry:

> I shall not be industrious to deny, what you are so good to declare, that I am buoy'd up by the greatest Wits, and finest Gentlemen of the Age; and Patroniz'd by the Great, the Sensible, and the Witty in the Opposition. Of such Patrons I shall always be proud, and to such shall be always glad of the Honour of owning an Obligation. Nor is it a small Pleasure to me, that my Heart is conscious of none to certain Persons who are in the Opposition to those Characters by which you have been pleased to distinguish my Patrons.

His closing argument is concise, witty, and energetic, and is doubly interesting because it offers a vision of England ruled by his Broad-Bottom patrons that materialized in part with the formation of the Broad-Bottom ministry between 1744 and 1746. He stresses that he has "not ridiculed Patriotism" but the perils of corruption, ridicules the idea that his plays have damaged England in the eyes of Europe, warns that the curtailing of freedom of the press could be justified by the same bad arguments the *Gazetteer* uses in favour of controlling the stage, and concludes:

> . . . I must beg Leave to say, without any Reflection on our present Ministry, that, I believe, there are now amongst those Gentlemen who are styled the *Opposition*, Men in Genius, Learning, and Knowledge so infinitely superior to the rest of their Countrymen, and of Integrity so eminent, that should they, *in process of Time*, be in the Possession of Power, they will be able to triumph over, and trample upon all the Ridicule which any Wit or Humour could level at them: For Ridicule, like *Ward's* Pill, passes innocently through a sound Constitution; but when it meets with a Complication of foul Distemper in a gross corrupt Carcase, it is apt to give a terrible Shock, to work the poor Patient most immoderately; in the Course of which Working, it is ten to one but he bes---ts his Breeches.

Three days later, on May 24, the Licensing Act was introduced in Commons, beginning a progress through both Houses that was inexorable, though there were many protests, including one of Chesterfield's finest orations in the Lords, a classic defence of literary freedom.[66] Fielding remained silent until June 4, just before the decisive Third Reading in Lords on June 6. Then he and *The Daily Gazetteer* fired simultaneous broadsides. "An Adventurer in Politics" addressed "Pasquin, in Common Sense, of May the 21st," treating the Licensing Act as a necessary shield against his libellous scurrility. As Aristophanes did by attacking the best men in Greece, Fielding has helped bring the law upon himself and others. This was the opening round of a barrage in favour of the Act and against Fielding continued in several issues of the *Gazetteer* (June 8, 11, 13, 15, for example), but it coincided with what I think was Fielding's last word on the subject in 1737.

Scholars have long assumed that if Fielding had chosen to continue defending himself he would have done so in Lyttelton and Chesterfield's *Common Sense*. But there are no more essays in *Common Sense* we can call his. Wilbur Cross vaguely observed that Fielding ceased to answer the *Gazetteer* after May 21, though he may in the next two years have contributed a few essays to *Common Sense* which we cannot identify. Since Cross, only Ioan Williams has even tentatively attributed any essays in *Common Sense* to him (those in nos. 31 and 32, September 3 and 10, 1737), and these are *certainly not* by Fielding, and in any case have no connection with politics or the Licensing Act.[67] However, it seems to me very likely that an essay that appeared in the *other* great opposition journal, *The Craftsman*, on June 4 was written by Fielding to serve as a dignified, reasoned valediction to the theatrical and censorial wars of 1737. Aside from the essay for December 20, 1735 (discussed earlier as possibly the first shot by Fielding in the battle that ended with the Licensing Act), I do not know whether or not he earlier or later contributed to *The Craftsman*. (The essay in that journal for April 30, 1737, which amusingly toys, in prose that suggests his, with the idea of a tax on urine in the spirit of the "Scene of the Politicians" in *The Historical Register*, is tempting.) However, the essay for June 4, 1747 is, I think, one of his rare pre-*Champion* flyers at journalism.

It says *exactly* what Fielding would have wished to say at this moment, about everything from the Licensing Act to the declining moral state of English society to Italian opera. It is also written in a style that everywhere suggests that of the "serious" essays in his later journals. The consistent use of "hath" is one indication; in addition, the prose has the same characteristics stressed in attributing the 1735 *Craftsman* essay to Fielding at the head of this chapter.[68] Perhaps the best argument, however, for those familiar with Fielding's essay style, is to cite some of it, a procedure justified by its present difficulty of access:

> . . . the *Immorality of the People* is so far from being owing to *the Licentiousness of the Stage*, that the *Licentiousness of the Stage* is immediately owing to the *Immorality of the People*, which flows from *Causes* too well known, and obliges *necessitous Writers* to comply with the prevailing Humour of the Times. Nay, the *Stage* hath been considerably reform'd of late Years, notwithstanding all the *Corruption*,

which hath been so wickedly introduced and encouraged amongst the *People;* for I may defy the severest Critick to point out half so many Instances of Debauchery, Prophaneness and Blasphemy, in any of our *modern Plays,* as are to be found in those of *Dryden, Etherege, Wycherly, Congreve, Vanbrugh,* and others. Some, indeed, are too gross to be quoted, though still extant in Print, and even represented on the Stage.

....

Besides, the Bounds of *Liberty* and *Licentiousness* are so ex- tremely nice, that it is very difficult to distinguish exactly between them; but it is certain there can be no *Liberty,* where there is no Room left of extending it too far. A few Inconveniences of this Kind are the Tax we pay for *Liberty,* and which cannot be had without them. We pay, at present, about *Seven Millions* a Year for our *Liberty;* and is This attended with no *Hardship,* or *Licentiousness?* Is there no Oppo- sition, or Possibility of Opposition, from the *Tax-gatherers* and *Soldiers,* who preserve this *Liberty* to us; or shall We part with *such watchful Guardians* of it, upon this Account? To prune *Liberty* of all *Licentiousness* is supposing a Thing to subsist, which is not capable of being abused; whereas the *best Things* are liable to *Corruption,* and nothing more than *Government* itself, which hath been prostituted to such wicked Purposes, that even the pious Doctor *Prideaux* makes a Doubt whether it hath not done more Mischief than Good in the World. But are We therefore to live in a State of *Anarchy,* lest *Govern- ment* should degenerate into *Tyranny* and *Oppression?* The same Question may be ask'd about *Religion,* or *any other good Thing,* which is equally subject to *Corruption,* and hath been equally *cor- rupted,* in all Ages.

....

However, if *this Bill* must pass; if the *Court* is still so short of Power, that it cannot support itself against the People, without taking away the *Liberty of the Stage,* or listing it intirely on *that Side;* I hope our *Italian Opera's* will fall the first Sacrifice, as they not only carry great Sums of Money out of the Kingdom, but soften and enervate the Minds of the People. It is observable of the *ancient Romans,* that they did not admit of any *effeminate Musick, Singing, or* Dancing, upon their Stage, till *Luxury* had corrupted their Morals, and the Loss of *Liberty* followed soon after.

....

The *Bill,* now under Consideration, was carried through *one House* with so much Expedition, and even Precipitancy, that I shall hardly have any Opportunity of speaking my Mind freely upon it again, unless it should be rejected in the *other;* but whatever may be its Fate, every *Englishman* hath a Liberty of proposing his Objections to any *Bill,* till it passes into an *Act,* and becomes the *Law of his Country.*

The writer of this essay—Fielding in my opinion—treats the Licensing Act as a *fait accompli.* Its last paragraph—"I shall hardly have any Op- portunity of speaking my Mind freely upon it again"—reads like a wistful farewell not to the stage, but to authorship. If so, Fielding was hinting his real plans for the foreseeable future. The Licensing Act received the Royal Assent and became law on June 21, 1737, without fur- ther comment from Fielding. For once he was probably able to live without writing for a time. The profits had been large from his successes of 1736 and 1737. Something may have remained of the 1735 Craddock inheritance of £1500. There was income from his part of the family estate at East Stour (sold in 1738 for £260).[69] His opposition patrons must also have done something for a schoolfellow who had lost much for them. Fielding stopped publishing, as far as anyone has discovered, for over two years. He did not publish unperformable plays, establish a journal, or contribute to established journals, though he had threatened to fight on in the press, and the opposition's campaign against Walpole continued.

Even in the theatre the assault went on. The government was fairly severe about enforcing the restriction of theatrical activities to the patent houses. But it was surprisingly loose about licensing plays with anti-ministerial content, so long as it was somewhat masked, and—one would guess—Henry Fielding, arch-offender, was not connected with them. Not until Henry Brooke's *Gustavus Vasa* of 1739 (the use of historical or foreign subjects as camouflage remained a protection against censorship) was a play refused a licence. James Thomson's subtler *Agamemnon* and *Mustapha* had not been bothered, but after *Gustavus Vasa* the censor looked more closely at plays by Broad-Bottom wits, also banning in 1739 Thomson's *Edward and Eleonora*, which celebrated Prince Frederick and suggested the need to supplant evil ministers. Though nothing like *The Historical Register* and nothing questionable by Fielding could have survived, the stage remained a political forum, reaching a post-Licensing Act peak with Thomson's "Britannia, Rule the Waves" in the *Masque of Alfred* of 1740. Theatrical audiences and the young Samuel Johnson fought the ministry. Johnson deplored the Licensing Act for permitting the Chamberlain "to do that *without* reason which *with* reason he could do before" in the ironical *A Complete Vindication of the Licensers of the Stage, from The Malicious and Scandalous Aspersions of Mr. Brooke, Author of Gustavus Vasa.* In 1738 the audience rioted, singing Fielding's "The Roast Beef of Old England" and closing the Haymarket, when the government allowed a troupe of French comedians to open at the theatre closed to Fielding by the Act.[70]

However, though his later writings show his adherence to the Broad-Bottom opposition was unaltered, Fielding remained silent from early June 1737 to the first number of *The Champion* on November 15, 1739. He enrolled as an unusually mature student of the law—following the tradition of his Gould ancestors—at the Middle Temple on November 1, 1737, and applied himself intensely to his studies.[71] One effect of the Licensing Act was to give England a scholarly lawyer who would serve with rare distinction as a magistrate. Another fortunate result was that he turned, when he could not resist writing any longer, from drama to prose and prose fiction. When the Licensing Act went into effect in June 1737, however, his admission to the Bar was three years away, and the publication of *Joseph Andrews* nearly half a decade in the future, an eternity for an ambitious man in his thirties starting a new life.

Chapter Four

The Final Assault on Walpole: 1739-42

Aside from the fact that he enrolled at the Middle Temple and studied assiduously, we know little about Fielding between mid-1737 and late 1739. A good decade behind most Templars, he must have been too busy to write much, even if he had the heart, after he left his family in the country and enrolled in the fall of 1737. He may have worked on *Liberty: to George Lyttelton, Esq.* and the *First Olynthiac of Demosthenes,* which read like political satires *circa* 1738-39, though they only appeared in the *Miscellanies* of 1743. But he published nothing until November 1739, nearly eight months before he was called to the Bar, unless he allowed the publication in the *Gentleman's Magazine* (December 1738) of one of his early poems to Walpole.[1]

Having failed to take his campaign against Walpole into the journals in 1737, he did so in 1739 as chief editor, principal essayist, and shareholder of *The Champion: or British Mercury.* This essay journal was published three times a week beginning on November 15, 1739: at first on Tuesday, Thursday, and Saturday mornings in a two-page format; after April 10, 1740 in the afternoons of the same days under the title, *The Champion: or Evening Advertiser,* in a four-page format. It survived until an obscure period well into the early 1740s, long after Fielding left it.[2] Financial need was surely one reason Fielding (and James Ralph, his old Haymarket partner, who shared the editorial and writing labours) signed on with *The Champion.* Savings from theatrical successes and inheritances, eked out by the sale of ancestral lands, probably were for a time sufficient to support Fielding's wife and daughters in the country and Fielding at the Middle Temple. Distress does not seem implicit in a surviving letter of July 9, 1739 in which he requested John Nourse, bookseller, to find him a London house with a lease for seven years at up to £40 *per annum.*[3] However, by late 1739 he had been living— presumably with at least minimal gentility—for over two years without income. Since writing was a natural activity that he must have missed, one imagines Fielding accepting with alacrity the proposal of a syndicate of booksellers that he contribute time and talent in return for "two-sixteenth shares" of the potential profits of *The Champion*. So long after the glory days at the Haymarket, James Ralph was probably glad to become (as circumstantial evidence suggests) a salaried assistant.

The booksellers were taking a risk backing a new journal in a crowded market. Fielding recalls in the essay for June 12, 1740 that his publisher anticipated the heavy competition that long kept *The Champion* on the very "Precipice of Oblivion." The booksellers and writers probably hoped that *The Champion*'s essays would appeal to an audience wider than those absorbed by politics. Unlike *The Craftsman* and *Common Sense*, it would frequently offer jocular and serious discussions of critical, literary, moral, religious, and social subjects, as well as political ones, blending the strengths of *Common Sense* with those of *The Grub-Street Journal* and *The Tatler* or *The Spectator*. The Steele-Addison connection was obviously implicit in the creation of both a comic *persona* for Fielding, Captain Hercules Vinegar, Esq. of Hockley-in-the-Hole (later of Pall Mall), and a Vinegar family of correspondents. Fielding would later sign essays "C" and "L," recalling a signature Addison had used, "Clio." As a master of masks and parody, Fielding gave *The Champion* far more humour and variety than its competition could boast, though this did not initially raise circulation.

The Champion also carried foreign and domestic news extracted from the *Gazetteer* and other dailies and "digested in a peculiar manner," annotated, often satirically, according to the pattern established in *The Grub-Street Journal*. Though the annotations added spice, one wonders how many readers were attracted by the news sections, which occupied (together with a variety of special features) much of the space between the lead essay and the closing obituaries, stock quotations, and advertisements: most of a page in the two-page format and more after April 10, 1740 in the four-page format. The news items were mere snippets, rather out of date since *The Champion*'s "quotation hunter" (said to be William Young, Fielding's later collaborator in translating *Plutus; or the God of Riches* and the supposed model for Abraham Adams) had to clip items from published newspapers, and give Fielding a chance to annotate them. What *The Daily Gazetteer* said on Saturday could only be repeated—in part—on Tuesday, and often news got even colder. A London reader, therefore, must have read more for the annotations than the news. Advertisements were a potential source of revenue once adequate circulation was achieved, but there are remarkably few in the earlier numbers except for works written by Fielding or published by printers associated with the journal. *The Champion* provided free space in lieu of profits.

The establishment of *The Champion* was obviously encouraged by the rising tempo of attack on the government triggered by the outbreak of the War of Jenkins' Ear with Spain despite Walpole's efforts to avoid it and his success in passing the unpopular, appeasing Convention of Pardo. Forcing Walpole toward war with Spain had for years been an opposition pastime. Success not only produced a euphoric sense of having beaten the "great Man," but opened up a new vein for his critics. George Lyttelton and others who had insisted on war could now call for a more vigorous military effort than was likely under the unenthusiastic Walpole, particularly at sea and in favour of trade, and to demand a speedy and cheap victory. Within a week after the declaration of war, Lyttelton (*Common Sense*, October 23, 1739) was arguing that Walpole would be responsible for all difficulties in the war, and demanding that he should win victories economically. Overarming would be a "Mark of Fear and Cowardice." Continental realities, including the Hanoverian involvements of King George, obliged Walpole to wage unpopular, expensive, inconclusive land campaigns, a practice followed also by his successors throughout the general European conflict into which the War of Jenkins' Ear blended, the War of the Austrian Succession. This made Walpole vulnerable, with a general election due in 1741. War was declared on October 19, 1739 and issue one of *The Champion* appeared on November 15, little more than three weeks later, absolutely the minimum time required to set up a high-quality journal.

It may seem odd that financial support from opposition politicians has not been mentioned as a stimulus to the establishment of *The Champion*, but I am convinced it did not enjoy any at first. It has always been assumed that, in Wilbur Cross's words, "Behind this undertaking were doubtless Fielding's friends in Parliament."[4] This would seem probable enough in the light of Fielding's closeness to Lyttelton and the anti-Walpole bias of *The Champion*. It is clear that support from political beneficiaries was normal for major political journals. We have seen in Chapter II examples of the considerable investment Walpole made in several journals in the earlier 1730s with secret service funds; certainly much more was spent to float and distribute *The Daily Gazetteer* after it took over as the "official" voice of ministry in 1735. As Fielding and others complained, thousands of copies of each issue were bought up by the ministry and distributed *gratis* throughout the nation by post, making the journal both profitable and formidable because widely read. In 1747-48 such a ministerial subsidy (his enemies mentioned 2,000 copies of each issue bought and distributed)[5] was a major element in the success of Fielding's *Jacobite's Journal*. Though the opposition could not match the ministry's subsidy-distribution capacity, influential opposition journals (always actually run by professionals, not "literary" lords) were supported in a similar way. The method was so efficient: the artificial, guaranteed sale of, say, a thousand copies of each issue paid the writers and booksellers while a thousand copies in coffee-houses, post-houses, and inns in London and the provinces spread the opposition's propaganda. It explains the influence and longevity of *The Craftsman* (originally sponsored by Lord Bolingbroke and William Pulteney), *Common Sense* (the project of George Lyttelton and Lord Chesterfield), and such journals of the 1740s as *Old England* and *The Remembrancer*. Subsidies were embarrassing secrets, but I would guess more copies of *Common Sense* were given away than sold, and that this had as much to do with its impact as its high quality.

However, largely circumstantial but very strong evidence indicates that *The Champion* was not subsidized before June 1740. In its first seven months or so it needled, then hammered ministerial targets in the hope of making enough noise to sell and attract patronage, not because it already was subsidized. It is unclear why this was so, for Fielding would not have hesitated to accept a subsidy. Most likely Lyttelton felt that backing *Common Sense* was enough, particularly since *The Champion* would compete with it. Then too the new journal, with its mixed content, was not quite ideal for a subsidy, though the political material in it was always perfectly in accord with the positions taken by Lyttelton, the Broad-Bottoms, and *Common Sense*. A man of taste, Lyttelton must have enjoyed the early *Champion* essays, but the politician in him may not have seen it as worthy of hire.

The pattern suggested—no subsidy of seven months, then a resolution of the problem—is not readily detectable by a reader of *The Champion* unless he is forewarned to look for unobtrusive signs. When they were subsidized, journals did not advertise the fact, and a journalist speaking as a devoted patriot could hardly complain about lacking a subsidy! The pattern is, however, strongly implied by a seemingly anomalous pattern in the response of *The Daily Gazetteer*. From mid-November, 1739 to early July, 1740 *The Champion* was almost totally ignored by *The Gazetteer*, while *The Craftsman* and *Common Sense* were "answered" and satirized in many issues. *The Champion* satirized the ministry as corrupt, inept, and traitorously eager to lose the war with Spain; Walpole as a thief, a boor, and an impotent lecher; and the staff of *The Gazetteer* as slanderous and illiterate hacks. But in the roughly 200 issues of *The Gazetteer* between November 15, 1739 and the end of June 1740, there is only *one* easily missed acknowledgement of the existence of *The Champion*. On December 22, 1739 a "letter" from "Farrol McGascoigne, Late Secretary of Hockley-Hole" (from which Hercules Vinegar then addressed his essays) to his "fellow-labourers," *The Craftsman* and *Common Sense*, vaguely teases *The Champion* and gloats that Fielding and Ralph (not named) have been forced into hack-work by the Licensing Act.

The puzzle thus posed is completed by an outburst of abuse directed at *The Champion* which begins *very suddenly* just after mid-year and grows *very rapidly* to the point where *The Champion* is more often attacked than *Common Sense* and *The Craftsman* combined. *The Gazetteer* opens fire on July 4 upon "those excellent Persons the Writers of the Craftsman, Common Sense, and the Champion, [who] have expressed their Resentments against us in very high and angry Terms." It goes on to rebut *The Champion*'s criticism of the government's conduct of the war on July 12, and expresses the hope before citing Shakespeare on July

16 that "the *Champion* will allow me to be acquainted with that author." On July 24 it expresses greater contempt and dislike for *The Champion* and another obscure journal than their older opposition compatriots: "I think the two mushroom Writers lately sprung up of the papers call'd the *Champion* and *Englishman's Evening Post*, the most incorrigible, crude and inconsistent. They would, 'tis supposed, be look'd upon as Auxiliaries to the two establish'd *Empirick's* of the Week, when in truth they deserve not to be rank'd amongst their Zanies and Pickleherrings. The *Vinegar Captain* attempts to be witty, but wants Genius . . . ." By the end of the month *The Champion* (attacked again and alone on July 29 and 30) obviously had replaced *Common Sense* and *The Craftsman* as the *Gazetteer's* principal concern. Through the end of 1740 the *Champion* continued to receive most attention from the *Gazetteer*, which attacked it on August 5 and 13, September 5, 12, 17, and 19, October 9, 17, 20, 23, 29, 30, and 31 (a flurry of abuse generated in part by the publication of the notorious "Remarkable Queries" in the *Champion* on October 7), November 5, 14, 19, and 26, and December 6 and 10.

Moreover, the *Gazetteer* treated *The Champion* as a new adversary, as though it was established in the early summer of 1740. We have seen it referred to on July 24 as "lately sprung up." On August 13 the *Gazetteer* spoke of the strengthening of the opposition "corps" by "a fresh supply of new-rais'd *Auxiliaries* that exceed, if possible, the *Veterans* themselves, in Speen or Malevolence." It accused "Vinegar," on September 12, of being the worst of opposition writers, a dangerous rabble-rouser: "A Man who writes a *Pasquin* may not be able to write a *Freeholder*, but a Man who has Malice enough to set a House on Fire, may, with the Assistance of Fortune, burn down a great City." It said on October 17, before beginning a point-by-point rebuttal of the "Remarkable Queries": "It is an Honour justly due to the Paper call'd the *Champion, or Evening Advertiser*, that tho' it set out *last*, yet it has outstripped all the *Vehicles* of *Sedition* in the Service of the Opposition."

Almost as peculiar as the *Gazetteer's* silence has been the silence of Fielding scholars about it. Only as I write has Bertrand Goldgar (on the basis of information supplied by Martin Battestin) noticed it.[6] Clearly, it has simply been assumed without a glance at the British Museum file of the *Gazetteer* that if Fielding fought with the ministerial journal he must have gotten a response or (better!) been responding to its scurrilities. Goldgar associates the *Gazetteer's* sudden increase in interest with a change in the tone and content of *The Champion* around mid-1740. But to explain the phenomenon *The Champion* would have had to change from a harmless journal into one more dangerous than *Common Sense* and *The Craftsman*. *The Champion* did undergo two evolutions in direction of greater concern with politics and harsher treatment of the ministry in its first year, but their timing is wrong. The moderately political *Champion* of roughly November 1739 through mid-February 1740 (itself offensive enough to deserve a response from the *Gazetteer*) gradually evolved into a more political journal, but the change was complete by mid-spring. In April, May, and June, *The Champion* was as partisan and potent as in July and August. In the early fall, beginning the first week in September, *The Champion* rapidly evolved into an almost single-minded smiter of ministry, the propaganda organ that would carry the "Remarkable Queries" on October 7 and the pamphlet-length *Address to the Electors of Great Britain* in serial form through all eleven issues in November.

Obviously, the threat any journal presented to the ministry and the pressure on the *Gazetteer* to respond to it varied according to three factors: (1) the degree of its political absorption and its aggressiveness; (2) its quality; (3) its influence (basically the amount and geographical spread of its circulation). *The Champion* deserved a black mark for content months before the *Gazetteer* acted, and it was from the first very witty, cogent, and pungent, the quality of its essays being rather higher *before* than after July 1. Only influence remains, and I suggest that *The Champion* was ignored for all those months because it had little circulation (and taking notice of it might encourage sales), and that its sudden importance in the *Gazetteer*'s eyes followed upon a sudden rise in its circulation and impact. This, in turn, is best accounted for as the result of its obtaining a subsidy in mid-run, surely from Lyttelton or those close to him, and probably in June 1740.

Other evidence points in the same direction. One would hesitate to press the fact that no copies of the earliest issues of *The Champion* have survived,[7] since *The Champion* is the classic bibliographical morass in Fielding's canon. But one may see significance in the scope of the reprint of the *Champion*'s early run, *The Champion: Containing a series of Papers Humorous, Moral, Political, and Critical*, published at the time of the general election in June 1741. It reproduces (with silent editing and some additions) most of the lead essays that appeared between November 15, 1739 and June 19, 1740, almost *exactly* the period when I have suggested no subsidy and very low circulation. What more natural than to republish high-quality journalism, not originally seen by most readers of opposition propaganda? There are also internal pointers. In early issues (see December 4 and 18, 1739) Fielding worries about low circulation. When, on June 28, Fielding resumed the "Voyages of Mr. Job Vinegar" series, begun on March 20, he devoted a good deal of his leader to recapitulating the first installment of the "Voyages." After such a lapse of time this may seem natural, but he justifies it in part by observing that several readers never saw the original essay and that he now has a wider acquaintanceship (that is, more readers) than in the past. More importantly, on June 12, 1740 (only a couple of issues before the reprint's cut-off date and just about the time an increase in circulation would have to have begun for the *Gazetteer* to feel and react to the new pressure by the first week in July) Fielding's lead essay is devoted to reflecting upon the *Champion*'s difficult past and relishing its secure present and future in a way that fits our theory. He recalls his bookseller's accurate prediction that sales would come hard in competition with established journals. The public and the coffee-houses hesitated to buy, and the most "unprecedented," "meanest" efforts of competitors (presumably the ministerial journals and possibly *The Craftsman* and *Common Sense*) prevented its sale. Hawkers denied its existence! For so long on the "Precipice of Oblivion," *The Champion* has now achieved success. Of course, Fielding does not attribute this to outside help or imply an *abrupt* upturn in the *Champion*'s fortunes; instead he suggests problems gradually overcome through hard work. He also reiterates his determination to offer "miscellaneous" fare, as opposed to a steady diet of politics, a promise he would keep until politics took over in the fall. But in the light of all the other evidence, this essay reads like an oblique reaction to sudden prosperity. Significantly, it ends by promising that "Dr. Lilbourne" (James Ralph) will give "Doses" of political medicine "as often as it is requisite" and is preparing a "grand Nostrum" for the electorate before the next election. Many years ago J. E. Wells quietly observed that this essay has the air of departure, of a "gathering up."[8] Wells, always a sensitive reader of Fielding, mistook a rebirth for an ending. Within a week the *Gazetteer* opened fire.

The journal's political orientation was always unambiguous. From its first issue to the fall of Walpole and beyond it was anti-ministerial, critical of corruption, the prodigal ineffectuality of the war effort (especially failures at sea and in defence of merchant trade), and the vulgar mendacity of government writers. But *The Champion* went through five distinguishable phases during the period of Fielding's editorship:

(1) From November 15, 1739 to about the latter half of February 1740, anti-ministerial satire was only moderately important in lead essays, though virtually every issue had some anti-ministerial touches (in other sections, if not the essay), and its political involvement grew.

(2) From roughly late February to June, politics became more important and the tone of the satire more cutting, making *The Champion* potentially dangerous although low circulation reduced its effectiveness.

(3) In the summer of 1740, newly subsidized, it was abused by *The Gazetteer* and replied, but it did not become more political or aggressive.

(4) From early September to about the end of 1740 it reached its political peak, and became the *Gazetteer*'s chief opponent, focussing upon the dangers of Walpolian electoral corruption, *the* issue as the general election of 1741 loomed.

(5) From December 1740 to June 1741 *The Champion* became less formidable in the eyes of the *Gazetteer*, perhaps because its subsidy was lost. Fielding seems to have withdrawn wholly or in great measure from his role as essayist, though he continued to publish anti-minis-

terial satire outside of the journal, and remained an active *Champion* partner, friendly with his colleagues. From this obscure period very few *Champion* essays have survived, none of them by Fielding.

While hostile to the ministry, *The Champion* was not originally an "opposition journal." One has to pick through the miscellaneous content of its earliest issues to determine its political tendency. Even late in the first phase, politics never really dominates for long in the lead essays of Fielding and Ralph (not yet the political specialist he would become in phase two). Still, there is some stringent political criticism, and we must never underestimate the anti-ministerial commitment implicit in the political ground-bass that played (on page two) behind even the most innocent essays. There were few issues indeed without anti-Walpole satire in the annotations to the "Home News" and "Foreign News," such special features as the "Rumours" and "Puffs" sections, and the one-joke political feature called "The Journal of the War." For example, even in the first issue, where Fielding's essay stresses that the *Champion* will strive for breadth of focus and open-mindedness, there is a sharp dig on page two at Walpole's supposed undermining of parliamentary independence. Joking about his ancestry on November 17, Captain Vinegar offers Swiftian equations, "Pickpockets or Lords, Highwaymen or Bishops, Thieves or Prime Ministers." Two days later, though his essay is innocent (on the theme *"Noscite Ipsum"*), he passes on the false rumour that once supplies are voted Parliament will be dissolved without dealing with grievances or corruption. The next essay —also apolitical—is followed by ridicule of "political Methodists" who believe in Walpole's divinity and the process of "touching for the King's Evil," meaning bribery ("touching" with gold), not a cure for scrofula. In the ninth issue the "Journal of the War" begins its sustained, implicit criticism of the war effort, a typical example being the entry for December 15, which contrasts five captures of English ships by the Spanish with "Ships taken by the English. NONE."

More occasionally, lead essays grew partisan. On November 24 the leader "puffs" Richard Glover's opposition poem, *London, or the Progress of Commerce*, and echoes its call for full exertion by the slothful ministry against Spain. More characteristic is James Ralph's first essay, published on December 1. It combines an apolitical warning against excessive wine and mirth with a "defence" of the ministerial writers, who make the government look foolish when they criticize Benjamin Heathcote and Glover, the darlings of London. Heathcote and Glover would again be praised together by Fielding in *Of True Greatness*. The essay is followed by abuse of the *Gazetteer* for opposing the Place Bill of 1740 (the first of many "puffs" for the bill; its defeat is lamented on January 31). On December 8, Hercules Vinegar notes that his club, which automatically beats rascals, is hard to control near the Treasury, and a "letter" by Ralph (a sort of secondary essay) argued that a Place Bill is as needed as naval victories and pressures M.P.s to heed instructions from constituencies to vote for it. The issue also "puffs" a print, *His Honour's Equipage*, satirizing Walpole and his "tools." On December 11 an apolitical essay is followed by a "letter" in which *The Champion*'s "Compositor" defends the journal's impartiality and promises eulogy of the ministry when deserved.

Such is the usual mixed pattern. For brief periods only is *The Champion* less hesitant, cases in point being the essays for December 13, 15, and 18. The first compliments Pope, the Muses' favourite, but complains of his failure to smite Walpole (a reaction to Pope's avoidance of politics since 1738). It also praises Glover ("the author of Leonidas") and George Lyttelton, and depicts Walpole bribing his way even onto the Hill of the Muses: ". . . with a shake of the hand" (a bribe) he brings "any person whatever to think, or speak, or do what he himself desired, . . . there was only one way to be secure against him, and that was by keeping your hand shut, for then his touch had no power." The essay for December 15 is a mock-scientific treatise on the "Art of Political Fishing," describing the clever use of many "Baits" (bribes) to catch different "Fish" (e.g., "Gudgeons" love "red Baits," Orders of the Bath) useful in "political Cookery." On December 18 *The Champion* is urged by a "correspondent" to continue wooing reluctant readers, the "State of the Nation" is mourned, and "the Citizens of London" are urged in extreme language to spurn ministerial corruption for the sake of trade and liberty. Such essays surely removed any ambiguity about *The Champion*'s political intentions (they elicited the *Gazetteer*'s one early response), but only in the latter half of February did political lead essays really begin to proliferate. Essays on such subjects as virtue and vice (January 22, 24, and 26) or charity and future rewards and punishments (February 16, 19, and 26) were still frequent. *The Champion* was not an all-out opposition organ, though a supporter of the ministry might have thought so on February 21 reading "The Art of War. After the Newest Receipt":

> First at *Freeman* and *Sydney*, the Gazetteer—Drums!
> Roar manfully out that, The Enemy comes!
> Then, during the Panic, urge Taxes good Store,
> Not barely enough, but some Twenty Times more.
> Next levy new Forces by Sea, and by Land,
> Give each pretty Fellow his Share of Command.
> Let Seamen be press'd and Embargo be laid,
> To **** the Merchants defending the Trade.
> Whole Herds dye *untimely* to victual the Fleet,
> No matter, tho' Carrion, if bought for good Meat.
> Hold Councils, send Couriers, despatch Plenipo's,
> Bribe some to be Friends, some not to be Foes.
> Make Earth groan with Armies, with Navies the Main,
> As *Europe* in league was the Second of *Spain*,
> And, when ev'ry Job, and Expedient is served,
> Let us *rest* on our Arms, till our Foes are all *Starv'd*.

In phase two *The Champion* remained "miscellaneous": the "Apology for the Clergy" series (March 29, April 5, 12, and 19) is an obvious example. On April 10, when it became an evening four-pager, Fielding promised roughly the same mixed contents as before:

> I. An Essay on the Manners or Politics of the Times.
> II. Frequently, new Articles of Intelligence.
> III. The News of Two Days, Foreign and Domestick, stated and digested in a peculiar Manner.
> IV. Extracts from, or Remarks upon such Books, Poems, Pamphlets, &c. as are worthy the Notice of the Publick.

However, things were changing: politics was absorbing more of Fielding's energies and almost all of James Ralph's. *The Champion* was now an opposition journal, though a more sprightly, less single-minded one than *The Craftsman* or *Common Sense*. In this phase, so much political material, presented in such a variety of forms, was carried by *The Champion* in the leaders alone that only a few of the more interesting essays can be mentioned. The second (after April 10 the last three) pages of each issue carried a wild variety of partisan material: the "Journal of the War," ceaseless ridicule of the *Gazetteer*, reviews of opposition (favourable) and ministerial (unfavourable) literature, songs, poems, extracts from pamphlets, and much more.

The element in the many political leaders that least needs discussion is Fielding's ridicule of Colley Cibber and his *Apology*. Presumably because literary scholars are more at home with satire on Cibber than on the ministry's war policies, the *Champion*'s attacks on Cibber have been well covered, especially in Bertrand Golgar's recent *Walpole and the Wits*. It is true that much of the abuse of Cibber (by Fielding and others) was inherently political, in part aimed at the minister who helped make Colley poet laureate. And political irritation obviously was mingled with personal annoyance when Fielding read Cibber's account in the *Apology* (April 1740) of the "Great Mogul's" excesses at the Haymarket in 1736 and 1737:

> . . . he produced several frank and free farces, that seemed to knock all distinctions of mankind on the head. Religion, Law, Government, Priests, Judges, and Ministers, were laid out flat at the Feet of this Herculean Satirist, this Drawcansir in Wit, that spared neither Friend nor Foe; who to make his poetical Fame immortal, like another Erostratus, set Fire to his Stage by writing up to an Act of Parliament to demolish it. I shall not give the particular Strokes of his Ingenuity a Chance to be remembered by reciting them; it may be enough to say, in general Terms, they were so openly flagrant, that the Wisdom of the Legislature thought it high Time to take proper Notice of them.[9]

The sheer bulk of the anti-Cibber material also lends it importance, there being examples in the issues for April, 1, 7, 15, 22, and 29, and May 3, 10, and 17, 1740, as well as in essays published during the summer. Still, politics was only one stimulus to satire on Cibber, and hitting him was a pretty innocuous way of getting at Walpole. One suspects ministerial wits read Fielding's jabs at Cibber with equanimity and amusement. Fielding fought more serious battles.

Far more important and less understood is James Ralph's role in the political effort of this phase. *The Champion* would have been radically different without Ralph's steady, sober political pounding, and one of the weaknesses of previous discussions of *The Champion* is that they hardly notice Ralph. Fielding and Ralph had complementary talents. Witty, humorous criticism was not Ralph's strength. We have seen that his first essay (December 1) alternates non-political and political material. However, most of his non-political essays come early in the run (e.g., the inept dream vision about pleasure and pain of January 19 and the "eastern tale" of February 23, 1740), and they show him at an uncongenial task. He is occasionally successful with playful irony: an instance being the essay for March 18 which treats the attack on libellous and ignorant authors in Shaftesbury's *On the Freedom of Wit and Humour* as a "Prophecy" of the "*Legion-Authors* of the *Gazetteer*." Perhaps on March 18 Ralph was in a gay mood. The great victory of Admiral Vernon at Porto Bello is celebrated on page two, and even the "Journal of the War" records two considerable English captures and no successes for the Spaniards! Ordinarily, Ralph excelled at soberly and energetically protesting ministerial policies and behaviour and exhorting electors and Parliamentarians to vote "patriotically," against Walpole. He was especially happy in warning of "Constitutional" perils with an air of scholarly patriotism, stressing, say, that Walpole's corruption of Commons disturbed the separation and balance of powers in "mixed government." The alteration in *The Champion*'s title, hour of publication, and size on April 10 coincided with the first of his many "Constitutional" essays over the signature "Lilbourne," with its serious, seventeenth-century political overtones. As "Lilbourne," Ralph was to deliver solid body blows while Fielding attracted readers with non-political delights and performed his ironical wonders at the expense of Walpole and his "Tools."

The "Lilbourne" of phase two is at his best and most typical in three published essays in May. On May 1 he lectures on the wonders of the English Constitution, particularly its elevation of law even above the power of the "sole Magistrate," whose power, naturally corruptive, is curbed by the legislature. The people must watch for the "encroachment of those at the Head of Affairs," a worse threat than foreign foes. The freedom of the legislature to resist even a king, if evil, must be guarded, for the chief function of Commons is "to keep a strict Eye on the Prerogative" and preserve the rights of subjects. The national wealth must never be at "the discretion of the Crown," for ministers will then really control it, a bad thing with good ministers, a disaster with corrupt, universally hated ones. The long battles over the prerogative in the seventeenth century are then rehearsed, their contemporary applications left implicit, unstated. This is quintessential Ralph, as is the essay for May 22, in which "Lilbourne" laments he has lived to hear "Whigs" say that

Parliament should be dependent on the crown and corruption is essential to the Constitution, and to hear a Place Bill treated with contempt despite the pleas of the great trading cities. This is a result of the "Craft, Power, and Insolence of *one Man*," Walpole, as Prime Minister. After the usual marshalling of scary and inspiring seventeenth-century examples, the essay ends with a plea for an effective Place Bill. It will be a necessary hedge against "Arbitrary Power" (the words are taken from a speech of 1680 by Sir Francis Winnington) since placemen and pensioners are a "distinct *middle Interest* between the King and the People: *And their Chief Business was to serve the End of some* great Minister of State, *tho' never so opposite to the true Interest of the Nation.*" Interestingly, this sort of argument would move Fielding to accuse Ralph of "Sedition" in 1748 when Ralph directed it at the Broad-Bottom ministry in *The Remembrancer*. The picture is rounded out by the extra-long essay for May 29, where "Lilbourne," a good Broad-Bottom, complains that factions have so long cursed the nation that writers who support the people are thought to be tools of yet another ambitious faction. To avoid such suspicions he will simply present facts and let the people decide merits. There follows a list of recent bills, arranged according to whether ministerial or anti-ministerial members proposed them. On the ministerial side are twenty bills, all calling for expenditure, all passed; on the other are twenty-three, only nine of which passed. The failures include gestures toward frugality, a motion to accept a petition from distressed merchants, "requests for papers" (the placement of confidential records before Commons, a staple opposition item), and, of course, the Place Bill. So faithful a mirror will be worth consulting, "Lilbourne" says, before the next election.

How different are Fielding's political essays in approach and method. Yet under the jests and ironies Fielding hits the same targets, takes the same points of view, and can be stringently personal. The difference is in touch and method. This shows best in the "April Fool's" essay which interrupts the "Apology for the Clergy" series on April 1. One "Vander Bruin" begins his "letter" by lamenting the declining taste of the nation (only *The Champion, Common Sense* and *The Craftsman* are readable, the theatres are decayed, and Cibber's *Apology* is out), but soon turns to "puffing" bear-baiting at "His Majesty's bear-garden in Hockley in the Hole" (the House of Commons) and ridiculing politics under Walpole. Two brother bears (Robert and Horatio Walpole) who have once before been baited (the Excise crisis?) will fight mastiffs (the opposition) while, for the first time, a group of curs (Walpole's tools and apologists) bark at the mastiffs to ingratiate themselves with the bears, knowing that the "great" bear will defend them. There is a conspiracy afoot among a "Majority" of the curs to betray the great bear to the mastiffs as he weakens. "Vander Bruin" praises the agile toughness of the "great Bear" (and the pleasing tameness of the other one, Horatio, "a dancing Bear"), argues against spoiling a good show by ruining him, and warns that he is strong enough, though old, to go another year. He remains very dangerous in his growled determination (in a neat pun combining the baiting stake and the Treasury) "to keep his POST." This is anything but straightforward, run-of-the-mill opposition satire. Far from uncomplicatedly admiring the mastiffs, as the Broad-Bottoms always were, it shows an unsureness about the likelihood of soon bringing down the able Walpole that would persist until the eve of his resignation, as is clear in *The Opposition: A Vision* of December 1741.

More typical in sounding standard opposition notes, but superimposing on them enough irony to make them funny and fresh, are the essays for February 14 and 28; they roughly mark the line between phases one and two of *The Champion*. The first ostensibly rejects increasing the political satire in *The Champion*, but is politically satiric and surely adds up to a doubly ironical promise of more to come. Nehemiah Vinegar details and resists the many arguments correspondents have used to persuade him to "apply myself to politics," rather than "amuse the town with essays of virtue and vice, words which have lost their ideas a great while." Some lament the ills of the land under Walpole: the death of trade, "a prodigous debt, a useless army, an immense fleet, and dreadful taxes to support them, when a dilatory war, formidable enemies, and suspicious allies hover over us." This *is* satire, not merely a list of possible targets. Ministerial correspondents urge a panegyric on a prosperous nation, with "as fine an army as men would desire to see on a summer's day," which "we are shortly to see encamped (on Hounslow Heath outside London], without going a great way for the sight." Each offers "different rewards: one of them reputation, honour, fame, and the like; the others ask me, if I have no love for my family, and talk of vacancies, good things, snug places, &c. One Mr. Forage [Walpole], particularly says, Do, do, do, Mr. Vinegar, write, write, write and I'll warrant you *** let me see but *** ay that will do *** depend ** but then *** through thick and thin ** my interest." This is the familiar bribing and promising Walpole; old wine is very cleverly rebottled. However, Nehemiah thinks there is too much good political writing already, "such a vast number of able hands employed in that excellent political paper, called the Gazetteer, which is published every day, and distributed gratis over the kingdom, at the expense, as some imagine, of the authors [here he means the minister beneath all the multiple insults], who are not content to club their wits, but club their purses also, for the good and instruction of their country." Indeed, even the *Gazetteer* often meets the Shadwellian fate of becoming toilet paper before it is read, "in common with other fundamental treatises." Here an author really worried about weak circulation and dying for a fight with the reluctant *Gazetteer* is revealed, but his playful instincts remain. Vinegar claims no skill in politics, which began when the Babel tower ("bearing an exact resemblance to most political schemes") was built by "a set of ministers." It is not to be understood. It is a great "mystery." How can he explain the ministry's mysterious military fumblings and expenditures, or guess the future of English trade? The evils every opposition writer laid at Walpole's door are all profound mysteries to Vinegar, and he *seems* to define the *Champion* "as a miscellaneous, not a merely political paper": ". . . consult others in politics; since I declare for my part, I am so far from knowing I cannot ever guess what we are about, what we intend to do, or what we shall be able to do." This determinedly anti-ministerial essay has an ironical and comic flair quite beyond James Ralph or any other journalist writing in 1740.

The sequel is a "letter" from "Nicodemus Bungle" to Nehemiah in the issue for February 28 (little known because it is not in the Henley edition, though it is obviously Fielding's), which denies that the true interest of England is anything but clear:

> The Interest of this Island, is, I believe, chiefly to preserve a perfect good understanding between the King and his People: to maintain a very small Army, and a very strong fleet; to keep up the strictest Alliance with the Maritime Powers without making too great Concessions to them on the Article of Trade: to ballance Power as equally as possible on the Continent, and to hold the Scale ourselves . . . [details of military and trade policies follow] to prevent the Growth of Luxury, and to take the Opportunity of every Hours Peace to lessen the Debt of the Nation.

This could have been written by Ralph, but Fielding soon asserts himself. Mr. Vinegar must mean "The art of Prime Ministering," a real mystery upon which Bungle (who here stands for Walpole) will lecture beginning "April next" (1741? or this may anticipate an early election, in 1740) when he will be "at leisure." The "Course of Lectures on the Elements of Prime Ministry, chiefly Natural; by Mr. Nicodemus Bungle" will include instruction in "certain kinds of Whispers," "a Broad Grin," "a Stare," "Promises of all Sorts and Sizes," "Slanders of the blackest Kinds," "Squeezes by the Hand [bribes], Bows, and Invitations to Dinner, illustrated by proper Emblems, the last of them by a Fellow baiting a Mouse-trap," "Bribery," and "The Art of Lie-Looking." There will be advice about concealing fear and shame, the former by such means as trousers which are proof against kicks from without and excrement from within, and the latter with the help of an "antipudorifick Lotion." The final touch is a footnote advising that the course be given abroad since in England "we neither have nor can have a Prime Minister." The office is not part of the Constitution, and the King should act in concurrence with all of his councils. This essay foreshadows the extraordinary richness and humour of the essay on "Trunks" of May 31, which, in a way that defies description, satirizes everything from bad sermons to scholarly pedantry, to Peter Walter's rapaciousness, to pagan superstition. It ends with a wild allegory in which Walpole is the great "Trunk," keeper of the King's treasures and sole avenue to the royal favour, applied to by eager supplicants who kiss his rump. It is a variation on the notorious "Vision of the Golden Rump" of 1737.

Even when his essays were not really focussed on politics, Fielding very often inserted some political satire. The essay for May 20 (another

Fielding piece, foreshadowing *The Jacobite's Journal* and *Tom Jones*, omitted by Henley) is a really funny "letter" from "H. Bottle," a comic "Country Squire," in praise of the grand art of drinking. But Bottle also wishes that the election due in 1741 will fulfill the hopes of Broad-Bottoms:

> . . . there hath been a Mixture of Liquors, as Tory Principles have lately been decanted into Whiggish Vessels; it is high Time to have a coalition of two Parties; and a coalition of all Parties who wish well to their Country I hope to see at the next Election, when our Toast shall not be a Tory, nor one of the Country Party, but those who *cannot be corrupted to betray us;* and of such only I hope always to see our House of Commons, or I hope to see none.

However, the most revealing example of Fielding's habit of slipping politics into non-political leaders is the essay for June 10, 1740, the last one before his expression of relief at obtaining a subsidy. It renders absurd the argument that the *Champion* was too mild to merit the *Gazetteer*'s enmity until July and August, and represents an extreme in Fielding's early political prose, generating a breathless, personal rhythm of vituperation against Walpole that Ralph and the authors of *Common Sense* never approached. It seems at first a classic instance of the brief moral disquisition in essay form at which Fielding excelled. It is a scholarly argument (beginning with a quotation from Terence's *Adelphi*, so influential upon *Tom Jones*, and including massed historical examples) in favour of teaching by "negative example." But in mid-essay Fielding settles upon Walpole, at the head of affairs and cynosure of all eyes, as the greatest of negative examples. There are not, even in Swift, many *single sentences* with such a freight of directed fury:

> Can there be a more instructive lesson against that abominable and pernicious vice, ambition, than the sight of a mean man, raised by fortunate accidents and execrable vices to power, employing the basest measures and the vilest instruments to support himself; looked up to only by sycophants and slaves and sturdy beggars [there is a note saying this is "Another name for Roberdsman," a reference to satiric etymological play on Walpole's given name in the essay for June 7), wretches whom even he must in his heart despise in all their Tinsel; looked down upon, and scorned and shunned by every man of honour, nay, by every man of sense, and those whom his rotten, rancorous heart must, in spite of himself, reluctantly admire; who knows that he is justly hated by his whole country, who sees and feels his danger; tottering, shaking, trembling; without appetite for his dainties, without abilities for his women, without taste for his elegances, without authority from his power, and without ease in his palace, or repose on his bed of down.

The Champion's third phase—roughly mid-June to early September 1740—differed from the second less in degree of political activity than in its circumstances. By this time, I have suggested, it was subsidized and widely read. There were adjustments in emphasis. Attacks on the newly responsive *Gazetteer* became a bit more frequent. *The Champion* always gave more than as good as it got. Next year's election steadily grew in importance—by late summer the later pages were full of reprints of nomination notices and candidates' advertisements. Even in April *The Champion* had complained about ministerial canvassing, but now the long campaign was gathering momentum. Generally, however, the *Champion*'s political emphases remained the same: no trade, national indebtedness, corruption always, Walpole's lack of enthusiasm for defeating Spain and jealousy of Admiral Vernon, the need for a Place Bill, the vulgar stupidity of Cibber (July 1 and August 12) and the "Gazetteer Legion." Many non-political essays by Fielding continued to lighten and vary the fare offered readers, and while James Ralph seldom strayed far from partisan concerns, other correspondents often did. As in the later spring, however, such purely innocent essays did not predominate, and they were always balanced by political satire in later pages. The essays on "Manners" promised on June 12 were provided, but politics mattered more.

The division of labour between Ralph and Fielding persisted. "Lilbourne" accused Walpole (June 19) of enmity to London and trade, of opposing the Place Bill, of waging war badly, and of resenting Admiral Vernon's victories. He stressed (July 29) Walpole's false greatness, depicting him as dishonest, inept, and universally hated, and threatened him (not for the first or the last time) with a noose: " 'Tis better that one Man should dye, than a whole Nation perish." Small wonder that at this juncture the *Gazetteer* tried to discredit Ralph by raking up his past as a Walpole hack in the earlier 1730s, eliciting a blend of confession and defiance in *The Champion*'s "Home News" section, where Ralph declares his readiness

> . . . to make Affidavit that he never writ a single line in the Gazetteer or in any other *ministerial Vehicle*, since that Paper was on foot [i.e., since 1735]; and that, tho' he was *unhappily* many Years ago, induced to write certain insipid *Things* in your Honour's [Walpole's] behalf *(for which he likewise takes Shame to himself)* he was far from *receiving* a Dismission, that, being upbraided by your Honour for the Neglect and lukewarmness in your Service, he *dismissed himself* with these, or the like remarkable Expressions, *It is impossible to do you any*.

Indeed, as "Lilbourne" grew more assured and skilled in his role as political specialist for a successful journal, he showed an ability to assess the rhetorical methods of partisans on both sides that foreshadows his later historical writings and the fine essays in *The Remembrancer*. Claiming that *The Champion* "disavows all Parties alike," the standard Broad-Bottom stance, he observes on August 30 that "Whig" and "Tory" are "Artifices of the *Wicked* to seduce the *Weak*," and urges electors to vote in 1741 without paying much attention to the continual mudslinging of both extremes. Ralph understood the business he was in:

> . . . at home, we are told by one set of Men, that a mercenary F____n [felon] has usurped the A____n [administration], monopoliz'd all the Power and Wealth of the Nation, engross'd the Royal Ear, defam'd the People to the Prince, and the Prince to the People; render'd Peace as chargeable and destructive as War, and War as tame and insignificant as Peace; traffic'd away our Honour, and sacrificed our Traffic; exhausted their whole Art and Address to plunder, and insolently deny'd all Redress: in short, debauch'd the very Morals of the People, made Corruption universal, and put all Possibility of a Reformation out of our Power, by making our own R____s [representatives] the Tools to enslave us, and vote the very Wealth, Armies, and penal Laws, they had Reason to fear were to be employ'd to undo us. —This is our miserable Condition, if we will believe one Party; and, if the other, a wicked, and inveterate Knot of Traitors are hurrying us onto Ruin, under the Pretence of endeavouring our Preservation: Under the Pretence of Liberty and Property, they mean to introduce Popery and Slavery, or Anarchy and Confusion: Not only discontented, but disaffected; complaining only to embarrass; pretending Public Spirit, and yet pursuing nothing but private Interest: In a Word, such as create the very Ills they expose, and are themselves greater Grievances than they would remove.

The key to this, of course, is that Ralph and Fielding identified with politicians whose chosen pose was superiority to faction even in the throes of anti-ministerial effort. And Ralph carefully gives it all an anti-ministerial twist, as well as a Broad-Bottom one, by observing that readers and electors faced with offsetting propaganda must remember that though they may *suspect* hypocrisy in opposition candidates, the ministerial candidate is *known* to be false. "Above all things," he urges, "avoid the Man already branded for having acted uniformly as a Slave."

Meanwhile, Fielding cultivated his more oblique mode, just as he had in the spring. On July 15, for example, an essay on oracles and astrological divination predicts the defeat in 1741 of Walpole, ironically eulogizing him as a great wartime leader ("a M____r the Wonder, and a War the Delight of all the World") while seriously praising Admiral Vernon. On July 5, he considers the wisdom of the academic philosophers in teaching men to believe nothing, but inevitably targets Walpole:

> If what I have here said be right, how glaring must that Truth be in which all Men concur, and if it should ever happen to be the Fate of any Man to have his Guilt so manifest, that a whole Nation should unanimously agree in thinking he deserves to be hanged, can that Man, if he hath any Modesty, tho' no Body else could touch him, refrain from hanging himself?

Then a passage applicable to Walpole in Jonson's *Catiline* is recommended as "well worthy the serious considerations of every Man in *Britain*, who has a vote to give at the Election of the Representatives of his Country." At the same time, however, Fielding began exploring a new vein in the third phase, the extended prose satire, comprising a series of essays forming a more or less connected whole. The thirteen parts of the "Voyages of Mr. Job Vinegar" are a kind of *Gulliver's Travels* in miniature (somewhat equivalent, say, to parts of Swift's "Voyage to Lilliput") crossed with elements of Pope's *Dunciad* and touched by Fielding's own verbal drollery. It anatomizes the vices and follies of the contemporary English, in describing the shallow, fickle, and amoral "Inconstants" visited by Job Vinegar. They worship "Mney" (Fielding achieves surprising humour by "disemvoweling" terms), lack honesty, public spirit, taste, even "Gd BRDNG," and are addicted to bribery, "DRNKNG, GMNG, SMKNG, WNCHNG," infidelity, hypocrisy, and other "Fashions." Such satire on England as degenerate is often rightly interpreted as inherently critical of Walpole, even when it is not explicitly political. And if the entire "Voyages" series is thus implicitly political, a few installments are explicitly so. If MNEY is the only religion, Walpole (as "Hum Clum") is its high priest and the inspirer of its most pernicious heretical form.

The "Voyages" series was begun twice. On March 20, well back in the second phase, Hercules Vinegar, alluding to *Robinson Crusoe* as well as *Gulliver*, printed "Some Extracts" out of the third chapter of the sixth book of "The Voyages of Mr. Job Vinegar," his ancestor. He promised more if they proved popular. The "Extracts" mock the legal system, drunken country squires, opera and sentimental comedy. Only near the close does Fielding find a direction when he turns to their worship of MNEY and its results. He introduces direct political satire and promises to follow that line in future. While he was in the land of the Inconstants, says Job Vinegar, there was a violent schism in the church of MNEY, which began when Hum Clum (Walpole) backed by three hundred disciples (his majority in Commons) claimed the right to control all the MNEY in the realm, and to give it only to those who pleased him. More about this was promised in the "next paper." However, the second "Voyages" installment did not appear until June 28. Wilbur Cross suggested Fielding may have saved the series for gradual release while he was following the summer assizes as a fledgling lawyer (he was admitted to the Bar in June).[10] If so, his vacation from writing must have been brief, for he contributed a good number of other essays during the summer. Fielding notes on June 28 that there have been petitions for more "Travels" and (offering the explanation that many present readers did not see the first installment, the significance of which has already been suggested) summarizes the essay of March 20. Then he outlines Hum Clum's strategy in the wars of MNEY. Hum Clum uses "CRTURS" and "TLS" (creatures and tools), inferior priestly orders distinguished by coloured badges (Orders of the Bath, Garter, and Thistle), to spread the Hum-Clumish heresy (the true articles of faith being, of course, merchant trade and the Constitution). His creatures fill all court places, and anathematize CNTR GNTLMN and MRCHNTS, who are denied preferment and called PTRTS (patriots), a name implying a shameful love for their "Earth" (land, the country) rather than MNEY. These enemies are still better loved by the people, the MRCHNTS being considered the original conveyors of the deity MNEY from above. "The Creed of a

Hum-Clumist'' (taken from a book called a GZTR [*Gazetteer*], spread abroad by CRTRS and TLS *gratis*) praises corruption and holds MNEY dearer than Liberty and Country, the false idols of PTRTS, who wrongly try to bring down Hum Clum by invoking the LWS of his CNTRY. Job suggests the superiority of the old way of worshipping MNEY called TRD and predicts the people will recognize this. The allegory neatly telescopes many of the anti-Walpole topics of *The Champion*.

The essay for July 17 concentrates on legal and social follies, but returns to overt political satire at its mid-point, where Hum Clum's oppression of the merchants and trade (the old way of ''worshipping'' money) is compared to quacks' opposition to true physicians. The ''Voyage'' essays for July 22 and 31 (the latter the only one not by Fielding, probably by Ralph),[11] August, 9, 16, 19, and 26, and September 4 are only explicitly political on occasion, however one assesses the anti-Walpole impact of their depiction of degenerate England. In fact, Fielding only really returned to concentrated political satire once, with the discussion of animal life unknown in Europe in the penultimate installment, September 13. Politically saturated, it is doubly interesting because, though obviously anti-ministerial, it ridicules the extreme ''Tory'' (or Country) faction as well as the extreme ''Whig'' (ministerial) faction. A companion piece to Ralph's Broad-Bottom essay of August 30, discussed earlier, it is yet another of the reminders that *The Champion* was not simply an opposition, but a Broad-Bottom opposition journal. The TRY and WHG are both five to six feet tall, venomous animals when a long time in sunlight (in power), savage when touched with a quill (satirized). They alternate between basking in the sun and howling in the shade. Though alike in essentials, they hate one another, and each has some peculiarities. Most Tories are larger (from feeding on malt) and love sitting on church steeples. A black sub-species, the ''PRSN'' (parson), like the female in dress but male enough physically, excels at crawling up steeples, and loves to flock on CTHDRL CHRCHS. The beautiful female TRY is more virulent than the male, hating female WHGS and excelling in PLLNG CAPS. The WHG is slightly smaller, prefers low, even ground, and hates churches and other high places, from which it always tries to pull down the TRYS, which in turn yell PARSONOLBOTHON (''The Church is in Danger!''). The black WHG, a DSSNTNG PRSN, is less dark than the black TRY, wears shorter skirts, is stiffer and more inclined to groaning. This even-handed parody of stereotypes is followed by a report that in the past the WHGS and TRYS began to flock together and lose their separate names at the very moment that a great monster, born overnight out of a dunghill (obviously Walpole, manipulator of faction), began to destroy both. The monster had 250 tongues (the Walpole voters in Commons), 50,000 little red fins—for show, not use—on its great claw (the idle army decried throughout *The Champion*), and a huge, unfillable belly which it stuffed with the insides of TRYS and the outsides of WHGS. It was caught (the Excise Crisis?) when TRYS and WHGS co-operated, but broke out again, and died of surfeiting on the inside of an overgrown Tory (the coming election?). In this laboured allegory, the "grand Coalition" of Broad-Bottom theory mingles with exhortation to assault Walpole as the common foe.

The fourth phase, roughly mid-September to the end of November 1740, was *The Champion*'s political climax. Non-political essays became rare as Walpole, the war effort, and the *Gazetteer* were steadily criticized, and patriots were continually urged to vote out the corrupter at the election. The few non-political leaders (aside from the two late "Voyages" essays) tend to be weak: examples are Fielding's skimpy effort of October 21 and the feeble condemnation of seducers by another writer of September 25. After the essay for September 6 (a discussion of envy with an anti-Walpole twist), Fielding strongly "puffed" a special election piece by an "eminent" outsider, not one of the regular contributors:

> N.B. We shall shortly present our Readers with some Papers addressed to the Electors of *Great Britain*, written by a very eminent Hand, who hath thought fit to honour us by the introducing them into the World thro' our Hands. As these are calculated to do public Service, we hope those who wish well to their Country will take all possible Care to spread them universally.

This promise was not soon fulfilled, probably because the "eminent Hand" failed repeatedly to deliver, forcing Fielding to fill in belatedly with *An Address to the Electors of Great Britain* in November. But the announcement signalled a great political push.

After September 6 began a surge of anti-ministerial, election propaganda that crested in the "Remarkable Queries" of October 7 (reprinted October 14, and again, with a false date, June 14, 1740, in the reprint of June 1741)[12] and Fielding's *Address*. The election "Papers" were promised again on September 8 and 11. When they failed to appear, the slack was initially taken up by essays satirizing the war effort and corruption, and warning that bribery would not save Walpole at the election. Soon, however, a piece addressed "to the Freeholders and Electors in Great Britain" really opened the fall campaign. Signed "Philopatriae," it was published in two parts (September 20 and 23), and was written, I am sure, by James Ralph. It may be the "extraordinary Nostrum" he was said by Fielding on June 12 to be preparing against the next election. On September 20 "Philopatriae" begins with one of the defences of a free press that were obligatory in opposition journals, just as quickly denied hints of tighter censorship were in ministerial ones. It makes the usual distinction between criticism of bad ministers and the crime of insulting the king: "whenever Majesty is mentioned by the Declaimers against the licentiousness of the Press, Minister is really meant . . . . That an Opposition to the Measures of the Administration is wounding the Sovereign thro' the Sides of the Minister:

. . . [is] a stale Piece of ministerial Policy, and has been so effectually exploded that nothing but Want of Argument and Sincerity in the Friends of the Ministry could induce them to revive it." The press must remain free to urge voters of all parties to preserve the trade and liberty of England by voting Walpole out of office. The Broad-Bottom Ralph rejects "Whig and Tory . . . *Shibboleths* that are now no more," and insists that "Jacobitism is now only a stalking-Horse, a mere puppet of Straw, to be set up and beaten down again just as it serves the turn of those in the Administration." He urges all to "lay aside . . . former animosities when the good of the Commonweal requires a Coalition." Vote, he says on September 23, according to facts, not slogans: the good candidate will not have a place or pension, will have a good estate, will be for triennial Parliaments, and will have voted against the Excise Bill. Neither strangers without parliamentary experience, nor those with unsound views on the war or standing armies or spending should be trusted. Reject any candidate who has voted against patriotic motions or bills. This is the last chance to save freedom, to deserve the name of "Preservers of your Country." Electors were fast becoming the only audience that greatly interested *The Champion*.

After the "Philopatriae" essays, the campaign went on without a break. Even on September 25, when the leader is non-political, it is followed by a "letter" (a secondary essay) from a repentent ex-ministerial writer ashamed of attacking the "City of L[*ondo*]n, W____m, tho' dead [William III], P[*ultene*]y, B[*arnar*]d, L[*yttelto*]n, C[*a*]r[*tere*]t . . . C[*hesterfiel*]d, Ar[*gyl*]l, and every great and honour'd Name in the Three Kingdoms." *The Champion* was calling the opposition's honour roll. More typically, the essays matched the political barrage in later pages. On October 4 Fielding even turned an admission that he once accepted money from Walpole into an attack on the Prime Minister. A "letter" from one "experto credo Roberto" offers "Captain Vinegar" a choice: change sides for money ("Pills") or "kiss my A____." The "Captain" (Fielding) says he has already turned down such offers,

> tho' I own, being in an ill State of Health [i.e., poor], I accepted a few to stop the Publication of a Book, which I had written against his Practice, and which he threaten'd to take the Law of me, if I publish'd; These Pills, tho' a mere matter of Bargain, he was pleas'd to consider as a great Obligation: But I can tell him, his Nostrums have now done so much Mischief, that whoever takes any Reward to him to secure his Practice any longer, deserves more to be hang'd, and is a more infamous Villain than any on the Records of the *Old Bailey*.

Clearly, this is a reaction to a confused story (that Fielding was bailed out of a country jail by Walpole, though he had written a libel against him, before he "set up for a playwriter") told in a pamphlet published in London at roughly the same time, *An Historical View of the . . . Political Writers of Great Britain*. What "Book" Fielding withdrew and what period he is referring to are both obscure, however. *Jonathan Wild* has been suggested by Bertrand Goldgar, on the grounds that it *may* original-

ly have been completed in 1740 (in a different form than appeared in the
Miscellanies of 1743) and withheld. *The Grub-Street Opera* of 1731 is far
more likely. It, unlike *Jonathan Wild*, is early enough to be described
vaguely as written before Fielding's stage career began. Its performance
was prevented by the censor and the company that would have performed it was harassed by the law. Its satire on the royal family was far
more likely to tempt Walpole to "take the law" than anything in
Jonathan Wild. Finally, Fielding did not allow its publication during his
lifetime (though it was pirated in 1731), so that it appeared only in
1755.[13] On the other hand, it is very possible that Fielding kept his
"Bargain" with Walpole and is referring to a work never published.

Certainly, there is no warrant for a recent suggestion that Fielding's
admission constitutes early evidence of the "change of parties" supposedly signalled in *The Opposition: A Vision* fourteen months later.[14] It
implies exactly the opposite, being a rededication to the assault on
Walpole. This is patent in context. The issue of October 4 also satirizes
those who take government bribes and anticipates Walpole's defeat in
the election. The very next essay is the "Remarkable Queries" (probably
by Ralph), the most potent attack on Walpole in *The Champion*'s run,
and the one that drew the most fire from *The Gazetteer*. The massing of
rhetorical questions was fairly common, but this is an extraordinarily
powerful, extended example. It treats the election as a decisive trial, the
"whole Nation Plaintiff" *versus* "one single Man Defendant," and the
last chance to cure corruption and preserve liberty. Then it addresses
twenty-seven questions to the nation-as-jury, bringing home every standard anti-ministerial topic of criticism. It questions the ministerial
record: the Excise Bill, penal laws, the Gin Bill, the large idle army, the
proliferation of places for members of Commons, the toleration of corruption in government departments and chartered companies, the ill
treatment of London, the neglect of trade, the constant increase in
government revenues, and the disastrous war policies of the ministry.
Would such ills be tolerated if electors and M.P.s were not corrupted *en
masse* and do they benefit even those corrupted in the long run? It
stresses Walpole's "personal" corruption. Does he not prosper through
public calamities? Does he not, having started with next to nothing,
spend £20,000 *per annum*, and own land yielding £10,000 *per annum* and
a house and gardens worth £250,000? Are not his sons wealthy, and his
brother richer in land and money by £300,000 plus £5000 *per annum*? It
warns of Constitutional dangers. Can a man so universally hated as
Walpole be innocent, and has he any refuge but the power of the Crown,
or any safety without increasing that power? Is the road to tyrannic
power not through the corruption of Parliament, and will another seven
years of parliamentary subservience not finish off Constitutional liberty
and even the rights of property? Can any bribe or consideration make it
worth the while of electors to choose representatives who will retain the
tyrant in power? Even in 1740 this was political dynamite.

During October Fielding was far from quiescent; on October 9 he threatened Walpole with hanging. Still, his energies were otherwise engaged: he contributed fewer essays than was his wont between mid-September and the end of October, some half a dozen (including two "Voyage" installments) out of nineteen. Ralph raged on, demanding on October 23 and 25, for example, that the king dismiss Walpole and "give him up to the Laws as a Peace-offering," and lamenting England's descent of the same path of corruption that doomed the Roman Republic. Meanwhile, Fielding was, I believe, writing the longest, most closely reasoned piece to appear in *The Champion*, and the longest formal political essay he ever wrote: *An Address to the Electors of Great Britain*. It appeared in eleven consecutive issues, November 1 to November 29, and was later published in Edinburgh as a 108-page pamphlet.[15] Its connectedness, particularly in the earlier installments (roughly through November 13), strongly suggests that it was written in great part before November 1, rather than hurried together three times a week in a race with the presses. Elections seemed to bring out the sober political debater in Fielding; the only other work in his canon comparable to the *Address* (though its thought is often radically different since he was a ministerial apologist) is his election pamphlet of 1747, *A Dialogue Between a Gentleman from London . . . and an Honest Alderman of the Country Party*.

There was also pressure to produce something impressive because of the failure of the "eminent Hand" to deliver the "Papers addressed to the Electors of Great Britain" promised on September 6 and 11. The "Philopatriae" essays of September 20 and 23 were no adequate substitute, and on September 23 and 25 there had been a second promise: "Our Readers are desired to take Notice that the Papers, relating to Elections, lately promised in the Champion, will be published in the Beginning of next Month." Finally, on Tuesday, October 28, it was announced that:

> On Saturday next we shall begin to publish the promis'd *Address to the Electors of Great-Britain;* which we hope, all *honest Men* will do their best to *forward* to the Persons to whom they are directed: Scarce *four Champions* in *Twelve* having at present, the good Fortune to find their Way by the *Post*, tho' the Superscriptions are written ever so legible.

This promise was fulfilled, but the series of delays unmistakably suggests repeated failure by some outside contributor. (If I had to hazard a guess, it would be George Lyttelton, the "eminent Hand" closest to Fielding; parts of his "Considerations on the Present State of Affairs" of 1739 are close in spirit to the *Address*.) That Fielding wrote the substitute piece is strongly suggested, as I have argued elsewhere,[16] by the style of the *Address* and certain external indicators. Even before it was understood that it originated in *The Champion*, the Edinburgh pamphlet was confidently attributed to Fielding by Frederick S. Dickson, first made suspicious by an ironical denial in the pamphlet of rumours that Fielding wrote it. Moreover, it was attributed with malicious certainty to him by Ralph Courteville, chief writer of the *Gazetteer*. Courteville was familiar with the shadow world of contemporary political journalism, and had followed closely the charade of promises and disappointments regarding the election "Papers":

> . . . some Weeks ago . . . the *Champion*, of the Patriots, threatened us with a Series of Papers on the Elections, written by a distinguish'd Hand, and Care was taken to prepossess the Town that this distinguish'd Person was a Man of great Parts, and also of great Quality. In consequence of this he made the Publick dance a long Attendance! now these Letters were to be inserted this Time, now that; nay, a sort of Running Footman ["Philopatriae"], an occasional Scribbler, was dispatch'd before him to stop People's Mouths with a few crude Sentences on the same Subject, till this distinguish'd Hand was at leisure . . . . Well, at length comes the Great Man, and who should it be but—Captain Vinegar himself . . . .

The *Address* is precisely what one would expect from Fielding, the scholarly lawyer and adherent of Bolingbroke's Broad-Bottom theories. It deplores present corruption, in detail and at length, as evil in its immediate effects and a danger in the long run to balanced government and Constitutional freedom. It lectures on the so-called "Whig theory" of the Constitution, stressing that no branch of government, but the three in concert, should wield the supreme power, and insisting that the most essential bulwark of liberty is a free House of Commons, unsapped by faction or the corrupting influence of the Crown. It traces the rise of the Constitution from Saxon times through 1688-89 and its decline under "Robinocracy." Always it urges voting for opposition candidates and shunning those tainted by Walpole, corruption, faction, and moneyed indifference to trade. The essays for November 8 and 11, for example, urge that, guided by love of country (Bolingbrokean "true Patriotism"), electors must follow the "Principle of Virtue" (voting for the best, most independent men) or the "Principle of Interest" (voting for men of sufficient standing and substance, especially landed wealth, to be above corruption) when faced with a choice between new, untried candidates. In choosing among those who have served before, they must choose only men who have voted in a way that distinguishes them from the creatures and tools of ministry. If they do their duty, an uncorrupted Commons will be "the impregnable Bulwark of the Nation, against which the *Gates of Hell*, the Malice of the Devil, or of his chief Engineer, a *First Minister*, shall never be able to prevail." Fielding had come a long way since the light, deft jabs at Walpole of November 1739.

If the *Address* was the climax to Fielding's political development as *Champion* essayist, it was also a long swan-song, and thereon hangs a mystery. The leader for October 21, 1740 used to be considered, surprisingly, his latest extant contribution, though he remained actively connected with *The Champion* until June 1741, and did not formally relinquish his shares until June 1742. The attribution of the *Address* to him probably moves the date of his last essay up to November 29, 1740, and adds eleven leaders to our harvest of his contributions (seven in original issues, the rest in the Edinburgh reprint), but the gap between December 1740 and June 1741 still yawns.[17] This has recently generated conjectures that he ceased writing for *The Champion* considerably earlier than June 1741, for political reasons.

There are two schools of thought on Fielding's departure from *The Champion*. One was elaborated in G. M. Godden's *Memoir* of 1910. Godden cites Fielding's own statement in the "Preface" to the *Miscellanies* of 1743: "I have long since (as long as from June, 1741) desisted from writing one syllable in the Champion, or any other public paper." She adds the minutes she discovered of a *Champion* shareholders' meeting for June 29, 1741, which Fielding attended, and at which he alone voted against the sale of 1000 copies of the 1741 reprint to another shareholder for resale. Though the apparent disappearance of the minutes once in Godden's possession is troubling (especially since she quotes them scantily and out of context), this constitutes an unanswerable case for Fielding's continued association with *The Champion*. However, it does not indicate how much *writing* he continued to do in the first half of 1741, and does not justify theories that Fielding left because he was at odds with his partners over the sale of the reprint copies.[18]

Since Godden's time the possibility that Fielding wrote much less after late 1740 (though remaining a shareholder) has always been just below the horizon of scholarly consciousness. The minutes of another shareholders' meeting (also cited by Godden)[19] held on March 1, 1742 record the transfer of Fielding's "two-sixteenth" shares to James Ralph on the grounds that he had failed to contribute "for above twelve months past." This seems to imply a withdrawal from the role of essayist before the end of February 1740, an implication not contradicted, to say the least, by the lack of extant Fielding essays from after the end of November 1740. Indeed, the only reason the lack of later Fielding contributions has not forced scholars to look beyond February 1740 in dating his withdrawal is the almost absurd scantiness of our file of *Champion* essays from the period: we have only six original issues, January 22, February 12, March 7, March 24, May 7, and May 19, and seven more essays that survived because they were reprinted in the *York Courant* for December 2, 9, and 23, January 27, March 3, and April 21 and 28.[20] With only thirteen essays of the more than seventy published, one cannot confidently theorize about the non-survival of even a single Fielding essay. Were there many more extant issues, and still none (or even one or two) by the man who wrote well over half the essays published between November 1739 and November 1740, a pattern of total (or almost total) withdrawal would clamour for recognition, the 1741 minutes and Fielding's "Preface" notwithstanding.

The possibility of an earlier withdrawal was hinted by Martin Battestin in 1960 (seconded in 1975 by Bertrand Goldgar), with an unfortunate political rider. Battestin suggests that Fielding may have stopped contributing as early as February 1741 because "he no longer wished to support the opposition, whose cause that paper was working to promote."[21] The problem is the unlikelihood of the assumption that Fielding withdrew for political reasons, whatever the date. Battestin came to the problem of the timing of Fielding's retirement as *Champion* essayist in attempting to strengthen the case, by extending the symptoms backward in time, for his "change of parties" reading of *The Opposition: A Vision* of December 1741 and *Joseph Andrews*. He did so at a time when the essay for October 21 seemed Fielding's latest extant contribution. Having assumed political motivation, he proceeded cogently: (1) stressing the March 1, 1742 minutes; (2) eliminating one difficulty by rightly suggesting that Fielding did not write *The Crisis: A Sermon*, of April 1741 (though he did *not* deal with the anti-ministerial material in *Shamela*, also published in April); and (3) arguing that February 1741 is the earliest possible date for Fielding's rupture with the opposition and *The Champion* because of the publication of the strongly anti-ministerial *Of True Greatness* and *The Vernoniad* in January.

But all revolves around the false assumption that Fielding stopped writing for *The Champion*—whenever he did so—because he was breaking with the opposition. Battestin and Goldgar only weakly support this assumption: suggesting that two jabs at Fielding in *The Daily Gazetteer* for March 11 and 30, 1741 imply he was "thinking of deserting his party," though each clearly treats him as a present as well as a former foe well after the date of his supposed break with the opposition and *The Champion*. The earlier *Gazetteer* depicts him as a Sisyphus trying to push the opposition up the hill to power, but letting it fall when the goddess, "Britannia," rebukes him and praises Walpole. The later has a message from "Hercules Vinegar":

> Having irredeemably mortgaged my share of the little Profit, arising from the Sale of the *Champion*, I have determin'd to bite the Mortgagee (I'm a Lawyer you know, and understand Trap) by withdrawing my propping Hand from that falling Paper; and intend for the future to dedicate the Strength of my surprising Genius to you. Publish what I have sent you therefore, as a Specimen of my Taste for collecting [a scurrilous attack on *The Craftsman* follows) curious Pieces of Wit and Humour.

The first is quite unexceptional anti-opposition satire, free of innuendoes about changing sides, though it does foreshadow the self-portrait of Fielding, among other "asses," trying to pull the opposition wagon in *The Opposition: A Vision*. It classifies "Vinegar" with the rest of the opposition writers ("that *sour Generation*") a month after his supposed defection. Though the implication that Fielding is joining the "Gazetteer Legion" is a joke, the second *Gazetteer* comment is more interesting, for the hints about disgust with "propping" the "falling" *Champion* may reflect a withdrawal from writing connected with a withdrawal of opposition subsidy which I will suggest below. But it is not at all what the

Gazetteer would have written if Fielding had changed sides as well as withdrawn from writing *Champion* essays. It treats him as an enemy, though it may also imply he was not earning his keep.

The evidence against the theory of political motivation is considerable. Fielding's continued friendship with George Lyttelton alone makes the notion that he turned his coat at the beginning (or even the end) of 1741 pretty untenable. Moreover, if we assume he left *for political reasons* in February, or slightly later, we must account for the anti-ministerial touches in *Shamela*, and swallow the idea that a man who had abandoned the opposition and *The Champion* in disgust could attend a *Champion* shareholders' meeting in June and hold his shares for another eight months. We must also face the fact that Fielding seems to have been regarded as a friend by his former *Champion* associates *as late as June 1742*, well after the fall of Walpole and the publication of *Joseph Andrews*. The *Champion* essay for June 29, 1742 is one of the tiny handful of survivals from the late run, printed precisely a year after the last shareholders' meeting Fielding is known to have attended and sixteen months after he supposedly broke with *The Champion* and the opposition. It is a dream vision that reflects the disgruntlement of those—including Fielding's patrons—left in opposition after Walpole's fall and the reconstruction of the ministry. In particular, it wishfully imagines the execution of Walpole, not the safe retreat he achieved with the connivance of those former opponents who entered the new ministry. It also contains a strong, unambiguously positive "puff" for the "*new* Translations of *Plutus the God of Riches*, from *Aristophanes*, by Fielding and Young," as a piece capable of providing an "Evening's Amusement." By itself, it seems to me, this invalidates a political explanation of Fielding's departure from *The Champion* or the theory that he "changed parties" at any time in 1741-42.

Once the assumption of political motivation is dropped, the case for an early withdrawal from writing becomes attractive. It is no longer necessary to assume a sudden, absolute cessation of contributions or a rupture between Fielding and his partners. It even becomes thinkable that Fielding's opposition patrons may have *encouraged*, positively or negatively, his withdrawal from writing for *The Champion*. Of course, the time-span within which he may have withdrawn is also widened since he could have worked on the opposition pieces of January 1741 after he stopped writing *Champion* essays. Indeed it seems more likely that he cut back or ceased writing for *The Champion* as early as December 1740, rather than later, with perhaps an occasional return in the next few months to help out Ralph, still a friend and still backing the same opposition faction. There are several reasons why he may have done so. After the early summer of 1740, Fielding's contributions to *The Champion* changed. In place of the one or two miscellaneous essays a week of the earlier run, the "Voyages" series incorporated a large portion of his contributions within an ongoing framework. Did the space and time limits of normal essay writing begin to pall for a writer whose tendency was not toward brevity? Was a change needed after eight months of unaccustomed literary grinding? By the time the "Voyages" ended, *The Champion* had entered a more consistently political phase, with little use for the kind of non-political essays that Fielding wrote so well. The climax of this political phase is the *Address*, which takes the "Voyage" pattern of elongation to extremes in eleven consecutive essays. In October and November, Fielding did unaccustomed labour that left him (if I read aright the descending quality of the writing and argument in the final three or four *Address* installments) drained and bored. Finally, to broaden our perspective even more, when he finished the *Address*, and thus his last extant essay, Fielding had already stayed with *The Champion* longer than any of his later journals would last: *The True Patriot* ran from November 1745 to the following June, *The Jacobite's Journal* from December 1747 to November 1748, and *The Covent-Garden Journal* from January to October 1752. Fielding had set a personal endurance record as a periodical drudge, and perhaps simply wanted a change.

The outburst of miscellaneous writing Fielding did between mid-fall 1740 and April 1741 has been treated as a sign that he needed money badly. Certainly, he had to borrow money in March 1741, and was in financial straits by 1742-43.[22] But the certain effects of Fielding's labours have been less considered than its possible causes. They must have conflicted with the ready performance of his duties as *Champion* essayist and may have precluded it. In October 1740 the translation of Adlerfeld's *Histoire militaire de Charles XII roi de Suède* was published, in January 1741 *Of True Greatness* and *The Vernoniad*, in April *Shamela*. Other projects may also have been absorbing time—*Jonathan Wild* and *Joseph Andrews*, for example—in the first half of 1741. A new career was in the making, and would gather momentum in the latter half of 1741 as *Joseph Andrews* took shape. Fielding's political friends and patrons may also have requested a change of pace near the end of 1740. Doubtless he was encouraged to write *Of True Greatness* and, especially, *The Vernoniad* and rewarded for doing so. His boast about refusing bribes from the ministry to change sides in the preface to the first poem was one more step in the game of suggesting, then rejecting such offers—real or imagined—begun by Fielding on October 4, 1740 and concluded on March 30, 1741 by the *Gazetteer*. But it was also a strong hint to George Dodington, to whom the poem is addressed, to reward its author:

> I have been obliged with Money to silence my Productions, professedly and by Way of Bargain given me for that Purpose . . . I have been offered my own Terms to exert my Talent of Ridicule (as it was called) against some Persons (dead and living) whom I shall never mention but with Honour . . . I have drawn my Pen in Defence of my Country, have sacrificed to it the Interest of myself and Family, and have been the standing Mark of honorable Abuse for so doing.

There is also what I take to be evidence that Fielding's patrons negatively influenced him to shift his efforts away from *The Champion*.

I have interpreted the peculiarities in the *Gazetteer*'s response to *The*

Champion in its first year as indicating the tardy provision, *circa* June 1740, of an opposition subsidy. Significantly, *The Gazetteer* abruptly lost interest in *The Champion* at about the time (early December) when I have suggested Fielding may have begun to withdraw from essay writing. In October and November 1740 *The Champion* obsessed *The Gazetteer* (it was satirized on October 8, 9, 17, 20, 23, 29, 30, and 31; November 5, 14, 19, and 26) while *The Craftsman* and *Common Sense* were only occasionally touched. Fielding's journal seemed the most potent "Vehicle of Sedition," as it was termed on October 17. But on November 14 (just when our file of *Champion* issues becomes so nearly empty) the *Gazetteer* vowed to ignore *The Champion* in future because of its negligibility and the present situation (read the approach of the election). *The Champion* is jabbed in an attack on Richard Glover in the *Gazetteer* for November 19, the "Hockley Hero" is briefly teased on November 26 (the last even mild satire specifically aimed at Fielding until March 1741), on December 6 the *Gazetteer* sharply criticizes the *Champion* essays for October 21, 23, and 25, and there is a final satiric aside on December 10. But after that the *Gazetteer* concentrates almost totally on *Common Sense* and *The Craftsman*. The pattern for the first two months of this "new policy," if compared with what we have seen in the fall of 1740, makes the point. On December 12, 20, 24, 26, and 31, January 9, 14, 16, 23, and 28, and February 4, 6, 9, 11, and 16 *The Craftsman* and *Common Sense* are hit, but only on January 28, February 11, and February 16 is *The Champion* mentioned, always together with the other two journals. Even these passing attacks seem stimulated not by what *The Champion* was doing, but by what it had done. The satire on January 28 and February 11 is very vague, not aimed at a specific issue, and on February 16 the *Gazetteer* is obviously interested in past performances. Later in the spring *The Champion* was sometimes attacked on its own, but single billing was a rarity, and, we have seen, the most noteworthy attacks suggest Fielding's discouragement (March 11) and disgust at working to maintain a "falling" journal (March 30).

The *Gazetteer*'s behaviour indicates *The Champion* was no longer a major threat, which seems to me, in turn, a strong circumstantial indicator of a withdrawal or sharp reduction (occurring somewhere between mid-November and early December 1740) of the support that abruptly made *The Champion* formidable the preceding summer. Perhaps its opposition backers hoped that the journal, now notorious, could remain a power without a subsidy. Whether this withdrawal was a cause or a result of Fielding's decision to turn to opposition poetry is impossible to determine—though I suspect the former. *The Champion* could not have been very profitable thereafter, as is perhaps indicated in the passage in *The Opposition: A Vision* depicting the opposition before the election of 1741: it specifies that James Ralph had not been "fed" since the "hard frost," and implies that Fielding, also ill rewarded, had ceased pulling his weight. Taking all the evidence together, there seems fair warrant for a theory that Fielding withdrew from the role of principal essayist, being replaced by Ralph, in December 1740, at about the time the journal lost its subsidy. In early 1741 he contributed very occasionally, if at all, though he did not fall out with Ralph, *The Champion*, or his friends in the opposition. This pattern is consistent with his attendance at the shareholders' meeting of June 1741, and with the precise wording of the explanation given on March 1, 1742 for the transfer of his shares (held "as Writer") to Ralph on March 1, 1742. It quietly distinguishes between acting as principal writer and assisting Ralph in the statement that he has "withdrawn himself from that Service (writing) for above twelve Months past and refused his Assistance in that Capacity since which time Mr. Ralph has solely Transacted the said Business."

The two heroic-couplet poems published in January 1741 offer no political surprises. *Of True Greatness*, published on January 7, resembles many essays in *The Champion*. Among its falsely great is the powerful but bad minister, flattered by sycophants (including writers so inept that people will not be paid to read them), living in "mock state" and hailing himself as "the Great." This is the Walpole described in *The Champion* for June 10, 1740 and mocked as "Hum Clum" in Job Vinegar's "Voyages." Trade, the London merchants, and their spokesmen, Barnard and Heathcote, are praised, while Walpole is said to denigrate them. More importantly, *Of True Greatness* is an extended compliment to the leaders of the opposition. Fielding insists "to no profession, party, place confined,/ True greatness lives but in the noble mind." Though this sounds non-partisan, his examples are an opposition roll-call (many of the names matching those praised, as noted earlier, in *The Champion* for September 25, 1740): George Dodington (treated as a prime exemplar of "true greatness," as improbable as it may seem), the Duke of Argyll ("supreme in all the arts of peace and war," the latest *grandee* to join the anti-Walpole forces), Lord Carteret, Lord Chesterfield, and, of course, George Lyttelton. Fielding compliments the 1st Duke of Marlborough as the type of the "truly great" military hero. He soon would defend Marlborough's duchess (who would leave large bequests to Chesterfield and William Pitt in honour of their "patriotism") against politically motivated assaults in the *Full Vindication of the Dutchess Dowager of Marlborough*. Finally, in the "Preface" to the poem (removed upon republication in the *Miscellanies*) Fielding may complain about the abuse brought upon him by his patriotic stance, but its main emphasis is on justifying Dodington in the face of similar attacks. Though notorious for political opportunism, Dodington was very important in the opposition. Close for years to the Prince of Wales and the Duke of Argyll, he was a natural ally in 1741 of Lyttelton and the other Cobhamites. After the election of 1741 he would strive mightly along with them to stave off the break-up of the opposition in a rush for places and a cynical accommodation with the weakened Walpole of the kind predicted in *The Opposition: A Vision.*

Though it is a splendid example of Fielding's genius for parody, politics is the soul of *The Vernoniad*. It is rooted in the mythology and rhetoric of opposition, its corrosive allegory focussing upon Walpole's supposed corruption and incapacity, even disinclination, to win the war with Spain. As soon as news of Admiral Vernon's conquest (November 1739) of Porto Bello in the Spanish West Indies reached England, the victory of this anti-ministerial admiral with a meagre fleet of "six ships only" became a reproach to a government that with huge resources did little. Throughout 1740 the government's slow reaction to his request for a fleet fit for a campaign in the Indies was a staple with opposition critics. Vernon asked for rapid naval reinforcement, indicating that land troops would do poorly in the hot and feverish islands. The ministry ponderously decided to send a Brobdingnagian fleet (25 ships of the line) and 9000 troops to reduce fortified positions, setting the stage for the fiasco of the assault on Cartagena in 1741. Only as *The Vernoniad* appeared did the fleet finally reach Vernon, political delays having been compounded by storms and west winds that kept the fleet in harbour. *The Vernoniad* telescopes the many complaints about naval inaction and ministerial negativity regarding trade and the war in *The Champion*, but its mood is that of the period when the reluctantly assembled men-of-war were windbound.

Fielding opens by celebrating the Porto Bello victory:

> Arms and the man I sing, who greatly bore
> Augusta's flag to Porto Bello's shore,
> On sea and land to much suffering, e're he won,
> With six ships only, the predestined town;
> Whence a long train of victories shall flow,
> And future laurels for Augusta grow.

The crucial point is not, however, what Vernon did, but Walpole's efforts to prevent him from doing more. The poem is focussed on its anti-hero, Walpole, not its admiral-Aeneas. Satan detests Augusta (a "Trojan" colony "within the mouth of Thames," inhabited by people "sturdy to foes and studious of their trade") as a threat to his beloved "Iberia" ("A country of Asia, near Armenia"), home of devilish Catholicism and the Inquisition. Satan calls on Mammon (Walpole, the great corrupter) who sits in "solemn melancholy pomp of state" in a "dome" that recalls the epic underworld and Walpole's Norfolk mansion. In particular it mocks the great lantern at Houghton and the huge collection of paintings that (as J. H. Plumb has stressed)[23] were Walpole's delight:

> A huge dark lantern hung up in his hall
> And heaps of ill-got pictures hid the wall.

Satan reminds Mammon: "No more our Lewis [Louis XIV] spreads the iron chain,/ For Europe's neck which Marlborough cut in twain;/ Charles [Charles XII of Sweden] who their bowels from vast empires

tore,/ Now sleeps and plagues the northern world no more." The fight
against freedom and true religion is only continued by Spain, threatened
by "Augusta's navy arms." This is anti-Spanish, anti-Catholic hate propaganda, but anti-Walpole animus dominates the rest of *The Vernoniad*.

Satan exhorts: "Haste, Mammon, haste, ascend the glittering bar,/
Haste, and obstruct the progress of the war." Mammon-Walpole, true to
his attachment to devil, Spain, and tyranny, does so. He flies to his dome
for a "mighty bag" of gold, the only metal, Fielding interjects, that can
threaten England, since her forces, led by "A___" (Argyll), can overcome Spanish steel. Walpole will not submit to the efficient, trade-
oriented conduct of a war he long opposed:

> Shall I let merchants triumph, and no more
> See their rich ships made booty on their shore?
> Merchants! whom I must envy; for their wealth
> Is by just means acquired, but mine by stealth.

Having seen him bested by London's merchants, he asks, who "will ever
kiss my ___ again?" To prevent Vernon from receiving reinforcements
in time to act effectively, Mammon appeals to Aeolus, god of winds, in a
palace suggesting Whitehall. This, of course, refers to the delay of the
fleet by contrary winds, but obviously Aeolus also represents Walpole in
his role of controller through corruption of Parliament. The winds under
his control represent the membership of Parliament in particular and the
might of England in general. Aeolus-Walpole rules the winds:

> Now bids them all be silent, and now blow,
> While all submissive watch his ay or no.

This alone prevents the defeat of Spain and Walpole-Aeolus' ejection
from office. If the winds were free (if Parliament were independent and
uncorrupted),

> . . . their resistless sway
> Would sweep the world before 'em in their way.
> ....
> The greatest man their fury would unhorse,
> Hurl from his saddle, and dash forth his brains,
> Regardless of his spurs, or golden reins.
> In vain long artful puzzling schemes of power
> The minister would lay; when in an hour
> The work of ages would be overthrown,
> And all the Babel project tumbled down.

However, the ruling god, Jupiter (this is one of only two places where
Fielding risked explicit criticism of George II), now uses Aeolus
(Walpole) to restrain the winds (Parliament) through corruption:

> But Jupiter . . .
> Restrained their fury by a bribing awe;
> Made Aeolus, dispenser of their meat;
> Ev'n winds subsist not long unless they eat,
> Gave them moreover vanity and pride
> [a desire for honours and titles as well as money]
> To be by Aeolus, alone, supply'd.

The compliant wind is rewarded, and the defiant "turned out" and replaced by "some poor breeze, of some ignoble race"; thus Aeolus is a kind of demi-king with "arbitrary sway."

To this lordly Aeolus (one aspect of Walpole) Mammon (another aspect) comes for help, careful as he enters his palace to "touch" (bribe) all he meets. In a long speech he states his principles (hatred of Vernon and Britain's naval power, love of Spain and her wealth) and his convictions that every "wise man's conscience always hath a price," that great rogues are admirable and small ones deserve punishment (the formula of the *Beggar's Opera* and *Jonathan Wild*) and that "Virtue's a name a bubble or a fart." Then he calls on Aeolus for contrary winds to stop Vernon's reinforcements. Mammon will pay any price to and through Aeolus while Jove (George II, here a dupe, as in *The Welsh Opera*) remains indifferently compliant:

> . . . as for Jove, he troubles not his head;
> But on his throne sips nectar, and then nods,
> And leaves the earth to us, his demy-gods:
> Cares not the affairs of wretched men to know,
> Indifferent where I plunder or you blow.

Naturally, Aeolus (who here represents both the Parliament, in Fielding's typically flexible allegory, and Walpole, its corrupter and a greedy speculator) accepts two purses from Mammon, one for the winds and a larger one for himself. Then, after a long speech on the total corruption of the world (Mammon's "puppet shew" in which he "bawlest and squeakest through each throat"), he looses winds that force the fleet to seek "the peaceful bay." The poem ends with the happy Mammon keeping "a three weeks feast" (one of Walpole's famed get-togethers with his cronies and dependants at Houghton in Norfolk, presumably during the Christmas recess of December 1740), and cursing Augusta.

With *The Vernoniad* Fielding had pretty well "shot his bolt" politically. Martin Battestin is right in denying that he wrote the one really partisan work from the spring of 1741 that has been attributed to him, *The Crisis: A Sermon* of April 1741. Only a dubious inscription (recorded in *Literary Anecdotes of the Eighteenth Century*) on the title page of a copy of *The Crisis* once in the possession of John Nichols connects Fielding and *The Crisis:* "This sermon was written by the late Mr. Fielding, author of *Tom Jones, &c.*, as the printer of it assured me.—R.B."[24] We know nothing about "R.B.," whose information was at least second-hand and gathered at the earliest in the 1750s. It has been argued that the content of *The Crisis* marks it as Fielding's: "a Sermon on Revelation xiv. 9-11. Necessary to be preached in all the Churches in England, Wales and Berwick upon Tweed, at or before the next General Election," it appeals to electors to shun the Prime Minister and his mark on the hand, a bribe. But though Fielding would have endorsed in 1741 all it says, many other writers were making the same points at the time. A more crucial claim is that its prose style matches Fielding's, but this does not stand scrutiny. It is said to be in Fielding's style mainly because it passes the "hath test" (the use of the obsolescent "hath," instead of "has"). This "test," however, not only is inherently inconclusive (other contemporary writers used it, though it was becoming unusual), but is virtually meaningless in a mock sermon where it would be natural to favour such an old-fashioned, biblical-sounding usage. Consider, to cite only one of many examples, the concluding sentence of the "Sermon," where other verbs are given the old-fashioned ending: "To Him, therefore, who besetoweth freedom and delighteth in it, may freedom lift up her voice, and ascribe, as is most due, all honour, praise, glory, might, majesty, and dominion for evermore. Amen." The "hath" usage aside, Battestin is right that the "solemn vehemence" of this sermon "in the rhythm of the Prayer book" (the phrases are F. Homes Dudden's and Wilbur Cross's) is very unlike Fielding.[25] I do not find that it anywhere has the "feel" of Fielding's prose. That leaves *Shamela*, which appeared on April 4, 1741, as the one publication of Fielding's between January and December 1741, the period of his labours over *Joseph Andrews*. Hugh Amory suggested some years ago that *Shamela* is a "political romance," replete with anti-Walpole allegories, the "*real* author" of which is Walpole.[26] However, his theories far outrun the evidence and probability. *Shamela* is only peripherally concerned with politics (*Pamela*, George Whitefield, and Cibber's *Apology* being its prime targets), though the political material in it is quite consistent with Fielding's Broad-Bottom opposition allegiance. His political attitudes had not changed; he was simply not concentrating on political satire.

The main body of *An Apology for the Life of Mrs. Shamela Andrews*, the correspondence between Shamela, Shamela's mother, Mrs. Jervis, Parson Williams, and Squire Booby, includes only a minimum of political material, though Shamela's description on the title page as a "young Politician" may have led some readers who knew its author to expect more. Even when material seems to cry out for political application Fielding does not always respond. Mrs. Jervis, for example, says that "*Robin* Coachman" is "intrusted by his master to carry on this Affair [the abduction of Shamela] privately for him" and goes on to vow that "we hang together . . . as well as any Family of Servants in the Nation" (Letter VII), but Fielding passes up the opportunity for political satire like that in *The Welsh Opera*. There are just enough political references in the main body of *Shamela* to mark it as the work of a Broad-Bottom writer during the election campaign of 1741.

When Mrs. Jewkes threatens to tell the Squire about Shamela's relationship with Parson Williams, Shamela declares that as long as Williams "hath a Vote for Pallament Men, the Squire dare do nothing to offend him" (Letter IX). Slightly later, Williams vows he "will vote the other Party" if he is refused a living by Booby; he owes the Squire £150, but tells Shamela, in her words, by the "Time the Election is past, I shall be able to plead the Status of Lamentations" (Letter X). We later learn that the Squire is Country-oriented, and the parson a secret favourer of the Court. Aside from this there is only the political comedy in Shamela's long, last letter, where after-dinner drinking merges into an informal meeting of the borough's electors. Williams and Booby differ over toasts, a disagreement Shamela sees as political, though the joke is really sexual, *"et cetera"* (note the "Borough:burrow" pun) meaning Shamela's pudenda. Hugh Amory's description of it as a reference to Laud's "et cetera" oath and a hint that Williams is a "crypto-Jacobite" is not convincing:

> After Dinner Mr. *Williams* drank the Church *et caetera;* and smiled on me; when my Husband's Turn came, he drank *et caetera* and the Church; for which he was very severely rebuked by Mr. Williams, it being a high Crime, it seems, to name any thing before the Church. I do not know what *Et cetera* is, but I believe it is something concerning chusing Pallament-Men; for I asked if it was not a Health to Mr. Booby's Borough, and Mr. Williams with a hearty Laugh answered, Yes, yes, it is his Borough we mean.

Shamela leaves, followed by the Squire, and the "whole Corporation" begins to make a night of it with wine, tobacco, and song. She tries to encourage Booby "to sit down and drink for his Country with the rest of the Company" (a hit at the bibulousness of Country electors like that Fielding indulged in from the early plays to *Tom Jones* and *The Covent-Garden Journal*). Booby's refusal shows he is a true Country candidate, opposed to the ministry and in favour of "Trade." He distrusts the hypocritical patriotism of the corporation and, not without cause, Parson Williams:

> . . . he refused, and desired me to give him some Tea; swearing nothing made him so sick as to hear a Parcel of Scoundrels roaring forth the Principles of honest Men over their Cups, when, says he, I know most of them are such empty Blockheads, that they don't know their right Hand from their left; and that Fellow there, who hath talked so much of *Shipping*, at the left side of the Parson, in whom they all place a Confidence, if I don't take care, will sell them to my Adversary.

A dupe elsewhere, Booby here enunciates Fielding's concerns. Parson Williams is an out-and-out scoundrel, rather than a libidinous fool with sound political principles. Predictably, Shamela has heard enough from him to know that he is a secret well-wisher to the ministry, pretending to stand with his benefactor. She apologizes to her mother for mentioning the Squire's outburst:

> I don't know why I mention this Stuff to you; for I am sure I know nothing about *Pollitricks,* more than Parson Williams tells me, who says that the Court-side are in the right on't, and that every Christian ought to be on the same with the Bishops.

The balance is loaded against the ministry and any who may sell out to it. Sharp satire on opposition hypocrites is normal in Fielding's anti-ministerial writing; it surfaces in his fleeting gesture at electioneering in *Shamela*.

The only other anti-ministerial satire in *Shamela* is in the prefatory material—where the barbs are sharpest. The parody of Cibber's *Apology* (stressed in the title and the name of the author, "Conny Keyber," a neat blend of Colley Cibber and Conyers Middleton, another target) may have inherent political overtones, though I am not enthusiastic about automatically assuming political intent in satire on Cibber. There are also two definite anti-ministerial items. Conny Keyber's dedication "To Miss Fanny" parodies Conyers Middleton's fulsome dedication of his *History of the Life of Marcus Tullius Cicero*, to "John, Lord Hervey, Lord Keeper of His Majesty's Privy Seal," a close political associate of Walpole. In line with the earlier attacks on Hervey by Pope (who calls him "Miss Fanny" in *The First Satire of the Second Book of Horace Imitated*, I, 6) and the characterization of Beau Didapper in *Joseph Andrews*,[27] the Keyber dedication touches on Hervey's partisanship (he errs in dancing by "leaning too much to one side"), but stresses his sexual inversion. Keyber implies that his visits at the dawn levees of Miss Fanny involve sexual as well as intellectual contact: ". . . I have constantly found you reading in good Books, and if ever I have drawn you upon me, I have always felt you very heavy." However, the most unequivocal and sharp political jab in *Shamela* is at Walpole himself in the letter from "John Puff" to the editor. It recommends a new biographical project for Keyber and, in the process, lewdly implies that Walpole and Mr. Williams are much alike, except that the minister lacks the robust genitalia of the parson. The author of *Shamela* "is able to draw every thing to Perfection but Virtue and I would recommend to him, in his next Performance, to undertake the Life of *His Honour*. For he who drew the Character of Parson Williams, is equal to the Task; nay, he seems to have little more to do than to pull off the Parson's Gown, and *that* which makes him so agreeable to *Shamela*, and the Cap will fit."

In 1741 political conflict intensified in stages that would be reflected in *The Opposition: A Vision* of December 1741. In February 1741 the famous motion calling upon George II to dismiss "Sir Robert Walpole from . . . his Presence and Counsels forever" was debated in Lords and Commons, supported by Carteret in a speech that "would not have disgraced Cicero" and by Argyll and Lord Bathurst in speeches fit for "the Roman senate before the ruin of that republic."[28] It was defeated by a large margin in Commons (290 to 106) because many Country members refused to support an attack on an individual and an unconstitutional encroachment on the King's right to choose his servants: 32 abstained and 22 voted with the ministry. Moreover, most of the dependants of the Prince of Wales (naturally unwilling to undermine royal prerogative) withdrew before the vote, though George Lyttelton, William Pitt, and the Grenvilles, the Cobhamite element in the Prince's orbit, helped force the doomed motion to a division.[29] This laid bare the radical disunion of the polyglot opposition, and deserved such rich mockery as the satiric prints known as "The Funeral of Faction," "The Acquittal," and "The Motion,"[30] the last of which foreshadows

Fielding's description in *The Opposition: A Vision* of the divided state of the opposition in early 1741.

More important was the election that followed. On April 25 Parliament rose, writs for new elections being called for by June 25. By mid-year it was clear that the exertions of the opposition and dissatisfaction with the war effort (though news of the Cartagena disaster arrived too late to affect the results) had resulted in a dangerous reduction of Walpole's Commons majority. John B. Owen[31] calculated that it had fallen as low as 18, and this was especially bad because a majority was liable to erosion when the House anticipated a ministerial failure. Majorities were "built" after and between (as much as chosen at) elections. Walpole was in peril unless his enemies quarrelled or a compromise could be negotiated with some element in the opposition before the fight over contested elections in the new Commons showed (and determined) that he was not in control. The way in which the election tide was turned (much of the difference between 1734 and 1741 being the opposition's strong performance in Cornwall and Scotland, thanks to the Prince of Wales and Argyll) and the opposition's post-electoral situation (much increased strength likely to be diluted by internecine intrigue) are essential backgrounds to *The Opposition: A Vision*.

After the election Fielding and his Broad-Bottom friends felt great hope. However, it was soon poisoned by dread of betrayal and then converted into despair and hate as William Pulteney and Lord Carteret moved toward the deal with the Walpole forces that in 1742 would leave the Broad-Bottoms in opposition. Until mid-1741 there was the worry, implicit in *The Champion*'s pleas to the electors, that Walpole would win a majority good for another seven years. The motion fiasco of February was also a reminder that the independent Country members were likely to be uncooperative in a crisis, though they were not hypocrites. After the election, euphoria was soon tempered by the fear that enough of his opponents would sell out to keep Walpole in power. This is reflected in Ralph's message "To the New Members" of Commons, prefaced to the June 1741 reprint of the early *Champion*. Ralph warns those who come in with "clean Hands" of Walpole's corruptive methods, then begs them not to waste this opportunity to revive Parliament, save the Constitution, and "for ever remove that grand Anti-Constitutional First Mover, a Prime M_____r." "Now is the Time," he warns, *"The Only Time."*

The key problem was that the election results were not decisive. They were just close enough to force Walpole to think of buying off a few enemies with places and a share of power, with a reasonable chance of succeeding. Chesterfield wryly assessed the effect of the election in a letter to Lyttelton (August 1, 1741): "It will raise the price of some individuals and he [Walpole] will be obliged to come up to it, and there's an end of the opposition."[32] Even if Walpole fell, would a wholly new ministry, bent on reform and including all of the best men in the present opposition (that is, oneself and one's friends), take over? A reform of Walpole's system, not just the replacement of Walpole with another prime minister at the head of a new faction, was the goal toward which the Broad-Bottoms claimed to be working. Or would a few turncoats take office, together with the remnant of Walpole's supporters (leaving the rest of the opposition and the idea of reform behind), and pursue the same policies in the same old way? Dodington was voicing his own fears, as well as attempting to allay the suspicions of the Country members, when he argued that the Country Tories must know that they were not "scaffolding" for "the 'Patriots' to climb to power, but brothers in pretension."[33] In fact, Walpole did not survive, but neither did the Country element and the Broad-Bottoms derive any benefits from his fall. With the Prince of Wales's blessing, Lord Carteret and William Pulteney joined with Henry Pelham and the Duke of Newcastle, Walpole's chief lieutenants, and a new coalition ministry nominally headed by Wilmington was formed. Walpole was allowed to retire as Lord Orford to the upper house, unimpeached, despite the determination of those elements of the opposition left out of the reconstructed ministry to punish him for his supposed crimes in office. However, from the election to early 1742, the nightmare of Walpole's continuance at the head of a ministry with a very slightly "broader bottom" (including, say, Carteret and Pulteney) disturbed Lyttelton, Chesterfield, Bolingbroke, Argyll, and Dodington, as well as the Country members and, of course, Fielding. It is precisely this nightmare around which Fielding built in December 1741 his satiric prophecy of the immediate future, *The Opposition: A Vision*, which has often been misconstrued because of unsophisticated assumptions about its political background.

The Opposition: A Vision was long near ignored because its satire on the opposition was troubling within the clear, bi-partisan "Whig myth." Wilbur Cross's avoidance of the issues typifies this. Cross noted that Fielding voluntarily acknowledged it in the "Preface" to the *Miscellanies*, though it might otherwise not have been attributed to him, a point that ought to be pondered by those who see it as a symptom of a sell-out to Walpole. But Cross really did not know how to fit it into his sense of party divisions in 1741. Though it would seem to imply "he had changed his politics," he observes, " 'The Opposition' was a good-natured rebuke of the leaders of his party like what had occurred in briefer form in 'Pasquin.' "[34] The *Pasquin* reference is a gesture in the right direction, however ludicrous the description of this bitter vision as "good-natured" may be, but neither *Pasquin* nor *The Opposition: A Vision* are explicable by anyone who believes Fielding ever belonged to a "party" called "the opposition."

More recently, the inadequacy of Cross's obfuscation has been recognized by Martin Battestin and Bertrand Goldgar, who believe that Fielding did indeed "change his politics" (or "change parties") in 1741 out of disgruntlement with the opposition—still seen as a party—and in return for money from Walpole.[35] This view is only slightly more adequate than Cross's, to which it is closer than it may seem. They share a bi-partisan view of contemporary politics. The essential difference is that

Cross is eager to acquit Fielding of abandoning the opposition party for the ministerial one, while Battestin is ready to convict him of it, with a plea of mitigating financial circumstances, on his way to a "change of parties" reading of *Joseph Andrews*. What *The Opposition: A Vision* needs is a close allegorical reading (not a glance on the way to more satisfying works) against the background of the intrigues, divisions, and distrusts within the opposition in 1741-42.[36] For the sake of clarity, we must examine separately Fielding's depiction of the divided and hypocrite-cursed opposition, his surprisingly favourable treatment of Walpole, and his supposed implication that he wrote it because he had taken money from Walpole.

Fielding's *Vision* begins by satirizing the state of the opposition in the period *preceding* the election of 1741. Stimulated by reading an absurd sentence ("Here I met the revolution.") in Colley Cibber's *Apology*, Fielding's persona dreams he meets the opposition, a "heavy-laden" wagon drawn by "asses . . . of different colours and sizes, and so extremely ill matched, to which the shagged coats of many did not a little contribute." The asses are, of course, the opposition's backbench voters (the shaggy ones being Country squires) in all the strange bedfellowship of the Commons minority. Though cheered by a mob, the wagon stands "quite still" because the several drivers (the opposition's competing leaders) do not know where they are trying to go. One passenger is "extremely cold, and begun [sic] to despair of ever moving again." He has no clearer idea of a destination than the drivers. Thus drawn and driven, heavily laden with a "vast trunk . . . inscribed . . . grievances" and a "huge box" marked "public spirit," as well as an unmarked trunk containing motions for the year 1741-42, this wagon perfectly symbolizes the amorphous, ineffectual pre-election opposition. The satiric print called "The Motion"[37] of March 1741 stresses its motleyness by depicting it as riding in a coach and four driven wildly by Carteret to destruction, while the Broad-Bottoms, the Country leaders, and Pulteney (who lags behind, leading opposition followers by the nose) are dismayed. Looking back in December, Fielding recognized gloomily the same truth that the ministerial artist had found so heartening.

The wagon's passengers—"scarce two of them looked the same way"—are ill-assorted. The asses (here representing the opposition's insufficient support in Commons) are not up to moving it. However, the head driver (Pulteney, one presumes) promises his restive backseat drivers that he awaits a "fresh supply of asses" (added votes after the election), with which he will "drive through thick and thin; for he was obliged to pass such abominable bad ways, that it would require immense strength to drive them through." Here Pulteney is made to state attitudes he had been suspected of concealing beneath patriotic rhetoric since the 1730s by a writer whose patrons rightly felt Pulteney was ready to betray them during the parliamentary session of 1741-42. As the picture of the ill-led, understrength pre-election opposition develops, one "honest gentleman" (presumably representing the leaders of the Coun-

try members—specifically William Shippen?—who could not stomach
the motion of February) gets off the wagon, declaring that he will not go
farther through such dirt, being so bespattered with the last motion "I
almost despaired of ever making myself clean again." Others fight for
his seat, protesting that they have been aboard longer than those who
joined at "Turnem Green" but who now sit before them, and that they
did not leave safe places (riding "behind a coach" for "wages") to sit
"in the tail of a wagon." Others call for new drivers more gentle with the
"asses" and more familiar with "the English roads" (more respectful of
Country prejudices). One wishes to reform the team so that the asses will
be of the same quality and kind, another wants to stop for a snack (accept some minor patronage), while others urge him to wait for the "dain-
ties" at the top of the hill they are climbing. One vows to go home if the
wagon does not move soon, while others cry out against desertion. The
"secession" of some passengers almost triggers a general exodus of those
near the rear, stopped by ineffectual whipping of the asses and halloaing,
led by a passenger near the front who assures the defectors that if they do
"not desert their friends" only a "few pulls more . . . will carry us to the
top of the hill."

This opposition is not a "party" in any meaningful sense. With the
"wagon . . . stuck, nor could the long-eared beasts move it an inch," one
cynical passenger urges that the huge trunk of grievances be jettisoned,
while others protest that it includes all the provisions for them and their
asses, affords seats (debating points) to most of the passengers, and occasions all the "huzzas which the mob gave them as they passed, or
rather whilst they stood still." The cynic says that there are better provisions on top of the hill, that they never meant to fatten their asses on arrival, and that the vulgar would cheer as hard if they were merely *told* the
trunk was there. Then they open the trunk, which contains a few
newspapers (the *Champion* and *Common Sense*, airers of *real*
grievances) and a few parcels with "something in them" at the bottom.
These, however, are not intended to be removed at journey's end and do
not really belong to Walpole, though they are addressed to him. This
stresses the intention of the opposition hypocrites to betray the principles
(a reform of "Measures," not just a change of "Men" or the destruction
of Walpole) and the hopes of the Country and Broad-Bottom oppositions. Pulteney and Carteret, with their goal of "conventional accommodation," Fielding recognized as the enemy within. Soon it is suggested
that the real drag may be the "immense box" marked "public spirit,"
the high-flown principles of "Patriotic" opposition. It is, but only
because it contains far heavier stuff: "ambition, malice, envy, avarice,
disaffection, disappointment, pride, revenge, and many other heavy
commodities." Bolingbroke could not have better mocked the hypocrite
exploitation of Patriot ideology.

The sly fellow who opened the trunk of grievances says the asses
ought to be able to pull lead, as well as true silver, if they are fed.
However, the asses (and here—*and only here*—Fielding, Ralph, and, by

extension, other opposition writers are included with the backbench voters in the team of asses) are starved and weak. There is one more attempt to drive them, but "though the drivers themselves put their shoulders to the wheels, the wagon could not be stirred." The failure brings despair, symbolizing that felt by many who feared Walpole would win the election of 1741. As he makes haste "over to the other side of the way," one passenger cries, ". . . by G____ you are stuck for seven years longer." Then, there is a reversal of fortune, symbolizing the crucial opposition gains in Scotland and Cornwall: "Lo! a sudden supply of asses appeared at the same time, one herd of which, I was informed, were of the Cornish breed, the other, by the particular tone of their bray, I soon discovered to come from far North."

Here the real, topical heart of *The Opposition: A Vision* is first approached: a vision of the withering of the strengthened post-election opposition by jealousy, greed, and ambition. The hypocrites show their natures the moment victory is in sight (as Bolingbroke, Lyttelton, and Chesterfield had warned one another they would since the 1730s) and, after the briefest pause to confront his enemies, Walpole returns triumphantly to the Treasure. With its augmented team the wagon begins "to move heavily through the dirt," drivers shouting, passengers halloaing, mob cheering, and asses braying, but after a few paces "the drivers offered to turn aside out of the great country road" (abandon Country principles). Those in the middle and tail of the wagon—the Country element and perhaps the Broad-Bottoms—try to get out but are abused and stopped, while the asses who flinch are whipped up so hard that the wagon leaves the dreamer and "great numbers of its followers" behind. We are finally at "time present," the period at the end of 1741 in which Fielding angrily wrote *The Opposition: A Vision*. Small wonder that the mob begins to mutter, and that Fielding, like his Broad-Bottom patrons, treats Walpole as superior to the opposition's drivers (the "riper Patriots") when the minister (the "fat gentleman") blocks their road to St. James's. At their threats, the "fat gentleman" only smiles, and one passenger in the wagon denounces the personal malice (rather than reforming zeal) and hypocrisy of the driver (Pulteney, presumably):

> Oh thou perfidious driver! dost not thou profess thyself a driver of the country wagon? Are not those words written in large characters upon it? Have not the passengers taken their places for the country? What will their friends who sent them, and bore the expenses of the journey, say, when they hear they are come upon their account and neglect the business of those who sent them? Will it be a sufficient excuse that thou hast misled them? And hast thou no more humanity, than to endeavour to trample on an honest gentleman, only because his coach stands in your way? As to asses, it's of little consequence where they are driven, provided they are not used to such purposes, as the honesty of even an ass would start at.

Those in the front seats laugh, and a dozen passengers ask to be dropped at the Admiralty, as many at the Treasury, the Exchequer, and similar destinations. But the "fat gentleman" asks whether their asses (forces in Commons) are likely to "stand against his high spirited horses" (the "Walpole corps"). When the drivers urge dragging the "gentleman" from his coach, because he stands "in their way," the result is an imagined, more decisive repetition of the motion fiasco of 1741: "the question is not only carried in the negative but many of them leap out of the wagon and swear they will travel no longer in such company." The opposition dissolves, and the "gentleman" is magnanimous in victory. In a passage some see as Fielding's acknowledgement of a bribe (but which actually seems to predict a general acceptance of Walpole's bounty by former opposition voters if he survives because of the disintegration of the opposition), he unharnesses the asses, turning them "into a delicious meadow, where they all instantly fell to grazing, with a greediness common to beasts after a long abstinence." Walpole's victory is completed as Pulteney and Carteret become powerless ministerial camp-followers, an ironical *dénouement* that might have been more sweet than bitter to Chesterfield or Lyttelton at the close of 1741: ". . . several of those who had been concerned in driving the wagon, whipped up behind the coach, where I was informed they had formerly rode many years, but had been turned away for demanding more wages than their services were worth." Though he was wrong in his prediction that Walpole would survive, Fielding was probably right in predicting that the shaky opposition coalition would not have been capable of surviving a ministerial victory won in the very jaws of defeat. As Chesterfield said, that would have put "an end to the opposition."

Fielding's satire on the opposition is not a sign of a "change of parties." Indeed, it can be viewed as an extreme expression in public of fears and suspicions about the near future that Lyttelton and the Broad-Bottoms confided to one another in private in the latter half of 1741. But what of the surprising vein of praise for Walpole in the later pages of the tract and the supposed hint that Walpole has paid Fielding better than the opposition? The statement that the few real grievances at the bottom of the trunk so marked do "not honestly belong" to Walpole is more a criticism of the non-reforming intent of his would-be successors than an exoneration of the minister. (The discovery of opposition journals, including *The Champion*, in the trunk implies that some of the "grievances" of 1739-41 were real). But the "fat gentleman" is also said to have "one of the pleasantest, best-natured countenances I had ever beheld," and the speaker who rebukes his attackers describes him as "an honest gentleman, only [threatened] because his coach stands in your way." This cannot be passed off as a sarcastic attack on Walpole. It sounds like it might have come from *The Daily Gazetteer*, and helps explain why that journal carried advertisements for *The Opposition: A Vision* (a fact Battestin and Goldgar have not noticed) four times between December 14 and 21, 1741. The magnanimity of the "gentleman" in feeding the asses is not, of course, unambiguous. He is "feeding"—buying off—the former opposition rank-and-file. Still, Fielding makes it clear he will not blame asses for "grazing" if Walpole wins, and before the vision ends Walpole is actually shown following the "country road" once the opposition is no more:

> . . . the coach having gained that place whence the waggon had devi-
> ated, struck directly into that very road whither the other had pre-
> tended it was going, at which the mob set up a universal shout, and
> swore they would burn the waggon and its furniture, for having so
> long obstructed the gentleman in his journey.

Describing Walpole as good-natured and generous is a striking reversal after the attacks in *The Champion* and even *Shamela*. But this more positive view of Walpole is probably closer to what Fielding really believed. From the 1720s to the 1750s he as often complimented him as insulted him, sometimes (in the unpublished mock-epic poem of 1729, the dedication of *The Modern Husband* and *The Journal of a Voyage to Lisbon*) in much the same way. When lambasting the minister (in *The Grub-Street Opera*, say, or *Pasquin*) he often treated him as more able and less contemptible than the hypocrites among his opponents. Fielding had it both ways with the great minister for years, professional author-ship and loyalty to patrons being exacting disciplines. But he probably always respected him more than William Pulteney.

Odd as it may sound, Fielding was not necessarily far from the posi-tion of his patrons when he compared Walpole so favourably to the men in the front of the opposition wagon and predicted his triumph over them. Indeed he may have been reflecting the precise point they had reached in their desperate assessment of the best horses to back in the ministerial crises of 1741-42. We have seen in Chapter One that Pulteney and Carteret became the successful rivals of the Broad-Bottoms during the ministerial reconstruction of early 1742 and remained their worst enemies through the later 1740s. Walpole, as Lord Orford, used his in-fluence in 1743 and 1744 to forward the intrigues that led to the ejection of Carteret from the ministerial coalition and the inclusion of the Broad-Bottoms as junior partners in the Broad-Bottom ministry. Horace Walpole was amused in January 1742, when his father was teetering on the brink of danger, at the greater hatred his would-be heirs felt for one another than for Sir Robert. "Lord Hervey, Lord Chesterfield and William Pulteney virtually live together," he wrote Horace Mann, but "hate one another more than any one they would proscribe had they the power."[38] More material is an item of gossip retailed years later in Richard Glover's *Memoirs*, suspect to some because Glover was a depen-dant of Carteret. It indicates that at the end of 1741, at about the time *The Opposition: A Vision* appeared, George Lyttelton was negotiating with Walpole, presumably on behalf of his faction, to guarantee the minister's safe retreat from politics after his resignation in return for places in the new political order.[39] This manoeuvre was soon abandoned, if, in fact, it ever was attempted. The Broad-Bottoms were left among those who remained in opposition and called for Walpole's impeachment in 1742. Their attempts to punish the fallen minister were balked by the refusal to pursue him of those, chiefly Pulteney and Carteret, who more successfully traded co-operation for places and honours. But if in December 1741 Fielding believed Walpole would survive and felt the urge to move toward him and away from Pulteney and Carteret, Glover's gossip indicates he may have been taking a line parallel to his patrons'. Thus, the compliments to Walpole may not only be part of a hyperbolic denunciation of the greater evil of the Pulteney-Carteret group (obviously the prime target of *The Opposition: A Vision*), but also a reflection of an obscure attempt at *rapprochement* between his patrons and Walpole that only bore fruit in 1743-44. The waters were murky indeed in 1741-42; by the mid-1740s Lyttelton would be very close to Henry Pelham, Walpole's *protégé*, and Fielding closer to Lyttelton than in 1740.

In the dynamic, broader context, sketched in Chapter One, of the Broad-Bottoms considering (winter of 1741-42), then attempting (1743), and finally consummating (1744) a coalition with the "Walpole corps" and the Pelhams, it may be possible to explain even the closing picture of Walpole entering upon the "great country road." This is the most extravagant and puzzling touch in *The Opposition: A Vision:* a description of a Walpole ministry without an opposition, supported or followed by most former opponents and pursuing an idealistic, "Country" program. However, aside from its leadership by Walpole, rather than his *protégés*, the Pelhams, it looks *very* like the Broad-Bottom coalition formed in 1744 with Fielding's friends as junior members and Fielding as potential (and after the fall of 1745, active) apologist. In short, this passage may be another of Fielding's erroneous predictions of what would happen in the 1742 session of the new Parliament. *The Opposition: A Vision* makes it obvious he thought Walpole would survive in office. He hoped he would do so by closing with the Broad-Bottoms and such associates as Argyll and Chesterfield, and by embracing elements of the "Country" or "Patriot" programs. As we will see in Chapter Five, even when the Pelhams were rebuilding their ministerial majority in early 1742, a variation on this arrangement (excluding Walpole, of course) was not totally unthinkable. George II later said that he considered the Broad-Bottoms as ministerial recruits before turning to Pulteney and Carteret.[40] It was that close, and less than two years later the Pelhams were reconsidering the bargain. If Fielding was wrong in December 1741 (two months before the new ministerial arrangements were made) he may have miscalculated little more than his patrons.

Finally, there is the problem of whether Fielding was paid by Walpole for writing *The Opposition: A Vision*, whether it acknowledges prior generosity. I think he was not. Its sentiments pleased *The Daily Gazetteer*. It may have moved Walpole to subscribe generously—ten copies—to Fielding's *Miscellanies* in 1743, though Walpole was a free spender in such circumstances, politics notwithstanding, and was relatively well-disposed to Fielding's patrons in the new opposition in 1743.[41] However, there are positive external indicators that Fielding was not considered a turncoat by his friends. As noted earlier, the simple fact that he remained close to Lyttelton and his group is one very strong one, and the Fielding "puff" in *The Champion* for June 29, 1742 (six months after his *Vision*), is another. On the negative side, William Coley is right to see significance in the fact that Horace Walpole, always quick to belittle Fielding, whom he obviously disliked, never mentioned that he sold out.[42] We should ponder this in the light of Horace's gleefully malicious reflections on the bargain struck by Fielding's Broad-Bottom patrons when they joined the Pelhams in 1744, even though his father favoured the coalition.

But we need not go so far afield, sifting indirect, external evidence. Read precisely, *The Opposition: A Vision* does not really imply that Fielding was rewarded by Walpole. It is chiefly a vision of the future, which means that even if we are to assume that Fielding is one of the asses released to graze in the "rich meadow" by the triumphant Walpole, this expresses a hope or a desire for patronage, not an acknowledgement of same. And the assumption that Fielding includes himself among the grazing asses may be based on a blurry reading of the allegory. The ill-kempt, ill-fed asses primarily represent the mass of the opposition's voters (Country gentlemen and others) in Parliament. This is obvious upon the first appearance of the wagon, as we have seen, and un-mistakable when the struggling asses are reinforced by the "fresh" (new-ly elected) asses from Cornwall and Scotland. The *only* time the basic equation of ass and minority voter broadens to include opposition writers is in a brief passage complaining about the ill-feeding (poor pay-ment) of Fielding and Ralph. This passage is slipped in just before the ar-rival of the Cornish and Scottish asses reinforces the basic Parliamentary equation:

> . . . they appear to me to be the worst fed asses I ever beheld; why there is that long-sided ass they call Vinegar, which the drivers call upon so often to gee up, and pull lustily, I never saw an ass with a worse mane, or a more shagged coat; and that grave ass yoked to him, which they name Ralph, who pulls and brays like the devil, sir, he does not seem to have ate since the hard frost. Surely, considering the wretched work they are employed in, they deserve better meat.

This perfectly captures the situation I have suggested in discussing *The Champion* in the first half of 1741, Ralph doing most of the writing without adequate rewards since the winter (the "hard frost"), and Fielding unwilling to become deeply involved again in essay writing. But there is little warrant for assuming that it means we must broaden the significance of the ass:voter equation elsewhere to include Fielding, or, specifically, that it obliges us to see him as one of the asses released into the "delicious meadow" of patronage by Walpole at the end of the *Vi-sion*. Much has been, and could be, said that would emphasize the wrongness of these assumptions, but one conclusive argument against them is that their acceptance would involve believing that James Ralph, Vinegar's starving "Yoke"-mate, also had taken money from Walpole by December 1741. No one familiar with Ralph's surviving *Champion* essays from 1741 to 1742 will easily forbear laughing at so preposterous a notion. This passage surely expressed Fielding's dissatisfaction at the inadequate financial rewards he and Ralph received for all their work on *The Champion*, but it does not indicate that *The Opposition: A Vision* was paid Walpole hack-work. Fielding did not "sell out," any more than "change parties," in 1741 or at any time between the formation of the Broad-Bottom faction in 1735 and the end of his career.

Chapter Five

Fielding and the "New" Opposition: 1742-44

We have seen that Fielding's last publication during Walpole's time in power, *The Opposition: A Vision*, reflected his expectation that Walpole would exploit divisions in the opposition and not only remain in office, but eliminate serious opposition. He had been proven wrong by February 22, 1742, the day *Joseph Andrews* was first published. However, his conviction that the opposition would be broken by intemperate ambition had been validated in a way that would influence his political writing through the mid-1740s. Opposition hypocrites had betrayed both their allies and the reform principles of Patriot and Country opposition, making themselves more hated than Walpole himself had been:

> Oh my poor Country, is this all
> You've gained by the long laboured Fall of Walpole and his Tools?
>   He was a Knave indeed—what then,
>   He'd Parts—but this new Set of Men,
>   Ain't only Knaves but Fools.[1]

English political life remained unreformed, Walpole went unpunished for his supposed crimes in office, and Fielding's patrons won none of the political spoils they had expected at his fall. Fielding's disappointment doubtless reinforced his apparent decision in 1741 to devote less energy to political propagandizing. It also left him even more contemptuous than he had been in the 1730s of hypocritical "Patriotism," though never "true Patriotism," which he continued to attribute to his Broad-Bottom patrons through the 1740s, in opposition and in place. Scorn for the revealed falsity of opposition turncoats became a dominant element in his work, as it did in the pronouncements of other voices of the "new" opposition that fought on after Walpole fell and the ministry was reconstructed.

Much that Fielding published in 1742 and 1743 testifies both to his transfer of enmity from Walpole to his successors, particularly William Pulteney (who became Lord Bath) and Lord Carteret, and to a partial withdrawal from involvement in political writing. This in no way reflects a "change of party,"[2] for his disappointed opposition patrons, Lyttelton, Chesterfield, Pitt, Bedford, and the other Broad-Bottoms, shifted aim in precisely the same way at precisely the same time, and in 1745-46 Fielding would vigorously serve the same patrons, now ministerialists. For a while the bitter close to the noble opposition to "Robinocracy" lessened the hopes that had stimulated his political satire since 1736, but the author of *Joseph Andrews* was a Broad-Bottom still, reacting, when he touched on politics, as a Broad-Bottom must.

It is unclear, as has been noted, whether in December 1741 George Lyttelton tried to obtain places for his faction at the price of protecting Walpole from impeachment *if and when he resigned*, an intrigue that must (assuming it occurred) have been blessed by the Prince of Wales, Lyttelton's patron. But around mid-January 1742, the Prince of Wales firmly rejected an offer of places for his dependants and a reconciliation at court with his father in return for supporting Walpole *in office*. The Earl of Egmont's diary for January 17 records that the King let it be known that if they came over to the court, the Prince's "Servants" would all be "well received and even preferred, even Mr. Lyttelton." Accepting Lyttelton and William Pitt, whom he detested, would have been unpleasant for the King, but the Leicester House group represented twenty-one votes in a Commons virtually deadlocked as a result of the close election of 1741.[3] They would have saved Walpole for the moment and assured a further increase in his majority as he won divisions on contested elections, and as those who had wavered when he was in danger returned to their duty. But the Prince could not so dishonour himself and his followers. Probably no leader of the old opposition could at this juncture have supported a ministry headed by Walpole, however ready he might be to abandon opposition principles and alliances in joining a ministry without the great minister, but based upon a partnership with his surviving lieutenants. There were degrees of dishonour, and the King found in January 1742 that Walpole must try to survive with present strength. No recruits were available: the opposition was poisoned by suspicion, but would not disintegrate until it brought Walpole down. Then all would scramble for berths in the new ministry.

Though some might pretend otherwise, all knew a thorough ministerial revolution was unlikely, Walpole or no Walpole. The "Walpole Whigs" (or "old Corps"), still led by Henry Pelham and the Duke of Newcastle, were roughly deadlocked with the less cohesive opposition coalition in Commons, and controlled the Lords. There would be no grand alteration in the policies of the new government, regardless of its precise membership. There would be no return to annual or triennial Parliaments, no exclusion of placemen and pensioners from Commons, no abandonment of land warfare on the continent in favour of naval warfare. King George would neither lose interest in Hanover nor become a Bolingbrokean Patriot King, ruling without the intermediary of a faction. The Country wing of the opposition was also sure to be little represented in the new arrangements, and to be left in opposition by whatever opposition leaders finally allied themselves with the Pelhams in office.

In effect, the real battle would be for office, and would pit those Walpole called the "riper Patriots" (William Pulteney, Lord Carteret, and their few personal followers) against the reasonably tight group formed by the Broad-Bottoms, Cobham, Chesterfield, Lyttelton, Pitt, the Grenvilles, and the Duke of Bedford, together with the Duke of Argyll and George Dodington, and their much more numerous following. The final decision of the Prince of Wales about which opposition group (that is, in effect, the kind of coalition ministry) to back would be of great importance and the King's decision would be decisive. Though heavily outnumbered, the "riper Patriots" commanded enough votes to eke out the Pelhams' majority (which would grow when it looked viable), and enjoyed great advantages after Walpole fell. Lyttelton probably was not very surprised in February that the "riper Patriots" succeeded in the fevered, cynical negotiations that followed Walpole's resignation, leaving the Broad-Bottoms and Fielding without reward or the slightest satisfaction in return for years of opposition striving.

Walpole was finally beaten in Commons on January 28 on a contested election. He absorbed one more contested election defeat, then resigned on February 2, ending an extraordinary era in which he had dominated and shaped English political life. The Prince of Wales agreed not to support attempts to impeach him. This must be regarded (though it was common sense for a man who expected to rule England) as the first step in the Prince's abandonment of the reforming element in the opposition and acquiescence in the realistic compromise favoured by Pulteney and Carteret. Since the King was determined to protect his minister, no one would achieve office without a similar capitulation, though the opposition journals might roar for Walpole's blood. The Broad-Bottoms would have left Walpole alone at the right price, but it would have been high, for their insistence over many years on a thorough clear-up of English politics made them less able than Pulteney or the Prince to drop the issue of Walpole's impeachment. This made them less attractive ministry-rebuilding material, but there was little they could do to change that.

In forming the new ministry, the King played the key role. Free within reason to choose ministers, he preferred Pulteney and Carteret over their competitors. They had always privately advocated a "conventional accommodation" with the Walpole forces once Walpole was brought down, though they indulged in reformist rhetoric in public, espousing elements of the "Country Party Programme" and the Patriot,

Broad-Bottom ideas of Bolingbroke. The Broad-Bottoms were also less sincerely dedicated than they pretended to reform, to radically altering the personnel and factious practices of the ministry and the nation's policies at home and abroad, and to imposing a higher political morality. But the Broad-Bottoms were more aggressive in pressing for change, not only in the composition of the ministry, but also in its maxims and behaviour, even in the jealously guarded royal preserves of patronage distribution and foreign affairs. They took a sterner line, partly because they thought it right, partly because they had talked their way into a position where it would be embarrassing to do otherwise, and partly because they controlled a considerable body of votes in both Houses, many more than the "riper Patriots," and felt strong enough to be rash. This could only repel both the King and the Pelhams, the heads of a vested interest. The old ministerial "Corps" remained mainly intact, aside from Walpole's departure. Pulteney and Carteret were more in tune with the times: "There is no instance [with the possible exception of Pitt's first ministry] concerning ministerial arrangements . . . between 1733 and 1763 where principles held by those lately in opposition were not either completely disregarded or severely compromised."[4]

A closely related factor was the price the King and the Pelhams would have to pay for the loyalty of the rival groups. The "lone wolf" orientation of Pulteney and Carteret meant they could deliver fewer votes, but only relatively few would be needed unless the compromise eroded the almost sufficient strength of the Pelhams. On the positive side, the recruitment of a faction ready to abandon opposition allies without regret involved much less redistribution of patronage and places. The price was moderate indeed. A Secretaryship of State went to Carteret, a post that he would in the short run parlay into great power. He would become something like an old-fashioned royal favourite and a dangerous rival of the Pelhams, as he and George II indulged their fascination with continental diplomacy and military strategy. Pulteney (perhaps partly in embarrassment at turning his coat after twenty years of calling for reform) settled for the politically emasculating glory of a peerage, becoming Lord Bath. He gave up office and his power base in Commons. When the leader of a faction changed sides without obtaining even a secondary cabinet post, he had cut his price astonishingly. Robert Walpole, now Lord Orford, is said to have observed as they took their seats in Lords for the first time: "Here we are, my Lord, the two most insignificant fellows in England."[5] In addition, only a few minor favours and posts were required for the dependants of Carteret and Pulteney.

The Broad-Bottom price would have been much higher. The Dukes of Argyll and Bedford, Lords Cobham and Chesterfield, Dodington and the Grenvilles, Lyttelton and Pitt were not apt to abandon one another as Pulteney abandoned them. They and their relatively numerous body of relatives and dependants would have required a mass of appropriate or at least respectable cabinet appointments, lesser places, honours, pensions, and sinecures. The King would have been forced to give up much, and the Pelhams (since a post in the cabinet or a government department for a recruit or a recruit's relative or friend necessarily meant taking one from an incumbent) much more. The Pelhams might even have found their grip on the Walpole "old Corps" loosened by resentment at the transfer of benefits to newcomers. The sheer number and level of patronage benefits required would probably have defeated the Broad-Bottoms even if other negative factors had not been operating. In 1744, when Fielding's patrons finally joined the ministry, as Carteret left office, they settled for such minor places that they were mocked for it.[6] But they were then older, wiser after the defeat of 1742, and less encumbered with senior colleagues.

Finally, the King liked Pulteney and Carteret better than their rivals, better than the Pelhams themselves. Between 1743 and the later 1740s the competition between Carteret, the King's favourite advisor, and the Pelhams would lead, in turn, to (1) embarrassment and ill feeling; (2) Carteret's dismissal in 1744 by an unwilling King; (3) an unseemly battle for the King's "confidence" between the fallen Secretary and the cabinet (1744-46); (4) the cabinet crisis and "forty-eight-hour ministry" of 1746. In 1742 George II was comfortable with Pulteney, an old-line, conventional politician (he had been a minister under George I), and delighted with Carteret, a fellow enthusiast in continental diplomacy. He hated Lyttelton, Pitt, and their friends as impudent upstarts, and resented the pride the great Duke of Argyll showed in negotiation. George II was exceedingly difficult to bully and determined to please himself in making appointments. Their rivals made Pulteney and Carteret look good, as George confided to Pulteney years later: "I saw that I had *two shops to deal with*, and I rather chose to come to you because I knew that your aim was only directed against my minister, but I did not know but the Duke of Argyll wanted to be king himself."[7]

Thus advantaged, after Walpole resigned Pulteney strove covertly with his opposition colleagues, who simultaneously attempted to overreach him and pressured him to insist loyally on places and patronage for them. He also competed for the support of the Prince of Wales for himself and Carteret in the inter-opposition contest. On February 13, eleven days into the post-Walpole era, Pulteney debated his enemies *en masse* before the Prince of Wales at the Fountain Tavern. He argued the case for a "narrow-bottomed" coalition ministry (the Pelhams, plus the "riper Patriots," excluding the rest of the old opposition) rather than a "broad-bottomed" one. And he urged the Prince to abandon the hopeless pretensions of his own Leicester House faction (including Pitt and Lyttelton), leave opposition, and return to court. On February 14 the Prince was reconciled with George II at St. James's Palace.[8] This was the end of all hope for the rivals of Pulteney and Carteret, the final precondition for a "conventional accommodation" between the latter and the Pelhams having been met the moment Frederick shifted his considerable weight.

The precise shape of the settlement had to be worked out, but its

general shape was clear. A few scraps were thrown to the defeated. Lord
Cobham won the belated reversal of his post-Excise loss of command,
becoming a Field Marshal and a cabinet councillor, as well as a Colonel
of the Grenadier Guards. Lord Gower got a token place, a sop to the
Country Tories, over whom he was naïvely supposed to exercise leadership. A cabinet post went to the Duke of Argyll, but he resigned as soon
as he saw it gave him no real power, but neutralized his capacity to oppose the ministry. For the rest of the opposition there was nothing. The
men Fielding had expected to do something handsome for him when
Walpole fell could do nothing for themselves.

The members of the old opposition not parties to the ministerial accommodation soon found they lacked the leverage and the heart even to
impeach Walpole. Their outmanoeuvred impotence in the months between the first and second edition (August 1742) of *Joseph Andrews* is
perfectly symbolized by the impeachment fiasco, last act in the cabinet
crisis of 1742. On March 9 a motion to form a secret committee of the
House of Commons to investigate "the conduct of public affairs" for
the past twenty years was narrowly defeated (242:240). A motion to investigate "the conduct of Robert, Earl of Orford" during the previous
ten years was passed by a small margin on March 23 (in the Lords,
significantly, one like it was heavily rejected, 109:57, the same day).
Walpole's Solicitor of the Treasury, Nicholas Paxton, refused to testify
before the committee on the grounds of possible self-incrimination and a
bill was introduced to grant immunity from prosecution to those testify-
ing. It passed the Commons, but was defeated in the Lords after a
brilliant debate. The committee found no grounds for impeachment during a single, 22-hour sitting, and dissolved. The committee was
dominated by men who had fought against Walpole (all but two earlier
had been considered opponents), but they lacked crucial testimony and
failed to scrape up the crimes and charges politicians usually can when
the circumstances are right.[9] Even among Walpole's bitterest opponents,
some doubtless realized that impeaching a fallen minister, seventeenth-
century style, was barbaric and constitutionally dangerous. This would
have been especially bad if it involved the use of immunity to force
witnesses to testify. Others saw their interest in letting Walpole (warmly
supported by George II) go unmolested into Lords. Still others were
either dispirited or less interested in revenge upon the powerless Walpole
than upon Pulteney and Carteret, now the chief targets of the "new" opposition (really the rump of the old one) and of writers like Fielding.

Joseph Andrews clearly reflects the impact on Fielding of the
extended drama of betrayal played out between the election of 1741 and
the summer of 1742. The sheer sparseness of political material (compared to its massive presence in his recent journalism) indicates his
withdrawal from an arena that had proven as unprofitable as it was
laborious. It is not a political work in any basic sense or in comparison

with works that chronologically flank it. However, the strokes of political satire woven into the two editions of 1742 reflect his increasingly bitter resentment as his friends were left out of office and Walpole escaped to the Lords. Finally there is one crucial item of panegyric that in itself invalidates the notion that Fielding's cynical appraisal of the hypocrisy of opposition "Patriots" was directed against those who *remained* in opposition in 1742 (a group that included all of the politicians to whom he had been closely, "personally" attached since the mid-1730s).[10] This is clear if one reads the eulogy of Lord Chesterfield in Book III, chapter ii (in all editions of *Joseph Andrews*) together with the satire on opposition hypocrisy in both 1742 editions, but particularly the second. Fielding moved from hope to angry disenchantment in drafting and revising *Joseph Andrews*, but moved parallel to his political patrons.

Much of the opposition satire in the novel could have been written in 1734 or 1737 or 1740. No one who knows Fielding's plays or *The Champion* will be surprised to learn that Joseph's "Father . . . had not Interest enough to get him into a Charity School, because a Cousin of his Father's Landlord did not vote on the right side for a Church-warden in a Borough Town" (I, iii), or that "There are certain Mysteries or Secrets in all Trades from the highest to the lowest, from that of *Prime Ministering* to this of *Authoring* . . . ." (II, i).[11] The same is true of Fielding's compliment to the electoral independence of Mr. Tow-wouse ("who notwithstanding his charity would have given his vote as freely as he ever did at an Election, that any other House in the Kingdom, should have had quiet possession of his Guest"—I, xiii) and one of the droll analogies to Trulliber's horror at learning that Adams has come to borrow, not buy: "Suppose a Minister should, instead of a good round Sum, treat my Lord _____ or Sir _____ or Esq; _____ with a good Broomstick" (II, xiv).

Only slightly more specific is the attack (II, xvii) on *The Daily Gazetteer* and the ministry (obviously Walpole's, though the same complaint would be made about its successor) for indifference to protecting English trade. The host of the ale-house who sets Adams straight about the "promising Squire" (whom I lack evidence to connect with Walpole, expert "promiser") recalls losing his ship to the Spanish in the period before the opposition forced Walpole to declare war on Spain: ". . . I was attacked by one of those cursed *Guarda-Costas*, who took our Ships before the beginning of the War." This momentarily fixes time present after 1739, but the satire that follows on *The Daily Gazetteer* (and, by implication, the ministry) for denigrating English trade reflects Fielding's views from the mid-1730s on. Adams observes that "Trade . . . as Aristotle proves in his first Chapter of Politics, is below a Philosopher, and unnatural as it is managed now." He later protests that he is "no Enemy to Trade, while it is consistent with Honesty," and that he values "the Tradesman" (proper attitudes for a Country-party clergyman), but his "philosophical" denigration of trade causes the host to ask "if he was one of the Writers of the *Gazetteers*'." The host goes on to describe *The Gazetteer* as "a dirty Newspaper . . . Which hath been given away all over the Nation for these many years to abuse Trade and honest Men, which I would not suffer to lie on my Table, tho' it hath been offered me for nothing." Nothing here distinguishes Fielding, the novelist, from "Pasquin" or the editor of *The Champion*. In the same vein is the allusion (IV, xii) to the decay of the woollen trade and resulting unemployment in Bristol and other manufacturing centres. Finally, there is the satire on the political corruption of the ridiculous Beau Didapper. This Martin Battestin has rightly treated as an attack on John, Lord Hervey, worded to parody the same fulsome dedication to him of Conyers Middleton's *Life of Cicero* mocked in *Shamela*.[12] Thus it recalls Fielding's political broadsides of the period before, rather than after, the election of 1741. It implies nothing about Hervey that Fielding might not have said (Conyers Middleton aside) years earlier: " 'Tho' he was born to an immense Fortune, he chose for the pitiful and dirty Consideration of a Place of little consequence, to depend entirely on the Will of a Fellow, whom they call a Great-Man; who treated him with the utmost Disrespect, and exacted of him a plenary Obedience to his Commands; which he implicitly submitted to, at the Expence of his Conscience, his Honour, and of his Country" (IV, ix).

More topical satire, related directly to Fielding's concerns after mid-1741, is rare in the first edition of *Joseph Andrews*. Indeed, there are only two passages that seem at all likely to fall in this category, and one of these may not actually belong in it. The doubtful item is the narrator's account (I, xvi) of the suspicions that Tom Suckbribe, the constable, was bribed to allow the thief who robbed Joseph to escape:

> It hath been said, that not being concerned in the taking the Thief, he could not have been entitled to any part of the Reward, if he had been convicted. That the Thief had several Guineas in his Pocket; that it was very unlikely he should have been guilty of such an Oversight [forgetting to guard the window]. That his Pretense for leaving the Room was absurd: that it was his constant Maxim, that a wise Man never refused Money on any Conditions: That at every Election, he always had sold his Vote to both Parties, &c.

This may reflect Fielding's expectation in the period preceding publication that Walpole might bribe his way through the crisis of 1741-42 or at least (as actually happened later in the year) that enough opponents might be bought to protect him from impeachment if he fell. But the passage may also indicate Fielding's more general fear of betrayal, revealed regularly from *Pasquin* onward, usually in combination with indignation about electoral corruption. In the first edition that leaves only its prime political set-piece, the account of Parson Adams' experience with the hypocritical Patriot squire in II, vii-ix. It centres around the "notable Dissertation by Mr. Abraham Adams; wherein that Gentleman appears in a political Light."

Almost as soon as they begin to talk, the squire turns a complaint about the slaughter of game by soldiers quartered in the neighbourhood into an attack on the inactivity and ineffectiveness of the army and the Cartagena fiasco of 1741, touched on in our earlier examination of *The Vernoniad*. " 'It is very probable,' cries Adams, 'for shooting is their Profession,' 'Aye, shooting the Game,' answered the other, 'but I don't see they are so forward to shoot our Enemies. I don't like that Affair of *Cartagena;* if I had been there, I believe I should have done other guess things; d--n me; what's a Man's Life when his Country demands it; a Man who won't sacrifice his Life for his Country deserves to be hanged, d--n me' " (II, vii). Adams applauds his patriotism while the reader scents hypocrisy. In chapter ix the squire brags that he "disinherited" as a coward "a Nephew who is in the Army, because he would not exchange his Commission, and go to the *West Indies*," and talks "much of Courage and his Country." When he hears Fanny's screams for help, however, he runs home, gun in hand, leaving Adams to fight her ravisher with his crabstick and his fists. This constitutes the most obvious thrust at the hypocrisy of some opposition patriots in the first edition. We must remember, of course, that Adams supports the Country Interest, approves of the squire's *principles*, and acquits himself bravely. This makes it clear that the incident is no general condemnation of the opposition (certainly not of the men Fielding had long abetted), any more than is the satire on corrupt Country electors and candidates in *Pasquin*.

Even closer to Fielding's concerns (and those of his friends) between the election of 1741 and the betrayal of 1742 is Adams' account, in the chapter preceding the squire's flight, of the ill-fortune he has had as a man able (he boasts with a comical sense of its importance) to influence the vote of an alderman, his nephew. Believing Mr. Fickle a sincere Country Patriot, Adams advised his nephew to vote for him rather than Colonel Courtly, the ministerial candidate, angering his rector and losing his curacy. Mr. Fickle left for London, forgetting the desires of his constituents. He became a ministerial placeman within two years, and at the next election urged Adams to support Colonel Courtly. Adams preferred to support Sir Oliver Hearty, a classic Country gentleman, but was soon dismayed by Sir Oliver's habit of hunting at home when he should have been in Commons voting with the Country minority (such truancy being, as P.D.G. Thomas has stressed,[13] a perennial opposition problem). At least Sir Oliver got the half-starved parson his curacy back and gave him, Adams says with a ridiculous air of having been well-treated, "eight pounds out of his own pocket to buy me a Gown and Cassock, and furnish my House." Then Sir Oliver died, and at the resulting (and latest) election Adams convinced his nephew to support Sir Thomas Booby, who has served more energetically in Parliament, but has never managed to find a living for Adams. Now his nephew is dead, and Adams cannot find a patron to procure ordination for his deserving, thirty-year-old son, even though "on all proper Seasons, such as the Approach of an Election, I throw a suitable Dash or two into my Sermons, which I have the pleasure to hear is not disagreeable to Sir Thomas, and other honest Gentlemen my Neighbours."

Such have been the rewards of labouring for the Country cause, and Fielding's own sense of having been ill rewarded in the post-*Champion*, post-election period when he completed *Joseph Andrews* is patent. But his resentment was not indiscriminately directed at the opposition, certainly not at the Broad-Bottoms or their allies. Fielding not only saw no illogic in including both Adams' political history and a eulogy of Lord Chesterfield (III, i) in the first (and every subsequent) edition, but was at pains to emphasize that Chesterfield had been a generous, affable patron to him:

> . . . I could name a Peer no less elevated by Nature than by Fortune, who whilst he wears the noblest Ensigns of Honour on his Person, bears the truest Stamp of Dignity on his Mind, adorned with Greatness, enriched with Knowledge, and embelished all with Genius. I have seen this Man relieve with generosity, while he hath conversed with Freedom, and be to the same Person a Patron and a Companion.

Chesterfield's political life is not stressed in a passage coupling him with the non-partisan philanthropist Ralph Allen, but he remained the intimate of Lyttelton and Bolingbroke, and would prove more energetic in the fight against Carteret in 1743-44 than he ever had been against Walpole. When Fielding wrote this and allowed it to stand in subsequent editions he signalled that he remained as loyal to his old opposition patrons as he was contemptuous of Pulteney and Carteret.

Fielding's most specific reactions in the novel to the betrayal of 1742 occur in two small but bitter touches added to the second edition of August 1742. In II, iv Fielding added a political barb to Lord Bellarmine's devotion to French tailoring, converting that untrustworthy fop for a moment into a symbol of Pulteney and Carteret (addition in my brackets):

> 'All *French*,' says he, 'I assure you, except the Great Coats; I never trust anything more than a Great Coat to an *Englishman;* you know one must encourage our own People one can, [especially as before I had a Place, I was in the Country Interest,] he, he, he! but for myself, I would see the dirty Island at the bottom of the Sea, rather than wear a single Rag of *English* work about me . . . !

Far more telling and obtrusive is a political post-script Fielding added to the chapters describing Adams' experience with the cowardly Patriot squire (II, vii-ix), giving the whole section a more specific slant. Having been saved from one she wrongly trusted, Fanny momentarily suspects Adams of designs on her honour even in the first edition. In the second edition, the passing notice of her fears in II, ix is augmented at the head of II, x, Fielding's sharpest attack in the novel on the betrayel of the old opposition and its principles:

> She began to fear as great an Enemy in her Deliverer, as he had delivered her from; and as she had not Light enough to discover the Age of Adams, and the Benevolence visible in his Countenance, she suspected he had used her as some very honest Men have used their

> Country; and had rescued her out of the Hands of one Rifler, in order
> to rifle her himself.

It was a commonplace in opposition propaganda, 1742-44, that Walpole
was certainly no worse than the erstwhile "Patriots" who replaced him.
Under the cloak of a desire to save the national honour, Carteret and
Pulteney had, as Bolingbroke predicted, merely prepared "one faction to
succeed another"[14] by the time the second edition of *Joseph Andrews*
went to press.

The rest of Fielding's publications in 1742 are politically in tune with
Joseph Andrews. The Duchess of Marlborough's *Account of Her Conduct from Her First Coming to Court till the Year 1710* ("digested" or
ghost-written by Nathaniel Hooke and published in early 1742) was attacked in several pamphlets as self-serving and mendacious. Fielding's
Full Vindication of the Dutchess Dowager of Marlborough (April 1742)
is an energetic defence of her memoir, character, and late husband. It is
not usually relevant to contemporary political conflicts, though it reflects
his Broad-Bottom involvements. The Duchess' memoirs are primarily
concerned with events long past, though partisans on both sides continued to draw shopworn debating points from the events of the reigns of
William III and Queen Anne, particularly the War of the Spanish Succession and the Treaty of Utrecht. Thus, Fielding's point-by-point answering of objections to the Duchess' version of past events in the unfriendly
pamphlet called *Remarks on the Account of Her Conduct . . . till the
year 1710* had a certain ancient-history quality even when published.
Whether the Marlboroughs were "Tories" under Anne or whether the
Duke was guilty of warning the French that the English were about to attack Dunkirk in 1692 (points discussed on p. 22 of the *Vindication*) must
have seemed pretty academic to politicians at a time when a new ministry
was squaring off against a new opposition. Indeed, Fielding and James
Ralph could take opposite sides in this affair (the latter refuting the
Duchess' arguments with his usual methodical effectiveness in *The Other
Side of the Question*) and yet remain friends, ranged on the same side in
the contemporary political wars through the mid-1740s. As mentioned
earlier, Ralph was to take time in an opposition essay in *The Champion*
for June 29, 1742 to "puff" Fielding and Young's translation of
Aristophanes' *Plutus*. In the *Full Vindication* Fielding avoided his old
collaborator's piece, concentrating on the anonymous *Remarks upon the
Account* (signed "Britannicus").[15] In Parliament there were bills and
motions on which men were expected to vote on factional lines, and
others where even the partisan might behave independently. There were
also topics—the Duchess' character being one of them—on which
political writers could differ without permanent estrangement.

In contemporary terms, the key element in the *Vindication* (and
another signal of Fielding's unchanged political stance in 1742) was its
celebration of the Duchess for devoting her resources, long after the
period covered by her memoirs, to the fight against Walpole, whom she

hated with all her inimitable capacity for spite. At moments interest shifts to the past decade rather than the reign of Anne:

> Had the Weight of the Duchess of *Marlborough* been lately thrown into the Scale of Corruption, the Nation must have sunk under it: But on the contrary, her whole Power hath been employed in Defense of our Liberties, and to this Power we in a very great Measure owe their Protection; and this, the barbarous and inhuman Exultations of the Corruptor [Walpole] and his chief Friends last Winter exprest on her Grace's dangerous Illness, and their eager Expectation of her Death, which they declared would do their Business sufficiently testify. So that this Nation may be truely said to have been twice saved within Forty Years by the glorious Conduct of this Illustrious Pair. (p. 38)

The scholars who believe Fielding became a Walpole man, bought and paid for, in December 1741 should ponder this outburst of April 1742, in which the Duchess is eulogized as a noble enemy of Walpole, the "Corrupter." He may have been paid by the Duchess (or some agent of hers) to defend her: his finances were precarious and she is said to have paid Nathaniel Hooke £500 for his fairly unimpressive compiling of her memoir.[16] But the most promising explanation of Fielding's decision to defend this waspish enemy of Walpole in 1742 was that she was well known to favour his Broad-Bottom friends in the old (and now the "new") opposition. On her death in 1744 she would bequeath to Chesterfield the astounding sum of £20,000 and her "best and most brilliant diamond Ring" and to the impecunious William Pitt £10,000 for "his Merit in the noble Defense he has made for the Support of the Laws of England, and to prevent the Ruin of his Country." I have suggested the eulogy of Chesterfield in *Joseph Andrews* indicates Fielding's continuing closeness to the Broad-Bottoms. Clearly his defense of the Duchess points in the same direction. I would not be surprised, though there is no evidence I know of, if Chesterfield paid Fielding to write the *Full Vindication*.

Fielding's slight ballad-opera farce in one act, *Miss Lucy in Town*, was staged and published on May 6, 1742. Apparently written in 1736 (it is a sequel to *An Old Man Taught Wisdom; or, The Virgin Unmasked* of 1735), it was then left unperformed, presumably because of its poor quality. In 1736 "Pasquin" did not need to proceed with so mediocre a farce, particularly since (as he says in the "Preface" to the *Miscellanies* of 1743) he had only "a very small share" in writing it.[17] However, in 1742-43 he was not too proud to empty his desk-drawer for profit. Politically (as well as artistically) the play is a nullity. A profligate peer (somewhat like Lord Richly in the *Modern Husband*) pursues Miss Lucy after her naïve footman husband lodges them in a cat-house by mistake on their arrival in London. When the footman denounces Bawble and town morals before taking his wife home, his rhetoric momentarily has a Country party tang: in the country "there is still something of Old England remaining." But the play is really apolitical, though it seemed personally insulting to one peer whose identity remains shadowy. The peer thought Lord Bawble was modelled upon him, and complained to the Lord Chamberlain, the Duke of Grafton, with the result that performance was suspended until the autumn, when the play was allowed again in slightly altered form. That there was anything really political in this murky infighting seems doubtful; indeed one would not even consider the possibility were it not for a very odd little pamphlet dealing with the affair, *A Letter to a Noble Lord, to whom alone it belongs* [i.e., the Duke of Grafton]: *Occasioned by a Representation at the Theatre Royal in Drury Lane, of a Farce called, Miss Lucy in Town* (London: T. Cooper). Apparently published in December 1742 (after Grafton allowed the play to reopen), it describes the peer's complaint and Grafton's reaction, then insults the Lord Chamberlain for pro-Hanoverian toadying, political venality and suppleness, and misuse of the powers given him under the Licensing Act of 1737: now there may be no "satire," only "filth and bawdry" on stage. Though this pamphlet attacks a man who had interfered with the staging of Fielding's farce (as well as enforced the repressive law that had for five years kept him from the stage), and though it takes the *Miss Lucy in Town* episode as a pretext for a political attack on Grafton, it is hard to believe Fielding was involved (or much interested) in the whole affair. The suggestion that Fielding himself wrote the *Letter to a Noble Lord*, advanced by F. Lawrence,[18] is absolutely absurd. This pamphlet should not tempt us to read partisan implications into the text or the stage history of *Miss Lucy*.

Only slightly less innocent from a political standpoint is *Plutus, the God of Riches, A Comedy, Translated from the Original Greek of Aristophanes . . . by Henry Fielding, Esq., and the Rev'd. Mr. Young* (London: T. Wallis; published May 31, 1742). The translated play seldom seems politically applicable, and only where the original allowed ample opportunity: a "Superintendant of the Publick Weal" is specified as an example of uselessness, and a greedy sycophant calls himself "an honest man and a Patriot." A somewhat artificial appearance of opposition is given to the play only by its dedication (written, apparently, by Fielding alone)[19] to Lord Talbot, cultured supporter of the reformist wing of the opposition, and by some notes (surely Fielding's) on the translation. The political implications of the dedication are stressed in one passage, which says that in *Plutus* Aristophanes satirized the enemies of his country "with a boldness and integrity which must endear his memory to every true and sincere Patriot." Fielding's anger at the turncoats of 1742 shows in a note on page 57: "TO MAKE USE OF POPULAR INTEREST, AND THE CHARACTER OF PATRIOTISM, IN ORDER TO BETRAY ONE'S COUNTRY, is perhaps the most flagitious of all Crimes."

These added touches re-emphasize that political harmony as well as old friendships lay behind James Ralph's puff in *The Champion* for June 29, 1742 for "the New Translation of *Plutus, the God of Riches . . .* by Fielding and Young" as a good "Evening's Entertainment." *The Champion*'s opposition orientation remained unchanged and the puff leads into a description of a dream vision that suggests Robert and Horatio

Walpole should have been hanged for having *"so long and grievously robb'd and injur'd"* the nation. Ralph was an unrelenting pursuer of Walpole. The opposition in Parliament gave up after 1742 (there was one more vain, symbolic call for an impeachment investigation in December), but Ralph still grumbled about the failure to punish Walpole in *A Critical History of the Administration of Sir Robert Walpole* in 1743.[20] Fielding also continued to be regarded with approval by Pope, who complimented his dramatic satires of the 1730s in Book IV of the *Dunciad* (lines 41-44) when it appeared as an individual poem in March 1742. In August 1742 a hack writer "fathered" on Fielding a crude attack on Pope, *Blast upon Blast and Lick for Lick, or, a new Lesson for P-pe. A Parody on the Fourth Chapter of Genesis*, which Horace Walpole accepted, probably with malice, as Fielding's.[21] A glance through it makes it clear he did not write it. He published nothing in 1742 after *Plutus*, and remained in sympathy with Pope and Ralph.

During the latter half of 1742, Fielding was involved in revising and composing the major and minor works that filled the three volumes of his *Miscellanies*, published by subscription the following spring. Subscriptions were probably being solicited during the winter of 1741-42, though they were first advertised in the *Daily Post* for June 5, 1742. Publication was promised in December 1742 and then on February 22, 1743 but copies were only delivered to subscribers on April 7.[22] The delays were obviously caused by the scope and complexity of the undertaking, compounded by personal and family health problems and financial pressures. Indeed, as we will see, Fielding finally had to send his work to the printer carelessly revised (one compliment to Lord Carteret as a member of the Patriot opposition, most inappropriate in 1743, survived), and with the promising long narrative, *A Journey from this World to the Next*, unpolished and unfinished.

Fielding was seriously ill (with his chronic gout, presumably) in the winter of 1741-42, and his wife and his daughter were more gravely afflicted. The child died. His wife temporarily recovered, apparently required a trip to Bath in the summer of 1742 that her husband could ill afford, worsened again in early 1743, and died in 1744. His financial problems, which probably had slowly worsened since he was forced off the stage, had become acute. By March 1741 he was in debt for the sum of £197 to one Joseph King, and it is probable that only the generosity of his patrons and Ralph Allen got him through the months of sickness, tragedy, and composition without current income preceding the publication of *Joseph Andrews*. The profits from the novel, his minor publications of 1742, and the rewards one assumes he got for his compliments to Allen, Chesterfield, and Talbot seem to have been soon exhausted. Joseph King had to sue for his money in July 1742. F. Homes Dudden's conjecture that Fielding was helped by a gift of £200 from Ralph Allen to pay King and escape the nemesis that hung over every debtor in the 1740s is plausible, if unproven.[23] The whole congeries of pressures that both impelled Fielding to devote himself to his *Miscellanies* and prevented their efficient completion is symbolized by his frank, manly apology in the "Preface" to the collection for the weaknesses of *The Wedding Day*, the old play he dusted off for performance in February 1743 and then placed in volume II. He gave himself no more than a week to revise it, only to be interrupted by a sudden crisis in his wife's condition, so that David Garrick and Andrew Millar, the printer of the *Miscellanies*, received it in lamentable condition. He exposed so "imperfect" a piece only because of an "urgent" need for money.[24] The hurried, harassed putting together of the *Miscellanies* explains why most of the political satire in it seems so dated. Some was written long before, in the earliest stages of his career. Some was written during Walpole's last years in office and printed in 1743 (when satire on Walpole was hardly a current item) with at most a perfunctory attempt at making it reflect the contemporary situation and the anti-turncoat animus of the "new" opposition. We have seen him adjusting *Joseph Andrews* to hit new political targets. Though published a year later, some of the political satire in the *Miscellanies* as obviously reveals awkward tinkering to make it fit post-Walpole realities.

During the latter half of 1742 the opposition was both furious and numbed by shock and suspicion. Its country gentlemen were less trusting of "whiggish" allies, Pulteney, Carteret, the Prince of Wales, and even Lords Cobham and Gower. The Broad-Bottoms had to convince the Country independents of Commons to grant them again at least provisional trust. As Archibald Foord has observed,[25] one very strong emphasis of the new Broad-Bottom journal, *Old England* (signed "Jeffery Broadbottom" and dominated by Lord Chesterfield from February 5, 1743 through December 1744) was to keep the public from tarring the "new" opposition with the same brush as Pulteney and Carteret. The "false Patriotism" of a few would soil the reputations of many if careful distinctions were not made between the different elements in the old opposition. This distancing from the turncoats was accomplished in the year or so after Walpole left Commons, though the Country group must have half-expected another desertion whenever the time was right for the Broad-Bottoms to enter the ministry.

Unity was dictated by common indignation against Pulteney and Carteret and chagrin that the new ministry was manned and behaved so much like Walpole's, and by common dismay at continental war policies seen as more beneficial to the Electorate of Hanover than to England. Factious schemers had gained power in the teeth of the Country gentlemen and the Broad-Bottoms. Both knew that unpopular diplomatic and military policies were the Achilles' heel of this ministry, as they had been of Walpole's and would be (if the Broad-Bottoms could see ahead to their days as ministerialists) of the next ministry. From the moment Walpole was forced to declare war on Spain in 1739, lukewarm effort and ill success gave the opposition an issue. As the War of Jenkins'

Ear expanded into the general European War of the Austrian Succession, with England the principal supporter of Maria Theresa against the threat of France and the on-again, off-again aggressiveness of Prussia, the war problem became more of a danger to ministry. The feeling that land war on the continent, as opposed to naval war in the Atlantic and Caribbean, had ceased to further the original objective of protecting and expanding English trade was general in opposition circles. It took on focussed bitterness in 1741 when George II declared the Electorate of Hanover neutral to prevent its being over-run by the French. In 1742 Lord Carteret talked the King into reversing this move, but George's diplomacy and military decisions continued to be affected in major ways by his determination to protect Hanover, in which he spent as much time as practicable. The Electorate was incapable of defending itself against determined assault, and fighting the war in a way that would not tempt the enemy to invade Hanover was self-defeating. It was also expensive, a fact rubbed into the English each time they were asked to approve the payment out of the English treasure of troops from neutral Hanover to fight an "unEnglish" and inglorious war.

When the *Miscellanies* appeared, the evil of "Hanoverian Measures" and the hypocrisy and Hanoverianism of Carteret had become the major emphases of opposition complaint. Such ministerialists as the Earl of Egmont (*Faction Detected by the Evidence of Facts*, 1743) countered by attacking as "treasonous" the anti-Hanoverianism of the opposition and its anti-Constitutional intention to force the King to employ (and dismiss) ministers against his will. But in issue after issue of *Old England* Chesterfield pressed both points, while William Pitt readied himself to mount explosive attacks on Carteret's Hanoverianism in the parliamentary winter session of 1743-44. Other issues receded from the foreground as the assault on Carteret and Hanoverianism warmed. Horace Walpole might cogently protest against this in *The Interest of Great Britain Steadily Pursued*, but Lord Chesterfield enjoyed real rhetorical advantages in his fine pamphlet, *The Case of the Hanover Forces in the Pay of Great Britain* (1743). Chesterfield argued that there had been little change in policy with the fall of Walpole, and that the opposition remained dedicated to the same goals it had pursued for twenty years: eliminating national corruption and reversing pernicious, Hanoverian foreign policies.[26] The first issue of *Old England* (February 5, 1743) risked charges of Jacobitism and got its printer arrested when it called for a new, untainted opposition and insinuated that if William III had treated England as a fief of Orange (the target being George's preference for Hanover) he would soon have been sent home.

As the opposition gathered momentum in 1743 and 1744, united by fury against Carteret and Hanoverianism, it achieved a formality and solidarity of organization never achieved under Walpole. This solidarity was more apparent than enduring. As hinted above, there were covert, abortive negotiations even in 1743 between the Broad-Bottoms and the Pelhams aimed at a coalition ministry that would permit the ejection of Carteret from office and the abandonment of the Country opposition, and such a coalition would be achieved in late 1744. However, unity briefly rendered the recently shattered minority more formidable than one might expect, particularly with the Prince of Wales in the ministerial orbit. By late 1743, opposition "Whigs" (including Lyttelton, Pitt, and the other Broad-Bottoms) and "Tories" were not only at the stage of meeting in an opposition equivalent of the ministerial get-togethers in the Cockpit before the convening of Parliament, but formed a kind of opposition shadow cabinet. It first included three Broad-Bottoms (Pitt, Waller, and Dodington) and three Country leaders (John Phillips, John Hynde Cotton, and W. Watkins Wynne). It expanded in 1744 to nine members of Commons and Lords, Dodington, Pitt, Waller, the Duke of Bedford, Lord Chesterfield, Lord Cobham, and George Lyttelton from the Broad-Bottom leadership, and John Hynde Cotton and Lord Gower representing (at least in their own minds) the "Country Interest."[27]

Fielding did not enter into the opposition assault with full vigour. The *Miscellanies* insult both Lord Bath and Carteret, but scarcely touch on the issue of Hanoverian policies. Only in late 1744, with very poor timing, would he contribute materially to the anti-Hanoverian barrage in *An Attempt toward the Natural History of the Hanover Rat*. Nonetheless, the *Miscellanies* volumes contain a fascinating variety of old and current political satire, the best of it biting, and indicate that he remained firmly aligned with the "new" opposition. It is dangerous to read too much into who subscribed to the *Miscellanies*, and for how many copies. As Henry Knight Miller has observed, Lyttelton, Chesterfield, Argyll, Cobham, Talbot, Dodington, Bedford, and the Prince of Wales (still Lyttleton's patron, though pro-ministerial) subscribed, but so did Lord Orford (down for ten copies on royal paper) and the Duke of Newcastle. The subscriptions of Orford and Newcastle do not indicate political cordiality, any more than does the subscription of Lord Bath (William Pulteney), who may have subscribed early in Fielding's canvassing, before he became an apostate. The *Miscellanies* were significant in the literary life of the time, and Walpole and Newcastle, who collected books along with all else that grandeur required, would have spent a few guineas on them without particular reference to the loyalties of *Joseph Andrews*. (The third edition of *Joseph Andrews*, the first carrying Fielding's name, was published in March 1743 to "puff" the *Miscellanies*.) Indeed, the inclusion of their names is probably less significant than the *exclusion* of Lord Carteret's.

The political interest of the "Preface" to the *Miscellanies* lies in its closing rejection of pieces "fathered" on Fielding, and sly hints that *Jonathan Wild* is applicable not only to Walpole, but to Pulteney and Carteret. Perhaps still angry over *Blast upon Blast*, Fielding insists he has written nothing since the end of June 1741 except "*Joseph Andrews . . . The Opposition: A Vision, A Defense of the Dutchess of Marlborough's*

Book, *Miss Lucy in Town* (in which I had a very small share)." He explicitly denies rumours that he has written for the *Champion* or another paper after that date or ever written a word in the *Daily Gazetteer*. As argued in the last chapter, his willing admission that he wrote *The Opposition: A Vision* seems inconsistent with a theory that it acknowledges a sell-out to Walpole in 1741. There is, however, pointed irony, mingled with truth, in the statement that Fielding's Jonathan Wild is no more a symbol for any other particular person than he is a "very faithful Portrait" of the real Jonathan Wild, and the hint that a reader insistent upon reading his satire as particular, contemporaneously topical, will "if he knows much of the Great World" see there is "more than one on whom he can fix the Resemblance." This prepares the reader to recognize that the obvious parallels between Wild as head of the "Prigs" and Walpole as Prime Minister are capable of more general application, and that in places (notably part II, chapter 12) they are applied obtrusively to William Pulteney.

Only a few of the forty-six pieces in Volume I of the *Miscellanies* have any political interest, and only two or three reflect the political situation in 1742-43. Some of the political pieces are dated survivors from the 1730s. "To Celia on her wishing to have a Lilliputian to play with" alludes to Pulteney and Walpole as they were then: "P--lt--y, who does for Freedom rage,/ Would sing confin'd within thy Cage:/ And W--lp--le, for a tender Pat,/ Would leave his Place to be thy Cat." The two poems to the "Right Honourable Sir Robert Walpole" were actually written (as I have argued in Chapter Two, in opposition to Hugh Amory's placement of their composition in the more recent past) in "The Year 1730" and "*anno* 1731." Their half-bantering hints about Fielding's readiness to accept patronage ("I'm fittest for _____ a Sinecure!") from Walpole, described as living in Arlington Street, from which he moved in 1732, suggest the young Fielding. The publication of a truncated version of one of the poems in the *Gentleman's Magazine* for December 1738 is not inconsistent with much earlier composition. The principal change Fielding made when he slipped the old poems into the *Miscellanies* was probably to add the information "Now Earl of Orford," after Walpole's name in the title.[28]

Also dated, though not so early, is "A Sailor's Song," a minor serio-comic example of the propaganda in favour of war with Spain (and possibly France) of the 1730s. It may well have been written in 1737 for the obscure, anonymous ballad opera called *The Sailor's Opera*.[29] The translation of *The First Olynthiac of Demosthenes* may have been intended in the late 1730s as an oblique attack on Walpole's peace policies. In 1737 and 1738 the use of loose translations and adaptations of Demosthenes to denounce Walpole's handling of Spanish aggression became so frequent that *The Daily Gazetteer* criticized it in a formal essay, "Of applying the Orations of Demosthenes," on February 22, 1738. The praise of the Duke of Richmond in the poem "Of Good Nature" was not politically significant when it was first published in *The*

Champion (November 27, 1739) and remained innocuous in 1743. From the early 1730s through the late 1740s Fielding praised Richmond's virtues, but never for political reasons. That is why Richmond's pro-Walpole alignment between 1735 and 1742 made no difference in Fielding's view, a fact that has vaguely troubled some scholars.[30] Finally there is *Liberty: to George Lyttelton, Esq.*, a poetic effusion in the manner of Thompson's *Liberty* of 1735-36. In it Fielding traces the growth of liberty through history (just as Thompson, Glover, Lyttelton did in the later 1730s), from the primitive swarm, through Greece and Rome, barbarism and renaissance, to Britain, where he prays it may survive despite ". . . Lords, and Ministers, and such sad Things;/ and . . . the Strange Divinity of Kings." It may have been written in 1737 when, in the face of the Licensing Act, Fielding threatened to carry his anti-Walpole campaign into the newspapers. His failure to do so may explain why the poem remained unpublished, and the intention to take up weekly journalism may be reflected in a pun:

> Accept the Muse whom Truth inspires to sing,
> Who soars, tho' *weakly*, on an honest Wing.[31]

In 1743, however, the chief significance of the poem was that it was addressed to Lyttelton, important in the new opposition, and thus showed precisely where Fielding still stood. Times had changed, but his personal allegiances and anti-ministerial orientation endured.

The same continued adherence to old Broad-Bottom patrons is clear in other works. His very early English version of Juvenal's *Sixth Satire* (it may originally have been done as early as 1725) is only vaguely political in its transference of the Roman's disdain for the luxury and absurdity of Rome to the absurdities and luxuries of Walpole's England: "when our old *British* Plainness left us,/ Of every Virtue it bereft us./ And we've imported from all Climes,/ All sorts of Wickedness and Crimes." However, Fielding inserted in it a compliment (1. 118) to the oratory of Lyttelton and William Pitt. Similar compliments, though without the explicit political associations of oratory, are found in the *Essay on Conversation* (composed no earlier than the winter of 1741-42), and the *Essay on Nothing* (not finished, there is evidence to show, until Fielding was in the final stages of putting together the *Miscellanies* in the winter of 1742-43).[32] The latter compliments Chesterfield as the "inimitable Author of a Preface to the Posthumous Eclogues of a late ingenious young Author," the *Love Elegies* of the late James Hammond, published in November 1742. The closing page of the *Essay on Conversation* lists among other kinds of innocent "True Raillery" ironical criticisms of men "for Vices and Faults which they are known to be free from. Thus the Cowardice of A[rgyl]l, the Dulness of Ch[esterfiel]d, the Unpolitness of D[oding]ton, may be attacked without Danger of Offense; and thus Lyt[telto]n may be censured for whatever Vice or Folly you please to impute to him."

Finally there is the poem, *Of True Greatness*, with which Fielding begins Volume I. It was first published in early 1741, and reprinted with only two changes in 1743: (1) the removal of the dedication to Dodington, a structural awkwardness in a collection and anachronistic in defending Dodington and Fielding himself from ephemeral slanders of 1740, and in complimenting the since-disgraced Pulteney; (2) the substitution of the name"H__cote" (Heathcote) for "G__schal" in a line celebrating the leaders of anti-ministerial London, Sir Robert Godschall having died in June 1742. *Of True Greatness* has been ana- lyzed politically in Chapter Four, but it is of interest that Fielding so cur- sorily revised it that he failed to delete a compliment to the "True Greatness" of Lord Carteret, absurd in 1742-43, normal in early 1741:

> . . . in any Sphere of Life she shines,
> Whether she blaze a Hoadley 'mid Divines,
> Or, an *Argyll*, in Fields and Senates dare,
> Supreme in all the Arts of Peace and War.
> Greatness with Learning deck'd *in Carteret* see,
> With Justice, and with Clemency in *Lee*,
> *In Chesterfield* to ripe Perfection come,
> See it in Littleton beyond its Bloom.

That this was sheer carelessness is obvious in the exclusion of Carteret from the very similar string of names (Argyll, Chesterfield, Dodington, Lyttelton) in the *Essay on Conversation*, written for the *Miscellanies*, not resurrected from beyond the divide of 1742.

The satire on political deceit in *An Essay on the Knowledge of the Characters of Men* ("political Great Men . . . lie under the Necessity of giving [promises] in great Abundance and the Value of them is so well known that few are so imposed on by them") could have been written at any point in Fielding's career, though the poem probably dates from the *Champion* period. Otherwise there is little more of interest in Volume I, with two important exceptions. (I pass over the unlikely suggestion[33] that when written, *circa* 1737, *An Interlude between Jupiter, Juno, Apollo and Mercury* was meant to insult King George and Queen Caroline, paralleling them with Jupiter and Juno. There seems no basis for it, though the failed farce *Eurydice* of 1737, first published in Volume II, preserves hints of a similar, dated parallel, Pluto-Proserpine:George-Caroline.) The poem "To John Hayes, Esq." (written, surely, in 1742), ends with an example that seems openly aimed at Lords Bath and Carteret:

> Thus while the Courtier acts the Patriot's Part,
> This [art] guides his Face and Tongue, and that [nature] his Heart.
> Abroad the Patriot shines with artful Mien
> The naked Courtier glares behind the Scene.
> What wonder then to Morrow if he grow
> A Courtier good, who is a Patriot now.

Some Papers Proper to be Read before the R---l Society, Concerning the Terrestrial Chrysipus, Golden-Foot or Guinea, by "Petrus Gualterus," parodies an account of the "Fresh-Water Polypus" presented to the

Royal Society in January 1742-43 and printed in the *Philosophical Trans-actions* on January 28. It was written rapidly and published in-dependently on February 16, 1743, then, with one significant addition, reprinted in the *Miscellanies*. The principal targets are scientific pedantry and style, usury, and Peter Walter ("Petrus Gualterus" is Peter Walter, Latinized), the model for Peter Pounce in *Joseph Andrews*. However, the discussion in the February version of the nature, reproduction, and distribution of the golden guinea (the Chrysipus being that coin, not an animal) twice touches upon the great political issue of 1743, the betrayal of English interests in favour of Hanoverian ones.

The covering letter from "Heer Rottenscrach in Germany" (a droll change not only in name, but in country, the model for the papers having been sent to the Royal Society by Sir William Bentinck from the Hague) says there may be "still some [Chrysipi, or guineas] *to be found in* England: *However, if that should be difficult,* it may be easy *to send some over to you; as they are at present very plentiful in these Parts.*" This sarcastic hint that England has been bled to enrich Hanover during the war echoes those of every opposition propagandist in 1743, and an-ticipates Fielding's *An Attempt Towards a Natural History of the Hanover Rat*. Even more overtly anti-ministerial and anti-Hanoverian is Petrus Gualterus' complaint about the difficulty of finding Chrysipi:

> . . . it is much to be feared the Species will soon be entirely lost among us: And indeed, in *England*, they are observed of late to be much rarer than formerly, especially in the Country, where at present there are very few of them to be found; but at the same time it is remarked, that in some Places of the Continent, particularly in a certain Part of *Germany*, they are much plentier; being to be found in great Numbers, where formerly there were scarce any to be met with.

Upon republication in the *Miscellanies* a *"Postscript"* from Gualterus was added. It mocks electoral corruption, in good Broad-Bottom style, though without specific reference to the politics of 1743, the next election being years in the future:

> Since I composed the above Treatise, I have been informed, that these Animals swarm in *England* all over the Country, like the Locusts, one in Seven Years; and like them too, they generally cause much Mischief, and greatly ruin the Country in which they have swarmed.

The second volume of the *Miscellanies* is slightly more politically ab-sorbed than the first, though only one of the three works in it is much concerned with politics. The two resurrected plays that fill out the volume, *The Wedding Day* and the damned farce of 1737, *Eurydice*, are all but innocent of politics. The former is a five-act comedy in the style of Fielding's youth (it may have been written as early as 1730), staged for six performances by Garrick between February 17 and 26, 1743, and apologized for by Fielding, as we have seen, in the "Preface" to the *Miscellanies*. It has seemed political to no-one. There was trouble with the licensing authority, but on the grounds of smuttiness (as one can believe, reading even the expurgated version that was performed and

printed), not political offensiveness. The Countess of Hertford, who
wrote to her son about the licensing problems on January 25 and after
the play's opening on February 19, assured him the comedy was "refused
by the Licenser, not as a reflecting one, but on account of its
immorality."[34] The published play includes only the barest minimum of
the kind of political allusions that were obligatory in the 1730s—a
reference to a fat bawd as "the first Minister of Venus" is typical.
Eurydice; a Farce: As it was damned at the Theatre Royal in Drury Lane,
the play hissed from the stage in February 1737, is not political, though
later in 1737 Fielding made brilliant political use of this setback in
Eurydice Hiss'd. Indeed, it seems astounding that Fielding wrote so
apolitical a piece in 1737, during his most aggressive phase as a dramatic
satirist. There is some vague satire on the absurdities of court and army
beaus (in 1737 the utter uselessness for war of foppish officers apparently
roused the hissing apprentices, though it is hard to see why), and we are
told that the devil is often seen "in or about" Westminster Hall. But the
only items that even in 1737 might have seemed politically potent are two
passages where Proserpine's ascendancy over Pluto might have suggested
the opposition's frequent claim (think of Fielding's own *Welsh Opera;
or, the Gray Mare the Better Horse*) that Queen Caroline dominated
George II: ". . . how could Hell be better represented than by supposing
the people under petticoat government?"; "He [Pluto] settled one half of
the government on me at my marriage, and I [Proserpine] have, thank
fate, pretty well worked him out of the other half." But satiric parallels
would never have been of major importance in the play, and would have
been pointless and in the worst taste after Queen Caroline's death on
November 20, 1737. By 1743 any political meaning had evaporated.

The lead piece in Volume II, *A Journey from This World to the
Next*, was written closer to publication day. There is some reason to
believe that its parts were hurriedly joined as it went to press, in a process
that combined elements written at different times and with different intentions. There is the narrator's opening Lucianic tour of the underworld, the best, freshest-feeling part of the *Journey*. Then comes the
long account of Julian the Apostate's transmigratory existences, uneven
in quality, with an unfinished feel. Tacked onto Julian's history (after a
mock-scholarly announcement that the suppposed manuscript broke off)
is an account of Anne Boleyn's life, surely not composed as part of a
gallery of histories of the dead, though made more or less to fit the
Journey in a revision so hurried that her story seems to have been sent to
the printer virtually without paragraph breaks. There is one short
paragraph at the beginning and one at the end. The rest of it is one immense, plodding block of print—a genuine oddity in Fielding's canon. It
seems very likely that the bulk of the *Journey* (Chapters I-XXV) was
written between 1740-41 and the spring of 1742. The story of Anne
Boleyn could have been written at any time and put aside as un-
publishable until Fielding saw a chance to use it to pad the *Journey*. In
addition, Fielding obviously added a few sneers at false Patriots to an ex-

isting manuscript in the year between the fall of Walpole and publication, when Pulteney and Carteret became prime targets. The *Journey* has a good deal of satire with the tang of the late Walpole years, updated with a few touches of post-Walpole satire. Fielding was more inclined to stress than hide this double, pre-1742, post-1742 pattern, hinting broadly about it in the footnote to the "author's" recollection, in the first sentence of Book I, that he died on December 1, 1741 (my italics):

> Some doubt whether this should not be rather 1641, which is a date more agreeable to the account given of it in the introduction: but then there are *some passages which seem to relate to transactions infinitely later, even within this year or two.*—To say the truth, there are difficulties attend either conjecture; so the reader may take which he pleases.

Fielding's history of Anne Boleyn seems utterly unconnected with politics after the sixteenth century. However, Julian's existences very frequently involved him in politics, as everything from a favourite slave to a court fool to a prime minister. His account stresses, in very general terms, the danger and prevalence of political corruption in all ages, the shaky tenure any politician has on power and glory. But this was readily applicable to England under George II and a good deal of it was originally aimed at Walpole (particularly the passages which stress the evil of rule through favourites or powerful, corrupt ministers, self-serving barriers between the ruler and the ruled), and was susceptible of application to his successors in 1743. In Chapter XVII, Julian recalls being the King of Spain. His description of the evils into which he was led by bad ministers would fit perfectly into a *Champion* lead essay:

> None, who hath not been himself a prince, nor any prince, till his death, can conceive the impositions daily put on them by their favourites and ministers; so that princes are often blamed for the faults of others . . . .
>
> To confess the truth, I had, by means of my ministers, conceived a very unjust opinion of my whole people, whom I fancied to be daily conspiring against me, and to entertain the most disloyal thoughts; when in reality (as I have known since my death) they hold me in universal respect and esteem. This is a trick, I believe, too often played with sovereigns, who by such means, are prevented from that open intercourse with their subjects, which as it would greatly endear the person of the prince to the people, so might it often prove dangerous to a minister who was consulting his own interest only at the expense of both. [Chapter XVII]

Julian also enjoyed "absolute dominion, under another name," as favourite of the Anglo-Saxon king, Edward:

> I had everything of royalty but the outward ensigns: No man ever applying for a place, or any kind of preferment, but to me only. A circumstance, which as it greatly enriched my coffers, so it no less pampered my ambition, and satisfied my vanity with a numerous attendance; and I had the pleasure of seeing those, who only bowed to the king, prostrating themselves before me . . . .

He recalls that he kept from the monarch all who were "capable of engaging or improving his affection; no prime minister, as I apprehend, esteeming himself to be safe while any other shares the ear of his prince, of whom we are as jealous as the fondest husband can be of his wife. Whoever, therefore, can approach him by any other channel than that of ourselves, is in our opinion a declared enemy, and one whom the first principles of policy oblige us to demolish with the utmost expedition" (Chapter XX). In earlier lives Julian encountered Eutropius, prime minister to an eastern emperor, who had perfected Walpole's trick of buying the honour of his tools with promises, then failing to fulfill or remember them (Chapter X), and was himself favourite to the Greek Emperor Zeno:

> A bow, a smile, a nod from me, as I passed through cringing crowds, were esteemed as signal favours . . . The smile of a court favourite immediately raises the person who receives it, and gives a value to his smile when conferred on an inferior: thus the smile is transferred from one to the other, and the great man at last is the person to discount it . . . . a very low fellow hath a desire for a place . . . . He therefore applies to A, who is the creature of B, who is the tool of C, who is the flatterer of D, who is the catamite of E, who is the pimp of F, who is the bully of G, who is the buffoon of I, who is the husband of K, who is the whore of L, who is the bastard of M, who is the instrument of the great man. Thus the smile descending regularly from the great man to A, is discounted back again, and at last paid by the great man.

Later, a servant achieved ascendancy over Julian when he was a court tailor saddled with a profligate mistress, and needed someone to run his business and find money to cover his massive expenses:

> . . . he was as absolutely my master, as was ever an ambitious, industrious prime minister over an indolent and voluptuous king. All my other journeymen paid more respect to him than to me; for they considered my favour as a necessary consequence of obtaining his. [Chapter XXII]

Small wonder King Minos informed Julian that "he always acquitted a prime minister" if he "could produce one single good action in his whole life," but made it a rule about Elysium that "no prime minister ever entered there."

   Reading such passages a contemporary could only cry, "Walpole!" I am certain they were written while Walpole was in office, probably before the death date of the narrator of the *Journey*, which we are told in its opening sentence was December 1, 1741.[35] However, one passage in Chapter XXIII obviously satirizes not Walpole, but William Pulteney. This unmistakably dates it as written after he defected for a peerage (and places for his associates) in 1742, then fell to defending policies and persons he had execrated in opposition. Julian became a leader of opposition in the reign of King John as a means of obtaining power. He opposed John's measures "whether right or wrong," though they usually were wrong (another sign that Fielding had not rejected the principles of the old opposition, only their false proponents), making "his opposition . . . justifiable enough . . . if my motive from within had been as good as the occasion from without." Julian admits, "in truth, I sought nothing but my own preferment, by making myself formidable to the king, and then selling to him the interest of that party, by whose means I had become so." This is Pulteney kicking away what Bolingbroke called the "scaffolding" of Broad-Bottom and Country allies as he grasped power.[36] To turn his coat, Julian demanded "a place, a pension, and a knighthood. All those were immediately concented to. I was forthwith knighted, and promised the other two." Substituting his peerage for the knighthood, this is precisely what Pulteney got in 1742. Julian then "mounted the hustings, and without any regard to decency or modesty, made as emphatical a speech in favour of the king as before I had done against him." But he found (this Broad-Bottom fantasy was fulfilled in 1746) his listeners were repelled by his hypocrisy. They cursed him and the king abandoned him. If much of the political satire in Julian's history sounds like leftovers from 1740-41, this is purest 1742-43.

The most entertaining and complex part of the *Journey* is the block of nine chapters in which the author dies, and travels through a series of allegorical realms (the "City of Diseases," the "Palace of the Dead," the place where transmigrating souls spin the "Wheel of Fortune" and draw lots for their roles in their next existences) to Elysium. Though its quality is higher, it is as Janus-like politically as the Julian or Anne Boleyn sections: some material seems to come from the Walpole period and some seems to have been added after Walpole's fall. The pattern is unmistakable though political satire is sparse in this part of the *Journey*, there being only two major political passages in nine chapters.

The oldest material in this section again obviously was written before the old opposition broke down, certainly not after the second half of 1741, most likely in Fielding's *Champion* period. Lucianic dream visions (often involving journeys to hell, paradise, or the "Hill of the Muses") were stock items in the *Champion*, and Chapters VI and VIII are so like some of Fielding's essays in *The Champion* in length and development, as well as approach and content, that it is by no means unlikely they began as journal leaders, never used for some reason, in 1740 or 1741. The first concerns the dead choosing identities for their next lives. They spin Fortune's Wheel, drink vials containing varying tinctures of the passions and intellectual powers, and draw lots on which the balanced goods and evils of their coming lives are written. Among ten drawn lots (others are "Poet, Contempt, Self-Satisfaction" and "Coach and six, Impotent jealous husband"), two tell us precisely where Fielding stood when he wrote the chapter:

> On a Seventh, *Prime Minister,*
> *Disgrace.*
> On an Eighth, *Patriot,*
> *Glory.*

The simple distinction between vicious Walpole and his virtuous Patriot foes had not yielded to 1742-43 complexities when this was written. A second antique survived in the graceful account of the narrator's dealings with the spirits of dead poets, musicians, actors, and scholars: Orpheus and Sappho, Homer, Madame Dacier, Pope, Virgil, Addison and Steele, Shakespeare, Betterton, Booth, and Milton. Before meeting these greats the narrator encounters Leonidas of Sparta, providing an opportunity for a compliment to Richard Glover's poem *Leonidas*, also praised in the *Champion* in 1740: "I acquainted him [Leonidas] of the honours which had been done him by a celebrated poet of our nation; to which he answered, he was very much obliged to him."[37] This passage is also like one of Fielding's *Champion* leaders.

Other touches surely were more recent, though hardly new. Compliments to the Duke of Marlborough and Ralph Allen's house that could easily have been inserted in revision presumably date from early 1742 when Fielding praised Allen in *Joseph Andrews* and defended the Marlboroughs. Allen's house is admired in a confused sentence describing the scenery along the Road to Goodness (as opposed to Greatness) in the underworld. On this Road the only "handsome" building resembles "a certain house by the Bath," suggesting that Allen is one of the few "truly Good" *and* "truly Great" eulogized in the "Preface" to the *Miscellanies*. In the Palace of Death tapestries depict the great battles of history, but there are none of Marlborough's victories like the "beautiful tapestries to be seen at Blenheim Palace." The skeleton of a Beefeater explains that "Lewis XIVth, who had a great interest with his most mortal majesty, had prevented any such from being hung up here; besides . . . [Death] hath no great respect for that Duke, for he never sent him a subject he could not keep from him, nor did he ever get a single subject by his means, but he lost 1000 others for him." Marlborough is an exception to the blood-stained "Greatness" of the military hero. The passage is a postscript to the *Full Vindication of the Dutchess Dowager of Marlborough* of April 1742.

In Chapter III we are told that the money on Lord Scrape's table was "desposed in several heaps, every one of which would have purchased the honour of some patriots, and the chastity of some prudes." This may have been aimed at the turncoats of 1742, but Fielding had always sneered at the venal in the old opposition. If it was written under Walpole, it was surely applicable to Pulteney and Carteret in 1743. Far more important and ambiguous is the description at the end of Chapter V of the spirits choosing between the hideous, popular Road to Greatness, and the lovely, little-travelled Road to Goodness. The roads recall the Country Road and the short-cut to Whitehall in *The Opposition: A Vision* of 1741, but the key political elements are the last two paragraphs of the chapter. The first is a noble oration by a spirit who has drawn the lot of a king in the next life, in response to the mockery with which the other spirits express their "contempt for earthly grandeur." He agrees that pride in royal grandeur is absurd, since it does not necessarily imply superior virtue, and involves more cares than pleasures. But he welcomes his lot, partly because it will give greater power to do good. Other monarchs may misuse their powers, refusing "happiness in the other world, and heaven in this, for misery there, and hell here." But not he:

> ". . . my intentions are different. I shall always endeavour the ease, the happiness, and the glory of my people, being confident that by so doing, I take the most certain method of procuring them all to myself." —He then struck directly into the road of goodness, and received such a shout of applause, as I never remember to have heard equaled.

The sentiments are worthy of a Bolingbrokean Patriot King, and meant to be read as such. However, the last brief paragraph ends the chapter on another note:

> He was gone a little way, when a spirit limped after him, swearing he would fetch him back. This spirit, I was presently informed, was one who had drawn the lot of his prime minister.

This passage is richly ambiguous political satire. There are three ways to read it. The first is as traditional anti-Walpole satire of the kind that rather insincerely distinguished between the basically good King (beloved by his subjects, even those in opposition) and the minister who fooled and manipulated him into evil courses, the cunning Walpole. If this was the original intention, the passage obviously was written before the fall of Walpole. It probably refers to the opposition's great disappointment of the 1720s, when George II, having associated himself with opposition as Prince of Wales and replaced Walpole at his father's death, soon returned Sir Robert to power. This version casts George II as the great disappointment of the age, and Walpole as his bad angel. A second, more plausible reading assumes that the passage is concerned with Frederick, Prince of Wales, William Pulteney, and Lord Carteret, and was written in two well separated stages. The long penultimate paragraph was composed first, probably before *The Opposition: A Vision*, certainly before February 1742, when the Prince shifted his support to the coalition dominated by Carteret and the Pelhams, and blessed by Pulteney. Up to that point the speech of the king-to-be (the heir to the throne) would have constituted a panegyric on Frederick, a reproach to his father, and a Patriot sermon. Frederick was expected to take the "Road to Goodness" (roughly the "Country Road" of *The Opposition: A Vision*) when power came to him. The short last paragraph, however, was added between February 1742 and publication. The "prime minister" represents Pulteney or Lord Carteret or both. The intention to divert the spirit from the "Road to Goodness" into the "Road to Greatness" both refers to Pulteney's seduction of the Prince in February 1742 and gloomily anticipates that Carteret will dominate royal councils when George II dies. Finally, both paragraphs may have been written in anger after the reversal of 1742. They may always have been meant to

function as a unit, the first to recall the noble pose of Patriotism that
Frederick assumed during the great years of the old opposition, the
second to undercut this false idealism. This reading is perhaps excessively
subtle, involving the writing of a ringing and lengthy Patriot oration by a
royal heir, free of apparent irony, to set up a brief undercutter.
However, Fielding may have been extra cautious since Lyttelton and Pitt
had not openly broken with the Prince, and this reading allows for
simultaneous composition of the two paragraphs in the twelve months
before the *Journey* was published. On balance, the second reading seems
most plausible, but either of the anti-Frederick, anti-Pulteney readings is
far more likely than an anti-Walpole reading that looks back to the winning of the new George II by Walpole in the 1720s.

One unmistakable attack on Pulteney and Carteret was certainly
written no earlier than the end of June 1742. In Chapter VII of the
Journey the gates of Elysium are thrown open to "our last Lord
Mayor." This must be Sir Robert Godschall, mentioned as one of the
"truly Great" in the original *Of True Greatness*, though replaced by
Heathcote in the version of the poem in the *Miscellanies*. Godschall died
during his term as Lord Mayor of London on June 26, 1742.[38] The
paragraph immediately preceding this compliment to Godschall depicts
the very different luck of the spirit of a political turncoat:

> A very stately figure now presented himself, and informing Minos that
> he was a patriot, began a very florid harangue on public virtue, and the
> liberties of his country. Upon which, Minos showed him the utmost
> respect, and ordered the gate to be opened. The patriot was not con-
> tented with this applause.—He said, he had behaved as well in place as
> he had done in opposition; and that, though he was now obliged to
> embrace the court measures, yet he had behaved very honestly to his
> friends, and brought as many in as was possible.—"Hold a moment,"
> says Minos, "on second consideration, Mr. Patriot, I think a man of
> your great virtue and abilities will be so much missed by your country,
> that if I might advise you, you should take a journey back again. I am
> sure you will not decline it, for I am certain you will with great readi-
> ness sacrifice your own happiness to the public good." The patriot
> smiled, and told Minos he believed he was in jest; and was offering to
> enter the gate, but the judge laid fast hold of him, and insisted on his
> return, which the patriot still declining, he at last ordered his guards to
> seize him and conduct him back.

If there were no other political passages in the *Journey*, this insult to
Pulteney and Carteret, succeeded by the compliment to Godschall,
would indicate with precision Fielding's "new opposition" orientation in
the latter half of 1742 and 1743.

Volume III of the *Miscellanies* contains one work, *Jonathan Wild*,
the most political, as well as the most considerable, piece in the collection. In the 1743 version, even more than the somewhat depoliticized
1754 version most moderns read, it is as laced with general and particular
political satire as Fielding's plays of the later 1730s or Gay's *Beggar's
Opera*, to which it is massively indebted. Its political satire falls into

three fairly distinct categories. First, *Jonathan Wild* is a general critique of political and military glory, of "Greatness" that is not "true," not combined or even compatible with "Goodness." This general critique applies to the "great Men" of Fielding's own times, George II, Prince Frederick, Walpole, and Carteret, but it equally applies to Alexander of Macedon or Charles XII of Sweden. It is the most pervasive variety of political satire in *Jonathan Wild*, present implicitly or explicitly on nearly every page. It is also timelessly applicable, a fact that doubtless explains the continued appeal of this work when most of Fielding's highly topical pieces are unread. At this broadest level, the confrontation between the "Great," evil Wild and the "Good," vulnerable Heartfrees, ending in the triumph of light over darkness, is a fable with combined moral and political significance. It is set at a level of abstraction that distances it from the narrower area of partisan conflict that has been denominated "politics" throughout this study. The existence and tendency of this level of political significance (heavily stressed by Fielding in his explanation of the "Good," the "Great," and the "Good and Great" man in the "Preface" to the *Miscellanies*) is too pervasive and obvious to require much exemplification. Readers interested in the subsumption of the political into the "fundamental ethical problem" in the work will find it well explained in W. R. Irwin's *The Making of Jonathan Wild*. From Chapter I (which initiates the ironical pattern of praising the ruthless evil of the "Great" Wild and mocking virtue as imperfection) to the end Fielding didactically stresses the misery which "Greatness" inflicts not only on humble men, but on the "Great Man" himself. He also stresses the resemblances between Wild and all the bloody-handed, corrupt, freedom-destroying "Great Men" of history. Wild and his prigs move unhappily toward the gallows, spreading ruin about them as they prey on London and vie with one another for dominance and profit, as did Alexander, Caesar, Wolsey, Charles XII, and, for that matter, Milton's Satan. Wild lectures the Count La Ruse on the relativity of ambition and "Greatness":

> I had rather stand on the Summit of a Dunghil, than at the bottom of a Hill in Paradise; I have always thought it signifies little into what Rank of Life I am thrown, provided I make a great Figure therein; and should be as well satisfied with exerting my Talents well at the Head of a small Party or Gang, as in Command of a mighty Army . . . . the same Genius, the same Inducements have often composed the States-man and the *Prig*, for so we call what the Vulgar name a *Thief*. The same Parts, the same Actions often promote Men to the Head of superior Societies, which raise them to the Head of lower; and where is the essential Difference if the one ends on *Tower*-Hill, and the other at *Tyburn*?[39]

Jonathan Wild is also permeated by narrower satire suggesting that Jonathan Wild, the chief of the "Prigs," is *very* like Robert Walpole at the head of his corrupt ministry. In some places the connection is made overtly but, as J. E. Wells pointed out long ago, this is only the tip of the iceberg. Once the hint was given, every ironical jab at "Greatness," every equation of "Great Man" and "rascal," every account of the vicious, amoral activities of Wild and his gang could be regarded as a dig at Sir Robert, even when the text made no specific connection between Newgate and Westminster.[40] Such multiplication of targets was a specialty of the age. Swift's Flimnap is Walpole as well as the type of the evil minister and a discussion of Wolsey in the *Craftsman* would be read doubly. Fielding had most skillfully cultivated such effects since 1731, when he converted *Tom Thumb* into *The Tragedy of Tragedies, or the Life and Death of Tom Thumb the Great*.

So clear is the anti-Walpole aspect of *Jonathan Wild* that the only real ambiguities about it stem from its date of publication, more than a year after Walpole fell (moving into the Lords and toward political irrelevance), and from some gestures toward blurring and reapplying the assault on Walpole. Fielding added the latter in revising his work before initial publication and again in preparing the version published in 1754. It is impossible to picture Fielding composing, after the spring of 1742, some of the more palpable hits on Walpole or the sections of the work most readily applicable to his behaviour in office. I must agree with scholars who have suggested earlier composition (in, say, 1740 or 1741), though no external evidence really solidifies the case for this.[41] The situation seems complicated further by *Jonathan Wild*'s unevenness of quality and doubleness of focus. The anti-Walpole account of Wild's life that takes up roughly half of the work is better than the melodramatic and rather turgid account of Wild's villainous behaviour to the Heartfrees. I believe it was composed earlier. A sharp, hard little political and moral satire was crossed as a second thought with something closer to Fielding's novels in tone and spirit (most like parts of *Amelia*), though not in quality. Moreover, I do not believe that the boring and pointless account of Mrs. Heartfree's travels was part, in anything like the form in which we have it, of the original plan or even of the Heartfree element imposed upon it. Fielding very seldom wrote narrative of such poor quality. My guess is that her story was written and tacked onto *Jonathan Wild* very late in a hurried process of revision and expansion to fill a volume carried out not very long before publication. It is the pattern of *A Journey from This World to the Next* all over again: there we move from the narrator's amusing tour of the underworld through Julian's dawdling history to the irrelevant history of Anne Boleyn, and here we slide from Wild-Walpole, to Wild *versus* Heartfree, to Mrs. Heartfree's travels. I suggest that the Wild-Heartfree material and the travels of Mrs. Heartfree were *successively* superimposed upon an already drafted, shorter life of Wild after the fall of Walpole had dated the latter. This roughly doubled the original length and made it approximate the form of a primitive novel as much as a satiric parody of a rogue's biography on the order of Defoe's life of Wild.

There are other complications. Two passages unquestionably were inserted after the spring of 1742 with the intention of extending the satire on Walpole to insult Lords Bath (Pulteney) and Carteret. Modern readers generally do not see the most obvious of these items, the last "Proverb" in Book II, Chapter 12, because the whole chapter was removed from the revised edition of 1754 that has since been the standard text of *Jonathan Wild*. As we will see, this "updating" of the 1743 version was not a result of pro-Walpole sentiment, but of anti-Carteret, anti-Pulteney animus. We must be careful of C. J. Rawson's over-simple explanation: ". . . Walpole had fallen by the time the novel was published, and . . . Fielding may have gone through a pro-Walpole phase after he had drafted the anti-Walpole part of the novel but before he prepared the whole novel for publication." I approve Rawson's concept of the process of composition, but not his simplified concept of its shifting political backdrop. There is not a shadow of "pro-Walpole" intent in *Jonathan Wild*.[42]

The ambiguities about the patterns of composition and alteration that gave us the 1743 version of *Jonathan Wild* seem impossible finally to resolve in the absence of manuscripts. But it is obvious that very little in it would have seemed at odds with the intention to treat Walpole as a political Wild if it had appeared in 1741. The passages that make general political satire and moral didacticism anti-Walpole are many and obtrusive. The Table of Contents alone would raise suspicion, in somewhat the way the subtitle and *dramatis personae* of *The Tragedy of Tragedies* did in 1731. It dwells on phraseology suggesting Walpole's nickname, the "Great Man": ". . . *those wonderful Productions of Nature called* GREAT MEN," "*The Birth, Parentage, and Education of Mr. Jonathan Wild the Great*," "*Shewing the Consequences, which attended* Heart-free's *Adventures with* Wild; *all natural, and common enough to little Wretches, who deal with* GREAT MEN." The text includes so many sharp, obvious hits at Walpole that only the high points can be mentioned. In Chapter 5, Count La Ruse asks: "Can any Man doubt, whether it is better to be a prime Minister, or a common Thief? . . . Doth it not ask as good a Memory, as nimble an Invention, as steady a Countenance, to forswear yourself in *Westminster-Hall*, as would furnish out a complete Ministerial Tool, or perhaps a prime Minister himself?" There was no identifiable "prime minister" in the coalition ministry put together in 1742 (or indeed in that constructed in 1744), and the pre-1742, anti-Walpole animus of this is patent. The same is true of the really angry verdict in Wild's rejoinder to La Ruse on the proper fate of an evil statesman, one of the many cries for Walpole's blood in his last years in power.[43] The gang leader, when caught, is hanged and forgotten, while the minister "is not only hated in Power, but detested and condemned at the Scaffold; and future ages vent their Malice on his Fame, while the other sleeps quiet and forgotten." The minister suffers in his conscience not from "having taken a few shillings or Pounds from a Stranger," but from "having betrayed a publick Trust and ruined the Fortunes of Thousands." The next morning Wild advises La Ruse to bribe his way out of captivity at the Snaps. On learning he is penniless, he recommends that he "make it up with promises, which he supposed he was Courtier enough to know how to put off." This is precisely the opposition's Walpole, briber and promiser of bribes. La Ruse hopes "to persuade him [Wild] to condescend to be a Great Man, for which he was so perfectly qualified."

Again and again the comparisons of the great criminal to other kinds of great men culminate in a parallel of prig and prime minister:

> Now suppose a *Prig* had as many Tools as any Prime Minister ever had, would he not be as GREAT as any Prime Minister whatsoever? [Book I, chapter 14] 'Tis the inward Glory, the secret Consciousness of doing great and wonderful Actions, which can alone support the truly GREAT Man, whether he be a CONQUERER, a TYRANT, a MINISTER, or a PRIG. [Book II, chapter 4]
> Have not whole Armies and Nations been sacrificed to the Humour of ONE GREAT MAN? Nay, to omit that first Class of Greatness, the Conqueror of Mankind, how often have Numbers fallen, by a fictitious Plot, only to satisfy the spleen, or perhaps exercise the Ingenuity of a member of that second Order of GREATNESS the *Ministerial!* [Book IV, chapter 4]

The reference to "ONE GREAT MAN" is pure anti-Walpole rhetoric, quite out of date after his fall. Each of the ministerial coalitions of the decade following 1742 took pains to stress that they were led by several great public servants, not a single "prime minister." We will find Fielding making this distinction very carefully in defending the Broad-Bottom ministry in 1747-48. We are seeing Walpole, before his fall, when we see Wild "setting himself at the Head of a Gang [the majority in Parliament or the other ministers?], which he had not any shadow of a Right to govern; . . . maintaining absolute Power, and exercising Tyranny over a lawless Crew, contrary to all Law, but that of his own Will" (Book IV, chapter 16). When Fielding wishes that all "GREAT MEN" might join Wild on the gallows (e.g., II,13; IV,15) we recognize a sentiment common in anti-Walpole propaganda, from the 1730s through Walpole's escape into Lords in 1742. At moments *Jonathan Wild* has the flow and tone of a *Champion* essay from 1740. The attack on schemes to gag the press in IV,2 sounds like "Hercules Vinegar, Esq." accusing *The Daily Gazetteer* of such intentions:

> There is one Misfortune that attends all great Men and their Schemes, viz. That in order to carry them into Execution, they are obliged in proposing their Purpose to their Tools, to discover themselves to be of that Disposition, in which certain little Writers have advised Mankind to place no Confidence: An advice which hath been sometimes taken. Indeed many Inconveniences arise to the said GREAT MEN from these Scriblers publishing without Restraint their Hints or Alarms to Society; and many great and glorious Schemes have been thus frustrated wherefore it were to be wished that in all well regulated Governments, such Liberty should by some wholesome Laws be restrained; and all Writers inhibited from venting any other Instructions to the People than what should be first approved and licensed by the said

GREAT MEN, or their proper Instruments or Tools; by which Means nothing would ever be published but what made for the advancing of their most noble Projects.

This kind of specific political satire in *Jonathan Wild* has the feel of the closing Walpole years. However, a third level of political significance is briefly apparent in *Jonathan Wild:* there are two isolated but crucial attacks on the betrayers of opposition after Walpole's fall, obviously added in 1742-43. These additions (one lengthy, the other brief and sharp) are unmistakably alien to the material surrounding them. A broadening of animus from Walpole to others is insisted upon, under the thinnest veil of irony, in the "Preface" to the *Miscellanies* (my italics):

> . . . as it is not a very faithful Portrait of *Jonathan Wild* himself, so neither is it intended to represent the Features of any other Person. Roguery, and not a Rogue, is my subject; and as I have been so far from endeavouring to particularize any Individual, that I have with my utmost Art avoided it; so will any such Application be unfair to my Reader, especially if he knows much of the Great World, since *he must then be acquainted*, I believe, *with more than one on whom he can fix the Resemblance.*

The point is that by 1743 Fielding wished to satirize more than one great rogue, and "Proverb XII" in Book II, chapter 12 ("Of Proverbs") all but names William Pulteney, newly Lord Bath: "debauching a Member of the House of Commons from his Principles, and creating him a Peer, is not much better than making a Woman a Whore, and afterwards marrying her." The whole chapter (removed *in toto* in 1754) was probably added late. It is unfunny and unmeaning, aside from the twelfth and last "Proverb," and extraordinarily unrelated to the rest of *Jonathan Wild* even by Fielding's digressive standards. But the blood drawn from Lord Bath probably seemed in 1743 to justify the chapter. Significantly, the narrator apologizes in the closing paragraph (immediately after "Proverb XII") for going on so long, and ironically hints his motivation: "Thus having . . . *staid somewhat longer on these Sentences than is agreeable to the Proportion of an Example,* and perhaps offended some, who will direct the Force of this Chapter (if it have any) where it was little meant; I now return to our Hero." Once again, the process of hurriedly updating political satire in preparing a lengthy piece for the *Miscellanies* left it structurally ragged.

Satire on Walpole also gives way to satire on the turncoats of 1742 (in this case it fits both Pulteney and Carteret) in the account of Wild's displacement of Roger Johnson as ruler of the Newgate prigs in Book IV, Chapter 2. Fielding went to unusual lengths in altering the facts to yield the pattern desired, converting Johnson, a partner of Wild's in fact, into his greatest rival. Though it is possible to read it as an account of Walpole's struggles with his rivals in the 1720s, as Wilbur Cross did, so distant an application seems most unlikely.[44] Instead, we must, in this one chapter, adjust our reading of the allegory, seeing Roger Johnson as equivalent to Walpole in his last years and the moment of his fall, while

Jonathan Wild represents both Pulteney and Carteret, urging reform with fine rhetoric until the old leader falls, then grasping for his "Place and Power." We have seen that varying allegorical equations was habitual with Fielding. Once entertained, this reading becomes more compelling with each paragraph in the chapter.

Roger Johnson, "a very GREAT MAN, had long been at the Head of all the Prigs" when Wild entered Newgate. This fits only Walpole, twenty years in power. Wild behaved as Pulteney had in Commons, representing Johnson "as a Fellow, who under the plausible Pretence of assisting their Causes, was in Reality undermining the liberties of Newgate." Having "by Degrees formed a Party against Roger," in a "florid" speech he accused Johnson of threatening the "Liberty of Newgate" and the "Privileges" (both those of Commons and Constitutional freedoms) of its inmates. They "have been long undermined and are now openly violated by one Man."[45] The speech is broken off (the only copy being defective, says the narrator) as Wild fulminates against Johnson's gaudy "silk Night-Gown," purchased with the liberties and blood of condemned prigs. One presumes it represents both the fortune Walpole was said to have stolen and the public money and patronage he controlled. Wild's speech, like so many of Pulteney's in its emphases as well as its floridity, leads to open rivalry for control of Newgate. The prison "was divided into Parties on this Occasion; the *Prigs* on each Side writing to one another [the activity of journalists, not felons], and representing their Chief or GREAT MAN to be the only Person by whom the affairs of *Newgate* could be managed with safety and Advantage." The Prigs were divided by self-interest, each side expecting "Plunder" on its leader's "Exaltation"; the two parties of the Prigs represent Walpole's group and the more cynical professionals in the old opposition. The debtors in Newgate also took sides with great violence in this basically "priggish" struggle. This obviously represents the involvement of the "Country gentlemen" and "honest" backbenchers as well as Fielding's Broad-Bottom patrons in the struggles of the 1730s and early 1740s.

At length, we are told, Wild won, as Pulteney and Carteret had, but the result was of benefit only to himself:

> . . . he succeeded to the Place and Power of *Johnson*, whom he presently stript of all his finery; but when it was proposed, that he should sell it, and divide the Money for the good of the whole; he waved that Motion, saying it was not time, that he should find a better Opportunity, that the Clothes wanted cleaning, with many other Pretences, and, within two days, to the Surprise of many, he appeared in them himself, for which he vouchsafed no other Apology than, that they fitted him much better than they did *Johnson*, and that they became him in a much more elegant Manner.

The debtors were "greatly incensed . . . particularly those by whose Means he had been promoted": the reaction of the Country and Broad-Bottom wings of the old opposition to the betrayal of 1742. However, a "very grave Man" with "much authority among them" (this fits several leaders of the "new" opposition; I favour Lord Bolingbroke or Lord Cobham)[46] pointed out their folly in believing the replacement of one gang of prigs (Walpole's faction) with another (the Pulteney-Carteret clique) would benefit them or reform Newgate. What was needed was a general change in "Manners" throughout the prison. He suggested that the debtors form an interest separate from either faction (always a key concept in Bolingbrokean Broad-Bottom theory, partially realized in 1743 when the Country/Broad-Bottom "shadow cabinet" was formed), and oppose not one prig, but priggism—corruption. "Liberty is consistent with no degree of Honesty inferior to this," and it is in their interest "to resolve bravely to lay aside our *Priggism*, our Roguery, in plainer Words, and preserve our Liberty." The debtors applauded this Broad-Bottom oration, but Wild continued "to strut openly in the Ornaments which he had stript from *Johnson*." The only consolation was that in this

> there was more Bravado than real Use or Advantage . . . . As for the Night-Gown, its Outside indeed made a glittering Tinsel Appearance, but it kept him not warm; nor could the Finery of it do him much Honour, since everyone knew it did not properly belong to him, nor indeed suited his Degree . . . . these Clothes . . . brought him more Envy, Hatred and Detraction, than all his deeper Impositions, and more real Advantages; afforded very little Use or Honour to the Wearer; nay, could scarce serve to amuse his own Vanity, when it was cool enough to reflect with the least Seriousness.

The mixture here of indignation, sour grapes, and hopes for early retribution (Wild's death warrant arrives in the first sentence of the following chapter!) is the quintessence of all the emotions felt by the Broad-Bottoms in 1743 as they contemplated Pulteney in the Lords and Carteret encouraging the King to carry on with policies he had criticized under Walpole.

Fielding left off writing for a surprising length of time after he got his *Miscellanies* through the press; presumably it earned him enough to afford a breathing space. The many signs of hasty compiling and revision in those three volumes probably indicate that he was already having difficulty focussing on the job in late 1742 and early 1743. The *Miscellanies* do not indicate much current enthusiasm for creation and the fact that he published as a means of escaping pressing financial difficulties indicates that he had grounds to doubt that literature was a route to a secure future. Perhaps he was again in the mood that silenced him in 1737-39. Then too the final deterioration of his wife's health, ending in her death in 1744, would have distracted a colder husband than we know him to have been. But the prime reason for his silence was no doubt just what he implied in the Preface to the second edition of his sister Sarah's novel, *The Adventures of David Simple*, his first publication since the *Miscellanies* when it appeared in the fall of 1744. Law seemed a better livelihood than writing, and it kept him very busy. This is said in the course of a declaration that he did not write the *Causidicade*, a pamphlet insulting to men at the top of the legal profession that had been "fathered" on him, but it is probably an accurate statement. Whatever the precise mixture of reasons, Fielding not only withdrew from writing for a year and a half, but then fell silent again until the early fall of 1745, after publishing the "Preface" to *David Simple* and the 23-page pamphlet called *An Attempt toward a Natural History of the Hanover Rat*, which appeared in November 1744. The "Preface" is unimportant and apolitical, unless one considers its disowning of the *Causidicade* a political gesture, and there seems no reason to do so. The *Attempt*, a violent, anonymous attack on Hanoverian foreign policies, crept so quietly into print that it was not attributed to Fielding until 1935. The publication of no more than a preface and a brief, obscure pamphlet in a period of almost two and a half years in the middle of the career of a prolific writer is the more amazing because there is no evidence that he was working on a major project, as he probably was (the first draft of *Tom Jones*) during his next quiet phase, mid-1746 to late 1747.[47]

The political world thus deprived of Fielding's satiric commentary should have been anything but unstimulating during his months of silence, especially to a writer with Broad-Bottom connections. The odd anti-ministerial pamphlet or *Old England* essay from Fielding would surely have gratified Lyttelton and Chesterfield, who blossomed into the most active and formidable of "new" opposition propagandists in 1743-44. His patrons were playing a complicated and exciting game of baiting the ministry in the hopes of forcing Carteret (backed by Pulteney, the King, and the Prince) out of the ministerial coalition and themselves into a new one with the Pelhams.[48] In 1743-44 Carteret was the enemy not only of his old opposition colleagues, but of his contemporary ministerial partners. Newcastle, Henry Pelham, Hardwicke, and the rest of the cabinet resented the growing power he derived from his position as the King's favourite foreign policy advisor and his habit of treating with scant respect the men who controlled the Parliamentary majorities necessary for acceptance and financing of the policies he and George II favoured.

The Pelhams often had an inadequate voice in the diplomatic decisions they had to defend in Commons. This was not an impossible situation when Carteret's schemes worked. In 1742 he talked George into reversing his declaration of Hanoverian neutrality of 1741 and obtained peace between Maria Theresa and Prussia, one of her encircling foes, at the moderate cost of guaranteeing Frederick's possession of Silesia, already in his hands, in the Treaty of Breslau. He concluded alliances with Sweden and Russia which were of considerable potential importance. He also laid the foundations for the so-called "pragmatic army," composed of English troops, Hessians and Hanoverians in English pay, Austrian and, finally, Dutch troops. It rendered the allies far more formidable in Germany, especially with the 30,000-man Prussian army no longer fighting alongside the French. After the battle of Dettingen in mid-1743, where the Pragmatic Army led by George II himself beat the French, England's position on the continent seemed stronger than it had for years.

However, the effect of this on Carteret was unfortunate. His ministerial colleagues remained in England, abused by the opposition, while Carteret and George played power politics in Hanover and elsewhere in northern Europe between May and December 1743. Barely informing them of his plans or actions, Carteret entered into a frenzy of negotiations, skillful, but so tortuous they had finally to backfire. Instead of following up Dettingen, he moved to the negotiating table. At Hanau he worked through the unreliable Prince William of Hesse to win over Charles VII, the virtually powerless Elector of Bavaria and Holy Roman Emperor. This irritated Frederick of Prussia, whose re-entry into the war against Austria in 1744 was a severe setback. Carteret also obtained an agreement between England, Maria Theresa, and Charles VII of Savoy, King of Sardinia, formalized in the Treaty of Worms of 1743, that was designed to counter Spanish aggression in southern Europe. But this accomplished little and was expensive. England agreed to pay £500,000 a year to Austria, out of which Austria would pay Charles VII £200,000 a year. The £500,000 had to be voted yearly by the English Parliament. When Carteret proposed adding a convention to the Treaty of Worms guaranteeing the yearly Austrian subsidy for the duration of the war, the Pelhams voted down the proposal in the Cabinet Council, nine to four. Without going into the extreme complexities of European power politics in 1743-44, we can observe the net effect of all of Carteret's schemings. In late 1744, after immense expenditures by the English, Austria was on the defensive again, assaulted by both France and Prussia, and the momentum of Dettingen had been permanently lost. England herself felt threatened by a Jacobite-French invasion which she would have been ill equipped to repel since 14,000 of her troops were tied up (along with virtually every mercenary she had hired in Germany) in the "pragmatic army."[49] The legacy of Carteret is perhaps symbolized by the fact that in 1745 England had nothing more tangible to take pride in than the courage shown by English troops under the Duke of Cumberland in the bloody defeat at Fontenoy. She also had to scramble to find enough reliable regiments to repel the advance of Charles Stuart's small, irregular Highland army upon London during the "Forty-Five." If France had joined in the Jacobite invasion, desperation might have become disaster.

At home, the effects of Carteret's schemes and behaviour were more immediately negative. His foreign policy was not easy to fault in 1742, though even then the payment of Hanoverians by England was protested. But in 1743, as we have seen, there was a growing outcry against Hanoverian measures, land warfare, and continental intrigue, rather than a straightforward, pro-trade, English naval strategy. It crested in the debates on retaining 16,000 Hanover troops in English pay during

December 1743 and January 1744. One can only imagine the uproar if the Pelhams had allowed the convention indefinitely granting £500,000 a year to Maria Theresa to reach the Commons! Foreign policy was the Achilles' heel of the coalition ministry, as it had been for Walpole. Carteret seemed determined to bring wrath down on himself and his colleagues, and George II was another problem. At Dettingen George won a victory that should have proven the wisdom of employing the Hanoverian troops. They were brave and well disciplined, whatever the opposition might say, and an essential constituent of the "pragmatic army." However, George inflamed public opinion by tactlessly wearing a yellow Hanoverian sash rather than a red English one at the head of his army.

Seven months of being ignored by the King and scarcely half informed by Carteret (whose dispatches and letters from Germany were few even when negotiations of the most essential kind were being carried out) taught the Duke of Newcastle (the other Secretary of State), his brother Henry Pelham, Hardwicke, and the rest of the ex-Walpolians that coexistence with Carteret was intolerable in the long run. They worked to solidify their position, aided quietly by the still influential Lord Orford. When the figurehead Wilmington died in July 1743, Carteret supported Pulteney's bid for Walpole's old post of First Lord of the Treasury. However, urged by Orford and pressured by the cabinet majority, the King appointed Henry Pelham, solidifying the latter's hold on Commons and beginning the process that would make him the most powerful politician in England by the later 1740s. The Pelhams also privately half-welcomed, as they publicly fought off, the opposition's assaults on Carteret's foreign policies and the Hanover troops. Carteret paid for his contempt for the abilities and influence of his colleagues. He left the cultivation of Parliament to them while he adventured in Europe: "What is it to me who is a judge or a bishop? It is my business to make Kings and emperors, and to maintain the balance of Europe."[50] Since control of Commons was at least as essential as royal favour, this attitude doomed Carteret as well as the coalition patched together in 1742. Carteret was over-confident, believing that "any man with the crown on his side can defy anything." Though their fates were long balanced on a knife-edge, the Pelhams would force him from the ministry in late 1744 and oblige the King to cease consulting him and support them fully in early 1746.

In 1743 and 1744, Chesterfield declaimed in pamphlets and *Old England* against Hanoverian measures and the "Hanover Forces in the Pay of Great Britain." William Pitt saw England as a "province to a despicable electorate" and hinted that the loyalty of the English to a German king was not inexhaustible. Lord Sandwich called for "a zealous opposition . . . to all destructive, particularly all Hanoverian Measures."[51] All this was a help, as well as an embarrassment, to the Pelhams and their allies. Carteret was the chief target of opposition anger. A turncoat in 1742, in 1743-44 he was to Pitt "one English minister without an

English Heart," a "Hanoverian troop-master" with 16,000 Hanoverian "place-men." Before the parliamentary winter session of 1743-44 the opposition Broad-Bottoms and the Pelhamite majority in the cabinet engaged in preliminary, abortive negotiations toward a Pelhamite/Broad-Bottom ministry, excluding Carteret and, as always, the Country element. The negotiations of 1743 were quietly encouraged by Lord Orford, backer of the Pelhams against Carteret, who urged his protégés to build their strength around his "old Corps" and "recruits from the Cobham squadron," to "Whig it with all that will parly," being carefully only to " 'ware Tory." In the end the negotiations failed since the Broad-Bottoms (particularly Lord Cobham) demanded too much, and the Pelhams had finally to defeat the opposition's campaign against the Hanover troops if they were to remain in office.[52] The Broad-Bottoms returned to the attack on Hanoverianism with renewed energy, but thereafter an accommodation bringing them places and unseating Carteret was never far from their minds. In late 1744 they would acquiesce in Hanoverian measures, though neither they nor the Pelhams would delight in them, once their price in places and other patronage was met and their spite against Carteret satisfied. Indeed, they would even set their price very low.

As the diplomatic and military successes of 1743 turned into the problems of 1744, Carteret's position became increasingly unstable. His colleagues hated him, and the public associated him with unpopular Hanoverian measures. The powerful backing of the King, the Prince, and Pulteney could not forever balance lack of influence in Commons. The Pelhams were weighing the dangers and irritations of coexisting with Carteret against the dangers of forcing the King to choose between them and Carteret. Once the former outweighed the latter, and they could be sure the Broad-Bottoms would join them at a price the King could be obliged to meet, Carteret would be forced from office. The opposition was applying pressure—in Parliament and in the press—that could only hasten the Pelhams along the road toward an open confrontation with Carteret and the King. The anti-ministerial shadow cabinet co-ordinated the campaign, while the fears of invasion by the French and the Jacobites, and the re-entry of Prussia into the War of the Austrian Succession provided grounds for complaint. In April, in the very act of supporting measures of defence against invasion from France, Pitt lambasted Carteret, while ignoring the Pelhams.[53] In the fall, the looming of another round of debates on the Hanover troops and various continental subsidies forced the Pelhams to act decisively.

The final steps leading to the fall of Carteret and the formation of a new ministerial coalition were taken deliberately, but inexorably. In August 1744, Bolingbroke advocated gentle treatment of the Pelhams in the coming winter session of Parliament if Carteret still survived when it opened, since the Pelhams would have to be confident of Broad-Bottom support before they could insist on his dismissal. Bolingbroke was convinced that Carteret's policies had proved disastrous, and that the

dismissal of "the madman, who brought us into this situation" and a
Broad-Bottom "junction with the Pelhams" were equally essential. How
odd to find Bolingbroke and Lord Orford on the same wave-length! By
September, the Earl of Marchmont detected a weakening of even Prince
Frederick's support for Carteret, and Carteret was defending his
diplomacy in the teeth of Henry Pelham, the Duke of Newcastle, and
Lord Hardwicke. Still, the Pelhams were loath to coerce a King stubborn
and independent in foreign affairs and the choosing of ministers, and
feared a failure of opposition support. Newcastle worried: "If we did
[force out Carteret], who could we take in his place? for the Opposition
won't join us but upon an alteration of measures, which the King will
never be easy with, or consent to." But to Chesterfield the only answer
was obvious: "Why don't the boobies [the Pelhams] see, that Carteret,
who has got the closet [the King's ear] will, when peace is made, not be
easy, till he is the domestic master too?" In October Lyttelton reported
that the Prince of Wales was confusedly dithering about the need not to
force the ministry to the wall over the Hanover troops in the coming session. Lyttelton was clearly ready to trade his relationship with Frederick
for a place whenever the Pelhams decided to act.

In late October and early November the Pelhams moved. They more
openly opposed the foreign policies of Carteret. Then they informed the
King "that the other part of his ministers or Carteret must go"
(November 6), and that "they could not serve with him; that he had
engaged them in measures, he himself must think ruinous" (November
8). They gave the King a week or ten days to consider this; in effect, to
see if Carteret could form a ministry without them. The inevitable
followed: royal rage, unsuccessful attempts by the King to woo individual ministers over to Carteret. George offered some magnates—including Cobham and Gower—places in a ministry dominated by
Carteret, but this they treated as an "opportunity to show the King, the
Prince and the World that they did not oppose for places . . . could not
serve with Lord Carteret . . . his schemes were so wild, so impracticable,
and so inconsistent with the interest of England, that they could not
possibly concur with them." Lord Chesterfield expressed the Broad-
Bottom attitude toward Carteret and his clique more succinctly: "Let
'em bleed." Threats from the King and the Prince did nothing. The last
expedient of all, an appeal to the great Lord Orford, brought only a
recommendation that the King accept the wishes of the cabinet majority
—hardly a surprise considering his quiet encouragement of a Pelham/
Broad-Bottom coalition for more than a year. Finally, on November 24
Carteret resigned his post, his ministerial epitaph provided by Thomas
Winnington, the foxy survivor: "Had he studied Parliament more and
Demosthenes less, he would have been a more successful minister."[54]

This defeat certainly did not mean that Carteret was without
political strength or that the new coalition, the "Broad-Bottom
Ministry," was secure. The ministry's parliamentary position was very
strong, in votes and debating strength, but the King still favoured

Carteret, especially as a foreign affairs advisor. Indeed he treated the ministers who had presumed to dictate to him with indignant and contemptuous brusqueness. The new ministry would not be safe until the ministerial crisis of 1746 taught George that a viable government headed by Lord Bath and Earl Granville (Carteret inherited the family title in 1744) was impossible. He learned he had to employ and fully trust the Pelhams and their colleagues and drop Granville. But that is a matter for the next chapter; here the crucial point is that Fielding's patrons, the Broad-Bottoms, were finally included in the ministry.

They were sneered at for turning their coats by the Country group and the disgruntled followers of Bath and Granville. Lyttelton and Pitt were dismissed by the Prince. They had to settle for relatively minor posts in the new ministerial arrangements announced before Parliament was recessed for Christmas. Henry Pelham (First Lord of the Treasury and Chancellor of the Exchequer), the Duke of Newcastle (Secretary of State), Hardwicke (Lord Chancellor), and other survivors kept the most senior posts, Lord Harrington taking Carteret's place as the other Secretary of State. George Lyttelton got a profitable but not very powerful appointment as a Lord of the Treasury (under Henry Pelham, First Lord), Richard Grenville got a place at the Admiralty, Chesterfield became Lord Lieutenant of Ireland and was sent on an important diplomatic mission to the Hague, Dodington became Treasurer of the Navy, and the Duke of Bedford became First Lord of the Admiralty. Lord Cobham (who in 1743 had resigned the Colonelcy of the 1st Horse Guards, which he was given in 1742, as a protest against Hanover measures) was appointed Colonel of the 1st Dragoons, accepting only on the assurance that henceforth Hanoverian interests would be subordinated to English ones. For William Pitt, hated by the King, there was nothing more than a promise of employment when the Pelhams could cajole or coerce the King to allow it. To complete the broadening of the ministry's "Bottom" Lord Gower became Lord Privy Seal.[55] But the Broad-Bottoms finally had something, after nine years of energetic opposition. For the immediate future they would prove loyal to the Pelhams. They would also accept the diplomatic strategies and military stumbling that characterized the closing years of the dismal War of the Austrian Succession, even though they hardly met the standards they had endorsed so recently in opposition. Even Pitt usually soft-pedalled his anti-ministerial, anti-Hanoverian diatribes to avoid embarrassing his friends in place and to keep alive his hope that the King would soon be ready to employ him. Pitt's opinions on foreign policy were strong and generally valid, but his hunger for office, profit, and the opportunity to shape events was as sharp as that of any other Broad-Bottom.

Fielding remained silent during all but the last phase of this great struggle of ministers. When he did join the chorus of anti-Hanover propagandists with the publication of *An Attempt toward a Natural History of the Hanover Rat* in the fall of 1744, he incorporated the standard anti-Hanover themes into a very funny, biting parody of scientific presentation, first cousin to *Some Papers Proper to be Read before the R---l Society* of 1743. Stylistically, it is vintage Fielding. However, the ill timing that forced him to revise *Jonathan Wild* and *A Journey from This World to the Next* after Walpole fell still afflicted him. He must have been thankful that he published the *Attempt* anonymously, having prepared the ground in the apolitical "Preface" to *David Simple*, where he withdrew the promise made in the "Preface" to the *Miscellanies* that he would in future publish only under his name. In November 1744, when *An Attempt* was in the bookstalls (his hand in it mercifully unrecognized),[56] the last steps leading to the fall of Carteret were being taken, and anti-Hanoverian rhetoric was about to become an embarrassment to his patrons in their new ministerial roles. In December 1743 Lyttelton would have loved *An Attempt*, and as Fielding completed it (presumably in September or October 1744) it must have seemed a useful contribution to the last barrage of anti-Hanoverianism that it was hoped would force Carteret toward the abyss and the Pelhams toward risking the reconstruction of the ministry. By mid-November, however, it was anything but timely, and after November 23 Fielding surely tried to forget he ever wrote it. At least, though his luck was unusually bad, Fielding was not alone in backtracking. Chesterfield had to move with extraordinary rapidity in December to sever his connections with *Old England*, which would, with a different staff and sponsorship, harass the Broad-Bottom ministry in the later 1740s as steadily as it had the Carteret-Pelham coalition. Its claim in those years would be that it, not the ministry, truly adhered to Broad-Bottom ideals.[57] A great reversal, a natural result of being on the ministerial side, had begun. Between 1746 and 1749 Fielding would equate acceptance of the Broad-Bottom ministry and its policies, foreign and domestic, with loyalty to King and country. He would associate precisely the kind of anti-Hanoverian opposition rhetoric found in *An Attempt* with Jacobitism and sedition.

An Attempt parodies the scientific manner in the spirit of *Some Papers*, but this time the political element momentarily present in the earlier work is utterly dominant. Substituting the "Hanover Rat" (rather than the guinea) for the polyp, Fielding drolly rehearses the anti-Hanoverian themes of Pitt, Chesterfield, and *Old England*. The learned "author" has studied these rats for thirty years (precisely the time that had elapsed since George I became the first Hanoverian King in 1714), and informs us the species is not "native to these Islands," but to the Electorate. However, they are so good at evading English traps (English law or parliamentary control) that "they must in Process of Time increase to such a Degree, that the Country would suffer extremely by them."[58] They notoriously are hungry for "Steel, Brass, Pewter, Tin, Copper, Silver, Gold (of the two last it is particularly fond)" (p. 8). Their appetite explains the scarcity of utensils (plate, sold to pay taxes to support the Court and the war) in the homes of country gentlemen, who say (p. 8), "They had such Things formerly, but the *Hanover Rat* hath snatched them away from them." (The perfect reversal of political attitude Fielding underwent after 1744 is symbolized when Squire Western reveals he is an opposition Country booby and perhaps a Jacobite by saying roughly the same thing in *Tom Jones*.) One passage looks specifically at the 16,000 Hanoverian troops in British pay: "There is a Gentleman of my Acquaintance very well versed in Political Arithmetic, who tells me there is no Possibility of being exact as to the number of them now in the Kingdom, but he computes that the feeding of 16,000 of them (including what they hoard, as well as what they devour) must cost the Publick as much as the Poor's Rates of all the Parishes in the Nation amount to" (pp. 8-9).

The rats' appearance is not unlike that of George II. Wide-mouthed, they have "Eyes of a light grey, something like those of *Horses* that are called wall-eyed" (p. 10), probably a reference to the protuberant eyes of the early Hanoverians. Closer yet, when the rat is in a passion it behaves like George, who was notorious for kicking courtiers in the rump and much ridiculed for "rumping": "it always strikes or kicks with its hind legs" (p. 12). They are afraid to fight (as was said of the Hanoverian troops), but the overgrown "Common English Rat" (the ministry) acts as their "Provider," searching out food (i.e., taxing) for them in every barn, warehouse, and cellar (pp. 13-14). In a passage that would in November 1744 have been understood as threatening the ministry with a renewal in the coming session of the troubles of December and January 1743-44 over the Hanover troops, the scientist observes ". . . that there will be a petition from the several Countries and Cities of *Great Britain* for leave to bring in a Bill for importing Rats-Bane free of Duty, it being the common Opinion that if these Providers were destroyed, the Losses which the Nation suffers by the voracious Quality of the Hanover Rats would soon cease" (p. 15).

Until something is done about them the rats will be a menace. Their providers are "assiduous and attentive . . . to the Looks and Motions of their Master." As soon as the rats arrived, they were surrounded by "these Agents or Ministers" and "fell to undermining a large building near the Thames" (Parliament) formerly thought to be on so "solid a Foundation that Nothing could hurt it . . . [that] had always before served as a safe Retreat for our *English Rats* when exposed to any extraordinary Danger" (p. 16). A more specific indictment of Pulteney and Carteret is implicit in the observation that the rats have been encouraged when men who should have trapped their "Providers" among the English Rats instead helped and defended them in their eagerness for a share of their hoards. The voice of the angry Broad-Bottom grows more strident near the end: "These Hanover Rats swarm to such a Degree, that we may truly say, the Farmer ploughs and sows, and the Industrious Part of the Nation labour to feed *Rats*" (p. 22). It closes (p. 23) with a declaration calculated to do the business of Fielding's patrons when written, but an embarrassment as they metamorphosed into ministerialists at virtually the moment it was published:

The Decay of Publick Spirit appears in nothing so much as in this, that we are wasting the little that is left us, in carrying on a War abroad, when, for our immediate Preservation, we should be hunting *Rats* at home.—I know there has been a great Noise about the exorbitant Power of France; but I will venture to assert, that the most effective Method to check the Growth of that Power, will be to destroy the Vermin that are eating us up within.—I speak it not without Grounds, that if this were done, and their hoard seized, a Treasure would be found not only for carrying on the War, but even for paying off a greater Part of the National Debt.

These were Fielding's last words as an opposition satirist.

Chapter Six

Fielding and the Jacobites, 1745-49: The True Patriot *to* Tom Jones

Fielding was probably again feeling the itch to write when Charles Edward Stuart, who had invaded the western highlands of Scotland on July 23, 1745 with seven followers, began the armed rebellion we know as the Jacobite "Forty-Five." Having rallied the clans and supplied himself with the nucleus of the army that would invade England in the fall, "Bonnie Prince Charlie" raised his standard and declared his father's right to the throne at Glenfinnan on August 19. Somewhat earlier Fielding published for the first time since the fall of 1744. The minor pamphlet entitled *The Charge to the Jury: or the Sum of the Evidence on the Trial of A.B.C.D. and E.F. All M.D.* has been little read since early July 1745, when it was advertised in London's *General Advertiser*. Fielding's biographers, following Wilbur Cross, declared it lost (though several copies are extant) and dated it incorrectly. It is not really political, though concerned with the medical arguments about the cause of death of a great politician, Lord Orford, on March 18. He died after taking (against advice) Dr. Junin's medicine for the "stone," and a pointless debate about the real nature of his ailment and the propriety of the care he had received was initiated by Dr. John Ranby, one signer of his *post mortem*. Fielding parodies the medical "paper war" that Ranby began, and concludes that Walpole died of his doctors, not the "stone."[1]

The *Charge* suggests the witty Fielding of old, and as it went to press events were creating a situation that would involve him as heavily in political journalism as he had been in 1740-41, this time on the ministerial side. For a patriotic Englishman with a background in political journalism and close ministerial connections, the "Forty-Five" was a strong stimulus. Suddenly the Establishment in Church and State

207

was threatened. Almost before the government could react, a minor uprising in Scotland (in the eyes of the French, a mere feint in the War of the Austrian Succession) had become a major invasion of England, and then a tense race with the English throne as prize, the highland army moving with surprising rapidity through the west-country while the authorities tried to scrape together enough steady troops in England and from the continent to destroy it. The ministry included every politician to whom Fielding had been close since the 1730s, except William Pitt. If the prospect of a bigoted, Catholic, absolutist Stuart returned to the throne with the assistance of the French and an army of wild highlanders was not enough to set Fielding writing, the urgings of his patrons had to do so. These urgings probably were in a tangible form. Fielding's biographers have been nervous about conjecturing that he received direct ministerial aid in getting out his anti-Jacobite journalism in the fall of 1745. There is no concrete evidence, and it is unlikely he was paid directly, by the issue. However, I am convinced that at least *The True Patriot* (the weekly four-page journal he began in November, after publishing a series of anti-Jacobite pamphlets in October) was subsidized in the usual way. As explained in Chapter Four, a ministry would buy up a certain number of copies and ensure their free distribution throughout the kingdom by post. It is hard to picture *The True Patriot*, which lasted nine months, as a profitable or even viable venture for author or publisher without a good deal of financial aid. The likelihood of this aid will become more apparent when, after considering the initially dominant patriotic function of Fielding's journal, we analyze his support of the ministry against its domestic opponents and the hints of ministerial alignment woven among Fielding's protests of non-partisanship.

Fielding burst into print in October and November 1745, just at the time that the seriousness of the invasion was clear. Having marched southeast across Scotland, gathering recruits, Charles Edward took Edinburgh on September 17, though the castle garrison held out. At Prestonpans on September 21 his highlanders routed the only English force of any size in Scotland, sending it and its commander, Sir John Cope, in panic flight toward the English border. Suddenly, Charles's invasion was not the mere annoyance it had been in July and August, but a danger taken seriously even by those who had been most inclined to slight it in favour of the main conflict with the French in Flanders. The year 1745 was a series of disasters for England. A deterioration in her military position abroad began in 1744, when Carteret's policies brought on a formal declaration of war on England by the French. It reached a real low with the defeat of the allied army, despite the extreme valour of the English and Hanoverians under the Duke of Cumberland, at Fontenoy on May 11, 1745. Then came the news of Jacobite successes in Scotland that left the way open for an invasion aimed at London. The militia was called out in several counties and the wealthy and great began recruiting amateur regiments. All available troops were sent north under General Wade, and the ponderous mechanism required to bring English troops and foreign mercenaries from Flanders was put in operation. Commons voted all but unanimously for energetic defence measures.[2] Significantly, even the so-called "Jacobite Tories" proved loyal when faced with the prospect of an actual Stuart restoration. As has been observed in earlier chapters, Jacobitism in England had been for two decades a way for opponents to express resentment against the "Hanover Rats" of Court and ministry, little connected with a desire to see a Stuart on the throne.

Beginning in early October, Fielding, erstwhile author of *An Attempt toward a Natural History of the Hanover Rat*, worked to rouse the populace and moderate its panic. He reprinted *The Old Debauchees*, stressing its rather nasty anti-Papism with a new subtitle, *Or, the Jesuit Caught*. He published a hurriedly written, propagandistic account of the early stages of the Rebellion called *The History of the Present Rebellion in Scotland*, supposedly "taken from the relation of Mr. James Mac-Pherson," a spy who had been held by Charles Edward's forces. In fact, it was mostly a *pastiche* of newspaper reports, with added appeals to defensive patriotism. Covering events through the defeat at Prestonpans on September 21, it was rushed to the booksellers by October 5. Its propaganda foreshadows the themes of Fielding's subsequent anti-rebellion exhortations. English liberties, Protestantism, and the safety of English men, women, and children are threatened by a Papist-absolutist, Franco-Caledonian invasion. Englishmen of all classes and parties should oppose it to the last drop of blood:

> I shall conclude these Papers, with exhorting every Man in this Kingdom to exert himself, not only in his Station, but as far as Health, Strength, and Age will permit him, to leave at present the Calling, which he pursues, and however foreign his Way of Life may have been to the Exercise of Arms, to take them up . . . HIS ALL IS AT STAKE. This is not the Cause of a Party. I shall be excused if I say it is not the Cause in which the King only is concerned, your Religion, my Countrymen, your Laws, your Liberties, your Lives, the Safety of your Wives and Children; the whole is in Danger, and for God Almighty's Sake! lose not a Moment in ARMING YOURSELVES for their Preservation.[3]

Such hysteria is rare in Fielding's work. But the situation was so dismaying that even the call for shopkeepers to take up arms in this relatively unimpressive pamphlet must have been music to his patrons in the ministry.

In October Fielding wrote two more shilling pamphlets, *A Serious Address to the People of Great Britain* and *A Dialogue Between the Devil, the Pope and the Pretender*, both printed by M. Cooper, subsequently publisher of *The True Patriot*. *A Serious Address* is the best of his Rebellion pamphlets, urging with some power that the Stuart-Papist-French-highland invasion threatens the liberty, property, and safety of the English, as well as the Present Establishment in Church and State. It also—a significant point, as we will see—condemns partisanship and calls for unanimous support of the ministry. Though good sense in the circumstances, this also justifies Rupert Jarvis' description of *A Serious*

Address as a "stern ministerial" piece.[4] The less impressive, though more
"literary" *Dialogue* was published on November 5, the same day as the
second edition of *A Serious Address* (to which was appended a ten-page
piece by another author called *A Calm Address to All Parties in
Religion*) and the first issue of *The True Patriot*. In the manner of *The
Old Debauchees*, it appeals to popular fear of Popery. The Pope
describes plans for England when the Pretender regains the throne that
contradict the manifestoes in which the Pretender had tried to allay the
fears of English Protestants. The Pope plans to bring the Inquisition to
England, assume control of all high ecclesiastical appointments, restore
the abbey lands secularized in the sixteenth century, and massacre all
"Hereticks." The Pretender will rule as a Stuart autocrat, controlled only by his own whim, the King of France, and the Pope. Finally, the Devil
mocks the idea that such plans can succeed in freedom-loving, Protestant
England.

Between its inception and the waning of the Jacobite threat in early
1746, *The True Patriot* usually cultivates the reasoned arguments of *A
Serious Address* about the effects of a Jacobite victory and echoes its
urgings toward national unity. But it also incorporates the emotionalism
and frank appeal to bigotry of the *Dialogue Between the Devil, the Pope
and the Pretender*. The double pattern of Fielding's anti-Jacobite
strategy is clear by the time one has read through the first three issues.
The Dialogue and *A Serious Address* are offered for sale in the only two
advertisements in issue 1, Tuesday, November 5, but the lead essay is,
amazingly enough, neglectful of the Rebellion. Instead, it emphasizes the
poor quality of the London newspapers and insists that the new journal's
editor, "The True Patriot," is of no party. It also teases the reader about
the editor's real identity in a passage we will need to recall when we en-
counter the metamorphosis of the "patriotic" journal into a ministerial
propaganda organ in its later run. The passage reminds us that *The True
Patriot* was covertly partisan, as "ministerial" as *A Serious Address*,
from its inception.

Supporting the Broad-Bottom ministers in a protracted power struggle against the King and his favourite, Granville, was always a very important intention of *The True Patriot*, though Fielding normally was
careful not to flaunt this in the first fifteen weekly issues. He could not
afford to appear to take sides, especially against the King's desires, until
the Jacobite invasion of England became a retreat through Scotland and
the ministry won out over Granville in the battle for the King's full support. However, in issue 1 he wittily advertised his alignment with the
ministry that included his patrons, and that probably was subsidizing his
efforts. The "True Patriot" coyly refuses to identify himself, but suggests some possibilities:

> It is very probable I am Lord B_____ke. This I collect from my
> Stile in Writing and Knowledge in Politics. Again it is as probable
> that I am the B_____p of ****, from my zeal for the Protestant
> Religion. When I consider these, together with the Wit and Humour

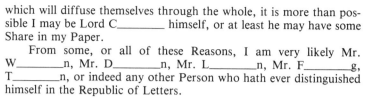

which will diffuse themselves through the whole, it is more than possible I may be Lord C_____ himself, or at least he may have some Share in my Paper.

From some, or all of these Reasons, I am very likely Mr. W_____n, Mr. D_____n, Mr. L_____n, Mr. F_____g, T_____n, or indeed any other Person who hath ever distinguished himself in the Republic of Letters.

Without stating it in so many words, Fielding could hardly have indicated more clearly his ministerialism and special affinity for the ministry's Broad-Bottom wing. Putting aside "Mr. F_____g" (Fielding) and the "B_____p of ****" (possibly Bishop Hoadly or Bishop Herring of York; I favour the latter), the list is politically supercharged. "Mr. W_____n" (Thomas Winnington) was Paymaster of the Forces and would be posthumously defended by Fielding in 1747 in *A Proper Answer to the Late Scurrilous Libel*. More significantly, "Lord B_____ke" (Bolingbroke) was the great theoretician of Broad-Bottom, and "Mr. D_____n" (George Dodington), "Mr. L_____n" (George Lyttelton), and Lord C_____ (Chesterfield) were all familiar Broad-Bottom heroes of Fielding's and members of the Broad-Bottom ministry. Dodington was Treasurer of the Navy, Lyttelton a Commissioner of the Treasury, and Chesterfield Lord Lieutenant of Ireland. All remained vociferously anti-Granville, as we will see, and critical of defensive delays in the fall of 1745. Even "T_____n" (obviously James Thomson) fits; he had been the chief poetic voice of the Broad-Bottoms since the 1730s and Lyttelton's grateful dependant. The difficulty is not in convincing oneself that Fielding is politically placing the journal here, and very precisely, but in understanding how anyone ever took seriously Fielding's half-mocking professions of political neutrality in this and other essays.

While Fielding waited for the appropriate moment to become overtly partisan—it came in February 1746—he worked to arouse patriotic feelings against the Jacobites and to moderate popular fears. Even when he turns from journalistic and political badinage to the Rebellion in issue 1 he is careful that there is no panic in his tone. He modulates easily between the reasonableness of *A Serious Address* and the extremism of the *Dialogue*, but the former predominates. The "Present History of Great Britain" is one of the major news sections (the other being the "Present History of Europe," mainly concerned with military and diplomatic events abroad) that take up most of pages 2 and 3 in each four-page issue. It relates the domestic news of the past week, mostly as it relates to the Rebellion or reflects loyal opposition to it. In issue 1, this section praises the raising of defence regiments by noblemen, canvasses the possible plans of the rebels, and reports that the 63rd birthday of George II, October 30, 1745, has brought forth an extraordinary show of "Loyalty at this Season." However, a humorous tale about the pleasure the trained bands take in searching carriages full of young ladies is also included. Only in the section called "Apocrypha, Being a Curious Collection of certain and true *We Hears* from the Newspapers" does Fielding approve, as a "generous and ingenious Diversion," a public display in the streets of Deptford that was perfectly in tune with the *Dialogue Between the Devil, the Pope and the Pretender:*

The Deptford Procession

1. A Highlander, in his proper Dress, carrying on a Pole a Pair of Wooden Shoes, with this Motto, *The newest Make from Paris.*
2. A Jesuit, in his proper Dress, carrying on the Point of a flaming Sword, a Banner, with this Inscription in large Capitals, *Inquisition, Flames and Damnation.*
3. Two Capuchin Friars, properly shaved, habited, and accoutred with flogging-Ropes, Beads, Crucifixes, &c. One of them bore on a high Pole, a Bell, Mass-book and Candle, to curse the British Nation with; the other carried a large Standard, with this Inscription:

Indulgences cheap as Dirt

Murder, ...Nine Pence
Adultery, ...Nine Pence Halfpenny
Reading the Bible, ...A Thousand Pounds
Fornication, ...Fourpence Halfpenny Farthing
Perjury, ...Nothing at All
Rebellion, ...A Reward or Drawback of
Thirteen Pence Halfpenny
Scots Money

4. The Pretender, with a green Ribbon, Nosegay of Thistles, &c. riding upon an Ass, supported by a Frenchman on the Right and a Spanniard on the Left, each dressed to the Height of the newest Modes from Paris and Madrid.
5. The Pope riding upon his Bull.[5]

Fielding's second leader (November 12) is also coolly reasonable. It denounces false patriotism, in terms that once more may cautiously imply Fielding's disapproval of the Granville-Bath faction in the King's councils and its struggles to embarrass and supplant the Broad-Bottom ministry. However, its overt theme is that the "truly Patriotic" will eschew partisanship and do nothing "to embarrass or distress the King and his Service, when the most perfect Unanimity is requisite." "Observations on the Present Rebellion," a long secondary essay serialized on page 4 of issues 1 through 3 (and surely Fielding's work) concentrates on opposing the Rebellion, but in a controlled way. It (the Rebellion) must concern all sensible patriots and Protestants, but should *not* be allowed to inflame religious and political divisions. In particular, the "Whole Body of the *Scottish* Nation" is not disloyal, merely a rabble of highlanders. Most Scottish aristocrats have been loyal, as have the Scottish legislators, the Protestant clergy in Scotland, and the Protestant, lowland majority of the common people, not to speak of the Scots who have died defending the kingdom. To Fielding's credit, he would never cease to insist on this, even when the vicious reprisals began after the battle of Culloden. Similarly, it would be wrong to express "a violent Animosity against all Roman Catholics." All should oppose "the

Establishment'' of Roman Catholicism ''under a Prince who is a known bigot, with the utmost Force and most animated Resolution.'' But most *English* Catholics will surely shun the Stuart cause. They may even oppose it as a threat to their liberties, property, and lives, considering the character of the highland banditti. All Catholics must be *suspect*, but not all are *guilty*, and no violence against them is justified while they remain quiet. The military situation is grave, but the odds are vastly on the side of the Present Establishment, and sure to improve once troops from Flanders take the field. Fielding treats as excessive claims that the government has not done enough, soon enough. The regiments raised by the Duke of Bedford, Lord Halifax, and Lord Gower, and a massive movement of English troops from Flanders, already ordered, are sure to end the danger in a reasonable time. This is the calming voice of a journalist attached to the ministry.

Such moderation could not consistently be maintained in November 1745. On November 8 the Jacobite army entered England. It had avoided General Cope, the loser at Prestonpans, and would evade General Wade, reaching Derby, more or less unfought, by December 5. London panicked, and the Church of England declared December 18 a solemn day of fasting and humiliation. On November 19, Fielding finally let the tension show in a lead essay. Under a motto describing the sack of Saguntum by Carthaginians, the essay represents one extreme in the journal. The ''True Patriot'' describes a horrible ''dream-vision'' he had about the aftermath of a Jacobite victory. Highland ruffians take him to Newgate through streets lit by burning buildings, dotted with the bodies of men, women, and children, and scoured by highlanders and Popish priests. At Smithfield he sees many of the ''most considerable Persons'' in the kingdom, including the Archbishop of York and the Bishop of Winchester, abused. The Court of King's Bench, now presided over by strange judges, is busy returning abbey lands. There he is tried for treason as editor of *The True Patriot*. A judge speaking broken English sweeps aside his defence, and he is condemned without a jury. A rascally Oratorian, now Ordinary of Newgate, reviles him during the three hours' grace he is allowed before execution. One prisoner says he was condemned for stealing bread after losing his estate (which was in the funds, rendered valueless by royal decree) and laments over his wife, ''dead of a broken Heart,'' and his unclothed, starving daughters. The ''True Patriot'' imagines the murder of his son and the rape of his daughter until the executioner comes. On the way to the scaffold he sees one of the aristocratic beauties of the capital fought over by two lusting Scots, screaming, half-naked, and blood-spattered. Bodies lie everywhere —''for there had been, I was told, a Massacre the Night before''—and Protestants roast in fires. Having urged his executioners to treat him as brutally as possible, a hypocrite priest pretends compassion, urges him to accept Holy Communion, then curses him when he refuses. At the gallows he sees a non-juror, ''who had lent considerable Assistance to the Pretender's Cause, out of Principle'' lamenting his folly and the fate of the Pretender's victims. Finally, as the rope is slipped around his neck, he is awakened from his nightmare by his little girl, come to tell him of the arrival of the new clothes he ordered for "his Majesty's Birthday." This is crude, "scare" propaganda, but "the Present History of Great Britain" in the same issue reports that a Jacobite army of 7000 men is before the walls of Carlisle, on the western route through England, while Wade waits, out-foxed, at Newcastle on the more easterly route. Though the news had not come, Charles Edward, styling himself Prince of Wales and Regent of England, entered Carlisle on a white charger with banners flying on November 17.[6] A vision of London ravaged by highlanders was not utterly mad on November 19, 1745.

Fielding was seldom moved to such stridency. Essay 4 ironically repeats the arguments of *A Serious Address* ("puffed" in the opening paragraph) about the effects of a Jacobite victory. Assuming the anti-Jacobitism of every "Protestant . . . attached to his Religion and his Liberties, or who hath any Estate or Property, either in Church Lands or in the Funds," Fielding addresses only the freethinkers, the abusers of the King's government, and men who live by selling themselves. The Romish church and a Stuart King will not tolerate freethinking or the abuse of "the King, Ministry and every Thing great, noble and solemn." And it will be hard to sell one's freedom when one is already a slave. The essay may indicate that a panicked populace seemed worse than an unaroused one. It also allowed Fielding a rare opportunity to mock the opposition to the ministry—the abusers of the government—at a time when his ministerial partisanship still had to be muted.

As the "Present History" section records in issue 7, the English situation reached its nadir in the week before it appeared. The Jacobites entered Derby on December 4. This turned out to be their deepest penetration into the country and the turning-point of the "Forty-Five." However, as Fielding stresses in *Tom Jones*, no one could be sure they would not continue to elude Wade and Cumberland and reach London. There was a report from Admiral Vernon that the French were loading troops at Dunkirk, which "struck such a terror into several public-spirited Persons, that, to prevent their money, Jewels, Plate, &c. falling into rebellious or French Hands, they immediately began to pack up and secure the same." Typically cool, Fielding devotes six paragraphs of his seventh leader to a general disquisition on man's foolish tendency to trade solid happiness for vanities, and only applies this to the political situation in paragraph seven. There he turns to the folly of the few English Protestants who are willing to trade the happy *status quo* for life "under the Protection of a bigoted *Popish* Prince, educated in the highest Principles of absolute Power, coming as a Conqueror, by the Assistance of the Arms of *France*." He goes on to urge the lukewarm, lightheaded, pleasure-loving, and cowardly to defend their liberties and happiness and to assure all that even if the rebels were ten times more numerous and "doubled by the Troops of *France* or *Spain*," the English have the power and spirit to win. Though the danger of defeat by a highland rabble "is (humanly speaking) impossible . . . should unfore-seen Accidents demand it, nothing but absolute Impotency from Age or Infirmity can excuse Attendance."

On December 17 there is finally grand news. The "Present History of Great Britain" announces that the rebels began on December 6 to retreat toward Scotland from Derby, after his officers forced Charles Edward to give up his determination to press on toward London. They are being pursued northward by the Duke of Cumberland. The lead essay, however, is a somewhat inappropriate "letter" from Abraham Adams attributing the amazing success the rebels have so far achieved to the intention of an angry God to punish the English for impiety and im-morality. Adams' insistence that the English must undergo "a total Amendment of Life" if the wrath of God is to be appeased is hardly a practical anti-rebellion gesture. Fielding now had leisure to moralize; the situation remained serious, but not critical, through January 1746. The Jacobites retreated steadily, though in order and undefeated. After a minor clash at Clifton on December 19, they got safely out of England. They marched to Glasgow, then Stirling, gathering a few reinforcements from the highlands and France, and even defeated General Hawley at Falkirk on January 17. Meanwhile, Cumberland gathered troops and ar-tillery, and closed in on the doomed Jacobites. The Jacobite withdrawal became flight only in February, ending in the neighbourhood of Culloden on February 19. Even then nearly a month passed before the fragmenting Jacobite army was smashed by Cumberland in the battle of Culloden Moor, which ended the Rebellion on April 16 and ushered in its aftermath: Charles Edward's fugitive adventures, Cumberland's butch-ery in the highlands, and the legal as well as military destruction of the clan system.

During the rest of December 1745 and January 1746 Fielding con-tinued to turn aside in his lead essays, as often as not, from military mat-ters, while covering them in detail in the news sections. The leader for December 24 discusses the characteristics of good and bad statesmen, on-ly mentioning the present crisis in closing:

> I have avoided making any Applications, during the Course of this Paper; I shall conclude with this general One, That if we have any Abilities left in this Country, I hope they will be now employ'd in those Stations to which they are adapted, since our present Situation requires their utmost and immediate Assistance. If we have a Man among us blest with all the Talents I have before described, (and such I know we have) GOD forbid that Pique, Envy, Jealousy, or any other Motive, should be able to exclude him from the Capacity of serving, I will say Saving, his Country.

This is all but openly a demand for the employment of the brilliant William Pitt at ministerial level, and conversely a criticism of his exclu-sion from office by the King. His exclusion was encouraged by Granville and Bath, against the wishes and to the considerable discomfiture of the whole ministry, not only Pitt's Broad-Bottom friends. The Pelhams feared Pitt's tongue and grasp of foreign affairs as an opposition orator.[7] These sentences are, therefore, clear, early signs of the coming metamorphosis of *The True Patriot* into an openly pro-ministerial (anti-Granville) journal, as well as an anti-Jacobite one. The metamorphosis would be complete by mid-February, 1746, its timing partly dependent on the waning of the military threat and partly on the course of the domestic struggle between the ministry and the King, Carteret, and Bath. Meanwhile, Fielding marked time.

On December 31 Fielding satirizes Italian Opera, as he had done regularly since 1730, but connects this attack with the Rebellion. Opera is inappropriately effeminate and luxurious at such a time. The retreat of the rebels to Carlisle is reported on page two and *A Serious Address* is advertised on page four, but the sense of crisis is gone. In this issue, a lengthy plan for the setting up of an effective national militia (by "a Person of great Property, as well as great *Abilities*") is begun. It continues for a number of issues as a secondary essay, but it really is a plan for preempting *future* crises. The effects of the easing of military tension are even apparent in the next essay, January 7, though it is the closest thing to the vision of the rape of London of November 19 in the rest of the run. In a letter dated December 24, 1745 a "correspondent" sends the *True Patriot* an "imaginary Journal of Events" in London, January 1 through March 17, following a Jacobite victory. It includes highland rapine, the oppression of Protestants, the destruction of Parliament, the dominance of Frenchmen and Jesuits, the burning of "hereticks," and the execution of Admiral Vernon. It ends with "Fresh Rumours of a Plot ----a Riot in the City----a Rising in the North----a Descent in the West---- Confusions, Uproars, Commitments, Hangings, Burnings, &c., &c.---- *Verbum non amplius addam*." But the events are so unlikely and the tone so inconsistent (the journal-keeper's son itches after he attends a review of the new Life-Guards regiment in its plaids) that the effect is more comical than frightening, and seems meant to be so. There is again a tendency to praise the ministry as well as defend the Present Establishment.

The "Present History of Great Britain" for January 7, obviously by Fielding, records the recall of his old hero, Admiral Vernon, from command of the fleet. Predictably, Fielding praises Vernon's great services to the nation during the long wars. However, he is careful to avoid criticizing the ministry for relieving Vernon. He fulsomely compliments the Duke of Bedford, formerly a Broad-Bottom ally of Lyttelton and Pitt in opposition, presently First Lord of the Admiralty, and in future a most generous patron of Fielding's:

> How he [Vernon] hath behaved in his present Command I shall not venture to say, since his recall is ascribed to a noble Duke, whose Character ought to be dear, nay even sacred, to every Englishman, as he certainly deserves every Honour his Country can bestow on it. In Cases of this kind, the only safe Way is to suspend our Judgment, till Time and Enquiry have set all Facts in a true and certain Light.

The man who wrote this might claim to be of "no Party"; it was normal to claim that allegiance to the Broad-Bottom ministry, supposedly a non-factious coalition of several factions, did not make one a partisan. But he was a skilled, cautious ministerial apologist nonetheless, moving closer to the moment when he would become one openly and in earnest. One is not surprised that in the "Apocrypha; Or, We Hear" section (which reprinted reports from other papers with Fielding's satiric or humorous commentary on them) Fielding cites a complaint about Vernon's recall in the *London Evening Post*, an opposition paper which he would savage in *The Jacobite's Journal*, and rebukes its author.

In the next few weeks the Rebellion became even less a source of exciting copy. On January 14 "Stephen Grub" is made to argue that loyalty to the Present Establishment is a good investment—patriotism, of course, being moonshine. Essays 13 and 15 (January 28 and February 11) satirize beaus and hoop petticoats. The reason for the lull is clear. The "Present History of Great Britain" in issue 14 observes that so little action in Scotland has been reported that the editor must reserve comment until there is more news. The anti-rebellion themes of the earlier issues are only dominant in two essays from this period. Essay 12 (January 21) is a "letter" from the Pretender to his son, supposedly left behind when the latter fled Penrith at Cumberland's approach. As usual, it details the most oppressive and bigoted plans for England, regardless of the promises in his manifestoes to the English,[8] but the fear has gone out of the hate themes of the fall. Fielding is amused and contemptuous. The "Present History" says that "All Accounts from the North agree, that the Rebels are far from being formidable"; the recent Jacobite victory at Falkirk was an "*inconsiderable skirmish.*"

More interesting is essay 14 (February 4) in which Fielding prepared to alter *The True Patriot* from a primarily anti-Jacobite to a determinedly pro-ministerial, partisan journal. Good writers "who meddle with politics" have often been vilified by "Ministers of State, who are generally the worst and wickedest of Men." But "a great Man of the Present Age" (Henry Pelham, one presumes) is above caring about partisan writers, friendly or hostile, presumably "from a Consciousness of his own Rectitude." To his "regard and serious Attention" the "True Patriot" wishes to "recommend" his journal. It was founded in a time of danger to rally the people, and has been conducted on "the true Principles of Liberty," in opposition to "Papists, Jacobites, and factious Malecontents" and to "Ministerial Slaves and Hirelings." It has never been a slavish apologist of the ministry or abused the ministry to serve the ends of a discontented clique, "clogging the Wheels of Government with needless Opposition, and raising dangerous Factions in the Community, when no actual Danger hath threatened it." He "hath not sought the Protection of any Party, by adhering rigidly to the Principles of any, farther than is consistent with the true Interest of his Country, which no Party . . . hath effectedly consulted at all Times." Indeed he believes the "absurd and irrational Distinction of Parties hath principally contributed to poison our Constitution." He has not sought "Places, Pensions and Rewards," which are won by "Flattery of Ministers, and the support of iniquitous Measures," not by defending one's Sovereign.

In short, the "True Patriot" claims to be non-partisan, and shows he is nothing of the kind. In issue 1 he said he was "of no Party," then hinted he might be a member of the ministry or one of its supporters. On February 4 he reiterates this claim, with a closing qualification that alters everything:

> I again declare, and I presume my Writings will bear the same Testi- mony, that I am engaged in no Party, nor in the Support of any, un- less of such as are truely and sincerely attached to the true Interest of their Country, and who are resolved to hazard all Things in its Preser- vation.

Supporters of the Broad-Bottom ministry always claimed not to be adherents of a traditional party. But we must not mistake Fielding's in- tent in protesting his superiority to party so excessively (one finds little in the earlier run describable as satire on "ministerial Slaves and Hirelings") and in terms so reminiscent of his essays or those of Bol- ingbroke or Lyttelton in the days of the Broad-Bottom opposition. He knew that a domestic political crisis was soon going to permit, even force, him openly to champion the present ministers and attack their enemies. When he wrote essay 14 Fielding was preparing to campaign either way, as a ministerialist if they remained in office, as an opposition writer if they moved into opposition. In fact, only two weeks later (the beau and hoop-petticoat essays intervening) essay 16 (February 18) would definitely mark the metamorphosis of *The True Patriot* into a ministerial journal. However, before we can understand Fielding's careful eschewing of ministerial propaganda—occasional hints aside—in the earlier run and his sudden shift to overt partisanship, we must understand the tense domestic battle against Lord Granville and the King that the ministry was engaged in during the most dangerous phases of the "Forty-Five."

We have already seen how the Pelhams forced Granville, formerly Lord Carteret, from office in late 1744, recruiting the Broad-Bottom wing of the "new" opposition in the process and forming the Broad- Bottom ministry. This ministry had good majorities and a near monopo- ly of debating talent. Even the excluded William Pitt moderated his op- position in the hope of a future place. But Granville still advised the King on foreign policy, and profited from King George's low opinion of his ministers. Between late 1744 and early 1746, and thus throughout the dark days of the "Forty-Five," the really serious enemies of the ministry were the King and Lord Granville (backed by Lord Bath and the Prince of Wales), not the weak opposition in Parliament. This was uncomfort- able in the first six months after Granville's fall. When Newcastle at- tended upon the King he could expect rude treatment, and he knew his opinion could not consistently outweigh Granville's. He and Henry Pelham might control Parliament, but it seemed at times as if their function was to obtain financing for the policies settled between the King and Granville, who had no official post and little weight in Parliament.

The situation worsened after Fontenoy, a disaster the ministry had to explain, though Carteret and the King were primarily responsible for the diplomatic and military policies that forced the English to fight at a disadvantage. Even before the defeat, Henry Pelham hinted an intention to resign if the King did not develop "a more favourable opinion of us." When the King, as usual, left to spend the warm months of 1745 in Hanover, it was clear that he planned to dismiss his ministers soon after his return, probably after he used them to put the essential money bills through Commons. This could only be followed by the formation of a new ministry dominated by Lords Granville and Bath, and filled out by their followers and those members of the present ministry with whom the King felt most comfortable. Lord Harrington (Granville's successor as Secretary of State in 1744) was one important example. The Pelhams and their ministerial colleagues prepared to resign before the King dismissed them, as soon as he returned and before supplies were voted for the year. Just at this point the Pretender's son landed, gathered an army, defeated Cope, and menaced the Establishment. Though George II was amazingly slow to recognize the seriousness of the situation, dismissal or resignation suddenly became impossible. Even the extreme "Country Tories," no friends to Granville or the Pelhams or Hanover, had to support His Majesty and his government at such a juncture. They were Englishmen and Protestants first, Tories second. The final battle between Granville and the King and the ministry was put off until the danger eased.

In the meanwhile, all had to cultivate an appearance of unity. This was rendered more difficult, typically enough, by a disagreement between the King, encouraged by Granville, and the long-suffering ministry about how to react to the Rebellion. The ministry was more inclined to take it seriously in the early stages, to contemplate massive troop shipments from Flanders and insist that the King return early from Hanover. The King and Carteret regarded the Rebellion as a feint in the War of the Austrian Succession, engineered by the French, and resisted bringing over troops needed in Flanders. The King returned only at the end of August, more than a month after Charles Edward began to gather strength in Scotland. He even considered forming a new ministry under Lord Harrington (who refused to hear of it) as late as September 17. George's attitude through September was that "the storm would soon blow over;" he was even cool to the idea of noblemen raising regiments for defence. Granville agreed, fearing that the continental position, his greatest interest, would be worsened by over-reaction to the Rebellion. One of his followers, Lord Tweeddale, a great power in Scotland, did amazingly little to oppose the Jacobites in the north: "thus, supporting an opinion of Lord Granville's perhaps," he for a time "lost the King one of his crowns."[9] The King's instinctive reaction to any news of the invasion was, "Pho! don't talk to me of that stuff!" and as late as September 28, a week after Prestonpans, the Prince of Wales saw the

Rebellion as an irritating interruption of "our schemes in Germany and on the continent." Well might Lord Bolingbroke pity the Broad-Bottom ministers, trying to save the throne of a King so unwilling to protect himself or listen to them:

> he felt the situation of those who acted as ministers without the King's confidence; that they laboured on through everything was up-hill work; that if they treated this affair as important, Lord Stair laughed at them, and Lord Tweedale gave no help at all; that he [Bolingbroke] wished they could do any good, and that animosities ought to be laid aside.[10]

The ministers could not complain publicly. How could they appear at odds with the monarch whose throne they were bent on preserving? In October they had to endure criticism in Parliament of their lack of initiative in opposing the Rebellion, when they had wished to do more all along. On October 23 William Pitt was joined by George Lyttelton, George Grenville, and George Dodington, junior ministerialists, in supporting a bill requiring that all troops be recalled from Flanders. This was an attack on the ministry, in one sense. Pitt spoke sharply against its behaviour, though he was fully aware that all but 2000 horse were already on their way home. It was also a sign of ministerial exasperation. The bill was defeated, but the fact that not only Pitt, but also junior ministers voted for it (without resigning or being punished), together with some of the "Old Corps" in Commons, indicates the cross-pressures of the time.[11] Although the King and Granville were responsible, the ministry was answerable not only to the Commons for lax defence, but to the King for defeating an insulting bill. A place of some importance for Pitt, the only way to quiet him, remained as unlikely as ever, given the King's attitude toward him.

Obviously, Henry Fielding, long attached to Lyttelton, Pitt, and their Cobhamite-Grenville associates, did not accidentally blossom into a defence-arousing pamphleteer at precisely the time that his patrons rose to urge the full exertion of England's might in the north. It is also not surprising that in his anti-Jacobite pamphlets and the early run of *The True Patriot* he avoided criticizing Granville, Bath, and Tweeddale, much less the King and the Prince. As long as the ministry was obliged to remain in office, Fielding had to act as if His Majesty, his heir, his advisors, and his ministers were perfectly unified in the face of armed sedition. Non-partisan, indeed anti-partisan, patriotism was the only possible stance. He let slip the odd item: the hints in essay 1, passing compliments to Bedford and Pelham, brief defences of the ministry against the charge of dilatory defence, the snarl against the exclusion of Pitt from office of December 24. Normally, however, he waited quietly for the moment when the ministry could *either* defeat Granville and force the King to back it fully (and employ Pitt) *or* move into unambiguous opposition and begin working to undermine the next ministry. Fortunately, the former eventually happened in February 1746, and Fielding became an overt ministerialist in issue 16.

By early February the Jacobites were all but finished, and the ministry was able to follow precisely the course outlined by the Duke of Newcastle as early as September 21, 1745:

> . . . nothing but a rebellion in the heart of the kingdom would or should hinder us from retiring from the most disagreeable and perhaps the most dangerous situation that ever ministers were in. And, as soon as that rebellion is in effect over, that will be our measure.[12]

Their retirement began on Monday, February 10, the day before Fielding published his time-marking essay on hoop-petticoats. Perceiving a "resolution to dismiss them at the end of the session," after they had carried the supplies, the Duke of Newcastle and the Earl of Harrington (the Secretaries of State, Southern and Northern Departments) resigned. They were followed by a succession of their colleagues, Henry Pelham (First Lord of the Treasury and Chancellor of the Exchequer), Bedford (First Lord of the Admiralty), Gower (Lord Privy Seal), Monson (First Lord of Trade and Plantations), and the Earl of Pembroke. Hardwicke, Devonshire, Grafton, Dorset, Richmond, Fox, and Winnington announced their intention to resign, though neither they nor Lyttelton got around to it during the amazingly short-lived confrontation. It was a planned, well-executed withdrawal *en masse* by those who controlled both Houses of Parliament, the only way of baulking the King's design to dismiss and replace them piecemeal and at his pleasure. The gamble was extreme. Fielding could not be sure on February 11 whether he would be an opposition writer (he surely would have become one if the King and Granville had prevailed) or a ministerial one by the following Tuesday. But it worked perfectly. Lord Granville was appointed Secretary of State and Lord Bath, First Lord of the Treasury, replacing the Pelham brothers. However, nothing the King could promise or threaten could induce anyone but the weak Earl of Carlisle (who agreed to be Lord Privy Seal) and the Earl of Winchelsea (First Lord of the Admiralty) to risk office under two politicians as unpopular and ill-supported in Parliament as Bath and Granville.

The embarrassing ministerial crisis, one of the turning points in Constitutional history, lasted only until February 14. Then the King, Granville, and Bath gave up, Bath muttering pathetically that it was the King's fault, since he had nursed "a faction by governing by a party." Granville and Bath began a descent into obscurity, and the King had to ask his old ministers to return to office. He also had to employ Pitt, whose insistence on office before the month of February was out (backed by the Broad-Bottom wing of the ministry) had helped determine the precise timing of the mass resignation. We have seen Fielding pressing Pitt's claims in late December. In January Pitt felt sure enough that the ministry would either bring him in or resign that he helped to silence opposition to the high military estimates for the year. He argued their necessity and expressed hope for success in arms and the dawning of a new trust in the ministry when "a certain fatal influence in his Majesty's

Councils'' (Granville) was removed. The King was not defeated on all fronts. Pitt did not even become Secretary at War (a relatively minor administrative post), but settled for a lucrative joint Vice-Treasurership of Ireland. In the near future George would also force the resignation of Harrington as Secretary of State. He had been the minister the King liked best; indeed he was brought in as Granville's replacement in 1744 as a sop to royal resentment. But his forthright refusal to betray his colleagues in September 1745 and the peremptory way he resigned in February 1746 made him *persona non grata* with a King outraged at having his constitutional right to choose his ministers infringed. Still, the Broad-Bottom ministers had won. Granville and Bath had proved impotent in the face of the Pelhams' control of Parliament. Horace Walpole said that they forgot ''one little point, which was to secure a majority in both Houses.'' From now on the King would have to repose confidence, at first grudgingly, in his ministers, and shun Granville. A period of instability was over; now the ministry faced only an opposition short on votes and ability.

Mrs. Elizabeth Montague wrote with glee of the ''comedy at St. James'':

> the *exeunt omnes* of our ministry and all their adherents. An interlude was played by Lord Granville, and the famed Earl of Bath, Lord Carlisle, and Lord Winchelsea; but, to act exactly according to the rules of criticism, their theatrical performance was confined to the space of twenty-four hours; at the expiration of that time they made their exit, and the Pelhams, and their followers, are again on the great stage . . . . Indeed it was an odd affair to see only two or three persons to fill all places and stations; it was the old blunder of the K⸺ and two fiddlers solus.[13]

In a similar vein, Fielding laughed at the *dénouement* of the crisis in issue 16, published on February 18, four days after the King asked the Pelhams to return. The essay signals the metamorphosis of *The True Patriot* into an overtly pro-ministerial, anti-opposition organ. It expatiates generally upon the instability and contemptibility of ''worldly'' or political greatness. However, this is from the first applied to the ''Forty-eight-hour Ministry'' fiasco. The epigram from Juvenal mocks the destruction of politicians who lust after ''Summus . . . Locus'' (the highest place), and the first example of the theme from modern literature is three lines from *Tom Thumb* (I, iv):

> Greatness (says a Burlesque writer) is a lac'd Coat from
>   Monmouth Street,
> Which Fortune lends us for a Day to wear;
> To-morrow puts it on another's Back.

Next Fielding adapts to his purpose lines from *Macbeth* (his capitals):

> Life's but a walking Shadow, a poor Player,
> THAT STRUTS AND FRETS HIS HOUR UPON THE STAGE,

> AND THEN IS HEARD NO MORE. It is a Farce
> Play'd by an Idiot, full of Sound and Fury,
> Signifying nothing.

He observes, "By Life here, is meant the Life of a Great Man. This appears as well by the Tenor of the Play, the Moral of which is levelled at Ambition . . . ." More specific and much funnier is the second turn of this Shakespearean screw, at once satiric of textual scholarship and the fallen would-be ministers. The lines preceding the "quoted" passage (in Theobald's edition, "And all our Yesterdays have lighted Fools/ The Way to dusty Death; out, out, brief Candle") should read:

> And all our Yesterdays have lifted Tools
> The Way to dusty Death. Out, out, brief Cabal.

Fielding then "critically interprets" the amended lines:

> Then addressing himself to his brief Cabal (where by the by, the Word *brief* may be either apply'd to the Paucity of their Number, or to the Brevity of their Duration) he says, *Out, out,* i.e. resign, go out before ye are kicked out, and brought to that *Dusty Death,* &c. He then proceeds very naturally to illustrate the life of *such Tools* by a Player, who puts on a false Appearance on the Stage, being indeed the very Reverse of what he seems, and who, after having strutted a few Hours in the Habit and Character of a great Man, reverts again to his primitive State, and becomes an inconsiderable Member of the Community. And here perhaps the Poet intended to insinuate, that none but an idiot, or a very silly Fellow, would be desirous of acting such a *strutting, fretting, sounding, furious, insignificant* Part.

Fielding caps his Shakespearean ridicule by comparing the dethroning of the two Kings of Brentford in Buckingham's *Rehearsal* and the fall of Granville and Bath:

> . . . had Mr. Bayes left *two such Fellows* in Possession of their great Chairs, his Piece would have been deservedly hiss'd off the Stage. These two Usurpers therefore, who are always personated by *two very ridiculous Actors*, having sat a little while in their Places, to the great Diversion of the Spectators, *sneak off* as comically and as absurdly as they enter'd . . . . For upon hearing of the Approach of the two whose Chairs they filled [the Pelhams], without any Thing having happened which they must not have foreseen, one of the Usurpers addresses the other,
>   *K. Usher.* Then, Brother *Phys.* 'tis Time we should be gone. (*Upon which they both steal out from their Chairs and run away.*) No human Wit can ever bring Greatness to a more farcical End.

Though the news and special feature sections in issue 16 report as fully as possible on the Rebellion, apologizing for the lack of "very material or certain information," the shift to ministerialism is also marked on pages 2 and 3. The first three paragraphs of the "Present History of Great Britain" report with laconic irony the resignations of Newcastle and Harrington and the appointment of Granville on February 10 and the reversal of this process on the 14th. The fourth stresses the universal lamentation at Lord Hardwicke's intention to resign and compliments him. In the seventh Harrington is eulogized. The fifth mocks a young lad from Carlisle (The Earl of Carlisle) who was left cooling his heels when "Will Waddle" (Bath, formerly William Pulteney) absconded "down a *Pair of Back Stairs.*" The sixth sneers at Lord Bath's innuendoes about the impropriety of the place given to William Pitt:

> We are inform'd that a certain Person, who is well known to have been in an Opposition for many Years, and to owe to that all the Reputation he ever had, hath lately affected, in Public Coffee-Houses, to decry all Opposition as unjust; and in particular hath declared, that the Promotion of a Gentleman, who hath exerted the highest Abilities, and most incorrupted Integrity, would give an encouragement to young Men for the future to display their Talents the same way.

It is no surprise that in the course of this "Present History" installment Fielding begins to speak as a semi-official voice of ministry, with inside information and some authority:

> Notwithstanding the Reports which have been spread of our sending 15,000 Troops abroad [since the Rebellion was under firm control, while the continental situation remained critical], *we assure the Publick no such measure is as yet determined; nor will be, unless Affairs should take such a Turn, as must make every honest Man in Britain to desire their Embarkation.*

In the ten issues between Fielding's horse laugh at the *"brief Cabal"* on February 18 and his delighted announcement in issue 26 (April 29) of the conclusive defeat of the Jacobites at the Battle of Culloden (April 16), he concentrated on partisan politics in the lead essays, praising the ministry and denouncing opposition. He also began the "Present History of Great Britain" sections with secondary essays that propagandize for the ministry soberly, seriously, even ploddingly. Some of them read like the *Gazetteer* essays mocked in *The Champion*. In May 1746, looking back at March and April, the *Gentleman's Magazine* rightly said that *The True Patriot* had "become a strenuous advocate for a ministry."[14] Issues 17 and 18 are headed by a complaint that indicates a strong opposition reaction to the metamorphosis of *The True Patriot:*

> Whereas we have been informed by several Persons, that they have not been able to procure the *TRUE PATRIOT* at any Rate: And we have great Reason to believe that many malicious and base Endeavours have been used to suppress the Sale of this Paper, by some who are concerned in imposing on the Public, by propagating Lies and Nonsense, which we have endeavoured to detect and expose. If any Hawkers, or others, will acquaint *Mr. A. Millar*, Bookseller, opposite *Katharine Street* in the *Strand*, with the Name of any Person who has bribed, or offered to bribe them to refuse delivering out the *TRUE PATRIOT* to their customers, they shall be well rewarded, and their Names, if they desire it, concealed.

Essay 17 makes it clear that Fielding was now an unembarrassed ministerialist. It ends with a eulogy of the ministers:

> . . . that glorious Body of Men who have shewn that the highest Dignity and Property in this Kingdom are accompany'd with the highest Honour; and that the Administration is in the Hands of Men who esteem Power and Preferment of no Value any longer than they can be preferred with a strict Adherence to the true Interest of their Country.

The secondary essay in this issue, obviously Fielding's, praises them at greater length and implicitly satirizes their enemies:

> . . . the most satisfactory Contemplation is, that the Administration of Affairs is now in the Hands of Men who have given such Proofs of their Integrity, that have at once convinced us we are free Men and may depend on being so under their Protection. It is indeed the rare Blessing of the Public, in the Present Age, to be convinced that their Friends are in Power; that the greatest Men in the Kingdom are at the same time the honestest; that the very Person [Henry Pelham] to whose Councils it is to be attributed, that the Pretender hath not been long since in Possession of this City, is at the Head of the Ministry; and that the greatest Enemies of the People [the Stuarts or Granville and Bath; the application is left ambiguous] are disabled from any longer hurting or oppressing them. Indeed it is now known in our Streets, to whom we owe the Preservation of our Kingdom, by the timely bringing our Troops from Flanders, and who they were who opposed and delayed that Measure.

The public must support such a ministry, and despite all opposition. Finally, Fielding introduces an equation that would be crucial through the rest of the run and then—in more extreme form—become the rhetorical keystone of all his anti-opposition satire through 1749:

> It is now therefore, that the Opposition is really and truly Faction; that the Names of Patriot and Courtier are not only Compatible, but necessarily conjoined; and that none can be any longer Enemies to the Ministry, without being so to the Public.

This is but one step from the disingenuous *Jacobite's Journal* formula: support of the ministry equals loyalty to the Present Establishment, while opposition equals Jacobitism.

Every succeeding issue offers more of the same. The "Present History" section in issue 18 celebrates the death of faction and party—that is, effective opposition—under the Broad-Bottoms, ushering in a "New Patriotism." The secondary essay in number 19 strongly favours the ministry, and its leader implies that the opposition is weak, untalented, and tainted with Jacobitism. Even when an essay is apolitical—number 21 is an example—Fielding remains partisan: non-political essays are possible, he observes, now that the nation is capably led and safe. However, the most energetically partisan of the issues from this period are numbers 24 and 26 (April 15 and 29). The lead essay in the former makes it certain that as a ministerialist Fielding plans consistently to employ the standard equation of Jacobitism and opposition. One senses some embarrassment when he maintains he is "not ashamed to own myself to have been one of the many who were imposed on by . . . Suggestions" that the "Apprehensions of a *Jacobite* Party in this

Kingdom'' expressed by ministerialists ''were counterfeited in order to form an Argument for the Support of a standing Army, or to excuse some other Ministerial Schemes; for that, in reality, the very Seeds of *Jacobitism* were destroyed, and rooted out from the Minds of every Protestant *British* Subject.'' Professing to believe in the Jacobite spectre was a reversal indeed for Fielding. *The Champion* had called Jacobitism a ''mere Stalking-Horse'' of ministry. He had himself flaunted every *supposed* symptom of Protestant Jacobite disaffection in *An Attempt Toward a Natural History of the Hanover Rat*, and he had been at pains earlier in the run of *The True Patriot* to stress the astounding lack of support in England for the Jacobite Rebellion. But for a ministerial propagandist the equation of opposition and Jacobitism was at least as irresistible as it had been in 1730, when Fielding contemplated using it to smear Swift, Pope, Bolingbroke, and Gay. Essay 24 vilifies Protestant Jacobites as too stupid for reasoned argument, and asserts that their beliefs have been so discredited by ''the Labours of the good Men, who have undertaken the Defense of the Revolution [that is the post-1688 *status quo*], that the Jacobites of this Age have no other Excuse left, but that of not being able to read.'' Fielding admits that there are few Jacobites in England at present: not to do so would have been absurd in the spring of 1746, the Jacobitism of 1745 having been an almost purely Scottish, indeed a Catholic and highland, phenomenon. But his intention is to revive the hoary ''Jacobite smear,'' and anachronisms are most apparent. The second half of the essay is a ''letter'' written by ''a Non-Juror to his Son at Oxford'' *in the reign of William III*, full of the tired arguments and slogans of old-time ''Jacobite Toryism,'' from ''Rump''-damning to toasting liberty and the exiled King. Fielding would re-use such material in the *Jacobite's Journal* and the political outbursts of Squire Western.

In issue 26 the ''Present History'' section offers a detailed account of the battle of Culloden. It begins by observing that the impatient must now be satisfied and concludes with elaborate praise of the Duke of Cumberland. He was close to the ministry, while his older brother, the Prince of Wales, had favoured Granville. The lead essay is more complicated. Obviously partly written before the news of Culloden reached London, it closes with praise for the victory that sounds like an afterthought. Its real point is to praise the foreign and military policies pursued by the ministry in the recent past and to denigrate the policies favoured by the fallen Granville. How terrible the situation looked a few months earlier: disaster for the allies opposed by Frederick of Prussia in Germany; defeat looming over the Sardinians in Italy; France threatening to overrun not only Flanders and Brabant, but even Holland; a dangerous rebellion striking into the heart of the nation and opposed by few regular troops; no trade, no credit, and no confidence in England. Now Prussia is at peace with Austria (a result of the Treaty of Dresden of late 1745), Sardinia has been propped up sufficiently to resist Spain, in Flanders an army has begun to gather that will impede the French, the rebellion is almost over, and trade, credit, and confidence have risen amazingly. True Englishmen can only praise God and those ministers who favoured and concluded the Treaty of Dresden, bringing peace between Austria and Prussia at the price of the cession to the latter of Silesia. They should curse those (Granville is obviously meant) who opposed the treaty. The ministers are "glorious," moreover, not only for concluding the treaty but for acting decisively to bring home enough troops from Flanders to save England from the Jacobites, against opposition from less patriotic men. Here again, looking back to the fall, "we . . . find the same glorious Persons pursing the same salutory Councils in Opposition to the same Cabal." If the Cabal—Granville and his supporters—had prevailed, the rebels might "have marched without Opposition to the Capital, have placed their Popish Pretender on the Throne of these Realms, and at one Blow have extirpated our Religion and Liberties for ever." This is what Fielding had wished to write for months, though he is careful not to mention that King George was at least as inclined to oppose the policies of his ministers in September 1745 as Granville! Having thus glanced as explicitly at recent political history as he ever does in *The True Patriot*, Fielding goes on to satirize the very idea of an opposition and also (again anticipating the techniques of 1747-48) to depict the opposition as an unholy and ineffectual amalgam of republicans, ambitious rogues, and Jacobites:

> What can give a Foreigner so contemptible an Idea of this Nation as to hear that . . . . while we are actually enjoying the *Blessings procured by them*, there should yet remain a Faction among us who dare avow an Opposition to such an Administration. I have mentioned a Foreigner; for as to ourselves, who know of how few and of what Persons this Opposition consists, it must surprize us very little to find that there are some few silly enough to maintain the Principles of Republicans and *Jacobites;* and others base enough to prefer their own private Views and Ambition to the true Interest of their Country.

After Culloden *The True Patriot*'s days were numbered. For three issues Fielding maintained momentum. Essay 27 (May 6) praises George II and the Duke of Cumberland, a true prince of the "BRAVE and ILLUSTRIOUS HOUSE of HANOVER." It describes the Prince of Wales, once again inclining toward opposition, as capable, though he "hath never yet had a Single Opportunity of carrying any great political or martial Quality into act." One could not say less about the heir to the throne, but Fielding avoids saying more and invites readers to detect sarcasm. A more or less innocuous essay in the issue for May 13 is followed by a "Present History" in which Fielding pleads in good Broad-Bottom ministerial fashion for the "utter Extinction of Parties" (that is, of factious opposition), and argues that this long-wished, hitherto impossible goal is conceivable under a leader (Pelham) who takes advice from others, shares power, and works to comprehend opposition:

> . . . we must not for the future ascribe our Mischiefs and Misfortunes to *Evil Ministers;* we must ascribe them to those who *oppose* and de-

feat the Designs of an Administration founded on the *best Principles*,
that is on the *Principles* of the BRITISH CONSTITUTION."

Finally, on May 20 a "humble Petition of the People Calling Themselves
the Opposition" asks the *True Patriot* not to "dissect" them as issue 26
had threatened. Some plead insanity, others sincere republicanism,
others hereditary Jacobitism, and some—the majority—poverty and
blind ambition. This is a preview of the concept of the opposition as an
amalgam of madmen, republicans, Jacobites, and hungry scoundrels
that Fielding would repeat through 1747 and 1748. The essay is rounded
out by a letter from a ministry-hating Tory called Oliver Oldcoat, one of
the ancestors of "John Trott-Plaid, Esq." and Squire Western:

> Don't tell me that the Ministry are Men of known Integrity, that they
> have distinguished themselves as such, that they have already preserved
> us in Times of the utmost Danger, that nothing can tempt them to go
> one Step beyond the true Interest of their Country, and that they have
> shewn it to demonstration, and such Stuff. I tell you all Ministers are
> alike, *and a Patriot is he who opposes the Ministry.*

After this the journal runs down. Probably both Fielding and the
ministry lost enthusiasm with Granville disgraced and the Pretender
beaten. Essay 30 denounces the treatment of the ministry as national
"whipping boys" for war problems not of their making. The next essay
mocks the self-destructive folly of Protestant Jacobites, again printing a
Jacobite letter from the reign of William III. Neither essay is impressive.
On June 10 (issue 32) the essay signals a real withdrawal of attention: it is
a non-political, unimpressive discussion of the fact that polished deceit is
often better received than sincere merit. The "Present History" sounds
like a valedictory justification of the conversion of *The True Patriot* into
a ministerial organ, arguing that a free press is necessary even if it calum-
niates a good ministry, but that a spirited defence is needed to turn the
freedom of the press to the good of the nation.

Of the thirty-third and last issue of the *True Patriot*, June 17, 1746,
only an abstract of the lead essay has survived, reprinted in the *London
Magazine and Monthly Chronologer* (XV, June 1746). It offers some insight into Fielding's emotions upon concluding his second periodical.
The tone of the lost essay was self-congratulatory. Now that Cumberland
has smashed the rebels, "this Paper, . . . entirely occasioned by [the] . . .
Rebellion, [must] cease with it." The "True Patriot" feels he has done
his duty, and takes pride that he has avoided general condemnations of
English Roman Catholics and the "*Scottish* Nation." He has also
avoided cruel references to those attainted for their part in the Rebellion
(including, in the year after Culloden, some eighty persons, the most
distinguished being Lords Balmerino, Cromarty, Kilmarnock, and
Lovat); he is sure they will be treated with perfect justice and whatever
clemency is practicable by Hardwicke, the Lord Chancellor, "whose
Goodness of Heart is no less conspicuous than those great Parts, which,
both in the Character of a Statesman and a Lawyer, are at once the

Honour and the Protection of his Country." This may be a cautious hint that Fielding was repelled by the cruelties committed by the English after Culloden. However, the confident placement of the rebels' future in Hardwicke's hands keeps the essay well within the bounds of ministerial fidelity.

The real interest of this farewell essay resides in Fielding's parting observation that his lenient "Temper" toward the loyal Catholics, Scots, and even captured rebels has been of a kind that will "seldom" recommend" a writer "greatly to the Party he espouses." It ought to compel some consideration from those on the other side (the opposition press?) for a "fair and honest Adversary." He goes on to say that having served his King and Country with "even a Decency to those who have (erroneously, I hope) embraced a Cause in Opposition to both, I shall now retire with the secret Satisfaction which attends right Actions, tho' they fail of any great Reward from the one, and are prosecuted with Curses and Vengeance from the other." The reference to abuse from the opposition is no surprise. Fielding would be abused through the publication of *Tom Jones* and beyond. But the hint that he has not received "any great Reward" from "King and Country" may be a quiet protest about the lack of a solid reward for his ministerial efforts during the troubles of 1745-46. He would finally become a magistrate with the help of George Lyttelton and the Duke of Bedford, but the process would not begin until mid-1747, or be completed until late 1748 or early 1749. Fielding had been poorly rewarded for political writing in 1737 and 1741-42. Though his loyalty to his patrons endured, his patience perhaps wore thin in June 1746 as he prepared to return to the law and to begin composing *Tom Jones*. There seems no cogency in Paul De Castro's suggestion that the *True Patriot* closed because Fielding was forced to pay all or part of a defaulted loan of £400, for which he had stood surety, according to a judgement dated June 6. The end of the crisis and presumably his journal's ministerial subsidy are far more likely causes, though acute financial pressure may have increased his sensitivity about being underrewarded.[15]

Presumably hard at work on *Tom Jones* as well as scraping a living from the law, Fielding published little in the next year. *A Compleat and Authentick History of the Rise, Progress, and Extinction of the Late Rebellion* (April 1747) is no longer attributed to him,[16] and only three minor publications from the period are known: *The Female Husband; or, The Surprising History of Mrs. Mary, alias Mr. George Hamilton, convicted for Marrying a young Woman of Wells* (November 1746), *Ovid's Art of Love Paraphrased* (February 1747), and some contributions to Sarah Fielding's *Familiar Letters between the Principal Characters in David Simple* (April 10, 1747).

The Female Husband is apolitical. Fielding's version of Ovid is generally so, aside from one passage that compliments King George as a "glorious" martial ruler and elaborately eulogizes Cumberland as one of the "greatest Commanders." He traces Cumberland's career, from Dettingen through Fontenoy to Culloden, and pictures him victorious over France in the near future: ". . . thou shalt conquer and to thy Conquest I dedicate my votive Prayers, prepared hereafter to resound thy Praise; when we shall see thee, most lovely Prince, returning, thy glories far outshining the Gold in which thou art attired. Thee shall Crouds [*sic*] of Youths and beauteous Virgins hail from their crowded Windows as thou passest, and universal Joy shall overspread each *British* Face on that blest day." Obviously Fielding had repressed any distaste he may have felt about the rape of Scotland by "Butcher" Cumberland, who was cultivated by the ministers and had been appointed Commander-in-Chief of the allied armies in the Netherlands a month earlier. Fielding's preface stresses that he published his adaptation of Ovid, begun "many Years ago," because it included a "Passage so justly applicable to the Glorious Duke of Cumberland, which cannot fail of pleasing every good Briton."

Fielding's contributions to the *Familiar Letters*—a preface and five letters, XL, XLI, XLII, XLIV, XLV—also have political overtones. Indeed, Fielding forced uncongenial material into the apolitical *Letters* to reassert his loyalty to his patrons and the ministry. The preface praises George Lyttelton as an author ("that inimitable writer," "master of style") and a good man. In Letter XL Valentine praises the ministry precisely as Fielding had in *The True Patriot* (and soon would again in pamphlets and *The Jacobite's Journal*), then compliments Lord Chesterfield's intellect and performance as Lord Lieutenant of Ireland between December 1744 and October 1746. The passage recalls the ministerial secondary essays in the "Present History" sections of *The True Patriot:*

> The Administration of our public Affairs is, in my Opinion, at present in the Hands of the very Men, whom you, and every honest Person would wish to be intrusted with it. Amongst those, tho' there is no absolute Prime Minister, yet there is one, whose Genius must always make him the Superior in every Society, as he hath joined to the most penetrating Wit, the clearest Judgement both in Men and Things, and the profoundest Knowledge of them, of any Man, whom perhaps the World ever saw . . . . What but a Genius of the highest Kind could have preserved *Ireland* in a perfect State of Tranquillity and Obedience during the late Troubles. Or what could have restored this Nation from that drooping and Languid Fit of Despair, which lately appeared in every honest Countenance, to those chearful Expectations, which the present Prospect of Things affords us.

A ministerialist particularly attached to those he had served in opposition Fielding clearly remained, even though, as William Coley has noticed, there may again be quiet hints in the *Familiar Letters* that Fielding was unsatisfied with the rewards he had received for his late political exertions: "there is no one Patron of true Genius, nor the least Encouragement left of it in this Kingdom" (Letter XL).[17] Chesterfield became Secretary of State in the fall of 1746, a member of the inner cabinet, and he had been close to Lyttelton for a decade. As will be seen below, during the next year Chesterfield would split over foreign policy with Henry Pelham and thus with George Lyttelton and the Duke of Bedford, the Broad-Bottoms who had most completely cast their lot with the Pelhams. He would leave the ministry in February 1748, and immediately be dropped by Fielding, whose real loyalty was to Lyttelton and, increasingly, Bedford. In the spring of 1747, however, there was no need to choose between Chesterfield and "personal" loyalties.

Fielding's full return to partisan authorship required another crisis. When the ministry faced the "Forty-Five" and Granville he had responded. He would respond to two more crises: the early election of 1747 and the negotiation and signing of the Peace of Aix-la-Chapelle in 1747-48. Odd as it may seem to a modern, aware of the complex ministerial evolutions of 1742, 1744, and 1746, the Parliament elected in 1741 was still in being and could have remained so under the Septennial Act until mid-1748. But it had to occur to the ministry in 1747 that its commanding majorities were not forever proof against certain pressures. The weak opposition had been encouraged in January 1747 when the Prince of Wales began openly to act as its patron and organizer, backed by Dodington and the Earl of Egmont, and by Lord Bolingbroke, on whose theories the Broad-Bottom ministry was ostensibly based. This gave the weak opposition some coherence and the capacity to embarrass the ministry with a close vote on the right issue in a thinly attended House of Commons. This happened on January 22, when a ministry-baiting motion for the investigation by a "Committee of the Whole House" of the Navy debt was defeated by a plurality of only forty-one, 184 to 143.[18] The war still was not going well and never would. The opposition would have an issue while the war lasted, yet a peace treaty (necessarily a poor one) was not an attractive alternative. The Duke of Newcastle was more inclined to fight on in the hope of victories and better terms. His brother, Henry Pelham, was inclined to take the best terms obtainable and escape the Continental morass. The campaign of 1747 would show that peace was essential, but meanwhile the ministry worried about the prospect of negotiating an unsatisfactory treaty to end a dismal war. It decided to call a general election a year early, lest the election required under the Septennial Act coincide with an unpopular treaty. In 1747 an unprepared opposition had no real chance to win, and peace negotiations would be far safer with a large majority in a Parliament with seven years ahead of it. Parliament was prorogued on June 17 and dissolved on June 18 by the King. Fielding soon returned to action.

In his election pamphlet, *A Dialogue Between a Gentleman from London, Agent for two Court Candidates, and an Honest Alderman of the Country Party*, Fielding shows himself a complete ministerialist. It is a longish dialogue between an honest and intelligent, but naïve Country adherent and a London friend who in the end successfully argues him into the ministerial camp. The latter's arguments are cogent, the former's not quite weak enough to emphasize his "straw-man" qualities. Argument is not the only level on which the *Dialogue* appeals; it also consistently treats the opposition as a contemptible alliance of Jacobites, republicans, and disgruntled "Whigs." This tactic is familiar from the later run of *The True Patriot* and would soon be the rhetorical key to the *Jacobite's Journal*. But in the *Dialogue* Fielding first perfected its use, and his opponents gave him some excuse for equating sedition and opposition. Having shown their real loyalty, actively or passively, during the "Forty-Five," the Country extremists resumed the "Jacobitical" (really anti-ministerial and anti-Court) excesses so dear to them. They were ready, once there was no danger of a change in dynasties, to denounce Hanover policies and "Hanover Rats," to toast the Stuarts and violently abuse the ministry. Since the Country element was even more preponderant than usual in the opposition minority after the formation of the Broad-Bottom in 1744, focussing on the "Jacobite" behaviour of its extremists was a very attractive means of defaming the whole opposition. Finally and most ironically, the opposition started a half-humourous, half-libellous cross-fire of Jacobite accusations to which the *Dialogue* was Fielding's first contribution.

Old England had become the premier organ of the opposition, assaulting its founder, Lord Chesterfield, and his colleagues in the name of "true" Patriot principles. It attempted to forestall the inevitable ministerial use of the Jacobite smear and reduce it to absurdity. On February 28, 1747, almost four months before the *Dialogue* appeared, *Old England* laid mock charges of Jacobitism against an opposition work, *The Taffydeis: an Humourous Heroic Poem, in Honour of St. David and the Leek* (the second edition of which is advertised in the same issue), basing these charges upon gross misinterpretations of its contents. On April 11 (two days after the execution of Lord Lovat, the most celebrated captured Scottish traitor of 1745-46) *Old England* energetically attacked Jacobitism in general and the Jacobitism of a specific author (unidentified, he apparently posed as a Dutchman). This was obviously an attempt to demonstrate its loyalty to the "Present Establishment." *Old England* needed to stress the distinction between loyalty to Hanover and support for the ministry.

That spring the opposition chose as a focus of confrontation with the ministry one of the clan-destroying measures pressed after the "Forty-Five," the "Bill for taking away and abolishing heritable Jurisdictions in . . . *Scotland*." It stripped Clan chieftains of their hereditary authority to administer justice in their districts, compensating them with money for this loss of "property," and was strongly opposed from its introduction on April 7 through the granting of Royal Assent on June 17, the last day of the session, roughly six days before the *Dialogue* was published. This resistance to the bill pleased Scottish members, whose support was needed to bolster the weak Commons minority, but lent credence to attacks on the Jacobitism of opposition. Moreover, on

March 19 the extremist Tory society called "The Independent Electors of the City and Liberty of Westminster" indulged in Jacobite toasts during its annual banquet at Vintner's Hall, and severely beat a man thought to have harboured a witness against Lord Lovat, whose trial ended the same day. As William Coley has recently noted, this was the immediate point of departure for Fielding's *Dialogue*. Advertisements say it is "Earnestly address'd to the Electors of Great Britain, particularly to the glorious Independent Electors of Westminster," though the title page does not carry the final specification of audience.[19] The anti-Jacobite broadside in *Old England* for April 11, three weeks after the Vintner's Hall incident and two days after the execution of Lovat, was an act of prudence. The Vintner's Hall incident became one of many occasions for swapping Jacobite innuendoes. The Commons ordered the same members who had managed the impeachment of Lovat to look into it, and George Lyttelton (a "manager") was asked embarrassing questions about the anti-Hanoverian, "Jacobite" behaviour of his opposition faction in 1743 by Lord Doneraile, a dependant of the Prince of Wales. This may explain why George Lyttelton was wrongly assumed by some opponents to have written *A Letter to the Tories*. The anonymous pamphlet, which appeared in June, at almost the same time as Fielding's *Dialogue*, warns the Tories not to tarnish their image by continuing to consort with Jacobites.

Thus, the *Dialogue* naturally alternates between straightforward political theorizing and argument and implications of opposition disloyalty in London and throughout the nation. It begins with a debate about the propriety of allowing placemen to serve in Commons (an evergreen issue, raised yearly by every opposition), the aldermen urging their exclusion, and the London gentlemen explaining that if men of ability could not be at once in place and in Commons, "We must have . . . a very sorry Parliament, or a very sorry Administration." Soon, however, it is revealed that one opposition candidate, "Mr. Toastem," is an unprincipled "Whig," who has joined forces with Sir *Thomas Leadenhead*," a *"known Jacobite,"* while the "honest Alderman" has long maintained "the most rigid Principles of a Republican." This is the same pattern mocked in the "Petition" of the opposition against "Dissection" in the *True Patriot* for May 20, 1746, and a precise anticipation of the graphic and verbal depictions in *The Jacobite's Journal* of the opposition as a rag-tag of republicans, Jacobites, and Whiggish scoundrels. The alderman argues, as Fielding would have before 1745, that "the Court . . . hath long cheated us with Names, the term *Jacobite* is a mere Bugbear." The gentleman's answer is consistent with Fielding's position in *The True Patriot*, no. 24: he treats as absurd the "Strange Doctrine which possessed many some Years ago, that the Spirit of *Jacobitism* was totally extinct among us," and says that the "Forty-Five" proved "*Jacobitism* is no empty Sound." When the alderman asks "what Assistance" the highlanders found "in England," the gentleman's half-humourous answer anticipates the ambiguities of *The Jacobite's Journal*, and mocks the "Independent Electors of

Westminster": "The usual Assistance which your Friends the *Jacobites* here lend to any Cause. It is true, indeed, they prudently refrained from drawing their Swords, but it is as well known how gloriously and openly they *drew their* Corks in the Pretender's Favour." Such jesting was not unusual throughout the period. In the 1730s Lord Bathurst admitted, "I go out hunting to show I am a Tory and drink bumpers to show I am a Churchman." And in 1749 the Earl of Egmont laughed at the Tory Thomas Rowney: ". . . It is remarkable of this man, who is a rough clownish country gentleman, allways reputed a rank Jacobite, and has drunk the Pretender's health 500 times, that when the Pretenders son came into England, he was frightened out of his wits—and ordered his chaplain to pray for King George which he never suffered him to do in his life before."[20]

The "Honest Alderman" admits in confidence that though he is a republican, he believes *"Redress of Grievances"* would be easier to obtain under the absolutist Stuarts. He declares he is "a *Jacobite upon Republican Principles*," which his friend says is a greater absurdity than "an *Atheist upon Christian Principles*." There follows a complicated debate, summarizing the arguments of several generations of controversialists about relative strengths of the divine and human, hereditary and legal claims of the Stuarts and Hanoverians to the Crown. The Gentleman of London and the Hanoverians prevail, but the point is that the debate is an *absolute red herring* with respect to the election of 1747. No one who mattered in England wanted the Stuarts back or believed in divine right to the point of acting to change the succession or thought anyone else who mattered believed such nonsense when sober. But a ministerialist always relished an opportunity to pretend ministry *versus* opposition was tantamount to Hanover *versus* Stuart.

The *Dialogue* next deals with opposition complaints that under the present ministry "Liberty is in Danger" and corruption is rampant. The first is dismissed as ridiculous under a ministry too lenient to invoke existing laws, much used under the Stuarts, against "Treason writ in our News-Papers; and talked and sung and toasted in our Taverns every day." *"Liberty being in Danger"* is a "Cant Phrase invented for the same seditious Purposes with that ever-memorable Cant Phrase of the Church being in Danger." The cry of corruption evokes a more complex and significant response. The alderman insists that pensions are corruptive. The gentleman first replies that this is only true when they are clandestinely given to M.P.s and declares that there is no present evidence of this, then attacks the opposition, and, in particular, Lords Granville and Bath. The word "corruption" should connote "every Thing which corrupts the Minds of the People." The opposition has corrupted the Public understanding, misrepresenting the ministry. In a perfect reversal of the "normal" equation of prime minister and chief corrupter, Granville and Bath are treated as the real corrupters:

. . . perhaps we need not search long to discover the Views of Men *who*

> *have formerly been in Opposition, have grown popular from being so,*
> *have succeeded from that Popularity: have obtained the Power which*
> *they had opposed, have been removed from it again by their Country,*
> *have again set on foot an Opposition, and have impudently applied a*
> *second time to their Country, hoping to corrupt even their Common*
> *Sense, and aspiring to a Second Establishment in Power.*

Finally, the gentleman reminds the alderman (in a passage that recalls the indirect bribery scenes in *Pasquin*) that the Country gentleman of opposition also bribe electors, using their great local leverage as landlords and important customers. Corruption is a national disease, not to be charged to the present ministry.

The alderman next suggests a "Place-Bill and the Bill for annual, or at most triennial Parliaments" as cures for corruption, both standard opposition demands. The gentleman argues that there are place restrictions already, and that no ministry has enough places in its gift to buy a majority in Commons, a half-truth, as we have seen in Chapter One. The removal of paid places and pensions for "men of business" in Parliament would simply result in more secret forms of remuneration, since they must be paid for their services if there is to be effective government. Such legislation cannot cure the flaws of human nature and, the gentleman suggests, "your republican or *Jacobite* Friends" would welcome the chaos resulting from a "universal Place Bill." Annual or triennial Parliaments would make effective government difficult, increase the degree of corruption, and make it vastly easier for the ministry to control Commons. Country gentlemen go so deeply in debt buying votes every seven years under the present system that one cannot imagine them surviving an annual or even triennial ritual. Then too a Commons with a short term might lose enough prestige and efficiency to upset the balance of government, thus endangering popular liberty. An elector "who sells his Vote once in seven Years, will be equally ready to sell it once in three," and the advantages the Court enjoys septennially would be multiplied under the annual or triennial systems. Balancing hope and cynicism, the gentleman says the corruption of Commons is "infinitely less than it hath been represented," though "the Corruption practised at Elections, is so known and certain, that I should think no Man deserved the least Credit who denied it." There is perhaps a degree of ministerial influence sufficient to encourage "a Majority on the Side of the Government, as will suffer public Business to go on, by placing some Confidence in the Administration, and by assisting the Crown in pursuing vigourous Measures, when such are necessary against its Enemies." However, the "Majority" does not "hearken implicitly to the Vote of a Minister without any Attention to the Good of the People."

The Fielding who produced this had certainly come a long way from the Fielding who, during the last election campaign, had treated corruption as the greatest of dangers to the Constitution and liberty in *An Address to the Electors of Great Britain*. The *Dialogue* and the *Address* are comparable in length, seriousness, and cogency, but their attitudes are diametrically opposed on such issues. Just how far he had come is symbolized by his justification in the *Dialogue* (reminiscent of Dr. Johnson's remark about "defensive pride") of "defensive" corruption. The gentleman says that "some Degree of Corruption always hath attended, and always will attend a rich and flourishing Nation." The present government neither caused nor can cure it. He unhesitatingly asserts that the present government must use corruption against a disloyal and corrupt opposition:

> To defend yourself with the same sort of Weapons by which you are attacked, hath always been held lawful; and even Corruption . . . becomes justifiable when defensive . . . . In this defensive Way only the present Government can be fairly said to apply to any Arts and Corruption; and in this sense, I sincerely think every honest impartial Man will own, that some degree of it may be necessary to preserve not only the King on his throne, but the Religion and Liberties of this Nation; all which are by the blackest Corruption attempted to be undermined.

The alderman next decries the war as "Hanoverian" and ruinous, and the gentleman recalls that it was begun at the insistence of men now in opposition and under the Walpole ministry, not the present one. He treats the alderman's preference for a "War only at Sea, and . . . let the Continent go to the Devil" as suicidal. It would leave England a prey to the power of France and Spain, probably backed in time by the fleets of the abandoned Dutch. "If your Friends mean to serve the Pretender," the gentleman observes, "they cannot advise a better policy" than total withdrawal from the continent. For his own part, the gentleman thinks the bad situation abroad might have been worse had the ministry not acted shrewdly and patriotically. He explains that the Treaty of Dresden (December 1745) has served British and allied interests, and that the treaty would have been lost if the ministry had not rejected Granville's anti-Prussian policies. The chances for early and successful peace negotiations will depend on strong support for the ministry at home. They must win the election:

> If the Opposition prevails, we have two things to fear; either a shameful and fatal Desertion of our Allies and Interests in the Continent, which is the Scheme of some who are engaged in that Opposition [i.e., the "Country" group], or a no less ruinous Forwardness to continue the War upon Objects or Passions in which the true Interest or Honour of *England* hath no real or weighty Concern, which the past Conduct of others who bear a principle Part in the same Opposition gives too much Cause to apprehend.

A vote for the ministry is a vote for a *good* peace treaty in the near future.

Fielding touches every other issue in a ministerial spirit. High taxes are justified by international circumstances, and Henry Pelham, First Lord of the Treasury, is eulogized for managing well during an expensive war and in the aftermath of a Rebellion that stopped trade. Granville and his associates are indicted for resisting measures needed to put down the Rebellion as Fielding praises Pelham's judgement. Pelham gave "early Advice . . . to bring over our Troops, without which that Rebellion would certainly have proved successful; when some who oppose him, and would be thought good Friends to the Government, affected to treat our Danger with Scorn, and the Measure of recalling our Troops to the Defense of their Country, as the Effect of a cowardly and pusillanimous Spirit." The gentleman defends the bill to abolish heritable jurisdictions on the grounds that those deprived of inherited legal authority are to be financially compensated. It will also remove a barrier between the people of Scotland and the justice of the Crown, rendering more consistent the legal status of subjects throughout the realm. He mocks the alderman for objecting to the early dissolution of Parliament. He has just argued vehemently for triennial or even annual Parliaments, and surely cannot object to His Majesty's desire to consult the will of the people in a general election after six years. The election will also show foreign allies and enemies that the ministry is well supported, "and that our King reigns in the Hearts of his People, contrary to the malicious Suggestions of *Jacobites*, both at home and abroad," who have "wickedly given out, that not only the present Administration but even the present Royal Establishment subsists only by a corrupt accidental Majority, in a Parliament almost expired."

The gentleman closes his anti-opposition argument with an utterly irrelevant comparison between universally loved King George and the Pretender, and a declaration that "The Republican doth indeed serve the Purpose of the *Jacobite*, as the Atheist doth that of the Papist: For to reduce this Nation to the Form of a Republic, is as wild a scheme as to reduce it to Atheism." He asks the alderman to vote for "honest Gentlemen, who will support an Administration which hath already preserved this Nation from Ruin, and under which the present Establishment, and of consequence our Religion and Liberties, will be always secure." The alternative is to vote for candidates who embody the disloyalty, stupidity, and hypocrisy of an evil opposition:

> One of them a notorious *Jacobite*, and as notorious a Blockhead. The other a Person of known profligate Principles; a *Whig* in Name, but in Heart a Slave as all wicked Men are; one who hath joined with this *Jacobite*, and would join with the Devil himself, to work himself into Employment, which he despairs of being let into under the present Administration.

Naturally, the "honest" alderman finally agrees to vote for the ministerialists and is congratulated for abandoning candidates who represent all that is worst in England:

> . . . the one would destroy the Administration at the Hazard of the Government, to introduce himself into Power; and other would destroy the Government, to introduce the *Pretender*. One or other of these Schemes is the real Motive of all the present Opposition, except among those who are merely the Dupes and Fools of the others.

The *Dialogue* was so pleasing to his patrons that the first step toward making Fielding a magistrate was taken roughly three days before it was published: a fiat nominating him Justice of the Peace for Middlesex was issued on June 20, 1747. Probably because he could not satisfy the property requirements, he did not fully qualify, take his oaths, and ascend the Middlesex Bench for over a year and a half, but his reward was in the works. Meanwhile, all of the issues and innuendoes aired in the *Dialogue* were revived after the government opened formal treaty negotiations with the French at the end of 1747 and Fielding returned to his duties as ministerial apologist and opposition-baiter. The negotiation of the treaty would pose the third and last serious threat to the stability of the Broad-Bottom ministry, mainly because the war had been so long and so costly, yet so unsuccessful, and the treaty had to be frustrating. As long as a decision could be put off, the ministry needed little defending. It had won the election of 1747 overwhelmingly; there were a mere 60 committed Tories, Lord Egmont grimly estimated, together with a trustworthy nucleus of about 40 adherents of the Prince in opposition. The King had come to respect and trust Henry Pelham, and with big majorities and a virtual talent monopoly in Commons, the ministry could leave Fielding to the law and *Tom Jones*. He probably completed the novel in first draft in 1747 at his residences in London and Twickenham, and in summer quarters near Bath or at the country estates of George Lyttelton or Ralph Allen, Hagley Park and Prior Park.[21] For five months the opposition carried on its side in the strange crossfire of Jacobite display and satire begun in the spring of 1747 by *Old England* and the Westminster electors and continued in Fielding's *Dialogue* and the *Letter to the Tories* of June. Fielding remained silent.

The west-country Tories indulged in Jacobitical and anti-ministerial displays that made the Westminster electors seem tame. They donned Scots-plaids, toasted the Pretender, and publicly damned Hanover and the ministry at fairs and race-meetings. They were not remotely interested in the return of the Stuarts, but their antics, together with a new rash of Jacobite displays by the denizens of Tory Oxford, seemed perfect validations of Fielding's *Dialogue*. Fielding must have been infuriated when, in August at the Lichfield races, the hot heads went further, rioting and horsewhipping the great Duke of Bedford. Bedford was an intimate of Lyttelton and the senior member of the Grenville "cousinhood" in the ministry. Then First Lord of the Admiralty, he would become a Secretary of State early the following year. He would also be a most important patron of Fielding's by 1748-49, worthy to share the honours with Lyttelton and Ralph Allen in the "Dedication" of *Tom Jones*. Meanwhile, *Old England* continued the Jacobite "paper war," pre-empting the themes of the ministerialist.[22] On August 8 *Old England* described the ministry just as the *Dialogue* had described the opposition: ". . . surely a *Coalition:* form'd of so many repugnant Parts, of *Whig*, of *Tory*, of *Republican, Jacobite* and *Jew*, was never heard of till in these our latter Days; so productive of Monsters in Politics, and extraordinary Events in the State.'' *Old England* could count on the public to remember that the kind of anti-Hanoverian speeches that Pitt, Lyttleton, and Chesterfield made in 1743-44 were as ''Jacobitical'' as anything said since by opposition parliamentarians. After all, *Old England* had been founded by Chesterfield, and had taken a line under his leadership that seemed openly ''Jacobite'' to Lord Orford. How *Old England* would have enjoyed penetrating the secret that Fielding wrote *An Attempt toward a Natural History of the Hanover Rat!*

On September 26 *Old England* implied that the ministry found the ''Forty-Five'' convenient; it lent patriotic colouring to its forcing itself upon the King. The Rebellion helped the ministers, and they purposely protracted it. This was patently false, but all was fair in the Jacobite ''paper war'' gathering momentum in the latter half of 1747. During the same month, a ministerial print depicted the ''Lichfield Jacobites'' as drunkards in plaids, toasting and swearing seditiously on horseback, while Bedford is horsewhipped.[23] This strikingly anticipates the woodcut that adorned the early numbers of *The Jacobite's Journal;* perhaps the same artist (Hogarth is often vaguely credited with the latter) did both. In *Old England* for October 10 (in a scene recalling the execution of Lord Lovat) a dream-vision essay depicted George Lyttelton (very thin; in his youth author of the *Persian Letters;* in 1746 thought to have written *A Letter to the Tories*) threatening loyal opponents with death as Jacobites. With him the dreamer saw Henry Fielding (whose *Ovid's Art of Love Paraphrased* had complimented ''Butcher'' Cumberland), helping his patron to choose victims:

> Immediately there issued out of a large Building, not unlike a certain *Chapel* of great resort, a tall, lank, meagre figure, much more resembling Death than the amiable God of Love, and excepting a *Persian* Bonnet which he wore on his Head, he was dressed like an *Executioner*, with an Axe in his right Hand and a Halter in his Left; the former of which he complained was blunted and wanted *whetting*. As he stalk'd along, his long lean Feet scraped up an exceeding deal of Dirt, which he kicked about and bespattered all Sorts of People, particularly, a Body of Men *that stood in his Way*, whom I heard somebody call *Whigs*. He was attended by a corpulent elderly Gentleman, who held a Map of *Staffordshire* in his Hand, and who every now and then whispered in *Cupid's* Ear and pointed to some of the poor, gaping Crowd, saying, such a one *is a Jacobite;* at which the Spectre, grinning a horrid and ghastly Smile, shook his Halter.

Finally, on October 24 *Old England* directly denounced Jacobite smearing: ''. . . whoever has not accepted a Place, nor asked for one, since the Date of the Coalition, is stigmatized for a Rebel.'' Even the Prince of Wales has been dishonoured ''in this civil Distribution of the term Jacobite.''

During the fall of 1747 Fielding published nothing in reply. His life was no doubt hectic enough; he married Mary Daniels during this period, three months before she bore their first child. In late November, however, the political tempo was raised by the onset of formal peace negotiations with the French. He began to set up a formidable, weekly vehicle for anti-opposition satire, *The Jacobite's Journal*, supposedly the work of a ridiculous, drunken Jacobite Tory, "John Trott-Plaid, Esq." The bustle of preparations preceding issue 1, published December 5, was surely followed closely by the opposition journalists, one of whom attempted to reduce the Jacobite theme to absurdity on November 30. *The Jacobite's Journal* was, in effect, answered in advance by the anonymous pamphleteer who wrote *An Apology for the Conduct of a late celebrated second-rate Minister*. Supposedly the political *apologia pro vita sua* of Thomas Winnington (a placeman under Walpole and his successors, and a member of the Broad-Bottom ministry at his death on April 23, 1746), it carries the anti-ministerial version of Jacobite satire to its drollest heights. "Winnington" recalls how he began his career as a secret Jacobite, and found that all of the ministries during his long political lifetime—including Walpole's and the Broad-Bottom—were equally determined to bring back the Stuarts. By mismanaging at home and abroad they hoped to disgust the people, weaken England, strengthen its enemies, and bring about a revolution. The pamphlet's ironies get wildly complex. It claims, for example, that the French secretly favour the inept Hanoverian regime, while pretending to support the Stuarts. But its most obvious pragmatic thrust is plain: To denigrate in advance as un-English, even anti-English, *any* treaty terms the ministry's representatives might obtain from the French. Its "anti-anti-Jacobite" approach is a pre-emptive parody of the humorously slanderous *Jacobite's Journal*.

Fielding's specific answer to the *Apology* was published on December 24, *A Proper Answer to a Late Scurrilous Libel entitled an Apology . . . Second-rate Minister*. It is inferior to the work it attacks, and its targets are precisely what one would expect: the evils of Stuart absolutism and bigotry, the falsity of the Jacobite slander levelled at Winnington and loyal ministers. It lauds the efforts of ministers to wage war effectively, resist the Pretender, and negotiate an honourable peace. For our purposes, the key fact is that it answers the Jacobite ironies in the *Apology* with more of the same, calling its author and the opposition disloyal and implying that the battle between ministry and opposition is really between Hanover and Stuart. The opening of the pamphlet reveals his strategy and centres it in the Jacobite paper war: "When Popery without a Mask stalks publicly abroad, and Jesuits preach their Doctrines in Print, with the same Confidence as when the last Popish Prince was seated on the throne, it becomes high time for every Man, who wishes well to his Country, to offer some Antidote to the intended Poison."[24] When he published this, Fielding had already gotten out three issues of *The Jacobite's Journal*. In the *Journal* he would exploit the Jacobite:opposition, pro-ministerial:pro Hanoverian equations more effectively than anyone had since 1715-16, when Addison perfected them in *The Freeholder*.

The opposition kept up its side of the Jacobite paper war during the run of *The Jacobite's Journal*, though it was unable to compete with

Fielding, Jacobite satire being inherently a ministerial weapon. *Old England* mocked Fielding's adoption of a Jacobite *persona* (January 2, 1748), complained bitterly about his Jacobite slander (March 5), and called him Lyttelton's "informing Jackcall" (March 26). In the *Gazetteer* (e.g., essay no. 261 by "The Fool") and *The London Evening Post* there was much "Jacobite" satire directed at Fielding and the ministry. On March 15, the latter called Fielding "the known pension'd Scribler" for a ministry avowedly opposed to freedom of the press, and suggested: "By this let Men judge *who* are the true *Jacobites*." The Jacobite jesting in *An Apology . . . Second-rate Minister* was carried on in such arch pamphlets as *A Free Comment on the Late Mr. W-G-N's Apology* and *The Patriot Analized* of February 1748. The latter implied that Fielding was just as Jacobite as the author of the *Apology*. This assertion changes meaning as often as one reconsiders it. It is topped by an insidious hint that Fielding may have written the *Apology* himself, then answered it: "What would you say, if the Apology had been wrote by the Answerer himself." In the *March to Finchley* of 1750, Hogarth would show a "Jacobite" vendor hawking both *The Jacobite's Journal* and the opposition's *Remembrancer*, attacked as seditious in *The Jacobite's Journal*, no. 17. Either Hogarth got confused (which I doubt) or was adding his own late twist to a dead paper war. The joke was compounded by ignorant "readers" of the print who saw the vendor as specializing in "opposition" journals.[25]

The closing opposition contributions to the war—aside from a brief revival of hostilities at the end of 1749 which will be looked at in Chapter Seven—were appropriately made by *Old England*, which began it. On June 11, 1748, looking back to the spring of 1747 (before Fielding's *Dialogue*), *Old England* brought the long war momentarily into focus when it reminded its readers that it had always been anti-Jacobite. It only stopped actively campaigning against Jacobitism when "the Subject-Matter became disgraced by the Hireling-Pen of a dirty Drawcansir, set up for the Coalition, at a weekly Allowance, to form new Distinctions among us, and brand every Pen with *Jacobitism* that refused Obedience to that Babilonian Image [the ministerial coalition], composed of so many different Materials." How perfectly the ironies had come full circle. Finally, on November 12, 1748 (a week after the last issue of *The Jacobite's Journal*) *Old England* argued that Fielding's Jacobite journalism was always ministerial propaganda. Even issue 1 of the *Journal* had "proved that *Argus* [Argus Centoculi, the editorial persona of *Old England*] and his patrons were to be the real objects of Trotplaid's venal Pen, in order to be humorized into *Jacobites*, as Occasion occur'd suitable to the Purpose of his Paymasters." The phrasing was perfect; everyone was "humourizing" his enemies "into Jacobites" in 1747-48.

Fielding's employment of Jacobite satire must not be allowed to obscure the specific occasion for the establishment of *The Jacobite's Journal*. This was the onset in the closing weeks of 1747 of peace negotiations with the French at Aix-la-Chapelle that would eventually end the

War of the Austrian Succession. In 1747 the Broad-Bottom ministry was as weak in the world of journalism as it was strong in Parliament. Secure ministries scanted propaganda; weak oppositions depended on it. Before *The Jacobite's Journal*, the opposition was backed by *Old England*, the *Gazetteer* (especially in the essay series signed "The Fool"), the *London Evening Post*, the *Westminster Journal*, and the *Craftsman*, while the ministry had no strong daily or weekly voice. This was an unsatisfactory situation from the moment in late November 1747 that the King announced to Parliament the opening of peace negotiations. The ministry faced a period of unusual vulnerability to criticism.

The opposition would be sure during the negotiations to insist vociferously on an early peace, an escape from the "ministerial" war, with terms far better than could conceivably be obtained. The dismal tendency of the long conflict had continued in 1747, when Bergen-ap-Zoom was lost. If a treaty was made, the opposition would as certainly denounce it as insufficient. It would stress English gains during the war, ignore losses, deplore every concession to the French or Prussians, and pretend that the terms it had been demanding could have been obtained. On the other hand, the worried ministry would not be able to reply effectively for a considerable period. The Duke of Newcastle had favoured continuing the war through the campaigning months of 1747, hoping to win victories and go to the conference table with the leverage to obtain a more palatable treaty. Henry Pelham (supported by Fielding's patrons) had favoured early negotiations. On July 11 Henry Pelham had observed to George Lyttelton that the favourable results of the election left only the question of war or peace as a major ministerial problem, and by September 24 he was discussing tentative plans for negotiations at Aix-la-Chapelle. Still, on the latter date even he had vague hopes that a victory somewhere would bring down the French King's demands.[26] By November it was obvious to all that an immediate attempt at a peace was the only course, if another year of—at best—expensive military stalemate were to be avoided.

In the event, the English and French agreed to a return to the *status quo ante bellum*, sweetened for the Prussians at the expense of the Austrians, and for England by French acceptance of the Hanoverian Establishment. The terms were reasonable and acquiesced in as such by all but opposition zealots. But it was impossible to be sure in late 1747 and early 1748 that a treaty acceptable to both France and England, as well as the other participants in the war, would be obtained at all, much less to predict with confidence when it might be obtained and what its precise terms might be. There were insecurities even after the outlines of the treaty, the "Peace Preliminaries," were clear and tentatively accepted by foreign foes and allies. The ministry waited through months of bargaining for extra concessions (in which George II was heavily involved in his Electoral role) before the final treaty was signed. Only then could it be officially revealed and justified to Parliament and the public. This presented a massive rhetorical problem. No ministerialist could too strongly argue the need for an immediate peace, lest the negotiations prove abortive. An attempt at peace negotiations had failed in 1746. Neither could he wax too confident about obtaining specific terms, lest some not be obtained and the opposition crow that the ministry had admitted they should have been. Too forthrightly to deny opposition's claims that given, desirable terms were obtainable would be to concede bargaining points too early to the French.

In short, the opposition could be specific and effective in criticizing the negotiations (winter and early spring, 1747-48), then the Peace Preliminaries (later spring through early fall, 1748), while ministerialists had to be vague or attempt to shift attention away from treaty expectations. This would become particularly difficult after the Preliminaries were signed on April 30, and the theoretically secret terms were reported and widely criticized by hostile London journals. The return to the French of Cape Breton, the capture of which had been one of the few English victories, is a case in point. It was well known that it was part of the treaty (balanced by French concessions), and it could not have been kept, given the overall situation. However, it was hard to deal with the wave of outrage that greeted it during the limbo period of over five months between Preliminaries and final treaty. This problem—having to skirt the issue of war and peace to a great extent, though it was the one great issue of the time—is a crucial determinant of the rhetorical approach and evolution of *The Jacobite's Journal*. Fielding adjusted his methods to fit the ministry's peculiar situation and the opposition's continuing vulnerability to half-humorous Jacobite smearing. He resumed on a weekly basis his side in the Jacobite "paper war" because he had no choice.

The first issue of *The Jacobite's Journal* (as well as a second edition of the *Dialogue*) appeared within days of the royal announcement about the negotiations. The journal would continue weekly for forty-nine issues, ceasing publication just over two weeks after the final treaty terms were officially revealed. Its value to the ministry is indicated by the elevation of Fielding to his London magistracy before it ceased publication, and the subsequent extension of his jurisdiction to Middlesex through the influence and generosity of George Lyttelton and the Duke of Bedford. The solid reward for loyalty that eluded him in 1737, 1741-42, and even 1746 and 1747 was finally given. Fielding's enemies repeatedly claimed that *The Jacobite's Journal* was heavily subsidized with secret service funds, channelled through Lyttelton, Fielding's "Paymaster." They said 2000 copies of each issue were bought up and distributed free by post.[27] There is, not surprisingly, no documentary evidence of this, and it was a charge meant to discredit Fielding. However, he never specifically denied it and I accept it. Whether the details were quite accurate—the precise number of copies, the role of Lyttelton—one cannot tell, but the pattern and the number seem plausible. As indicated in earlier chapters, such a subsidy would have been normal for an important, overtly ministerial organ. It would have made the journal at once profitable for Fielding and, by increasing circulation, a formidable propaganda voice. Normal circulation would not have been high, given its partisan content and inefficiency as a news medium—the "news," like that in Fielding's other journals, consisted of snippets from rival papers. Fielding's finances must have been strained in December 1747: *Tom Jones* would not bring in any money for another half-year, and he was newly married and expecting the first installment of a second family. Lyttelton may have done something for Fielding upon his remarriage, though wedding a pregnant servant, no matter how fine a woman, had to seem to him more an embarrassment than a cause for felicitation. Rumours that Lyttelton "gave away" the bride were surely meant to insult him,[28] and when Fielding wrote to congratulate Lyttelton on his very different second marriage (the letter dated August 26, 1749) he obviously had not met his patron's bride. Fielding could not have worked so hard and so long as he did on *The Jacobite's Journal* without pay, let alone convince booksellers to absorb losses for the good of the ministry. Obviously, the burden of proof lies with anyone who doubts that *The Jacobite's Journal*, or any comparable ministerial journal of the reign of George II, was not well subsidized.

Given the convenience of the "Jacobite smear"[29] during the touchy peace negotiations, and Fielding's prior involvement in the Jacobite "paper warfare" of the time, its employment in his new journal was natural. During the early run Fielding could pose as a ridiculous Jacobite and ridicule the opposition in "red herring" essays, while quietly undercutting opposition criticism of the negotiations and military matters in the remainder of his four-page issues. He was soon tempted to a more direct approach by attacks on himself and his patrons and other factors, but he never went all out defending the treaty until the final version was signed, and never really ceased to cultivate the ironical equation of Jacobite and opposition. In fact, reviving the Jacobite technique proved especially helpful during long periods in the later run when the delay between Preliminaries and treaty stretched out excruciatingly, forcing him to mark time for months. Conveniently, the abandonment by the French of the lost Stuart cause in the treaty allowed him to conclude his journal by drawing its pro-treaty, pro-ministerial, and anti-Jacobite strands together. Fielding's intention to use Jacobite satire like that in the *Dialogue* was made clear to readers of the first twelve issues even before they began the lead essays. These were headed by a woodcut succinctly associating opposition with Jacobitism, republicanism, and the drunken buffoonery of the stock Tory squire. A cassocked Jesuit on the left, signalling silence with a finger alongside his nose, uses a tasty copy of the opposition's "London Evening Post" to coax along an ass. On the ass are a huzzahing Tory squire, drink in hand, and his roaring wife, brandishing a sword, both wearing Scots-plaids. The backdrop is the London skyline, and the complex grouping and insult in the foreground is completed on the right: a copy of "Harrington" (that is, the notorious republican book, *Oceana*), absurdly decorated with three French *fleurs-*

de-lis, is tied to the tail of the ass. This opposition-blackening woodcut is even more deft and complete than the "Lichfield Jacobites" of September.

The first essay, under the perfect Horatian motto, *"Ridiculum acri/ Fortius et melius,"* sets the pattern of the new journal's rollicking slanderousness. It treats opposition Tories as drunken, disloyal, cowardly, and proudly imbecilic. It implies that the rest of the opposition, its "republicans" and "whigs," are *pro tem*, opportunist Jacobite "fellow travellers." Fielding made the far-from-original technique work well; this and some of the other early *Jacobite's Journal* essays are comic gems, for all their dated topicalities. Trott-Plaid introduces himself with a brag that he is a Jacobite, observing that such openness is the current fashion in "Taverns, in Coffee-Houses, and in the Streets." He and his proud brethren were born Jacobites (*"Jacobita nascitur, non fit"*), and need or heed no rational arguments for their Stuart loyalties ("we scorn to regulate our Conduct by the low Documents of Art and Science, like the Whigs"). Reason can only make a man loyal (read a supporter of the government or the ministry), while Jacobites (read Tories or the opposition) glory in unreasoning rejection of the *status quo*. Jacobites have hitherto been more secretive, Trott-Plaid explains, for a variety of reasons, all reflecting on the character and brainpower of the opposition Tories and the hypocrisy of their ambitious allies. Revealed disloyalty "might be some Objection to them in their Pursuit of Court Favours, or Preferment." Cries against encroachments on Liberty "would not come with so proper a Weight from Men who profest the Tenets of indefeasible, hereditary Right, arbitrary Power, and prostrate Non-Resistance." Loyalty to the Stuarts, Papist bigots and absolutists, might not attract opposition republicans and non-conformists. Worst of all, an open Jacobite might be asked for a rational justification or explanation of his principles, which are "NOT FOUNDED ON ARGUMENT," and about which few Jacobites know anything:

> In all Mysteries, such as Jacobitism is, Faith is sufficient, without the least Knowledge: And whoever wears a Plaid Waistcoat, roars at Horse-Races and Hunting-Matches, and drinks proper Healths in Bumpers, is a good and worthy Jacobite, tho' he should not be able to assign any Reason for his Actions, nor even to tell what he would be at.

Finally, Jacobites were too cowardly before the "latter End of last Summer" (before the general pardon proclaimed in June 1747) to show themselves. They drink, never fight:

> . . . true English Jacobites fear Blood, as well as they love almost everything else which is liquid. This fear . . . is so extensive that the least shedding or sprinkling of Blood will disperse the greatest Numbers of Jacobites in a Moment; whereas they always appear more or less, in this Nation, in Times of a mild and bloodless Administration.

Trott-Plaid vows to abuse the ministry, to outdo the "Jacobite" *Old England* and *London Evening Post*, and to be "laughed at for the Good of my Country."

Subsequent issues cleverly elaborate this kind of ridicule of Jacobites, Jacobitism, the opposition, and the opposition press. Essay 2 announces that Trott-Plaid's drunken wife will contribute Jacobite wit to his paper, and notes that she has authored "several of the most acute unintelligible Articles which have been, from time to time, published in the *London Evening Post*, to the great Entertainment and Edification of our Party." Essay 3 ridicules "Mysteries" or "Doctrines" of "Protestant Jacobitism":

> *That all Kings are by Divine Appointment. That the Regal Right being divine, is consequently indefeasible. That Passive Obedience and non-Resistance must be preserved by Subjects to the Prince, tho' he should endeavour to erect a Tyranny in a limited Monarchy or to Extirpate the established Religion of the Country. That a Popish Prince may be the Defender of a Protestant Church.*

The crucial point is the insistence that anyone who calls himself a "Jacobite" (here the term includes the whole opposition, seen as a Jacobite faction) "must, and doth, and will maintain" these doctrines "in Defiance of all the Argument or Reason which hath, or may be, urged against them." In the fifth issue *"The Creed of a* Female Jacobite" blends the mindless anti-Whig, anti-Court, anti-Hanover rhetoric of extreme Tory opposition with the argument that the Church of England, as well as "the merry Days of old *English* Hospitality," would revive under the Catholic Pretender ruling with the help of "all the Popish Powers in Europe." The following week "Jacobite" and "Bacchus" (associable not only with wine, but beer, "the Liquor chiefly used in the celebration of the *English* Mysteries") are etymologically related, and the race-meeting brawls of the previous summer described as Bacchanalian orgies.

The Jacobite reverse irony often thins almost to the vanishing point, but the fiction that Trott-Plaid is defending "Jacobitism" always reasserts itself. In essay 12 he complains of those who have denied "that I should in Earnest hold the Principles I have asserted; and this for no other Reason, but because they are directly repugnant to common Sense." He suggests that the sources of Jacobitism are the same as the sources of the ancient myths described in the Abbé Banier's *Mythology and Fables of the Ancients Explain'd* (a translation of which, put out by Millar, is advertised in this and other numbers of *The Jacobite's Journal*): vanity and obstinacy, illiteracy, the thoughtless passing on of beliefs from father to son, the "false Eloquence" of demagogues, the "lies of Travellers," ignorance of philosophy, "misunderstanding Sacred Scriptures, and Ignorance of History." Trott-Plaid admits that no Protestant Englishman could prefer the Stuarts unless he knew nothing of their history. But he closes by refusing, with the absurd energy of Buckingham's Drawcansir, to allow his knowledge of the absurdity of his position to change it: "I am resolved to be a Jacobite, and will be so in spite of all the Reason and Evidence in the World. I was born a Jacobite, and I was bred one. My Father was a Jacobite before me, and so have been all our Family, and so am I, and so I will always be, because I will, and because I dare.''

After issue 12 the satiric woodcut was not used. Perhaps it broke or proved an embarrassment in some way I cannot fathom. (Fielding's later complaints that it was misunderstood are, of course, ironical). Possibly its removal was an early symptom of a change in tactics Fielding would announce in essay 17. In any case, Trott-Plaid's droll commentary in issue 13 on the misinterpretation of the "Emblematical Frontispiece so long prefixed to my Paper" carries on the pattern of reverse irony: he brags that the ass was a "Figure [for] the whole Body of Jacobital Doctrine" and an appropriate symbol of "a Protestant Jacobite." Subsequent issues go the same way. In essay 15 (March 12) letters from "Jacobite Correspondents" deftly combine ironical ridicule of Jacobites and scorn for the opposition: "Cambr. Britannicus" takes pride in the "Genealogy of a Jacobite:"

> The Devil begot Sin, Sin begot Error, Error begot Pride, Pride begot Ignorance, Ignorance begot blind Zeal, blind Zeal begot Superstition, Superstition begot Priest-craft . . . Lineal Succession . . . Indelible Character . . . Blind Obedience . . . False Worship . . . Infallibility . . . the Pope and his Brethren in the Time of *Egyptian* Darkness . . . Purgatory . . . Auricular Confession . . . Renouncing of Reason . . . Contempt of the Scriptures . . . Implicit Faith . . . Carnal Policy . . . unlimited Passive Obedience . . . Non-Resistance . . . Oppression . . . Faction . . . Patriotism . . . Opposition to all Measures of the Ministry . . . Disaffection . . . Discontent . . . Discontent begot a Tory, and a Tory begot a Jacobite on the Body of the Whore of *Babylon*, when she was deem'd past Child-bearing.

This genealogy symbolizes perfectly the use of Jacobite satire while the peace talks dragged on: it is clever, sharp, and an absolute "red herring." The resulting frustration may explain why the overworked writer, doing a weekly journal and finishing and revising *Tom Jones*, kept himself even more bustlingly busy. He involved himself, under the pseudonym "Madame de la Nash," with a Punch and Judy show in Panton Street that ran from March 28 to June 2, and was "puffed" on March 7 in the *General Advertiser*. It is unclear whether the show had political overtones, though Fielding's political enemies teased him about it. He also published, during April, the pamphlet called *The Important Triflers: a Satire*, by "Captain Cockade," only one passage in which is at all political.[30]

Naturally, while Fielding blackened the opposition, its press corps turned the Jacobite jest back on him, as we have seen, and hammered the ministry and its policies, foreign and domestic, especially the issues of war and peace. From the first, Fielding had to rebut their attacks in the second, third, and fourth pages of each issue. The opposition attacks were too numerous to allow even a fair sampling, but the aggressive essay in *Old England* for December 26, 1747 is typical. It notes that the late Speech from the Throne promised an active campaign by the laggard Dutch allies and announced the onset of negotiations. It insists on the need for naval, not land, warfare and the absolute necessity of retaining Cape Breton and all other gains in Canada. It sarcastically maintains, "There is no Foundation for saying our present Rulers are Bunglers and Blockheads, because the Country is impoverished, our Honour gone, *Flanders* lost, and *Holland* at the Eve of Ruin." The safest, simplest way for Fielding to respond was to quote bits of such criticism in the news sections, and then treat them as "Jacobite" nonsense. In special feature sections following the annotated news the treatment of opposition statements as "Jacobite Doctrine" sometimes became elaborate:

ARTICULI JACOBICI:

Or, Articles of Jacobite Faith invented and spread for the Use of our Party; and which every good Jacobite is either to believe or say he does.

I. That the Ministry are desirous of making a bad Peace when we are able to carry on an advantageous War.

II. That they are desirous of carrying on a disadvantageous War in order to purchase a bad Peace.

III. That all the bad Consequences which have attended the War, the Burden of Taxes at home; the Infidelity and Weakness of our Allies abroad, &c. are all justly to be charged on the same Ministry.

IV. That a Desire of obtaining the best Peace in their Power . . . is to be imputed as a Crime by those who clamour against Evils which we suffer by the War.

V. That a Great Peer [Chesterfield] is about to resign his Place, and a Great Commoner [Pitt] is gone discontented to Bath.

Such things as these can never be inculcated too often by those Jacobites who are not afraid nor ashamed to serve their Party at the trifling Expence of Modesty and of Truth. [January 9, 1748, p. 3]

Jacobitism aside, this is not an entirely unfair paradigm of the propaganda in the *London Evening Post* and *Old England*.

The need to defend the ministry more directly soon affected lead essays. Essay 4 (December 26) is a "letter" that stresses the absurdity of Jacobitism and the quality and security of the Broad-Bottom ministry: "We have an Administration not consisting of one absolute Prime Minister, supported only by his Tools and Dependents, and obnoxious to the Great Men in the Nation, but an Administration composed really of all the Great Men, whose abilities of any Kind make them worthy of any Place in it; supported by both Houses of Parliament, and, as appears by the last Election, by a vast Majority of the whole People." This is pretty straight ministerial writing, parallel to much in *The True Patriot* and the *Dialogue*. John Trott-Plaid claims that he printed it only to show he was not afraid to do so. The leader in issue 7 consists of excerpts from an anti-opposition pamphlet, *An Historical Essay upon the Ballance of Civil Power*, probably by Samuel Squire. Published a week earlier, *circa* January 9,[31] it satirizes the opposition as an alliance of Jacobites, republicans, and ambitious Whigs.

There is more direct anti-opposition satire in essays 8, 9, and 10. The first scorns opposition writers who "have attacked the present Administration during a Course of Years, and have never touched upon a single Excellence in the bright Characters of a *Pelham* or a *Hardwicke*." Essay 9 "praises" the opposition's "Art of Contrariety," or "abusing on both Sides of the Question":

> . . . if the Ministry, when abused for having involved us in the Miseries of War, answer, that they did not begin it; that they lament the Calamities it hath brought upon us and the Ruin with which it threatens us, and are therefore desirous of putting an End to it; we immediately turn our Accusation to the direct Contrary, and libel them with endeavouring to procure a disadvantageous and dishonourable Peace.

Essay 10 is a consistent, straightforward attack on the opposition and its press and a defence of the "Present Administration" and its attempt to obtain an "honourable Peace." Fielding cites a ministerial pamphlet, *The Case Restated* (January 1748), and his own *Dialogue*, totally abandoning Jacobite irony. The ministry includes the best men in the Kingdom. They inherited terrible difficulties, many of them the results of Granville's policies. They are trying to obtain a fair peace in difficult circumstances, while the opposition attempts to subvert them and the national interest. The highest honours will be due to "that Person who shall give a tolerable Peace to this bleeding Country." This was as far as Fielding dared go in praising the search for peace in February, nearly three months before the announcement of the signing of the Peace Preliminaries. He may have been encouraged by indications that the achievement of a treaty was becoming more likely. *The Daily Advertiser* carried a rumour during the same week to that effect, cited with a satisfied, "Jacobite" comment by Fielding in the "Domestic News" section:

> We hear that the Propositions made by France, &c. to his Majesty for a General Peace, will soon be laid before both Houses of Parliament. D.A.
> *I heard an impudent Whig, on reading this paragraph, wish the glorious Ministry, who signed the Peace of Utrecht, had been as honest as the present.*

An openly pro-ministerial essay may also have been Fielding's way of re-emphasizing his loyalties. Though he does not mention it, on the day essay 10 appeared, February 6, Lord Chesterfield resigned as Secretary of State for the Northern department, albeit not with the intention of joining the opposition. Chesterfield's enmity toward Newcastle and his discomfort in office had been common gossip for months. Chesterfield's place was taken by the Duke of Bedford, who would be a major patron of Fielding's for the rest of his life. The sudden interest Fielding showed in Bedford at this time (he is praised in *The Jacobite's Journal* for January 30, February 20 and June 11) was no doubt a reaction to his new eminence, but it may also indicate that patronage had already begun to flow in Fielding's direction. At some point before

December 19, 1748, when he resigned the post, Fielding apparently was appointed High Steward to the Warden of the New Forest by Bedford, who had been Warden since 1746. The date of appointment as High Steward is not known, but a recently recovered letter by Fielding, dated April 3, 1748, seems to reflect business dealings with Bedford, his agent, Robert Butcher, and Richard Birt, deputy Steward of the New Forest.[32]

Fielding was also under strong personal attack. *Old England*'s lead essay for March 5 is a sustained, personal affront to Fielding, signed "Porcupinus Pelagius." In *The Jacobite's Journal*, No. 11, Fielding had ridiculed him as the author of "a Panegyri-Satyri-Serio-Comi-nonsensi-unintelligi-Poem, called *The 'Piscopade'*." In return he calls Fielding a ministerial "Press informer" and a "Scavenger of Scandal" employed by Newcastle. He has Fielding describe his ministerial employment as a sanctuary won after years in which he

> . . . hunted after Fortunes and lived on Kept Mistresses for a while; scored deep at the Taverns, borrow'd Money of my Landlords and their Drawers, burrough'd in privileg'd Places among the Flatcaps of the town, stood Bully for them, and p*x'd them all round; abused my Benefactors in the Administration of public Affairs, of religious Dispensations, of Justice, and of the Stage; hackney'd for Booksellers, and News-Papers; lampooned the Virtuous, wrote the Adventures of *Footmen*, and the *Lives of Thief-Catchers;* crampt the Stage, debas'd the Press, and *brought it into Jeopardy;* bilked every Lodging for Ten Years together, and every Alehouse and Chandler's shop in every Neighbourhood; defrauded and revil'd all my Acquaintance, and being quite out of Cash, Credit and Character, as well as out of Charity with all Mankind, haunted by Duns and Bumbailiffs, hallow'd, hooted at and chased from every side, and by every Voice, I escap'd with whole Bones indeed, but d--bly mangled into these Purlieus of Safety, where no venemous Creatures dare enter.

Perhaps encouraged by an open defence of Lyttelton in *The Jacobite's Journal* for April 2, *Old England* would maintain on April 23 that Fielding's "Paymaster," Lyttelton, was paying him a "weekly stipend." It would close, however, by laughing at Fielding's involvement with the Panton Street puppet show and repeating the very nasty story that his second wife, his first wife's maid, was mistaken for a shabby trull and refused admittance to the boxes in the theatre by the box-keeper. The opposition was hitting low, and would continue to do so through the end of the run and beyond, mocking his morals and his wife, his poverty and political apostasy, his supposed illiteracy and drunkenness, his puppet show, his snuff-taking, and his long jaw. In 1751 Smollett would sneer at Fielding's marriage to his "cook-wench" and mock Lyttelton for giving the bride away, in the first edition of *Peregrine Pickle*. The following year, he would vilify Fielding with nearly insane venom in *A Faithful Narrative of the base and inhuman Arts . . . practised upon the Brain of Habbakuk Hilding*.[33]

In the "Court of Criticism" section in issue 15 (March 12) Fielding pillories "Porcupine Pillage" as a scurrilous extremist who threatens freedom of the press by abusing that freedom. On March 15 the *London Evening Post* says Fielding: ". . . the known pension'd Scribler for the M--try, the Author of the *Jacobite's Journal*, has this Day openly thrown off the Mask, and declar'd himself an Advocate for taking away the *Liberty of the Press*." Perhaps the opposition writer knew something. After a week's pause, Fielding abandoned his pretence of Jacobitism in essay 17. He explains that he is tired of impersonating idiotic Protestant Jacobites, and that Jacobitism has become too serious for jesting indirection. It is poisoning the minds of university youth (Jacobites misbehaved again at Oxford on February 23), polluting the press, and spurring on the mob. In fact, Fielding had other reasons for abandoning his Jacobite pose at just this time. The Peace Preliminaries would not be signed by all parties for more than a month, but it was clear that an agreement had been reached. Fielding also identifies as a major precipitating factor the appearance of a dangerous "new" opposition writer: a "Drummer of Sedition" who recruits for the "Pretender's Cause," calling on the "People to take Arms against the Government, with this Motto on their Banner, *Nil Desperandum*." He pretends to do this "in the Name of his present Majesty," but really "fights in the Cause of Popery and Slavery, under the Standard (as he pretends) of the Constitution." The writer thus singled out was James Ralph, Fielding's old friend and partner between 1736 and 1741. Ralph's impressive opposition journal, *The Remembrancer*, had begun publication on December 12, 1747 (it would run until June 1751), only a week after *The Jacobite's Journal*, and thus was hardly new in late March. However, though even the introduction to the recent Wesleyan-Oxford edition implies that the months-old journal was the irritant, Fielding singled out Ralph for attack on March 26, after ignoring him for sixteen weeks, because the first twelve *Remembrancer* essays were republished the same week as a shilling pamphlet: *The Remembrancer, by George Cadwallader, Gent., Consisting of the First Twelve Essays from the Weekly Paper*, printed for "W. Owen, at Homer's-Head near Temple Bar." No doubt the idea was to get twelve very potent attacks on the ministry before a public that may not have bought the individual issues. Only the pamphlet bears the motto *Nil Desperandum* (though each essay had another classical or modern motto), so that Fielding's stress on this "Banner" precisely identifies the target of his attack.[34]

Ralph's essays reveal the same skill as his best *Champion* leaders, blending scholarship and invective. He depicts the ministry as a dangerous super-faction, composed of opposition turncoats and the rump of Walpole's faction, interposed between the manipulated King, his true friends, and the people. He calls for real non-partisanship and a Patriot King, for true Broad-Bottom measures, not those of a false Broad-Bottom ministry (see especially essays 1-3). This had particularly to gall Lyttelton, Bedford, and Pitt, now facing an opposition backed by their old patron, the Prince of Wales, and Lord Bolingbroke, the fount of Broad-Bottom theory. Bolingbroke's *Good Queen Anne Vindicated* appeared in the spring of 1748, reminding all that this opponent thought up the supposed principles of the ministry. His *Idea of a Patriot King* (written 1735-38, but never before authorially published, though Pope and others pirated it) finally came out with his blessings in 1749. On the eve of publication George Lyttelton, in great embarrassment, had to ask Bolingbroke to remove the anachronistic dedication of this work to him. The cross-pressures and anomalies were extreme for the Broad-Bottoms and Fielding and even for Ralph: within five years Ralph would be editing *The Protester*, a pro-Bedford, opposition journal (the Prince having died and Bedford having left the ministry) that lasted twenty-four issues in 1753, and dining with Fielding at George Dodington's. The power of Ralph's writing in the pamphlet of March 1748 sometimes suggests the hey-day of the *Craftsman* (Horace Walpole called *The Remembrancer* the "Craftsman of the present age"), while the violence of his rhetoric seems deliberately to invite Fielding's attack.[35]

Ralph depicts the King as in the toils of an evil, hypocrite, factious administration, corrupt and desirous of a bad peace. The balance of government is nearly gone, leaving "the usurped dominion of an Oligarchy." The utter destruction of the Constitution looms (essay 12). The holy hope of the people is the "H[*ei*]r A[*p*]p[*aren*]t." They must rise against the ministry, "freeing" the King and saving the nation. The later essays in the pamphlet border on sedition. The wonder is not that Fielding rounded on Ralph on March 26, but that he had ignored him for so long and would generally ignore him thereafter, concentrating on *Old England*, the *London Evening Post*, and the *Gazetteer*. Presumably he retained some regard for his old friend. Conveniently, Ralph's more extreme essays could be misconstrued as "Jacobite" sedition. The motto *"Nil Desperandum"* (part of the speech in which Teucer vows to return from exile in Horace—*Odes*, I.vii, 27-29) was particularly easy to misconstrue this way; one simply had to associate Teucer and the Pretender. Fielding would again suggest as much in *Tom Jones*, where Partridge, a Jacobite, cites Teucer's words and for a moment represents James Ralph of *The Remembrancer*.

The quickening of the opposition campaign of personal invective, the progress of the peace talks, and the appearance of Ralph's pamphlet were not the only determinants of Fielding's rhetorical *volte face* in essay 17. His strongest loyalties were always to George Lyttelton and the rest of the Grenville "cousinhood." At this precise juncture both Lyttelton and the Grenville brothers, Richard and George, were under opposition attack to an extent that made ambiguous, ironical Jacobite ridicule an inadequate response. These attacks were not important enough in the broad movement of party warfare greatly to concern a writer merely "ministerial" in his orientation. But they bulked very large in Fielding's narrower view, impinging on the "personal" loyalties that underlay and determined his ministerial orientation, just as they once had his opposition orientation. Having branded Ralph and seditious grumbling during delicate negotiations carried forward by "the best of Governments," and having abandoned the "Character of a Jacobite," Fielding immediately turned to the defence of his "personal" patron and his associates.

The anonymous *Letter to the Tories* of June 1747 was still awaking reverberations in the spring of 1748. Though he probably did not write it—however he may have approved of its contents—George Lyttelton was thought by many to be its author. *A Second and Third Letter to the Whigs* were published anonymously on March 26, the day that Fielding dropped his Jacobite pose. Their author (Horace Walpole, though Fielding did not know it) abused Lyttelton for writing the *Letter to the Tories*. It accused "Selim" (the name of Lyttelton's persona in the *Persian Letters*) of the grossest political hypocrisy, stressing particularly alterations in later editions of the *Persian Letters* to bring it in line with Lyttelton's changing alignments in the earlier 1740s. It also said he was immoral, scurrilous, and irreligious, guilty of open sedition in the past, determined at present to limit freedom of the press. Walpole's charges resemble those obliquely pressed in *A Modest Apology for My Own Conduct*, an anti-Lyttelton pamphlet "fathered" upon Lyttelton in 1748 by some opposition writer. As we will see, the confusing crossfire was completed somewhat later by Edward Moore, whose *Trial of Selim the Persian* is a mock trial of Lyttelton that actually defends him. Fielding had to rebut Walpole's charges more quickly and directly. Essay 18 insists that Lyttelton never "saw, or heard of" the *Letter to the Tories* "till he read it in Print." It says all three *Letters to the Whigs* (the first published on July 23, 1747) show their author's ignorance and malice. Neither Lyttelton nor anyone else in the ministry favours new limitations on freedom of the press: "The Abuse of the Press, so far as it is personal to themselves, they see with Contempt: If it offends in a higher Manner, there are Laws in Being to punish those Offenses, and *let those Laws take their Course:* but let nothing be done, even for the Security of Government, by which Liberty can be hurt." Fielding rounds out his rebuttal in the "Court of Criticism" section in issue 18. There he declares that "no Man who hath the least acquaintance" with Lyttelton's "public or private Character, can read this Letter without being equally astonished at the Malice and Folly" of the author of the *Letters to the Whigs*.

The Grenville brothers, Richard and George, were under heavy attack in the press and in Parliament over a fairly minor matter that was made a debating point by the opposition as a way of getting at the ministry. Richard Grenville, as local magnate and M.P., brought a bill into Commons on February 19 to move the summer assizes from Aylesbury to Buckingham, infuriating the former town. This move was designed to increase the Grenville's power in the district, where they were rivalled by the Willes family. In Commons the bill (finally passed, 155 to 108) was denounced as an abuse of power, even an attempt at infringing Royal Prerogative, by men with ministerial backing. Both the Grenvilles and Henry Pelham, who supported them, were criticized in *Old England*, the *London Evening Post*, and other opposition organs. Horace Walpole observed that the usually calm Pelham was moved almost to tears of rage in Commons.[36] Eager to honour his "personal" as well as his ministerial loyalties, Fielding devoted his second "post-Jacobite" essay (number 19, April 9) to defending the Grenville position in this squabble. He characterized assaults on the bill as examples of the "Art of Perversion," the product of envy, malice, and jealousy, though "no Ministers since *Adam* have, I believe, given less Food to these malignant Passions in their Enemies than the present." Then he reprinted with minor alterations the text of a three-page pamphlet, *The Case of the Town and County of Buckingham: Reasons for Passing the Bill now depending for fixing the Summer Assizes at the antient Country-Town, where they have usually been holden*, which it is not inconceivable he wrote himself.[37] The extraordinarily long leader ends with a defence of the Grenvilles and a eulogy of Pelham as a political paragon, who has "in this Instance, as in all others . . . maintained the Dignity of his high Station, and of his higher Character."

Having done his duty by his patrons, in essay 20 Fielding completed the broadside made possible by dropping his Jacobite mask. He complains at length at the "load of Scandal [that] hath been cast, upon me" since undertaking *The Jacobite's Journal*, observing that he has been pursued even "*into private life, even to my boyish years.*" (In fact, on September 24 even the decades-old scandal of his father's second marriage would be dredged up by *Old England* and related to Fielding's second marriage.) He disingenuously asserts that he has done little to deserve the enmity of the opposition press, and that he was attacked because he defended the Present Establishment, irritating writers in "the Pretender's Interest." He offers as proof the "fact" that: "much of this Scurrility was cast on the Author of the *Jacobite Journal*, before he had even touched on a single Ministerial Question. Nay even to this Day, so very little of the kind hath been made the Subject of this Paper, that those who will call it Ministerial, must acknowledge, that to defend the King and the present Administration, are one and the same Thing." This is, of course, a variation on the rhetorical fiction Fielding had employed since the later run of *The True Patriot*. Its resumption may indicate a regret that the need to answer Ralph and defend Lyttelton, the Grenvilles, and himself had obliged him to relinquish Jacobite reverse irony three weeks earlier. In any case, having made his personal complaint, he goes on in the essay to indict the author of the *Letters to the Whigs* and *The Remembrancer* again, and to print "letters" praising his decision to attack Jacobitism openly.

In subsequent essays, Fielding perforce returned to lambasting Jacobites while waiting for the official announcement of the signing of the Preliminaries. Essays 21, 22, and 23 are concerned with the ill effects of Jacobite infiltration of the educational system, a theme encouraged by the continuing Jacobite excesses at the universities.[38] There is a certain apologetic, anachronistic air to them. Essay 21 begins with the observation that "The Reader will perceive that the following Letters have lain by me some Time, and were received before I threw off the Mask of Jacobitism." Fielding only takes fire at a passing chance to praise the ministry: "The administration is at present happily in the Hands of Men of more sensible and more liberal Principles; of Men who have been and are the Guardians of those Liberties, which these poisonous Doctrines endeavour to undermine." (Essay 22) Not until May 14 (essay 24) was Fielding free to praise the ministry for achieving a peace.

The English, Dutch, and French signed the Peace Preliminaries at Aix-la-Chapelle on April 30. The King first proclaimed this fact on May 5 and announced it in his prorogation speech to Parliament on May 13. The Sardinians and Austrians at first refused to sign, though the Austrians finally gave in on May 25. The substance of the 24 articles soon was generally known (abstracted in the newspapers between May 12 and 14 and reprinted from them by Fielding in his foreign news section on May 14): basically a return to the *status quo ante bellum* for the French and English, with Cape Breton going back to the French and the Hanoverian Establishment being recognized by the French. Steady, specific opposition attacks began immediately. Fielding had to take the position that the terms were not public property and would remain subject to minor changes until the final treaty was signed. He would for months normally confine himself to a defence couched in generalities, when he mentioned the Preliminaries at all. However, it was a great moment for the ministry, after years of frustrating warfare and months of worry, and Fielding made the most of it on May 14. His essay stresses the happy alteration in the national situation and credits it to the ministry. The first paragraph recalls the essay of thanksgiving after the victory of Culloden in *The True Patriot*, no. 26:

> Whoever will be pleased to cast his Eye backward for one Month only, and recollect the gloomy Prospect which the situation of public Affairs then presented; the dreadful Apprehension which prevailed in every Mind, and discovered itself in every Countenance; arising from the daily Decline of National Credit, from the apparent Strength of our Enemies, and from the manifest Weakness or Perfidy of our Allies, must be obliged to own, when he compares it with the pleasing Scene now shifted on the Stage, that no Nation hath ever had a quicker Transition from Evil to Good. Now as this happy Alteration of our Affairs is intirely owing to the Preliminaries of Peace lately signed, surely we ought, with one Accord, to cry BLESSED ARE THE PEACE-MAKERS.

Fielding goes on to predict that a nation sick of war will embrace the peace and honour "those glorious Patriots who have obtained a Blessing for us." Jacobites, who have long hoped that failure in the war would "introduce the Pretender to the throne," will lose all hope. Ambitious opposition hypocrites will be more chagrined:

> All the hopes of these men lie only in Change, and their End is to accomplish it. The Means consequently are to cry out against the Things that be. If we are engaged in a War, then is the War to be undertaken upon unjust or weak Grounds, to be carried on in an improper Man-

ner, to be attended with intolerable Expence, and to be dangerous and ruinous to the Nation. If we make a Peace, then is it is base, dishonourable, injurious: Our Successes in the War are magnified, in Defiance of manifest Truth and Experience, and in direct Contradiction to what they themselves had just before asserted; and to make the Terms we have accepted disadvantageous, we are in a Moment elevated to a Situation of giving Laws to all *Europe*.

The essay defends the agreement with irony, and without risking a listing and justification of the 24 specific clauses of the Preliminaries. It will not resemble the treaty Henry V forced upon the humbled French in 1420, giving the English king reversionary rights to the throne of France. It will not (and the anti-Tory irony drips) be the kind of peace that "*might* have been obtained . . . at . . . Utrecht" in 1713. France will not concede all and England nothing, while Prussia smiles acquiescence. It will be "very desirable . . . if Matters are restored by it to a kind of Status quo," and it will be an occasion for honouring the Ministers responsible for it.

Even amid the rejoicing and self-congratulations on May 14 one can see Fielding facing up to an embarrassing situation: his inability to speak forthrightly or with an air of knowledge about the treaty until it is finalized, signed, and announced. He argues that "whatever terms our Ministers may have obtained" will be satisfactory, declares his ignorance of terms generally known (and reprinted on the next page!), and refuses to "venture to praise, tho' others have been rash and foolish enough to condemn, in the Dark." This awkwardness is the key to the rhetorical peculiarities of many later essays. For, amazing as it may seem, after the one great pro-treaty statement in essay 24, Fielding returned doggedly to Jacobite satire and the task of generally vilifying the opposition and its press. Meanwhile, a flood of journal essays and pamphlets criticized the peace terms—particularly the return of Cape Breton—and the Pelhams. Good examples are the essays in *Old England* for May 7, 14, and 20, June 25, July 30, August 6 and 13, and September 3, and in the *London Evening Post* for August 18 and 23, September 8, 15, and 17, and such pamphlets as *Observations on the Probable Issue of the Congress at Aix-la-Chapelle, Remarks on the Preliminary Articles of Peace as they were Lately Transmitted to us from the Hague* (both published in May), and *The Finesse of Rantum Scantum, A New Diverting Dialogue Between Tom and Harry* [Newcastle and Henry Pelham], *Fratres Fraterrimi* (August).

From this Fielding turned aside. Essay 25 drolly compares the Jacobites and the Jews, while essays 26 and 27 satirize Grub-Street slander of good and great men (the ministry) and university Jacobitism. Small wonder that on June 11 Fielding's anti-Jacobitism is denounced once more in *Old England* as ministerial and as so polluting the issue that no honest patriot can touch it. In number 28 Fielding returns to abusing the *Three Letters to the Whigs* (comparing the false charge against Lyttelton with those against Socrates), snarls about the horsewhipping of Bedford (a "Nobleman of the highest Rank and Dignity" and "distinguished Bravery"), and again defends the Grenvilles over the Buckingham-Aylesbury assizes. At this point Fielding was missing no chance to praise his patrons without raising the peace question; on June 18 in the "Court of Criticism" section his glowing notice of *The Castle of Indolence*, by James Thomson, George Lyttelton's dependant, particularly praises the "extremely just" eulogy of Lyttelton in stanzas 65 and 66. Essay 29 resumes the assault on *Old England*, the "Fool" (in the *Daily Gazetteer*), and the *London Evening Post*, proposing the establishment of a "Hospital for Sc-ndr-ls" to house them, and essay 30 is a letter from "Honoria Hunter" that takes us back to the most light-hearted, wittily distanced days of the *Journal:* her Tory father refuses to let her marry a fine young man because his great-grandfather voted for the Whiggish Exclusion Bill in 1681. Its innocuousness is particularly striking if one compares it to the *Old England* essay for the same day, which not only attacks the peace and the Pelhams severely, but insults Fielding as John Trott-Plaid and "Master Punch" in Panton Street, then sneers at "his Wife—or his Maid, if the Reader pleases." (This was part of an ongoing pattern: *Old England* returns to the puppet show on August 27 and six days later emphasizes that Fielding's wife was first his "Cookmaid.") During this stage in the run, aside from the annotated news and regular jabs in special sections, Fielding mainly deals with the peace debate in the "Court of Criticism." In issues 26 and 27 the "Court" tries two opposition pamphlets of the previous month, *Observations on the Probable Issue of the Congress of Aix-la-Chapelle* and *Remarks on the Preliminary Articles of Peace.* Even in this forum Fielding normally stressed neutral issues. In issues 29-32 it is taken up by a sober plea for "a charitable Provision for the Widows and Children of the poor Clergy," a subject also touched in passing in *Tom Jones.* One could not get much farther from partisan debate and the treaty.

The peace process dragged on through July, August, and September, the opposition at once criticizing clauses in the Preliminaries and complaining at the delay in signing the final treaty. It was insinuated, not wholly inaccurately, that attempts by George II (in Hanover with the Duke of Newcastle) to win new concessions beneficial to the Electorate were causing the delays. The English and their allies and enemies were involved in the most complex manoeuvers toward final concessions, as is clearly evident, to cite but one source, from the hectic overseas correspondence of Lord Chancellor Hardwicke.[39] While Europe haggled, Fielding continued the rhetoric of delay and barbed semi-relevancy for a dozen more issues; only two essays from this period, numbers 35 (July 30) and 41 (September 10) touch on the treaty. His patrons apparently were pleased. On July 30 they revived the plan of placing him on the Bench (begun with the London-Westminster fiat in June 1747), nominating him for a Westminster magistracy. Lord Hardwicke did the appointing as Lord Chancellor, and Lyttelton surely provided the original impetus for this reward. However, Bedford was the principal landowner in the area around the Bow Street Court, and the owner of the house in which Fielding and other contemporary Bow Street Justices lived and worked. He probably was the key to the arrangement. Normally, Hardwicke would have appointed in the district according to Bedford's wishes. Fielding would not fully qualify for and assume the position of Bow Street magistrate for some months, but it must have been heartening to take another step forward toward professional security, especially since London and Westminster magistrates, unlike Middlesex Justices, did not have to meet the £100 property qualification.[40]

Fielding's writing during the long delay reflects both loyalty and great ingenuity. On July 2 he ridiculed the venal impudence of the "Fool," the particular irritant being an attack on Pelham as a corrupter of Parliament that appeared in the *London Evening Post* for June 18, as well as in the *Gazetteer*. On July 9 Abraham Adams presented a mock etymology of the word "Jacobite," indicating that Jacobites (opposition members) have no principles, only a desire to "supplant" the present government. (The suggestion that William Young, the supposed original for Adams, may have written this essay does not convince me, and there is no real evidence to support it. It is not even certain that Young was Fielding's assistant at the time.)[41] The next essay (July 16) compares the Jacobites and Milton's lying, despairing fallen angels, a particular target being *Old England*. The same day he waxed doubly ironical in the "Court of Criticism" upon a work that pretended to attack Lyttelton, but actually defended him: Edward Moore's *The Trial of Selim the Persian for Divers High Crimes and Misdemeanors*. The publisher, M. Cooper, stands accused of "taking in" those who believed Moore was really hostile to Lyttelton, though the piece was actually a reductive parody of opposition attacks on Lyttleton. On May 31, 1748 Henry Pelham had congratulated Lyttelton on the *Trial of Selim*, and a year later Fielding would write to cajole Lyttelton into extending aid to the distressed Moore.[42]

England's diplomatic crisis seems far away in essay 34, which recounts the ill effects on the family of a civil servant named "Supple" of taking in a Jacobite clergyman as boarder. It stresses, among other things, the utter hypocrisy of the ambitious in the opposition and the sins of the *Three Letters to the Whigs*. It ends by identifying Supple's wife, "Anna Maria Supple," as the author of *Old England*, the "Fool" essays, and the *London Evening Post*, the last also carrying poems by her eight-year-old son. In this issue the "Court of Criticism" is adjourned for the summer so that the Grub-Street authors can take menial harvest work in the country, which may, as has been suggested more than once, be an oblique announcement that Fielding was leaving for the country. Tradition has him reading *Tom Jones* aloud during the summer of 1748 at the country estates of Lyttelton and Ralph Allen. Up to July 4 he was obviously in the vicinity of London and on the job (perhaps acting as High Steward of New Forest as well as John Trott-Plaid), since a recently discovered letter to Robert Butcher, the Duke of Bedford's agent, was dated that day from Twickenham.[43] Thereafter, a move is possible, but a lot of the evidence for his reading *Tom Jones* to distinguished audiences is vague and recorded long after the fact. As we will see, he was paid for the copyright to *Tom Jones* on July 11 and could have afforded country recreation. The only thing we know definitely is that he was at Hagley Park on August 21, for he wrote a letter from there that day. On the whole, I am dubious about a very extensive summer holiday, since I do not see marked lowering of energy and quality in his *Jacobite's Journal* copy for the summer,[44] though there are a few shaky lead essays.

The essay for July 30 centers around a fictitious letter in which an "honest Quaker" denounces Jacobitism and disloyalty to a good government in difficult times, but it also defends the peace, stressing the need to end the war and the difficulty of getting even "tolerable Terms of Peace" from the French. This is a lonely exception. The next essay is a reprint of Addison's sixteenth *Freeholder* (March 26, 1716). The next is a reaction to Addison's themes, which becomes an argument proving that the failure of 1745-46 should convince even Jacobites that their cause is lost and loyalty necessary—as if this was a live issue or anyone doubted it! It is difficult to read these two essays as other than filler. They perhaps support the theory that Fielding was out of town before the third week in August, and they are very clear signs that Fielding was marking time until something decisive happened abroad. Succeeding issues are better written, but not much more relevant to current issues. On August 20, Fielding traces the plaids worn by Jacobites to the garb of Roman jockeys and the parti-coloured suits of professional fools. Only the fact that Fielding does not pretend to be a Jacobite distinguishes it from the earliest essays in *The Jacobite's Journal*. Three weeks later, essay 42 lambasts Jacobites, this time as partisan automata, who know no more why they take the direction they do than a clock's hands: "The Clock goes by the Weight of Lead; the Jacobite generally goes by the Weight of Liquor." In between, essays 39, 40, and 41 mock *Old England*, the *London Evening Post*, and the "Fool." In essay 39 the wife of the man replaced when Anna Maria Supple took over *Old England* offers her husband's services to *The Jacobite's Journal*. Essay 40 argues that the opposition writers are really ghosts, taking shape under their pen-names and haunting "the First Commissioner of the Treasury," Henry Pelham. It is only because Fielding so carefully avoided the peace question for so long that one's attention is caught in essay 41 by a passing mention of the Preliminaries in a note supposedly sent by the author of the *London Evening Post:*

> If you had taken me into your Paper this Mischief might have been stopt; but now 'tis all over, and I shall speak my Mind. The Pr__l__-m__ry A__t__cles for the G__n__l Peace shall be treated in a new Manner in my next; and you shall find that I can go near to prove, that the D__e of _____, and the E__l of _____, and Mr. _____, and a certain Person that shall be nameless, are no better than S____ls, and that they deserve a G__b__t.

Finally, on September 24, more than four months after his first—

and only earlier—real defence of the peace, Fielding's patience snapped. The *London Evening Post* had mounted an intensified assault on him that would continue through the end of *The Jacobite's Journal*'s run; he was attacked on September 11, 15, 20, 27, 29, October 6, 11, 15, 25, and November 8. The ministry may also have been growing nervous under pressure. The *London Evening Post* for September 15 imagines "Selim Slim" (Lyttelton) warning Fielding of the loss of his weekly stipend if he does not defend the peace. Was he not given "Peace for a Theme? Did I not order a Panegyric on Modern French Sincerity? Wert thou not to prove that *Cape Breton* would be a useless Incumbrance?" Fielding seems to be responding to this in the later pages of issue 43, where he ridicules *Old England* and the *London Evening Post* for objecting to the delay of the final treaty and argues that the ministers have done very well in obtaining "a Peace, which no Nation ever more wanted, more desired, or hath, more loudly called out for." Even here Fielding concentrates on denouncing the opposition press and praising the ministry:

> It is, indeed, as clear as the Sun, that we never had a more extensive Administration than at present. That in the Circle of this Administration are contained Men of the most known Abilities, of the longest Experience in Business, of the largest Property, and of the most confirmed Integrity that are to be found in the whole Kingdom. I might add, what I firmly believe, that the Honourable Gentleman [Henry Pelham], who is generally suppos'd to have the Lead, as he is known to possess the most solid Parts, and the most thorough Experience in public Affairs, so he is one of the best and worthiest Men in the Nation.

The treaty was not signed until October 18 and the terms were not publicized until October 24. As a result, the defence of the treaty and its makers seemingly begun in essay 43 did not continue immediately. The essay for October 1 is a lengthy excerpt (pages 3-11) from an anti-Tory pamphlet called *Manchester Politics: A Dialogue between Mr. True-blue and Mr. Whiglove*, published in London in September.[45] On October 8 the subject is the vice of ingratitude (black examples are opposition attacks on Henry Pelham), and the next essay "proves" that men—and especially Jacobites—love "Slavery." Only on October 22, four days after the final treaty was signed at Aix-la-Chapelle, did Fielding directly celebrate it, and even then he stressed that he had not yet seen its 24 articles. Essay 47 reflects on the unique difficulties the ministers, "glorious Saviours of the Kingdom," have faced in the last few years. The "Forty-Five" had to be put down, he hints, not without domestic opposition. Then, albeit ambiguously, he reflects on the difficulties both he and the ministry have had in bringing England through the peace crisis without indiscreetly exposing her weaknesses to her enemies.

It has been hard for Fielding to defend an administration without revealing "dangerous Wounds" (factious divisions) it is "endeavouring to heal." He has suffered as an advocate would if restrained "from fully defending his Client, when he hath it in his Power," and it has been an "extremely arduous . . . Task . . . to do Justice to the most deserving Ministry, without sacrificing the Good of the Public in their Defense." The need to scant the negotiations, then to ignore or vaguely defend the preliminary terms in the past ten months are obviously the circumstances about which Fielding is rueful here at the end of the run. Fielding recalls that "public Incendiaries" have "traduced the Preliminaries, before they were known: and afterwards upon the most random and uncertain Informations," and accused the ministry of "basely and wickedly" surrendering "Cape Breton, a Fortress of the utmost Consequence to the Trade and Navigation of *Great Britain*, without asking any Equivalent in Return." Now he can defend the ministry against such malice. Though he remains ignorant of "every particular Article of this Peace," he needs only to urge his readers to judge the wisdom of concessions in the light of circumstances, remembering that it can never be wrong to free the "Country from Danger, at the Expence of an honorary Concession" or to "give up a Part to save the rest . . . a Peace may be advantageous to the other which received Them." The "true Question . . . is . . . , Was this Peace necessary or convenient to us or no, and were we or were we not in a Condition of hoping to beat *France* into a better?"

The 24 articles were summarized in the *Daily Advertiser* for October 24; Fielding's essay for October 29 justifies the treaty with sprightly wit. He again explains that it has been very difficult to do full justice to the ministry that has saved the nation from a ruinous war without exposing her weaknesses to foreign enemies. He imagines what a French opposition writer (if such freedom were allowed in France) would say against the very generous concessions made in the treaty to the nearly defeated English. The Frenchman describes the peace as what the English "could have expected, or even demanded three years ago [that is, before the "Forty-Five," in early 1745], when their Armies were in the Heart of *Flanders*, and the *Dutch* Barrier remained entire." All France has gotten, instead of conquest of "all Flanders, Brabant, Zealand, I may say Holland; nay, I may say, *England* itself," is "*Cape Breton*. One single Fortress in all *America*." The French have lost the peace; they were winning the war. Fielding emphasizes that his "French" essay parodies those in the *London Evening Post*—"I have imitated . . . the Stile of the worst of all *English* Writers." Such writers make even the glorious blessing of freedom seem an evil at times, though never enough of a problem to justify considering a limitation of freedom of the press. They are not really able to betray their country to foreigners, who are hardly likely to understand their imbecile jargon, impenetrable by most Englishmen. George Lyttelton agreed with Fielding's Frenchman: "had we been in the situation of France, and France in ours, I will venture to say no English ministers would have dared to sign such a peace, not even the ministers who signed the peace at Utrecht."[46] Fielding and Lyttelton knew that they had weathered the peace crisis of 1747-48, the third and last great test of the stability of the Broad-Bottom ministry.

Satisfaction and confidence are everywhere obvious in the last

Jacobite's Journal essay, number 49, published on November 5. Fielding ties together the rhetorical strands of his journal in masterful fashion, aided by the treaty clause in which the French recognized the Hanoverian Establishment. After 1746 this was largely a symbolic gesture, but it was a concession the English had tried unsuccessfully to wring from the French since the negotiations toward the Treaty of Utrecht of 1713. Fielding recalls the "strange Spirit of Jacobitism" that infected the nation. He says—most insincerely—that this encouraged the French to hope for another Jacobite rebellion. *The Jacobite's Journal* set out to eliminate Jacobitism through ridicule, even though he knew Jacobitism to be "hereditary; and complicated with Folly." Despairing of converting the Jacobites, he is now ready to cease publication, convinced that the dangerous "Spirit of this Party [has] . . . become the Object only of Derision and Contempt since by that happy Peace which the present glorious Administration have, so much to their own Honour and the public Good, secured to this Nation, the Hopes of this Party are, in a Manner, plucked up by the very Root." The Jacobites have been depressed since the Preliminaries and in utter dejection since the "definitive Treaty." This is "the only Measure that . . . could have frustrated them." Fielding's real point—Jacobitism aside—is that the treaty has rendered the ministry secure and the weak opposition impotent. Fielding closes with a ringing and ironical defiance of the Jacobites, meant to taunt an opposition faced with years in the wilderness under a ministry unshakably secure:

> In short, if Reason, Honour, Liberty, Duty, and every worldly Interest, nay, the express Commands of Scripture, cannot engage their Fidelity *to the Powers that be;* I hope they will, at least, become faithful and good Subjects, from a perfect Assurance that *these Powers* will most certainly *continue to be*, in Defiance of all which the Courts of Rome or Hell can devise against them.

The opposition would continue to fulminate against Fielding and the treaty in 1749. The pamphlet warfare over the treaty indeed really peaked in early 1749 as the balked opposition vented its frustrations. A considerable exchange of "answers" and "counter-answers" was generated by one powerful pamphlet written by the Earl of Egmont (though published anonymously), *An Examination of the Principles, and an Enquiry into the Conduct of the Two B*****rs; in Regard to the Establishment of their Power and their Prosecution of the War, 'till the Signing of the Preliminaries.* *Old England* hinted on March 25, 1749 that Fielding might be responsible for one rebuttal of Egmont, *A Genuine Copy of the Tryal of J[ohn] P[erceva]l, Esq.; Commonly Called E[arl] of E[gmont]*, but there seems no reason to believe this. The opposition press naturally mocked Fielding's retirement, touching familiar issues. For example, on November 12, 1748 *Old England* blends satire on Lyttelton, political apostate, with mockery of Fielding, puppeteer and lately Lyttelton's weekly pensioner, "2000 of his weekly Performances" bought up and "distributed by the Clerks of the *General Post Office* through *Great Britain* and *Ireland gratis*." Early in 1749 a new level of vulgarity was reached in the scatalogical "Epitaph on John Trottplaid, alias J_____ F_____ [Justice Fielding]":

> But ah, alack!
> He broke his Back,
> When Politicks he try'd:
> For like a Fart
> He play'd his Part,
> Crack'd loudly, stunk, and dy'd.[47]

This was all impotent noise, however, and Fielding's fortunes were rising. *Tom Jones* was finished, some minor polishing aside, and in the first stages of printing, though it would not finally be on sale until early January, 1749. Andrew Millar had paid £600 for the copyright of its six volumes; Fielding gave a receipt for the money on July 11, 1748. The novel would make so much money for Millar that, according to Horace Walpole, he would voluntarily give Fielding another £100 in 1749.[48] Moreover, Fielding was already beginning to enjoy the reward given him by his ministerial friends for his aid over three years and through three crises. Political writing no doubt delayed the completion of *Tom Jones*, but it earned him his magistracy. The reward was a long time in the granting, partly because meeting the property qualifications of £100 in property in Middlesex was not simple for Fielding. As noted earlier, he was first nominated (the fiat dated June 20, 1747) a Middlesex Justice just before *A Dialogue* was published, but he did not complete the process of property qualification and oath-taking necessary before ascending the Bench until 1749. In the meanwhile, he established *The Jacobite's Journal* and, no doubt with the help of Lyttelton and the Duke of Bedford, was nominated Justice for the City of London and Borough of Westminster in a fiat dated July 30, 1748. He very probably was also High Steward of the Warden of New Forest, a post held by Bedford, by this time. Again, however, his appointment to the magistracy hung fire for some time, even though no property requirement was in force in the jurisdiction. He did not take the oaths and become Bow Street Magistrate until October 26. He was signing recognizances in that capacity three days before the final issue of *The Jacobite's Journal*.

The original appointment as Middlesex Justice, necessary both to render his judicial work effective and to provide a competent income for a middle-aged man raising a second family, had still not been taken up. There is some evidence that he originally planned to take the Middlesex oaths, as well as the London oaths, in late October, but he had to scrape together sufficient property to qualify. In a surviving letter, dated December 13, he begged Bedford for help in the form of twenty-one year leases in London. Six days later he wrote Robert Butcher, Bedford's agent, in terms that indicate that his request had been granted, and resigned his High Stewardship, as was required if he was to be Middlesex magistrate. After some obscure difficulties on January 11 (perhaps the result of doubts about the validity of his property claims), he was sworn as Middlesex Justice on January 12 and the writ was filed on January 13. Even then the process remained technically uncompleted, for there are records of his taking the Sacramental Test on March 26, the Oath of Allegiance, declaring loyalty to George II and abjuring the Stuarts, on April 5, and a second property oath (required because Bedford desired an exchange of leases in May) on July 13, 1749. For all the delays, however, Fielding's appointments as magistrate were permanent, deserved, and honourable rewards, good for him and a crime-ridden city.[49] At some later point his income would be augmented by a pension, arranged by Bedford, as he recalled in the *Journal of a Voyage to Lisbon*.[50] Fielding had reason to praise the generosity as well as the characters of Lyttelton and Bedford in *Tom Jones*.

When Fielding closed *The Jacobite's Journal* he was turning his back upon day-to-day political journalism. Most of his subsequent writing would be less obviously partisan, even though he remained close to Lyttelton and Bedford, and would zealously serve the latter during the riotous Westminster election of November and December 1749. *Tom Jones* was apparently completed by the fall of 1748, aside from some final polishing and, possibly, the composition of the later introductory chapters, the "Dedication," and other prefatory matter. There are, indeed, indications that the first three volumes (of six) were printed in September and available to insiders by November. It is not primarily a political work. It appealed not to partisans, but a broad spectrum of readers fascinated by its moral and social insights, impressed by its formal and narrational finesse, and charmed by its rich comedy and stylistic sophistication. Still, Fielding flaunted his gratitude and loyalty to his political patrons in the "Dedication." It thanks Lyttelton: "without your Assistance this History had never been completed." Stressing that Lyttelton "first recommended" him to Bedford's "Notice," it declares that "Gratitude for the princely Benefactions of the Duke of *Bedford* bursts from my Heart." In the novel itself, Fielding compliments Henry Pelham and George Dodington (XI, ix), William Pitt (XIV, i), and Lord Hardwicke (IV, vi). This ministerial roll-call excludes the Duke of Newcastle, unless a possible compliment to his cook qualifies. However, George Lyttelton and Bedford had for several years aligned themselves with Henry Pelham when the Pelham brothers differed on issues and Fielding had never been inclined to eulogize Newcastle. Even the fact that Fielding does not mention Lord Chesterfield fits the pattern, though Martin Battestin has described it as "curious."[51] When Chesterfield resigned from the ministry in February 1748, he departed without a kind farewell from Fielding and was replaced as Secretary of State by Bedford. He had ceased to be a politician whom a writer with Fielding's loyalties would notice.

Aside from these compliments, which politically "place" Fielding with great precision, most of the novel lacks really partisan political material. There are sneers at the cowardice of the French and the unreliability of the Dutch in the late war, and compliments to the shrewdness of Frederick of Prussia.[52] Aunt Western is a stock, silly "Court Whig" and Squire Western is a stock "Country Tory" boobie, extremes always scorned by the Broad-Bottoms. However, there is in their political outbursts and interactions—with a few exceptions, which will be stressed below—little that Fielding could not have written in 1736 or 1743 as well as 1748. More pointed and up-to-date satire is to be found in the novel, but it is restricted to a few chapters in the central third of the novel, Books VII-XII. I believe it was inserted after all or most of the novel had been completed in draft, in the course of a revision carried out by Fielding during the run of *The Jacobite's Journal*. This revision was probably performed hastily and certainly did not involve very extensive changes to more than a few chapters. Nonetheless, it not only added anti-opposition satire of the "Jacobite" variety, but also made *Tom Jones* a "quasi-historical" novel, to the extent that it is one, its central action set in the darkest days of the "Forty-Five."

Fielding suddenly and rather cavalierly announces in *Tom Jones*, VII, xi, that the Jacobite "Forty-Five" is in progress. Tom encounters a company of infantry and learns that it is marching north to help "the glorious Duke of Cumberland" fight the rebel army. The narrator observes, "the Reader may perceive (a Circumstance which we have not thought necessary to communicate before) that this was the very Time when the late Rebellion was at its highest; and indeed the Banditti were marched into *England*, intending as it was thought, to fight the King's Forces, and to attempt pushing forward to the Metropolis." This announcement has two effects. It places the novel in a hitherto unsuspected, specific historical context. Tom meets the soldiers in the last week of November or the first week in December 1745, when the Pretender's army was near Derby. It also disrupts violently the novel's much-praised chronological consistency, for the chapter headings to Books VI and VII indicate that exactly three weeks and one day elapse between this meeting and the night of Allworthy's recovery which is described as "a pleasant Evening in the latter part of June." Later references to cold nights and heavy frosts in the novel's central books (in the final six books the weather is unspecified) also suggest an autumnal setting, but a discrepancy of four months has bothered readers since the eighteenth century. Recently this has encouraged Martin Battestin to theorize, unconvincingly, that Fielding had reached this point in 1744 when the process of composition was interrupted by the outbreak of the "Forty-Five," and that he picked up the novel again after the "Forty-Five," around mid-1746.[53]

This violation of chronology underlines the peculiarity of the sudden introduction of the "Forty-Five." Together with other evidence, it may indicate that Fielding decided to impose the background of the

"Forty-Five" on the novel in the course of a partial revision after its main action had been elaborated. The obvious objection is that the encounters with soldiers in the central books are too organic to allow us to believe that they were inserted as an afterthought. But surely Fielding would have had no difficulty explaining the presence of troops on the Bristol-London road during the War of the Austrian Succession, assuming he did not specify that they were marching northward. On the positive side, there are other indications that revision is a likely hypothesis. Many important characters seem aware nowhere in the novel that the "Forty-Five" is in progress. Though Squire Western is fascinated by politics, is normally viewed as a Jacobite, and lives within one hundred miles of Derby, he never once seems aware of the "Forty-Five." His archetypically "political" sister also seems unaware, except possibly in VI, iv, where she turns from an exposition of the latest *Gazette* to inform her brother that "Things look so well in the North, that I was never in a better Humour." This lonely, vague allusion is probably either a reference to military or diplomatic affairs in northern Europe (in the fall of 1745 the situation in the north of England was grim) or simply a ridiculous example of her "politic" rant. It recalls the meaningless gossip of Aunt Western's closest relation in Fielding's canon, Sir Politic Wouldbe in the *Coffee House Politician* of 1730: "I am not satisfied at all with the Affairs in the North: the Northern Winds have not blown us any Good lately; the Clouds are a little darker in the East than I could wish them" (Act V, sc.ii). Significantly, her remark elicits no response from her brother. Even more striking is the oddly intermittent interest in the Rebellion shown by those characters who are aware of it. Tom Jones evinces no astonishment on meeting the troops in VII, ix and volunteers for patriotic service. But he does not earlier seem aware of the Rebellion and completely forgets it after he finds Sophia's pocketbook, even though—if the novel's chronology is taken seriously—he marries (December 1745) well before the battle of Culloden. Partridge too seems aware of the Rebellion only on the road. Sophia and Honour seem aware of the Rebellion only occasionally. Not a single character, including the narrator, alludes to the "Forty-Five" in Books I-VI (except for Aunt Western's vague allusion in VI, iv) or, more surprisingly, Books XIII-XVIII.

Fielding claims total control over his "new Province of Writing" (II, i), including the right to manipulate characters and divulge information to the reader when and as he sees fit. However, his rejection of the restrictions of narrowly defined "realism" seems an inadequate explanation of such anomalies in structure, chronology, and characterization. I also cannot accept the theory that Fielding composed Books I-VI before the "Forty-Five," then returned to the novel after closing *The True Patriot* and, beginning in Book VII, added the background of the Rebellion. The most obvious reason for rejecting it is the utter disappearance of the "Forty-Five" after Book XII. In addition the Jacobite material in the central books not only reflects the themes and techniques of *The Jacobite's Journal*, but is opposed in implication to much in *The True Patriot*. In 1746 Fielding was at great pains to stress the lack of support for the Jacobite cause in England, as opposed to Scotland. Some years ago, I argued that the most adequate hypothesis is that these anomalies resulted from a partial and hasty revision, involving the middle third of the novel and carried out in 1748, subsequent to the completion of the original draft of the whole novel. Hugh Amory has very recently joined me in arguing against Battestin's scenario. He demonstrates that the last third of the novel also shows manifold signs of revision, presumably carried out in 1748, upon a text drafted in later 1746 and 1747. Amory's detailed discussion does not shed new light on politics in the novel since the changes to Books XIII-XVIII were not politicizing ones. However, our arguments seem to me to rule out the theory of seriatim but interrupted composition beginning in early 1745.[54]

Once one hypothesizes a politicizing revision of the central books, much supporting evidence is apparent. Most importantly, the anti-Jacobite satire in *The Jacobite's Journal* mode is as consistently and anomalously confined to the central books as the specific historical background. Though he is usually regarded as the novel's most effectively reductive Jacobite, Squire Western does not "become" a Jacobite until about the same point (VII, iv, v) that the "Forty-Five" is introduced (VII, xi). Earlier he curses courtiers, Whigs, and "Hanover Rats," and laments that his land taxes are used to enrich Hanover and to fight a continental land war that benefits the Electorate rather than England, but little in his characterization up to VII, iv would have convinced a contemporary, in the absence of other evidence, that he was a Jacobite rather than merely an extreme Country Tory. The political attitudes and anti-Hanoverian rhetoric of this former candidate for Parliament in the "Country Interest" are those of the anti-Court but loyal Country Tories in the 1740s. They can, as we have seen, be matched in the speeches of Pitt from 1743 and 1744 and in Fielding's own *An Attempt toward a Natural History of the Hanover Rat* of 1744.

The contemporary reader would doubtless have viewed Western's diatribes in the first third of the novel as does Aunt Western. She never accuses her brother of disloyalty. Instead, she ridicules his "country Ignorance" with the scorn of a Whig courtier for an ignorant and bigoted Tory squire. Two of their interchanges well illustrate the pattern. In VI, xiv Western, goaded by his sister's contempt for his political sagacity, rants in a manner that might suggest Stuart sympathies: "Pox! the World is come to a fine Pass indeed, if we are all Fools except a Parcel of Roundheads and *Hannover* rats. Pox! I hope the Times are a coming when we shall make Fools of them, and every Man shall enjoy his own . . . I hope to *zee* it, sister, before the *Hanover* rats have eat up all our Corn, and left us nothing but Turneps to feed upon." This sounds seditious enough, but when Aunt Western replies that his outburst is "perfectly unintelligible," his rejoinder indicates that he is hoping for a revolution in administrations, not ruling families: "I believe . . . you

don't care to hear o'em [his arguments], but the Country Interest may
succeed one Day or other for all that.'' When the Squire later roars that
he is ''a true *Englishman*, not of your *Hannover* Breed, that have eat up
the Nation,'' Aunt Western rebukes him not as a Jacobite uttering sedition during a Rebellion, but merely as a member of a faction that renders
the successful prosecution of the War of the Austrian Succession more
difficult: ''Thou art one of those wise Men . . . whose nonsensical Principles have undone the Nation; by weakening the Hands of our Government at home, and by discouraging our Friends, and encouraging our
Enemies abroad'' (VII, iii).

In fact, the only hints that the squire is a Jacobite as well as an extreme Tory before VII, iv are the names of his favourite horses, ''The
Chevalier'' and ''Miss Slouch'' (V, ii), which may allude to Charles Edward Stuart and Jenny Cameron. It is also just possible that the name of
his favourite tune, ''Old Sir Simon'' (mentioned in the same chapter)
alludes to Sir Simon Fraser, Lord Lovat, who was executed for his part
in the ''Forty-Five.'' This idea is somewhat strengthened by what *may* be
a reference in II, vi to the harsh treatment of the Jacobite lords.[55]
However, it should be noted that the cases of Sir Simon and the other
Jacobite lords were news between 1746 and the spring of 1747, not the
period of the Rebellion. Aside from such unobtrusive details, it is first indicated that Western is a Jacobite in VII, iv, shortly before the announcement (VII, ix) that the ''Forty-Five'' is on. There we learn that
Western's late wife used to stay at his dinner table only long enough ''to
drink the King over the Water.'' Moreover, the *last* definite indication in
the novel that Western is a Jacobite occurs in the very next chapter (VII,
v) where the Squire very tardily recognizes the possibility that his anti-
Hanoverian rantings may be construed and reported by his Whig sister as
disloyal: ''She may 'dite me of a Plot for any Thing I know, and give my
Estate to the Government.'' Thereafter, Western reverts to loud ''Country Toryism'' for the remainder of the novel. Such an anomaly in
character development may not prove that the Tory was converted into a
Jacobite in revision, but it is noteworthy that the renaming of two horses
(and perhaps a song) and the deletion of a few words from two adjacent
chapters in Book VII would eliminate all evidence of Western's
Jacobitism.

The characterization of Partridge, the other major Jacobite
character, reveals a somewhat similar pattern. Partridge only appears
briefly as Tom's supposed sire in the first third of the novel, and is not
regarded in a political light until he joins Tom on the road. His illogical
and credulous Jacobitism is revealed in VII, ix; X, vi; and XII, vii, in
passages that greatly resemble the ''reverse irony'' essays in *The
Jacobite's Journal*. Elsewhere, he is not at all political and his Jacobitism
never affects the plot. In VIII, ix, Jacobitism is abruptly added to his
characterization when he absurdly maintains, on the word of a Catholic
priest, that the Young Pretender is a good Protestant and that a Stuart
victory would not imperil the Established Church. His folly elicits from

Tom a scornful reproof and an eloquent sermon on the benefits of Hanoverian rule. It draws from the narrator the revelation that Partridge is a secret Jacobite who has mistaken his new master for a kindred spirit. However, since Partridge manages to hide his secret from Tom at the last moment, his indiscretion changes nothing. If this political digression was added in revision it did not require adjustments even to adjoining chapters. Similarly, the comically satiric incident early in X, vi, in which Partridge refuses to drink to King George, though he is marching to fight against the Pretender, would leave no perceivable hiatus in the novel or even the chapter were it omitted. The lengthy argument about the Stuart claim in XII, vii, in which Partridge and the Jacobite's attorney's clerk (who is encountered only in this chapter) illogically argue their bottle companions into acquiescing in that claim or at least into toasting the Pretender, is just as digressive from the point of view of plot. These passages could be eliminated (or, conversely, could have been added) without difficulty or inconsistency, and they obviously recall the satire in many issues of *The Jacobite's Journal*.

Aside from the passages in which Partridge and Western are revealed as Jacobites, only three sections of the novel include anti-Jacobite satire. Each is a "set piece" satire on Jacobitism placed in a digressive context and digressive even within that context. The closing section of the "Man of the Hill's Tale," in which the misanthropic veteran of Monmouth's Rebellion receives with incredulity the news that the latest of a series of attempts to restore the Stuarts is in progress, seems digressive even within the context of the "Tale." It allows Fielding to mock the absurdity of "Protestant Jacobitism" in the spirit of *The Jacobite's Journal*, but it robs the "Tale" of even the relative structural shapeliness of Wilson's tale in *Joseph Andrews*. The "Jenny Cameron episode" is developed in a series of interruptions (XI, ii, iii, vi, viii) of Mrs. Fitzpatrick's lengthy and digressive "history." The account of the political history of the "Egyptians" and the ensuing lecture by the narrator on the relative merits of the various forms of government in XII, xii constitute the final attack on Jacobitism in the novel.[56] So digressive has the whole Gypsy episode seemed to some that its inclusion has been justified on the weak grounds that it allows Sophia to reach London before Tom. Its lengthy political epilogue is again doubly digressive, for it is only minimally related even to the account of Partridge's apprehension *in flagrante delicto* and "his Egyptian Majesty's" Solomonic judgement. Its omission would no more disrupt the "Gypsy episode" than the omission of the whole episode would the novel. Significantly and very atypically, the narrator apologizes for this "long Digression" on government in the first paragraph of the next chapter (XII, xiii). He justifies it on the grounds that it was necessary to qualify the approval of absolute, Divine Right monarchy which might have seemed implicit in the history of the "Gypsy Commonwealth." The doubly digressive quality of such anti-Jacobite "set pieces" does not prove that they were inserted in revision. The habit of indulging in digressions within digressions is constant in Cervantes, Fielding's principal model in the central books. Nonetheless, it is most suggestive that virtually all anti-Jacobite satire in the novel could be eliminated (or could have been inserted) by three very minor changes in the treatment of Western, and by the omission or insertion of three doubly digressive segments and the three passages in which Partridge speaks as a Jacobite.[57]

Assuming that Fielding revised the novel in the ways suggested, there seems every reason to assume he did so during the *Jacobite's Journal* run. Squire Western and Partridge have been correctly described as highly reminiscent of the Jacobites ridiculed as ignorant, drunken, illogical, illiterate, and cowardly as well as seditious bumpkins in the journal's early issues. Such similarities even were taken by Wilbur Cross to "indicate nearly if not quite simultaneous composition." We may dismiss as logically inconsistent with this suggestion Cross's conjecture that *Tom Jones* was composed more or less continually and "seriatim" between some time in 1746 and its publication.[58] It is most unlikely that Fielding wrote the last twelve Books of the novel between late 1747 and the fall of 1748, a period when he was heavily involved in political journalism. Working from his own, non-political evidence Hugh Amory firmly and correctly concludes that the novel (not begun until after the "Forty-Five") was complete in first draft before the end of 1747, and that thereafter Fielding worked at revising and polishing it. The characterization of Western and Partridge aside, the resemblances between the political material in the novel and *The Jacobite's Journal* are often striking. Immediately after revealing in VII, iv that drinking "the King over the Water" was, and perhaps still is, a habit at Western's dinner table, the narrator describes the "Conversation" there as consisting "chiefly of Hollowing, Singing, Relations of sporting Adventures, B-d-y, and Abuse of women and of the Government." Aunt Western rebukes her brother's principles (VII, iii) as those that ". . . have undone the Nation, by weakening the Hands of our Government at Home, and by discouraging our Friends and encouraging our Enemies abroad." Her remark might be paralleled with many in the *Journal*, and recalls, even verbally, the description of the "Jacobites" (i.e., the opposition) in Fielding's *A Proper Answer to a late Scurrilous Libel* (December 1747) as men who take "every Opportunity to weaken the Hands of the Government at Home, and the Reputation of it Abroad."

Parson Supple hypocritically and venally toadies to Squire Western. His name recalls that of Anna Maria Supple, the fictitious lady identified ironically in *The Jacobite's Journal*, no. 34 (July 23, 1748) as the author of several actual opposition papers. She writes not out of conviction, but to earn a meagre living. The jubilant cry "Old England forever!" of the "famous Jacobite Squire" in *Tom Jones*, XI, ii, at the rumour that the French have invaded recalls the title of *Old England*, one of the journals most often attacked in *The Jacobite's Journal*. Squire Western is, of course, a reader of the *London Evening Post* (VII, ii). Two details in Fielding's treatment of Partridge recall specific skirmishes between

Fielding and the opposition press between December 1747 and March 1748. *An Apology for the Conduct of a late celebrated second-rate Minister* (c. December 1, 1747) ironically explained the actions of members of the present government and past Whig administrations as the result of secret Jacobitism, and the opposition more than once pretended to take Fielding's Jacobite pose seriously in early 1748. Partridge almost surely is meant to stand for the opposition writers who took part in the Jacobite "paper war," when the narrator explains his erroneous assumption in VIII, ix that Tom Jones is a secret Jacobite as a result of his persuasion that ". . . the whole Nation were of the same inclination in their hearts; nor did it stagger him that *Jones* had travelled in the Company of Soldiers; for he had the same Opinion of the Army which he had of the rest of the People." Three chapters earlier (VIII, vi), in the process of assuring Tom that he will serve him without remuneration, Partridge quotes a line from Horace, *"Nil Desperandum Teucro duce et auspice Teucro"* (*Odes*, I, 7). As Fielding stressed on March 26, 1748 (*Jacobite's Journal*, No. 17) James Ralph affixed the motto "Nil Desperandum," to the pamphlet reprint of the first twelve *Remembrancer* essays. The obvious likelihood is that Fielding inserted this detail at roughly the same time that he attacked Ralph as a Jacobite "Drummer of Sedition."

In short, everywhere in the satirical, anti-Jacobite passages in the central books one senses the author of *The Jacobite's Journal* at work, making minor changes and adding topical barbs. Every attack on Jacobitism or Jacobites in the novel is thematically and rhetorically paralleled in the journal. A final example, which seems to date Fielding's labours on a section of the central books more definitely than the "Nil Desperandum" thrust, is a curious verbal echo in XII, xiii, the chapter immediately following the conclusion of the Gypsy episode. As noted, the opening paragraph of this chapter justifies the "long Digression" on government in the previous chapter as necessary to prevent the ideal qualities of absolute monarchy among the Gypsies from lending support to the "pernicious" doctrine of Divine Right. The chapter then describes the resumption of Tom's pursuit of Sophia, the narrator conjecturing that Tom would have caught her at St. Albans had he not spent the night with the Gypsies. Otherwise, Tom would "most probably have overtaken his *Angel at the aforesaid Place*" (my italics). Issue 25 of *The Jacobite's Journal* (May 21, 1748) similarly ridicules Divine Right, particularly the notion that an angel brought a "divine Commission" to James II at Whitehall on his coronation day, and that in 1688: ". . . the *aforesaid Angel* . . . convey'd away the King, together with his Commission . . ." (my italics). This convergence of theme and word may indicate direct cross-fertilization in May 1748. It is perhaps no coincidence that only a few chapters earlier (X, v-vi) Fielding obliquely defends his puppet show in Panton Street, which was in operation and under opposition attack from March 28 to June 2, 1748.

Fielding's politicizing revision of *Tom Jones* was part of the sustained campaign of Jacobite satire on the opposition and its press which he carried on in 1748. It made the novel serve the cause of the politicians he went on to praise when he composed the "Dedication." *Tom Jones* is not primarily a partisan work despite the changes to its middle third. But taking a last chance to praise ministers and ridicule their enemies, a last shot in the Jacobite "paper war" of 1747-48, was a fitting close to the thirteen years in which Fielding most actively supported Lyttelton, Bedford, and the other Broad-Bottoms in their strivings first to obtain and then to hold office.

Chapter Seven

The Final Phase:
1749-54

The political pressures that had kept Fielding so active in 1747-48 were gone in the months following the publication of *Tom Jones*. In the fall of 1749 there would come a crisis—minor, but very close to home—as the Duke of Bedford and Fielding's old opposition foes of 1747, the "Independent Electors of Westminster," fought an election, literally and figuratively, in the streets in front of his Bow Street court and residence. Generally, however, the Country opposition and Leicester House, *Old England*, *The London Evening Post*, the *Gazetteer*, and the *Remembrancer* were impotently critical. The ministry had confidence, talent, and big majorities, and the peace crisis was behind it. The *Gentleman's Magazine* noticed that: "Politics, which some years ago, took up a large field is now reducible into small compass . . . a change, though very sensibly felt by those who still pursue this subject at a loss, not at all to be regretted by the public."[1] Fielding wrote neither *Stultus versus Sapientem* nor the *Trial of J____ P____*, political pamphlets of this period that have in the past been associated with his pen. Quiescence was now possible, and he probably agreed with the unknown author of *A Satire of All Parties* (1749) that the overly partisan on both sides were merely trouble-making. Primarily, however, Fielding wrote less because battling crime and vice in London became the absorbing, exhausting focus of his life from the moment he qualified as a magistrate. In this battle he remained dependent on the wealthy and politically powerful to implement reforms, pass needed laws, and appoint the right men as magistrates (John Fielding became one in 1751) and constables. He also continued to seek from them preferments and favours to augment the income from his Middlesex and London-Westminster magistracies. But though it was not always separable from his commitments to those who had helped place him on the Bench, his commit-

273

ment to the demands of Bow Street and the amelioration of London life
was prime and absolute.

Without going into detail about his day-to-day activities in apprehending and trying criminals, well chronicled in the newspapers and
canvassed by Fielding's biographers, it is clear that Fielding soon became
an outstanding and successful Justice. A letter he wrote to the Duke of
Richmond (in years past praised in the dedication of *The Miser* and the
poem "Of Good Nature") on April 28, 1749 shows him in the thick of
the fight against crime in his early months as magistrate. His energy and
ability, as well as his connection with Bedford, the dominant landowner
in the Bow Street jurisdiction, resulted in May 1749 in his selection by
fellow Justices as chairman of the Quarter Sessions of the Peace for the
City and Liberty of Westminster. He would be so honoured repeatedly,
six times in all, until the collapse of his health forbade such activity. His
first selection led directly to one of his two major publications in the year
following *Tom Jones*. "At the unanimous request of the Grand Jury"
and "by Order of the Court," his *Charge Delivered to the Grand Jury, at
the Sessions of the Peace Held for the City and Liberty of Westminster,
&c. On Thursday the 29th of June, 1749* was published, *circa* July 20, by
Andrew Millar.[2]

It is unclear whether the Duke of Bedford, concerned with crime
and immorality in London not only as local magnate, but as Secretary of
State, underwrote this publication, but Fielding was much concerned to
please him in performing his duties. Bedford had helped to appoint and
qualify Fielding. Thereafter, he helped him to a pension, and allowed
him not to pay the rent of £30 per annum for his Bow Street residence
and court through the last six years of his life. Enough letters have survived to suggest that from the first Fielding worked very closely with
Bedford and his agents in performing his magisterial duties, and regularly asked him for favours and patronage.[3] Fielding's *Charge* urges the
Grand Jury to act as "censors of this nation" (anticipating his self-
denomination as "Knt. Censor of Great Britain" in *The Covent-Garden
Journal*) and to enforce strictly the laws against brothels, dance-halls,
and gaming houses. However, moral elevation did not wholly preclude
partisan touches. He hints the need to curtail the licentiousness of the
stage and newspapers which "promote idleness, extravagance and immorality, among all sorts of people." A call for tighter control of the
stage is surprising, coming from the chief victim of the Licensing Act of
1737, though Fielding had been ridiculed on stage by Samuel Foote and
had retaliated in *The Jacobite's Journal*. His call for more enforcement
of the anti-libel laws—as tending to cause quarrels, riots, and murder—
does not specify political targets. Nonetheless, he stresses that men deserving of public praise and honour—one almost expects him to say
ministers—are often injured by the libeller, "a Viper, which men ought
to crush where-ever they find him, without staying 'till he bite them."
Though Wilbur Cross saw its response as unfair,[4] *Old England* had some
excuse for treating this, coming from Fielding, as a sly continuation of

the assault on the opposition press in *The Jacobite's Journal*. On August 5 *Old England* parodied the *Charge*, accusing Fielding of all the vices and crimes arraigned in it, particularly of libelling the great in his plays and journalism before he became a ministerialist and an advocate for limiting the freedom of the press.

The first real test of Fielding's mettle as a magistrate had been passed before the *Charge* appeared, though its aftermath would briefly involve him in partisan writing. On Saturday evening, July 1, three sailors from a man-of-war were robbed in a bawdy-house in the Strand. They returned with reinforcements, demolished the house, abused its inmates, and burned the debris in the street, to the delight of a mob that was dispersed only after the guards were called from Somerset House and the Tilt-yard. The following night a massive gathering of sailors rioted again, backed by a mob, freeing the only two prisoners taken the first night. The rioters were dispersed by Saunders Welch, Fielding's chief constable, and a body of soldiers. Several ringleaders were confined. At this point, Fielding, who had been out of town, returned to deal with the rioting.

A mob waited outside his Bow Street court and home intent on freeing the prisoners when they were brought there on Monday from prison for examination. Fielding wrote Bedford twice during the day from Bow Street, letters that give a sense of the way matters moved from disturbance to a potentially very dangerous peak in this third and final day of rioting. The first letter most peculiarly, yet typically, begins with a request for preferment, then moves to the riot. The second shows Fielding cool in a crisis. Presumably, he felt his courage and energy—much of the property likely to be destroyed being Bedford's—might encourage the Duke to oblige him once more.

> My Lord,
>> The Protection which I have been honoured with receiving at the Hands of your Grace, and the Goodness which you was pleased to express some time since towards me, embolden me to mention to your Grace that the Place of Solicitor to the Excise is now vacant by the Death of Mr. Selwyn. I hope no Person is better qualified for it, and I assure you, my Lord, none shall execute it with more Fidelity. I am at this moment busied in endeavouring to suppress a dangerous Riot, or I would have personally waited on your Grace to solicit a Favour which will make me and my Family completely happy.

> My Lord,
>> I think it my Duty to acquaint your Grace that I have received repeated Information of upwards of 3000 Sailors now in Arms ab.^{t} Wapping and that they threaten to march to this End of the Town this Night, under Pretence of demolishing all Bawdy Houses. I have an Officer and 50 Men and submit to yr Grace what more Assistance may be necessary. I sent a Messenger five Hours ago to the Secretary at War [Henry Fox] but have yet no Answer.

Meanwhile, Fielding and Saunders Welch tried to reason with the mob, the Justice addresing them from his window and the fearless Welch exposing himself among them. In the afternoon Fielding had the arrested ringleaders brought to Bow Street and committed nine of them to Newgate, where they were sent with a strong escort. The night was tense throughout the city, as mobs roamed, but the soldiers who were brought in and supervised throughout the night by Fielding, Welch, and their commander kept matters under control and finally ended the violence.

However, the riot spawned a legal dispute that eventually became a political issue during the Westminster by-election of November and December 1749. One of the prisoners committed by Fielding to Newgate, Bosavern Penlez, was arrested as a rioter on Sunday night while in possession of a bundle of female linen, caps, aprons, and the like, alleged to belong to the wife of Peter Woods, supposedly a "victualler," actually proprietor of a tavern that doubled as a house of ill-repute and was destroyed by the mob. In August, Penlez was condemned to death, along with one John Wilson, under the Riot Act, Mr. and Mrs. Woods and a servant having identified him as one of the rioters who attacked their house. Though he had also been indicted for burglary because of the bundle of linen, he was not tried on this charge. Both before and after his conviction he (with Wilson) became the object of widespread pity and a focus of resentment against the government. Petitions to the King and Newcastle won Wilson a reprieve, then a pardon. Fielding later said that he made efforts of his own to save Wilson. But though his supporters claimed he was only a minor participant in the disturbances, motivated by wine and a noble desire to destroy brothels, Penlez was hanged on October 18, and this severity was widely protested. *The Case of the Unfortunate Bosavern Penlez* described Penlez's good character, and the accidental nature of his involvement, while intoxicated, in the attack upon Peter Woods's disreputable tavern. It also argued that, since the Riot Act was not read on the scene, the law under which he was condemned did not apply. The theft of the linen bundle was scanted, and the indictment for burglary (a felony) was treated as trumped-up. In November and December, the case was used as a means of blackening the ministerial candidate in a Westminster by-election. Lord Trentham had refused to sign the petition to the Duke of Newcastle on behalf of Wilson and Penlez. Trentham was also vilified for having sponsored a troupe of French comedians at the Haymarket and using violence against "patriots" who attempted to prevent them from performing on November 14.[5]

Fielding had urgent reasons for becoming involved in the election and the accompanying paper war. Trentham was up for re-election as M.P. for Westminster because he had been placed on the Admiralty Board (a general election was not due until 1754), so that opposing him was a double slap at the ministry. He was also the Duke of Bedford's brother-in-law, and surely owed his new appointment to Bedford, Secretary of State and former First Lord of the Admiralty. To ensure his election Bedford was prepared to use his money and leverage in the district, including the energies and votes of Fielding and his fellow magistrates. *Old England* was vociferous in the anti-Trentham cause, and Sir George Vandeput, Trentham's opponent, was the candidate of the "Independent Electors of Westminster," whose antics had provided the immediate occasion for Fielding's *Dialogue* during the 1747 general election. Fielding's part in the election has only recently been made clear.[6]

In September, well before Penlez was executed (October 18), Fielding's *True State of the Case of Bosavern Penlez* had been printed (in a first run of 1000 copies) by William Straham. Obviously, there was no chance of a reprieve. In it Fielding justifies the severity shown to Penlez and defends the ministry against accusations of cruelty and an inclination to favour brothel-keepers. His argument is two-pronged and half-convincing. He stresses the dangerous, wantonly destructive nature of the riot. He denounces mob law regardless of ostensible purpose, but insists that this mob was as bent on pillage as reform. On the slippery grounds that a better felony case could have been made for theft of the linen, he justifies the execution of Penlez, despite the inherent shakiness of the case against him under the difficult-to-apply Riot Act. He asserts he has no qualms about the execution of this thief and rioter though he worked to save young Wilson. The *True State* would not have seemed too strongly partisan, or at all related to the election, if it had been published when printed, or even immediately after the execution. However, it was held in reserve, ready-printed, in the knowledge that a Westminster election (the appointment of Trentham to the Admiralty Board was in the works by August) was soon to take place, and that the case was sure to be used against Trentham, who had been unsympathetic to the condemned. The *True State* was an election tract though it says not one word about the election. The September printing was not put on sale until November 18, in the opening days of the election campaign, and there was a second printing in November, published on December 16. One of the oddities of the whole affair is that the *True State*, when first printed in September, was not only a justification of the death of a man with weeks to live, but also a most efficient answer to *The Case of the Unfortunate Penlez*, published on November 7.

On November 14 opponents of Trentham rioted against the French Comedians at the Haymarket. The opposition later claimed that Trentham used his sword against unarmed men in the theatre and hired a squad of fifteen bullies led by John Haines, a tavern-waiter, to overawe "true Britons." On November 15, Trentham resigned his seat, his appointment to the Admiralty Board having been made, and on November 16 he declared his candidacy for the same seat. Two days later Fielding published his *True State*, and on November 20 Trentham began to protest in print his innocence in the theatre incident. Later, though it is doubtful they were right, opponents accused Fielding of writing Trentham's protestations and an appeal to voters that he issued on November 16.

The election began on November 22. On November 24, the first polling day, there was a battle in front of St. Paul's, Covent Garden, between supporters of Trentham and adherents of Vandeput and the "Independent Electors," led by the minor writer Paul Whitehead. It resulted in the arrest of Benjamin Boswell and his group of ministerial toughs, and their confinement in the Roundhouse. The same day one William Davison declared in an affidavit that he knew Trentham had hired Haines and his henchmen to bully the enemies of the French Comedians on the 14th. On the 24th the Duke of Bedford paid to print 10,000 copies of an electioneering broadsheet, *Ten Queries submitted to every Sober, Honest, and Disinterested Elector for the City and Liberty of Westminster*, that Martin Battestin convincingly attributes to Fielding, who personally certified William Strahan's bill. The *Ten Queries* are conveniently reprinted by the Battestins and need not be reproduced here; basically they treat Vandeput as a nobody and a Dutchman (though the family had been in England since the sixteenth century), stress the innocence of Trentham in the Haymarket broil, and plead for votes for Trentham. In "Queries" 4 and 6 Fielding insinuates that Trentham's opponents are Jacobites and the tools of Jesuits, though these innuendoes are slanderous "red herrings." This was another dying echo of the long Jacobite paper war traced in Chapter Six. A few days later (it was printed on November 29 by Richard Franklyn) another handbill, *Reasons for Voting for Lord Trentham*, was distributed. Martin Battestin suggests this too may be Fielding's work, though there is no firm evidence. It is very short (three terse questions) and insignificant.

On November 25 Fielding released Boswell and his toughs from the Roundhouse. He would be arraigned for protecting Trentham's "Bruisers" by *Old England* on December 9 and in a pamphlet called *The Two Candidates: or, Charge and Discharge*. As late as June 1751 Fielding would be abused for this in a pamphlet, *The Case of the Hon. Alexander Murray*, by Paul Whitehead, the leader of the opposition group that had fought with Boswell's gang in Covent Garden. On November 25 Fielding was reported to have found no visible injuries upon the supposed victims of his assault before he admitted Boswell to bail. But this report came from George Ward, one of Bedford's attornies. Certainly Bedford was angry at the arrests, and Fielding and Bedford's lawyers agreed in seeing Boswell as an innocent, injured party. Ultimately, on December 14, Fielding received a tardy and somewhat suspicious affidavit (preserved in the Bedford Estates Office) by William Bayley, which declared that Boswell was an innocent bystander with his hands in his pockets, attacked and forced to go to the Roundhouse by Whitehead and his followers.

On November 26, Haines, the leader of Trentham's bullies at the Haymarket on November 14, according to Davison's affidavit of November 24, swore an affidavit of his own before Fielding, denying the "false, scandalous and malicious" charge against him. It was repeatedly printed in the newspapers on the next few days, over Fielding's name, and Bedford paid to have it printed as a handbill to the extent of 12,000 copies on November 27 and 28. On November 27 Fielding went to the polls, together with John Hiatt, one of the election agents for Bedford's candidate. He cast his vote for Trentham, as did seventy-six of the eighty-five Westminster magistrates. Serving the government on the Westminster Bench and voting Bedford's way were virtually equivalent in 1749. On the nights of November 26, 27, and 30 Fielding also hosted the treating of electors in three London taverns, the Old George and Punchbowl in Drury Lane, the White Bear in Bow Street, and the Sun, Longacre, authorizing their proprietors with his signature to bill Bedford for something over £26 in all.

It has been suggested that Fielding had a hand in one of the later election broadsheets, the *Covent-Garden Journal. No. 1 . . . . By Paul Wronghead of the Fleet, Esq.*'' This is a parody of an essay-journal, not the first issue of one; the promise "To be publish'd Once every Month, during the present *Westminster Election*'' is part of the parody and a witty comment on the unusual length of the election. It has intrigued students of Fielding's later *Covent-Garden Journal* since the time of G. E. Jensen, who concluded that Fielding had no "connection with it,'' and assumed (missing the irony) that it was anti-Trentham. In fact, it was an election hand-out printed and distributed at Bedford's expense, to the tune of 13,000 copies, a very large number for the time in one district, at a cost of nearly £25. Aimed at Paul Whitehead (formerly an inmate for debt in the Fleet Prison) the piece greatly pleased Lord Trentham, who urged its wide distribution. Even before the election Whitehead had invited satire from Fielding; in 1747 he had abused Lyttelton and Pitt as turncoats in the poem *Honour: A Satire*. The *Covent-Garden Journal* includes—in absurdly abbreviated form—the standard features of an essay-journal: a lead (in this case, "Introductory") essay, "Foreign Affairs'' and "Home Affairs'' sections, an "Advertisement,'' and even a comic booksellers' imprint: "Printed for T. Smith, R. Webb, and S. Johnson, and sold by all the People of *London* and *Westminster*, where Persons who bring Advertisement or Letters to the Authors are taken in.'' It mocks opposition themes, including the supposed ministerial threat to "Liberty,'' the Penlez affair, and the Haymarket riot. It satirizes the "Independent Electors,'' "Dutch'' Vandeput and the impecunious Whitehead, and also—under "Foreign Affairs''—adds the usual barbs about opposition Jacobitism and Jesuits. Given Fielding's heavy involvement in electioneering and love of parody, and given the fact that *Old England* accused him of "penning the *Covent-Garden Journal* for the Service of the Faction'' on December 9 and parodied it as "The Bowstreet Journal; or, Covent-Garden Advertiser. By Hercules Vinegar'' on December 16, I am convinced that Martin Battestin is correct in suggesting that the style of the "Introductory Essay'' (not the rest of the broadsheet) completes a fairly strong case for Fielding's authorship.

After the *Covent-Garden Journal. No. 1* Fielding remained silent, presumably because he fell ill with the gout that killed him in 1754. The election ended on December 8 and Trentham won, though the opposition appealed the results on the grounds of irregularities and delayed his seating. During the post-election period Fielding continued to be attacked. On December 16 and 30 *Old England* accused him of ghost-writing Trentham's publications and misusing his position to ensure Trentham's election. He was accused repeatedly of sacrificing Penlez because he had a financial interest in bawdy houses. *Old England* and the *London Evening Post* both did so on November 25, the day Fielding released Boswell, and *Old England* repeated the charges on December 2, 9, and 16 and on March 3, 1750. As late as May 15, 1750 Fielding needed to keep the peace when the final confirmation of Trentham's victory was announced. He promised to do so ("I shall preserve the Peace on that Occasion") in a note to Bedford, the point of which was unclear until the Battestins gave it a context. In fact, the very last chapter in the Westminster election paper war was not written until over a year after Trentham got his seat. The riotous behaviour of the opposition extremist Alexander Murray (one of the few real Jacobites in the opposition) upon the confirmation of Trentham's election led to his impeachment. He was sentenced to ask pardon on his knees at the bar of the House of Commons, repeatedly refused to do so, was imprisoned, and finally fled to France. Paul Whitehead treated him as a "martyred patriot" in *The Case of the Hon. Alexander Murray*, published on June 27, 1751. It criticized Parliament for hounding Murray and abused Bedford, Trentham, and Fielding (the politicians' tool) for their behaviour during the 1749 election. Fielding strove to repress Whitehead's satire, the authorities having banned its sale. On June 28, according to the *Whitehall Evening Post* for July 2, 1751, Fielding committed a female hawker of the pamphlet to Bridewell for a month, and had the *Case* publicly condemned and burnt "in the Street before his own Door, and in the Presence of upwards of a hundred people."[7]

Fielding remained very active in the cause of reform, as a magistrate and an essayist. Since the reforms he favoured were being actively pursued by the ministry, particularly Lord Hardwicke, his campaign against crime and vice had inherent political overtones. On July 21, 1749 he had sent Lord Hardwicke a draft of suggestions for a law to reduce street robberies, apparently at the Lord Chancellor's request, and he began in 1751 by publishing (around mid-January) his first major socio-legal tract: *An Enquiry into the Causes of the Late Increase of Robbers, with some Proposals for Remedying this Growing Evil. In which the present Reigning Vices are impartially Exposed, and the Laws that relate to the Provision for the Poor, and the Punishment of Felons are largely and freely examined.* The appearance of the *Enquiry* was obviously timed to coincide with the declaration in the Throne Speech at the opening of Parliament on January 17 that the government intended to suppress "outrages and violences, which are inconsistent with all good government, and endanger the lives and properties of . . . subjects." In 1750 the government for the first time really enforced a law of 1743 designed to limit the sale and consumption of gin; Fielding was doubtless involved in the fining of more than 4000 unlicensed sellers of gin. The 1751 Throne Speech was the signal for the beginning of an extended attempt to reform the legal apparatus for combatting vice and crime. It would produce significant new legislation in the following year, even though several Bills favoured by the ministry would fail to survive Parliamentary scrutiny. As early as October 9, 1750 the *Enquiry* was so specifically and accurately "puffed" in the *General Advertiser* that we may assume Fielding was well along in the process of composition, though it was published when it would do the most to support the planned reforms. Helped along by Fielding and by Hogarth's horrifying "Gin Lane" engraving (first published on February 1), the government took the first steps two weeks later with the introduction of the new Gin Bill. This would become law as the Gin Act on June 25, 1751, when it received Royal Assent. The new Gin Act revoked existing gin distillers' licences to sell their product retail, and allowed the granting of no new ones. It forbade the giving or selling of gin in jails, prisons, houses of correction, workhouses, or other refuges for the impoverished. Only taverns, alehouses, inns, and coffeehouses offering food would in future be licensed to sell gin, and the licensing fees and tax on gin were raised. Magistrates were also given new powers to enforce the Act. Though gin remained a popular, cheap, and relatively available drink, the number of outlets and consumption were considerably reduced. Slower in coming were other reforms proposed by Fielding in the far-ranging *Enquiry*.[8]

The *Enquiry* is never specifically partisan, but it supported a programme of reforms intended by the ministry, led in this direction by Lord Chancellor Hardwicke. One presumes Bedford had a particular interest in reform legislation. In the past four years Bedford had been mobbed and horsewhipped at Lichfield and seen sailors and opposition bullies fighting in the London streets and threatening his property. Fielding's diagnosis centres upon the rage of the lower orders for "luxury." The poor no longer are frugal and hardworking. They gamble and are able to remain in a dangerous state of idle drunkenness because of cheap gin, the "diabolical liquor." They steal and intimidate to support their vices. The availability of gin must be lessened and gaming houses closed. In addition, the poor laws need reforming, so that the poor who are able to work can be made to do so rather than being incarcerated in ill-run Bridewells where they learn every variety of vice and crime. The relatively few who really need alms and cannot work can subsist better on private charity. Magistrates need broad new powers to compel idle and impecunious vagabonds to return to their home parishes or face severe punishment. To deal with those who have made the change from idle poverty to crime, the legal system must be made more efficient. The open activities of receivers of stolen goods—successors of Jonathan Wild —must be stopped. A more efficient system of policing than the present system of thief-takers (outnumbered and often in fear of their quarry) is needed, and the public must help to apprehend and prosecute criminals. The government must take on the financial burdens of prosecution, change the rules of evidence so that the testimony of accomplices may weigh more heavily against defendants, and be less ready to pardon the convicted. And the Roman holidays at Tyburn, felons going out in a blaze of glory to a cheering mob, must be replaced by execution soon after conviction and in fearful privacy. There is much to make a modern civil libertarian cringe in all of this, but it would have made the streets and highways safer if it had been carried through *in toto* and with vigour.

The *Enquiry* was well received in such neutral quarters as the *Gentleman's Magazine*. There were attacks on its singling out of the poor —never the rich—for reform and its potentially dangerous recommendation that the rules of evidence be loosened in felony cases. There were also personal sneers at Fielding; remembering the Penlez riots, one writer asked why he did not urge the closing of brothels as well as gaming houses and dram shops. But the praise drowned out the complaints and the government not only introduced the Gin Bill, but set up a Commons Committee, including Pitt and Lyttelton, "to revise and consider the laws in being, which relate to felonies and other offenses against the peace." It also offered £100 rewards for apprehending a felon in London and an area five miles around it, together with pardons for accomplices, other than those themselves guilty of murder, who turned in persons found guilty of a felony.[9]

Fielding's day-to-day labours against crime remained hectic in 1751, and the bits of his correspondence that have survived indicate that he continued to work with political leaders in this connection. On January 15 he successfully urged Newcastle to appoint one of his best constables, William Pentlow (who had apprehended a gang of robbers), Keeper of the new Clerkenwell Prison, and on May 23 stood surety in the amount of £100 for Pentlow's behaviour in that post. At the same time Fielding reorganized his eighty constables, and encouraged the composition of a treatise on the duties of constables by Saunders Welch. Though so incapacitated by his gout that he could not walk, in May Fielding pressed Bedford (as is clear from a surviving letter to Robert Butcher, dated May 7) for a new appointment or perhaps the mysterious pension ("on my obtaining which depends the future Happiness of my Life"). On June 12 he wrote Butcher regarding a request from Bedford to prevent someone from obtaining a licence, presumably to sell gin, and closed by asking Butcher to remind "his Grace" to send him some venison in season as he apparently had in 1750. The patron-petitioner relationship with Bedford obviously remained very strong.[10]

The rest of the measures recommended in Fielding's *Enquiry* were not enacted as rapidly as the Gin Act. The activities of the Commons committee to study the larceny problem did not begin to produce specific legislative action until November 14, 1751, when the Throne Speech at the opening of the 1751-52 session indicated an intention to pass a new Robbery Act. The wording of the King's speech suggests the stresses of

Fielding's pamphlet with some precision: "I cannot conclude without recommending to you, in the most earnest manner, to consider seriously of some effectual provisions to suppress those audacious crimes of robbery and violence, which are now become so frequent, especially about this great capital; and which have proceeded, in a great measure, from that profligate spirit of irreligion, idleness, gaming and extravagance." A bill was introduced and passed on March 26, 1752, and the Royal Assent was soon given to an "Act for the better preventing of Thefts and Robberies and for regulating places of public Entertainment, and punishing Persons keeping disorderly Houses." It required a sizeable licensing fee from proprietors of places of entertainment, limited their hours, made the prosecution of brothel and gaming-house keepers easier, empowered Justices to imprison and return vagabonds to their legal parishes, and offered financial aid to poor prosecuters of felons. All of this was in line with Fielding's ideas, implicit in *Jonathan Wild* and explicitly urged in the *Enquiry*. The same was also true of other provisions of the Act: it made advertising a reward for stolen goods, no questions asked, an offence, rendering the advertiser, the publisher, and the printer liable to a fine of £50. Wilbur Cross was wise to doubt that Fielding was involved in writing the bill itself, and the details of legal history relevant to Fielding's activities in 1751-52 more recently drawn together by Hugh Amory reinforce the dangers of overestimating Fielding's influence on the course of legal reform. However, Cross was right to treat the *Enquiry* and the draft of a robbery bill sent to Hardwicke in 1749 as the obvious and substantial relatives of the bill introduced by Sir Richard Lloyd. Though the patterns of influence are hard to settle, there may even be substance in Cross's contention that Lloyd's bill was a revised version of a revised version of the 1749 draft prepared by Fielding. Whatever the precise truth, seldom has a writer so directly affected major criminal legislation.[11]

Fielding's *A Plan of the Universal Register Office* (February or March 1751, though dated 1750) has no political significance. However, at around the time it was published a fascinating political drama, with farcical as well as tragic overtones, was being played by those in power and those hungry for power in the next reign. It had a strong negative effect on Fielding, precluding any considerable return to partisan writing for the rest of his life. Early in the morning of March 21, 1751 Prince Frederick died, nearly a decade before the hated father he expected to succeed, to the confusion of many in the ministry and in the opposition. The Leicester House faction was utterly confounded. As A. M. Newman has made clear, the Earl of Egmont, George Dodington (back in opposition with the Prince), and the rest of the Prince's dependants were far advanced in the most elaborate plans for excluding virtually all of the present ministers from office—the Pelhams and Broad-Bottoms alike—and determining their own entrenchment in power. They had written plans detailing day by day the change in ministries. Their extreme care was motivated by the memory of the disaster of 1727, when the Leicester

House dependants of the new George II were left out of office, after a short period of doubt, and Walpole and his henchmen were asked to continue. The death of the Prince made these plans a hollow jest.

Whether any other arrangements would have been honoured if the King had predeceased Frederick is dubious, given the organized determination of the Leicester House faction to have exclusive enjoyment of the spoils. However, various elements in the ministerial coalition were hopefully negotiating with the Prince and his dependants when he died. The Duke of Newcastle did so very actively in 1750, anticipating that the Prince might soon succeed his aged father. The "reversionary" possibilities weighed more heavily against the present enjoyment of office with every passing year. It had affected the thinking of skilled politicians since the 1730s. In the 1750s it was a major consideration. The Pelhams feared the Leicester House faction might oust them despite their parliamentary power. Newcastle's goal was some kind of agreement, secret while George II lived, that would lead toward an alliance with Frederick's dependants after his accession. Such an agreement would have left the Broad-Bottoms in opposition. At the same time, William Pitt, backed by Bedford, Lyttelton, and the other Broad-Bottoms, worked to revive their former connection with the Prince and obtain a secret agreement with Leicester House that would keep them in office (and perhaps higher office than they had under the Pelhams) upon the Prince's accession. This would have involved the dismissal of the Pelhams.

The surviving documents indicate that Egmont, Dodington, and the Prince were agreed about the need to sacrifice *both* the Pelhams and the Broad-Bottom element when the time came for a change in government. However, this did not preclude leading on both groups of intriguing ministerialists while George II lived. According to good "family faction" habit, Pitt, Lyttelton, and their associates negotiated with their old patron, Frederick, through Thomas Ayscough, D.D., Clerk of the Closet to Frederick, first preceptor to the future George III, and the husband of one of George Lyttelton's sisters. So seemingly successful were these negotiations that Lyttelton and Pitt felt—rightly or wrongly—that they had made matters up with the Prince and ensured their futures at just the point when he suddenly died. Indeed, Horace Walpole noted with amusement that Lyttelton lamented in a letter to his father the terrible timing of this sad event because the connection with Frederick had just been renewed, and that this embarrassing letter fell into the hands of Henry Pelham and the King. The Broad-Bottoms not only lost an apparent opportunity to rise to new levels of power under a friendly monarch, but were exposed as intriguers. When the dismissal of Ayscough from his posts was planned, the "Grenville Cousins" tried to save him, but had not that degree of influence, and he ended up the Dean of Bristol.[12]

In the aftermath of the Prince's death, which left Henry Pelham and Newcastle even more firmly in control, Lyttelton and Pitt were allowed to scramble back into the Pelhams' good graces and retain their relatively minor posts. They had no further room for manoeuvre and remained quietly loyal through the death of Henry Pelham in 1754. The Duke of Cumberland also had problems to work out with the leading minister. He strove with them briefly, angered that he was not named a regent for the young royal heir, still nearly a decade from his accession as George III, and was supported in this by Pitt. But he also soon resumed peaceful relations with the Pelham brothers. There really was no practical alternative. Thus the death of the Prince did not create a ministerial crisis, though it did alter the political future and the goals of politicians. Indeed, the ministry remained unchanged, with one exception, for Fielding a very important one. The Duke of Bedford was forced from office. Bedford was the Broad-Bottom with the greatest wealth and personal power and by far the highest cabinet post. He had become unsatisfied, well before Frederick's death, with his role as subordinate Secretary of State, his influence and power far outweighed by the Duke of Newcastle's, though they were nominally roughly equal in the cabinet as well as in the peerage. The great Dukes were pretty open rivals by 1750-51. When the Prince died and the junior Broad-Bottoms clung to their places, Bedford was dangerously isolated. He may have been unwilling to swallow his pride, supported by wealth and rank, and accept the domination of the Pelhams, as the situation and their far greater power dictated. Newcastle may have been far less willing to forgive a grandee with a major inner cabinet post than he was to tolerate the foibles of Lyttelton and Pitt, talented and realistic junior colleagues. On June 18, 1751, Bedford resigned his Secretaryship, followed into the wilderness only by Sandwich. It was the first major break in the ministerial façade since Chesterfield resigned his Secretaryship and was replaced by Bedford in early 1748. (Serving as co-Secretary with Newcastle was obviously a very uncomfortable position for a peer with ambition.) In this case, unlike that of Chesterfield, the outgoing Secretary moved into opposition, albeit futile, ineffectual opposition.

This situation was most awkward for Fielding. He had been a firm supporter of the almost unaltered ministry for years, and it was in the process of working toward the socio-legal reforms that were his passion. The man who had for the better part of two decades been his closest political friend, George Lyttelton, remained in office, along with Pitt and the Grenvilles. Fielding also admired Henry Pelham, though his opinion of Newcastle may have been less favourable. It is impossible to say what he might have done had all the Broad-Bottoms resigned from the ministry, but as things stood he could not conceivably consider opposing the ministry. James Ralph would blossom into an opposition journalist in the Bedford interest by 1753, when he turned out the twenty-four issues of *The Protester*. Ralph had none of Fielding's close ministerial ties, held no official position like Fielding's magistracy, and was merely trading the shattered Leicester House interest that had stood behind the *Remembrancer* for another opposition patron with money. On the other hand, Fielding owed Bedford so much: his nominations to the magistracy, the very roof over his head (with the annual rent forgiven), the pension obtained for him during Bedford's period in power and still paid annually, many personal and administrative favours, even venison in the fall. Obviously, Fielding could not turn his back on Bedford, and the evidence is overwhelming that he never did. He virtually died thanking him, and for years after Fielding's death, his brother, John Fielding, his widow Mary, and his son William continued to call on the generosity of the Duke. Undesirous of altering his ministerial orientation, but hardly eager to eulogize ministry or to smite opposition with his wonted fervour, obligated both to men in the ministry and to Bedford outside of it, Fielding did the only thing possible after Bedford's resignation. He cut back partisan material to a very slender minimum in subsequent works, though he was careful to maintain his anti-opposition orientation when he indulged in partisanship. He also straddled political fences in his social life. Between August 6, 1751 and July 12, 1752 Fielding dined nine times with George Dodington, the archetypical Leicester House intriguer during the Prince's lifetime. On at least four occasions Mrs. Fielding accompanied him. Most significantly, they were joined on September 14, 1751 by James Ralph, who wrote the *Remembrancer* with the support of Dodington and Leicester House, and was rebuked for it in *The Jacobite's Journal*, and who would in 1753 become the voice of the Bedford opposition.[13]

Amelia is a far less partisan novel than *Tom Jones*, eschewing both open assault on the opposition and eulogy of the present ministry, even though it is more concerned with political problems, in the super-partisan sense, than any of his major fiction with the exception of *Jonathan Wild*. Its London setting; its concentration on the neglect and oppression of brave officers, women, and children by those in authority; its concern with needed legal reforms and corruption, civil and military, with crime, with the ill-treatment of debtors, and the venal injustice of many law courts would all have lent themselves to a multitude of partisan touches, especially if Fielding had decided to support Bedford against the ministry. In fact, the novel sometimes implies that the nation's "governors" have much to answer for, but does not imply that the present government is in any particular way to blame for the corrupt state of the nation. Many of the reforms Fielding calls for were favoured by the ministry when *Amelia* was published.

It is obvious, when one compares *Amelia* and *Tom Jones*, that in the former Fielding avoided eulogy of contemporary politicians. He also technically placed the bulk of the action in 1734. Though one tends to forget it, the political abuses, the corrupt politicians, the influential, seducing peers and their pimps are, theoretically, evils of the age of Walpole, not that of Henry Pelham and the Broad-Bottom ministry. This is so even though parts of the action seem—somewhat irrationally—placed in the early 1740s and parts seem roughly contemporary, so explicitly so that the Universal Register Office is mentioned in the novel.[14]

Thus, the faults of England in the world of the novel may be attributed to an earlier age, before the best of ministries, the present one, took shape, though Fielding never puts into words this obvious, pro-ministerial potential theme. We will see that he comes close to doing so in one political chapter (XI, ii), and he ironically notes that the practices of the Justice Thrashers began to be reformed in 1749 (when he became active in Bow Street), but that is all. With one patron in opposition and others in the ministry, Fielding was avoiding all political risks without relaxing his opposition to prevailing corruption and abuses, threading his way between Scylla and Charybdis. One assumes both Lyttelton and Bedford, who remained close "familially," though they were separated temporarily by the vagaries of inter-ministerial competition, understood and even encouraged his caution. This time there could be no eulogies of Pelham, Lyttelton, Pitt, Hardwicke, or the present administration in Fielding's novel, nor could there be a word of gratitude to Bedford, for all his continued generosity. The novel is dedicated to Ralph Allen, as a moral leader and a lover of mankind. Allen had shared the praise with Lyttelton and Bedford in 1749. In 1751 he had it all.

The mockery by contemporaries of accidental absurdities in the first edition of *Amelia* (the oversight about her missing nose and the rest) and its supposed immorality and actual inferiority to *Tom Jones* has been described too often to require discussion. The intrinsically assault-inviting nature of the novel's anatomy of sexual vices, so like those of the *Modern Husband*, also maligned as smutty, explains much of the criticism. But some attacks were motivated by resentments generated during Fielding's ministerial heyday, 1747-49. One obvious example is a mock advertisement in *The Drury-Lane Journal* for January 16, 1752. The latter suggests a reaction to *Amelia* very like Fielding's reaction to *Pamela* (perhaps its author knew the secret of Fielding's authorship of the parody of Richardson):

> Shamelia, a Novel.
> Printed for the Major General
>   Where may be had,
> The Works of Hercules Vinegar Esq;
> The True Patriot.
> N.B. These are proper to be bound with the
> lucubrations of Sir Alexander Drawcansir.
>   Likewise,
>   Several d__mn'd Farces.
> A Bundle of Political Pamphlets, by the same
>   hand, pick and chuse for a Penny.
>   The Complete Justice of Peace.

Fielding remained fair game after *The Jacobite's Journal* and the election free-for-all of 1749. His aggressive, high-profile behaviour as a magistrate, encouraging legal reforms sought by the ministry, insured that he remained associated with ministerialism even when he was careful to seem neutral, and the novel regularly urges reforms of this kind.

However, there is little in *Amelia* that would have encouraged politically motivated attack if such pressures had not been operative. Jacobites and their women are momentarily ridiculed in an early chapter, and Mrs. Mathews' father is praised as "a well-wisher to the present government" (I, vi, vii). There is no more in the first half of the long novel. Later, a hack making up news and parliamentary speeches for the papers is said to be a member of the opposition (as is the bailiff, Mr. Bondum, who holds him) and the opposition's cries of "Liberty," "Freedom," and the "Constitution" are mocked (VII, ii). Another passage laments the fact that poetry does not pay now, when booksellers buy scandalous and abusive trash by the page, then indicates that more money can be earned and less time is used up *per* page writing opposition speeches (VIII, ii, v). Fielding had given the opposition more grounds for feeling offended in the annotated news sections alone of one typical *Jacobite's Journal* issue than in all of *Amelia*.

The "government" and "great men" are far more often criticized than the opposition, though never in a partisan or very topical way, especially in the last hundred pages or so of the novel. Fielding is indignant about the amorality of great men and the system by which preferments in the civil service and armed forces are given. In places the satire aims more precisely at the use of corruption by those in power to enhance and extend their control. However, we must hold firmly in mind Fielding's placement—technical and erratic as it is—of the action in the 1730s, in the years after the siege of Gibraltar of 1727. The grounds for doing this are strong because the novel's satire on corruption and corrupters recalls that in Fielding's early plays and journalism. The rampant immorality and the stalking of wives by a nobleman in the novel recall *The Modern Husband* of 1732. Political corruption in general and the acquiescence of so many with some degree of power or authority in a system badly needing reform are the real targets, not the Pelhams or Cumberland, at the head of the armed forces. As Fielding said in the *Dialogue* of 1747, the Pelhams did not create and could not wholly cure corruption. This perception and the placement of the action nearly twenty years in the past must condition our interpretation of much of the novel's gloomy anatomy of corruption: the boys in command while tried officers starve on half-pay, the disgraceful delays in paying pensions to the families of the war-dead, the sale of places by the "tools" of "great men," the "touching" or bribery. Fielding did not mean to affront the Pelhams, Hardwicke, or Cumberland, much less the ministerial Broad-Bottoms, by calling on "great men" to feel ashamed (XI, iv, v). When he indicates that not only corruption, but promises, often unkept (V, iii), are the weapons of a great man he is reviving one of the clichés of anti-Walpole satire in the 1730s. Fielding speaks as a moralist and "true patriot" on the nation's ills, deploring "the great State Lottery of Preferment" (XII, ii) as harshly as degenerate sexual *mores* and duelling, but his condemnations could as easily have been written in 1731 or 1741 as in 1751. Indeed, in 1751 much of his satire was tacitly supportive of the reform plans of Hardwicke and the ministry.

The one place in the novel where Fielding seems to have approached the limits of the permissible in criticizing ministerial acceptance and employment of corruption is Book XI, chapter ii, entitled "Matters Political." Significantly, before exposing us to political and potentially dangerous material in the chapter, Fielding carefully re-emphasizes the placement of the action, a meeting between Dr. Harrison and a ministerial nobleman, in the fairly distant past (roughly 1734) and under an earlier ministry. It is specified at the head of the chapter that the nobleman, whose help in getting Booth a posting Harrison goes to re-quest, was known (my italics) "to have a very considerable interest *with the ministers at that time.*" This specifically precludes contemporary ap-plication, and the chapter may hint that the corruption current under Walpole has been lessened by the *present* ministry.

The dialogue between Harrison and the nobleman is a rather static set-piece, somewhat reminiscent of the much longer *Dialogue* of 1747, though Harrison denounces a rationalization of corruption akin to those in the pamphlet. Harrison requests an assignment for the deserving, needy Booth. The nobleman replies that Harrison is in a position "to ask a greater matter than this," though assignments are not usually affected by "personal merit." Harrison's influence is needed to win the post of mayor in the clergyman's home town for one Colonel Trumpington, "a mere stranger, a boy, a soldier of fortune, . . . of a very shallow capacity, and no education," who is running against Mr. Fairfield, "a neighbour-ing gentleman of a very large estate, a very sober and sensible man, of known probity and attachment to the true interest of his country." This is extraordinarily like the electoral satire not only in *Pasquin*, but in *Don Quixote in England* of 1734, the year in which Harrison supposedly con-fronts the nobleman. Harrison recommends that Trumpington stick to the military profession, more fitting for an "illiterate." The nobleman responds predictably: "Well, sir, . . . if you are resolved against us, I must . . . tell you plainly I cannot serve you in your affairs . . . if I should mention his name with your recommendation after what you have said, he would perhaps never get provided for as long as he lives."

To Harrison's objections the nobleman cynically replies that many as meritorious as Booth are suffering on half-pay, and always will be. Harrison denounces this as "an infamous scandal on the nation," and proposes that room be made for men of merit by ceasing to "suffer a set of worthless fellows to eat their bread." The nobleman laughs at this as "mere Utopia . . . the chimerical system of Plato's Commonwealth, with which we amused ourselves at the university; politics which are inconsis-tent with the state of human affairs." It is wrong to "apply maxims drawn from the Greek and Roman histories," unless from "those times" of the degenerating Roman republic "that were most like our own." England now "is as corrupt a nation as ever existed under the sun," and it is impossible to govern it "by the strict principles of honesty and morality." Harrison calls for healing the moral sickness of the British

republic before it goes the way of the Roman, a sentiment worthy of Hercules Vinegar or Thomson's *Liberty*. The nobleman argues that the process of change is irreversible. The political degeneracy of England must
be accepted and used. He asks, ". . . do you really think, doctor, . . .
that any minister could support himself in this country upon such principles as you recommend? Do you think he would be able to baffle an opposition unless he should oblige his friends by conferring places often
contrary to his own inclinations and his own opinion?"

Fielding never stated such a view so baldly even in the *Dialogue* of
1747. He sneered at such rationalizations in his years as critic of
Walpole's methods, just as Dr. Harrison does. Harrison agrees that a
minister acquiescing in a bad, factious, and corruption-dominated *status
quo* would have "to baffle opposition . . . by these arts," but goes on to
propose that a minister with reforming, "national" (rather than factious), Broad-Bottom aims need not:

> . . . if . . . he will please to consider the true interest of his country, and
> that only in great and national points, if he will engage his country in
> neither alliances nor quarrels but where it is really interested; if he will
> raise no money but what is wanted, nor employ any civil or military
> officers but what are useful, and place in these employments men of
> the highest integrity, and of the greatest abilities; if he will employ
> some few of his hours to advance our trade, and some few more to
> regulate our domestic government, if he would do this, my Lord, I
> will answer for it he shall either have no opposition to baffle, or he
> shall baffle it by a fair appeal to his conduct.

This could have come from Bolingbroke in an optimistic mood or
Fielding's *Address to the Electors* of 1740. It seems little relevant to the
period from the mid-1740s to 1751. Indeed, a sly compliment to the present ministry, a contemporary application, seems half to surface when
the nobleman asks: "And do you believe . . . there ever was such a
minister, or ever will be?" and Harrison tersely rejoins, "Why not?"
Given the strange displacement caused by placing the dialogue a decade
before the formation of the Broad-Bottom and the rise of Henry
Pelham, this hint about a "future" cure for corruption and faction may
"look forward" to a better ministry. If so, it is most interesting that
Fielding does nothing to make the compliment more specific or em-
phatic, though there were easy ways to do so. A footnote to the effect
that Harrison has been proved right would have been a typical Fielding
touch. I cannot imagine that Fielding would have failed somehow to
capitalize politically at this point had *Amelia* been published before the
ministerial battle with Newcastle that led to Bedford's resignation in
June 1751. If placing *Tom Jones* in late 1745 allowed the addition of
anti-opposition satire, placing *Amelia* in Walpole's time made it possible
to criticize corrupt government without being offensive to the present
ministry.

For all its technical placement in the past, *Amelia* propagandizes for
the legal and moral reforms that were favoured by Fielding and the

ministry while it was composed. As soon as the action begins in Justice Thrasher's court the novel becomes in part a tract by Fielding, the reformer. He deplores corrupt courts, horrid prisons that encourage vice and crime, luxury, irreligion, gaming, sexual licence, legal loopholes, and rules of evidence that protect rogues and fences. The novel exemplifies every argument of the *Enquiry* and his other reformist tracts, earlier and later. In *Amelia* Fielding avoided offending either an opposition patron or the ministry, while propagandizing for Lord Hardwicke's reforms. The robbery bill was introduced in Commons a few weeks before *Amelia* appeared and signed into law on March 26, 1752 as "An Act for the better preventing Thefts and Robberies, and for regulating Places of Publick Entertainment, and punishing Persons keeping disorderly Houses."

When *Amelia* was published on December 18, 1751 plans for Fielding's fourth periodical, *The Covent-Garden Journal* by "Sir Alexander Drawcansir, Knt. Censor of Great Britain," were well advanced. In the *London Daily Advertiser* for November 1, its first issue had been promised for November 23. A delay was belatedly announced in advertisements at the end of the second volume of *Amelia* and in the *London Daily Advertiser* for December 18. The first issue appeared on January 4, 1752. Though it was at first a twice-weekly journal, unlike the thrice-weekly *Champion* and weekly *True Patriot* and *Jacobite's Journal*, it had the usual format: four pages, with a sizable lead essay, news foreign and domestic, culled from the newspapers and annotated, proceedings of a mock court (the "Censorial Court" is not very different from the "Court of Criticism"), advertisements, notices of births, marriages, deaths, stock quotations, and special features. In the first four issues there was also a "*Journal* of the Paper War." It detailed the supposed combat (in the manner of the *Battle of the Books*) between Drawcansir's forces and those of Grub-Street, between Fielding and Dr. John Hill, prolific hack and editor of the *Inspector*. This was abandoned by Fielding after the fourth issue, though other writers would mock both Fielding and Hill for months. Fielding presumably withdrew because the reasonably playful, circulation-stimulating war was turning personal and nasty. For our purposes, however, the crucial fact is that *The Covent-Garden Journal* is relatively free of partisan political satire and panegyric. *Amelia* is much less partisan than *Tom Jones*, but *Tom Jones* is itself not often or obstrusively partisan. The change in Fielding's level of aggression between 1748 and late 1751 is far more dramatically symbolized by a comparison of *The Jacobite's Journal* and *The Covent-Garden Journal*. The extreme difference heavily underscores Fielding's new concern to avoid partisanship in the years when he had to avoid offending either Bedford or the ministry.

Generally, *The Covent-Garden Journal* focusses on literary and critical, social and moral matters, not political ones. Many of its essays seem close to the non-political leaders in the *Champion*'s early run, and in *The Covent-Garden Journal* they are not followed by partisan material in news or special feature sections. As editor of Bedford's opposition organ, *The Protester*, James Ralph would show in 1753 that he had not lost any of his aggressiveness. But that Fielding had is apparent throughout *The Covent-Garden Journal*. The sinfulness of adultery and atheism, the dangers of luxury, the silliness of beaus and coquetes, the vanity and hypocrisy of society snobs, bad manners, the need and duty of charity, the ignorance and spite of modern authors, the danger of mob rule, the state of the theatre, the public's behaviour in theatres, manners and morals are major concerns. The relative merits of the ministry and its critics are not. Normally one puts little faith in the declarations of non-partisanship of eighteenth-century journalists. As often as not they are the first indications of partisanship—the *True Patriot* is a classic example. However, Fielding adheres with considerable consistency to the promise in issue 1 that he will avoid "any Dealing in Politics," particularly ". . . that great political Cause between WOODALL OUT, and TAKEALL IN, Esqs . . . in which the Nation in general are as greatly interested, as they were in the late Contest between Thomas Kouli Kan, and the Sophy of Persia."

Much of the political material in *The Covent-Garden Journal* carries on the quasi-ministerial legal and moral reformism of his serious social tracts. In issue after issue reports from Bow Street stress the need for reforms. Essay 2 touches on the problem of making provision for the poor, as do essays 36, 50, and 54. Essay 17 recalls the stress on reform in the throne speech of "George the Good" in 1751, and essay 25 "puffs," in a weirdly equivocal way, the execution of felons in private. Essay 30 identifies corruption, luxury, and immorality as the sources of crime and vice in the manner of the *Enquiry*, then humorously argues that both bribery and robbery would decline were the use of money abolished. Essay 57 attacks Bridewells in familiar terms ("Bridewell . . . is, a School rather for the Improvement, than for the Correction of Debauchery" to which one hesitates to send a woman with any residual decency). Essay 66 treats recent anti-gaming laws as signs that his hatred of gaming is shared by the "whole Nation," especially "all the greatest Men in it." The implicit compliment to the ministry in the last example would two or three years earlier have been expanded into a paragraph of the most excessive praise of Pelham, Hardwicke, and the rest. It is typical of the Fielding of 1752 to hint an ambiguous compliment and drop the matter. Drumming up support for reforms also favoured by ministers was a political act, particularly when Fielding did it, but it was hardly partisan.

The insistence in essay 1 that WOODALL OUT *versus* TAKEALL IN will be avoided is restressed in other early issues. Essay 3 sneers, in good Broad-Bottom fashion, at faction, the ambitious, and the existence of party, reiterating his scorn for WOODALL OUT and TAKEALL IN. However, Fielding does not twist this neutral-sounding stance into an attack on the opposition (as a faction opposed to a ministry above party) as he would certainly have done from 1746 to 1749. Essay 4, the "Modern Glossary" (a gem of Fielding journalism), is painstaking in its evenhandedness. The only political definitions are:

PATRIOT.	A Candidate for a Place at Court.
POLITICS.	The Art of getting such a Place.
ROGUE.)	
)	A Man of a different Party from yourself.
RASCAL.)	

After this point, specific protestations of political disinterest cease (presumably because the point was well made), aside from a compliment in essay 41 to Drawcansir for avoiding not only private slander, but "any servile Flattery to the Great." But Fielding's super-partisan stance was maintained in the very clever dialogue between Elizabethans in essay 54. They view seats in Parliament and places as onerous public duties. They even corrupt county electors not to vote for them and saddle them with London expenses.

Nonetheless, Fielding remained a supporter of ministry. He was still inclined—Bedford aside—to look down on opposition and especially to dislike the opposition writers who continued to malign him and the ministry. Sometimes this shows fleetingly or implicitly. Essay 5 announces the end, from Fielding's point of view, of the paper war with Dr. John Hill and the *Inspector*. This paper war was generally non-political, as G. E. Jensen has observed.[15] However, in ending it Fielding reflects that such wars are kept going because men tend to side with the weaker opponent, just as the London mob sides with the political opposition and hoots great men; for a moment the anti-opposition, anti-mob animus of 1749 is there. Similarly, writings in favour of "Disaffection" (a favourite word while Fielding was a detector of opposition "Jacobitism") are specified as popular custard wrappings in essay 6. One example of the techniques of bad writers in essay 18 is the "disemvoweling" of significant words: "M--nst-r, L--d, B-sh-p." In essay 60 Drawcansir proposes to write a new *Dunciad*, noting that he is compiling a list of hacks who have written against the government, as well as religion and morality. The censure of the licentiousness of contemporary writing that runs through the journal periodically verges upon hinting the need for tighter censorship, a staple theme of ministerialists, and even the curtailment of abused civil liberties. Essay 55 stresses in passing that the English enjoy a "pure and perfect State of Liberty . . . in a degree greatly superior to every foreign Nation." Essay 23 recalls that laws, now obsolete, once punished "Libels against the Government," as well as blasphemy and private slander. The pattern is perfectly captured in essays 8 and 9, where Fielding ridicules the Robin Hood Society (a middle-class debating society) for debating the "first Principles of Religion and Government." Essay 8 is the fragmentary minutes of a debate, in Robinhoodian spelling, of "Important Questions cunsarning Relidgin and Gubermint." The fragment is almost wholly taken up with an absurd discussion of the "Question . . . whether Relidgin was of any youse to a Sosyaty." The absurdities attendant upon political debate among such ignoramuses are not exemplified. There is merely a hint at the end of the supposed fragment of their minutes that this *could* have been done, which was as far as Fielding was ready to go in the cautious mood that perforce dominated *The Covent-Garden Journal:*

> *Question*. Whether, in the Opinion of this Society, the Government did Right in _____
> Here ends this valuable Fragment, on which I shall give my Comment in my next Paper.

Besides the essays already mentioned, only four (numbers 16, 42, 50, 59) are politically significant. An elegy on the late Frederick, Prince of Wales (surely not by Fielding) in issue 28 has no partisan content and would have had no dangerous implications thirteen months after the death of the Prince and the utter evaporation of Leicester House as a threat to ministry. These four essays constitute the most obtrusively political material in *The Covent-Garden Journal*, but it is typical that all but one strikes a very careful political balance. Essay 50 considers the growing threat of the London mob, pinpointing the Elizabethan poor laws as one historical cause. It suggests that a false idea of "Liberty" encourages mob violence, and that the mob is held in check by fear of magistrates and soldiers. This sounds like the basis for a blast at opposition rabble-rousing. However, Fielding is careful explicitly to insist that the mob is encouraged by politicians on *both* sides for their own partisan purposes. In essay 42, one paragraph could come straight out of *The Jacobite's Journal*. Fielding considers how a learned man rendered unworldly by living in dreams of classical Greece and Rome would react to Country Tories:

> . . . convey [him] to a Hunting-Match, a Horse Race, or any other Meeting of Patriots. Will he not immediately conclude from all the Roaring and Ranting, the Hallowing and Huzzaing, the Gaming and Drinking, which he will there observe, that he is actually present at the Orgia of Bacchus, or the Celebration of some such Festival? How then will he be astonished to find he is in the Company of a Sett of honest Fellows, who are the Guardians of Liberty, and are actually getting drunk in the Service of their Country.

However, the previous paragraph imagines the learned man at court:

> How will he be puzzled when he is told that he hath before his Eyes a Number of Free-Men? How much more will he be amazed when he hears that all the Servility he there beholds, arises only from an eager Desire of being permitted to serve the Public.

The political balance is perfect.

A letter from "A true Englishman" (unquestionably by Fielding) in issue 58 constitutes the one major unambiguous and unbalanced thrust at opposition in the *Journal*. The target is familiar, the "Independent Electors of Westminster," though the occasion is obscure. The "true Englishman" reports a dialogue overheard in an Alehouse between members of the "fourth Estate" (the mob), who are beginning "as usual to exert themselves'' with "the Approach of a new Election for Westminster." The next election was not due and was not held until 1754; until then Viscount Trentham remained in the seat for Westminster which he obtained with such struggle in 1749-50. Perhaps Fielding expected an early election, like that of 1747. In any case, the alehouse debaters were in ludicrous full cry. Jobson, a cobbler, prated out a pointless speech with "frequent Repetitions of the Words Liberty and True Englishman," declaring his right to vote even for "Stroud" (a notorious swindler, not a candidate or a politician)[16] if he chose. This gave his listeners "a great Idea of the Dignity and Independency of the Speaker." Mr. Sneerwell drily complimented Jobson for "suffering in the Great Cause of Independent Liberty." His wording and the capitalization point clearly at the "Independent Electors of Westminster," men at home in an alehouse, as well as at Vintner's Hall, scene of their misbehaviour in 1747. This quip is followed by a debate about which candidate will bribe and treat and buy from their shops most generously, though "Liberty was in all their Mouths, and served like Lillaburlero, as a kind of Burthen to close the End of every Speech." The "true Englishman" hopes their liberty will not be lost as was that of the Greeks and Romans: ". . . by extending it to such an intolerable Degree of Licentiousness, and ungovernable Insolence, as to introduce that Anarchy which is sure to end in some Species of Tyranny or other." Fielding perhaps openly attacked an opposition group in this one instance because the interests of the ministry and the Duke of Bedford coincided in the Westminster constituency. Though the Duke was in opposition, he was Viscount Trentham's brother-in-law. Against this we may place the fact that in 1754 Trentham became member for Lichfield.[17]

The final and most significant political instance is essay 16. Fielding begins it by complimenting the valour of the English at Fontenoy and their commander, the Duke of Cumberland: "our glorious General as he deserved no less, so would he have gathered no less Laurels, than the most successful of his Predecessors had ever been crowned with." This compliment to a man groomed by both the ministers and Bedford, but despised by opposition, was political indeed. Equally so are the essay's denigration of the "Spirit of Party" and insistence that the ministry and the best writers now shun factious battle, leaving the dregs of society (the opposition press) to feed the taste for "Scandal and Scurrility." Axylus, whose "letter" is the centre of the essay, considers himself blest to live in an age of political peace and prosperity under the leadership of Henry Pelham:

> I often express great Gratitude to the Almighty, that I was born in a Country where I can reflect with constant Pleasure on the Freedom, the Wealth, and indeed every political Happiness of the People . . . I look up with unfeigned Gratitude to the Authors, under Heaven, of these Blessings to us. With these views I frequent the Court, and a certain Levee in Arlington Street, with more Devotion than any of the Candidates for Preferment.

This recalls the fulsome eulogies of other patrons of 1746-49, and the next paragraph re-emphasizes the political benefits of the Broad-Bottom ministry: "Of all my Life, I think, I never enjoyed so happy a Winter as this last, in which there hath been such perfect Unanimity among all Parties, and the sole Attention of all our great Men seems to have been the Good of the Public." Even here, however, I believe that Fielding maintained the Bedford-ministry balance. Axylus notes that he has been warmed recently by the generosity of a Duke, who has made a "private Family" happy. The only commentary on this passage rather vaguely directs the compliment to the Duke of Hamilton,[18] but I doubt any contemporary of Fielding's aware of his close patron-dependant relationship with Bedford would have hesitated long in reaching the correct conclusion: Bedford was the "Duke" and the "private family" was Fielding's. Given what the Battestins and M.P.G. Draper have shown us about Fielding and Bedford, we need not do so. Axylus' remarks reveal the excess typical of Fielding's flattery of political patrons:

> Within this last Fortnight too, I have been extremely delighted. The Happiness which within that Time hath accrued to a private Family, hath almost intoxicated me, with Joy. That noble, generous, Duke! How worthy of the highest Blessings of Life! In my Opinion how sure of them!

What Bedford did for Fielding in February 1752 is not clear. But in thanking him so publicly, even without naming him, Fielding was ensuring that Bedford would not be offended by his compliments in other paragraphs to the ministry.

Fielding's political balance in *The Covent-Garden Journal* was maintained in the face of attacks that stressed his ministerial allegiances and unsuccessfully attempted to draw him into partisan skirmishes. The paper war with John Hill, carried on by Fielding in the earliest issues and echoed in the trial of Hill in the last issue had no intended political significance, for all that we may wish to attribute such significance to any paper war in which Fielding was engaged. It began as a literary conflict, ridicule of Grub Street, designed by both Fielding and Hill, I would guess, to encourage sales of the *Covent-Garden Journal* and the *Inspector*. Because it proved good copy, it went on after Fielding found the abuse worse than the fun or profits could justify. Fielding's involvement in the theatrical war between Drury Lane and Covent Garden was also non-political. Nonetheless, there were attacks on Fielding during the run of *The Covent-Garden Journal* that were partisan in content and motivation.

The best known of these is Smollett's disgracefully personal *A Faithful Narrative of the base and inhuman Arts that were lately practised upon the Brain of Habbakuk Hilding, Justice, Dealer and Chapman, who now lies at his own House in Covent-Garden, in a deplorable State of Lunacy; a dreadful Monument of false Friendship and Delusion.* This twenty-eight-page pamphlet, published on January 15, 1752, accuses Fielding of literary theft from Smollett, scandal-mongering, and smuttiness, ridicules his marriage to Mary Daniels, and declares him a drunken madman. It also attributes his establishment of *The Covent-Garden Journal* and declaration of war on other authors, including Smollett, to the influence of George Lyttelton. "Gosling Scrag" (the long, lean character of that name had represented Lyttelton in *Peregrine Pickle*) has turned poor Hilding (Fielding) into a lunatic and bribed him to return to the political fray to suit his own partisan and abusive purposes. Just what Smollett saw as grist for Lyttelton's mill in the first three or four issues of Fielding's journal is unclear, though Smollett was mildly and apolitically teased (the account of a battle with "Peeragrin Puckle" and "Rodorick Random") in the "Journal of the present War" in issue 2.

In any case, *Old England* preceded Smollett in picking a political fight with Fielding. On December 21, two weeks before *The Covent-Garden Journal* appeared, *Old England* "hoped" it would not deal with politics. On January 9, five days after issue 1, *Old England* anticipated Smollett by printing a farce ("not intended for the Press, tho' now acting") in which *Harry Foolding*, senile writer of dirty novels, was depicted as having established the new journal at the behest of George Lyttelton ("Littlebones") to calm the political fears of Henry Pelham ("Harry Peg'em") and hoodwink the people. Peg'em does not believe that Foolding will dare try another journal, "since the People hiss'd down his *Jacobite* Buffoonery," but Littlebones brings Foolding before him, tobacco quid in his cheek, ready to run a puppet show or write a weekly journal for his political masters as long as there is profit in it. The farce ends with the decision to call it "The Covent-Garden Journal, by Sir Alex. Drawcansir, Censor of Great Britain, Knt." Though the essay never specifies the precise partisan purposes or themes of the *Journal* (as indeed it could not, since Fielding's first issue was so carefully non-partisan), it strongly and falsely asserts that Fielding's every move is politically motivated and paid for by Lyttelton and Pelham. G. E. Jensen was correct in saying that *Old England* and Smollett wished to tempt Fielding into a partisan paper war that could only benefit the opposition at a time when the ministry was secure and politics boringly peaceful, but that Fielding was determined not to be drawn in.[19] The attempt was in some ways like Fielding's extended, eventually successful attempt to draw the unwilling *Gazetteer* into attacking the new *Champion* in 1739-40. In 1752 Fielding's unbroken silence frustrated his enemies.

Fielding's other publication of 1752, *Examples of the Interposition of Providence in the Detection and Punishment of Murder*, is only political in the non-partisan sense of supporting reforms actively promoted by Hardwicke and the ministry. During the previous month a new Act had become law "for preventing the horrid Crime of Murder," incorporating some of the legal reforms indicated in Fielding's *Enquiry*. The Act required immediate sentencing of convicted murderers and execution two days after sentencing, directed that the condemned be fed bread and water and denied liquor unless ordered by a physician, and consigned their bodies to use as medical cadavers. The new Robbery Act and the Murder Act were complementary and put through Parliament almost simultaneously.[20] Though published over a year apart, Fielding's *Enquiry* and the *Examples* were nearly as interrelated.

A Clear State of the Case of Elizabeth Canning, published on March 20, 1753, is also without real political intent or interest. It distinguishes between "licentiousness" and "liberty" of the press, as Fielding often did in sniping at opposition writers, but it never applies this or its other social and moral criticism in partisan ways. However, his major publication of 1753, *A Proposal for Making an Effectual Provision for the Poor, for Amending their Morals, and for Rendering them Useful Members of the Society* (published by Millar, January 19, 1753), is not without political significance. The *Proposal* suggests the weaknesses of the present poor laws and system of punishing and rehabilitating budding criminals. It also analyzes the social, economic, and spiritual ills that underlie a situation in which the deserving poor suffer and many of the potentially useful poor are a burden and a curse on the nation. Its "Proposals for Erecting a County Workhouse" are the core of a disquisition that sums up all of Fielding's concerns about the socio-economic and legal *status quo* that offended him daily as Bow Street magistrate. For our purposes, there is less interest in Fielding's attitudes and suggestions than in the fact that he was once again propagandizing for the reform efforts of Hardwicke and the ministry, and perhaps pressing the nation's leaders along the paths of reform. When he wrote it, bills intended to continue the process of legal reform carried forward in the Gin Act and the Robbery and Murder Acts of 1752 were under consideration. Much of the ministry's programme would not survive and be enacted as law due to the same current of ignorant and bigoted resistance that later caused difficulties with the forward-looking Marriage Act and forced the disgraceful repeal of the Jew Naturalization Act.[21] When Fielding called for laws to discourage crime and immorality, he was obviously, if obliquely, supporting the ministry in the face of actual or anticipated resistance.

This is surely the reason Fielding dedicated the strongly reformist *Proposal* to "the Right Honorable Henry Pelham, Chancellor of His Majesty's Exchequer," not Ralph Allen or the Bishop of Worcester. The dedication is a quite specific declaration of continuing ministerial loyalty. Fielding expresses his sense of high obligation to Pelham, then suggests that the busy minister may have time to read his proposals now that the "Ship of State" has been skillfully navigated to a safe anchorage. This testimonial to Pelham's skill implies strong approbation of the formation of the Broad-Bottom ministry (and emasculation of opposition) between 1744 and the Treaty of Aix-la-Chapelle of 1748. It lauds the ministerial and parliamentary *status quo* as well as Pelham. Fielding suggests that his proposals will, if followed, entail repairs to the well-anchored ship of state that will increase both posterity's sense of obliga-

tion to the reformers of the present age and the praises it will heap on
Henry Pelham. There is not an explicit hint of satire on the opposition,
but the denial that there *is* any real opposition was potent, implicit
mockery. Farther Fielding could not go, given the fact that he may have
written the *Proposal* and its dedication in the Bow Street house provided
rent-free by the Duke of Bedford. Bedford became a more active opponent of the Pelhams in 1753 than he had been since his resignation in
1751. With Bedford's backing, James Ralph's anti-ministerial journal,
The Protester (appearing weekly, June 2 to November 10, 1753) called
for vigorous opposition as a needed safeguard for the Constitution and
criticized the Broad-Bottom ministry upon "true" Broad-Bottom
patriotic principles.[22] Fielding was prepared to signal his continuing
loyalty to the ministry, and even to imply the ineffectuality of the opposition Bedford was vainly trying to reinspirit. However, he could do no
more while Bedford opposed. Fielding closes the *Proposal* with the comment that he is near death, without ambition and avarice, but happily
possessed of enough to live on and to keep his family out of the
workhouse when he is gone. That this was so was in great part due to
Bedford's generous patronage.

During 1753 Fielding remained very active as a magistrate, hearing
cases and dispatching constables to enforce the law. Bits of his correspondence survive: three items addressed to Newcastle (two letters
regarding the Canning case and a memorial complaining about the non-
payment of rewards to seven special constables) and a letter urging Lord
Chancellor Hardwicke to nominate Saunders Welch as Justice of the
Peace. This is, of course, the merest tip of an iceberg of legal-judicial
business. In August the gout that had tormented him for years returned
in so dangerous a form that he was advised to go to Bath. Unfortunately,
he was required to remain in London by the Duke of Newcastle to
oversee an extraordinary and temporarily successful campaign against
robbery and murder that the Secretary of State had thought up. He
would recall in the "Author's Introduction" to *The Journal of a Voyage
to Lisbon*[23] that this finally destroyed his health. By the end of 1753 he
was an invalid, trying to rally against jaundice as well as gout. It was the
beginning of the end.

As a literary man, he revised older works, in hopes of augmenting
the inheritance of his wife and second family. *Amelia* was already
thoroughly revised, though there was not a sufficient market to warrant
republication in his lifetime. He revised *Jonathan Wild* for publication as
a separate work. Its content was relevant to his anti-crime commitment,
and it did not deserve to survive only in the obscurity of the third volume
of the *Miscellanies*. Politically, the 1754 version of *Jonathan Wild* is only
significant in a negative way. Fielding polished away some of the dated
vilification of Walpole, and eliminated the parts of the work (principally
Book II, chapter 12 in the 1742 version) that contained the most stringent
and specific double assaults on Walpole and his "false Patriot" successors in 1742. Such satire was antique and irrelevant in 1754, and com-

paring Walpole's and Wild's gang of "prigs" was not calculated to please Henry Pelham, Walpole's protégé and successor. Fielding's depoliticizing deletions and mollifications are quite consistent with the cautious political blandness he cultivated in the 1750s.[24] In 1743 Fielding added thrusts at Walpole's successors to make a dated manuscript timely, and in 1754 he had to revise in the opposite direction to adapt the book to changed times.

When Henry Pelham died on March 6, 1754, Fielding himself was on the brink of dissolution, having begun to endure the hideous process of tapping fluid from the distended trunk so specifically described in the posthumous *Journal of a Voyage to Lisbon*. Before mid-year his brother John Fielding took over in Bow Street, while Henry retired to Fordhook to work on his refutation of Lord Bolingbroke's deist writings. He left Fordhook on June 26 to embark for Lisbon, which he reached in early August, three months before his death on October 8, 1754. The fragment of his answer to Bolingbroke is apolitical, as are the other minor works printed after his death.[25] In 1754 he concentrated on Bolingbroke's deism, ignoring the important political works included in Mallet's recent edition, contenting himself with a single political jest: a man who played with the liberty and property of all Europe in his youth might well play with Man's hope of eternal happiness in his old age.

On the other hand, though it certainly does not focus on political matters and is non-partisan, *The Journal of a Voyage to Lisbon* is not devoid of political interest. It is often political in the broad sense characteristic of Fielding's latest period. He defines the duties and standards of a good magistrate, denounces corruption among those responsible for minor public works, deplores the mob and its misunderstanding of liberty, calls for the revival of laws forcing vagrants to work for reasonable wages, and expresses horror at the Circean brothels visited by sailors. He is indignant about discrimination between "low" and "high" people by Justices of the Peace, witch-hunting, and the luxury and impiety of the upper classes. He declares the laws governing marine commerce insufficient and calls on the Legislature to improve them, and he urges the encouragement of fisheries and a scheme to feed the poor with fish.

Exposure to nautical life and to the strengths and weaknesses of the great maritime trading systems revived the old patriot's enthusiasm for trade and naval power, though not the partisan animus that often accompanied it under Walpole and Carteret. Trade, he declares, is essential to England's glory. In the "Author's Introduction" Fielding also discusses the income of an honest Bow Street Justice: "little more than three hundred pounds" a year, most "of which remained with my clerk," He adds in a footnote that he has "received from the Government a yearly pension out of the public service money; which I believe, indeed, would have been larger had my great patron been convinced of an error, which I have heard him utter more than once, that he could not indeed say that the acting as a principal justice of peace in Westminster was on all accounts

very desirable, but that all the world knew it was a very lucrative office."
Only in this moment of death-bed honesty did Fielding publicize the extent of his financial dependence on both Bedford and the government.
The Duke seems to have remained generous to Fielding's family,[26] and
his admission that he would have been distressed without extra income
was probably one last way of appealing for such generosity.

Finally, Fielding expressed in his last major political statement the
admiration for the great Sir Robert Walpole that partisanship had usually prevented him from voicing. Fulminating against the ugly, freedom-
threatening, brawling presence of encamped troops seen on shore, he
reflected that the fleet in Spithead at least gave the nation "a fine sight
for their money" in the time of Sir Robert, "one of the best of men and
ministers." Henry Pelham would have warmed to this sentiment if he
had lived to read it, but the dying Fielding unquestionably was sincere in
his admiration for the greatest politician of the earlier eighteenth century
in England. The observation was an appropriate and shrewd last word at
the end of a full life as a political writer.

Notes

Notes to Introduction

1 This situation persists despite the publication (between the completion and publication of the present study) of Brian McCrea's *Henry Fielding and the Politics of Mid-Eighteenth-Century England* (University of Georgia Press, 1980). It is far too brief, covering summarily only a portion of Fielding's political writing. It is very lightly researched: for example, it discusses *The Champion* and *The Jacobite's Journal*, but it is clear that Professor McCrea has not seen the original sheets of *The Champion* and has not read the *Gazetteer* or *Old England* for the relevant periods. Its dependence on often untrustworthy secondary scholarship is a serious weakness.

Worst of all, as Donald Greene has said (*Times Literary Supplement*, September 11, 1981, p. 1028), the book is naïve and unconvincing when it deals with the political background. McCrea sees all of Fielding's career as affected by his "Whiggism," as opposed to the "Toryism" seen as the key in Vern D. Bailey's unreliable, unpublished dissertation on "Fielding's Politics" (University of California, Berkeley, 1970). As will certainly be apparent to anyone who reads the present study, dealing vaguely in "Whigs" and "Tories," "Whiggism" and "Toryism" is an impossible approach to Fielding's career. McCrea does not seem aware of the crucial, twenty-year relationship between Fielding and important members and allies of the Broad-Bottom (or Cobhamite or Young Patriot) faction within what he would probably call the "Whig" camp. Fielding's closeness to George Lyttelton is only noted in the chapter dealing with the later 1740s, and there the implication is that Fielding closed with Lyttelton because both followed Henry Pelham.

I applaud McCrea's rejection of the "Tory View" of Fielding's career. But the "Whig" view is no better, and the failure to grasp the basics of Fielding's political situation and orientation (1735-54) undermines every phase of McCrea's interpretation. McCrea's book is not referred to in my text or notes. If I had written with it before me, I would have been constrained to query or reject his analysis of the political tenor and intention of virtually every work he discusses.

Notes to Chapter One

1 Much of this chapter will be based on Wiggin and Foord. For Lyttelton and his correspondence see Phillimore. Cf. R. M. Davis, *The Good Lord Lyttelton* (Bethlehem, PA, 1939).
2 Samuel Johnson's *Life* leaves it rather vague when Lyttelton entered Commons: ". . . in 1728 he began his travels and saw France and Italy. When he returned he obtained a seat in parliament." (*Lives of the Poets*, ed. G. B. Hill [1905], III, 447.) Cf. Phillimore, I, 43.
3 Term used in Foord. George Lyttelton said in *Considerations on the Present State of Affairs* (London, 1739, pp. 44-45): "I pity those, if there are any such, who think the *removing an ill Minister* is a Point of consequence, if with him the *Maxims* and *Measures* of his Government . . . are not also expelled."
4 Wiggin, 86-87; Phillimore, I, 72.
5 Bolingbroke's Patriot ideas were aired in the "Dissertation upon Parties" (published in the *Craftsman*, then in pamphlet form) and developed in *Letters on the Spirit of Patriotism* and *The Idea of a Patriot King*. The *Idea* circulated in manuscript by December 1738, but was only published in an unauthorized edition in 1743 and in

authorized, revised form in 1749. In 1749 Lyttelton had to ask Bolingbroke to remove the once-appropriate dedication of *The Idea* to him. It would have been embarrassing to a junior member of the "Broad-Bottom ministry," opposed by both Bolingbroke and Prince Frederick.

6   The title came from part of Fielding's *Pasquin*, "The Life and Death of Common Sense."

7   Grundy, 213-45.

8   A letter to his father expressing satisfaction at a ministerial foreign policy success indicates that Lyttelton still favoured Walpole in November 1734 (Phillimore, I, 61-63), though he may have been humouring his placeman father.

9   Pitt was Frederick's "Groom of the Bed-Chamber" (with an annual stipend of £400) and George Lyttelton his Secretary (at £866 13s. 4d.).

10   Cleary, "Case," 308-18.

11   Chesterfield's printer was apprehended over the seditious character of the first issue of *Old England*. Ironically, *Old England* would continue to use "Jacobitical" rhetoric against Chesterfield after he became a ministerialist. Fielding accused it of "Jacobitism" in *The Jacobite's Journal*. Cf. Cleary, "Paper War," 1-11.

12   Cleary, "Jacobitism," 239-51.

13   W. B. Coley, "Fielding's Two Appointments to the Magistracy," *Modern Philology* 63 (1965), 144-49; B-B, "Bedford," 143-85.

14   In less-full houses and on relatively non-controversial issues Walpole's majority was secure. The Country Tories usually supported government bills that did not seem partisan or corruptive. They were more inclined to absenteeism during sessions than any other element in Commons, leaving the opposition short of votes. The attendance at the larger meetings Walpole held in the Cockpit before parliamentary sessions (there was also a smaller meeting for the inner circle, the ministry's "men of business") seems to indicate that his firm "Corps" numbered roughly 150, a majority in a thin House, but not enough (roughly 250) in a full one (Thomas, 105-26). Walpole's skilled use of patronage to maintain strong Commons majorities (Lords being safely packed) has been well explored up to 1734 in Plumb. Owen and Foord have filled in the picture with reference to the older Walpole and his successors. A very telling, though biased picture of the Walpole system is provided by the division list on the controversial Convention of Pardo of 1739 (one of Walpole's last efforts to avoid the war with Spain demanded by the opposition), published in the *Gentleman's Magazine* for June 1739. Its annotations indicate the patronage enjoyed by voting members and their families: over £200,000 *per annum* among "aye" (ministerial) voters; only £11,000 *per annum* for "nay" voters. Nevertheless, of the 262 "aye" voters (the "nays" numbered 234) 52 enjoyed no "incentive" discernible even by the partisan annotator of the list and those specified for another 34-40 seem dubious.

15   B-B, "Bedford," 143-85. He also arranged a pension for Fielding at some point and aided the writer's brother, widow, and son after 1754.

16   Ralph edited the pro-Bedford journal called *The Protester* from June 2 to November 10, 1753. He had earlier attacked the ministry in *The Remembrancer* (December 12, 1747—June 1, 1751) and been rebuked in Fielding's *Jacobite's Journal* (especially no. 17).

17   In addition to Wiggin, Foord, Plumb, Thomas, and Owen, the following studies help clarify the proto-party complexities under George II (as well as the process of party fragmentation and rebirth in earlier and later reigns): Sir Lewis B. Namier, *The Structure of Politics at the Accession of George III*, 2 vols. (London, 1927; 2nd Ed., 1957); Romney Sedgwick, ed., *Letters from George III to Lord Bute, 1756-1766* (London, 1939); _____, *The History of Parliament: The House of Commons, 1715-54* (London, 1970); Herbert Butterfield, *George III, Lord North and the People* (London, 1949); Richard Pares, *King George III and the Politicians* (Oxford, 1953); Robert Walcott, *English Politics in the Earlier Eighteenth Century* (Cambridge, MA, 1956); Geoffrey Holmes, *British Politics in the Age of Anne* (London, 1967); John Brooke, *The Chatham Administration, 1766-68* (London, 1956); J. H. Plumb, *The Rise of Political Stability, 1675-1725* (London, 1967); John W. Wilkes, *A Whig in Power: The Political Career of Henry Pelham* (Evanston, IL, 1964); Isaac Kramnick, *Bolingbroke and His Circle: The Politics of Nostalgia in the Age of Walpole* (Cambridge, MA, 1968); Sheila Lambert, *Bills and Acts: Legislative Procedure in Eighteenth-Century*

England (Cambridge, MA, 1971); Wolfgang Michael, *Englische Geschichte im achtzehnten Jahrhundert*, 5 vols. (Berlin, Hamburg, Basel, 1896-1955); Reed Browning, *The Duke of Newcastle* (New Haven, 1975); B. W. Hill, *The Growth of Political Parties, 1689-1742* (London, 1976). Michael's study is badly dated; Browning and Hill move rapidly over vast territory and sometimes employ bipartisan terminology inappropriately and vaguely. Plumb's *The Rise of Political Stability* is a brilliant assault on the validity of the extreme Namierite, "anti-party" view of the period before 1725 (developed by Walcott and others). However, the assault becomes less determined and meaningful as Plumb moves into the 1720s and toward the factious reign of George II. The richest sense of the day-to-day politics from the 1720s through 1754 is still provided by William Coxe's classics: *Memoirs of the Life and Administration of Sir Robert Walpole, Earl of Orford*, 4 vols. (London, 1816) and *Memoirs of the Administration of the Right Honourable Henry Pelham*, 3 vols. (London, 1829). In recent years, a series of historical works have refined the perceptions of post-Namierite historiography on issues of interest to the student of Fielding's politics, though they have not materially affected my interpretation of his career or its background. Fielding's Broad-Bottom associates were members of a faction that fits into neither the old Whig-Tory, bipartisan concept of politics under George II nor the qualified redactions of it that now are becoming popular. Some outstanding examples (in addition to Hill's *The Growth of Political Parties*) are: Paul Langford, *The Excise Crisis: Society and Politics in the Age of Walpole* (Oxford, 1975); John Brewer, *Party Ideology and Popular Politics at the Accession of George III* (Cambridge, 1976); Linda Colley, "The Loyal Brotherhood and the Cocoa Tree: the London Organization of the Tory Party, 1727-1760," *Historical Journal* 20 (1977), 77-95; H. T. Dickinson, *Liberty and Property: Political Ideology in Eighteenth-Century Britain* (London, 1977).

Notes to Chapter Two

1   *The Norfolk Gamester: Or, The Art of Managing the Whole Pack, Even King, Queen, and Jack* (London, 1734), 5.
2   Grundy, 213-20.
3   George Lyttelton wrote a letter from his father's government office in November 1734 (Phillimore, 61-62) that seems to imply approval of the ministry's diplomatic activities (specifically the negotiations that led to the Third Treaty of Vienna in 1738) and relief at a lull in continental conflicts "so dangerous to the ministry."
4   I am indebted to John B. Shipley for the information that Ralph (though he "converted" to opposition in 1735) supported ministry as editor-writer of the *Weekly Register* from January 1731 to late 1733 and continued to write non-political material for it until it ceased publication in 1735. He may also have written for the ministerial *Daily Courant* in 1733.
5   L. Hanson, *The Government and the Press* (Oxford, 1936), 109-14. Hanson notes that the use of the post office and government funds was attacked sharply in William Pulteney's *A Review of the Excise Scheme* (1734). Later, more, surely, was spent on *The Daily Gazetteer*. (Fielding's objections to this in the *Champion* and *Joseph Andrews* are well known.) I will argue that Fielding's *True Patriot* was probably subsidized, and that the *Jacobite's Journal* must have been (perhaps to the extent of 2,000 copies a week).
6   Howard P. Vincent, "Early Poems by Henry Fielding," *N&Q* 184 (March 13, 1943), 159-60.
7   *Love in Several Masques* (Dublin: S. Powell, 1728), 14.
8   *The Historical Register and Eurydice Hissed*, ed. W. Appleton (Lincoln, NE, 1967), p. 13.
9   Grundy, 215. (Page references on subsequent pages are also to Grundy.) J.R. Brown's "Four Plays by Henry Fielding" (unpublished Ph.D. dissertation, Northwestern University, Evanston, IL, 1937) confusingly discusses only the plays that can be made to fit his thesis that there was an increase of anti-Walpole animus from *The Welsh Opera* through *The Historical Register*. Brown's subsequent article, "Henry Fielding's 'Grub-Street Opera' " (see note 32 below), is excellent.

10   G. R. Levine reads the *Modern Husband* dedication as ironical (*Henry Fielding and and Dry Mock*, [The Hague, 1967], 146, n. 3), but he did not know of the poems Grundy has discovered. The anti-opposition bias of the fragment of 1729 is also apparent in "An Epistle to Mr. Lyttelton," written in 1733. The poems of 1729 and 1733 and the Walpole dedication of 1732 undermine Hugh Amory's suggestions that the two *Epistles to Walpole* (dated 1730 and 1731; published in the *Miscellanies* of 1743) were written much later and were wholly ironical ("Fielding's *Epistles to Walpole: An Reexamination*," *P.Q.* 46 [1967], 236-47.). Amory says the poem dated 1730 was written in 1740 and revised in 1742 to adjust it to Walpole's situation that year, and that the poem dated 1731 is (as printed in the *Miscellanies*) "a reply dated 1731 to a libel dated 1740." However, it is now clear that these poems are precisely what Fielding might have written for private amusement and distribution in 1730 and 1731 and dusted off (part of one of them having been published in 1738) in 1743.

11   Grundy, 232 note.

12   Grundy, 239 note. Gay discusses his experiences in the preface to *Polly;* cf. Gay's *Letters*, ed. G. F. Burgess (Oxford: Clarendon Press, 1966), 78. On Fielding's "ministerial" reputation, see Charles B. Woods, "Fielding's Epilogue for Theobald," *P.Q.*, 28 (1949), 423.

13   Woods, *AF*, xii-xiii.

14   Morrissey, *TT*, 5-6.

15   "The Significance of Fielding's *Temple Beau*." *PMLA* 55 (1940), 440-44.

16   In the original edition (London, J. Watts) it is printed after the play (a frequent practice). Perhaps significantly, a note says it was sung by a Miss Thornowets, not included in the cast list.

17   Woods, *AF*, xiii-xiv.

18   Morrissey, *TT*, 1.

19   Baker, 221-231; Woods, *AF*, xv note. (References to *The Author's Farce* of 1730 are to Woods's edition.)

20   Morrissey, *TT*, especially 4-5. Morrissey covers the same ground at greater length in "Fielding's First Political Satire," *Anglia* 93 (1972), 325-48. There he says (p. 330) that "Fielding's expansions and omissions establish the political satire in the revised play," but often writes as if this were not true.

21   Godden, 315; Cross, I, 103; *The Tragedy of Tragedies*, ed. James T. Hillhouse (New Haven, 1918), 9; Mabel Hessler, *The Literary Opposition to Sir Robert Walpole, 1721-1742* (Chicago, 1936), 125; Dudden, I, 64-69.

22   Cross, I, 90-91; Dudden, I, 69-74; Bertrand A. Goldgar, "The Politics of Fielding's *Coffee-House Politician*," *P.Q.* 49 (1970), 424-29 and *Walpole and the Wits* (Lincoln, NE, 1976), 105-110. Goldgar's political reading is less full and more tentative than mine.

23   *Rape upon Rape; or, The Justice Caught in His Own Trap* (London: J. Watts, 1730), 1. (All citations are from this edition.)

24   *The Free Briton* always treated opposition as factious, libellous, even Jacobitical, but the crossfire warmed when the *Craftsman* (May 30 and June 6) maintained that the throne speech implied the king saw a "great part of his Subjects as *disaffected* to his Person and Government." *The Free Briton* replied with charges that the opposition was seditious and insulting to the royal family: e.g., June 4 and 11, July 16, October 15 and 22, November 5, December 3 and 31. Fielding's *Welsh Opera* (1731), James Miller's *Vanelia; or, the Amours of the Great . . .* (1731) and *The Norfolk Gamester* (1734) all ridicule the royal family.

25   *DNB; Proceedings at the Sessions of the Peace and Oyer and Terminer for . . . London and Middlesex against Francis Charteris, esq. for committing a rape on the body of Anne Bond, of which he was found guilty* (London, 1730).

26   Cited in the introduction to Swift's *Ballad* in *The Poems of Jonathan Swift*, ed. Harold Williams, 2nd ed. (Oxford, 1958), II, 516. Goldgar (pp. 105-107) relates the play to the Charteris case and cites contemporary satires on Walpole based on that rape and its aftermath. He cites Swift's description of Charteris as "that continual favourite of Ministers," but ignores the Irish rape.

27   The *Free Briton* devoted much space to defending the treaty against the *Craftsman* and *Mist's Weekly*. From April through late June, 1730, when *Rape upon Rape* opened, diplomacy obsessed journalists on both sides.

28 Compare his "I am not satisfied at all with the Affairs in the North: the Northern Winds have not blown us any Good lately; the Clouds are a little darker in the East too than I could wish them" (Act V, sc. ii, p. 63) with the political Aunt Western's vague reference to affairs "in the north" in *Tom Jones*, VI, iv.

29 Phillimore, 34. Cf. note 3 above.

30 Loftis, 105.

31 *The Letter Writers: or, a New Way to Keep a Wife at Home* (London, 1731). Besides one vague compliment to the *Grub Street Journal* (p. 14) it has very few political touches: desultory mockery of the trained bands, the observation of Risque, the pimp, that if Rakel had employed "half the Dexterity" he has shown in amourous pursuit "in the Service of a Great Man, I had been a Captain or a Middlesex Justice long ago" (p. 10), and one politico-medical joke (p. 40): ". . . mending our Wives is like mending our Constitutions, . . . often . . . we would be glad to return to our former State."

32 The known facts about *The Grub-Street Opera*'s repression and the performance and publication history of the various versions—*The Welsh Opera, The Genuine Grub-Street Opera*, and *The Grub-Street Opera*—are surveyed in J. Brown, "Henry Fielding's *Grub-Street Opera*," *MLQ* 16 (1955), 32-41; Roberts, *GSO*, especially xiv ff.; and Morrissey, *GSO*, 13-14. Cf. *The Daily Post*, June 12 and 14, 1731. Morrissey demonstrates that *The Welsh Opera* and (in August) *The Genuine Grub-Street Opera* were pirated by J. Rayner, who obtained scripts or prompt copies from someone at the Haymarket.

33 Plumb (p. 131) notes the ridicule of George I during the preceding reign for employing Turkish body servants.

34 Roberts, *GSO*, xvii.

35 Plumb, 168. The King got £800,000 a year, plus the surpluses of all taxes appropriated to the Civil List, roughly £100,000. Lord Hervey's aspersions on Frederick's potency are notorious (*Memoirs*, II, 614-18).

36 According to the Earl of Egmont's *Diary* (I, 92), in 1730 Prince Frederick paid £1500 to a hautboy player named La Tour for this reason; this is cited in Roberts, *GSO* (29) as a gloss on Molly's reaction to Mr. Apshones' statement that Owen seduced a fiddler's daughter. Molly replies that it was the fiddler's fault for he "sold his daughter and gave a receipt for the money." Others mocked the Prince's sexual follies: James Miller's *Vanelia* scandalously exploited the relationship between Frederick and Anne Vane. Though Lord Hervey and others "confessed" to having fathered her bastard son, who was buried in the Abbey on February 26, 1736, it was said to be Frederick's. *Vanelia* went through six editions.

37 Roberts, *GSO*, xviii-iv. Cf. *DNB*. Before coming to England in 1728, Frederick vainly courted Wilhelmina, another Prussian princess. Cf. Peter Quennel, *Caroline of England* (New York, 1940), 106; Reginald Lucas, *George II and His Ministers* (London, 1910), 46; and Egmont, I, 208, 235-36.

38 Roberts, *GSO*, xix. Roberts' observation that "despite the impudent political burlesque, which would have pleased Walpole's opponents, an examination of the *Grub-Street Opera* does not indicate that Fielding had made a total commitment to the Opposition" does not go far enough. The anti-ministerial is unmistakable, but sufficiently balanced with anti-opposition material to make it clear that Fielding had *no* commitment to opposition.

39 Roberts, *GSO* (xi), was possessed only of negative evidence, basically that the play was not advertised in 1731 and that the supposed 1731 edition seemed to have a "relatively modern typographical appearance." Five years later L. J. Morrissey (Morrissey, *GSO*, 18-23) demonstrated that the 1731 ("J. Roberts") edition was actually published by Andrew Millar in 1755 with a misleading title page. Fielding did not publish the banned play during his lifetime, though he could not prevent piracy in 1731.

40 J. R. Brown, "Henry Fielding's *Grub-Street Opera*," *MLQ* 16 (1955), 39-40.

41 Cross, I, 112.

42 Roberts, "Fielding's Ballad Opera *The Lottery* and the English State Lottery of 1731," *Huntington Library Quarterly* 27 (1963), 39.

43 *The Lottery: A Farce* (London, 1732), 14. The song is on p. 26. On the Charitable Corporation scandal see the entries for the named M.P.s in Romney Sedgwick, *The History of Parliament: The House of Commons, 1715-54* (1970); cf. *British Museum*

Catalogue of Prints and Drawings, III, 12-13 for graphic satire on the directors. Ironically, a new lottery was established in 1733 to provide funds to aid the victims of the Corporation frauds.

44 Cross, I, 119; Dudden, I, 100. The letter (September 4, 1730) to Lady Mary says: "I hope your Ladyship will honour the Scenes . . . with your perusal. As they are written on a model I never yet attempted, I am exceedingly anxious lest they should find less Mercy from you than my lighter Productions. It will be a slight compensation to the modern Husband that your Ladyship's Censure will defend him from the Possibility of other Reproof . . . ." Fielding may have shown the play to Lady Mary again in the process of preparing it for performance in February 1732. See *The Complete Letters of Lady Mary Wortley Montagu*, ed. Robert Halsband (Oxford, 1966), II, 93, 96. Lady Mary would have been pleased by the dedication to Walpole.

45 *The Modern Husband: A Comedy* (London, 1732), 9. All citations in the text are to this edition.

46 Plumb, especially 98-100.

47 Morrissey, *TT*, 3.

48 Cross, I, 123. Cross (123-41) gives a good account of the campaign of the Grub-Streeters against Fielding in 1732. He also cites the "Philalethes" letter in full. I have noted a favourable or neutral allusion to Fielding's *Tom Thumb* in *The Grub-Street Journal* for June 11, 1730. There was no venom in other teasing notices of *Tom Thumb* through the fall of 1730. In the two years between the founding of the *Grub-Street Journal* and the assault on Fielding of 1732, its treatment of him was not favourable, but not very pointedly antagonistic. To cite a typical example, Fielding's *Tom Thumb* is paired in passing with "mad" Johnson's *Hurlothrumbo* on April 15, 1731 in an ironical reading of a print (B.M. Print No. 1869) with the same point. It is treated on June 10, 1731 as worthy of its Grub-Street associations, but I think Brown ("Henry Fielding's *Grub-Street Opera*," p. 34) is wrong to treat this as a sign that the play was seen as an attack on the journal.

49 Cross, I, 124.

50 Baker, *PAF*, 226-28. The epilogues Fielding wrote in 1732 for Charles Johnson's *The Modish Couple* (January) and *Caelia* (December) were apolitical. He was merely helping out a Drury Lane colleague.

51 Grundy, 242.

52 The first London edition of Swift's *On Poetry: A Rapsody* (1733) contains a passing shot at Fielding. Other editions do not. A footnote in the 1735 Faulkner edition says Swift never intended to satirize Fielding. The idea that Swift or a friend (Pope?) intended to mock Fielding in 1733 is more attractive if we assume that rumours about Fielding's "Epistle to Mr. Lyttelton" were abroad in 1733.

53 Fielding sided with John Highmore of Drury Lane against those who left (led by Theophilus Cibber) for the Haymarket. Theophilus Cibber is represented by the new character in the revised *Author's Farce* of 1734, Marplay Jr. See Arthur H. Scouten, *The London Stage*, Part III (Carbondale, 1961), LXXXIX-XCIII for an account of the theatrical dispute of 1733-34.

54 Dudden, I, 26, 45, 126.

55 Ibid., 126.

56 Ibid., 123-25.

57 *The Intriguing Chambermaid: A Comedy of Two Acts* (London, 1734).

58 Woods, *AF*, xv.

59 His massive borrowings and indebtedness, in part to finance electioneering, were notorious by the 1730s. Recently, a whole volume (Ray Kelch, *Newcastle, A Duke Without Money*, 1974) has been devoted to his tortuous finances.

60 See note 42 above. Woods (*AF*, 95) rightly assumes that the Director who dickers with Charon in the Act III was added to capitalize on the Charitable Corporation scandal.

61 *Don Quixote in England: A Comedy* (London, 1734), A2. Citations in the text are to this edition.

62 Loftis (138-39) gives a good account of Barnard's bill for "restraining the Number of Houses for playing of Interludes" in April 1735. Cf. P. J. Crean, "The Stage Licensing Act of 1737," *Modern Philology* 35 (1937-38), 243. It was intended to eliminate irregular theatres, especially Goodman's Fields, which was in the "City." Walpole's amendment was seen as "enlarging" the Lord Chamberlain's powers "with

regard to the Licensing of Plays" (Richard Chandler, *The History and Proceedings of the House of Commons* [London, 1743] IX, 94). *The Gentleman's Magazine* (V [1735], 777 ff.) records debate on the bill; it was possible for Walpole and William Pulteney to speak for it at different stages.

63 Coley, *JJ*, 24 ff.

64 Cross, I, 159-61; Dudden, I, 133-34. Both try vainly to link this gesture toward opposition with his activities of 1736-37. The latter vaguely observes that "the author's implied offer of service was duly noted by the 'Patriot' leaders, who were glad to avail themselves of it later on." As Cross notes, *The Grub-Street Journal* ceased attacking Fielding in 1734, probably because of his satire on the ministry and his compliments to Chesterfield. It even half-heartedly defended him against a poem called *The Dramatic Sessions; or the Stage Contest* of 1734.

65 Goldgar, 100-101.

66 Dudden (I, 153) suggests *The Universal Gallant* was hissed solely because of its poor quality. There is not hint of a political motivation.

67 *DNB;* Charles Spencer, Third Duke of Marlborough, was a member of the "Liberty Club." On February 13, 1734, he introduced in the House of Lords a bill (defeated 100 to 12) to prevent the deprivation of military officers of their commissions except by courts martial or as a result of an address from either House of Parliament. This was an opposition ploy, a reaction to Lord Cobham's loss of his Colonelcy in the King's Own Horse and other like punishments after the Excise Crisis. It was also an insult to the King and Walpole. By 1737, the year before he accepted a place, the twisty Marlborough became close to the Prince of Wales.

Notes to Chapter Three

1 Cross, 173-74. Her will was executed on February 8 and proved February 25, 1735.

2 Ibid., 172.

3 Rich's refusal is alluded to in the "Dedication to Mr. John Lun" prefixed to *Tumble-Down Dick;* rejection by Fleetwood is pondered by Cross (I, 178) and Dudden (I, 170).

4 *Seasonable Reproof, A Satire in the Manner of Horace* (London, 1735), 7.

5 Cross, I, 173.

6 Samuel Shellabarger, *Lord Chesterfield and His World* (Boston, 1951), especially 170-79; *DNB*, XVIII, 914. On September 5, 1733 Chesterfield married Petronilla Melusina von der Schulenburg, illegitimate daughter of George I and the Duchess of Kendal (*nee* Schulenburg). This displeased George II, and the Prince of Wales congratulated Chesterfield. He married for her money—£50,000, plus £3000 per annum and other expectations—and they seldom cohabited, though they remained on good terms. The *DNB* says, with slight exaggeration, that "Chesterfield seems to have celebrated the union by taking into his keeping a new mistress, Lady Frances or Fanny Shirly." By 1735, at the latest, he had entered into a lasting liaison with Fanny. After his marriage, he lost so much gaming at the Duchess of Kendal's that she refused him credit.

7 For relevant discussion of Fielding's essay style see: Henry Knight Miller, *Essays on Fielding's Miscellanies* (Princeton, 1961); "Some Functions of Rhetoric in *Tom Jones*," *P.Q.* 45 (1966); and *Henry Fielding's Tom Jones and the Romance Tradition, English Literary Studies*, no. 6; Thomas R. Cleary, "Henry Fielding as a Periodic Essayist," doctoral dissertation, Princeton, 1970, 101 ff.; and "The Case for Fielding's Authorship of *An Address to the Electors of Great Britain* (1740) Reopened," *Studies in Bibliography* 28 (1975), 308-318.

8 There is a playful reference to "scribendi Cacoethes" in the *Covent-Garden Journal*, no. 40; the jest originated in Juvenal's *Satire VII*.

9 Pope associates Swift with Cervantes and Rabelais in the *Dunciad*, I, 19-22.

10 Sheridan Baker, "Henry Fielding and the Cliché," *Criticism* I, 1959, 354-61.

11 *The Persian Strip'd of his Disguise; Or, Remarks on the Late Libel, intitled, Letters from a Persian in England to his Friend in Ispahan* (Dublin, 1735), p. 3. It slanders Lyttelton and Bolingbroke as Jacobites, republicans, and "Roundheads."

12 This appears in the "Prologue." The "Epilogue" urges: "Quit either Faction, and, like Men, unite/ To do . . . King and injured Country Right." See Loftis, 121-22.

13   In Rome warring wits attached epigrams to statues called Pasquin and Marforio.
     Fielding's play was answered by a piece called *Marforio*, staged at Covent Garden on
     April 10, 1736. Cross notes (I, 199) that during the same spring *Political Dialogues be-
     tween the Statues of Pasquin and Marforio* kept the joke warm. In 1722 there had been
     a ministerial journal called *Pasquin* (Loftis, 87).
14   Foord. (145-46) provides a brief résumé of Broad-Bottom Patriot writing. Isaac
     Kramnick's remarks (*Bolingbroke and His Circle*) on the political background of such
     works are not always adequate.
15   *Diary*, March 25, 1737; cf. Laprade, 376-77.
16   Henley, XI, 173. All references to *Pasquin* will be to this edition.
17   This is strikingly apparent upon scanning the British Museum's print catalogue. The
     point is stressed in Atherton.
18   Loftis, 115.
19   *Diary*, March 25, 1736; cf. Laprade, 376-77. The theme of "petticoat government"
     in "The Election" reflects the opposition's belief that Walpole influenced George II
     through Queen Caroline. The parallels in *Pasquin* are never as blatant as those in *The
     Welsh Opera:* typical is the scene where Lord Place urges the mayoress to influence the
     mayor. Opposition complaints about the corruptive use of clerical and military
     patronage are reflected when "a most delicate piece of black wax" is said to be ideal
     material for a chaplain in the King's Own Regiment. Cross (I, 183) notes that an essay
     by Chesterfield in *Fog's Weekly Journal* for January 17, 1736 described the idle army
     as "an army in Wax work."
20   *Letters on the Spirit of Patriotism*, ed. A. Hassal (Oxford, 1926), 25.
21   Cross, I, 182.
22   The letter was dated from Argeville, May 6, 1740; cited in Phillimore, 142-45.
23   Cross, I, 187-89. Even *A Key to Pasquin*, published in London in March, reflects this.
24   "Some of the lines were pertinent to the pending bills." *Diary*, March 25, 1737; cf.
     Laprade, 377. *The Grub-Street Journal*, no. 328 (April 8, 1736) treated parts of the
     tragedy rehearsed in *Pasquin* as reflecting on the attempt by Bishop Gibson to kill the
     Mortmain Bill and the Quaker Bill.
25   A. D. McKillop, "Ethics and Political History in Thomson's *Liberty*," *Pope and His
     Contemporaries: Essays Presented to George Sherburn* (Oxford, 1949), 219.
26   Cross, I, 190-91. We have only the version with the "New and very deep Things."
27   Cross, I, 189-90.
28   Baker (*PAF*, 228-31) correctly treats some of the play's satire, including its closing
     song, as applicable to Walpole. But his argument that memories of a ballad of 1731,
     "The Stateman's Fall, or Sir Bob in the Dust," would have made the play of 1736
     seem generally anti-Walpole is unconvincing. He assumes without strong evidence that
     Harlequin represents Walpole as well as Rich, and that parody of Orator Henley and a
     mention of Doctor Faustus add up to anti-ministerial satire.
29   Henley, XII, 7-8.
30   Dudden, I, 181; cf. John Jackson, *A History of the Scottish Stage* (London, 1793),
     367-38.
31   Cross, I, 194.
32   Wiggin, 87; Foord, 124; Phillimore, 72; Laprade, 378. For this Pitt lost his Cornetcy
     of Horse in Cobham's old regiment.
33   At times the parallel is there. For example, in *The Historical Register* Medley com-
     pares the trickery of Quidam (Walpole) to that of the "great Lun." But there is not a
     consistent, automatic parallel.
34   Cross, I, 187-88, 203.
35   Cross, I, 198.
36   Reproduced in Henley, XI, p. 164.
37   Cross, I, 198-99.
38   *The Champion*, February 26, 1740. Thomas Davies recalled Fielding's affection for
     Lillo, and said the Fielding revised *The Fatal Curiosity* and wrote a prologue for it.
     "The Life of George Lillo," *The Works of George Lillo*, ed. T. Davies (London,
     1775), I, xv-xviii.
39   Loftis, 124.
40   Cross, I, 202-203.
41   Loftis, 117-18.

42 Emmett L. Avery summarizes events at the Haymarket in the spring of 1737; "Field-
    ing's Last Season with the Haymarket Theatre," *Modern Philology* 37 (1939), 283-92.
    A very brief synopsis of Avery's discussion is provided in Appleton; all citations will
    be from Appleton.
43 Dudden, I, 193.
44 Appleton, 62-64.
45 *The History of Miss Betsy Thoughtless* (London, 1751), I, 76-77. Cross (I, 207-10)
    discusses the plays that preceded *The Historical Register* at the Haymarket.
46 Appleton, xii.
47 Morrissey, *TT*, 1.
48 Cross, I, 211-13.
49 *Diary*, March 22, 1737.
50 This was a standard opposition complaint; Fielding raised the point in *Pasquin*, as
    noted, *Joseph Andrews* (II, xvii), and *The Champion* for January 3, February 14 and
    21, and June 28, 1740.
51 The trick of placing one's action in faraway places and past (or future) historical
    epochs was cleverly employed as a screen against censorship and prosecution and as an
    extra comic-satiric resource. The richest cross-section of the variations on the tech-
    nique is found in the *Craftsman*. Cf. Kramnick, *Bolingbroke and His Circle*. Hanson
    (25-26) notes that the *Craftsman* began to use history in this way in the essays by Bol-
    ingbroke signed "Humphrey Oldcastle" and reprinted as *Remarks on the History of
    England*.
52 Cross, I, 211-13. Colley Cibber's alteration of *King John* was rehearsed in 1736, but
    withdrawn amid protests from the players. It was not performed until 1745. Fielding's
    Haymarket company put on Shakespeare's play on March 4, 1737. Apollo has been
    associated with Charles Fleetwood of Drury Lane and Walpole, as well as Theophilus
    Cibber. At various points a case can be made for each identification. Moria has been
    vaguely associated with Maria Skerrett, Walpole's mistress and second wife.
53 Medley says (45) his "two *Pollys*" were "damned at my first rehearsal [i.e., the first
    performance of this rehearsal play], for which reason I have cut them out."
54 Appleton (48) cites the verdict of Thomas Davies in *Garrick* (London, 1780, II, 205)
    that Quidam represented Walpole.
55 *Diary*, April 14, 1737. Dudden (I, 203) sees it as "wishful thinking," a vision of
    Walpole's fall.
56 See notes 25 and 51 above. Fielding exploits the Wolsey parallel in *The Champion* for
    May 8, 1740.
57 Here the Walpole-Harlequin parallel is intended. The identification of Honestus as
    Lord Scarborough (Lord Hervey's *Memoirs*, ed. J. W. Croker [London, 1884], I, 154;
    cited in Appleton, p. 59 note) is not convincing. Honestus represents the Broad-
    Bottom Patriots as a group.
58 P. J. Crean, "The Stage Licensing Act of 1737," *Modern Philology* 35 (1938), 239-
    55. Emmett L. Avery, "Fielding's Last Season with the Haymarket Theatre," *Modern
    Philology* 36 (1939), 283-92, should be read together with Crean. The Act is placed in
    wider perspective in Loftis, 138 ff.
59 Reproduced and discussed in Atherton.
60 Cross, I, 219. This assumption seems based on Fielding's supposed implication in the
    "Dedication to the Public" of his two plays of 1737. It "refutes" the "opinion of too
    many, that a certain person is sometimes the author, often the corrector of the press,
    and always the patron of the *Gazetteer*." However, the "certain person" may be
    Walpole, though he did not write *Gazetteer* essays or the letter from "An Adventurer
    in Politics."
61 He also stresses Fielding's ignorance of foreign affairs, and defends Walpole's
    policies.
62 Most obviously, *The Opposition: A Vision* expresses a preference even for Walpole
    in comparison with Carteret and Pulteney, who abandoned principle in the scramble
    for office during Walpole's last days in power.
63 Presumably "Thomas" suggested Thomas Pelham-Holles, Duke of Newcastle, and
    "John," John, Lord Hervey. Thus Walpole, Hervey, Newcastle, and the devil were
    associated.
64 Gifford, manager of the Lincoln's Inn, Fielding's theatre, was allowed to evade the

ban on non-patent theatres in the Licensing Act. It is possible that he and Walpole encouraged the writing of *The Golden Rump*, but there is obvious bias behind the implication in the *Apology for the Life of Mr. T... C... Comedian* [Theophilus Cibber]
(1740) that Walpole arranged for its composition and presentation to Gifford. I do not
accept Cross's suggestion (I, 282) that Fielding may have helped write the *Apology*.

65   Crean, 239-55; Cross, I, 229; Loftis, 142-50.
66   Pulteney abused the ministry for pretending to protect morals while silencing dissent.
     In Lords, Chesterfield's oration, admired by both sides for its wit and eloquence,
     made the same point and defended the right of men with "wit" (their "property") to
     employ it freely for the good and glory of the nation.
67   The essays are reproduced in *The Criticism of Henry Fielding* (London, 1970), 325-
     34; Williams admits that certain stylistic peculiarities suggest Chesterfield, not
     Fielding. But she is encouraged by similar critical opinions in them and other pieces by
     Fielding. The opinions were commonplaces in the period, and the style of the
     essays—the use of "hath" and a few other touches notwithstanding—is unlike
     Fielding's.
68   I have argued the strong negative and the less strong positive force of the "hath test"
     —in use since the time of Keightly. This essay "passes" the test, but the force of this is
     weakened since in 1737 "hath" is used in a few other essays in *Common Sense* that are
     surely not Fielding's. Those not very familiar with Fielding's essay style should consult
     the works cited in note 7 above.
69   Cross, I, 239-41. Ironically, the estate later fell into the hands of Peter Walter, the
     usurer satirized in *Joseph Andrews* and *Some Papers Proper to be Read before the
     R---l Society*. Slightly later in 1738, Fielding's uncle, Lieutenant-Colonel George
     Fielding, left reversions of certain annuities to his brother's children, though Fielding
     probably got nothing until a lawsuit over the will was settled in 1745, if then.
70   Loftis, 149-50.
71   Cross, I, 234-35.

Notes to Chapter Four

1   Miller, *Misc*, xxx-xxxi, xlii; Hugh Amory, "Henry Fielding's *Epistles to Walpole:* A
     Reexamination," *P.Q.* 46 (1967), 236-47.
2   The best available guide to the bibliographic problems of the *Champion*, including the
     date of its demise, is John F. Speer's unpublished dissertation, *A Critical Study of the
     "Champion"* (University of Chicago, 1951).
3   Dudden, I, 242-43. In the event, Fielding took lodgings.
4   Cross, I, 250.
5   E.g., *Old England*, November 12, 1748, where it is said that Lyttelton arranged for
     the purchase of "2000 of his weekly Performances . . . distributed by the Clerks of the
     General Post Office through *Great Britain* and *Ireland gratis*." Cf. Coley, *JJ*, liv.
6   Goldgar, 191-92.
7   Numbers 1-5 (November 15, 17, 20, 22, 25, 1739) are extant only in the two-volume
     reprint of *The Champion* published in June, 1741 and mentioned below.
8   "The 'Champion' and Some Unclaimed Essays by Henry Fielding," *Englische
     Studien* 46 (1913), 363.
9   *An Apology for the Life, Actions, and Writings of Mr. Colley Cibber* (London,
     1740), 164. The most recent example of the emphasis on Cibber is Goldgar, 193-96.
     Fielding's biographers stress the attack on Cibber.
10   Cross, I, 259. The series is conveniently available in S. J. Sackett, ed., *The Voyage of
     Mr. Job Vinegar from The Champion*, Augustan Reprint Society, No. 67 (Los
     Angeles, 1958).
11   Sackett, vii.
12   W. B. Coley, "The 'Remarkable Queries' in the *Champion*," *P.Q.* 41 (1962), 426-36.
13   Goldgar, 197-98; Roberts, *GSO*, xi; Morrissey, *GSO*, 18-23. Cf. Notes 32, 37, and 39,
     Chapter II above.
14   Goldgar, 197-98.
15   *An Address to the Electors of Great Britain* bears this information on its title-page:

"Edinburgh, Printed by Drummond and Company, in *Swan's* Close, a little below the Cross-well, North Side of the Street, 1740."

16 Cleary, "Case," 308-18. Dickson's attribution (dated March 19, 1923) is written on the fly-leaf of a copy he donated to the Yale Library. Debate was carried on in: Gerard E. Jensen, "*An Address to the Electors of Great Britain . . .* Possibly a Fielding Tract," *MLN* 40 (1925), 57-58; A. Leroy Greason Jr., "Fielding's *An Address to the Electors of Great Britain,*" *P.Q.* 33 (1954), 347-52; William B. Coley, "The Authorship of *An Address to the Electors of Great Britain* (1740)," *P.Q.* 36 (1957), 488-95. Greason connected the *Address* with *The Champion* and Coley noted an important statement, cited below, in the *Gazetteer*.

17 John B. Shipley claims to have found a somewhat later Fielding essay reprinted in *The Dublin Evening Post* for December 30–January 3, 1739/40. However, the evidence is too weak to support assigning it to *The Champion*, much less Fielding; "A New Fielding Essay from the *Champion*," *P.Q.* 42 (1963), 417-22.

18 Godden, 115-16. John B. Shipley has unconvincingly argued that Fielding left as a result of an argument over "puffing" one of the partners' pieces in *The Champion;* "Fielding's *Champion* and a Publisher's Quarrel," *N&Q* 200 (1955), 28. Shipley and W. B. Coley have vainly sought the minutes once held by Godden.

19 Godden, 138-139.

20 John B. Shipley, "Essays from Fielding's *Champion*," *N&Q* (1953), 468-69.

21 Battestin, "FCP," 47-48.

22 Battestin, "FCP," 42-44. Court records show that Fielding borrowed £197 on March 27, 1741 from a Joseph King, who sued for payment in 1742.

23 Plumb, 93-94.

24 John Nichols, *Literary Anecdotes of the Eighteenth Century*, VIII (London, 1814), 446.

25 Dudden, I, 308; Cross, I, 296; Battestin, "FCP," 48.

26 Hugh Amory, "*Shamela* as Aesopic Satire," *English Literary History* 38 (1971), 239-53; cf. Eric Rothstein, "The Framework of *Shamela*," *English Literary History* 35 (1968), 381-402.

27 Middleton's dedication is reprinted in *Joseph Andrews and Shamela*, ed. Douglas Brooks (Oxford, 1970), 359-64. The Hervey-Didapper connection is made in Martin Battestin, "Lord Hervey's Role in *Joseph Andrews*," *P.Q.* 42 (1963), 226-41.

28 Tobias Smollett, *A History of England*, IV, 40-44.

29 Wiggin, 95.

30 *British Museum Catalogue of Political Prints*, nos. 2479, 2486, 2487.

31 Owen, 6-7; cf. Foord, 201-203.

32 Phillimore, 188-89.

33 Foord, 207-208.

34 Cross, I, 298-99.

35 Battestin, "FCP," 39-49; Goldgar, 197-208.

36 This sort of reading was suggested by William B. Coley: "Henry Fielding and the Two Walpoles," *P.Q.* 45 (1966), 157-78. Goldgar has read such historians as Archibald Foord, but accepts in practice the view of party politics that misled Battestin.

37 British Museum print no. 2479. See note 30 above. Interestingly, one anti-Walpole print from the same period—"The Grounds" (i.e., for the motion), no. 2484—shows Walpole's placemen dragging a huge chest full of money, crushing liberty, trade, and honest men.

38 Phillimore, 193.

39 Richard Glover, *Memoirs by a Celebrated Literary and Political Character* (London, 1814), 4-5 note. Phillimore (102-202) and Wiggin (96-97) doubt the accuracy of Glover's story. Phillimore argues that there are no traces of such an intrigue in the Hagley MSS., and that Glover was anti-Broad-Bottom and heard about the intrigue in 1747 from a prejudiced source, the Prince of Wales. Still, what Frederick described to Glover is very plausible and would have been covered up. Phillimore is as prejudiced in favour of Lyttelton as Glover was against him, and Wiggin seems to have accepted Phillimore's position too readily.

40 Foord, 221.

41 Owen, 771 ff.; Coxe, *Pelham*, I, 91 ff.; Wiggin, 109 ff.

42 "Henry Fielding and the Two Walpoles," 157-58.

Notes to Chapter Five

1   Laprade, 435.
2   See Chapter One, *passim*, and the discussion in Chapter Four of Fielding's departure from the *Champion* and *The Opposition: A Vision.*
3   Owen, 79. Owen's is the best general account of Walpole's fall. Richard Glover's story—described earlier—about Lyttelton's flirtation in December 1741 with Walpole is suspect because it was recorded long after the fact by a man prejudiced in favour of Carteret. However, Glover's story is not implausible. See note 39, Chapter Four above.
4   Wiggin, 30-31. Cf. Owen and Foord. Only one of Walpole's cabinet colleagues, Sir Charles Wager, First Lord of the Admiralty, left the cabinet to make room for a newcomer (Wiggin, 99).
5   Phillimore, 209.
6   Wiggin, 109. On December 24, 1744 Horace Walpole said they were selling out for "profit—power they get none."
7   Foord, 221.
8   Foord, 220-28; Owen, 79-99.
9   Owen, 96-125; Foord, 220-29; Leonard W. Levy, *Origins of the Fifth Amendment* (New York, 1968), 328-29. I am indebted to Professor Donald Greene for valuable guidance on the impeachment fiasco.
10 See Chapter One on the distinction between "personal" and "party" or "ideological" allegiances.
11 *Joseph Andrews*, ed. Martin C. Battestin (Middleton, CT and Oxford, 1967), 24, 89. All future quotations will be from this edition, cited by book and chapter in my text.
12 Ibid., xxiii, n.2., 213. Cf. Martin C. Battestin, "Lord Hervey's Role in *Joseph Andrews*" *P.Q.* 42 (1963), 226-41.
13 *The House of Commons in the Eighteenth Century* (Oxford, 1971), 210.
14 Letter to George Lyttelton, May 6, 1740; Phillimore, 142-43.
15 All three pamphlets were published in London. There were several other attacks on the Duchess' memoir, including *Her Grace of Marlborough's Party-Gibberish Explained* (T. Cooper), *An Account of the Conduct . . . A Review of the Late Treatise*, and *A Continuation of the Review . . .* (both J. Roberts).
16 Dudden, I, 393; *A True Copy of the Last Will and Testament of Her Grace, Sarah, Late Duchess Dowager of Marlborough* (London, 1744), 27.
17 Miller, *Misc*, 15. Charles B. Woods has suggested Garrick as his collaborator; "The Miss Lucy Plays of Fielding and Garrick," *P.Q.* 41 (1962), 294-310.
18 F. Lawrence, *Henry Fielding* (London, 1855), 168. Cf. Dudden, II, 214, 1141.
19 Dudden, I, 158, 398.
20 James Ralph, *A Critical History . . . Walpole* (London, 1743), 18-21.
21 *The Letters of Horace Walpole*, ed. Toynbee, I, 274. Cited in Dudden, I, 402.
22 The sources for this and many other facts are Miller, *Misc*, and Miller's rich *Essays on Fielding's Miscellanies* (Princeton, 1961).
23 Dudden, I, 408, 412. Samuel Derrick said in 1763 that Allen once sent Fielding £200. Dudden conjectures that this may refer to the aid Allen is thanked for in *Joseph Andrews* or to a sum to cover the judgement of £197 in King's favour.
24 Miller, *Misc*, 6-8; all citations from the first volume will be to this edition.
25 Foord, 237-38.
26 *The Case of the Hanover Forces . . .* (London, 1743), e.g., 28.
27 Owen, 197-98. One source (P. Yorke's notes) substitutes George Lyttelton for Phillips in the first shadow cabinet.
28 Hugh Amory, "Henry Fielding's *Epistles to Walpole*: A Reexamination," *P.Q.* 46 (1967), 236-47. Cf. J. E. Wells, "Fielding's First Poem to Walpole and His Garret in 1730," *MLN* 29 (1914), 29-30.
29 Miller, *Misc*, 67. *The Sailor's Opera* was performed several times, beginning on May 3, 1737; *The London Stage, Part III*, ed. Arthur H. Scouten (Carbondale, IL, 1961), II, 666-70.
30 Miller, *Misc*, xiii; William B. Coley, "Notes Toward a 'Class Theory' of Augustan

Literature: The Example of Fielding," *Literary Theory and Structure*, ed. Frank Brady (New Haven and London, 1973), 141-42; Mary M. Stewart, "Henry Fielding's Letter to the Duke of Richmond," *P.Q.* 50 (1971), 135-40.

31 Miller (*Misc*, 36) parallels the line with line 197 of Pope's *Essay on Criticism* ("That on weak Wings, from far, pursues your Flights"). There is no basis for Cross's (I, 384) suggestion that the poem following *Liberty, To a Friend on the Choice of a Wife*, was written in 1742 to compliment Lyttelton's marriage.

32 Miller, *Misc*, xlv.

33 William Peterson, "Satire in Fielding's *An Interlude between Jupiter, Juno, Apollo, and Mercury*," *MLN* 65 (1950), 200-202.

34 Miller, *Misc*, 7. Cf. Helen S. Hughes, *The Gentle Hertford* (New York, 1940), 238, 242. All quotations from the three works in Volume Two, *The Wedding Day, Eurydice*, and a *Journey from this World to the Next*, will be from the Henley edition, located by act and scene or chapter in the text.

35 The discussion of composition and revision in Dudden (I, 431, 444-46) takes this as one evidence of early composition, followed by revision and expansion for inclusion in the *Miscellanies*. But Dudden's reasoning is sometimes confused and he wrongly argues that in I,i Fielding must have been complimenting Humphrey Parsons (died March 21, 1741), rather than Sir Robert Godshall (died June 26, 1742). He ignores the compliment to Godshall in the original *Of True Greatness*.

36 Cited in Maud Wyndham, *Chronicles of the Eighteenth Century* (London, 1924), II, 92-93.

37 One of several examples is the *Champion* for March 8, 1740.

38 Miller, *Misc*, 25. Cf. note 35 above.

39 All quotations are from the "World Classics" edition of *The Life of Jonathan Wild* (Oxford, 1932), which conveniently reproduces the 1743 version with a list of 1754 variants. Most other modern editions follow the politically blander 1754 text. Citation will be by book and chapter in the text.

40 J. E. Wells, "Fielding's Political Purpose in *Jonathan Wild*," *PMLA* 28 (1913), 1-55; cf. Cross, I, 409-10; Mabel Hessler, *The Literary Opposition to Sir Robert Walpole, 1721-1742* (Chicago, 1936), 124-51; Irwin, especially pp. 36-42.

41 In Chapter Four I have rejected Goldgar's identification of *Jonathan Wild* as the work Fielding said (*The Champion*, October 4, 1740) he withheld because he was paid to do so by Walpole and threatened with legal action. This does not mean that some version of *Jonathan Wild* may not have been in existence in October 1740, but I suspect even the Wild-Walpole element of the work was begun later.

42 C. J. Rawson, *Henry Fielding and the Augustan Ideal under Stress* (London, 1972), 103, 225. Book II, chapter XIII in the 1743 version becomes chapter XII in 1754. There were other changes that removed dated satire.

43 Laprade (432-33) summarizes the cries for Walpole's blood in 1742; as has been noted, Ralph still grumbled about Walpole's escape in 1743.

44 J. E. Wells ("Fielding's Political Purpose . . . ," 20) equates the Wild of Newgate with Pulteney. W. R. Irwin prefers Carteret, and equates the Newgate election with that of 1741. The weak Walpole-Townshend reading is to be found in Cross, I, 409. Aurelian Digeon's suggestion (*Les Romans de Fielding* [Paris, 1923], 146) that Wild represents Wilmington, figurehead First Lord of the Treasury, is wrong. See Irwin, 40-42, 118-19.

45 Thomas emphasizes the importance members placed upon the "privileges" of the House. It was a loaded word.

46 Irwin (119, 190) suggests William Shippen. However, the speech is a perfect example of Broad-Bottom rhetoric, not the "forthright," Tory rhetoric of Shippen. Irwin notes similarities between the "Grave Man's" attitudes and those Shippen expressed in the "Motion crisis" of 1741, but the Newgate revolution is obviously parallel to the more important cabinet crisis of 1742.

47 The attribution was made by G. E. Jensen, "A Fielding Discovery," *The Yale University Library Gazette*, 10 (1935), 23-32. I will argue in Chapter Six below against Martin Battestin's suggestion (made in the introduction to the Wesleyan-Oxford *Tom Jones*) that a good deal of the novel (roughly a third) was drafted before the outbreak of the Jacobite "Forty-Five."

48 The manoeuvres of 1743-44 are covered in detail in Owen (especially 190-245); useful

subsidiary accounts are in Foord and Wiggin. A sense of the tense day-to-day confrontations and negotiations can be gotten from the relevant sections of Coxe, *Pelham* and the Earl of Marchmont's diary (Marchmont, especially 55-90).

49 Owen, 160-89; Sir Richard Lodge, "The Hanau Controversy in 1774 and the Fall of Carteret," *English Historical Review* 38 (1923), 384-411, 509-36.

50 Marchmont, II, 63.

51 Foord, 243-45.

52 Owen, 185 ff. Cf. Wyndham, 185-56. Once the King had acted in foreign affairs, embarking on a military campaign or signing a treaty, his ministers had no other alternatives than to get Commons to finance his plans or leave office.

53 Phillimore, 231.

54 The events of the fall of 1744 I have briefly summarized can be followed in detail in Marchmont, II, 57-88. Cf. Owen, 230 ff.

55 Owen (242-43) summarizes the changes made in December 1744 and January 1745.

56 It is not a work he could or did acknowledge as a friend to ministers or (from mid-1745) an "anti-Jacobite." However, I unhesitatingly accept Jensen's attribution. He may have found that he had mistimed his satire too late to quash it, but soon enough to conceal all signs of his authorship. His enemies would have stressed his authorship of such a "Jacobitical" piece.

57 Chesterfield dominated it from February 5, 1743 to December 1744. It continued under its original title, *Old England; or, the Constitutional Journal*, ("By Jeffrey Broadbottom, of Covent-Garden, Esq.") until September 27, 1746. It then ran as *Old England: or, the Broadbottom Journal*, "by Argus Centoculi," until 1751. In 1747-48 "Argus Centoculi" was one of the major targets of Fielding's pro-ministerial *Jacobite's Journal*. The journal survived from 1751 to 1753 as *Old England: or, the National Gazette*.

58 *An Attempt towards a Natural History of the Hanover Rat* (London, 1744), 5. Subsequent references to this edition will be made in the text.

Notes to Chapter Six

1 R. C. Jarvis, "The Death of Walpole: Henry Fielding and a Forgotten *Cause Célèbre*," *MLR* 41 (1946), 113-30. Cf. *TJ* Battestin, I, xxiv-xxv, where it is suggested that this affair lies behind the dispute between Captain Blifil's physicians in *Tom Jones*, II, ix.

2 Owen, 277-93.

3 An authoritative overview of Fielding's Forty-Five pamphlets is provided in R. C. Jarvis, "Fielding, Dodsley, Marchant, and Ray: Some Fugitive Histories of the '45," *N&Q* 189 (1945), 90-92, 117-20, 138-41; "Fielding and the Forty-Five," *N&Q* 201 (1956), 391-94, 479-82; 202 (1957), 19-24. Earlier discussions must be regarded with scepticism. The question of government subsidy for these pamphlets is difficult. If the size of the press runs is any indication (the information comes from the records of William Strahan, the printer) the *Dialogue* (500 copies) and *History . . . Rebellion* (1000 copies) probably were not subsidized. The superior *Serious Address*, on the other hand, had two runs (3000 and 1000 copies) and this may indicate support. See Coley, *JJ*, 2.

4 *N&Q* 201 (1956), 392.

5 Locke, *TP* 37. All quotations are from this edition.

6 Dudden (I, 510-19) and Wilkes (149-160) briefly outline the rebellion.

7 Owen (239-301) best describes the complex evolutions forced upon Pitt, his ministerial Broad-Bottom friends, and the Pelhams; cf. Wilkes, 115-160; Wiggin, 109-136.

8 The Stuart proclamations issued in Scotland, England, and abroad are surveyed in George Hilton Jones, *The Main Stream of Jacobitism* (Harvard, 1954); cf. Sir Charles Petrie, *The Jacobite Movement: the Last Phase, 1716-1807* (London, 1950). Both studies should be used with extreme caution; Petrie argues that the Pretender would have revived the Church of England!

9 Marchmont, I, 107. Marchmont's daily notes (I, 98-103) for September and October record the royal resistance to action in the north. The Reverend Thomas Birch summed up the problem in a letter to Lord Hardwicke, dated September 14, 1745: ". . . would

you imagine that in this dangerous situation Lord Granville and his friends have taken no small pains to treat the affair of Scotland as a fiction or a mistake, and as of no other importance than to give a handle to their antagonists in the ministry to draw off our troops in Flanders, and by that means defeat the great schemes which might be executed on the Continent." The militant Bishop of York wrote that the danger to his diocese came from Westminster, not the north, and it was bitterly said at the end of September "that nothing need be done to arrest the Advance of the Rebels but to read a Proclamation." Yorke, Hardwicke, I, 417-65.

10 Marchmont, 108.

11 Owen, 285.

12 Owen, 282-83.

13 Locke, *TP*, 150. Locke also cites *The Surprising History of a Late Long Administration* (reprinted in the *Foundling Hospital for Wit*, v [1746], 58-61), which says the ministry "lasted forty-eight hours; three quarters, seven minutes, and eleven seconds."

14 The remark introduces a summary of the leader in *The True Patriot*, number 29, the "Humble Petition" of the opposition. Noted in Locke, *TP*, 235.

15 J. Paul De Castro, "Fielding and the Collier Family," *N&Q*, 12th Series, No. 1 (August 5, 1916), 104-106.

16 Rupert C. Jarvis, "Fielding and the 'Forty-Five,' " *N&Q* 201 (1956), 391-94, 479-82; 202 (1957), 19-24.

17 Coley, *JJ*, xxii-xxiii.

18 Owen (309-14) describes the Prince's movement into opposition. The navy debt division is stressed in Coley, *JJ*, xxiii.

19 Coley, *JJ* xxix-xxx. Coley (1 note) also notes that *A Dialogue* had a large press run, impressions of 3,500 and 1000 copies, more even than the *Serious Address* of 1745. This may indicate that it was bought up and distributed by the ministry, as I believe *The True Patriot* and *Jacobite's Journal* were.

20 Foord, 137; Aubrey N. Newman, "Leicester House Politics, 1750-60, from the Papers of John, Second Earl of Egmont," *Camden Miscellany*, Vol. XXIII; Camden 4th series, Vol. 7 (London: Royal Historical Society, 1969), 149-50.

21 For Egmont's calculations—he estimated similarly in both 1747 and 1749—see Manuscripts of the Earl of Egmont (London: H. M. Stationery Office [1920-23]), 220, 277. The point about the winning over of London between 1746 and 1754 is made by Lucy Sutherland, "The City of London in Eighteenth-Century Politics," *Essays Presented to Sir Lewis B. Namier*, ed. R. Pares and A.J.P. Taylor (London, 1956), 49-74. Dudden (II, 592-94) discusses Fielding's possible movements during the completion of *Tom Jones*.

22 This running battle between Fielding and the opposition press is traced in Cleary, "Paper War." A contemporary view of the Jacobite boisterousness of the summer of 1747 is provided in Smollett's *A History of England from the Revolution to the Death of George II*, III, 18 ff. Cf. Coley, *JJ*, lxiii-lxv, 93 n.

23 *British Museum Catalogue of Political Prints*, no. 2863; cf. nos. 2864 and 2865. One anonymous writer made fun of Bedford's role in this incident; "The Lichfield Defeat," *The Foundling Hospital for Wit*, Vol. v (London, 1748), 1-6.

24 Apparently this pamphlet had a very small press run (two 500-copy impressions), which may indicate that it (as opposed to *A Dialogue* of June, 4500 copies) was not ministerially subsidized. See Coley, *JJ*, 1.

25 Coley, *JJ*, liii, n. 4.

26 Phillimore, 256-59.

27 Coley, *JJ*, xv.

28 Smollett's *Peregrine Pickle* (first edition of 1751 only) treats Fielding as a sycophant, rewarded with a "trading" Westminster magistracy by Lyttelton, who gave "the bride away" when Fielding married "his own cook-wench." Fielding's marriage took place at the Church of St. Benet's, Paul's Wharf on November 27, 1747; their son, William, was baptized at Twickenham on February 25. Mary Daniels was 26 in 1747.

29 The term is used by Coley, *JJ*. Where possible, quotations will be from this edition. Items Coley excludes will be cited from the original issues in the Bodleian Library.

30 Martin C. Battestin, "Fielding and 'Master Punch' in Panton Street," *P.Q.* 45 (1966), 191-208. The one political thrust in the pamphlet is a lady's comment that she is

bored by certain papers: " 'London Evening's ___ a Dog: the *Gazette* is quite dull: Th' *Advertiser*—a Liar; *Gazetteer*—a mere *Fool*.' " *The Important Triflers. A Satire: Set forth in a Journal of Pastime a-la-mode* (London, 1748), 6.

31 Coley, *JJ*, 130. Squire was Newcastle's chaplain. The citation is from Squire's dedication "To the Freeholders, Burgesses, and other Parliamentary Electors of *Great Britain*" (xxv-xxx).

32 B-B, "Bedford," 146, 176.

33 Dudden, I, 543, II, 936-38. In the *Continuation of the Complete History of England* (1766), Smollett complimented Fielding's novels (II, 160).

34 Coley, *JJ*, 213-15. I am indebted to John B. Shipley, most knowledgeable of Ralphians, for information on the *Remembrancer* and its backers, the Prince of Wales, Dodington, and their associates.

35 Wyndham, 236-37.

36 Coley, *JJ*, 226-27.

37 Coley (p. 227) feels that Fielding would have republished the *Case* before April 9 if it had been his own. (Presumably it was published as a pamphlet before the Bill was accepted in Commons, March 15, or at least Lords, April 6.) However, republication after the fact seems less odd if we remember that Fielding was intent on justifying his patrons, not getting the Bill through—that was never in doubt. Fielding was still fulminating about the Buckingham-Aylesbury dispute and the abuse of his patrons in essay 28, June 11. The case "reads" like Fielding in one of his legalist moods.

38 Coley, *JJ*, lxiv, lxvi-lxviii, 212. As Coley points out, Oxford was probably more pointedly satirized by Fielding than Cambridge in part because of a current legal furor over Jacobite pranks at the former, but also in part because the latter was favoured by the ministry. Newcastle became its Chancellor in December 1748. There had been Jacobite rioting in the streets of Oxford as recently as February 23, 1748.

39 Yorke, Hardwicke, 658 ff.

40 B-B, "Bedford" reproduces 17 letters (found in the Bedford Estate files) from Fielding to Bedford and his man-of-business, Butcher (1748-51), as well as letters from John and Mary Fielding to Bedford (1755), from William Fielding to Robert Palmer, and Sir John Fielding to Bedford (1770). It illuminates Fielding's elevation to the magistracy and traces his involvement in the Westminster election of 1749. Cf. Coley, "Fielding's Two Appointments to the Magistracy," 144-49; "Henry Fielding and the Two Walpoles," 1.

41 Coley, *JJ*, 330.

42 The letter, dated August 29, 1749, is quoted in Cross, II, 246.

43 B-B, "Bedford," 176-77. The letter of August 21 from Hagley Park (to William Lyttelton) is in Phillimore, I, 265-66. Its existence and other indicators that he was away in the summer are noted in *TJ*, Battestin, xxxii-xxxiii.

44 Cross, II, 91-95, 109-114.

45 Coley, *JJ*, 398-99.

46 Phillimore, 269.

47 Reprinted in *The Foundling Hospital for Wit*, vol. VI (London: W. Wells, 1749). There is an abusive, scatalogical acrostic based on "Trott-Plaid" in the *London Evening Post*, March 19, 1748; reproduced in Coley, *JJ*, lxxviii-lxxix.

48 Letter to George Montague, May 18, 1749, *Correspondence*, ed. W. S. Lewis (New Haven, 1941), IX, 84.

49 B-B, "Bedford," 146-52.

50 *The Journal of a Voyage to Lisbon* (1755), "Introduction." Fielding complains at length about the cost to him of performing his Bow Street duties more honestly than his "trading magistrate" predecessors. This "reduced an income [based on fees from those before the court] of about 500l. a year of the dirtiest money upon earth, to little more than 300l." He thanks Bedford for augmenting his income through "a yearly pension out of the public service-money." It is not clear when Bedford made this arrangement: it could have been at any time between late 1748 and mid-1751, when Bedford left the ministry. After Fielding's death Bedford's patronage was extended to John Fielding, Mary Fielding, and his son William, the premature fruit of the 1747 marriage. See B-B, "Bedford," *passim*.

51 Battestin, *TJ*, I, xxviii.

52 E.g., V, vii, xi, xii; VI, ii; VII, iii; IX, v; XII, xiv; XV, vi; XVI, iv; XVII, vii.

53 *TJ*, Battestin, I, xxxv-xlii, cf. Dudden, II, 603-608.
54 Cleary, "Jacobitism"; Hugh Amory, "The History of the Adventures of a Foundling: Revising *Tom Jones*," *Harvard Library Bulletin* 27 (1979), 277-303.
55 *TJ*, Battestin, I, 102, note 1.
56 Martin C. Battestin, "Tom Jones and his 'Egyptian Majesty,' " *PMLA* 82 (1967), 68-77.
57 Tom's patriotic attacks on Jacobitism would also be eliminated, for the most part (for example, in VII, ix, xiv, vi). Assuming that the Jacobite background and the anti-Jacobite satire were added at the same time (logic all but requires this, if they were added in revision), the remainder of Tom's political speeches (VII, xii and XII, iii) must have appeared as a result of this alteration.
58 Cross, II, 98-99, 101.

Notes to Chapter Seven

1   *Gentleman's Magazine*, "Preface" to the 1749 volume.
2   Cross, II, 230-33. Mary M. Stewart, "Henry Fielding's Letter to the Duke of Richmond," *P.Q.* 50 (1971), 135-40.
3   My discussion of Fielding's activities in 1749 and relationship after 1748 with the Duke of Bedford is heavily indebted to B-B, "Bedford." Correspondence between Bedford and his agents, and Fielding and his family (preserved in the Bedford Estates Office) clarifies the relationship of writer and patron and Fielding's part in the Westminster election of 1749.
4   Cross, II, 233.
5   Cross, II, 235 ff.
6   B-B, "Bedford," *passim*.
7   Ibid., 159.
8   Cross, II, 255-56, 274-76. On the literary and legal aspects of Fielding's major social tracts see Malvin Zirker, *Fielding's Social Pamphlets; A Study of . . . An Enquiry . . . and A Proposal . . .* (University of California Press, 1966); he argues (30-42) that Cross exaggerated Fielding's influence on legislation and government policy. It has recently come to light that Fielding was involved in the apprehension, *circa* late November 1750, of three gaming-house keepers who conspired to murder Lord Hardwicke; see M.P.G. Draper, "Letters of the 4th Duke of Bedford," *ECS* 12 (1978-79), 206-208.
9   Cross, II, 268 ff.
10 B-B, "Bedford," 181-82.
11 Cross, II, 276-85. Hugh Amory, "Henry Fielding and the Criminal Legislation of 1751-52," *PQ* 50 (1971), 175-92.
12 Aubrey N. Newman, "Leicester House Politics, 1748-1751," *English Historical Review* 76 (1961), 577-89; "Leicester House Politics, 1750-60, from the Papers of John, Second Earl of Egmont," *Camden Miscellany*, Vol. XXIII, Camden 4th Series, Vol. 7 (London: Royal Historical Society, 1969), 85-228; Wyndham, 260-63. Cf. Phillimore, Foord, Wilkes, William Irwin, "Prince Frederick's Mask of Patriotism," *P.Q.* 37 (1958), 368-84.
13 B-B, "Bedford," 144-52, 182-84. Lewis M. Knapp, "Fielding's Dinners with Dodington, 1750-1752," *N&Q* 197 (1952), 565-66. He also dined at Dodington's (with "Messrs, Furnese . . . & Cary") on April 28, 1750.
14 The pattern of temporal anomalies is well set out in Cross, II, 323-39.
15 *The Covent-Garden Journal*, ed. G. E. Jensen (New Haven, 1915), I, 6-7.
16 Ibid., II, 251.
17 Gerrit P. Judd, *Members of Parliament, 1734-1832* (New Haven, 1955), 255 (No. 2763), 359.
18 Jensen (*Covent-Garden Journal*, II, 194) suggests that the compliment may have been to the Duke of Hamilton because he married, and thus made a family happy, at the right time.
19 Ibid., I, 39-98.
20 Cross, II, 269-80.
21 Ibid. On the Marriage and Jew Naturalization Bills of 1753 (the latter passed *and* repealed that year) see Basil Williams, *The Whig Supremacy*, 2nd. ed. (Oxford, 1962),

136-37 and G. Hertz, *British Imperialism in the Eighteenth Century* (London, 1908), 60-109.

22 Foord, 280.

23 Henry Fielding, *Jonathan Wild and The Journal of a Voyage to Lisbon*, ed. A. R. Humphrey (London, 1973), 191-94. Cf. Cross, III, 7-9.

24 See Chapter Five above; cf. Irwin, *The Making of Jonathan Wild*.

25 The most important of these is *The Fathers. or, the Good-natured Man, A Comedy*, published December 12, 1778. Mallet's edition of Bolingbroke's works appeared on March 6, the day Henry Pelham died.

26 B-B, "Bedford," 152, 182-85; Henley, xvi, 189.

Selective Bibliography

Addison, Joseph. *The Freeholder, or Political Essays*. London, December 23, 1715-29, June, 1716.

Adlerfeld, Gustavus. *The Military History of Charles XII, King of Sweden*. London, 1740.

The Advantages of the Difinitive [sic] *Treaty*. London, 1749.

An Account of the Conduct [of the Duchess of Marlborough] . . . A Review of a Later Treatise. London, 1742.

An Address of Thanks to the Broad-Bottoms, for the Good Things They Have Done, and the Evil Things They Have Not Done, since Their Elevation. London, 1745.

The Affecting Case of the Queen of Hungary. London, 1742. (Often attributed to George Lyttelton).

Amory, Hugh. "Henry Fielding's *Epistles to Walpole:* A Reexamination," *P.Q.* 46 (1967), 236-47.

_____. "Henry Fielding and the Criminal Legislation of 1751-52." *PQ* 50 (1971), 175-92.

_____. "The History of 'The Adventures of a Foundling': Revising *Tom Jones*." *Harvard Library Bulletin* 27 (1979), 277-303.

_____. "*Shamela* as Aesopic Satire." *English Literary History* 38 (1971), 239-53.

An Apology for the Conduct of a late celebrated second-rate Minister. London, 1747.

An Apology for the Life of Mr. T... C... Comedian. London, 1740.

An Apology for the Welch Knight, and a View of the Principles . . . of the Chiefs of the Broad-Bottoms. London, 1745.

Aristophanes. *Plutus, The God of Riches*. Translated by Henry Fielding and William Young. London, 1742.

Atherton, Herbert M. *Political Prints in the Age of Hogarth*. Oxford, 1974.

Austen-Leigh, R. "William Strahan and His Ledgers," *The Library* 4th series, 3 (1923), 261-87.

Avery, Emmett L. "Fielding's Last Season with the Haymarket Theatre." *Modern Philology* 37 (1939), 283-92.

Bailey, Vern D. "Fielding's Politics." Unpublished doctoral dissertation. University of California, Berkeley, 1970.

Baker, Sheridan. "Fielding and 'Stultus versus Sapientem.' " *N&Q* 198 (1953), 343-44.

_____. "Henry Fielding and the Cliché." *Criticism* 1 (1959), 354-61.

_____. "Political Allusion in Fielding's *The Author's Farce, Mock Doctor*, and *Tumble-Down Dick.*" *PMLA* 77 (1962), 221-31.

Banerji, H. A. *Henry Fielding, Playwright, Journalist and Master of the Art of Fiction: His Life and Works.* Oxford, 1929.

Banier, Antoine. *The Mythology and Fables of the Ancients Explain'd from History.* 4 vols. London, 1739-40.

Barker, R. H. *Mr. Cibber of Drury Lane.* New York, 1939.

Battestin, Martin C. "Fielding and 'Master Punch' in Panton Street." *P.Q.* 45 (1966), 191-208.

_____ (with Battestin, R. R.). "Fielding, Bedford, and the Westminster Election of 1749." *Eighteenth-Century Studies* 11 (1977/78), 143-85.

_____. "Fielding's Changing Politics and *Joseph Andrews*," *P.Q.* 39 (1960), 39-55.

_____. "Lord Hervey's Role in *Joseph Andrews.*" *P.Q.* 42 (1963), 226-41.

_____. "Pope's 'Magus' in Fielding's *Vernoniad:* The Satire of Walpole." *P.Q.* 46 (1967), 137-41.

_____. "Tom Jones and his 'Egyptian Majesty.' " *PMLA* 82 (1967), 68-77.

Beattie, Allan, ed. *English Party Politics.* Vol. I. London, 1970.

Blast upon Blast and Lick for Lick, or, a New Lesson for P-pe. London, 1742.

Bolingbroke, Henry St. John, Viscount. *A Dissertation upon Parties: in Several Letters to Caleb D'Anvers.* 2nd ed. London, 1735.

_____. *Good Queen Anne Vindicated.* London, 1748.

_____. *The Idea of a Patriot King.* London, 1749.

_____. *Letters on the Spirit of Patriotism*, Ed. A. Hassal. Oxford, 1926.

_____. *Remarks on the History of England.* Dublin, 1743.

_____. *Works.* Ed. D. Mallet, 5 vols. London, 1777.

Boyce, Benjamin. *The Benevolent Man: A Life of Ralph Allen of Bath.* Cambridge, MA, 1967.

Brewer, John. *Party Ideology and Popular Politics at the Accession of George III.* Cambridge, 1976.

Brooke, John. *The Chatham Administration 1766-68.* London, 1956.

_____. *George III.* London, 1972.

Brooke, Henry. *Gustavus Vasa.* London, 1739.

Brown, J. R. "Four Plays by Henry Fielding." Unpublished doctoral dissertation. Northwestern University, Evanston, IL, 1937.

_____. "Henry Fielding's *Grub-Street Opera.*" *Modern Language Quarterly* 16 (1955), 32-41.

Browning, Reed. *The Duke of Newcastle.* New Haven, 1975.

Buckingham, George Villiers, 2nd Duke of. *The Rehearsal.* London, 1672.

[Burgh, James?]. *Britain's Remembrancer.* 4th ed. London, 1747.

Butterfield, Herbert. *George III, Lord North and the People.* London, 1949.

The Case of the Town and County of Buckingham. London, 1748.

[Chesterfield, Philip Dormer Stanhope, 4th Earl of]. *The Case of the Hanover Forces in the Pay of Great Britain.* London, 1743.

_____. *Private Correspondence of Chesterfield and Newcastle, 1744-46.* Ed. Sir Richard Lodge. London, Royal Historical Society, 1930.

The Case Restated. London, 1748.

Catalogue of Prints and Drawings in the British Museum, Division I: Political and Personal Satires. 4 vols. London, 1870-73.

Cibber, Colley. *An Apology for the Life, Actions, and Writings of Mr. Colley Cibber, Comedian and Late Patentee of the Theatre Royal.* London, 1740.

Cleary, Thomas R. "The Case for Fielding's Authorship of *An Address to the Electors of Great Britain* (1740) Re-opened." *Studies in Bibliography* 28 (1975), 308-318.

_____. "Henry Fielding and the Great Jacobite Paper War of 1747-49." *Eighteenth-Century Life* 5 (1978), 1-11.

_____. "Jacobitism in *Tom Jones:* The Basis for an Hypothesis." *P.Q.* 52 (1973), 239-51.

_____. "Henry Fielding as a Periodical Essayist." Unpublished doctoral dissertation, Princeton University, 1970.

Cochrane, James A. *Dr. Johnson's Printer; the Life of William Strahan.* London, 1964.

Coley, William B. "The Authorship of *An Address to the Electors of Great Britain* (1740)." *P.Q.* 36 (1957), 488-95.

_____. "Fielding's Two Appointments to the Magistracy." *Modern Philology* 63 (1965), 144-49.

_____. "Henry Fielding and the Two Walpoles." *P.Q.* 45 (1966), 157-78.

_____. "Notes Toward a 'Class Theory' of Augustan Literature: The Example of Fielding," *Literary Theory and Structure.* Ed. Frank Brady. New Haven and London, 1973.

_____. "The 'Remarkable Queries' in the *Champion.*" *P.Q.* 41 (1962), 426-36.

_____. "Fielding and the Two 'Covent-Garden Journals.' " *Modern Language Review* 57 (1962), 386-87.

A Collection of State Flowers. London, 1734.

Colley, Linda. "The Loyal Brotherhood and the Cocoa Tree: The London Organization of the Tory Party, 1727-1760." *Historical Journal* 20 (1977), 77-95.

Common Sense, or the Englishman's Journal. London, February 5, 1737—November 16, 1743.

Considerations upon the Present State of Our Affairs at Home and Abroad. London, 1739.

A Congratulatory Letter to a Certain Right Honourable Person [Lord Bath] upon his Late Disappointment. London, 1743. (Often attributed to Lord Bolingbroke.)

A Compleat and Authentick History of the Rise, Progress and Extinction of the Late Rebellion. London, 1747.

The Conduct of the Two B-----rs Vindicated. London, 1749.

The Conduct of the Government with Regard to Peace and War, Stated. London, 1748.

A Continuation of the Review of a Late Treatise [The Duchess of Marlborough's *Account of her Conduct*]. London, 1742.

The Country Journal: or the Craftsman. London, December 15, 1726—September 15, 1750. (The first 44 issues are entitled *The Craftsman: Being a Critic on the Times.*)

The Convention Vindicated from the Misrepresentations of the Enemies of our Peace. London, 1739.

Conybeare, John. *True Patriotism. A Sermon preach'd before the hon. House of Commons.* London, 1749.

Coxe, William. *Memoirs of the Administration of the Right Honourable Henry Pelham.* 3 vols. London, 1829.

_____. *Memoirs of Horatio, Lord Walpole.* London, 1802.

_____. *Memoirs of the Life and Administration of Sir Robert Walpole, Earl of Orford.* 4 vols. London, 1816.

The Craftsman. 14 vols. London: R. Francklin, 1731-37.

Crean, P. J. "The Stage Licensing Act of 1737." *Modern Philology* 35 (1938), 239-55.

The Crisis: A Sermon. London, 1741.

Cross, Wilbur. *The History of Henry Fielding.* 3 vols. New Haven, 1918.

The Daily Gazetteer. London, 1735-48.

The Daily Post. London, 1719-46.

Davis, Rosemary M. *The Good Lord Lyttelton*. Bethlehem, PA, 1939.

Davies, Thomas. *Garrick*. London, 1780.

The Debates and Proceedings of the British House of Commons during the . . . sessions . . . 1743-1774. Ed. J. Almon, *et al*. 11 vols. London, 1766-75.

De Castro, J. Paul. "Fielding and the Collier Family." *N&Q* 12th Series, No. 1 (August 5, 1916), 104-106.

_____. "The Printing of Fielding's Works." *The Library* 4th *series*, Vol. 1 (1923), 257-70.

The Deposing and Death of Queen Gin, with the Ruin of Duke Rum, Marquee de Nantz, and the Lord Sugarcane. London, 1736.

Dickinson, H. T. *Liberty and Property: Political Ideology in Eighteenth-Century Britain*. London, 1977.

The Dictionary of National Biography. Ed. Sir Leslie Stephen and Sir Sidney Lee. 22 vols. London, 1937-38.

Digeon, Aurelian. *Les Romans de Fielding*. Paris, 1923.

The Dictionary, An Ode to Mr. P----m. London, 1752.

Dodington, George Bubb. *Diary of the late George Bubb Dodington*. Ed. H. P. Wyndham. Salisbury, 1784.

Dodsley, Robert. *The King and the Miller of Mansfield*. London, 1737.

Draper, M.P.G. "Letters of the 4th Duke of Bedford." *Eighteenth-Century Studies* 12 (1978-79), 206-208.

Du Crocq, Jean. *Le Théâtre de Fielding: 1728-1737 et ses Prolongements dans l'oeuvre Romanesque*. Paris, 1975.

Dudden, F. Homes. *Henry Fielding, His Life, Works and Times*. 2 vols. Oxford, 1952.

Eardley-Simpson, L. *Derby and the Forty-Five*. London, 1933.

Egmont, John Perceval, 2nd Earl of. *Diary of Viscount Perceval, Afterwards Earl of Egmont*. 3 vols. London, 1920-23.

_____. *An Examination of the Principles, and an Enquiry into the Conduct of the Two B*****rs; In Regard to the Establishment of their Power, and their Prosecution of the War, 'till the Signing of the Preliminaries*. London, 1749.

_____. *Faction Detected by the Evidence of Facts*. London, 1743.

_____. *Manuscripts of the Earl of Egmont*. London: H. M. Stationery Office, 1920-23.

_____. *A Second Series of Facts and Arguments; tending to Prove that the Abilities of the two b-----rs are not more extraordinary than their Virtues*. London, 1749. (If there was a *First Series*, it seems not to have survived.)

Ellis, K. *The Post Office in the Eighteenth-Century*. Oxford, 1958.

An Expostulary Epistle to the Welch Knight, on the Late Rebellion in Politics. London, 1745.

The Fatal Consequence of Ministerial Influence: Or the Difference between Royal Power and Ministerial Power Truly Stated. London, 1736.

Feiling, Keith. *The Second Tory Party, 1714-1832*. London, 1938.

Fielding, Henry. *An Address to the Electors of Great Britain*. Edinburgh, 1740.

_____. *Amelia*. 4 vols. London, 1751.

_____. *An Apology for the Life of Mrs. Shamela Andrews*. London, 1741.

_____. *An Attempt toward a Natural History of the Hanover Rat*. London, 1744.

_____. *The Author's Farce* (original version). Ed. Charles B. Woods, Lincoln, NE, 1966.

_____. *The Author's Farce; with a Puppet-Show call'd the Pleasures of the Town*. London, 1750.

———— [*et al.*], *The Champion*. London, November 15, 1739—?

———— [*et al.*]. *The Champion: Containing a Series of Papers, Humourous, Moral, Political and Critical*. London, 1741.

————. *A Charge Delivered to the Grand Jury*. London, 1749.

————. *The Charge to the Jury: or the Sum of the Evidence*. London, 1745.

————. *A Clear State of the Case of Elizabeth Canning*. London, 1753.

————. *The Coffee House Politician; or, The Justice Caught in His Own Trap*. London, 1730.

————. *The Complete Works of Henry Fielding, Esq*. Ed. W. E. Henley. 16 vols. London, 1903.

————. *The Covent-Garden Journal*. London, January 4—November 25, 1752.

————. *The Covent-Garden Journal. No. 1 . . . By Paul Wronghead of the Fleet, Esq*. London, 1749.

————. *The Covent-Garden Journal*. Ed. G. E. Jensen. 2 vols. New Haven, 1915.

————. *The Debauchees; or, the Jesuit Caught*. October, 1745.

————. *A Dialogue Between a Gentleman from London, Agent for two Court Candidates, and an Honest Alderman of the Country Party*. London, 1747.

————. *A Dialogue Between the Devil, the Pope and the Pretender*. London, 1745.

————. *Don Quixote in England: A Comedy*. London, 1734.

————. *An Enquiry into the Causes of the Late Increase of Robbers with some Proposals for Remedying this Growing Evil*. London, 1751.

————. *Examples of the Interposition of Providence*. London, 1752.

————. *The Fathers. Or, the Good-natured Man*. London, 1778.

————. *The Female Husband*. London, 1746.

————. *A Full Vindication of the Dutchess Dowager of Marlborough*. London, 1742.

————. *The Genuine Grub-Street Opera*. London, 1731.

————. *The Grub-Street Opera*. London [dated 1731, actually published 1755?].

————. *The Grub-Street Opera*. Ed. Edgar V. Roberts. Lincoln, NE, 1968.

————. *The Grub-Street Opera*. Ed. L.J. Morrissey. Edinburgh, 1973.

————. *The Historical Register and Euridyce Hissed*. Ed. W. Appleton. Lincoln, NE, 1967.

————. *The Historical Register for the Year 1736. To Which is Added a Very Merry Tragedy called Eurydice Hiss'd, or, a Word to the Wise*. London, 1737.

————. *The History of the Present Rebellion in Scotland*. London, 1745.

————. *The Important Triflers: A Satire: Set forth in a Journal of Pastime a-la-mode*. London, 1748.

————. *The Intriguing Chambermaid*. London, 1734.

————. *The Jacobite's Journal*. London, December 5, 1747—November 5, 1748.

————. *The Jacobite's Journal and Related Writings*. Ed. W. B. Coley. Middletown, CT and Oxford, 1975.

————. *Jonathan Wild and the Journal of a Voyage to Lisbon*. Ed. A. R. Humphrey. London, 1973.

————. *Joseph Andrews*. Ed. Martin C. Battestin. Middletown, CT and Oxford, 1967.

————. *Joseph Andrews and Shamela*. Ed. Martin C. Battestin. Boston, 1961.

————. *Joseph Andrews and Shamela*. Ed. Douglas Brooks. Oxford, 1970.

————. *The Journal of a Voyage to Lisbon*. London, 1755.

————. *The Letter Writers: or, a New Way to Keep a Wife at Home*. London, 1731.

————. *The Life of Mr. Jonathan Wild the Great: A New Edition with Considerable Corrections and Additions*. London, 1754.

————. *The Life of Jonathan Wild*. Oxford, 1932.

_____. *The Lottery: A Farce*. London, 1732.

_____. *Love in Several Masques*. Dublin, 1728.

_____. *Miscellanies, by Henry Fielding Esq., Volume One*. Ed. Henry Knight Miller. Middletown, CT and Oxford, 1972.

_____. *Miscellanies*. 3 vols. London, 1743.

_____. *Miss Lucy in Town*. London, 1742.

_____. *The Modern Husband*. London, 1732.

_____. *Of True Greatness*. London, 1741.

_____. *The Opposition: A Vision*. London, 1741.

_____. *The Old Debauchees*. London, 1732.

_____. *Ovid's Art of Love Paraphrased*. London, 1747.

_____. *Pasquin: A Dramatick Satire on the Times*. London, 1736.

_____ [with John Fielding]. *A Plan of the Universal Register Office*. London, 1751.

_____. *A Proper Answer to a Late Scurrilous Libel*. London, 1747.

_____. *A Proposal for Making an Effectual Provision for the Poor*. London, 1752.

_____. *Rape upon Rape; or, the Justice Caught in His Own Trap*. London, 1730.

[_____?] *Reasons for Voting for Lord Trentham*. London, 1749.

_____. *A Serious Address to the People of Great Britain*. London, 1745; 2nd edition, London 1745 (together with anonymous, *A Calm Address to All Parties in Religion*).

_____. *Some Papers Proper to be Read before the R---l Society, Concerning the Terrestrial Chrysipus, Golden-Foot or Guinea*. London, 1743.

[_____?] *Ten Queries submitted to every Sober, Honest, and Disinterested Elector for the City and Liberty of Westminster*. London, 1749.

_____. *Tom Jones*. Ed. Martin C. Battestin. Middletown, CT and Oxford, 1979.

_____. *Tom Thumb and the Tragedy of Tragedies*. Ed. L. J. Morrissey. Edinburgh, 1970.

_____. *The Tragedy of Tragedies*. Ed. James T. Hillhouse. New Haven, 1918.

_____. *The True Patriot*. Ed. Miriam Locke. Baton Rouge, 1964.

_____. *A True State of the Case of Bosavern Penlez*. London, 1749.

_____. *Tumble-Down Dick; or, Phaeton in the Suds*. London, 1736.

_____. *The Universal Gallant; or, the Different Husbands*. London, 1735.

_____. *The Vernoniad*. London, 1741.

_____. *The Voyages of Mr. Job Vinegar from the Champion*. Ed. S. J. Sackett. Augustan Reprint Society, no. 67, Los Angeles, 1958.

_____. *The Wedding Day*. London, 1743.

_____. *The Welsh Opera*. London, 1731.

_____. *The Works of Henry Fielding, Esq*. Ed. Arthur Murphy. 12 vols. London, 1762.

Fielding, Sarah. *The Adventures of David Simple*. 2nd ed. London, 1744.

_____. *Familiar Letters between the Principal Characters in David Simple*. London, 1747.

The Finesse of Rantum Scantum, A New Diverting Dialogue Between Tom and Harry, Fratres Fraterrimi. London, 1748.

Fitzmaurice, Lord. *Life of William, Earl of Sherburne, Afterwards Marquis of Landsdowne*. 2 vols. London, 1912.

Fink, Zera Silver. *The Classical Republicans*. Evanston, 1962.

Fog's Weekly Journal. London, 1728-37.

Foord, Archibald. *His Majesty's Opposition, 1714-1830*. New Haven, 1964.

The Foundling Hospital for Wit. Vols. 5-6. London, 1746-47.

The Free Briton. London, December 4, 1729—June 26, 1735.

A Free Comment on the Late Mr. W--G--N's Apology. London, 1748.

Fritz, Paul. *The English Ministers and Jacobitism between the Rebellions of 1715 and 1745.* Toronto, 1975.

Gay, John. *The Poetical, Dramatic, and Miscellaneous Works of John Gay.* 6 vols. New York, 1970.

_____. *Letters.* Ed. G. F. Burgess. Oxford, 1966.

The General Advertiser. London, March 12, 1744—November 3, 1752 [thereafter *The Public Advertiser,* 1752-1794].

The Gentleman's Magazine; or, Monthly Intelligencer. Vols. 1-25, London, 1731-55.

A Genuine Copy of the Tryal of J--- P--l, Esq.; Commonly Called E--- of E-----. London, 1749.

Glover, Richard. *Leonidas.* London, 1737.

_____. *London.* London, 1739.

_____. *Memoirs by a Celebrated Literary and Political Character from the Resignation of Sir Robert Walpole in 1742, to the Establishment of Lord Chatham's Second Administration, in 1757.* London, 1814.

Godden, G. M. *Henry Fielding: A Memoir.* London, 1910.

Goldgar, Bertrand A. "The Politics of Fielding's *Coffee-House Politician.*" *P.Q.* 49 (1970), 424-29.

_____. *Walpole and the Wits.* Lincoln, NE, 1976.

The Grand Question, Whether War, or No War, With Spain, Impartially Consider'd. London, 1739.

Greason, A. Leroy Jr. "Fielding's *An Address to the Electors of Great Britain.*" *P.Q.* 33 (1954), 347-52.

Greene, Donald. *The Politics of Samuel Johnson.* New Haven, 1960.

The Grub-Street Journal. London, January 8, 1730—December 29, 1737.

Grundy, Isobel M. "New Verse by Henry Fielding." *PMLA* 87 (1972), 213-45.

Guthrie, Dorothy A. and Grose, Clyde L. "Forty Years of Jacobite Bibliography." *Journal of Modern History* 11 (1939).

Haig, Robert L. *The Gazetteer, 1735-1797: a Study in the Eighteenth-century English Newspaper.* Carbondale, IL, 1960.

Hanbury-Williams, Sir Charles. *Works.* 3 vols. London, 1822.

Hanson, L. *The Government and the Press.* Oxford, 1936.

Hatfield, Glenn. *Henry Fielding and the Language of Irony.* Chicago, 1968.

Henderson, Alfred James. *London and the National Government, 1721-42.* Durham, NC, 1945.

[Henley, John]. *The Hyp Doctor.* London, 1730-39.

Her Grace of Marlborough's Party-Gibberish Explained. London, 1742.

Hertz, G. *British Imperialism in the Eighteenth Century.* London, 1908.

Hervey, John, Lord. *Memoirs.* Ed. J. W. Croker. 2 vols. London, 1884.

_____. *Some Materials Towards Memoirs of the Reign of King George II.* Ed. Romney Sedgewick. 2 vols. London, 1931.

Hessler, Mabel. *The Literary Opposition to Sir Robert Walpole, 1721-1742.* Chicago, 1936.

Heywood, Eliza. *The History of Miss Betty Thoughtless.* London, 1751.

Hill, B. W. *The Growth of Political Parties, 1689-1742.* London, 1976.

Hill, Sir John. *The Inspector.* 2 vols. London, 1753. [Collected essays, originally published in *The London Daily Advertiser, and Literary Gazette,* 1751-52.]

Hillhouse, James T. *The Grub-Street Journal.* Durham, NC, 1928.

An Historical View of the . . . Political Writers of Great Britain. London, 1740.

The History and Proceedings of the House of Commons of Great Britain . . . from the Death of Queen Anne (to the dissolution of the eighth Parliament in 1741). 7 vols. London, 1741.

The History and Proceedings of the House of Commons from the Restoration to the Present Time. 14 vols. London, 1742.

Hogarth, William. *Hogarth's Graphic Works*. Ed. Ronald Paulson. Rev. ed. 2 vols. New Haven, 1970.

Holmes, Geoffrey. *British Politics in the Age of Anne*. London, 1967.

Horatius, Flaccus, Quintus. *The Odes*. Ed. A. H. Allcroft and R. J. Hayes. London, 1899.

House of Commons Sessional Papers of the Eighteenth Century. Ed. Sheila Lambert. Vols. 1-52 (Introduction and list; 1701-1750). Wilmington, 1975-76.

Hughes, Helen S. *The Gentle Herford*. New York, 1940.

The Humours of a Country Election. London, 1734.

The Importance of an Uncorrupted Parliament Considered in Three Letters Addressed to the Electors of Great Britain. London, 1740.

The Interest of Great Britain Steadily Pursued. In Answer to . . . the Case of the Hanover Forces. London, 1743.

Irwin, William. *The Making of Jonathan Wild*. New York, 1941.

———. "Prince Frederick's Mask of Patriotism." *P.Q.* 37 (1958), 368-84.

Jackson, John. *A History of the Scottish Stage*. London, 1793.

Jarvis, R. C. "The Death of Walpole: Henry Fielding and a Forgotten *Cause Célèbre.*" *Modern Language Review* 41 (1946), 113-30.

———. "Fielding, Dodsley, Marchant, and Ray: Some Fugitive Histories of the '45." *Notes and Queries* 189 (1945), 90-92, 117-20, 138-41.

Jarvis, Rupert C. "Fielding and the Forty-Five." *Notes and Queries* 201 (1956), 391-94, 479-82; 202 (1957), 19-24.

Jensen, Gerard E. "*An Address to the Electors of Great Britain . . . Possibly* a Fielding Tract." *Modern Language Notes* 40 (1925), 57-58.

———. "A Fielding Discovery." *Yale University Library Gazette* 10 (1935), 23-32.

Johnson, Charles. *The Modish Couple*. London, 1732.

———. *Caelia*. London, 1732.

Johnson, Samuel. *A Complete Vindication of the Licensers of the Stage, from the Malicious and Scandalous Aspersions of Mr. Brooks, Author of Gustavus Vasa*. London, 1739.

Jones, B. M. *Henry Fielding: Novelist and Magistrate*. London, 1933.

Jones, George Hilton. *The Main Stream of Jacobitism*. Harvard University Press, 1954.

Judd, Gerrit P. *Members of Parliament, 1734-1832*. New Haven, 1955.

Keightley, Thomas. *The Life and Writings of Henry Fielding, Esq*. Ed. F. S. Dickson. Cleveland, 1907.

Kelch, Ray A. *Newcastle, A Duke Without Money*. London, 1974.

Kern, Jean B. *Dramatic Satire in the Age of Walpole 1720-1750*. Ames, Iowa, 1959.

A Key to Pasquin. London, 1736.

Knapp, Lewis M. "Fielding's Dinners with Dodington, 1750-1752," *Notes and Queries* 197 (1952), 565-66.

Knox, William. *Extra Official State Papers*. London, 1789.

Kramnick, Isaac. *Bolingbroke and His Circle: The Politics of Nostalgia in the Age of Walpole*. Cambridge, MA, 1968.

Lambert, Sheila. *Bills and Acts: Legislative Procedure in Eighteenth-Century England*. Cambridge, MA, 1971.

Langford, Paul. *The Excise Crisis: Society and Politics in the Age of Walpole*. Oxford, 1975.

Laprade, William T. *Public Opinion and Politics in Eighteenth-Century England, to the Fall of Walpole*. New York, 1936.

Largmann, Malcolm G. "Stage References as Satiric Weapon: Sir Robert Walpole as Victim." *Restoration and 18th Century Theatre Research.* IX/1 (May 1970), 35-43.

Lawrence, F. *Henry Fielding.* London, 1855.

A Letter from a Traveling Tutor to a Noble Young Lord. London, 1747.

A Letter to a Noble Lord, to whom alone it belongs: Occasioned by . . . a Farce called, Miss Lucy in Town. London, 1742.

A Letter to the Author of the Examination of the . . . Two Br----rs. London, 1749.

A Letter to the Most Noble Thomas, Duke of Newcastle, on Certain Points of the Last Importance to this Nation. London, 1749.

A Letter to the Tories. London, 1747.

Levine, G. R. *Henry Fielding and the Dry Mock.* The Hague, 1967.

_____. "Henry Fielding's 'Defense' of the Stage Licensing Act." *English Language Notes* 2 (1965), 193-96.

Levy, Leonard W. *Origins of the Fifth Amendment.* New York, 1968.

Lillo, George. *The Works of George Lillo.* Ed. T. Davies. 2 vols. London, 1775.

Lodge, Sir Richard. "The Hanau Controversy in 1744 and the Fall of Carteret." *English Historical Review* 38 (1923), 384-411, 509-36.

_____. *Studies in Eighteenth Century Diplomacy, 1740-48.* London, 1930.

Loftis, John. *The Politics of Drama.* Oxford, 1963.

The London Daily Advertiser. London, April 18, 1751—June 30, 1753 [originally published as *The London Advertiser and Literary Gazette*, London, March 4—April 17, 1751].

The London Evening Post. London, 1727-1806.

The London Magazine and Monthly Chronologer. London, 1736-46. [Earlier entitled *The London Magazine; or, Gentleman's Monthly Intelligencer*, established 1732; after 1746 it reverted to the original title.].

L--d B----k Speech on the Convention. London, 1739.

Lynch, Francis. *The Independent Patriot.* London, 1737.

Lyttelton, George, 1st Baron. *Considerations upon the Present State of Our Affairs at Home and Abroad.* London, 1739.

_____. *Farther Considerations upon the Present State of Our Affairs.* London, 1739.

_____. *A Letter to a Member of Parliament from a Friend in the Country.* London, 1738.

_____. *Letters from a Persian in England to His Friend in Ispahan.* London, 1735.

_____. *Works.* 2 vols. Dublin, 1774.

McCrea, Brian. *Henry Fielding and the Politics of Mid-Eighteenth-Century England.* Athens, GA, 1980.

McKendrick, Neil, ed. *Historical Perspectives: Studies Presented to J. H. Plumb.* London, 1974.

McKillop, A. D. *The Background of Thomson's Liberty.* Houston, 1951.

_____. "Ethics and Political History in Thomson's *Liberty*." *Pope and His Contemporaries: Essays Presented to George Sherburn.* Oxford, 1949.

Mack, Maynard. *The Garden and the City: Retirement and Politics in the Later Poetry of Pope, 1731-43.* Toronto, 1969.

Mallet, David. *Eurydice.* London, 1731.

Manchester Politics. A Dialogue between Mr. True-blue and Mr. Whiglove. London, 1748.

Marchmont, Earls of. *A Selection from the Papers of the Earls of Marchmont.* Ed. Sir G. H. Rose. 3 vols. London, 1831.

Marlborough, Sarah, 1st Duchess of [with Nathaniel Hooke]. *An Account of Her Conduct from Her First Coming to Court till the Year 1710.* London, 1742.

_____. *A True Copy of the Last Will and Testament of Her Grace, Sarah, Late Duchess Dowager of Marlborough*. London, 1744.

Michael, Wolfgang. *Englische Geschichte im achtzehnten Jahrhundert*. 5 vols. Berlin, Hamburg, Basel, 1896-1955.

Middleton, Conyers. *A History of the Life of Marcus Tullius Cicero*. 2 vols. London, 1741.

Miller, Henry Knight. *Essays on Fielding's Miscellanies*. Princeton, 1961.

_____. "Fielding's *Miscellanies:* A Study of Volumes I and II." Unpublished doctoral dissertation. Princeton University, 1953-54.

_____. "Henry Fielding's *Tom Jones* and the Romance Tradition." *English Literary Studies* 6 (1977).

_____. "Some Functions of Rhetoric in *Tom Jones*," *P.Q.* 45 (1966), 209-35.

Miller, James. *Vanelia; or, the Amours of the Great (in three Acts) as it is acted by a private Company near St. James'*. London, 1732.

Mist's Weekly Journal. London, 1725-28.

Mitchell, A. A. "London and the Forty-Five." *History Today* 15 (1965), 719-26.

Mitchell, Joseph. *A Familiar Epistle to Walpole*. London, 1735.

A Modest Apology for My Own Conduct. London, 1748. [Supposedly George Lyttelton's political autobiography; by one of his enemies.]

Molière. *Select Comedies of Molière*. 8 vols. London, 1732.

The Monosyllable If! A Satire. London, 1748.

Montagu, Lady Mary Wortley. *The Complete Letters of Lady Mary Wortley Montagu*. Ed. Robert Halsband. 3 vols. Oxford, 1965-67.

Morgan, McNamara. *The Causidicade*. London, 1743.

Moore, Edward. *The Trial of Selim the Persian*. London, 1748.

Morrissey, L. J. "Fielding's First Political Satire." *Anglia* 93 (1972), 325-48.

_____. "Henry Fielding and the Ballad Opera." *Eighteenth-Century Studies* 4 (1971), 386-402.

Mountfort, Richard. *The Fall of Mortimer: An Historical Play, Reviv'd from Mountford*. London, 1731.

Namier, Sir Lewis B. *The Structure of Politics at the Accession of George III*. 2 vols. 2nd ed. London, 1957.

J. H. *The National Alarm*. London, 1745.

The Natural Interest of Great Britain, in its Present Circumstances, Demonstrated. London, 1749.

Newman, Aubrey N. "Leicester House Politics, 1748-51." *English Historical Review* 76 (1961), 577-89.

_____. "Leicester House Politics, 1750-60, from the Papers of John, Second Earl of Egmont." *Camden Miscellany*, Vol. XXIII, Camden 4th Series (London: Royal Historical Society, 1969), 85-228.

Nichols, Charles W. "Social Satire in *Pasquin* and *The Historical Register*." *P.Q.* 3 (1924), 309-17.

Nichols, John. *Illustrations of the Literary History of the Eighteenth Century*. 8 vols. London, 1817-58.

_____. *Literary Anecdotes of the Eighteenth Century*. 9 vols. 2nd ed. London, 1812-16.

The Norfolk Gamester: Or, The Art of Managing the Whole Pack, Even King, Queen, and Jack. London, 1734.

Observations on the Probable Issue of the Congress at Aix-la-Chapelle. London, 1748.

O'Gorman, Frank. *The Rise of Party in England: The Rockingham Whigs, 1760-82*. London, 1975.

Old England: or, the Constitutional Journal by "Jeffrey Broadbottom, of Covent Garden, Esq.," London, February 5, 1743—September 27, 1746.

[Continued as *Old England: or, the Broadbottom Journal* by "Argus Cen-toculi" until 1751, and then as *Old England: or, the National Gazette* until 1753.]

Owen, John B. *The Rise of the Pelhams*. London, 1957.

Oxford Honesty: or, a Case of Conscience. 2nd ed. London, 1749.

P., P. T. "Woodfall's Ledger, 1736-37." *N&Q* 11 (1855), 418-20.

Pares, Richard. *King George III and the Politicians*. Oxford, 1953.

The Patriot Analized. London, 1748.

Percival, Milton. *Political Ballads Illustrating the Reign of Sir Robert Walpole*. Oxford, 1916.

The Persian Strip'd of his Disguise . . . Dublin, 1735.

Perry, Thomas W. *Public Opinion, Propaganda and Politics in Eighteenth-Century England: A Study of the Jew Bill of 1753*. Cambridge, MA, 1962.

Peterson, William, "Satire in Fielding's *An Interlude between Jupiter, Juno, Apollo, and Mercury*." *MLN* 65 (1950), 200-202.

Petrie, Sir Charles. *The Jacobite Movement: the Last Phase, 1716-1807*. London, 1950.

Phillimore, Robert. *Memoirs and Correspondence of George, Lord Lyttelton*. 2 vols. London, 1845.

The 'Piscopade. A Panegyri-Satiri-Serio-Comical poem. London, 1748.

Plumb, J. H. Review of Walcott, *English Politics in the Early Eighteenth Century*. *English Historical Review* 72 (1957), 126-29.

_____. *The Rise of Political Stability, 1675-1725*. London, 1967.

_____. *Sir Robert Walpole: the King's Minister*. London, 1961.

_____. *Sir Robert Walpole: the Making of a Statesman*. London, 1956.

The Political State of Great Britain. 58 vols. London, 1712-1740.

Pope, Alexander. *The Poems of Alexander Pope*. Ed. John Butt *et al.* London and New Haven, 1950-69.

Posthumous Letters from Various Celebrated Men. Ed. George Colman. London, 1825.

The Present Condition of Great Britain. London, 1746.

The Present State of Politics in Europe. London, 1739.

Pritchard, ?. *The Fall of Phaeton*. London, 1736.

Proceedings at the Sessions of the Peace and Oyer and Terminer for the City of London and County of Middlesex held at Justice Hall in the Old Bailey, on Friday the 12th February last . . . upon a bill of indictment found against Francis Charteris, esq., for committing a rape on the body of Anne Bond, of which he was found guilty. London, 1730.

Pulteney, William. *An Answer to One Part of a Late Infamous Libel*. London, 1730.

_____. *The Politicks on Both Sides*. London, 1734.

_____. *A Review of the Excise Scheme*. London, 1734.

Radzinowicz, Leon. *A History of English Criminal Law and its Administration from 1750*. Vol. 1. London, 1948.

Ralph, James. *The Case of Authors by Profession or Trade (1758) together with the Champion (1739-1740)*. Ed. P. Stevick. Gainesville, FL, 1966.

_____. *A Critical History of the Administration of Sir Robert Walpole*. London, 1743.

_____. *The History of England during the Reigns of King William, Queen Anne, and King George the First*. 2 vols. London, 1746.

_____. *Of the Rise and Abuse of Parliaments: in Two Historical Discourses*. London, 1744.

_____. *The Other Side of the Question*. London, 1742.

_____. *The Protester, on Behalf of the People*. London, June 2–November 10, 1753.

_____. *The Remembrancer (or, National Advocate)*. London, December 12, 1747—June 1, 1751.

_____. *The Remembrancer, by George Cadwallader, Gent., Consisting of the First Twelve Essays from the Weekly Paper*. London, 1748.

Rao, Amanda Vittal. *A Minor Augustan: being the Life and Works of George, Lord Lyttelton, 1709-1733*. Calcutta, 1934.

Rawson, C. J. *Henry Fielding and the Augustan Ideal under Stress*. London, 1972.

Realey, C. B. *Remarks on the Account of Her [the Duchess of Marlborough's] Conduct . . . till the Year 1710*. London, 1742.

_____. *Remarks on the Preliminary Articles of Peace*. London, 1748.

Roberts, Edgar V. "Fielding's Ballad Opera *The Lottery* and the English State Lottery of 1731." *Huntington Library Quarterly* 27 (1963), 39-52.

Roberts, S. C., " An Eighteenth-Century Gentleman." *London Mercury* II (1925), 290-97.

Robin's Panegyric: or, the Norfolk Miscellany. London, 1731.

Rogers, Pat. *Henry Fielding*. London, 1979.

Rogers, Winfield. "The Significance of Fielding's Temple Beau." *PMLA* 55 (1940), 440-44.

Rothstein, Eric. "The Framework of *Shamela*." *English Literary History* 35 (1968), 381-402.

A Satire on All Parties. London, 1749.

The Scandalizade, A Panegyri-Satiri-Serio-Comi-Dramatic Poem. By Porcupinus Pelagius. London, 1749.

Scouten, Arthur H., ed. *The London State, Part III*. 2 vols. Carbondale, IL, 1961.

Seasonable Reproof, A Satire in the Manner of Horace. London, 1735.

Sedgwick, Romney, ed. *The History of Parliament: The House of Commons, 1715-54*. London, 1970.

_____. *Letters from George III to Lord Bute, 1756-1766*. London, 1939.

Seventeen Hundred and Thirty-Nine . . . A Satire . . . inscribed to . . . Philip, Earl of Chesterfield. London, 1739.

Seymour, Mabel. "Fielding's History of the '45." *P.Q.* 14 (1935), 105-25.

Shellabarger, Samuel. *Lord Chesterfield and His World*. Boston, 1951.

Shepperson, Archibald B. "Additions and Corrections to Facts about Fielding." *Modern Philology* 51 (1954), 214-19.

Shipley, John B. "Essays from Fielding's *Champion*." *N&Q* 198 (1953), 468-69.

_____. "Fielding and 'The Plain Truth' (1740)." *N&Q* 196 (1951), 561-62.

_____. "Fielding's *Champion* and a Publishers' Quarrel." *N&Q* 200 (1955), 28.

_____. "A New Fielding Essay from the *Champion*." *P.Q.* 42 (1963), 417-22.

_____. "On the Date of the Champion." *N&Q* 198 (1953), 441.

Smollett, Tobias. *The Adventures of Peregrine Pickle*. 1st edition. London, 1766.

_____. *A Continuation of the History of England*. London, 1766.

_____. *A Faithful Narrative of the base and inhuman Acts that were lately practised upon the Brain of Habbakuk Hilding*. London, 1752.

_____. *A History of England, from the Revolution to the Death of George II*. 5 vols. London, 1827.

Spanish Insolence Corrected by English Bravery. London, 1739.

Speer, John F. "A Critical Study of the 'Champion.' " Unpublished doctoral dissertation. University of Chicago, 1951.

[Squires, Samuel]. *An Historical Essay upon the Ballance of Civil Power*. London, 1748.

The State of the Nation. London, 1745, 1746, 1747, 1748.

Steven, D. H. *Party Politics and English Journalism, 1702-1742.* Menasha, WI, 1916.

Stewart, Mary M. "Henry Fielding's Letter to the Duke of Richmond." *P.Q.* 50 (1971), 135-40.

Stultus versus Sapientum. London, 1749.

Sutherland, Lucy. "The City of London in Eighteenth-Century Politics." In Richard Pares and A.J.P. Taylor, eds. *Essays Presented to Sir Lewis B. Namier,* 49-74. London, 1956.

_____. "Samuel Gideon and the Reduction of Interest, 1749-50." In *Economic History Review* 16 (1946), 15-29.

Swift, Jonathan. *Correspondence.* Ed. Harold Williams. 5 vols. Oxford, 1963-65.

_____. *The Poems of Jonathan Swift.* Ed. Harold Williams, 2nd ed. 3 vols. Oxford, 1958.

The Taffydeis: an Humourous Heroic Poem, in Honour of St. David and the Leek. 2nd ed. London, 1747.

A Tale of Two Tubs. London, 1749.

Theobald, Lewis. *Orestes.* London, 1731.

Thomas, P.D.G. *The House of Commons in the Eighteenth Century.* Oxford, 1971.

Thomson, James. *Agamemnon.* London, 1738.

_____. *Edward and Eleanora.* London, 1739.

_____. *The Castle of Indolence.* London, 1748.

_____. *Liberty: A Poem.* London, 1735-36.

_____ [with Mallet, D.]. *The Masque of Alfred.* London, 1740.

_____. *The Plays of James Thomson.* Ed. P. G. Adams. New York and London, 1979.

[Thornton, Bonnell?]. *The Covent-Garden Journal Extraordinary.* London, 1752.

_____. *Have at You All: or, The Drury Lane Journal.* London, January 16–April 9, 1752.

Towers, A. R. Jr. *An Introduction and Annotations for a Critical Edition of "Amelia."* Unpublished doctoral dissertation. Princeton University, 1952.

T[ren]t[ham]m and V[an]d[epu]t A Genuine and Authentick Account of the Proceedings at the Late Election for the City and Liberty of Westminster. London, 1750.

A True and Impartial Collection of Pieces in Prose and Verse, which have been written on both Sides of the Question during the Contest for the Westminster Election. London, 1749.

Turner, E. R. "The Excise Crisis." *English Historical Review* 42 (1927), 34-57.

The Two Candidates or, Charge and Counter-Charge. London, 1749.

Van Der Voorde, Frans P. *Henry Fielding: Critic and Satirist.* Gravenhage, 1931.

Vincent, Howard P. "Early Poems by Henry Fielding." *Notes and Queries* 184 (March 13, 1943), 159-60.

_____. "Henry Fielding in Prison." *Modern Language Review* 36 (1941), 499-500.

The Voice of Liberty; or, a British Phillipic: A Poem, in Miltonic Verse. Occasion'd by the Insults of the Spaniards. London, 1738.

Walcott, Robert. *English Politics in the Early Eighteenth Century.* Cambridge, MA, 1956.

Walpole, Horace. *The Interest of Great Britain Steadily Pursued.* London, 1743.

_____. *A Letter to the Whigs.* London, 1747.

_____. *Letters to Horace Walpole.* Ed. Lord Dover. 4 vols. London, 1834.

_____. *Memoirs of the Last Ten Years of the Reign of George II.* 3 vols. London, 1822.

_____. *A Second and Third Letter to the Whigs*. London, 1748.

_____. *The Yale Edition of Horace Walpole's Correspondence*. Ed. W. S. Lewis. 42 vols. New Haven, 1937-80.

Ward, W. R. *Georgian Oxford: University Politics in the Eighteenth Century*. Oxford, 1958.

Wells, J. E. "The 'Champion' and Some Unclaimed Essays by Henry Fielding." *Englische Studien* 46 (1913), 363.

_____. "Fielding's *Champion*—More Notes." *Modern Language Notes* 35 (1920), 18-23.

_____. "Fielding's First Poem to Walpole and His Garret in 1730." *Modern Language Notes* 29 (1914), 29-30.

_____. "Fielding's Political Purpose in *Jonathan Wild*." *PMLA* 28 (1913), 1-55.

_____. "Henry Fielding and The Crisis." *Modern Language Notes* 27 (1912), 180-81.

The Westminster Journal; or, New Weekly Miscellany. London, 1742-1810.

Whitehead, Paul. *The Case of the Hon. Alexander Murray*. London, 1751.

_____. *Honour: A Satire*. London, 1749.

Wiggin, Lewis M. *The Faction of Cousins: A Political Account of the Grenvilles, 1733-63*. New Haven, 1958.

Wilkes, John W. *A Whig in Power: the Political Career of Henry Pelham*. Evanston, IL, 1964.

Williams, Basil. *Carteret and Newcastle*. Cambridge, 1943.

_____. *The Whig Supremacy*. 2nd ed. Oxford, 1962.

Williams, Ioan. *The Criticism of Henry Fielding*. London, 1970.

Woods, Charles B. "Cibber in Fielding's *Author's Farce:* Three Notes." *P.Q.* 44 (1965), 145-51.

_____. "Fielding and the Authorship of *Shamela*." *P.Q.* 25 (1946), 248-72.

_____. "Fielding's Epilogue for Theobald." *P.Q.* 28 (1949), 423-28.

_____. "Notes on Three of Fielding's Plays." *PMLA* 52 (1937), 359-73.

Wyndham, Maud. *Chronicles of the Eighteenth Century*. 2 vols. London, 1924.

Yorke, P. C. *The Life and Correspondence of Philip Yorke, Earl of Hardwicke*. Cambridge, 1913.

Zirker, Malvin. *Fielding's Social Pamphlets: A Study of . . . An Enquiry into the Causes of the Late Increase of Robbers and A Proposal for Making an Effectual Provision for the Poor*. University of California Press, 1966.

Index